The Essential Guide to Physics for Flash Games, Animation, and Simulations

Dev Ramtal
Adrian Dobre

friendsof

DESIGNER TO DESIGNER™

an Apress® company

The Essential Guide to Physics for Flash Games, Animation, and Simulations

Credits

President and Publisher:
Paul Manning

Lead Editor:
Chris Nelson

Technical Reviewer:
RJ Owen

Editorial Board:
Steve Anglin, Mark Beckner,
Ewan Buckingham, Gary Cornell,
Jonathan Gennick, Jonathan Hassell,
Michelle Lowman, James Markham,
Matthew Moodie, Jeff Olson, Jeffrey Pepper,
Frank Pohlmann, Douglas Pundick,
Ben Renow-Clarke, Dominic Shakeshaft,
Matt Wade, Tom Welsh

Coordinating Editor:
Corbin Collins

Copy Editor:
Nancy Sixsmith

Compositor:
Apress Production (Christine Ricketts)

Indexer:
SPI Global

Artist:
SPI Global

Cover Artist:
Anna Ishchenko

Cover Designer:
Corné van Dooren

To my mother, who made me possible; and to my wife and daughter, who supported me in making this book possible.

–DR

To my family who have been so understanding while I have been away from them working on this book.

–AD

Contents at a Glance

Contents

Contents

Part II: Particles, Forces and Motion

Contents

Part III: Multi-particle and Extended Systems

About the Authors

 **Dev Ramtal** has been coding physics for more than 20 years. Alongside his academic research background in mathematical and computational physics, he has a long history of web development experience since building his first website back in 1997. Dev has been working with the Flash platform for the past six years, using it as a research and teaching tool, for general web programming, and just for some serious fun. He is also increasingly interested in game programming. Dev has a BSc and a PhD in Physics from the University of London. He lives in the UK where he works as a research scientist in academia. He can be contacted at `www.physicscodes.com`.

 **Adrian Dobre** has more than 15 years of experimental and computational modeling experience in fluid dynamics. His experience in scientific research and teaching brought his attention to ActionScript and Flash, where programming combines with nice visual output. From here his dedication over more than five years for using Actionscript as a tool to model physical processes and create virtual laboratory platforms. Adrian holds a BSc in Aeronautical Engineering from University *Politehnica* in Bucharest, Romania and a PhD in Engineering Science from the University of Western Ontario, Canada. He currently lives in Bucharest, Romania, with his family.

About the Technical Reviewer

 **RJ Owen** is a senior software architect at Effective UI. RJ has been working with Flex since version 2 and has worked on many projects of varying sizes and complexities, but always favors those with great user interfaces. He is a regular blogger and has spoken at many events including 360|Flex, Adobe MAX, and O'Reilly's Web 2.0. RJ enjoys advocating for teaching developers how to design and branch into skills beyond software. He has an MBA degree in Physics and Computer Science and lives in Colorado with his family.

About the Cover Image Artist

 **Corné van Dooren** designed the front cover image for this book. After taking a brief hiatus from friends of ED to create a new design for the Foundation series, he worked at combining technological and organic forms, the results of which now appear on this and other book covers.

Corné spent his childhood drawing on everything at hand and then began exploring the infinite world of multimedia—and his journey of discovery hasn't stopped since. His mantra has always been, "The only limit to multimedia is the imagination"—a saying that keeps him constantly moving forward.

Corné works for many international clients, writes features for multimedia magazines, reviews and tests software, authors multimedia studies, and works on many other friends of ED books. You can see more of his work at and contact him through his website at **www.cornevandooren.com**.

Acknowledgments

We are extremely grateful to all the individuals, at Apress and elsewhere, who have helped turn this book from an idea into physical reality. An enormous amount of work goes into producing a book, of which writing it is only one part. We were fortunate to have the support of such a fantastic team—we won't mention any names for fear of missing anyone.

We are also grateful to the Flash and programming community for sharing their knowledge and expertise so openly through blogs, forums, websites, and books. It is a great pleasure to be able to give something back after having gained so much from the community.

Finally, we would like to thank our respective families for their constant support and patience during the intense period of writing this book.

Preface

We hope you will enjoy reading this book as much as we enjoyed writing it. Doing physics with Flash is a lot of fun—there is a sense of satisfaction in writing a few lines of code and then seeing how they make objects behave like they do in the real world. The ability to do this gives us great power as programmers. The aim of this book is to provide you with tools that will make you feel that sense of power. Whether you want to build convincing animations, games that behave realistically, or accurate simulators, you will find herein plenty of tools, examples and ideas that should be of help.

The inspiration for this book came from the excellent book authored by Keith Peters, *Foundation ActionScript Animation*. This was the first book we read when we were still getting acquainted with Flash and ActionScript several years ago. The book contained a good amount of physics-related topics and showed us the power of Flash in creating interactive animations with physics that were as fun to code as they were to play with. Since then we became addicted to Flash and ActionScript, using them to create numerous physics-based simulations and other applications. Along the way we learned or figured out a lot of things that seemed worth sharing with the Flash community. Keith Peters's book provided a great introduction to physics-based animation. But it seemed to us that there was also a need for a book that explored physics further and in greater depth, and that catered for more demanding applications such as accurate simulators or more complex game programming. After all, there are several "game physics" books written for other programming languages such as C++ and Java, so why not ActionScript? The present book is meant to fill this gap.

We should make it clear at the outset that this is primarily a book about physics, and secondarily about Flash. Therefore, the focus is less on producing attractive animations, and more on modeling real physics using the Flash environment. Some of the simulations in the book may not be very pretty or smooth from a visual perspective, but they do contain a lot of physics goodness! The approach we adopt attempts to make serious physics accessible. But although we don't shy away from going into technical stuff, with all the accompanying math, we hope to have done so in a way that is simple and straightforward.

Inevitably, due to space and time restrictions, there are topics that we were not able to include or that we didn't explore in detail. Nevertheless, the book covers an awful lot of ground, taking you from coding a simple bouncing ball animation in a few lines of code in the first chapter to a highly accurate simulation of the solar system in the final chapter. We hope you enjoy the journey in between!

What this book will (and won't) teach you

The Essential Guide to Physics for Flash Games, Animation, and Simulations teaches you how to include physics into your programming. It does not teach you how to program. It does not teach you ActionScript. And though this book teaches you how to implement physics into your games (as well as other projects), it is not about game programming *per se*.

We assume that you have at least some programming experience with ActionScript 3.0 (AS 3.0) as well as familiarity with an authoring tool for building Flash applications in AS 3.0, such as Adobe Flash (version CS3 or above) or Adobe Flash Builder (formerly Adobe Flex Builder). This book does not teach you how to use those authoring tools. If you don't have this background we highly recommend picking up one of the many excellent introductory books on Flash and ActionScript available, such as *Foundation ActionScript 3.0 for Flash and Flex* by Darren Richardson and Paul Milbourne. We also highly recommend *Foundation ActionScript 3.0 Animation: Making Things Move!* by Keith Peters.

We do not assume any previous knowledge of physics, and only assume basic school level math knowledge. One chapter is dedicated to explaining some of the more difficult math concepts and tools that you are likely to need in the book. All the physics concepts and knowledge you will need are explained in a self-contained way. Numerous applications are given throughout the book with full source code to illustrate the application of the principles learnt.

Overview of this book

This book is divided into four parts.

Part I: "The Basics" (Chapters 1-4) introduces the necessary background in basic math and physics concepts upon which the rest of the book builds. For completeness, it also covers selected topics in ActionScript 3.0 that are most pertinent to physics programming.

Part II: "Particles, Forces, and Motion" (Chapters 5-10) begins by formulating the laws of physics that govern the motion of particles under any type of force (Chapter 5). The next chapters then apply those laws to make objects move under the action of a large variety of forces including gravity, friction, drag, buoyancy, wind, springs, central forces, and many more. The main focus in this section is on simulating the motion of individual particles and other simple objects.

In Part III: "Multi-Particle and Extended Systems" (Chapters 11-13), we show you how to model more complicated systems, including multiple interacting particles and extended objects. In these systems the constituent particles and objects do not simply co-exist but interact with each other, mutually influencing their motion. These interactions include collisions, short-range forces, and long-range forces. This part includes a discussion of particle systems, rigid bodies, and deformable bodies.

Part IV: "Building More Complex Simulations" (Chapters 14-16) is devoted to building more complex simulations, where accuracy and/or realism is especially important, not just visual effects. This part includes a discussion of numerical integration schemes and other numerical and technical issues such as scale modeling and 3D. Part IV ends with a chapter including some example simulation projects.

Source code and examples

All the code for this book can be downloaded from the book's page on the Apress website: www.apress.com.

Source code in the book will work with Adobe Flash (version CS3 onwards; a few examples require CS4) and Adobe Flex/Flash Builder (version 3 onwards). All the code is pure ActionScript. We do not use MXML or the Flex framework.

We encourage you to modify and build upon the example codes given. While doing the technical review of this book, RJ Owen suggested it would be interesting to have a website where readers could share their codes to see what people can build with the tools given in this book. We thought it was an excellent suggestion, and have therefore set up the following page on our website where you can find and contribute more code and examples: www.physicscodes.com/as3book.

Part I

The Basics

Chapter 1

Introduction to Physics Programming

Because you picked up this book, we assume that you are interested in implementing physics into your programming projects. But why would you want to do that? What can it do for you? And how difficult will it be? This chapter will provide answers to these questions.

Topics covered in this chapter include:

- **Why model physics?** This section will explain some of the reasons why you might want to add physics to your projects.

- **What is physics?** Here we lift the veil of mystery and explain in simple terms what physics is. We also tell you, in a nutshell, what you'll need to know.

- **Programming physics.** Thankfully, programming physics is not as difficult as you might imagine, once you understand some basic principles. This section explains what you'll need to do.

- **A simple example.** As a concrete example, we'll code up a simple animation involving physics, using a minimum of code.

Why model real physics?

There are a number of reasons why you might be interested in modeling physics using Flash. Here are some of the most common reasons.

Creating realistic animation effects

One of the main strengths of working with Flash is the ability to create animations easily. With a little ActionScript and some physics, it is also possible to make animations that look and behave like the real thing. For example, suppose you are animating a scene in which someone kicks a ball and it bounces off the ground. If you're working with Adobe Flash, you could try and fake the animation with tweens, but however hard you might try it would probably look less than realistic. With just a little bit of coding and some knowledge of simple physics you could produce a far more realistic animation. And if, like the authors, you are programmers rather than designers, you might even find it easier! We'll show you just how easy it can be in the example at the end of this chapter.

Creating realistic games

Flash games are ever so popular on the Web. As the capabilities of the Flash Player continue to improve, better and more powerful games can be built. Hardware acceleration and native 3D support are just two of the recent developments that have the potential to improve the gaming user experience dramatically. But apart from performance and appearance, it is equally important for games to feel realistic. If you are throwing a ball, it has to fall according to the law of gravity; if you fire a torpedo underwater, it must move differently from a ball falling in air. In other words, your game needs to know physics.

How do you build physics awareness into your games? This book will show you how.

Building simulations and models

A *computer simulation* or *computer model* is a program that attempts to imitate certain key aspects of a system. Simulations vary in completeness or accuracy, depending on purpose and resources. Let's take a flight simulator program as an example. One would expect a flight simulator designed for training pilots to be much more comprehensive and accurate than one designed for a game. Simulations are extremely common in e-learning, training and in scientific research. In the final chapter of this book, you'll build simulations, including a submarine, a basic flight simulator, and a model of the solar system. In fact, many of the coded examples throughout the book are simulations, even if generally simpler.

Generating art from code

Generative art has gained popularity in recent years. ActionScript and Processing are popular tools used by artists to generate art from code. A lot of fun can be had with some simple physics—for example, elaborate effects and motions can be produced using particles and different kinds of forces.

We will explore the world of generative art and provide additional tools and algorithms that can be used to create original and interesting effects.

Can't I just use a physics engine?

You probably can. Physics engines are certainly useful for a lot of situations. But they may not necessarily be the panacea for all your problems. Here are a few reasons why the time you invest in learning how to program physics can pay off:

- You'll have more flexibility to do what you want. Physics engines cannot do everything.

- In some cases, it may be simpler to write code from scratch rather than to use a physics engine.

- Knowing how to use a physics engine doesn't guarantee that you'll know what physics to use for a particular application.

- Sometimes things may not work quite as they should with a physics engine. For example, problems may arise due to numerical instability or inaccuracy in some situations.

- You'll be able to build your own physics engine, matched to your own needs.

- It's fun!

The bottom line, though, is that it should not be an either/or lifetime decision whether to choose between a physics engine and coding your own physics. Experiment with both, and you'll become better at both: being able to code up your own physics will give you a deeper understanding of how physics engines work and how to use them more effectively; conversely, experimenting with physics engines should give you plenty of ideas that you can implement into your own coding.

There are now a number of Flash physics engines out there. Here is a brief list of some of them:

- **Box2DFlash**: Also known as Box2DAS3, this is an ActionScript 3.0 (AS3.0) port of Box2D, an open source 2D physics engine written by Erin Catto in C++. Box2DFlash is primarily a rigid body library, but with a host of other features. It is a popular choice among Flash game developers. Because Box2DFlash closely resembles Box2D, users can get help from the Box2D forums.

- **FOAM**: Another 2D rigid body physics engine. In the words of its creator, FOAM trades efficiency for modularity and extensibility, allowing a savvy developer to extend and repurpose FOAM to his own ends. FOAM is released under the MIT license.

- **Fisix**: The Fisix engine is an AS3.0 verlet-based physics engine aimed for use in games and relatively CPU-intensive applications. The website pledges to give good documentation and help, and states that the engine is currently free for both commercial and noncommercial applications until the next release.

- **APE**: APE stands for *Actionscript Physics Engine*, another AS3.0 open source 2D physics engine written by Alec Cove and released under the MIT license.

- **WOW-Engine**: This is an AS3.0 open source 3D physics engine written by Jerome Birembaut. It uses the Sandy library for all its 3D math computations and handles collisions and physics by extending APE, the 2D physics engine created by Alec Cove (see the previous bullet).

- **JiglibFlash**: This is another AS3.0 open source 3D physics engine, ported from the C++ physics engine Jiglib. The engine has support for Away3D, Papervision3D and Sandy3D. Documentation appears sparse, but it seems to have an active forum.

> *A disclaimer: The selection and ordering of the list are essentially random and do not constitute a recommendation to use any of them in preference to any other.*

What is physics?

Physics is the most fundamental of the sciences. In a broad sense, physics is the study of the natural laws that govern how things behave. More specifically, it concerns itself with space, time and matter (defined as any "stuff" that exists in space and time). One aspect of physics is to formulate general laws that govern the behavior of matter, its interactions, and its motion in space and time. Another aspect is to use these laws to make predictions of the way specific things move and interact—for example, the prediction of eclipses from the laws of gravity or how airplanes are able to fly from the laws of aerodynamics.

Physics is a vast subject, and in a book of this nature we cannot do more than scratch the surface. Fortunately, most of the physics that you will probably need to know fall within a branch known as *Mechanics*, which is one of the easiest to understand.

Everything behaves according to the laws of physics

Without getting too philosophical, it is fair to say that the laws of physics are truly universal, as far as physicists have been able to observe. What this means is that everything *must* behave according to physics. This is different from say, the laws of biology, which pertain only to living things. A stone thrown in the air, a planet orbiting the Sun, the workings of the human body, and the operation and motion of a man-made machine must all obey the laws of physics. Moreover, many seemingly diverse phenomena are governed by the same subset of laws. For example, a falling stone and a planet orbiting the Sun both obey the laws of gravity.

The laws can be written as math equations

The great thing is that the laws of physics can be written as mathematical equations. Okay, that may not sound too great if you don't like math! But the point here is that for a law to be useful, it has to be made precise. And math equations are as precise as anything can be. There is no possible ambiguity in how to apply a law that is expressed mathematically, in contrast with the laws that are fought over in courtrooms! Second, this means that centuries of developments in mathematics prove to be applicable to physics, making it possible to solve many physics problems. Third, and what is of most relevance for us: math equations are readily convertible into code.

Predicting motion

Let's get more specific. As an ActionScript programmer, you are mostly interested in how things move. Much of physics deals with how things move under the action of different types of influences. These "influences" can be from other things and from the environment. In physics we have a special name for these influences: they are called *forces*. The really good news is that the forces have simple mathematical forms. Although the motion of objects is usually complicated, the underlying mathematical laws that describe the forces are usually quite simple.

The general relationship between force and motion can be written schematically as follows:

motion = function{**forces**}

This is a cause-and-effect relationship. Forces cause objects to move in different ways. In practical terms, it means this: specify the forces acting on an object and put them in a mathematical equation, and then you can calculate the motion of the object. Simple isn't it?

> *Motion is effect. Force is cause. The motion of an object is the result of the forces acting on it. The mathematical relationship between force and motion is known as the "Law of Motion."*

Now to be able to put this principle to use, we need to know the following:

- **Definitions**. The precise definitions of *motion* and *force*.

- **The law of motion**. In other words, the precise mathematical form of the function that relates a force to the motion it produces.

- **Force laws**. In other words, how to calculate the forces. There are equations that tell you how to calculate each type of force.

So there are two kinds of laws you need to know about: laws of motion and force laws. You will also need to know the proper concepts (known as *physical quantities*) to describe and analyze motion and forces and the relationship between them. Finally, you will need to know the mathematics for manipulating and combining these quantities.

Programming physics

So, how do you code up physics? Do you program the motion or forces, or both? And what does it involve?

Once you know some basic physics (and some simple math), coding it is not much different or more difficult than what you are used to as a programmer—provided you do it in the right way. Let us take some time to explain what this "right way" is.

The difference between animation and simulation

Some wise guy once said "A picture is worth a thousand words" or something like that. One could extend this by saying "A movie is worth a thousand pictures". A movie (or *animation*) adds so much more to our perception than a static image because it includes the element of change in time, an extra dimension. But there is a sense in which an animation is still static rather than dynamic. No matter how many times you play it, it has the same beginning and the same end. Everything happens in exactly the same way. In terms of capturing the real world, while things become more realistic in progressing from written words to visual images to animated movies, there is still something missing: the power to interact with the medium and to influence the outcome in a way that duplicates the behavior of things in real life. This next step is what we call *simulation*. In the sense we use the word in this book, simulation entails realism and also interactivity. When you simulate something, you don't just depict how it behaves under one set of conditions; you allow for many, even infinitely many, conditions. Building interactive simulations including physics makes things behave like they do in the real world: interacting with the environment and with the user to produce diverse and complex outcomes.

There is more. If you really pay attention to accuracy, you can even build a simulation that is so realistic it can be used as a virtual lab. You'll be able to experiment with it to learn how things actually work out there in the real world, on your computer! In fact, you will build such simulations in this book.

The laws of physics are simple

We have already said that the laws of physics are mathematical equations. The good news is that most of the laws (and hence the equations) you'll come across are actually quite simple. The apparently bad news is that these simple laws can produce very complex motions. In fact, that is probably a good thing, too; otherwise the Universe would have been a rather boring place.

For example, the laws that govern gravity can be written down as just two simple-looking equations (they are given in Chapter 6). But they are responsible for the motion of the Moon around the Earth, the motion of planets around the Sun, and the motion of stars in the Galaxy. The net effect of all these motions, plus the gravitational interactions between different celestial bodies, create very complicated motions that arise from just two simple equations.

Hence, they can be readily coded up!

We are now in a position to answer the questions asked at the beginning of this section. Here is a no-brainer. The laws of motion and forces are simple; the actual motions they produce are complex. If you know the laws, you can calculate the motions under different conditions. Would you rather code up the forces or the motions they produce?

Okay, let's spell it out. Animation attempts to reproduce the motion of an object directly. Simulation is to program the laws of motion and then to *derive* the motion of the object. It is much easier to code up the cause of motion than its effect. Moreover, an animation generally depicts a single scenario. But a simulation can potentially handle an infinite number of different scenarios.

> *Simple laws of motion and simple force laws can give rise to complex motions. It is generally easier to code up the laws rather than the motions themselves. Hence, paradoxically, simulation can be easier than animation.*

Simulation is like playing God. You re-create a virtual world, not by blindly duplicating all the behavior you see, but by reproducing the laws that govern the way things behave and then letting it all happen.

The four steps for programming physics

The process of programming physics can be broken down into four steps, as shown schematically in Figure 1-1.

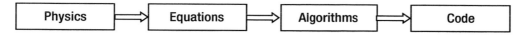

Figure 1-1. Steps in programming physics

The first step is to identify the physics principles that apply to the situation you are modeling. This can be tricky if you have no physics background. This book will help you: it is not just a how-to book but is also intended to actually teach you some physics. The second step is to recall, research, or derive the relevant equations. Obviously, this step involves some math. Don't worry; we'll give you all the help you need! The third step is to develop *algorithms* to solve the equations. Sometimes the equations can be solved *analytically* (we'll explain what that means in later chapters), in which case the algorithms are pretty simple. More often, one needs to employ *numerical methods*, which can be simple or less so, depending on the problem and on the desired level of accuracy. Although the first two steps may seem obvious, the third step is often overlooked. Indeed, many developers may even be unaware of its existence or necessity. Again, we'll spend some time on this aspect, especially in Part IV of the book. The fourth and last step is to write the code in your favorite programming language. You are already good at this, aren't you?

A simple example

To see how all this works in practice, we will now look at a simple example. We'll set ourselves the task of simulating the motion of a ball thrown to the ground, using just a few lines of code.

To start with, let's try and picture the scenario that we are trying to model, the way it behaves in reality. Suppose you throw a volleyball in the air. How does it move? You've probably noticed that such a ball does not move in a straight line, but traces out a curved path. Moreover, the ball appears to move slowly at the top of the curve and quickly at the bottom, near the ground. When it hits the ground it usually bounces, but always reaches a lesser height than that from which it fell. Before we try to reproduce this motion, let us look more closely at the physics that is causing it.

A bouncing ball: the physics

As you already know by now, forces are what cause things to move. So the first clue to understanding why the volleyball moves the way it does is to find out what forces are acting on it. As you'll learn later, there are generally many forces acting together on objects in everyday situations. But in this case there is one force that is much more important than any other. It's the force of gravity that the Earth exerts on the ball.

So let us assume that gravity is the only force acting on the ball once it has been thrown in the air. Thankfully, gravity acts in a very simple way. Close to the Earth's surface, as in the present example, it is a constant force that points vertically downward. Its effect is therefore to pull objects downward, making them *accelerate* as they do so. Accelerate? Yes, that means it increases the speed of the object. As we'll discuss in much greater detail in later chapters, gravity increases the vertical speed of an object by a constant amount in each second. But because gravity acts downward, it does not affect the horizontal speed of an object.

Every time the ball hits the ground, the latter exerts a *contact force* on it. This force acts upward for a very brief time. Unlike gravity, it is not easy to model this contact force directly. Therefore, we'll simplify things and model its effect instead. Its effect is to reverse the motion of the ball from downward to upward while reducing the speed of the ball.

Coding up a bouncing ball in 2D

To simplify things, we'll pretend we're living in a 2D world. An object in 2D can move along two independent directions: horizontal and vertical. We'll denote the position of the ball at any given time by two numbers, x and y, where x refers to the horizontal position, and y refers to the vertical position. We'll denote the speed at which the ball is moving along these two directions as **vx** and **vy**.

According to what we said, each time the clock ticks, gravity will cause **vy** to increase by a constant amount, but **vx** will remain the same.

Because **vx** and **vy** are speeds, they tell us how much the object moves each time the clock ticks. In other words, at each tick of the clock, x increases by an amount **vx**, and y increases by an amount **vy**.

This takes care of the effect of gravity. To implement the effect of the ground, what we have to do is reverse the sign of **vy** and reduce its magnitude each time the ball hits the ground. And, believe it or not, that's pretty much it.

Some code at last!

The code for Figure 1-2 is included in the `BouncingBall.as` file. Note that the frame rate in the source files has been set to 30 fps to produce a smooth animation. Here is the code that does it all.

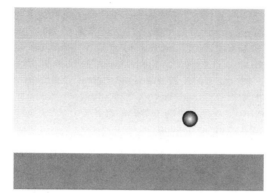

Figure 1-2. How to code up a bouncing ball

```
package{
        import flash.display.Sprite;
        import flash.events.Event;

        public class BouncingBall extends Sprite {

                private var g:Number = 0.1; // acceleration due to gravity
                private var vx:Number = 2;  // initial horizontal speed
                private var vy:Number = 0;  // initial vertical speed
                private var ball:Ball;

                public function BouncingBall() {
                        init();
                }
                private function init():void {
                        ball = new Ball();.
                        ball.x = 50;.
                        ball.y = 75;.
                        addChild(ball);
                        addEventListener(Event.ENTER_FRAME,onEachTimestep);
                }

                private function onEachTimestep(evt:Event):void{

                        vy += g  // gravity increases the vertical speed

                        ball.x += vx; // horizontal speed increases horizontal position
                        ball.y += vy; // vertical speed increases vertical position

                        if (ball.y > 350){  // if ball hits the ground
                                vy *= -0.8;  // its vertical velocity reverses and reduces
                        }

                }
        }
}
```

If you are not entirely comfortable with AS3.0 classes, don't panic. We'll explain all the elements of the code fully in the next chapter. The important bits that contain the physics are the lines with the comments next to them. The variable g is the acceleration due to gravity. Here we've set a value that will give an animation that looks visually correct. The next two lines set the initial horizontal and vertical speeds of the ball. All the physics action is taking place in the aptly named function onEachTimestep(), which is executed at the frame rate set for the movie. Here we increase vy but not vx because gravity only acts vertically. Then we update the ball's position by increasing x and y by amounts vx and vy, respectively. The final piece of code takes care of the bouncing.

Run the code and see the result. It looks pretty realistic, doesn't it? How does the ball know how to behave with so few instructions? This is like magic. We challenge you to create the same effect using tweens!

Is it really that simple? Wait! We've barely scratched the surface of what's possible. This is a good start (give yourself a pat on the back). There are plenty of ways to improve the simulation to make it even more realistic, but they require more physics and more coding. For example, you could add friction so that the ball's horizontal speed reduces as it touches the ground. Suppose you are building a game that includes balls moving around. You might want the ball to feel the effect of air resistance and to be blown by wind in addition to moving under the effect of gravity. You might want it to behave properly if thrown into water, sinking and then rising, and oscillating on the water surface before coming to rest and floating. There might be lots of balls colliding. Or you might want to create an accurate simulation that school students can use to learn about gravity. In that case, you would need to pay careful attention to implement proper boundary effects as well as accurate and stable time-stepping algorithms. By the time you finish the book, you will be able to do all these and more. And you'll know what you are doing. We promise.

Summary

Physics encapsulates the laws of nature in mathematical form. These laws are simple and can be readily coded up. Hence, it is generally easy to create effects that look realistic.

Programming physics involves four steps: identifying what physics principles you need, writing down the relevant equations, devising a numerical algorithm for solving the equations, and writing the code. So it involves knowledge and skills in four different areas: physics, math, numerical methods, and programming. This book gives you help in the first three areas; you are assumed to have some proficiency in the fourth: general programming in ActionScript.

Having said this, the next chapter will provide a rapid overview/review of selected topics in ActionScript 3.0, emphasizing aspects that are especially relevant for physics programming.

Chapter 2

Selected ActionScript 3.0 Topics

ActionScript 3.0 is very different from the previous versions of the language. This chapter will give a brief review of the elements of AS3.0 that we will make most use of in the rest of this book. It is not meant to be a comprehensive tutorial on ActionScript; instead, it is a summary of what you need to know to understand the code examples in the book. The other aim of this chapter is to cover relevant aspects of Flash and ActionScript that will set the context for applying physics.

This chapter was written with the assumption that the reader would have at least a basic knowledge of Flash and ActionScript. If you are an experienced AS3.0 programmer, you could safely skip most of this chapter, perhaps skimming over some of the material at the end on ActionScripted animation and collision detection. On the other hand, if you haven't done any programming with ActionScript before, we suggest you pick up one of the books mentioned in the summary at the end. If you have programmed in an earlier version of ActionScript, or maybe need a refresher of AS3.0, you will benefit from going through the chapter in some detail. While the overview on its own won't make you a proficient AS3.0 programmer, it should enable you to use and build upon the code examples in the book without much difficulty.

Topics covered in this chapter include the following:

- **ActionScript 3.0 classes**: Classes and objects are the basic building blocks of object-oriented programming (OOP). "Things" in the real world are represented as objects in ActionScript. Objects have properties. They can also do things by using methods.

- **ActionScript 3.0 language basics**: For completeness, the basic constructs of AS3.0 and their syntax are reviewed, such as variables, data types, arrays, operators, functions, math, logic, and loops.

- **Events in ActionScript 3.0**: The event framework in AS3.0 is very different from what it was in previous ActionScript versions. We briefly review some basic concepts and syntax, giving examples of how to make things happen in response to changes in the program or user interaction.

- **The Flash coordinate system**: This is the equivalent of space in the Flash world. Objects can be positioned on the stage in 2D and 3D using code. We review the differences between the Flash coordinate system and the usual Cartesian coordinate system in math.

- **The Flash drawing API**: The ability to draw things using only code is a powerful tool, especially when combined with math and physics. Some of the most common methods of the AS3.0 drawing API, which will be used throughout the book, are briefly reviewed here.

- **Producing animation using ActionScript**: We review different methods of producing animation using code, and explain the main method we'll use for physics-based animation in the rest of the book.

- **Collision detection**: In any game or other project involving motion, things are inevitably going to bump into each other. Collision detection algorithms tell you when this has happened so that you can program the appropriate response.

ActionScript 3.0 classes

If you've programmed using an earlier version of ActionScript before version 3.0, chances are you haven't worried too much about classes. However, in AS3.0 it is impossible to ignore classes, because they are built into the very structure of the language. So what is a class?

A *class* is a fundamental construct of *object-oriented programming (OOP)*. It is an abstract specification of an object that you want to create. An *object* is anything that exists in your movie at runtime.

Now that sounds pretty abstract, so let's look at an example. Suppose you want to create particles in a project, and the particles will be the objects. How will Flash know how to make particles? Well, you'll first have to tell it what a particle consists of, how it should look, what it can do, and so on. This is done by creating a class for the particle object called Particle, for example (by convention, class names start with an uppercase letter). Then each time you want a particle, you invoke the Particle class. The following sections describe how to produce an object from a class, create a class, and understand what it consists of.

Classes and objects

Let's take another look at the BouncingBall class from the last chapter. The function init() contains an example of how to produce an object from a class:

```
private function init():void {
        ball = new Ball();.
        ball.x = 50;.
        ball.y = 75;.
```

```
        addChild(ball);
        addEventListener(Event.ENTER_FRAME,onEachTimestep);
}
```

The `ball` object is an *instance* of the `Ball` class, and is created (or *instantiated*) by this code:

```
ball = new Ball();.
```

The ball is subsequently made visible (technically added to the *Display List*) by the `addChild` command:

```
addChild(ball);
```

Note that the Flash movie is made from a class. (See the listing in Chapter 1 for an example.) In Flash CS3 to CS5, this is called the *document class*. In Flex Builder 3 and Flash Builder 4 (used for a pure ActionScript project), it is generally called the *main application class* or something similar.

Structure of an AS3.0 class

Okay, you now know how to produce an object from a class, but what does a class actually look like in AS3.0? Here is a simple example of a perfectly valid class that does nothing:

```
package{
        public class DoNothing {

                public function DoNothing() {

                }

        }
}
```

Note that the class specification is enclosed within a `package{}` statement. A *package* is a bit like a folder; it is used to organize related classes. The default package has no name, as in this example. But you could give it any name you want, for example `package mypackage{}`.

The class is then declared using `public class DoNothing{}`, where *DoNothing* is the name of the class in this example.

This class ships with a *function* (more precisely a *method*) with the same name as that of the class: the DoNothing() function. This function is called the *constructor* of the class.

The keyword `public` sets the scope of a class, function, or property (we'll introduce properties shortly). This means that the class `DoNothing` and function `DoNothing` can be accessed from outside the class. It is also possible for a class to have *private* functions, which can be accessed only from within the class; or *protected* functions, which can also be accessed by its subclasses (see the following section on inheritance). We'll show examples of private and protected functions soon.

The next few sections explain some of these concepts in a bit more detail.

Functions, methods and constructors

As you've just seen in the last subsection, an example of a function is the constructor of a class. The code within the constructor is automatically executed whenever the class is instantiated as an object using the new keyword.

In the `BouncingBall` example, the function `init()` is called from within the constructor. Note that `init()` has private scope, so it is accessible (and therefore callable) only within the class `BouncingBall`. Why do we need a separate function `init()` in this example? Couldn't the code in `init()` be placed directly inside the constructor? The answer is that code placed in the constructor is interpreted, whereas code placed anywhere else is compiled—and so runs faster.

Notice the use of the function *type* `void` (this was `Void`, with a capital *V* in AS2.0). This means that this function does not return any value. It is possible for functions to return different kinds of things; for example, this function returns a random number between 0 and 100:

```
private function randomNumber():Number {
        return(Math.random()*100);
}
```

As in AS2.0, functions (and, therefore, methods and constructors) can have arguments or parameters (values that we can feed into them). For example, this function adds two numbers supplied as arguments and returns the value as another number:

```
private function addNumbers(x:Number,y:Number):Number {
        return(x+y);
}
```

Similarly, as in AS2.0, public methods of a class can be accessed using dot notation. For example, suppose a `Car` class has a public function `move()`. If `car` is an instance of `Car`, `car.move()` will invoke the `move()` function.

Properties

The splendid example of a class that we gave earlier is not very useful as it stands. Let us make it useful by making it do something, such as adding two numbers, for example.

This is how we might do it:

```
package{
        public class DoSomething {

                        private var x:Number = 2;
                        private var y:Number = 3;
```

```
public function DoSomething() {
        var z:Number;
        z = x + y;
        trace(z);  // write to output console
}

    }
}
```

There is a lot happening here. First, we created *properties* x, y, and z. In AS3.0, properties need to be *defined* or *declared* first. This is done using the var keyword.

Note that we declare the properties x and y as private. This means that they are accessible within the class but not outside of it. "Within the class" means that any function in the class can access them.

Did you notice a difference in the way z is declared? There is no private keyword. That's because it is declared within a function—in that case, it is accessible only within that function. So it cannot be declared as private because private properties are accessible from anywhere within the class.

How do you know whether to declare your properties and functions as private or public? The simple rule is to keep them private unless you really have to make them accessible from outside the class. This stops any outside code from potentially messing with your code.

Just as functions, public properties in AS3.0 can be accessed using dot notation. For example, ball.x gives the horizontal position of the ball object because x is a built-in public property of display objects such as MovieClips and Sprites (note that in AS2.0, this was denoted _x, with a leading underscore).

Static methods and properties

The methods and properties we've looked at pertain to objects, but it also is possible to have methods and properties for classes. This means that the class does not have to be instantiated to invoke the property or method.

An example is Math.random(), which is a class method from the Math class that generates a random number.

We use the static keyword to declare class level properties and methods. Static properties and methods are called using the class name, not an instance name. For example, suppose you have the following static method in a class called Physics:

```
static public function calcGravity(mass:Number,g:Number):Number {
        return(mass*g);
}
```

Physics.calcGravity(4, 9.8) would then give you the gravity force on a 4kg object on planet Earth.

Inheritance

An important concept in OOP is that of inheritance, which allows you to build new classes from existing classes. The new class is called a *subclass*, and the old class is called a *superclass*. This is done using the extends keyword.

For example, to create a subclass called Electron from a Particle class we'd do this:

```
package{
        public class Electron extends Particle {

                public function Electron() {
                        // Electron code goes here.
                }
        }
}
```

The subclass Electron has access to all the non-private properties and methods of the Particle superclass, as well as those of its own. To invoke the superclass constructor, one simply calls super().

Note that the BouncingBall class extends the Sprite class. Every document class must extend either Sprite or MovieClip. To do so, one must first use an import statement to import the class or package, as done in BouncingBall.as.

ActionScript 3.0 language basics

Classes are clever concepts but, as the last section showed, they are pretty useless by themselves. In this section, we'll review the code elements that do all the groundwork. Special emphasis is placed on their relevance to math and physics.

Variables and constants

Remember the var keyword that we used to declare properties? The keyword var stands for *variable*. A variable is a container that holds some value. Here value might mean different things. For example, the following variable x is defined to hold values that are numbers (we are omitting private keywords):

```
var x:Number;
```

Subsequently, x may only be *assigned* values that are numbers. For example:

```
x = 2;
```

This assignment can be done together with the following variable declaration or anywhere else in the code:

```
var x:Number = 2;
```

One can also perform arithmetic on x; for example, the following code multiplies x by a number, adds the result to another variable y, and assigns the result to a third variable z:

```
z = 2*x + y;
```

This resembles algebra, with some notable differences. The first difference is purely a matter of syntax: We use the operator * to multiply 2 and x. More about operators soon.

The second difference is more subtle and relates to the meaning of an assignment. Although the preceding code may look superficially like an algebraic equation, it is important to note that an assignment is not an equation. The difference can be highlighted by considering an assignment like this one:

```
x = x + 1;
```

If this were an algebraic equation, it would imply that 0 = 1—an impossibility! Here, what it means is that we increase the value of x (whatever it is) by 1.

The word *variable* entails that we can change the value stored in a variable any time. If we want the value of a variable to be fixed, it might be a good idea to define it as a constant instead:

```
const gravity:Number = 1;
```

The value of a constant can be assigned only when it is defined. This is because declaring a `const` effectively prevents any subsequent assignment to be made in the rest of the code. There is no absolute need to use constants, but it may be a good idea to protect values that should not really be changed.

Variables in ActionScript can have values other than numeric values. The type of value that a variable can hold is called its *data type*.

Data types

There are a number of different data types in AS3.0, and they may broadly be classified as *primitive* and *complex*. Primitive data types are the most basic types in AS3.0. ActionScript stores them in a manner that makes them especially memory- and speed-efficient. Complex data types, on the other hand, are made up of or reference primitives. They are more resource-intensive, but provide a lot of flexibility for programmers. Tables 2-1 and 2-2 list some of the more common data types in each category.

Table 2-1. Primitive Data Types

Data Type	Description
Boolean	Has two possible values: true and false, or 1 and 0
int	32-bit integer
Number	64-bit double-precision floating-point number

Data Type	Description
String	A sequence of 16-bit characters
uint	32-bit unsigned integer

Table 2-1 continued.

Table 2-2. Complex Data Types

Data Type	Description
Object	Defined by the Object class, which is the base class for all class definitions
Array	Holds a list of data of any type
Vector	Variant of Array that holds data of the same type
Sprite	A display object without a timeline
MovieClip	An animated movie clip display object
Bitmap	A non-animated bitmap display object
Shape	A nonanimated vector shape object
ByteArray	An array of binary data
TextField	A text field object

The Number, int, and uint primitive data types will be described in the subsection that follows, but let's say a few words about the remaining two primitive data types listed in Table 2-1: String and Boolean.

A String is group of characters. For example, the following

```
var str:String = "Hello there!";
trace(str);
```

would give this output: Hello there!

Note that the value of a String must be enclosed within quotes (single or double).

A Boolean can have only one of two values: true or false. For example:

```
var bln:Boolean = false;
```

Note that the value true or false is not enclosed within quotes; it is not a string.

Among the complex data types, objects and arrays are particularly useful in terms of programming. The Array data type is described in a separate section that follows. The Object data type is defined by the Object class, which serves as the base class for all classes in ActionScript. The Object class by itself does not do much, but it is powerful because it is *dynamic*: it can be extended at runtime with new properties and methods. Objects can also be used as associative arrays, which are arrays that store values using strings as keys (normal arrays store values using numeric indices —see the "Arrays" section that follows).

Because we'll be using numeric data types and arrays an awful lot, let's discuss them in a bit more detail.

Numeric data types

Numeric data types include `Number`, as discussed previously in the section "Variables and constants," `int`, and `uint`.

The `Number` type is a double-precision 64-bit floating-point number according to the IEEE 754 specification. It is able to store both positive and negative real numbers (i.e. not only whole numbers, but those with fractional parts, too). The maximum value that `Number` can store is 1.8×10^{308}. Given that the number of atoms in the visible universe is estimated to be "only" 10^{80}, this should be enough even for the biggest scientific calculations!

The `Number` class also includes the following special values: `NaN` (not a number), `POSITIVE_INFINITY`, and `NEGATIVE_INFINITY`.

`NaN` signifies that a numeric value has not been assigned. You'd get `NaN` if you look at the value of a `Number` variable that has not been given a value. You'd also get `NaN` as a result of a mathematical operation that produces non-real or undefined results (for example, by taking the square root of −1 or dividing 0 by 0).

Infinity is the result of dividing a non-zero number by 0. You will get positive or negative infinity depending on the sign of the number you are dividing by zero.

The `int` type is a signed 32-bit integer. This means it can represent both positive and negative integers (including zero) between −2,147,483,648 and 2,147,483,647.

The `uint` type is similar to `int` except that it can only be positive or 0. Its range of values is from 0 to 4,294,967,295. It is most often used for counting, as you might imagine.

Arrays

An array is an object that holds a collection of items. Suppose you have to keep track of a number of particles in your movie. You could do that by naming them individually as particle1, particle2, particle3, and so on. That might work fine if you have a few particles, but what if you have 100 or 10,000? That's where an array comes in handy. You can just define an array called `particles`, for example, and put all the particles in there.

A simple way to create an array is by specifying the array elements as a comma-separated list enclosed by square brackets:

```
var arr:Array = new Array();
arr = [2, 4, 6];
trace(arr[1]); // gives 4
```

As the preceding code snippet shows, the resulting array elements are then accessed by `arr[n]`, where n is an unsigned integer called the *array index*. Note that the array index starts from 0, so that the first array element is `arr[0]`.

There are several other ways of creating arrays. There are also lots of rules to do with the manipulation of arrays and array elements. We'll come across examples of those soon.

It is also possible to create multidimensional arrays. This is done by creating arrays whose elements are also arrays. The following example creates a two-dimensional array from two one-dimensional arrays:

```
var xArr:Array = new Array();
var yArr:Array = new Array();
xArr = [1,2];
yArr = [3,4];
var zArr:Array = new Array(xArr,yArr);
trace(zArr[0][1]); // gives 2
trace(zArr[1][0]); // gives 3
```

Note that we've created the third array in a different way, by passing the array elements directly to the constructor of `Array()`.

It is possible to add different types of objects into the same array. That's because arrays in ActionScript are not typed, unlike in some other languages like C++ and Java. The **Vector** data type (available in Flash Player 10 or above) is a variant of **Array** that *is* typed. Vectors generally perform faster than arrays.

Operators

You can perform basic arithmetic with numbers with the usual operators (+, -, * and /, respectively) for adding, subtracting, multiplying, and dividing numbers.

There are also a number of other, less obvious operators. The modulo operator % gives the remainder when a number is divided by another. The increment operator (++) increases the value of a number by 1, and the decrement operator (--) reduces the value of a number by 1.

```
var x:int = 5;
var y:int = 3;

trace(x%y); // gives 2

var z:int;
z = x++; // assigns the value of x to z, then increments x
trace(z); // gives 5
z = ++x // increments the value of x, then assigns it to z
trace(z); //gives 7
```

Operators can also be combined with assignment. For example:

```
var a:int = 1;

a = a + 1;
trace(a); // gives 2
```

```
a += 1; // shortened form of a = a + 1
trace(a); // gives 3
a = 4*a;
trace(a); // gives 12
a *= 4; // shortened form of a = a*4
trace(a); // gives 48
```

Math

Besides the basic operators described in the last section, the Math class contains many more mathematical functions.

Table 2-3 gives some common examples of Math functions and what they do. In the next chapter you will encounter many more Math methods, such as trigonometric, exponential, and logarithmic functions.

Table 2-3. Math Methods

Method	What it returns
Math.abs(a:Number)	absolute value of a
Math.pow(a:Number,b:Number)	a to the power of b
Math.sqrt(a:Number)	square root of a
Math.ceil(a:Number)	smallest integer that is larger than a
Math.floor(a:Number)	largest integer that is smaller than a
Math.round(a:Number)	nearest integer to a
Math.max(a:Number,b:Number,c:Number,…)	largest of a, b, c, …
Math.min(a:Number,b:Number,c:Number,…)	smallest of a, b, c, …
Math.random()	a pseudo-random number n, where $0 <= n < 1$

The last method, Math.random(), is an interesting one. It generates a random number between 0 and 1, including 0 but excluding 1. Strictly speaking, it is pseudo-random because it follows an algorithm. But it is good enough for most purposes you're likely to use it for.

Here is an example of how to use the Math.random() method. In BouncingBallsRandom.as, we have made a simple modification so that each time the swf runs, the ball has a different initial velocity. We do this by the following two lines in init():

```
vx = Math.random()*5;
vy = (Math.random()-0.5)*4;
```

The first line sets the initial horizontal speed to be between 0 and 5. The second line sets the vertical speed to be between –2 and 2. What does a *negative vertical speed* mean? It means a speed in the direction opposite to the direction of increasing y. Because in the Flash coordinate system y increases as we go down (as we'll see later in this chapter), negative vertical speed means that the object moves upward. So each time you start the swf you'll see the ball initially move up or down with a different horizontal and vertical speed.

Logic

In any programming language, logic is an essential part of coding. Logic enables code to take different actions based on the outcome of some expression.

The simplest way to implement logic in ActionScript is through a basic *if statement*, which has the following structure:

```
if (logical expression){
        do this code
}
```

An `if` statement basically checks if a logical expression is true.

For example, in the `BouncingBall.as` code, there is the following logic:

```
if (ball.y > 350){
        vy *= -0.8;
}
```

This tests whether the ball's vertical position is greater than 350 pixels and, if so, multiplies its vertical speed by –0.8. In this example, the logical expression to be tested is `ball.y > 350`, and `>` is a *logical operator* that means "greater than."

Other commonly used logical operators include `<` (less than), `==` (equal to), `<=` (less than or equal to), `>=` (greater than or equal to), and `!=` (not equal to). There is also a strict equality operator `===`, which differs from the equality operator `==` in that it takes the data type into account when comparing two variables.

Care must be taken not to confuse the equality operator `==` with the assignment operator `=`. This is a common source of mistake and consequent debugging frustration!

There are also `&&` (AND) and `||` (OR) operators that enable you to combine conditions:

```
if (a < 10 || b < 20){
        c = a+b;

}
```

There are more elaborate forms of the `if` statement. The *if else* statement is of this form:

```
if (logical expression){
        do this if expression is true
} else {
        do this if expression is false
}
```

You can also use an *if else if ... else* statement to check for different possibilities:

```
if (a == 0){
        do this if a is zero
} else if (a < 0 ) {
        do this if a is negative
} else if (a > 0) {
        do this if a is positive
} else {
        do this if a is NaN
}
```

Other logical constructs include the *switch* and the *ternary conditional operator*, but we won't be using them much in this book.

Here is an exercise: modify the `BouncingBallRandom.as` code to recycle the ball so that when it disappears at the right boundary, it starts again at the initial location but with a new random velocity. The answer is in `BouncingBallRecycled.as`.

Loops

Just like logic, looping is an essential ingredient of programming. One of the things that make computers useful is their capability to repeat operations over and over again, much more quickly than humans, and without ever getting bored. They do it by *looping*.

In ActionScript there are several kinds of loops. We'll review just a couple of those here.

The *for loop* is the one that we'll make most use of. Here is an example of a for loop, used for summing the first 100 positive integers:

```
var sum:Number = 0;
for (var i:int = 1; i <= 100; i++) {
        sum += i;
}
trace(sum);
```

The first line initializes the value of the variable `sum` to 0. The next line sets up the loop—the variable `i` is a counter, set to start at 1 (you could start it from 0 or any other integer), up to and including 100, and told to increment by 1 (`i++`) on each step. So the loop executes 100 times, each time adding the current value of `i` to `sum`.

Looping over elements of an array is an especially useful technique. Suppose you want to animate five bouncing balls rather than one. To see how you'd do it, take a look at the code in `BouncingBalls.as`.

The main idea is to modify the `init()` function so that we create a bunch of balls, give each one a position and velocity (we've added `vx` and `vy` as public properties in the `Ball` class), and put them into an array named `balls` (which is defined as a private variable, so can be accessed later in another part of the code) using the `push()` method:

```
        private function init():void {
                balls = new Array();
```

```
        for (var i:uint=0; i<5; i++){
                var ball:Ball = new Ball();
                ball.x = 50;
                ball.y = 75;
                ball.vx = Math.random()*5;
                ball.vy = (Math.random()-0.5)*4;
                addChild(ball);
                balls.push(ball);
        }
        addEventListener(Event.ENTER_FRAME,onEachTimestep);
}
```

Naturally, the event handler is also modified to loop over all the balls:

```
private function onEachTimestep(evt:Event):void{
        for (var i:uint=0; i<5; i++){
                var ball:Ball = balls[i];
                ball.vy += g;

                ball.x += ball.vx;
                ball.y += ball.vy;

                if (ball.y > 350){
                        ball.y = 350;
                        ball.vy *= -0.8;
                }
        }
}
```

Don't worry that the balls just pass through each other when they meet. That's because your code doesn't know about collision detection yet! We'll fix that later.

Note that in order to use a for loop, you need to know exactly how many times you want to loop. If you don't, then there are other options, such as *for ... in*, *for each ... in*, and *while loops*. We won't describe the first two as we don't make use of them in this book.

In a while loop, you tell the loop to execute as long as some condition is true, no matter how many times you need to loop. The basic structure of a while loop is as follows:

```
while (some condition) {
        do something
}
```

For example, suppose you want to know the minimum number of consecutive integers you must sum, starting from 1, to obtain at least 1000. Here is a while loop to do this:

```
var sum:Number = 0;
var i:int = 1;
while (sum < 1000) {
        sum += i;
        i++;
}
trace(i-1);
```

You can also use a while loop in the same way as a for loop, to perform an operation a fixed number of times, for example, to sum the first 100 positive integers:

```
var sum:Number = 0;
var i:int = 1;
while (i <= 100) {
        sum += i;
        i++;
}
trace(sum);
```

Be careful with while loops —if the condition is always true, you'll end up with an infinite loop and the code will never stop executing!

A variation is a *do ... while* loop, in which the condition is checked after the loop instead of before. This ensures that the code within the loop executes at least once:

```
do {
        do something
} while (some condition);
```

Events in ActionScript 3.0

An *event* allows a given course of action to be replaced by a different course of action. Events contribute in a major way to making interactive media as interesting as they are. AS3.0 has quite an involved event framework. We won't go into details of the event framework and how it works under the hood, but will just take a very practical approach by simply reviewing the code syntax for tracking and responding to events. Also we focus here only on a few examples that we'll use frequently in our physics applications.

Event listeners and handlers

There are two aspects to event management: tracking events and responding to events. In AS3.0, *event listeners* "listen" to events, and *event handlers* take the appropriate action.

The syntax for setting up an event listener is as follows:

```
addEventListener(event_type, handler);
```

Here `handler` is simply a function that is called whenever an event of type *event_type* happens. `BouncingBall.as` contains an example:

```
addEventListener(Event.ENTER_FRAME, onEachTimestep);
```

Here the event type is `Event.ENTER_FRAME`, a static property of the `Event` class. It is automatically triggered at a rate set by the frame rate of the movie. So if the frame rate is 20 frames per second (fps), `Event.ENTER_FRAME` is triggered every 50 milliseconds. In response, the function `onEachTimestep()` is called and executed immediately each time the event is triggered. Note that the function `onEachTimestep` takes an argument of type `Event` `(evt:Event)`.

You can also remove an event listener in exactly the same way, replacing `addEventListener` by `removeEventListener`. For example:

```
removeEventListener(Event.ENTER_FRAME, onEachTimestep);
```

Events and user interaction

There are many other classes that deal with events besides the `Event` class. For example, the `MouseEvent` class deals with mouse events and the `KeyboardEvent` class deals with, well, keyboard events.

Mouse and keyboard events are great because they allow the user to interact with the Flash movie. For example, suppose we want to pause the BouncingBall animation when the user clicks and holds down the mouse, and resume it when the mouse is released. This can be achieved easily using the `MouseEvent.MOUSE_DOWN` and `MouseEvent.MOUSE_UP` events. Just add the following lines to the `init()` method:

```
addEventListener(MouseEvent.MOUSE_DOWN,stopAnim);
addEventListener(MouseEvent.MOUSE_UP,startAnim);
```

and include these event handlers:

```
private function stopAnim(evt:MouseEvent):void{
        removeEventListener(Event.ENTER_FRAME,onEachTimestep);
}

private function startAnim(evt:MouseEvent):void{
        addEventListener(Event.ENTER_FRAME,onEachTimestep);
}
```

The code is in `BouncingBallPause.as`. Note that you need to import the class `flash.events.MouseEvent`.

Note that the `addEventListener()` is actually a method of an object such as a sprite or movie clip. Therefore, you can do something like this:

```
ball.addEventListener(MouseEvent.MOUSE_DOWN,stopAnim);
```

In this case, the animation will stop only if the ball object is pressed. If no object is specified, `stopAnim()` is called whenever the mouse is pressed anywhere on the stage.

Drag and drop

Drag and drop is easy with AS3.0, using the aptly named `startDrag()` and `stopDrag()` methods. To illustrate the use of `startDrag()` and `stopDrag()`, we will modify the bouncing ball code yet again, so that now you can click the ball, move it anywhere on the stage, and then release it again.

To do this, make the following changes. First, remove the following line from `init()`:

```
addEventListener(Event.ENTER_FRAME, onEachTimestep);
```

Replace it with the following two lines:

```
ball.addEventListener(MouseEvent.MOUSE_DOWN,drag);
ball.addEventListener(MouseEvent.MOUSE_UP,drop);
```

They set up listeners, and the corresponding event handlers are these:

```
private function drag(evt:MouseEvent):void{
        removeEventListener(Event.ENTER_FRAME,onEachTimestep);
        ball.startDrag();
}

private function drop(evt:MouseEvent):void{
        addEventListener(Event.ENTER_FRAME,onEachTimestep);
        ball.stopDrag();
}
```

You will also need to set the initial values of **vx** and **vy** to zero, the initial value of `ball.y` to 350 (so that it is initially stationary on the ground), and `ball.x` to any suitable value so that it is visible on the stage. The modified code is in `BouncingBallDrag.as`. Try it out!

The Flash coordinate system

In the real world things exist in space. In the Flash world the equivalent is that objects exist on the stage. To know how to position objects on the stage, it is necessary to understand the Flash coordinate system.

2D coordinates

Flash's coordinate system is somewhat different from the usual Cartesian system of coordinates in math. In normal coordinate geometry, the x-coordinate runs from left to right, and the y-coordinate runs from bottom to top (see Figure 2-1b). In Flash, however, the y-coordinate runs in the opposite way, from top to bottom (see Figure 2-1a). The origin is in the top-left corner of the visible stage.

The usual Cartesian system is called a *right-handed coordinate system* because if you hold your right hand with your fingers closed and your thumb pointing out of the paper, your fingers will point from the positive x-axis to the positive y-axis. By implication, Flash's coordinate system in 2D is a *left-handed coordinate system*.

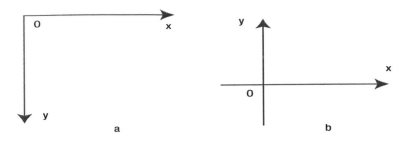

Figure 2-1. 2D coordinate systems compared: (a) in Flash and (b) math

Another oddity in the Flash coordinate system is that angles are measured in a clockwise sense from the direction of the positive x-axis (see Figure 2-2a). The usual convention in math is that angles are measured counterclockwise from the positive x-axis (see Figure 2-2b).

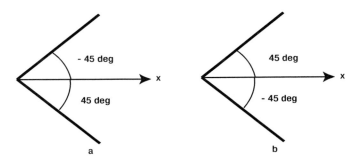

Figure 2-2. Angles as measured in (a) Flash and (b) math coordinate systems

3D in Flash

From Flash Player 10, 3D is supported natively. This means that it is possible to position and manipulate objects in 3D space using built-in AS3.0 properties and methods. To be sure, the capabilities of additional third-party 3D engines for Flash such as Papervsion3D or Away3D far exceed the native 3D capabilities of Flash Player. However, the availability of native 3D means that it is now extremely easy to perform basic tasks in 3D.

3D means that there is a third axis: the z-axis. In Flash, the direction of increasing z points into the screen. Any display object such as a sprite has a property z that fixes the z-coordinate of the object on the screen. Note that the position on the screen matches the x- and y-coordinate values only if the z-coordinate is zero.

Figures 2-3a and 2-3b show the corresponding coordinate systems in 3D. Note that the usual right-handed Cartesian system used in math is frequently pictured with the y-axis pointing into the screen and the z-axis pointing upward. The 3D coordinate system used in Flash 10, however, has the y-axis pointing down (as in the 2D version) and the z-axis pointing into the screen. However, the two coordinate systems are, in a sense, equivalent because the Flash 10 3D coordinate system is also right-handed. In fact, if you rotate it by 90 degrees clockwise about the positive x-axis you recover the usual orientation of axes used in math.

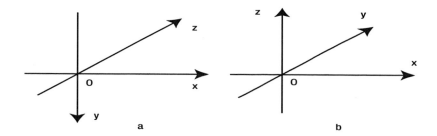

Figure 2-3. 3D coordinate systems compared: (a) in Flash and (b) in math

Rotation is also possible around the three axes. An object's rotation is specified by the properties `rotationX`, `rotationY`, and `rotationZ`, which are measured in degrees. The convention for the orientation of angles in 3D is again opposite to that in math, with angles about an axis being measured in a clockwise sense while looking in the positive direction along that axis.

To show how straightforward it is to incorporate basic 3D, we have modified the bouncing ball code to make the ball bounce off the four walls inside an invisible box. To achieve this, we invoked the third coordinate `ball.z` and introduced a corresponding velocity component `vz`. We initialize the values of these variables in `init()`. Then in the `onEachTimestep()` function, we update `ball.z` in exactly the same way as `ball.x`:

```
ball.z += vz;
```

The velocity component `vz` remains unchanged except when the ball bounces off a wall perpendicular to the z direction. This is because the z direction is also horizontal in this context, and gravity does not act horizontally.

The remaining additions in the code implement bouncing at the walls, following the same logic as that for bouncing at the ground (and taking into account the size of the ball).

This is what the updated `onEachTimestep()` method looks like:

```
private function onEachTimestep(evt:Event):void{

        vy += g;      // gravity increases the vertical speed

        ball.x += vx; // horizontal speed increases horizontal position
        ball.y += vy; // vertical speed increases vertical position
        ball.z += vz;

        if (ball.y > 350){ // if ball hits the ground
                ball.y = 350;
                vy *= gfac;    // its vertical velocity reverses/reduces
        }
        if (ball.x > 550 - w){
                ball.x = 550 - w;
                vx *= wfac;
        }
        if (ball.x < w){
```

```
                    ball.x = w;
                    vx *= wfac;
            }
            if (ball.z > 200){
                    ball.z = 200;
                    vz *= wfac;
            }
            if (ball.z < -200){
                    ball.z = -200;
                    vz *= wfac;
            }
      }
```

The full code is found in `BouncingBall3D.as`. There you are—a ball bouncing inside an invisible 3D box! Never mind if you can't see the box yet; we'll fix that soon.

The Flash drawing API

The Flash drawing *application programming interface (API)* allows you to draw things such as basic shapes and fills using ActionScript. Technically, this is possible because all display objects have a `graphics` property that can access the methods of the drawing API.

Drawing lines and curves

There are four methods that you need to know to be able to draw lines and curves: `lineStyle`, `moveTo`, `lineTo`, and `curveTo`.

- The `lineStyle(width, color, alpha)` method takes three arguments: the width of the line to be drawn, the line color, and its transparency.

- The `moveTo(x, y)` method moves the cursor to the specified location `(x, y)` without drawing anything.

- The `lineTo(x, y)` method draws a straight line from the current location to the new location `(x, y)` specified in its argument.

- The `curveTo(x1, y1, x2, y2)` method draws a curve from the current location ending at the new location specified by `(x2, y2)` and with a control point at `(x1, y1)`. The control point determines the curvature of the curve.

For example, to draw a straight line from the point (50, 100) to (250, 400), you would do something like this:

```
graphics.lineStyle(1,0x000000,1);
graphics.moveTo(50, 100);
graphics.lineTo(250, 400);
```

As an exercise, why not draw a grid using these methods? See the code in `Grid.as`.

There are also a few very useful methods for drawing primitive shapes such as circles and rectangles. For example, drawCircle(x, y, radius) draws a circle with a center at (x, y) and the specified radius; drawRect(x, y, width, height) draws a rectangle with the upper-left corner located at point (x, y) and with the specified width and height.

Creating fills and gradients

Producing fills is straightforward. The beginFill(color, alpha) method sets the fill to the specified color and alpha, to be applied to all objects drawn thereafter and until an endFill() is encountered. The following code snippet will produce a green rectangle without a border:

```
graphics.lineStyle(1,0x000000,0);
graphics.beginFill(0x00ff00);
graphics.drawRect(10, 10, 20, 30);
graphics.endFill();
```

Creating gradients is a bit trickier. To do the job, the method beginGradientFill() needs no fewer than eight arguments, although some have default values, so they don't necessarily need to be specified:

- type:String: a value that specifies which gradient type to use: GradientType.LINEAR or GradientType.RADIAL.

- colors:Array: An array of RGB hexadecimal color values used in the gradient.

- alphas:Array: An array of alpha values for each color in the colors array; valid values are from 0 to 1.

- ratios:Array: An array that specifies where to center each color; values range from 0 to 255.

- matrix:Matrix (default = null): A transformation matrix that tells Flash how to fill the shape.

- spreadMethod:String (default = "pad"): A value that specifies which spread method to use; chosen from SpreadMethod.PAD, SpreadMethod.REFLECT, or SpreadMethod.REPEAT.

- interpolationMethod:String (default = "rgb"): A value from the interpolation method that specifies which value to use: InterpolationMethod.LINEAR_RGB or InterpolationMethod.RGB.

- focalPointRatio:Number (default = 0): A number that controls the location of the focal point of the gradient; valid values are between -1 and 1.

The parameters you are most likely to need to change are the first five. Note that the last four parameters are optional because they have default values. A full description of all these parameters and what they do is outside the scope of this book, but we refer the reader to Adobe's online AS3.0 documentation for full details: http://livedocs.adobe.com/flash/9.0/ActionScriptLangRefV3/.

Back in Chapter 1 we built a Ball class (that we didn't talk much about) that we used to create the ball object in BouncingBall.as. It's time now to take a look at the code in Ball.as. Based on the explanations in this section, most of the code should be self-evident. The less-obvious part of the code is the creation of the gradient fill, which is done with the following three lines:

```
var matrix:Matrix = new Matrix();

matrix.createGradientBox(_radius,_radius,0,-_radius,-_radius/2);

graphics.beginGradientFill(GradientType.RADIAL,[0xffffff,_color],[1,1],[0,255],matrix);
```

After creating a matrix object, we used the `createGradientBox()` method, which takes five arguments: width, height, rotation, horizontal shift, and vertical shift. We set these parameters in relation to the radius of the ball to create a nice effect—feel free to experiment with alternative values. The final line invokes `graphics.beginGradientFill()` using a radial gradient, a two-color array (one of which is white), alphas of 1 for each, locating the center of each color at the two extremes 0 and 255, and the matrix object we created to fill the shape.

Example: Bouncing ball in a box

Okay, let's now put together what we discussed in the last two sections (Flash 3D and the drawing API) to create something useful: let's build that 3D box!

The code is in `BouncingBall3DWalls.as` and the final result is shown in Figure 2-4.

```
package {
        import flash.display.Sprite;
        import flash.events.Event;

        public class BouncingBall3DWalls extends Sprite {
                private var g:Number=0.1; // acceleration due to gravity
                private var vx:Number;  // initial horizontal speed
                private var vy:Number;  // initial vertical speed
                private var vz:Number;  // lateral speed
                private var ball:Ball;
                private var w:Number;
                private var gfac:Number=-0.99;
                private var wfac:Number=-0.99;

                public function BouncingBall3DWalls() {
                        init();
                }
                private function init():void {
                        setWall(0,200,250,300,400,-90); // left wall
                        setWall(550,200,250,300,400,90); // right wall
                        setWall(275,200,400,548,400,0); // far wall
                        vx = Math.random()*5;
                        vy = (Math.random()-0.5)*4;
                        vz = 4;
                        ball = new Ball();
                        ball.x = 100;
                        ball.y = 75;
                        ball.z = 0;
```

```
                    w = ball.width/2;
                    addChild(ball);
                    addEventListener(Event.ENTER_FRAME,onEachTimestep);
                    setWall(275,200,100,550,400,0,0x0000ff,0.2); // near wall
            }

            private function setWall(pX:Number, pY:Number, pZ:Number, pW:Number,↪
    pH:Number, pAngle:Number, pCol:uint=0x586cbf, pAlp:Number=1):void{
                    var wall:Wall = new Wall(pW, pH, pCol, pAlp);
                    wall.x=pX;
                    wall.y=pY;
                    wall.z=pZ;
                    wall.rotationY=pAngle;
                    addChild(wall);
            }

            private function onEachTimestep(evt:Event):void{

                    vy += g;        // gravity increases the vertical speed

                    ball.x += vx; // horizontal speed increases horizontal position
                    ball.y += vy; // vertical speed increases vertical position
                    ball.z += vz;

                    if (ball.y > 350){ // if ball hits the ground
                            ball.y = 350;
                            vy *= gfac;     // vertical velocity reverses and reduces
                    }
                    if (ball.x > 550 - w){
                            ball.x = 550 - w;
                            vx *= wfac;
                    }
                    if (ball.x < w){
                            ball.x = w;
                            vx *= wfac;
                    }
                    if (ball.z > 400){
                            ball.z = 400;
                            vz *= wfac;
                    }
                    if (ball.z < 100){
                            ball.z = 100;
                            vz *= wfac;
                    }

            }
        }
    }
}
```

Here's how we do it. First we create a Wall class. If you look at the code in Wall.as, you see that this is very straightforward. We basically draw a filled rectangle using values for the width, height, color, and alpha that are supplied via the constructor. Then in the main code BouncingBallBox, we define a function setWall() that basically creates a wall object, positions it, and rotates it in 3D space. This function setWall() takes eight arguments, the last two of which (color and alpha) are optional. The remaining six arguments set the location, size and orientation of the wall.

The final thing is to invoke setWall() four times in init() to create the four walls. Note that three of the walls are created before the ball instance is created and the fourth (the near side one) is created after. This is because there is no automatic depth sorting in Flash 3D, and objects are simply given a depth based on the order in which they are placed on the stage.

> You need Flash Player 10 or above to view this movie and Flash CS4 or above to work with the source code.

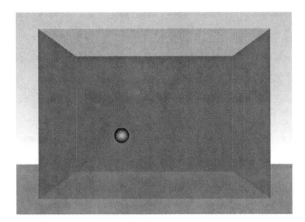

Figure 2-4. A ball bouncing inside a 3D box

Producing animation using code

There are a number of ways to produce animation using code in AS3.0. For example, there is a Tween class that can be used to move, resize, and fade movie clips. However, our focus is to produce physics-based animation. We basically know how to move objects. What is needed is a method to measure the advancement of time. We need a clock.

Using the built-in frame stepping as a clock

We've already been using a clock: the ENTER_FRAME event. Let's now take a closer look to see how good a time-keeper the ENTER_FRAME event is.

Suppose the frame rate of a movie is 50 fps. This means that, in theory, the Event.ENTER_FRAME event is triggered once every 1/50 seconds (every 20 milliseconds). We said "in theory" because the frame rate in the Flash Player is notoriously inaccurate and depends, for instance, on the capabilities of the machine running the movie. What effect can this inaccuracy have on the animation?

To answer this question, we'll need to do some simple math. Suppose that we want to move an object at a constant velocity of 100 pixels per second, and suppose that the frame rate of the movie is 50 fps. Let's increment the object's horizontal position by vx per frame as in the bouncing ball example:

```
private function onEachTimestep(evt:Event):void{
        ball.x += vx;
}
```

In other words, vx is the horizontal velocity in units of pixels per frame. What value must we give vx? Well, the velocity in units of pixels per second is 100, and there are 50 frames per second. So the value of vx is 100/50 or 2. In general, we have the following relationship:

(Velocity in pixels per second) = (Velocity in pixels per frame) × (Frame rate in fps)

Okay, so if we set vx = 2, we should see the ball moving at 100 pixels per second. The speed in pixels per second is what we actually perceive on the screen. However, there is no guarantee that the frame rate at which the movie runs will be exactly the frame rate that is set. Suppose that your machine is slow or there are other things running on it, so that the actual frame rate is closer to 30 fps. This gives an actual velocity of only 60 pixels per second. Your object appears to be moving slower. What's more, if you republish your movie at a different frame rate, the velocity of the ball will be different.

Clearly we need a better alternative than a clock that depends on the actual frame rate at which the movie runs.

Using the Timer class

So we just decided that Event.ENTER_FRAME is not reliable for timekeeping. Is there an alternative? Yes, one alternative is the Timer class (found in the flash.utils package), together with the related TimeEvent class (found in the flash.events package).

What a Timer does is not actually that different from Event.ENTER_FRAME. It "fires" an event at a specified rate. But Timer is a lot more reliable than Event.ENTER_FRAME. To set up a timer you need to do the following. First, create a timer object:

```
timer = new Timer(10, 1000);
```

As you can see, a Timer() takes two arguments. The first one is the time delay, in milliseconds, between timer events. The second, optional, argument is the number of times that the timer event fires. If the second argument is set to 0, or not specified, the timer will fire indefinitely.

The next step is to set up an event listener that detects timer events:

```
timer.addEventListener(TimerEvent.TIMER, onEachTimestep);
```

and the corresponding event handler that responds to the timer event:

```
private function onEachTimestep(evt:TimerEvent):void{
        ball.x + = vx;
}
```

The other crucial thing is to start it! You see, unlike an enterframe, a timer does not exist or tick by default. So after you create it, you have to actually start it. This is easy enough with the `start()` method:

```
timer.start();
```

Moreover, you can stop a timer at any time using the `stop()` method:

```
timer.stop();
```

This is neat because it allows you to stop and restart your animation at will, without having to remove and add the event listener (which is not very elegant).

One thing you have to remember with a timer is that it does not update your screen. So, if your frame rate is lower than your timer rate, you may not see the update until after the next frame event. For example, suppose your timer delay is 10 milliseconds, but your frame rate is only 10 frames per second. Your frames will be updating every 0.1 seconds, or 100 milliseconds —every 10 timer events. This will make your animation appear "jumpy" despite the high timer rate. To fix this, use the `updateAfterEvent()` method to force a screen update after every timer event:

```
private function onEachTimestep(evt:TimerEvent):void{
        ball.x + = vx;
        evt.updateAfterEvent();
}
```

Although `Timer` is a big improvement on `Event.ENTER_FRAME`, it is not without its shortcomings. One of the main problems is that the actual time interval between timer events actually includes the time it takes to execute all the code within the event handler on top of the specified delay. If there is a lot of code in your event handler, it might mean your timer ticking rate is substantially slower than what you specified.

Using getTimer() to compute elapsed time

Bad timekeeping can really mess up your physics. For really accurate timekeeping, what we need is a way to measure actual elapsed time. Keith Peters, in his book *Foundation ActionScript Animation*, gives a great way to do this: using the `getTimer()` function.

The `getTimer()` function, found in the `flash.utils` package, returns an integer equal to the number of milliseconds that have elapsed since the Flash Player has initialized. So, if you call `getTimer()` twice, in different parts of the code, and work out the difference in the returned value, that would give you the time that has elapsed between those two calls.

How does that help us with animation? The point is that we can calculate the actual time that has elapsed since the object's position was last updated. Then we can use that time to calculate the amount by which to move it.

To see this in action, `TimerExample.as` animates the motion of a ball moving at constant horizontal velocity **vx**. Here is the modified event handler:

```
private function onEachTimestep(evt:TimerEvent):void{
        // time elapsed in seconds since last call
        var dt:Number = (getTimer() - t)/1000;
        t = getTimer(); // reset t
        ball.x += vx*dt;
        evt.updateAfterEvent();
}
```

We added two lines here. The first line works out the time elapsed `dt` (this notation will become clear in the next chapter) since the last time the call to `onEachTimestep()` was made. Here `t` is a private variable initialized to `getTimer()` before the start of the animation. The next line resets `t` so that it can be used for the next call.

You'll see also that we modified the code that updates the ball's position. We're now adding an amount **vx*dt** to the ball's current position instead of **vx**, as before. What's going on here? Well, this is the whole point of calculating the elapsed time `dt`. You see, previously we were interpreting the velocity **vx** as pixels moved per frame (if using `Event.ENTER_FRAME`) or per tick (if using `Timer`). The assumptions we were making in doing so were that the frames or ticks were of fixed duration, and that duration was just what we specified in the frame rate or timer delay parameter. As long as those assumptions work, we can use frames or timer ticks as a good proxy for time, and thinking of velocity in terms of pixels per frame or timer tick is a good idea. But here what we're saying is this: let's get back to thinking about velocity in the correct way, as pixels moved per second. Therefore, in `dt` seconds, the distance moved is **vx*dt**, so that the new position is this:

```
ball.x += vx*dt;
```

The advantage of going back to the real meaning of velocity is that the motion is always computed correctly, independently of the frame rate or timer tick rate. This technique will come in handy when we start looking at more complex physics.

Here is the code for `TimerExample.as` in its entirety:

```
package {
        import flash.display.Sprite;
        import flash.utils.Timer;
        import flash.events.TimerEvent;
        import flash.utils.getTimer;

        public class TimerExample extends Sprite {
                private var vx:Number=100; // velocity in units of pixels per second
                private var ball:Ball;
                private var timer:Timer;
                private var t:int;

                public function TimerExample() {
                        init();
                }
```

```
private function init():void {
        createBall();
        setupTimer();
}

private function createBall():void{
        ball = new Ball();
        ball.x = 50;
        ball.y = 100;
        addChild(ball);
}

private function setupTimer():void{
        timer = new Timer(20);
        timer.addEventListener(TimerEvent.TIMER,onEachTimestep);
        timer.start();
        t = getTimer(); // initialise value of t
}

private function onEachTimestep(evt:TimerEvent):void{
        // time elapsed in seconds since last call
        var dt:Number = (getTimer() - t)/1000;
        t = getTimer(); // reset t
        ball.x += vx*dt;
        evt.updateAfterEvent();
}
        }
}
```

Precalculating motion

As you'll now be aware, the methods for animating objects with code we're using work by calculating updates to the object's position "on the fly." It might also be possible to precalculate the motion of an object and animate it afterward. This can be done by using a for or while loop to represent time-stepping, calculating the particles position at each step and saving the position coordinates in an array. You can even save the values in an external file (if using Adobe AIR) to be used by another movie.

Why would you want to do that? It can be useful, for example, if calculations take too long to perform and cannot fit within a reasonable frame rate.

The downside of this method is that it doesn't work with interactivity. Because user interaction is usually an important aspect of physics-based applications, we won't generally use this approach.

Collision detection

Collisions are an inevitable fact of life in an animated world. So far, the movies we created do not know how to detect when two objects have collided or what to do when they do. This section focuses on the first issue: collision detection. Responding properly to collisions will be treated in detail in Chapter 11.

In general, collision detection can be a tricky problem, but if the objects to be tested are rectangular in shape, there is a very simple built-in method: `hitTestObject()`.

Using the hitTestObject() method

The `hitTestObject()` method determines whether two display objects (such as sprites or movie clips) are in collision:

```
object1.hitTestObject(object2);
```

The outcome is a `Boolean`: it returns `true` if they do and `false` it they don't. So you'd typically use it as a condition in an if statement, writing code to handle the collision if it returns `true`.

What `hitTestObject()` actually does is to check whether the bounding boxes of the two display objects overlap or not. If the objects are rectangular in shape, obviously their bounding boxes coincide with their visible area, and `hitTestObject()` works like a dream. However, if one or both of the objects is any other shape (for example, a circle), that wouldn't be true, and `hitTestObject()` might return `true`, even in some cases when the objects are not actually touching.

Using the hitTestPoint() method

The `hitTestPoint()` method checks whether a given point is touching a display object. It takes two mandatory parameters and one optional parameter and returns a `Boolean`:

```
object.hitTestPoint(x:Number, y:Number, shapeFlag:Boolean = false);
```

The first two parameters specify the coordinates of the point to be tested against the object. The `shapeFlag` option tells Flash whether to test against the visible area of the object (if set to `true`) or against its bounding box (if `false`, the default).

With `shapeFlag=true`, this method is especially handy if one of the objects is quite small (think projectile), even if the other object has a complicated shape (think spaceship): boom!

Distance-based collision detection

This method involves checking the distance between two objects explicitly and is simplest to formulate for circular objects. We have already used a variant of this method when checking for collisions of a bouncing ball with the ground or walls. Basically, you work out, using simple geometry, the minimum distance the objects can be before they touch. Let's assume we have a circular ball with the registration point located at its center. Then the minimum distance the ball can be from a wall is equal to its radius. For example, to check if a ball hits a wall on the right side, the test would look like the following, where `_wallx` is the location of the wall and `_radius` is the radius of the ball:

```
if (ball.x >= _wallx - _radius){
        code to handle collision
}
```

If you're testing whether two circles (of radiuses r1 and r2) are colliding, you need to check if the distance between their centers is less than or equal to r1 + r2. Why the sum of their radiuses? Because that's always how far their centers are whenever there're touching. Okay, but how do we calculate the distance between the centers of the circles? This boils down to a common problem in elementary geometry—the formula for the distance between two points. Lucky for us, a Greek guy called Pythagoras worked that out a long time ago. It's called Pythagoras's Theorem. We'll take a closer look at that theorem in the next chapter. For now, here is the formula:

```
dist = Math.sqrt((x2 - x1)* (x2 - x1) + (y2 - y1)* (y2 - y1));
```

This gives the distance between two points with coordinates (x1, y1) and (x2, y2). So you take the difference between the x-coordinates and square it, do the same with the y-coordinates, add the results, and then take the square root.

Now if you're talking about two circles, (x1, y1) and (x2, y2) will be the coordinates of their centers, and are in fact equal to their x and y properties if their registration points are in the center. So, here is our condition for detecting collisions between two circles:

```
if (dist  <= (r1 + r2)){
        code to handle collision
}
```

Before you rush off to code this up, you can simplify things a bit. That Math.sqrt() is not entirely necessary, and could eat up lots of CPU time in a timer or enterframe loop. And things would get much worse if multiple objects were involved. The trick is to check for the square of dist instead:

```
rSquare = (r1 + r2)*(r1 + r2);
...
distSquare = (x2 - x1)* (x2 - x1) + (y2 - y1)* (y2 - y1);
if (distSquare  <= rSquare){
        code to handle collision
}
```

Note that if you only have two objects, or if all the objects have the same radius, the square (r1 + r2)*(r1 + r2) needs to be evaluated only once, outside of the time-stepping loop.

The formula for distSquare can easily be generalized to 3D:

```
distSquare = (x2 - x1)* (x2 - x1) + (y2 - y1)* (y2 - y1) + (z2 - z1)* (z2 - z1);
```

The formula for rSquare remains the same in 3D, of course.

When multiple objects are involved, you still need to check every pair of objects using the same formula.

The file CollidingBalls.as modifies BouncingBalls.as to implement this collision-detection method. Take a look at the code and have a play with the swf, but don't worry too much about the physics to deal with the collisions for now. We shall handle that in Chapter 11.

Advanced collision detection

You are now well equipped to detect collisions between to rectangular objects ((using `HitTestObject`), a point or small object and another object of arbitrary shape (using `HitTestPoint` with the `shapeFlag` option set to `true`), and two circular or spherical objects (using Pythagoras's Theorem). But what about more complex shapes?

Several clever techniques exist for testing for collisions between irregular objects. One of them is by looking at individual pixels of `BitmapData` objects. We refer the interested reader to Chapter 1 of Keith Peters's *Advanced ActionScript 3.0 Animation*.

Summary

Wow! This chapter has been a whirlwind tour through vast stretches of Flashland. Hopefully, you've now gained an appreciation of how different aspects of ActionScript can be useful for physics-based animation.

If you've struggled with any of the material in this chapter, we highly recommend that you brush up on your knowledge of Flash and ActionScript 3.0. Here are a couple of books that we particularly recommend for beginners:

- *Foundation ActionScript 3.0 for Flash and Flex*, by Darren Richardson and Paul Milbourne (Apress, ISBN: 978-1-4302-1918-7).

- *Foundation ActionScript 3.0 Animation: Making Things Move!*, by Keith Peters (Apress, ISBN: 978-1-59059-791-0).

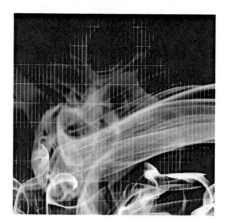

Chapter 3

Some Math Background

Programming even the simplest physics will inevitably involve some math. Therefore, we assume that readers of this book will be comfortable with math notation and have at least some math knowledge. This knowledge need not be very sophisticated; familiarity with basic algebra and simple algebraic manipulations of equations and formulas is the most important requirement and will be assumed without review. In addition, some appreciation of coordinate geometry and the basics of trigonometry and vectors would provide a good foundation. In case you need it, this chapter provides a review or refresher of these topics. Prior knowledge of calculus is a bonus, but is not essential; similarly for numerical methods. We provide an overview of the basic concepts on these topics at a level sufficient to apply them in physics programming.

Here is what we'll cover:

- **Coordinates and simple graphs**: Math functions and their graphs crop up constantly in physics applications. We review some common math functions, and plot their graphs using a custom ActionScript graph plotting class. We also show how to make an object move along any curve described by a mathematical equation.

- **Basic trigonometry**: Trigonometry crops up a lot in graphics and animation in general, and is pretty much an indispensable tool in physics-based animation. In this section, we'll review some trigonometry essentials that will be used in later chapters. We'll also get to play with trig functions such as sin and cos to produce some cool animation effects.

- **Vectors and vector algebra**: Vectors are useful because physics equations can be expressed, manipulated, and coded up more simply using them. After a review of vector concepts, we'll construct an ActionScript 3.0 (AS3.0) **Vector2D** class that will be used throughout the rest of the book.

- **Simple calculus ideas**: Calculus deals with things that change continuously, including motion. It is, therefore, a natural tool to apply to physics. Calculus is usually considered part of advanced math. So we'll give only an overview of the basic concepts here to show how they can be implemented in physics equations and in code.

Although this chapter consists of review material, much of it covers application of the math in ActionScript and physics. Therefore, even if you have a solid math background, we recommend that you at least skim through this chapter to see how we apply the math.

In our attempt to illustrate the application of otherwise abstract math concepts to physics, we have picked some examples of physics concepts that will be explained more fully in later chapters. So don't worry if you don't immediately get everything that we'll cover here; you can always come back to this chapter as needed.

Coordinates and simple graphs

Coordinate geometry provides a way to visualize relationships expressed as mathematical functions or equations. This section will review some things you'd have covered in your school math classes, but mixed with a lot of ActionScript code to emphasize the application of those math concepts.

To get started, let's remember how to plot functions on graphs. Say you want to plot the graph of the function $y = x^2$. The first thing you must do is to decide what range of values you want to plot. Suppose you want x to range from −4 to 4. Then what you might have done at school is to tabulate the values of x and the corresponding values of y that you get by using $y = x^2$. The next thing you might have done is to plot each (x, y) pair of values as a dot on graph paper and then join the dots to make a smooth curve. Don't worry; we won't ask you to do this here. Instead of reaching out for graph paper, let's do it with ActionScript!

Building a plotter: the Graph class

The **Graph** class is a custom class we created that does just what its name suggests: draw graphs. You're welcome to have a look at the code, but what it does is quite simple: it has public functions that draw a set of axes and major and minor grid lines using the drawing API. It also has a public function to plot data. The **Graph** class takes eight arguments in its constructor:

```
Graph(xmin, xmax, ymin, ymax, x0, y0, xwidth, ywidth)
```

The first four arguments (xmin, xmax, ymin, ymax) denote the minimum and maximum desired values of x and y. The next two parameters (x0, y0) denote the coordinates of the origin in the Flash coordinate system, in pixels. The final two parameters specify the width and height of the graph object in pixels.

The public function **drawgrid()** takes four arguments that specify the major and minor divisions:

```
drawgrid(xmajor, xminor, ymajor, yminor)
```

It draws corresponding grid lines and labels the values at the relevant major grid locations.

The public function **drawaxes()** takes two optional arguments that specify the text labels on the axes. It draws the axes and labels them, the default labels being **"x"** and **"y"**.

```
drawaxes(xlabel:String="x", ylabel:String="y")
```

An example will make the usage clear. Suppose we want to plot the function $y = x^2$ over the range of values specified for x from –4 to 4. Then the corresponding range of values of y would be from 0 to 16. This tells us that the graph should accommodate positive and negative values for x, but only needs to have positive values for y. If the stage is 550 by 400 pixels (the Flash default), a good position to place the origin would be at (275, 380). Let's choose the width and height of the graph to be 450 and 350 so that it fills most of the stage. The range in x and y (xmin, xmax, ymin, ymax) can be chosen to be (-4, 4, 0, 20). Sensible choices for (xmajor, xminor, ymajor, yminor) are (1, 0.2, 5, 1):

```
var graph:Graph = new Graph(-4, 4, 0, 20, 275, 380, 450, 350);
graph.drawgrid(1, 0.2, 5, 1);
graph.drawaxes('x','y');
addChild(graph);
```

The code is in **GraphExample.as**. Go on, have a go yourself and change the parameters to see the effect. It's not really hard, and you'll soon get the hang of it.

Plotting functions using the Graph class

What we've done so far is to make the equivalent of a piece of graph paper, with labeled axes on it. To plot a graph, we use the public method **plot()** in the **Graph** class. This method plots pairs of values of x and y, optionally joining them with a line of specified color:

```
public function plot(x:Array, y:Array, color:uint, dots:Boolean=true, line:Boolean=true)
```

As you can see, the values of **x** and **y** are to be specified as separate arrays in the first two arguments. The last two parameters, **dots** and **line**, are optional. If **dots** is **true** (the default), a small circle (radius 1 pixel) is drawn at each point with the specified color. If **line** is **true** (the default), the points are joined by a line of the same color. If you look at the code, you'll see that the dot is drawn using the **drawCircle()** method, and the line is drawn using the **lineTo()** method of the **Graphics** class.

Let's now plot the graph of $y = x^2$:

```
var xvals:Array = new Array(-4,-3,-2,-1,0,1,2,3,4);
var yvals:Array = new Array(16,9,4,1,0,1,4,9,16);
graph.plot(xvals, yvals, 0x0000ff);
```

There's our graph, but it looks a bit odd and not a smooth curve at all. The problem is that we don't have enough points. The **lineTo()** method joins the points using a straight line, and if the distance between adjacent points is large, the plot does not look good.

We can do better than that by computing the array elements from within the code. Let's do this:

```
var xA:Array = new Array();
var yA:Array = new Array();
for (var i:uint=0; i<=100; i++){
        xA[i] = (i-50)*0.08;
        yA[i] = xA[i]*xA[i];
}
graph.plot(xA, yA, 0xff0000);
```

We've now used 101 values instead of just 9. The result is shown in Figure 3-1. As you can see, the plot gives a smooth curve. This particular curve has a shape called a *parabola*. In the next few sections, we'll use the **Graph** class to produce plots for different types of math functions.

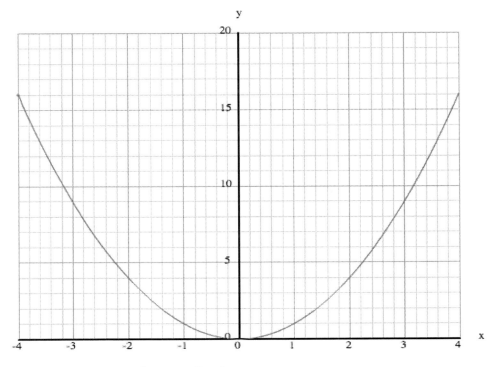

Figure 3-1. Plotting the function $y = x^2$ using the **Graph** class

Straight lines

We'll start with linear functions, such as $y = 2x + 1$. Type the following code or copy it from **GraphFunctions.as**:

```
package{
        import flash.display.Sprite;

        public class GraphFunctions extends Sprite{
```

```
public function GraphFunctions(){
        init();
}
private function init():void{
        var graph:Graph = new Graph(-4,4,-10,10,275,210,450,350);
        graph.drawgrid(1,0.2,5,1);
        graph.drawaxes('x','y');
        addChild(graph);
        var xA:Array = new Array();
        var yA:Array = new Array();
        for (var i:uint=0; i<=100; i++){
                xA[i] = (i-50)*0.08;
                yA[i] = f(xA[i]);
        }
        graph.plot(xA,yA,0xff0000,false,true);
}
private function f(x:Number):Number{
        var y:Number;
        y = 2*x+1;
        return y;
}
    }
}
```

Note that we've moved the actual math function to a function called $f()$ to make things slightly easier to see and modify.

The graph is a straight line. If you wish, play around with different linear equations of the form y = ax + b, for different values of a and b. You'll see that they are always straight lines.

Where does the line meet the y-axis? You'll find that it is always at y= b. That's because on the y-axis, x = 0. Putting x = 0 in the equation gives y = b. The value b is called the *intercept* on the y-axis. What is the significance of a? You'll find out later in this chapter, in the section on calculus.

Polynomial curves

You've already seen that the equation $y = x^2$ gives a parabolic curve. Experiment with **GraphFunctions.as** by plotting different quadratic functions of the form $y = ax^2 + bx + c$, for different values of a, b and c, for example:

`y = x*x - 2*x - 3;`

You may need to change the range of the graph. You'll find that they are all parabolic. If the value of a is positive, you will always get a bowl-shaped curve; if a is negative, the curve will be hill-shaped.

Linear and quadratic functions are special cases of polynomial functions. In general, a polynomial function is made up by adding terms with different powers of x. The highest power of x is called the *degree* of the polynomial. So a quadratic is a degree 2 polynomial. Higher polynomials have more twists and turns; for example, this polynomial will give you the plot shown in Figure 3-2:

`y = -0.5*Math.pow(x,5) + 3*Math.pow(x,3) + x*x - 2*x - 3;`

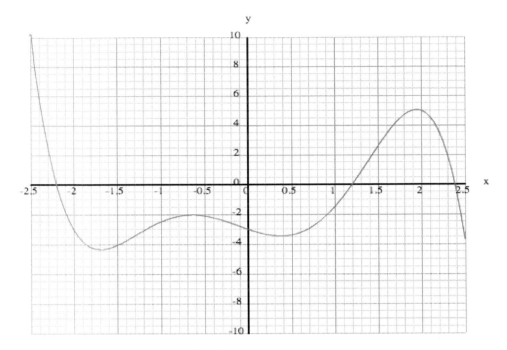

Figure 3-2. A polynomial curve y = −0.5 x⁵ + 3x³ + x² − 2x − 3

Things that grow and decay: exponential and log functions

There are many more exotic types of functions that do interesting things. One interesting example is the exponential function, which crops up all over physics. It is defined mathematically by

$$y = e^x$$

You might be wondering what e stands for. It's a special number approximately equal to 2.71828. In this respect, e is a math constant like π, which cannot be written down in exact decimal form, but is approximately equal to 3.14159. Constants such as π and e appear all over physics.

The exponential function is also sometimes written as exp(x). AS3.0 has a built in **Math.exp()** function. It also has a **Math.e** static constant with the value of 2.71828182845905.

Let's plot **Math.exp(x)** then!

As you can see from Figure 3-3, the graph of exp(x) goes to zero as x becomes more negative and increases more and more rapidly as x becomes more positive. You've heard of the term *exponential growth*. This is it. If you now plot exp(−x), you'll see the reverse: as x increases from negative to positive values, exp(−x) decays rapidly to zero. This is *exponential decay*. Note that when x is 0, both exp(x) and exp(−x) are exactly equal to 1. That's because any number to the power of zero is equal to 1.

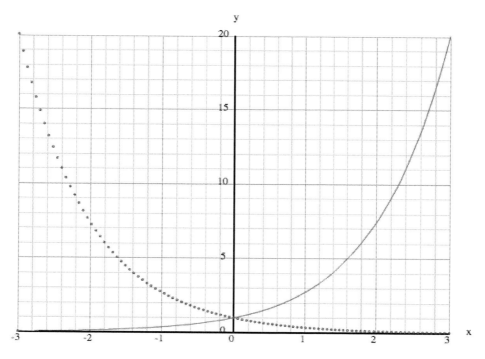

Figure 3-3. Exponential growth function exp(x) (solid curve) and decay function exp(–x) (dotted curve)

Nothing stops us from combining functions, of course, and you can get interesting shapes by doing this. For example, try plotting the exponential of $-x^2$:

$$y = \exp\left(-x^2\right)$$

This gives a bell-shaped curve (technically it's called a *Gaussian curve*), as shown in Figure 3-4. It has a maximum in the middle and falls rapidly toward zero on either side. In Figure 3-4, the curve appears to fall to zero because of the limited resolution of the figure. In reality, it never gets to exactly zero because $\exp(-x^2)$ becomes vanishingly small for large positive and negative values of x, but never actually becomes exactly zero.

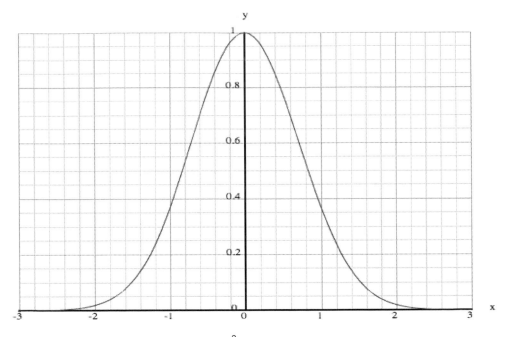

Figure 3-4. The bell shape (Gaussian) function $\exp(-x^2)$

Making an object move along a curve

Here is a fun thing to do. Can you make a ball move along a curve? To do this, we added three new functions to **GraphFunctions.as** and called the new code **MoveCurve.as**:

```
private function placeBall():void{
        ball = new Ball(6);
        ball.x = xA[0]/xscal+ xorig;
        ball.y = -yA[0]/yscal + yorig;
        addChild(ball);
}
private function setupTimer():void{
        timer = new Timer(5);
        timer.addEventListener(TimerEvent.TIMER,moveBall);
        timer.start();
}
private function moveBall(evt:TimerEvent):void{
        ball.x = xA[n]/xscal + xorig;
        ball.y = -yA[n]/yscal + yorig;
        evt.updateAfterEvent();
        n++;
        if (n==xA.length){
                timer.stop();
                timer.removeEventListener(TimerEvent.TIMER,moveBall);
        }
}
```

The function `placeBall()` is called after `plotGraph()` in `init()` and simply places a `Ball` instance at the beginning of the curve. Then `setupTimer()` is called after `placeBall()`, and it does exactly what its name suggests. The event handler `moveBall()` runs at every timer event and moves the ball along the curve, stopping the timer and removing the event listener when it reaches the end of the curve.

Fun with hills

You can try this with any function you like; for example $y = x^2$. But let's go crazy and try something more fun, such as this degree 6 polynomial:

```
y = 0.2*(x+3.6)*(x+2.5)*(x+1)*(x-0.5)*(x-2)*(x-3.5);
```

You can see that this is a degree 6 polynomial because if you expand out the factors, the term with the highest power of x will be $0.2\ x^6$.

Run the code with this function to see the animation. Does that give you any ideas? Perhaps you could use a curve to represent a hilly landscape and build a game where you try and push a ball over the hills? The only problem is that the curve shoots off to very large values at the ends. This is inevitable with polynomials. The reason is that for large positive or negative values of x, the highest term (in this case, $0.2\ x^6$) will always dominate over the rest. So, in this example, we'll get very large values because of the effect of the $0.2\ x^6$ term. In the jargon, the curve "blows up" in those limits.

Let's try and remedy this by multiplying the whole thing by a bell function of the type $\exp(-x^2)$, which, as you know, tends to zero at the ends:

```
y = (x+3.6)*(x+2.5)*(x+1)*(x-0.5)*(x-2)*(x-3.5)*Math.exp(-x*x/4);
```

Figure 3-5 shows what we get. Cool. The bell function flattens the curve at the ends, solving our problem. Note that we've divided the x^2 within the `exp()` by 4. This is to broaden the bell shape; otherwise it would kill off the polynomial too quickly, leaving fewer hills. Remove the 4 or replace it by 2 to see what we mean. Try also changing the 4 to 5 or 6 to see the opposite effect.

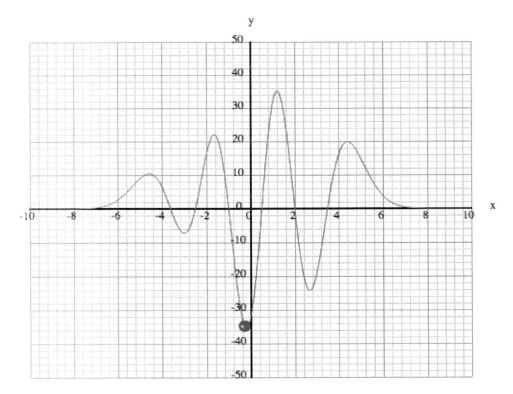

Figure 3-5. Animating a ball on a curve made by multiplying a polynomial and a Gaussian

Here is another way you can modify the curve: multiply it by another factor of x (and an appropriate number to keep it within the range being displayed):

```
y = 0.5*x*(x+3.6)*(x+2.5)*(x+1)*(x-0.5)*(x-2)*(x-3.5) *Math.exp(-x*x/4);
```

This modifies the curve in a different way. Because x is small near the origin and large away from it, by multiplying the function by x, we tend to reduce the hills closer to the origin and increase the relative height of the hills farther away. You might notice another change: the value of y for large negative x is now negative, and the landscape starts with a valley instead of a hill because by introducing that extra factor of x, the dominant term in that function is now $0.5\,x^7$. Compare that with the previous $0.2\,x^6$. When the power of the dominant term is odd, it will be negative for negative values of x. But when the power is even, it will be positive even if x is negative. Check this out by multiplying by another factor of x to get this:

```
y = 0.1*x*x*(x+3.6)*(x+2.5)*(x+1)*(x-0.5)*(x-2)*(x-3.5) *Math.exp(-x*x/4);
```

If you multiply the function by a negative number, you'll reverse the whole curve.

There is clearly enormous flexibility in what you can do with functions to create different types of shapes. Hopefully you might find some use for them! Perhaps build that game that shoots balls over hills. Or maybe get rid of the graph and curve to produce some cool math-based animations without giving away how you've done it.

Beyond its use for plotting known functions, the **Graph** class will come in handy as a useful diagnostic tool to help you visualize what your code is actually calculating, more intuitively and in much greater detail than the humble **trace()** can do. It can help you to understand the logic or physics in your code, and to identify any potential problems. Think of it as a dashboard or instrument panel like the ones in a car or plane, and soon you'll be using it more than you think!

The trouble with circles

Let's now try and move an object around a circle using the same method. That should be simple enough, right? First, we need the equation of a circle. You can find this in any elementary geometry textbook.

The equation of a circle of radius r and with origin at (a, b) is given by this:

$$(x-a)^2 + (y-b)^2 = r^2$$

If you try to do things in exactly the same way as before, you'll want to have y as a function of x. Recalling your algebra, you should be able to manipulate the preceding equation to get this:

$$y = b + \sqrt{r^2 - (x-a)^2}$$

To keep things simple, choose a = b = 0, and r = 1 (center at the origin, radius of 1):

$$y = \sqrt{(1-x^2)}$$

Now let's plot the graph. You'll want to use the same scaling on both axes so that your circle does not look distorted. If you do just that and run the code, you'll get something that looks half-good, but with a couple of strange problems. The first problem is that you only end up with a semicircle, not the whole circle. The second problem is that there are extra bits outside the circle. Figure 3-6 shows the resulting plot.

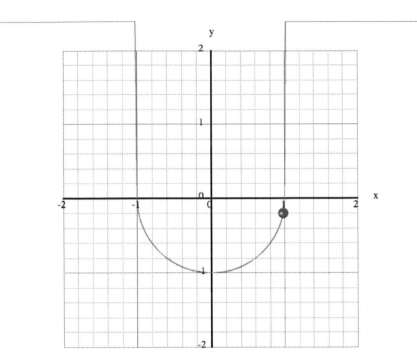

Figure 3-6. First attempt to plot a circle

Let's deal with the latter problem first. These "extra bits" are there because we've gone outside of the range for which the equation makes sense. If you look at the preceding equation, you'll see that if the magnitude of x is larger than 1, we have the square root of a negative number, which does not give you a real number.

In contrast with the functions you saw previously, a circle is confined to a limited region of the plane. In math jargon, the function is not defined outside of that range. Let's fix the code by calculating the value of the function only for values of x in the range −1 <= x <= 1. This is easily done in the loop that calculates the values of the function. Take a look at **MoveCircle.as**. This is the modified code that ensures that x is restricted to the correct range:

```
for (var i:uint=0; i<=1000; i++){
        xA[i] = (i-500)*0.002;
        yA[i] = f(xA[i]);
}
```

The first problem is trickier. It arises because when we take the square root to get the previous equation, we should have included the negative as well:

$$y = \pm\sqrt{\left(1 - x^2\right)}$$

The trouble is that you can't have a function returning two different values at the same time. There is another problem, this time to do with the animation. You might have noticed that the ball appears to move quickly along some parts of the circle and slowly elsewhere. This isn't usually what we want to see. It arises because we have been incrementing x in equal amounts. But where the curve is "steep," the same increment in x leads to a larger increment in y compared with where the curve is more "level."

Usually we'd want to make an object move in a circle at a uniform rate. Is there a way to know how the position of the ball depends on time and the rate of rotation? There is. It's time to learn about parametric equations.

Using parametric equations

The basic problem we had in the last section was that we know y as a function of x, but do not know how either x or y depends on time. What we are after is a pair of equations of this form, where f(t) and g(t) are functions of time:

$$x = f(t)$$

$$y = g(t)$$

They are called *parametric equations* because x and y are expressed in terms of another parameter t, which in this instance represents time. From those, it should be possible to recover the equation connecting x and y. But the reverse is not necessarily true. Parametric equations are not unique; there might be different pairs of parametric equations that work.

We'll give you an answer here. Although it won't make full sense until you've done some trigonometry and we've covered the concept of angular velocity (in the next section), here it is (where r is the radius of the circle and ω is the so-called angular velocity, which is basically a rate of rotation around the circle):

$$x = r\sin(\omega t)$$

$$y = r\cos(\omega t)$$

We're fully aware that we are using concepts that will be fully explained only later in this chapter. Therefore, although the concepts might not be completely clear now, they should become so soon enough.

Let's choose r = 1 and w = 1, and modify the code to compute x and y accordingly (see **MoveCircleParametric.as**):

```
for (var i:uint=0; i<=1000; i++){
        var t:Number=0.01*i;
        xA[i] = Math.sin(t);
        yA[i] = Math.cos(t);
}
```

This does the job perfectly (see Figure 3-7). The multiplicative factor that computes time **t** from the counter **i** is chosen to produce at least one complete revolution. Of course, you don't have to do it this way. You can get rid of the arrays and the loop altogether and just compute x and y on the fly in a timer or enterframe event handler. But it's just good to know that there *is* another way to animate an object with code apart from computing its position on the fly. This method can prove useful, for example, if the computations are too time-consuming; they could then be done and the positions stored in an array (as done previously) during an "initialization" period, to be animated subsequently in the usual way.

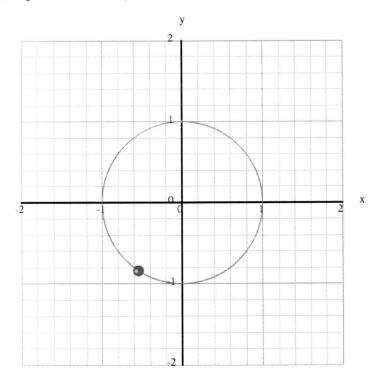

Figure 3-7. Moving an object around a circle using parametric equations

You should be able to do this in 3D easily. And while you're at it, why not add a constant drift in the third dimension so that you get a helical motion?

In `HelicalMotion.as`, we did this and also included a negative exponential factor to give a decaying helical (spiral) motion. Here is the event handler with the relevant code:

```
private function onEachTimestep(evt:TimerEvent):void{
        var dt:Number = (getTimer() - t)/1000; // time elapsed in seconds since last call
        t = getTimer(); // reset t
        theta += omega*dt;
        ball.x = 100*Math.cos(theta)*Math.exp(-theta/20) + 200;
        ball.z = 100*Math.sin(theta)*Math.exp(-theta/10) + 200;
        ball.y += vz*dt;
        evt.updateAfterEvent();
}
```

Distance between two points

A common problem is to find the distance between two objects given their locations, which is needed in collision detection, for example. Some physics laws also involve the distance between two objects. For example, Newton's law of gravitation (covered in Chapter 6) involves the square of the distance between two objects.

Fortunately, there is a simple formula, based upon Pythagoras's Theorem, which allows us to calculate the distance between two points. Pythagoras's Theorem is actually a theorem about the lengths of the sides of triangles. Specifically, it applies to a special type of triangle known as a *right-angled triangle*, which has one angle that is 90 degrees. The longest side of the triangle, called the *hypotenuse*, is always opposite the 90-degree angle (see Figure 3-8).

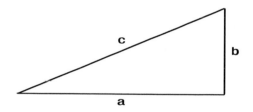

Figure 3-8. A right-angled triangle

Pythagoras's Theorem states that if we take each of the other sides, square their lengths, and add the result, we would get the square of the length of the longest side. In formula form, it is the following, where c is the length of the hypotenuse, and a and b are the lengths of the other two sides:

$$a^2 + b^2 = c^2,$$

Figure 3-9 shows how we use this formula to calculate the distance between two points: by drawing a right-angled triangle. If the coordinates of the two points are (x1, y1) and (x2, y2), the length of the two shorter sides are (x2 − x1) and (y2 − y1), respectively.

Therefore, the length of the hypotenuse, which is actually the distance between the two points, is given by this:

$$d^2 = (x2 - x1)^2 + (y2 - y1)^2$$

That's it. What's more, this formula can be readily generalized to 3D to give the following:

$$d^2 = (x2 - x1)^2 + (y2 - y1)^2 + (z2 - z1)^2$$

Note that it does not matter if we take $(x1 - x2)^2$ instead of $(x2 - x1)^2$, and similarly for the other terms because the square of a negative number is the same as that of the corresponding positive number.

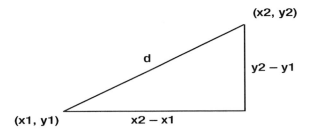

Figure 3-9. Using Pythagoras's Theorem to calculate the distance between two points

Basic trigonometry

Trigonometry is a branch of math that technically deals with the properties of triangles and the relationships between the lengths of their sides and their angles. Put this way, trigonometry may not sound very special, but it is, in fact, an indispensable part of your toolset as an animation or game programmer. For example, we used trigonometric functions previously in the parametric equations that produced uniform motion around a circle.

You probably remember the basics from your school days, such as the theorem that the sum of interior angles in a triangle is 180 degrees. But perhaps you may not remember what a sine function is. This section will review the essentials of the subject.

Degrees and radians

Everyone knows that there are 360 degrees in a complete revolution. Far fewer people know that 360 degrees equal 2π radians (or maybe have never even heard of a radian). So let's start by explaining what a radian is.

The short answer is this: a *radian* is a unit of angular measure (just like a degree is). Here's how the two measures are related:

2π radians is equal to 360 deg

so π radians is equal to 180 deg

so 1 radian is equal to 180/π deg, which is approximately 57.3 degrees

Now you might not feel very comfortable with this. Why do we need such a weird unit for angle? Don't we all know and love the degree? Well, the point is that the degree is just as arbitrary—why is there 360 degrees in a circle? Why not 100?

In fact, the radian is in many ways a more "natural" unit of angle. This follows from its definition: the angle subtended at the center of a circle by an arc that is equal in length to its radius. See Figure 3-10.

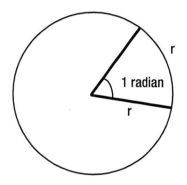

Figure 3-10. A radian is the angle subtended at the center of a circle by an arc of length equal to the circle's radius

The bottom line is that radians are here to stay. In fact, the AS3.0 trigonometric functions that we shall introduce shortly, such as **Math.sin()**, take angles in radians as arguments. Shall we give up degrees then? Unfortunately, it's not that simple. In Flash, the **rotation** property of objects is measured in degrees. So we need both in Flash. The consequence is that you will frequently need to convert between them. So, here is the conversion formula:

(angle in degrees) = (angle in radians) x 180 / π

(angle in radians) = (angle in degrees) x π / 180

The sine function

The trigonometric functions are defined in terms of the sides of a right-angled triangle. Referring to Figure 3-11, you know that the hypotenuse (let's call it *hyp* for short) is the longest side of the triangle and is opposite the right angle. Pick one of the other angles, say x. Then, in relation to angle x, the far side that does not touch x is called the opposite (*opp*). The near side that does touch x is called the adjacent (*adj*). Note that opposite and adjacent are in relation to your chosen angle (x in this case). In relation to the other angle, the roles of opposite and adjacent are reversed. On the other hand, the hypotenuse is always the longest side.

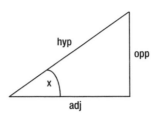

Figure 3-11. Definition of hypotenuse, adjacent and opposite sides of a right-angled triangle

The sine function is defined simply as the ratio of the length of the opposite side to that of the hypotenuse:

$$\sin(x) = \frac{\text{opp}}{\text{hyp}}$$

Now you could draw lots of right-angled triangles for different angles x, measure opp and hyp, calculate their ratio, and tabulate and plot sin (x) to see what it is like. But surely you'll prefer to dig out that **Graph** class and plot **Math.sin()**. This is what we've done in **TrigFunctions.as**.

Figure 3-12 shows what we get. We've plotted between –720 deg (–4π radians) and 720 deg (4π radians) to show the periodic nature of the function. The period (interval over which it repeats) is 360 deg, or 2π radians. The curve is like a smooth wave.

Note that sin (x) is always between –1 and 1. It can never be larger than 1 in magnitude because opp can never be larger than hyp. We say that the peak *amplitude* of a sine wave is 1. The value of sin (x) is zero at 0 degrees and every 180 deg thereafter and before.

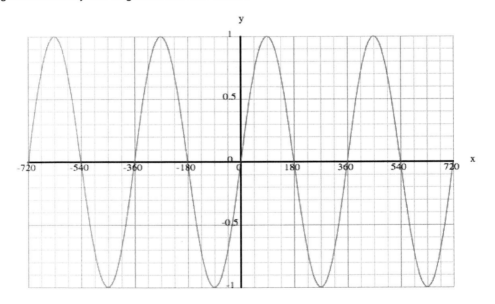

Figure 3-12. The graph of a sine function

The cosine function

Similar to sine, the cosine function is defined as the ratio of the length of the adjacent side to that of the hypotenuse:

$$\cos(x) = \frac{\text{adj}}{\text{hyp}}$$

The graph shown in Figure 3-13 is similar to that of sin (x), except that cos (x) appears to be shifted by 90 degrees with respect to sin (x). In fact, it turns out that cos (x − π/2) = sin (x). Go ahead and prove it by plotting this function. This shows that cos and sin differ only by a constant shift. We say they have a *phase difference* of 90 degrees.

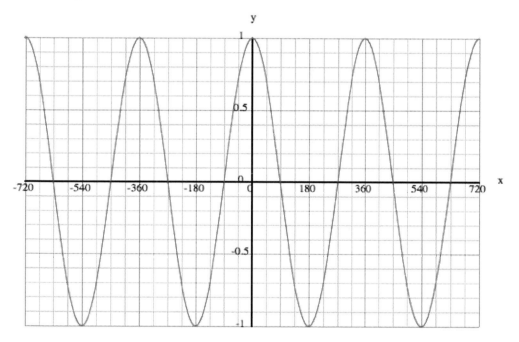

Figure 3-13. The graph of a cosine function

The tangent function

A third common trig function is the tangent function, defined as follows:

$$\tan(x) = \frac{\text{opp}}{\text{adj}}$$

63

This definition is equivalent to this:

$$\tan(x) = \frac{\sin(x)}{\cos(x)}$$

If you try and plot the graph of tan x, it might look a bit weird at first sight (see Figure 3-14). Ignore the vertical lines at 90 deg, and so on. They shouldn't really be there. The graph is still periodic, but it consists of disjoint branches every 180 deg. Also, tan (x) can take any value, not just a value between –1 and 1. What happens at 90 deg is that tan (x) becomes infinite. Going back to the definition of tan (x), this is because for 90 deg, adj is zero, so we end up dividing by zero.

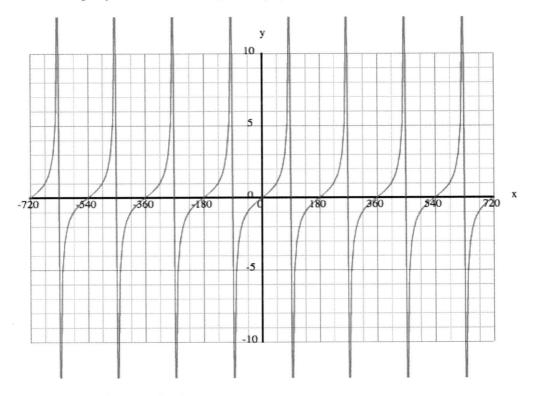

Figure 3-14. The graph of a tangent function

You probably won't use tan nearly as much as sin and cos. But you will definitely use its inverse, which we'll introduce next.

The inverse trig functions

It is frequently necessary to find an angle given the value of the sin, cos, or tan of that angle. In math, this is done using the inverse of the trig functions, called arcsin, arccos, and arctan, respectively.

In the AS3.0 `Math` class, these functions, which are called `Math.asin()`, `Math.acos()`, and `Math.atan()`, take a number as argument. Obviously, the number must be between –1 and 1 for `Math.asin()` and `Math.acos()`, but can be any value for `Math.atan()`.

Note that the inverse trig functions return an angle in radians, so you have to convert to degrees if that's what you need.

There is another inverse tan function in AS3.0: `Math.atan2()`. What is the difference, and why do we need two of them?

`Math.atan()` takes a single argument, which is the ratio opp/adj for the angle you are computing. `Math.atan2()` takes two arguments, which are the actual values of opp and adj, if you happen to know them. So, why is `Math.atan2()` needed—can't you just do `Math.atan(opp/adj)`?

To answer your question, do the following:

```
trace(Math.atan(1)*180/Math.PI);
trace(Math.atan2(2,2)*180/Math.PI);
trace(Math.atan2(-2,-2)*180/Math.PI);
```

All three have an opp/adj ratio of 1, but what you'll find is that the first two will return 45 deg, while the third will return -135 deg. What's going on is that the third option specifies that the angle points upward and to the left, and because angles are measured in a clockwise direction from the positive x-axis in Flash, the angle is actually -135 deg (see Figure 3-15). Now, you'd have no way of telling this to the `Math.atan()` function because it takes only one argument: 1, the same as for 45 deg.

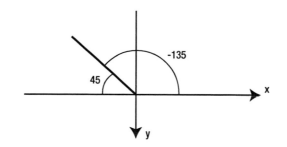

Figure 3-15. Understanding the result of Math.atan2(-2,-2)

Using trig functions for animation

You've already seen how sin and cos can be used for making an object move in a circle. They are also especially useful for producing any kind of repeating or oscillating motion. But before we get into animation using trig functions, let's introduce some new terms.

Wavelength, period, frequency and angular frequency

Take a look again at Figure 3-12, in which we show the graph of the sine function. If x represents distance in space, we have a sine wave in space that repeats at regular interval. That interval is called the *wavelength* of the wave. It is the distance between adjacent similar points, for example, the distance between successive crests.

If we instead plot the sine function against time, the repeating interval is a time scale called the *period* of the wave. For example, if this were a ball that's moving up and down, the period (denoted by the symbol T) would be the time it takes to return to its initial position. Let's call this a *cycle*.

Now, suppose that a cycle takes 0.5 seconds, i.e. T = 0.5 seconds. How many cycles does the ball complete in 1 second? Well, obviously 2. That's how many half-seconds there are in a second. This is called the *frequency* of the motion (denoted by the symbol f).

It is not difficult to see that, in general, the frequency is given by the reciprocal of the period:

$$f = \frac{1}{T}$$

Now, it turns out that you can always think of the up-and-down motion of the ball as the projection of the position of another imaginary ball that is moving at a constant rate in a circle (see Figure 3-16). One cycle in an oscillation then corresponds to a complete revolution around the circle. Thinking in terms of the angle moved by the circling ball, that's 2π radians. Because the ball moves f cycles per second, and each cycle is 2π radians, this means that the ball goes through $2\pi f$ radians per second. This is called the *angular frequency* or *angular velocity* of the motion (usually denoted by the Greek letter ω, omega). It tells you the angle, in radians, through which the circling ball moves in each second.

$$\omega = 2\pi f = \frac{2\pi}{T}$$

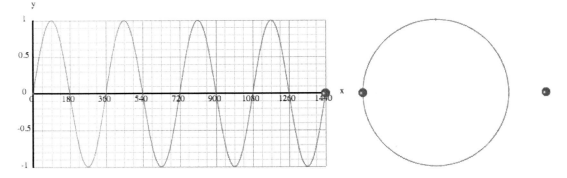

Figure 3-16. Relationship between oscillation, circular motion and a sine wave

Finally, because ω is the angle through which the imaginary ball moves per second, in t seconds the ball will have moved through ω t radians. So, if it starts out at an angle of 0 radians, at t seconds its projected displacement is equal to sin (ω t):

$$y = \sin(\omega t)$$

If we know the angular frequency of the oscillation, we can calculate the position of the ball at any time if its initial position is known. Of course, if we know the period or frequency instead, we can work out the angular frequency from the preceding formula.

Let's look at some examples. For these examples, we're using **TrigAnimations.as**, which is a modification of **MoveCurve.as**. We will now show, side by side, a 2D animation as well as its 1D version, in which you just move an object along one direction.

Oscillations

Basic oscillations (wave motion in 2D) are pretty straightforward to achieve with just a sine or cosine function. Such an oscillation is called a *simple harmonic motion (SHM)*. The oscillation consists of a wave with a single frequency. Try it out with **TrigAnimations.as**:

```
private function f(x:Number):Number{
       var y:Number;
       y = Math.sin(x*Math.PI/180);
       return y;
}
```

You can produce waves of different frequencies by multiplying the argument by different factors.

Damped oscillations

Oscillations with a sine wave go on forever. If you want to make them die out with time, you can just multiply the sine by an exponential with a negative coefficient:

```
y = Math.sin(x*Math.PI/180)*Math.exp(-0.002*x);
```

You can experiment by changing the coefficient 0.002 to a smaller or larger number. Figure 3-17 shows a typical pattern you might see.

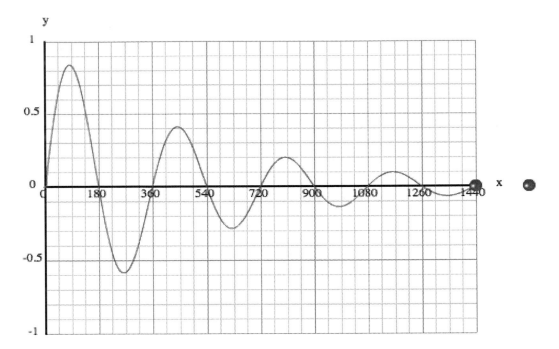

Figure 3-17. Damped oscillations using sin(x) and exp(–x)

Combining sine waves

You can produce all kinds of exotic effects by combining sine and cosine waves. Here's an example of a combination:

```
y = Math.sin(x*Math.PI/180) + Math.sin(1.5*x*Math.PI/180);
```

Or try two sine waves with nearly the same angular frequency:

```
y = 0.5*Math.sin(3*x*Math.PI/180) + 0.5*Math.sin(3.5*x*Math.PI/180);
```

This gives you a "beats" motion; a rapid oscillation upon which is superimposed a slower oscillation (see Figure 3-18).

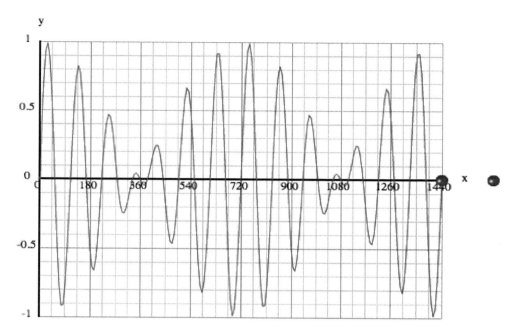

Figure 3-18. Pattern produced by superimposing two sine waves of nearly equal frequency

It is possible to produce all sorts of repeating patterns using a combination of sine waves. There is a mathematical technique called *Fourier analysis* that allows you to work out what combination of sine wave you need to produce a particular pattern. The resulting sum of sine waves is called a *Fourier series*.

For example, you can produce something that looks like a square wave (step function wave) by adding sine waves in the following way:

```
y = Math.sin(x*Math.PI/180) + Math.sin(3*x*Math.PI/180)/3 + Math.sin(5*x*Math.PI/180)/5;
```

The more waves you add, the closer it will be to a square wave. For example, add the next term in the series (`Math.sin(7*x*Math.PI/180)/7`) to see what you get.

We wrote a little function, **fourierSum(N,x)**, that computes the Fourier sum to N terms for the square wave.

```
private function f(x:Number):Number{
        var y:Number;
        y = fourierSum(10,x);
        return y;
}
private function fourierSum(N:int,x:Number):Number{
        var fs:Number=0;
        for (var nn:uint=1; nn<=N; nn=nn+2){
                fs += Math.sin(nn*x*Math.PI/180)/nn;
        }
        return fs;
}
```

Figure 3-19 shows what you get with N = 10. With a value of N = 1000, the curve is an almost perfect square wave.

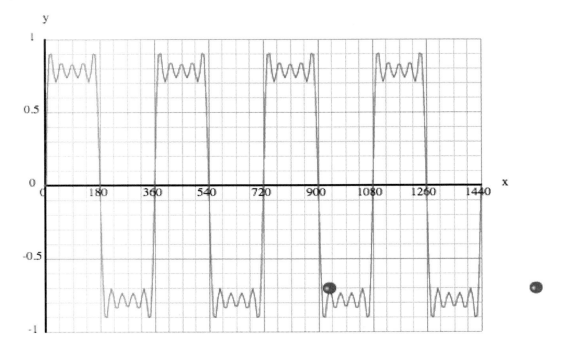

Figure 3-19. Fourier series pattern for a square wave with N = 10

Vectors and basic vector algebra

Vectors are useful math constructs that simplify how we need to deal with many physical quantities like velocity and force, which will be discussed in detail in the next chapter. You've already met vectors informally, when you dealt with velocity components. Let's now see what we were really doing.

What are vectors?

Vectors can be most intuitively illustrated using the example of displacements. The concept of displacement will be covered in detail in Chapter 4, but essentially it refers to movement for a given distance and in a given direction. Here is an example.

Suppose that Bug, the ladybug, is crawling on a piece of graph paper. Bug starts at the origin and crawls for a distance of 10 units; then he stops. Bug then resumes crawling for a further distance of 10 units before stopping again. How far is Bug from the origin? One might be tempted to say 20 units. But what if Bug crawled upward the first time and to the right the second time? (See Figure 3-20). Clearly 20 units is the wrong answer. By using Pythagoras's Theorem, the answer is actually $\sqrt{(10^2 + 10^2)}$, or roughly 14.1 units.

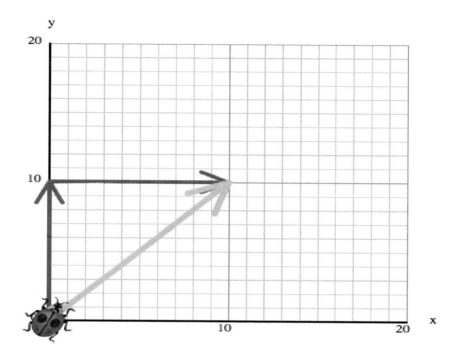

Figure 3-20. The direction of displacement matters!

You can't just add the two distances because you also need to take into account the direction in which Bug moves. To analyze displacements, you need a magnitude and a direction.

In math we abstract this idea into the concept of a vector, which is a quantity that has a magnitude and a direction.

Displacements are not the only vectors. Many of the basic concepts of motion, such as velocity, acceleration, and force, are vectors (they will be discussed in the next chapter). This section outlines the algebra of vectors as abstract mathematical objects, regardless of whether they are displacements, velocities, or forces. With a little grasp of vector algebra, you can simplify calculations by reducing the number of equations that you have to deal with. This saves time, reduces the likelihood of errors, and simplifies life.

Vectors and scalars

Vectors are often contrasted with *scalars*, which are quantities that have a magnitude only. Distance or length is a scalar—you need only one number to specify it. But displacement is a vector because you need to specify the direction of the displacement. Pictorially, vectors are often represented as directed straight lines—a line with an arrow on it.

Note that a vector is characterized uniquely by its magnitude and direction. That means that two vectors with the same magnitude and direction are considered to be equal, irrespective of where they are in space (see Figure 3-21a). In other words, the location of a vector does not matter. There's one exception to this rule, however: the *position vector*. The position vector of an object is the vector that joins a fixed origin to that object, so it's a displacement vector in relation to a fixed origin (see Figure 3-21b).

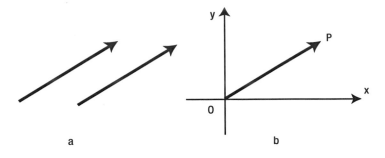

Figure 3-21. (a) Parallel vectors of equal length are equal; (b) Position vectors relate to the origin.

Adding and subtracting vectors

In the Bug example, what is the sum of the two displacements? The natural answer is that it is the resultant displacement as given by the vector that points from the initial to the final position (refer to Figure 3-20). What if Bug now moves a distance of 5 units downward? You might say that the resultant displacement is the vector that points from the beginning (the origin, in this case) to the destination. This is the so-called head-to-tail rule:

> To add two or more vectors, join them so that they are "head-to-tail," moving them
> around if necessary (as long as their direction does not change, i.e. they remain parallel
> to their original direction). The sum or resultant vector is then the vector that joins the
> starting point to the ending point.

To subtract a vector from another vector, we just add the negative of that vector. The negative of a vector is one with the same magnitude but pointing in the opposite direction.

Subtracting a vector from itself (or the sum of a vector and its negative) gives you the *zero vector*—a vector of zero length and arbitrary direction.

Let's look at an example. Suppose that after Bug has moved 10 units upward, he decides to move 10 units at an angle of 45 degrees instead (see Figure 3-22). What is the resultant displacement? Now that is trickier: you can't directly apply Pythagoras's Theorem because you don't have a right-angled triangle any more. You could use some more complicated trigonometry, or draw the vectors accurately and take a ruler and measure the resultant distance and angle.

In practice, that's not how you'll be doing it, though. Adding and subtracting vectors is much easier using vector components. So let's take a look at vector components now.

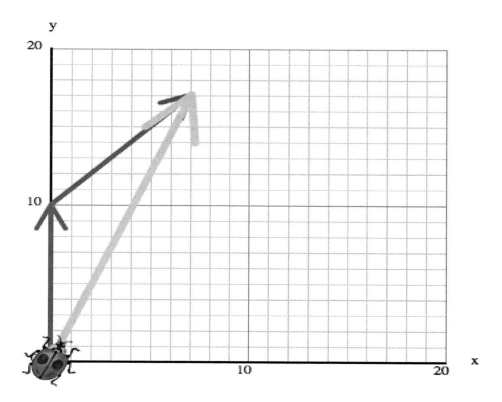

Figure 3-22. Addition of vectors

Resolving vectors: vector components

As mentioned before, a vector has a magnitude and a direction. What this means in 2D is that you need two numbers to specify a vector. Take a look at Figure 3-23. The two numbers are the length r of the vector and the angle θ that it makes with the positive x-axis. But we can also specify the two numbers as the extent of the vector in the x- and y- direction, denoted by x and y respectively. These are called the *vector components*.

The relation between (r, θ) and (x, y) can be obtained with the simple trigonometry discussed in the last section. Looking at Figure 3-23 again, we know this:

$$\cos(\theta) = x/r$$
$$\sin(\theta) = y/r$$

This gives the following:

$$x = r\cos(\theta)$$
$$y = r\sin(\theta)$$

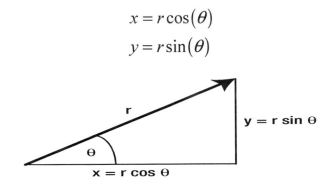

Figure 3-23. Vector components

Working out the vector components in this way from the magnitude and angle of a vector is known as "resolving the vector" along the x- and y-axes. Actually, you can resolve a vector along any two mutually perpendicular directions. But most of the time, we'll be doing that along the x- and y-axes.

There are lots of different notations for vectors, and it's easy to get bogged down with notation. But in ActionScript you just have to remember that a vector has components. So any notation that makes you remember that is just as good as any other. We'll use the following notation for compactness, denoting vectors using bold letters and denoting their components by enclosing them using square brackets:

$$\mathbf{v} = \begin{bmatrix} a, b \end{bmatrix}$$

In 3D, you need not two, but three, components to specify a vector, so we write this:

$$\mathbf{v} = \begin{bmatrix} a, b, c \end{bmatrix}$$

Position vectors

The position vector of an object is a vector pointing from the origin to that object. Hence, we can write the position vector in terms of the coordinates of the object:

$$\mathbf{r} = \begin{bmatrix} x, y \end{bmatrix} \text{ in 2D}$$

$$\mathbf{r} = \begin{bmatrix} x, y, z \end{bmatrix} \text{ in 3D}$$

Adding vectors using components

Here's how you add two vectors using components:

$$[a, b] + [c, d] = [a+c, b+d]$$

Pretty simple, isn't it? Why this is so should be clear from Figure 3-24. You separately add the horizontal components and the vertical components of the two vectors you're adding. This gives you the components of the resultant vector.

As an example, applying this to the Bug displacement problem shown in Figure 3-22 gives this displacement, which you can easily verify on the graph:

$$[0, 10] + [7, 7] = [7, 17]$$

Feel free to practice doing vector additions with pen and paper; after going through a few, it should become obvious and help you build your intuition about vectors and vectors components.

Similarly, vector subtraction using components is simply this:

$$[a, b] - [c, d] = [a-c, b-d]$$

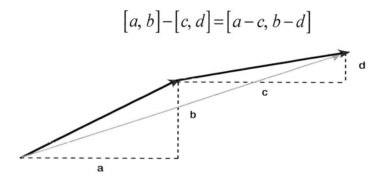

Figure 3-24. Adding vectors using components

Multiplying a vector by a number

Multiplying a vector by a number just multiplies each of its components by that number:

$$4[a, b, c] = [4a, 4b, 4c]$$

In particular, if we multiply a vector by –1, we get this, which gives the negative of that vector:

$$-\left[a,\,b,\,c\right]=\left[-a,\,-b,\,-c\right]$$

Dividing a vector by a number N is just the same as multiplying the vector by the reciprocal 1/N of that number.

Vector magnitude

The *magnitude* (length) of a vector is given by applying Pythagoras's Theorem to its components:

In 2D, the magnitude of [x, y] is $\sqrt{x^2+y^2}$; or in ActionScript code:
`Math.sqrt(x*x+y*y)`.

In 3D, the magnitude of [x, y, z] is $\sqrt{x^2+y^2+z^2}$; or in ActionScript code:
`Math.sqrt(x*x+y*y+z*z)`.

Note that if we divide a vector by its magnitude, we get a vector of length one unit in the same direction as the original vector. This is called a *unit vector*.

Vector angle

Calculating the angle of a vector from its components is no more difficult than calculating its magnitude. In ActionScript, this can be done most easily using the `Math.atan2()` function.

The angle of a vector [x, y] is given by `Math.atan2(y, x)`. Beware—you need to specify the arguments as y first and then x.

Multiplying vectors: Scalar or dot product

Is it possible to multiply two vectors? The answer is yes. Mathematicians have defined a "multiplication" operation called *scalar product*, in which two vectors produce a scalar. Recall that a scalar only has a magnitude and no direction; in other words, it is basically just a number. The rule is that you multiply the corresponding components of each vector and add the results:

$$\left[x1,\,y1\right]\bullet\left[x2,\,y2\right]=x1\cdot x2+y1\cdot y2$$

The scalar product is denoted by a dot, so it is also called the *dot product*.

Expressed in terms of vector magnitudes and direction, the dot product is given by the following, where θ is the angle between the two vectors, and r1 and r2 are their lengths:

$$[x1, y1] \bullet [x2, y2] = r1 \cdot r2 \cdot \cos(\theta)$$

The geometrical interpretation of the scalar product is that it's the product of the length of one vector with the projected length of the other (see Figure 3-25).

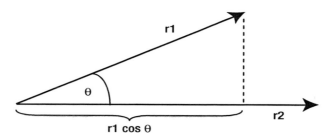

Figure 3-25. The scalar product between two vectors

This is useful when you need to find the angle between two vectors. In ActionScript, you just do this:

```
angle = Math.acos((x1*x2+y1*y2)/(r1*r2))
```

Note that if the angle between two vectors is zero (they are parallel), cos (θ) = 1 and the dot product is just the product of their magnitudes.

If the two vectors are perpendicular, then cos (θ) = cos (π/2) = 0, and so the dot product is zero. This is a good test to check if two vectors are perpendicular or not. All these formulas and facts carry over to 3D, with the dot product given by the following:

$$[x1, y1, z1] \bullet [x2, y2, z2] = x1 \cdot x2 + y1 \cdot y2 + z1 \cdot z2$$

Scalar products crop up in several places in physics. We'll come across an example in the next chapter, with the concept of *work*, which is defined as the dot product of force and displacement. So, although the dot product may appear somewhat abstract and mysterious as a math construct, it will hopefully make more intuitive sense when you come across it again in an applied context in Chapter 4.

Multiplying vectors: Vector or cross product

In 3D, there is another type of product known as the *vector product* because it gives a vector instead of a scalar. The rule is quite a bit trickier.

If you have two vectors **a** = [x1, y1, z1] and **b** = [x2, y2, z2], and their vector product is given by a vector **c** = **a** x **b** = [x, y, z], the components of **c** are given by the following:

$$x = y1 \cdot z2 - z1 \cdot y2$$
$$y = z1 \cdot x2 - x1 \cdot z2$$
$$z = x1 \cdot y2 - y1 \cdot x2$$

Now this is not exactly intuitive, is it? There sure is some logic to it, as with everything in math. But trying to explain it would be too much of a diversion. So let's just accept the formula.

The vector product is also called the *cross product* because of the "cross" notation used to denote it. The vector product of two vectors **a** and **b** gives a third vector that is perpendicular to both **a** and **b**.

In terms of vector magnitudes and directions, the cross product is given by this:

$$\mathbf{a} \times \mathbf{b} = a\,b\sin(\theta)\,\mathbf{n}$$

where θ is the smaller angle between **a** and **b**, and **n** is the unit vector perpendicular to **a** and **b** and oriented according to the right-hand rule (see Figure 3-26): hold your right hand with the forefinger pointing along the first vector **a**, and your middle finger pointing in the direction of **b**. Then **n** will point in the direction of the thumb, held perpendicular to **a** and **b**.

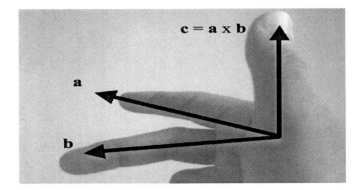

Figure 3-26. The right hand rule for the vector product

Note that the cross product is zero when θ = 0 (because sin (0) = 0). Hence, the cross product of two parallel vectors gives the zero vector.

Like the scalar product, vector products appear in several places in physics; for example in rotational motion.

Building a Vector class with vector algebra

Flash CS4 and CS5 ship with a **Vector3D** class with vector algebra built in using appropriately named functions. Here are some examples:

```
var vec1:Vector3D = new Vector3D(1,1,1);
var vec2:Vector3D = new Vector3D(1,1,0);
trace(vec1.length); // magnitude of vec1
trace(vec1.lengthSquared); // magnitude squared of vec1
trace(vec1.dotProduct(vec2)); // returns dot product of vec1 with vec2
trace(vec1.crossProduct(vec2)); // returns cross product of vec1 with vec2
trace(Vector3D.angleBetween(vec1,vec2)*180/Math.PI); // static method that returns the angle
//between two vectors
```

Have a look at the AS3.0 documentation to see all the methods available.

(By the way, there is another AS3.0 class called **Vector**. This **Vector** class has nothing to do with the math vectors we're talking about here. The AS3.0 **Vector** class is basically an indexed array whose elements must all be instances of the same class.)

Unfortunately, there is no corresponding built-in **Vector2D** class in AS3.0. Of course, you could just use Vector3D and set the third component to zero, but if you're only going to do 2D, a **Vector2D** class would save on unnecessary calculations. So we built a lightweight **Vector2D** class. Here is the code (see **Vector2D.as**). The method names have been chosen to correspond to those of **Vector3D**.

```
package {
    public class Vector2D {
        private var _x:Number;
        private var _y:Number;
        public function Vector2D(px:Number,py:Number):void {
            _x = px;
            _y = py;
        }
        public function get x():Number{
            return _x;
        }
        public function set x(px:Number):void{
            _x = px;
        }
        public function get y():Number{
            return _y;
        }
        public function set y(py:Number):void{
            _y = py;
        }
        public function get length():Number{
            return Math.sqrt(lengthSquared);
        }
        public function get lengthSquared():Number{
            return _x*_x + _y*_y;
        }
```

```
        public function clone():Vector2D {
                return new Vector2D(_x,_y);
        }
        public function negate(vec:Vector2D):void {
                _x = - _x;
                _y = - _y;
        }
        public function normalize():Number {
                if (length > 0) {
                        _x /= length;
                        _y /= length;
                }
                return length;
        }
        public function add(vec:Vector2D):Vector2D {
                return new Vector2D(_x + vec.x,_y + vec.y);
        }
        public function incrementBy(vec:Vector2D):void {
                _x += vec.x;
                _y += vec.y;
        }
        public function subtract(vec:Vector2D):Vector2D {
                return new Vector2D(_x - vec.x,_y - vec.y);
        }
        public function decrementBy(vec:Vector2D):void {
                _x -= vec.x;
                _y -= vec.y;
        }
        public function scaleBy(k:Number):void {
                _x *= k;
                _y *= k;
        }
        public function dotProduct(vec:Vector2D):Number {
                return _x*vec.x + _y*vec.y;
        }
        static public function distance(vec1:Vector2D,vec2:Vector2D):Number{
                return (vec1.subtract(vec2)).length;
        }
        static public function angleBetween(vec1:Vector2D,vec2:Vector2D):Number{
                return Math.acos(vec1.dotProduct(vec2)/(vec1.length*vec2.length));
        }
    }
}
```

The usage of the class **Vector2D** is similar to that of **Vector3D**. The file **VectorExamples.as** contains some examples.

Simple calculus ideas

As stated at the beginning of this chapter, we do not assume that all readers will have a background in calculus. If you do, that is certainly handy; but we still recommend that you skim through this section, especially the code examples and the section on discrete calculus, to see how we apply calculus in code. If calculus is completely new to you, this section is designed as a gentle overview of some of the basic concepts. So although you won't be able to "do" calculus just by reading this section, you will hopefully gain enough understanding to appreciate the meaning of physics formulas that involve calculus. Additionally, you will be introduced to discrete calculus and the subject of numerical methods, which will provide a foundation for approaching more complex physics simulations.

So what is calculus? In one sentence, it's a mathematical formalism for dealing with quantities that change continuously with respect to other quantities. Because physics deals with laws that relate some quantities with other quantities, calculus is clearly relevant.

Calculus consists of two parts. Differential calculus (or *differentiation*) deals with the rate of change of quantities. Integral calculus (or *integration*) deals with continuous sums. The two are related by the fundamental theorem of calculus, which states that integration is the reverse of differentiation.

That all sounds very mysterious if you've never come across calculus before, so let's start from something you know to give you a gentle introduction to the subject. By the end of this chapter, these statements will make much more sense to you.

Slope of a line: gradient

The idea of rate of change is an important concept in physics. If you think of it, we are trying to formulate laws that tell us how, for example, the motion of a planet changes with time; how the force on the planet changes with its position, and so on. The key words here are "changes with." The laws of physics, it turns out, contain the rate of change of different physical quantities such as position, velocity, and so on.

Informally, "rate of change" tells us how quickly something is changing. Usually we mean how fast it's changing in time, but we could also be interested in how "fast" something changes with respect to some other quantity, not just time. For example, as a planet moves in its orbit, how quickly does the force of gravity change with its position?

So, in math terms, let's consider the rate of change of a quantity y with respect to another quantity x (where x could be time t or some other quantity). To do this, we'll use graphs because that will help us visualize relationships more easily.

Let's start with two quantities that have a simple, linear, relationship with each other; that is, they are related by

$$y = ax + b$$

As you saw in the coordinate geometry section, this implies that the graph of y against x is a straight line. The constant b is the y-intercept; the point at which the line intersects the y-axis. We'll now show that the constant a gives a measure of the rate of change of y with x.

Look at Figure 3-27. Of the two lines, in which one is y changing faster with x?

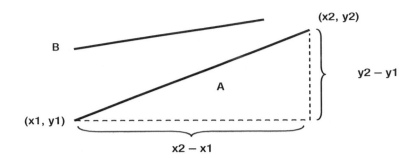

Figure 3-27. The gradient (slope) of a line

Clearly it's A because it is "steeper," so the same increase in x leads to a larger increase in y. The steepness of the slope of the line therefore gives a measure of the rate of change of y with x. We can make this idea precise by defining the rate of change as follows:

Rate of change = (change in y) / (change in x)

It is customary to use the symbol Δ to denote "change in", so we can write this:

$$\text{Rate of change} = \frac{\Delta y}{\Delta x}$$

Let's give the rate of change a shorter name; let's call it *gradient*. Here's the idea: take any two points on the line with coordinates (x1, y1) and (x2, y2), calculate the difference in y and the difference in x and divide the former by the latter:

$$\text{Gradient} = \frac{y2 - y1}{x2 - x1}$$

With a straight line, you'll find that no matter which pair of points you take, you'll always get the same gradient. Moreover, that gradient is equal to a, the number that multiplies x in the equation y = ax + b.

This makes sense because a straight line has a constant slope, so it should not matter where you measure it. This is a very good start. We've got a formula for calculating the gradient or rate of change. The only problem is that it is restricted to quantities that are linearly related to each other. So how do we generalize this result to more general relationships (for example, when y is a nonlinear function of x?)

Rates of change: derivatives

You already know that the graph of a nonlinear function is a curve instead of a straight line. Intuitively, a curve's slope is not constant—it changes along the curve. Therefore, whatever the rate of change or gradient of a nonlinear function might be, it is not constant but depends on x. In other words, it is also a function of x.

Our objective now is to find this *gradient function*. In a math course, you'd do some algebra and come up with a formula for the gradient function. For example, you can start with the function y = x² and show that its gradient function is 2x. But because you're not in a math course, let's do that with code instead. But first, we need to define what we mean by the gradient of a curve.

Because the gradient of a curve changes along the curve, let's focus on a fixed point P on the curve (Figure 3-28).

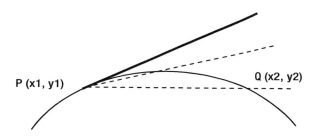

Figure 3-28. The gradient of a curve

Then let's pick any other point Q near point P. If we draw a line segment joining P and Q, the slope of that line approximates the slope of the curve. If we imagine that Q approaches P, we can expect the gradient of the line segment PQ to be closer and closer to the gradient of the curve at P.

What we are doing, in effect, is using the formula for the gradient of a line we had before and reducing the intervals Δx and Δy:

$$\text{Gradient} = \frac{\Delta y}{\Delta x} = \frac{y2 - y1}{x2 - x1}$$

We can then repeat this process at different locations for the point P along the curve to find the gradient function. Let's do this now in **GradientFunction.as**:

```
package{
        import flash.display.Sprite;

        public class GradientFunction extends Sprite{

                private var numPoints:uint=1001;
                private var numGrad:uint=250;
                private var xRange:Number=6;
                private var xStep:Number;

                public function GradientFunction(){
                        init();
                }
                private function init():void{
                        var graph:Graph = new Graph(-4,4,-10,10,275,210,450,350);
```

```
                    graph.drawgrid(1,0.2,2,0.5);
                    graph.drawaxes('x','y');
                    addChild(graph);
                    var xA:Array = new Array();
                    var yA:Array = new Array();
                    // calculate function
                    xStep = xRange/(numPoints-1);
                    for (var i:uint=0; i<numPoints; i++){
                            xA[i] = (i-numPoints/2)*xStep;
                            yA[i] = f(xA[i]);
                    }
                    graph.plot(xA,yA,0xff0000,false,true); // plot function
                    // calculate gradient function using forward method
                    var xAr:Array = new Array();
                    var gradA:Array = new Array();
                    for (var j:uint=0; j<numPoints-numGrad; j++){
                            xAr[j] = xA[j];
                            gradA[j] = grad(xA[j],xA[j+numGrad]);
                    }
                    graph.plot(xAr,gradA,0x0000ff,false,true); // plot gradient function
            }
        private function f(x:Number):Number{
                    var y:Number;
                    y = x*x;
                    return y;
            }
        private function grad(x1:Number,x2:Number):Number{
                    return (f(x1)-f(x2))/(x1-x2);
            }
        }
}
```

The relevant lines are the ones that compute the gradient function in **init()** and the function **grad()**. This function simply computes the gradient (y2 – y1) / (x2 – x1) given x1 and x2 as input. The line that decides which points to use is the following:

```
gradA[j] = grad(xA[j],xA[j+numGrad]);
```

Here **numGrad** is the number of grid points that Q is away from the point P (the point at which we are evaluating the gradient). Obviously, the smaller the value of **numGrad**, the more accurate the calculated gradient will be.

We have used a total of 1,000 gridpoints in an x-interval of 6 (from -3 to 3). That gives us a step size of 0.006 units per gridpoint. Let's use **numGrad=1** to start with. This is the smallest possible value. Running the code plots the gradient function alongside the original function $y = x^2$. The graph of the gradient function is a straight line passing through the origin. When x = 1, y = 2, when x = 2, y = 4, and so on. You can probably guess that the equation of the line is y = 2x. Now any calculus textbook will tell you that the gradient function of $y = x^2$ is y = 2x. So this is good. You've successfully calculated your first gradient function!

Now change the value of **numGrad** to 50. You'll see that the computed gradient function line shifts a bit; it's no longer y = 2x. Not too good. Try reducing **numGrad**. You'll find that a value of up to about 10 gives you something that looks very close to y = 2x. That's a step size of 10 x 0.006 = 0.06. Anything much larger than this and you'll start losing accuracy.

Let's finish off this section by introducing some more terminology and notation. The gradient function is also called the *derived function* or *derivative* with respect to x. We'll use these terms interchangeably. The process of calculating the derivative is called *differentiation*.

We showed that the ratio Δy/Δx gives the gradient of a curve at a point provided that Δx and Δy are small. In formal calculus, we say that Δy/Δx tends to the gradient function as Δx and Δy go to zero.

To express the fact that the gradient function is really a limiting value of Δy/Δx, we write it like this:

$$\frac{dy}{dx}$$

This is the standard notation for the derivative of function y with respect to x. Another notation is y' ("y prime"); or if we write y = f(x), the derivative can also be denoted by f' ("f prime").

There is nothing stopping you from calculating the derivative of a derivative. This is called the second derivative, and is written as follows:

$$\frac{d^2y}{dx^2}$$

In fact, as you'll find out in the next chapter, velocity is the derivative of position (with respect to time), and acceleration is the derivative of velocity. So acceleration is the second derivative of position with respect to time. In the notation, v = dx/dt, a = dv/dt, so a = d^2x/dt^2.

We calculated the derivative of a scalar function, but you can also differentiate vectors. You just find the derivative of each vector component separately.

For example, vx = dx/dt, vy = dy/dt, and vz = dz/dt are the three velocity components. We can write this more compactly in vector form as follows, where **v** = [vx, vy, vz] and **r** = [x, y, z]:

$$\mathbf{v} = \frac{d\mathbf{r}}{dt}$$

Discrete calculus: difference equations

What we did while calculating the gradient function in the preceding code is an example of discrete calculus: calculating the derivative using *numerical methods*. A numerical method is basically an algorithm for performing a mathematical calculation in an approximate way using code. This is needed if we don't have an exact formula for the quantity we are calculating.

In the preceding example, we had y = x² and needed to calculate y' using the discrete form of the derivative:

$$y' = \frac{dy}{dx} \approx \frac{\Delta y}{\Delta x}$$

To do this, we used a *difference equation* of the form:

$$y'(n) = \frac{y(n+1) - y(n)}{x(n+1) - x(n)}$$

This is called a forward difference scheme because we are calculating the derivative at step n by using values of the function at the next step n+1.

There are many other difference schemes. Let's try a central difference scheme:

$$y'(n) = \frac{y(n+1) - y(n-1)}{x(n+1) - x(n-1)}$$

It's called a central difference scheme because we're picking a point on either side of the point P at which we're evaluating the gradient. Here is the code that does this:

```
// calculate gradient function using centered method
        var xArc:Array = new Array();
        var gradAc:Array = new Array();
        for (var k:uint=numGrad; k<numPoints-numGrad; k++){
            xArc[k-numGrad] = xA[k];
            gradAc[k-numGrad] = grad(xA[k-numGrad],xA[k+numGrad]);
        }
```

If you run this code, you'll see that it gives you the same answer as the previous scheme for **numGrad** = 1 (recall that **numGrad** is the number of gridpoints between P and Q, and that the smaller it is, the more accurately the computed gradient will be). But if you now try larger values of **numGrad**, you'll find that it's still pretty accurate for a value as large as 250, which amounts to a grid size of 1.5. Compare that with the maximum step size of 0.06 for the forward difference scheme—it's 25 times larger!

This shows that the central difference scheme is much more accurate than a forward scheme. Figure 3-29 shows the derivatives calculated by the two methods for **numGrad** = 50. Note that we are plotting two different kinds of things on this graph: the original function y and its gradient function dy/dx. Hence, the labeling on the y-axis. The line that passes exactly through the origin is the gradient function obtained by using the central difference scheme. With your knowledge of coordinate geometry, you should be able to deduce that it's a plot of the function 2x. In other words, dy/dx = 2x. Anyone who's done any calculus will instantly recognize 2x as the gradient function of y = x², our original function—so the central difference scheme is doing very well. The other line, which is computed using the forward difference scheme, has a bit of an offset, though, which means it will have an error associated with it. This is called a *numerical* *integration error*. Of course, there is an error associated with all numerical schemes. But in this case, the error due to the central difference scheme is so small that it is not visible on the plot. We'll go into much more detail on numerical accuracy in Chapter 14.

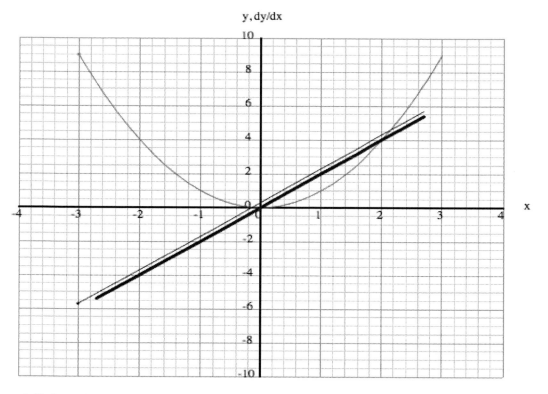

Figure 3-29. Derivatives computed by the forward (thin line) and central (thick line) difference schemes.

Doing sums: integrals

Now we ask this question: Is it possible to do the reverse? Suppose we know the derivative of a function; can we find the function? The answer is yes. This is called *integration*. Again, usually in math you'll do that using analytical methods. But here we'll integrate numerically by using code.

As an example of numerical integration, let's reverse the preceding forward difference scheme to find y(n+1), which gives this:

$$y(n+1) = y(n) + y'(n) \cdot \left[x(n+1) - x(n) \right]$$

Now y' is given, so we can calculate y(n+1) from the previous y(n). So you can see that this will be an iterative process in which we increment the value of y. It's a sum, and that's what integration is. The result of integration is called the *integral*, just like the result of differentiation is called the *derivative*.

Let's apply this to the derivative y' = 2x. We should be able to recover the function y = x². Here's the code that does this:

```
package{
        import flash.display.Sprite;
        public class Integration extends Sprite{
                private var numPoints:uint=1001;
                private var numGrad:uint=1;
                private var xRange:Number=6;
                private var xStep:Number;

                public function Integration(){
                        init();
                }
                private function init():void{
                        var graph:Graph = new Graph(-4,4,-10,10,275,210,450,350);
                        graph.drawgrid(1,0.2,2,0.5);
                        graph.drawaxes('x','y');
                        addChild(graph);
                        var xA:Array = new Array();
                        var yA:Array = new Array();
                        // calculate function
                        xStep = xRange/(numPoints-1);
                        for (var i:uint=0; i<numPoints; i++){
                                xA[i] = (i-numPoints/2)*xStep;
                                yA[i] = f(xA[i]);
                        }
                        graph.plot(xA,yA,0xff0000,false,true); // plot function
                        // calculate gradient function using forward method
                        var xAr:Array = new Array();
                        var gradA:Array = new Array();
                        for (var j:uint=0; j<numPoints-numGrad; j++){
                                xAr[j] = xA[j];
                                gradA[j] = grad(xA[j],xA[j+numGrad]);
                        }
                        graph.plot(xAr,gradA,0x0000ff,false,true); // plot gradient function
                        // calculate integral using forward method
                        var xAi:Array = new Array();
                        var integA:Array = new Array();
                        xAi[0] = -3;
                        integA[0] = 9;
                        for (var k:uint=1; k<numPoints; k++){
                                xAi[k] = xA[k];
                                integA[k] = integA[k-1] + f(xA[k-1])*(xA[k]-xA[k-1]);
                        }
                        graph.plot(xAi,integA,0x00ff00,false,true); // plot integral
                }
                private function f(x:Number):Number{
                        var y:Number;
                        y = 2*x;
                        return y;
                }
```

```
private function grad(x1:Number,x2:Number):Number{
        return (f(x1)-f(x2))/(x1-x2);
}
private function integ(x1:Number,x2:Number):Number{
        return (f(x1)-f(x2))/(x1-x2);
}
    }
}
```

The full source code is in **Integration.as**. One thing you'll notice is that you have to specify the starting point. This is clear from the preceding equation because y(n+1) depends on y(n), you need to know the value of y(0) (and x(0)) to begin with. This is called an *initial condition*. You always have to specify an initial condition when you are integrating. In the code we did that by specifying that x(0) = −3 and y(0) = 9. Try another initial condition and see what you get; for example, x(0) = −3, y(0) = 0.

This example might appear artificial, but in fact it describes an actual physical example: throwing a ball vertically upward. The function f(x) denotes the vertical velocity, and its integral is the vertical displacement. In fact, the derivative f'(x) is the acceleration. If you compute it (as we've done in the code), you'll find that it's a constant—a straight line with the same value of y for all x, like the acceleration due to gravity is constant. And in case you haven't guessed what x stands for in this example, it represents time. The initial condition x(0) = −3, y(0) = 9 represents the initial position of the ball. Now, it's clear why you need an initial condition in the first place and why different initial conditions give different curves. Of course, with x representing time, you'd probably start with x(0) = 0. If you feel so inclined, go ahead and animate a ball using the integrated values of y to show that it really produces a ball thrown upward. One thing you'd need to do is to scale y so that it extends over enough pixels on the stage.

You could start with the constant acceleration f'(x) and integrate it to get the velocity and then integrate the velocity to get the time. In fact, this is what we did, in a simplified way, in the first example of the book: **BouncingBall.as** back in Chapter 1.

The forward scheme that we used in this example is the simplest integration scheme possible. In Chapter 14, we'll go into considerable detail on numerical integration and different integration schemes.

Summary

Wow! Well done for surviving this chapter. You now have a remarkable set of tools at your disposal. Hopefully, you can begin to see the potential for applying these ideas and methods. No doubt you have many ideas of your own.

In case you've had difficulty with some of the material in this chapter, don't worry. Things will become much clearer when you see them applied in practice in later chapters. You might want to come back to this chapter again to refresh your memory and reinforce your understanding.

You're now ready for physics. So take a well-deserved break and, when you feel ready, let's move on to the next chapter.

Chapter 4

Basic Physics Concepts

In the previous two chapters, we have covered a great deal of background material in ActionScript coding and math tools. This chapter will provide a gentle overview of basic physics in order to establish some key concepts. Along the way, we will illustrate some of these concepts using ActionScript examples and will build some useful physics classes that will be used throughout the book.

Topics covered in this chapter include the following:

- **General physics concepts and notation**: Physics deals with measurable quantities. This brief section reviews some basic facts about the nature of physical quantities and their units, and explains the use of scientific notation for expressing the values of physical quantities.

- **Things—particles and other objects in physics**: Things in physics are modeled using idealized concepts such as *particles*. We build an AS3.0 `Particle` class that implements appropriate particle properties and methods, as well as related classes.

- **Describing motion—kinematics**: This section explains the concepts and methods needed to describe and analyze motion. It contains some essential definitions and formulas that any prospective physics programmer must know.

- **Predicting motion—forces and dynamics**: To predict motion, you need to understand what causes it: force. Dynamics is the study of force and motion. By specifying the forces acting on an object, you can compute its motion.

- **Energy concepts**: Energy is a powerful concept in physics and enables some otherwise tricky problems to be solved in a simple way.

General physics concepts and notation

This short section reviews some general concepts and establishes some essential terminology and notation that apply across all of physics.

Physical quantities and units

In physics, when you talk about length or mass or energy, you want to be as precise as possible. Ideally, you want to be able to measure or calculate the things that you talk about. For example, the size of an object is not just a quality; it's a quantity. Physical quantities are measurable properties. They can be given a numerical value, or magnitude.

There is something else that a physical quantity must have: a unit. For example, we don't just say that the length of a particular table is 2; we say it is 2 *meters*. Meter (m) is the unit. Why do we need a unit? A unit does two things. First, it tells us what kind of thing we are talking about. Meter tells me I am dealing with a length, not a temperature or something else. Second, the unit establishes a reference against which we are comparing the magnitude of the quantity. When we say that a table's length is 2m, what we are really saying is that the length is twice as long as that of a reference that we call the meter. All measurements are only meaningful against some reference that we compare with.

As you might imagine, there are different choices of units. For example, to measure lengths or distances, you can use meters or feet. The usual unit of length in scientific literature is the meter (m) and its subdivisions and multiples, such as centimeter (cm) and kilometer (km). The key thing is to use consistent units, not mix different types of units. Otherwise, we can use any system of units that is appropriate. For example, in Flash graphics and animation work, we usually measure distances in pixels.

In the last chapter, you came across scalars and vectors. Just to recap briefly, a *vector* is a mathematical object that has a magnitude and a direction, whereas a *scalar* is one that only has a magnitude. Physical quantities can be scalar quantities or vector quantities. An example of a vector quantity, referred to in the last chapter, is displacement. You'll come across more examples later in this chapter.

Scientific notation

One frequently encounters very large as well as very small numbers in physics. For example, the speed of light is approximately 300 000 000 m/s. Instead of writing all these zeros, we usually write this as 3×10^8 m/s. The 10^8 ("ten to the power of 8") is 1 followed by 8 zeros, which equates to 100 million. This is known as *scientific notation*. The idea is to write large or small numbers in this form, where A is greater or equal to 1 but less than 10, and B is a positive or negative integer:

$$A \times 10^B$$

As shown in the example, if B is positive, 10^B is 1 followed by B zeros. What if B is a negative integer? In that case, we place the 1 in the Bth position after the decimal place, with zeros before it: for instance, 10^{-4} is the same as 0.0001.

As an example, the mass of an electron (the tiny particle that circles the center of atoms) is approximately 9.1×10^{-31} kg.

In ActionScript, you write this as 9.1e-31 and the velocity of light as 3e8. The "e" here must not be confused with the number e introduced in the last chapter, which is `Math.e` in ActionScript. Here, e is used to denote the power of 10 by which we multiply the number preceding it.

Things: particles and other objects in physics

To describe and model the real world, physics has to have some representation of physical things. The theories of physics are conceptual and mathematical models of reality. They consist of concepts that are idealizations from the things that exist in real life. One such idealization is the concept of a particle. Although we'll focus exclusively on particles in this section, to put them in context, here is a list of the variety of "things" you'll come across in this book:

- **Particles**: Starting from this section, much of this book will deal with *particles*. We say more about particles shortly, but in a nutshell they can be thought of as indivisible units that exist at discrete points in space. Therefore, they are distinguished from more complex objects that can be extended or can consist of multiple parts. Particles move in a simple way: they can basically just change their position. This is also known as *translation*.

- **Rigid bodies**: A *rigid body* is an extended object whose size and shape cannot be changed easily, such as a table or car. Rigid bodies can move by translation like particles, but in addition they can undergo rotation. Rigid body motion will be covered in Chapter 13.

- **Deformable bodies**: Like rigid bodies, *deformable bodies* can translate and rotate, but in addition their shape and/or size can also change. Examples include a rubber ball, a rag doll, or a piece of cloth. An approach to model deformable bodies will be discussed in Chapter 13.

- **Fluids**: *Fluids* differ from the objects described previously in that they have no well-defined size or shape, but have the ability to flow from one part of space to another. Because any part of a fluid can move, it is much more difficult to simulate fluid motion accurately. But sometimes it is possible to "cheat" by modeling fluids using particles. This is the approach we take in Chapter 12 to create some interesting fluid visual effects.

- **Fields**: Fields are more abstract entities. In a broad sense, a *field* is some physical quantity that exists continuously over space. For example, we will introduce the concept of a *force field* in Chapter 10.

What is a particle?

Because we are going to do lots of things with particles, let's discuss them a bit more. What are particles? Probably the first things that might come to mind are tiny entities such as electrons. In physics these are called fundamental or elementary particles. That's not necessarily what we are talking about here.

The sense in which we are going to use the word *particle* is as a mathematical idealization for any physical object whose inner structure or composition is not important for the problem that we are considering. This might include atoms, or billiard balls, or even stars in a galaxy! In that sense, a particle is basically just a bunch of properties that characterize the object as an individual thing.

Particle properties

Let's be more precise about what we mean by that last statement. What properties are we talking about? A particle has the following properties:

- **Position**: It has to be somewhere! That means it must have coordinates x, y, z.

- **Size**: It exists in space, so it must have a size.

- **Velocity**: Things move, so they have a velocity. We define velocity formally in the next section; for now just note that it is a vector with components such as position.

- **Mass**: As a physical thing, it must also have mass.

- **Charge**: Some elementary particles, such as electrons, also have a property called an *electric charge*, which makes them experience an interesting type of force known as the electromagnetic force. Because we'll play with that force in this book, we want to give our particles a charge property, too.

- **Others (spin, lifetime, and so on)**: There are other properties we could include, taking inspiration from elementary particles in physics. But for now, we'll stick with the five properties listed here.

This background gives us enough ingredients to actually start building some ActionScript classes to represent particles and their behaviors, although some of the particle properties and motion concepts introduced as we do so will be covered in greater depth only as we progress through the chapter.

To start with, we will create an AS3.0 `Particle` class that implements the particle properties described above. We will then create a `Mover` class that will allow `Particle` instances to move, and update the `Particle` class with public methods that implement motion behaviors. We will then create a `Ball` class that extends `Particle`, drawing graphics so that `Particle` instances actually look like particles. Finally, a `MultiMover` class will be created that extends `Mover` so that multiple particles can be moved together.

Building a Particle class

It makes sense to first create a `Particle` class by extending a display object class; in doing so, we inherit the position properties `x`, `y`, `z` and the size properties `width` and `height`. Let us extend `Sprite`. So, our `Particle` class begins life looking something like this:

```
package com.physicscodes.objects {
        import flash.display.Sprite;
        public class Particle extends Sprite{

        }
}
```

You'll notice that we're placing the `Particle` class in the package `com.physicscodes.objects`. We'll soon start accumulating classes, so it's time to get organized!

Particle already has inherited properties **x**, **y**, **z**; and **width** and **height**. In addition, we need to create properties based on the physical properties such as mass, charge, and velocity described in the last section. These should be able to be read as well as modified. Table 4-1 shows the properties we want to create.

Table 4-1. Properties of the Particle class

Property	Type	Possible Values and Meaning
mass	Number	Any positive value (default 1)
charge	Number	Any value: positive, negative or zero (default)
xpos	Number	Any value; x-component of position
ypos	Number	Any value; y-component of position
zpos	Number	Any value; z-component of position
vx	Number	Any value (default 0); x-component of velocity
vy	Number	Any value (default 0); y-component of velocity
vz	Number	Any value (default 0); z-component of velocity
pos	Vector3D	Any **Vector3D** value; 3D position vector
velo	Vector3D	Any **Vector3D** value; 3D velocity vector
pos2D	Vector2D	Any **Vector2D** value; 2D position vector
velo2D	Vector2D	Any **Vector2D** value; 2D velocity vector

The choice of some of these properties and their possible values requires some explanation. It is clear that **mass** cannot be negative or zero because every particle has mass. As you will see in Chapter 10, **charge** can be positive, negative, or zero. A particle with a charge of zero would behave as if it had no charge at all.

You may wonder why we need to have the additional properties **xpos**, **ypos**, and **zpos** for position components given that **Particle** already has inherited position properties **x**, **y** and **z**. The reason is that Flash stores position coordinates (and everything else that uses pixels) in units of twips, which are 1/20 of a pixel. That means **x**, **y**, and **z** will always be multiples of 0.05. Therefore, if you require accuracy in your calculations, relying on these as position coordinates is not a good idea. In contrast, the variables **xpos**, **ypos**, and **zpos** are defined to **Number** precision—similar to the velocity components **vx**, **vy**, and **vz**.

Having extolled the virtues of vectors in the last chapter, we'd be hypocrites not to use them. Therefore, we create position and velocity vectors **pos** and **velo** as **Vector3D** objects from their respective components. We also create **Vector2D** versions **pos2D** and **velo2D**. Note that if you are using Flash CS3, the **z** components and **Vector3D** versions won't work, so you'll have to comment out the relevant pieces of code.

The implementation of these properties proceeds as follows. To begin with, we use getters and setters instead of public variables. For example, showing only the code relevant for the mass property, we have this:

```
package com.physicscodes.objects {
        import flash.display.Sprite;

        public class Particle extends Sprite{
                private var _mass:Number;
        }
        public function get mass():Number{
                return _mass;
        }
        public function set mass(pmass:Number):void{
                _mass = pmass;
        }
}
```

Hence, we use a private variable **_mass** that is accessed through **get mass()** and **set mass()**. Through these accessors, you can get or set the mass property of a **Particle** instance called **particle** simply by typing **particle.mass**. It could be argued that, in this case, the getter/setter is not doing anything useful, and we might as well use a public property. But we've followed this technique to be consistent with best practices.

We would also want to be able to set the mass and charge of our particles when we create them, so it makes sense to use a constructor and feed those as parameters in the constructor:

```
public function Particle(pmass:Number=1, pcharge:Number=0){
        _mass = pmass;
        _charge = pcharge;
}
```

The **mass** and **charge** properties are optional parameters, with default values of 1 and 0 respectively.

There are getters and setters for all the other variables. For example, here are the getters and setters for the x-components of position and velocity, **xpos** and **vx**:

```
private var _x:Number;
private var _vx:Number=0;
public function get xpos():Number{
        return _x;
}
public function set xpos(px:Number):void{
        _x = px;
        x = _x;
}
public function get vx():Number{
        return _vx;
}
```

```
public function set vx(pvx:Number):void{
      _vx = pvx;
}
```

Internally, **xpos** is using the private variable **_x**, and **vx** is using the private variable **_vx**. Note that the setter for **xpos** additionally includes a line that assigns the value of **_x** to the **x** property of the **Particle** instance. With this setup, all calculations involving position can therefore be done using **xpos** (and **ypos** and **zpos**), with the **x** (and **y** and **z**) property set accordingly so that the **Particle** instance is positioned at the calculated location. Hence, in this case the getter/setter pair is actually doing something quite valuable.

Similarly, here are the getters and setters for the **pos** and **velo** properties:

```
private var _pos:Vector3D;
private var _velo:Vector3D;
public function get pos():Vector3D{
      return new Vector3D(_x,_y,_z);
}
public function set pos(ppos:Vector3D):void{
      _x = ppos.x;
      _y = ppos.y;
      _z = ppos.z;
      x = _x;
      y = _y;
      z = _z;
}public function get velo():Vector3D{
      return new Vector3D(_vx,_vy,_vz);
}
public function set velo(pvelo:Vector3D):void{
      _vx = pvelo.x;
      _vy = pvelo.y;
      _vz = pvelo.z;
}
```

Setting **pos** will automatically position the **Particle** instance at the new location specified by the **pos** vector.

Have a look at **Particle.as**. We also created 2D versions of these properties, called **pos2D** and **velo2D**. In fact, we'll mostly use the 2D versions in this chapter. It should be straightforward for you to modify the example codes if you want to do 3D. We added a couple of public methods, **multiply(k:Number)** and **addScaled(vec:Vector2D, k:Number)**, to the **Vector2D** class (which is now in the **com.physicscodes.math** package). Doing **vec1.multiply(k:Number)** multiplies vector **vec1** by the scalar **k**. Doing **vec1.addScaled(vec:Vector2D, k:Number)** adds **k** times **vec** to **vec1**.

For example, to update the position of a **Particle** instance called **particle**, do this:

```
particle.pos2D = particle.pos2D.add(particle.velo2D.multiply(dt));
```

Or do this, which involves a single method call **addScaled()** rather than the two method calls **multiply()** and **add()**.

```
particle.pos2D = particle.pos2D.addScaled(particle.velo2D, dt);
```

These are equivalent to the component form:

```
particle.xpos += particle.vx * dt;
particle.ypos += particle.vy * dt;
```

Moving particles: the Mover class

We now have a **Particle** class with all the properties we need. But the particles that will be instantiated from this class won't know how to *do* anything (move, for example). There are two options for handling this: we can write code externally to make it move, or we can create a method that will make it move. We'll show an example of how to do both of these things shortly. But before we do that, let's try and take advantage of object-oriented programming (OOP). With both methods, we want to move an object repeatedly in time. So let's first create a **Mover** class that we'll use with either method.

The task of the **Mover** class is to make particles realize that they need to move at the velocity they possess. **Mover** also has to introduce time. The simplest way to do this is to use the enterframe event. Better still is to use the **Timer** class with the **getTimer()** function, as described in Chapter 2. Here is a basic **Mover** class that does this:

```
package com.physicscodes.motion{
        import flash.events.TimerEvent;
        import flash.utils.Timer;
        import flash.utils.getTimer;
        import com.physicscodes.objects.Particle;
        public class Mover {
                private var _particle:Particle;
                private var _time:Number;
                private var _t0:Number;
                private var _dt:Number;
                private var _timer:Timer;

                public function Mover(pparticle:Particle):void {
                        _particle = pparticle;
                }
                public function startTime(ptimestep:Number=20,psteps:Number=0):void {
                        _timer=new Timer(ptimestep,psteps);
                        _timer.addEventListener(TimerEvent.TIMER,onTimer);
                        _timer.start();
                        _time = 0;
                        _t0 = getTimer();
                }
                public function stopTime():void {
                        _timer.removeEventListener(TimerEvent.TIMER,onTimer);
                        _timer.stop();
                }
                public function killTime():void {
                        stopTime();
                        _timer=null;
                        if (_timer && _timer.running) _timer.stop();
                }
```

```
            public function get time():Number {
                    return _time;
            }
            public function get dt():Number {
                    return _dt;
            }
            private function onTimer(pEvent:TimerEvent):void {
                    _dt = 0.001 * (getTimer() - _to);
                    _time += _dt;
                    _to  = getTimer();
                    moveObject();
                    pEvent.updateAfterEvent();
            }
            protected function moveObject():void {
                    _particle.pos2D = _particle.pos2D.addScaled(_particle.velo,_dt);
            }
        }
    }
}
```

Most of the code deals with setting up the time-keeping, as described in Chapter 2, and should therefore be familiar. The public function **startTime()** sets up a timer and an event listener, taking two optional parameters, which are the usual **Timer** parameters. The public method **stopTime()** removes the event listener and stops the timer. The event listener increments the time and also calls the protected method **moveObject()**, which simply increments the position of a particle passed as a parameter in the constructor of the class, using the velocity of the particle and the time increment. The reason for declaring **moveObject()** as **protected** is to make it available to subclasses of **Mover**. We'll soon be extending it and will need to override the **moveObject()** method to modify its functionality. There are also getters for **time** and **dt**, which are useful for using with outside code.

Having created the **Mover** class, life is now extremely simple. Now you can forget about **Timer** or **getTimer()**, and all the hassle associated with that time-keeping procedure. By simply instantiating **Mover**, you never have to worry about doing any of that stuff again.

To use **Mover**, you just need the following two lines, where **particle** is a previously created **Particle** instance:

```
var mover:Mover=new Mover(particle);
mover.startTime()
```

The method **startTime()** on the second line could take two optional parameters, as described previously. That's the first, external, method of animating a particle.

The second method is even simpler. We begin by adding the following public methods to the **Particle** class itself:

```
public function move(ptimestep:Number=20,psteps:Number=0):void{
        _mover = new Mover(this);
        _mover.startTime(ptimestep,psteps);
}
public function pause():void{
        if (_mover){
```

```
                        _mover.stopTime();
            }
    }
    public function resume():void{
            if (_mover){
                    _mover.startTime();
            }
    }
    public function stop():void{
            if (_mover){
                    _mover.killTime();
                    _mover = null;
            }
    }
```

The public method **move()**, with the two optional **Timer** parameters, does just what we did before; it creates a **Mover** instance and calls its **startTime()** method. We also created **pause()**, **resume()**, and **stop()** methods. To make a particle move according to its current velocity, you therefore only need a single line of code:

```
particle.move();
```

And to make it stop:

```
particle.stop();
```

Can it get any simpler than this?

Extending the Particle class

What we've done in the last section is great stuff, but you haven't seen anything yet. That's because our particles are currently invisible. The **Particle** class has deliberately been kept to a minimum level of complexity. It's time now to extend it and include something that we can see. To do this, we'll reinvent the **Ball** class by making some modifications to the old version that we used in previous chapters.

The Ball class

The first modification is to extend **Particle** instead of **Sprite**. Doing this means that **Ball** inherits the properties of **Particle**, such as velocity and velocity components. So we don't need to create them in **Ball** again. Here is the class definition and constructor:

```
public class Ball extends Particle{
        private var _radius:Number;
        private var _color:uint;
        private var _gradient:Boolean;
        private var _sprite:Sprite;

        public function Ball(pradius:Number=20, pcolor:uint=0x0000ff, pmass:Number=1,
    pcharge:Number=0, pgradient:Boolean=true){
                this.mass=pmass;
                this.charge=pcharge;
```

```
                _radius=pradius;
                _color=pcolor;
                _gradient = pgradient;
                _sprite = new Sprite();
                drawBall();
        }
}
```

As you can see, the constructor takes five optional arguments: **radius**, **color**, **mass**, **charge** and **gradient**. The actual drawing now takes place in a private method **drawBall()**, which looks as follows:

```
private function drawBall():void{
        with (_sprite.graphics){
        if (_gradient){
                var matrix:Matrix = new Matrix();
                matrix.createGradientBox(_radius,_radius,0,-_radius,-_radius/2);
                beginGradientFill(GradientType.RADIAL,[0xffffff,_color],[1,1],[0,255],matrix);
        }else{
                beginFill(_color);
        }
                drawCircle(0,0,_radius);
                endFill();
        }
        addChild(_sprite);
}
```

As you can see, the **Boolean gradient** option determines whether the ball is drawn with a gradient fill (the default) or a simple fill.

Two new public functions, **clone()** and **clear()**, have been added: **clone()** creates a copy of the **Ball** object, whereas **clear()** clears all the graphics and removes the **particle** instance from the display list. Finally, getters and setters have been added for **radius**, **color**, and **gradient**. When these properties are changed, the **Ball** instance is redrawn with the new **radius**, **color**, or **gradient** option. Pretty neat!

Using the Ball class

Using the **Ball** class is quite straightforward. This code snippet creates a **ball** object, initializes its position and velocity, and then moves it:

```
var ball:Ball;
ball = new Ball();
ball.pos=new Vector3D(150,50,0);
ball.velo=new Vector3D(30,20,0);
addChild(ball);
ball.move();
```

This piece of code produces a bunch of particles of random size, color, location, and velocities (see Figure 4-1):

```
var numBalls:Number = 10;
for (var i:uint=1; i<=numBalls; i++){
        var ball:Ball;
```

```
        var radius:Number = (Math.random()+0.5)*20;
        var color:uint = Math.random()*0xffffff;
        ball = new Ball(radius,color);
        ball.pos=new Vector3D(Math.random()*550,Math.random()*400,0);
        ball.velo=new Vector3D((Math.random()-0.5)*100,(Math.random()-0.5)*100,0);
        addChild(ball);
}
```

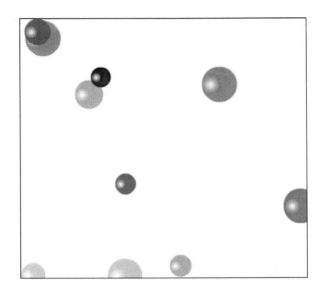

Figure 4-1. A multicolored bunch of **Ball** objects

To animate the balls, you could do **ball.move()** after the **addChild(ball)** line within the for loop. This will make each particle move individually, using its own timer. However, this is a bit of a waste of resources. Even with a relatively small number of particles, things might slow down noticeably.

It makes more sense to use a single **Mover** instance to handle the motion of all the balls. We can do this by putting all the **Ball** instances into an array that we'll then pass to a modified version of **Mover**, which we'll call **MultiMover**. Here is the code that puts the balls into an array:

```
var numBalls:Number = 10;
var balls:Array = new Array();
for (var i:uint=1; i<=numBalls; i++){
        var ball:Ball;
        var radius:Number = (Math.random()+0.5)*20;
        var color:uint = Math.random()*0xffffff;
        ball = new Ball(radius,color);
        ball.pos=new Vector3D(Math.random()*550,Math.random()*400,0);
        ball.velo=new Vector3D((Math.random()-0.5)*100,(Math.random()-0.5)*100,0);
        addChild(ball);
        balls.push(ball);
}
```

You then pass the array **balls** as an argument in the constructor of a **MultiMover**:

```
var multimover:MultiMover = new MultiMover(balls);
multimover.startTime();
```

The code for this animation is in **BallTest.as**.

Let's now take a look at the **MultiMover** class. We could just have modified **Mover** and saved it as a different class called **MultiMover**. But a smarter thing to do is to extend the **Mover** class and change only the bits that need changing. Here's the full code for **MultiMover.as**:

```
package com.physicscodes.motion {
        import com.physicscodes.motion.Mover;
        import com.physicscodes.objects.Particle;
        import com.physicscodes.math.Vector2D;

        public class MultiMover extends Mover{
                private var _particles:Array;
                public function MultiMover(pparticles:Array):void{
                        _particles = pparticles;
                        super(null);
                }
                override protected function moveObject():void{
                        for (var i:uint=0; i<_particles.length; i++){
                                var particle:Particle = _particles[i];
                                particle.pos2D = particle.pos2D.addScaled(particle.velo2D,dt);
                        }
                }
        }
}
```

MultiMover takes an array of particles as argument instead of a particle object as **Mover** does. Then it overrides the **moveObject()** method of **Mover**, and its new **moveObject()** method instead loops over the particles in the array, moving each one in turn.

You can, of course, use **MultiMover** for a single particle if you ever fancy doing that: simply pass the particle within an array. This is for a **Ball** instance named **ball**:

```
var mover:MultiMover=new MultiMover([ball]);
```

In all these examples, the balls move at the same constant velocity. The really interesting stuff is when the velocity changes; we'll do that soon in this chapter.

Describing motion: kinematics

In this section, we will start to describe motion more formally using precise concepts, equations, and graphs. The description of motion is called *kinematics*. In kinematics, we are not concerned with what causes motion, but only with how to describe it. The next section, dynamics, will look at the cause of motion: force.

Concepts: displacement, velocity, speed, acceleration

Up to now, we've talked about things like velocity and acceleration rather loosely. It's time now to say precisely what we mean by these quantities.

Here are the main concepts that require definition in kinematics:

- **Displacement**

- **Velocity** (and the associated concept of **speed**)

- **Acceleration**

These physical quantities rest upon more fundamental concepts that are taken as self-evident and do not require definition: position, distance, and time. For vector quantities, there is a fourth basic concept: angle, which defines a direction in space.

Displacement

Displacement is a vector quantity associated with the motion of an object. To be more precise, it's the vector connecting the initial position with the final position of the object. Remember the example of Bug from the last chapter? Bug moves a distance of 10 units along the y-axis from the origin—that's a displacement. From there, it then undergoes another displacement of 10 units to the right (in the +ve x direction).

In the above example, the net or resultant displacement of Bug is then √(200), or approximately 14.1 units at an angle of 45 degrees. But the net distance it moves is, of course, 20 units. This example illustrates the difference between displacement and distance. In general, an object might move along any complicated trajectory: the distance moved would then be the length along the trajectory, whereas the displacement would always be the vector joining the initial position to the final position of the object (see Figure 4-2).

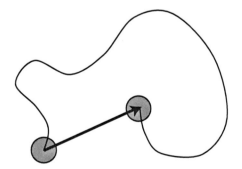

Figure 4-2. Displacement vector (arrow) contrasted with distance along trajectory

Displacement is usually denoted by the symbol **s** or **x**, and its magnitude as s or x. The usual unit of displacement (and distance) is the meter and its multiples (for example, km) and fractions (cm, mm, and so on). In Flash, where you've got a stage on a computer screen rather than real space, you'll think of distance and displacement in terms of pixels, which we'll often abbreviate as px.

Velocity

Velocity is defined as the rate of change of displacement with time. It tells you how quickly something is moving, but also in what direction it is moving. Hence, velocity is a vector quantity.

The usual symbol for velocity is **u** or **v**; for its magnitude, u or v.

Remember what rate of change means in calculus? It's the gradient function, or derivative. Therefore, velocity is the derivative of displacement with time. In calculus notation we write this as

$$\mathbf{v} = \frac{d\mathbf{s}}{dt}$$

Again, this derivative is the limit of the ratio $\Delta\mathbf{s}/\Delta t$ as the time interval Δt (and therefore also the displacement change $\Delta\mathbf{s}$) becomes small. So, for finite intervals, we can write

$$\mathbf{v} = \frac{\Delta\mathbf{s}}{\Delta t}$$

This gives us the average velocity over the time interval Δt, whereas v = ds/dt gives us the instantaneous velocity at a given time. In the special case when velocity is constant, the average velocity is equal to the instantaneous velocity at any time.

As mentioned before, the usual unit for velocity in physics is meters per second (m/s), although km/hr and miles/hr are commonly used in everyday life. In Flash, the measure of time is still the second, but the measure of distance is the pixel. So, you'll usually think of velocity in terms of pixels per second (px/s).

In a computer code, we are always dealing with discrete intervals, so we are really dealing with average velocities. But if we use a small enough time interval, the average is close to the instantaneous value. One can rearrange the last equation to give $\Delta\mathbf{s}$ in terms of **v** and Δt:

$$\Delta\mathbf{s} = \mathbf{v}\,\Delta t$$

This equation tells us that the displacement increment is given as the product of velocity and the time interval. This is exactly what we do in the **moveObject()** method of the **Mover** class:

```
particle.pos2D = particle.pos2D.add(particle.velo2D.multiply(_dt));
```

You might also recognize this as being equivalent to integrating in time using the forward scheme (refer to Chapter 3). That makes perfect sense—because velocity is the derivative of displacement with time, displacement is the integral of velocity with time. We'll use this integration scheme, specifically known as a *Euler scheme*, until we get to Part IV of the book.

Speed

Speed is the scalar version of velocity; it has no direction. *Speed* is defined as the rate of change of distance with time, or, in other words, as distance moved per unit time. The unit of speed is the same as that of velocity.

The average speed of an object is the total distance travelled divided by the total time taken:

$$\text{average speed} = \frac{\text{total distance travelled}}{\text{total time taken}}$$

In this book, most of the time we'll be dealing with velocity and velocity components rather than speed.

Acceleration

Acceleration is defined as the rate of change of velocity with time. It tells you how fast an object's velocity is changing. If you're driving a car at a constant velocity of 20 m/s (approx 45 miles/hr) in a straight line, you're not accelerating—the acceleration is zero. But if you apply the accelerator and increase the car's speed from 20 m/s to 30 m/s in 10 seconds, the average acceleration is (30 – 20)/10 m/s per second, or 1 m/s^2. This means that the velocity increases by 1 m/s in each second. Acceleration can also be negative; in that case, the velocity magnitude decreases.

The calculus definition of acceleration is

$$\mathbf{a} = \frac{d\mathbf{v}}{dt}$$

and the discrete version is

$$\mathbf{a} = \frac{\Delta \mathbf{v}}{\Delta t}$$

These equations are similar to those for velocity, with displacement replaced by velocity. Like the corresponding equations for velocity, $\mathbf{a} = \Delta v/\Delta t$ gives us the average acceleration over the time interval Δt, whereas $\mathbf{a} = dv/dt$ gives us the instantaneous acceleration at a given time.

> In the special case when acceleration is constant, the average acceleration is equal to the instantaneous acceleration. We'll illustrate this fact in the next section.

Reversing the above equation gives this:

$$\Delta \mathbf{v} = \mathbf{a}\ \Delta t$$

Interpreted as a discrete equation, this gives us an integration scheme for updating velocity given the acceleration. This is how you would code it up in ActionScript using **Vector2D**:

```
particle.velo2D = particle.velo2D.add(_acc.multiply(_dt));
```

or

```
particle.velo2D = particle.velo2D.addScaled(_acc, _dt);
```

Here **_acc** is a private variable representing acceleration. It is a **Vector2D** object. Suppose we use a fixed value:

```
private var _acc:Vector2D=new Vector2D(0,10);
```

This will make our particles accelerate downward at a rate of 10 px/s^2, simulating the effect of gravity.

Because acceleration is the rate of change of velocity, it is non-zero if the direction of motion changes, even if the speed is constant. A common example is that of an object moving at constant speed in a circle. Because the object's direction of motion changes, its velocity changes. Therefore, its acceleration is not zero. We'll look at this situation in detail in Chapter 9.

Combining vector quantities

Because displacement, velocity, and acceleration are vector quantities, it goes without saying that they must be combined (added or subtracted) using vector methods. You saw an example of how this is done in the previous chapter, so we won't repeat it here.

Why would you want to combine these quantities? You'll frequently want to add displacements and velocities to calculate their total (also known as their *resultant*). Again, you saw an example of resultant displacement in the last chapter. An example of a situation in which you would want to add velocities is that of a boat on a flowing river. The resultant velocity of the boat is then given by the vector sum of its velocity in the water with the velocity of the water current (see Figure 4-3).

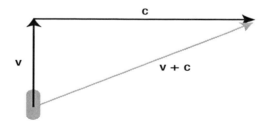

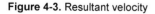

Figure 4-3. Resultant velocity

You'll need to use vector subtraction when calculating relative velocities. Suppose you have a spaceship A chasing another spaceship B, moving at different velocities **a** and **b** in space (see Figure 4-4). What is the velocity of B relative to A? That's the velocity of B from the point of view of A. In other words, it's the velocity of B in a frame of reference in which A is not moving (we say it's *at rest*). A little quiet thinking should convince you that it's given by the velocity of B minus that of A, in a vector sense: **b − a**. Figure 4-4 shows you what **b** − **a** means geometrically: it's the same as **b** + (−**a**), and because (−**a**) points opposite to **a** with the same magnitude, we end up with **b** − **a** pointing in the direction shown. This is the velocity of B as seen by A from its point of view.

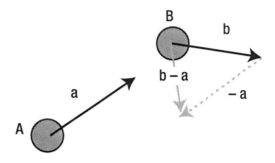

Figure 4-4. Relative velocity

Describing motion using graphs

The motion of an object can be represented graphically in different ways. For a particle moving in two dimensions, you can plot its y-coordinate against its x-coordinate at different times. The resulting graph would, of course, just give you the trajectory of the particle.

You can also plot the components of displacement, velocity or acceleration against time. These graphs can tell us useful things about how the particle moves.

You will soon see examples in which we make use of the **Graph** class that we introduced in the last chapter to create such plots.

Equations of motion for uniform acceleration

For the special case of motion under constant acceleration (also known as *uniform motion*), it is possible, starting only from the definitions of velocity and acceleration, to arrive at a very useful set of equations. These equations of motion can be used to analyze problems in which the acceleration is constant, including the motion of bodies falling under gravity and the motion of projectiles.

We could just state the equations of motion and ask you to accept them. But you might understand them better if you see where they come from. And it's not really difficult; you just need to do a tiny amount of algebra. The starting point is the definition of average acceleration:

$$\mathbf{a}_{av} = \frac{\Delta \mathbf{v}}{\Delta t}$$

If the acceleration is constant, $\mathbf{a}_{av}$ is also equal to the instantaneous acceleration **a**—it is true at any time t.

Let's now establish our initial conditions by saying that at time t = 0 (initially), **s** = 0 (zero initial displacement), and **v** = **u** (the initial velocity is denoted by **u**).

Therefore at time t, we have $\Delta \mathbf{v} = \mathbf{v} - \mathbf{u}$, and $\Delta t = t - 0 = t$, so that

$$\mathbf{a} = \frac{(\mathbf{v} - \mathbf{u})}{t}$$

It is now easy to change the subject of this formula to get this:

$$\mathbf{v} = \mathbf{u} + \mathbf{a}\,t$$

This formula gives us the velocity $\mathbf{v}$ at any time t, given the initial velocity $\mathbf{u}$ and the (constant) acceleration $\mathbf{a}$.

It would be nice to have a similar equation for displacement too. Can it be done? Yes, you just need to apply the same trick, this time starting from the definition of average velocity:

$$\mathbf{v}_{av} = \frac{\Delta \mathbf{s}}{\Delta t}$$

Now we have $\Delta \mathbf{s} = \mathbf{s} - 0 = \mathbf{s}$, and $\Delta t = t - 0 = t$, which gives

$$\mathbf{v}_{av} = \frac{\mathbf{s}}{t}$$

Because the velocity increases linearly, the average velocity $\mathbf{v}_{av}$ is just ½ ($\mathbf{u}$ + $\mathbf{v}$)—the average of the initial and final velocities. Substituting into the preceding equation gives

$$\mathbf{s} = \frac{1}{2}(\mathbf{u} + \mathbf{v})t$$

Now you can use the formula already derived ($\mathbf{v} = \mathbf{u} + \mathbf{a}$ t) to substitute for $\mathbf{v}$. Do this and simplify, and you should get this:

$$\mathbf{s} = \mathbf{u}\,t + \frac{1}{2}\mathbf{a}\,t^2$$

Now sit down and admire this remarkable result of your hard work. What you have here is a formula that tells you the displacement $\mathbf{s}$ of a particle at any time t, in terms of the initial velocity $\mathbf{u}$ of the particle and the (constant) acceleration $\mathbf{a}$.

This will equal the position vector of the particle at time t if it starts out at the origin at time t = 0. In general, if the particle starts out at location **pos0** = (x0, y0, z0) at time t = 0, its position vector **pos** = (x, y, z) at time t will be given by this, in pseudocode:

```
pos = u * t  + 0.5 * a * t * t + pos0
```

This gives you the position of the particle as an exact analytical equation. There is no need to use numerical integration in this case.

You can code up this solution directly in vector form (as we do), or split it into components if you prefer. In pseudocode, you get this:

```
x = ux * t + 0.5 * ax * t * t + x0
y = uy * t + 0.5 * ay * t * t + y0
z = uz * t + 0.5 * az * t * t + z0
```

Before we leave this section, let's mention that there is a third formula that sometimes proves useful. The two formulas derived previously (**v** = **u** + **a** t, and **s** = **u** t + ½ **a** t^2) give you the velocity **v** and the displacement **s**, each as a function of time t. If you eliminate the time t between these two equations, you can get an equation for v and s in terms of each other:

$$v^2 = u^2 + 2\,\mathbf{a} \bullet \mathbf{s}$$

Note that this one is a scalar equation, not a vector equation.

> *We repeat: the equations of motion derived in this section are valid only for constant acceleration. If the acceleration changes with time, they will give the wrong answer.*

Applying the equations to projectile motion

It's time for an example. Let's apply the preceding equations to model the motion of a projectile such as a cannonball. To do this, we'll neglect all other forces except gravity. In that case, the force on the projectile at any time during its flight is constant. This will give it a constant acceleration (you'll understand fully why in the next chapter).

We do not model the explosive force that shoots the cannonball in the first place. That force is very brief, and its effect is to impart an initial velocity **u** to the cannonball.

In this special case, the equations for the position of the projectile in component form reduce to this, in pseudocode:

```
x = ux * t + x0
y = uy * t + 0.5 * g * t * t + y0
z = uz * t  + z0
```

Because the acceleration due to gravity points vertically downward, its x and z components ax and az are zero and ay = g. If you use vectors, you simply need to specify the acceleration vector as (0, g, 0) in 3D and (0, g) in 2D in the equation **pos = u * t + 0.5 * a * t * t + pos0**.

Let's use these formulas to code a simple projectile simulation. To do this, we'll extend **Mover** again. The new class is called **Projectile**.

Here is the full code of **Projectile.as**:

```
package{
        import com.physicscodes.motion.Mover;
        import com.physicscodes.objects.Particle;
        import com.physicscodes.math.Vector2D;

        public class Projectile extends Mover{
                private var _particle:Particle;
                private var _acc:Vector2D;
                private var _pos0:Vector2D;
                private var _velo0:Vector2D;
                private var _euler:Boolean;

                public function Projectile(pparticle:Particle, ppos0:Vector2D,
                pvelo0:Vector2D, pacc:Vector2D, peuler:Boolean=true):void{
                        _particle = pparticle;
                        _acc = pacc;
                        _euler = peuler;
                        _pos0 = ppos0;
                        _velo0 = pvelo0;
                        super(pparticle);
                }
                override protected function moveObject():void{
                        if (_euler){
                                super.moveObject();
                                updateVelo();
                        }else{
                                useAnalyticalSoln();
                        }
                }
                private function updateVelo():void{
                        _particle.velo2D = _particle.velo2D.addScaled(_acc,dt);
                }
                private function useAnalyticalSoln():void{
                        _particle.pos2D =
                        _pos0.addScaled(_velo0,time).addScaled(_acc,0.5*time*time);
                }
        }
}
```

As you can see, the constructor of **Projectile** takes five arguments. The first one is a particle object, which is passed to the **Mover** constructor via **super()**. The next three arguments take the initial position, initial velocity, and acceleration of the particle as **Vector2D** objects. The final argument is a **Boolean** parameter **euler** with a default value of **true**. We override the **moveObject()** method of **Mover**. If the euler parameter is **true**, we call **super.moveObject()**, which invokes the Euler numerical scheme implemented in **Mover** for updating the position of the particle. We also call the private method **updateVelo()**, which implements the Euler integration scheme (as discussed in the section on velocity) for updating the velocity by adding the acceleration times the current time interval **dt**.

If the **euler** parameter is **false**, a private method **useAnalyticalSoln()** is called instead, which assigns a new current position to the particle based on the exact analytical formula **pos = u * t + 0.5 * a * t * t + pos0**. No numerical approximation is then involved.

Let's see both methods in action. **ProjectileTest.as** creates two balls and moves one using the numerical Euler scheme and the other one using the exact analytical solution. Here is the full code:

```
package{
        import flash.display.Sprite;
        import com.physicscodes.objects.Ball;
        import com.physicscodes.math.Vector2D;

        public class ProjectileTest extends Sprite{
                public function ProjectileTest():void{
                        init();
                }
                private function init():void{
                        var pos0:Vector2D = new Vector2D(100,350);
                        var velo0:Vector2D = new Vector2D(20,-80);
                        var gravity:Vector2D = new Vector2D(0,10);

                        var ball:Ball;
                        ball = new Ball(15,0x000000);
                        ball.pos2D = pos0;
                        ball.velo2D = velo0;
                        addChild(ball);

                        var ball1:Ball;
                        ball1 = new Ball(15,0xaaaaaa);
                        ball1.pos2D = pos0;
                        ball1.velo2D = velo0;
                        addChild(ball1);

                        var projectile:Projectile=new Projectile(ball,pos0,↵
velo0,gravity,true);
                        var projectile1:Projectile=new Projectile(ball1,pos0↵
,velo0,gravity,false);
                        projectile.startTime();
                        projectile1.startTime();
                }
        }
}
```

The two balls (one grey and one black) are initially positioned at the same location (100, 350), have the same initial velocity (20, -80), and are subjected to the same downward acceleration (0, 10) to simulate gravity. If you run the code, you'll see both balls start off together and move in a parabolic path like projectiles are supposed to do. As the simulation progresses, you'll see them begin to separate, as pictured in Figure 4-5, because of numerical errors due to the Euler scheme.

The grey ball is exactly where it should be because it follows the exact analytical solution of the equation of motion. Now you probably won't normally care about the difference. But if you're building an accurate simulation of projectiles or a game of billiards, you would. The difference in position shown in Figure 4-5 is after only about 15 seconds of run time. If you run this for a few minutes and include bouncing or collisions with other particles, your particle will soon be in places it shouldn't be.

So, what can be done about this if your simulation or game requires high accuracy? If your simulation is simple enough for an analytical solution to exist (as in the present example), using that solution would solve the problem. However, in the vast majority of scenarios, analytical solutions do not exist. In those cases, you need to use a more accurate integration scheme than the Euler scheme.

Chapter 14, in Part IV of the book, is devoted entirely to more accurate integration schemes. But before we get there, we will use the Euler scheme in most of the examples because Euler is the simplest and quickest scheme, and our main aim in much of the book prior to Part IV is to demonstrate physics effects without necessarily worrying too much about absolute accuracy. As we go along, we will point out examples in which the lack of accuracy may be especially important, although we will defer any solutions to Chapter 14.

The choice of integration scheme is not the only consideration if you are worried about numerical accuracy. Another possible source of error is how numbers are stored or handled—for example, this is why we chose to use **Number** variables like **xpos** instead of using the built-in **x** property when building the **Particle** class earlier in this chapter. Errors can also arise due to the algorithms for dealing with sudden changes such as bouncing and collisions. Chapter 15 will include a discussion of these other sources of error and how they can be dealt with.

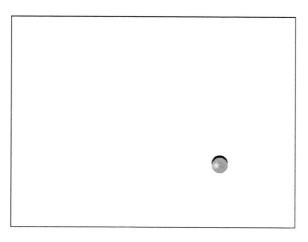

Figure 4-5. Simulating the motion of a projectile with both numerical and analytical solutions

More motion-related concepts: inertia, mass, and momentum

So far, we've been limited to a few motion concepts, and the progress we can make just with those is rather restricted. The greatest power comes with the notion of forces and how it affects motion. We'll introduce that approach in a conceptual way in the next section and then develop it fully in the next chapter.

Before we do so, we need to introduce two new concepts that act as a connection between motion and the forces that produce them: *mass* and *momentum*.

Let's start with mass. In physics, mass has a very specific meaning: it is a measure of inertia. *Inertia* (literally "laziness") is resistance to motion. The more massive an object is, the more it resists motion—it is more difficult to push a car than a bike. So, we say that the mass of a car is larger than that of a bike. The usual unit of mass in physics is the kilogram (kg). The usual symbol for mass is m.

In physics, the mass of an object is not the same as its weight. Weight is actually a force, the force of gravity that the Earth exerts on it. Mass is a scalar; weight is a vector. We'll come back to this in the next section.

The momentum of an object, denoted usually by the symbol **p**, with magnitude p, is defined as the product of its mass and its velocity. It is a vector quantity.

$$\mathbf{p} = m\,\mathbf{v}$$

Because it is equal to a scalar (mass) times velocity, it has the same direction as that of the velocity vector.

Informally, momentum is a measure of the "quantity of motion" that a body possesses—for the same velocity, a car has "more motion" than a bike because it is more difficult to stop the car. Momentum is important for two reasons: it is intimately connected with force, and there is a law known as the *law of conservation of momentum* that's very useful for solving problems such as collisions between particles. We'll take a close look at momentum and its conservation in the next chapter.

Predicting motion: forces and dynamics

In the last section, we could "solve" the projectile problem by obtaining a formula for the position of the projectile as a function of time. That was possible because we knew the acceleration—it was constant and was equal to g, the acceleration due to gravity.

The problem of predicting the motion of an object basically boils down to calculating the acceleration at each time **a**(t), whether by some analytical formula or by some numerical procedure. Once we know **a**, we know how to do the rest—we can integrate numerically (using the Euler or some other scheme) or use an analytical solution if one exists.

In the case of gravity near the Earth's surface, you now know that a = g, so that's nice and simple. But how can we calculate the acceleration of an object in general? Before we can give the answer, we need to talk a bit more about forces.

The cause of motion: forces

A *force* is an abstract concept in physics that denotes "something" that makes things move. To be more precise, if a bit mysterious, forces change the way things move. The meaning of this statement will be made clear in just a moment.

Intuitively, you can think of a force as some kind of push or pull. Gravity is a force; it pulls you toward the Earth. Friction is another type of force; it pushes against a moving object.

Forces can be measured and calculated. The unit of force is the newton, denoted by the symbol N.

Forces are useful because knowing the forces acting on a body allows prediction of its motion. How this is done will be explained next.

The relationship between force, mass, and acceleration

Let's go back to the question we asked at the beginning of this section. How can we work out the acceleration of an object? The answer turns out to be surprisingly simple. Without further ado, here it is:

$$\mathbf{F} = m\,\mathbf{a}$$

F is the total force acting on an object, m is its mass, and **a** is the acceleration that's produced by the force. That's it. This is a most remarkable formula, probably the most important formula in this book. It's remarkable because it connects motion (more precisely, acceleration) with its cause (force) in probably the simplest way you can imagine.

The equation **F** = ma is a special case of Newton's second law of motion. It's the most common form of this law. In the next chapter, we'll look at the general form of the law.

You can rewrite the formula as follows, which you can now use to calculate the acceleration **a** given the mass m of an object and the force **F** acting on it:

$$\mathbf{a} = \frac{\mathbf{F}}{m}$$

As we discussed in Chapter 1, the motion of an object is a function of the forces acting on the object:

motion = function{forces}

Well, **a** = F/m is exactly what that means. That's our function. Forces cause acceleration; they cause the velocity of an object to change. And that's how we calculate that change in motion.

This formula is consistent with our conceptual idea of force and mass as causing and resisting motion, respectively. For a given force, the acceleration produced is less for a larger mass because we'll be dividing the force by a larger number.

The next question is this: how do we know the force F? Well, in fact, there are many different types of forces. Luckily, there are formulas for each type of force. The formulas come from physics theories or experiments. For us, it does not matter where they come from, of course. The point is that we can calculate all the forces acting on an object at any time and then add them all up to give the total or resultant force **F**. We then divide this total force **F** by the mass m of the object; that gives us the acceleration **a** of the object. Problem solved.

Types of forces

In Part II of the book, we'll be looking at different types of forces in a lot of detail. Here are some quick examples.

Gravity is perhaps the most obvious example of a force. The force of gravity acting on an object is also known as its weight. The Earth (or any other planet or star) exerts a gravitational force on any object near it that is in proportion to the mass of that object. So the weight of an object of mass m is given by

$$\text{Weight} = m\,\mathbf{g}$$

where **g** is a vector that points vertically downwards with constant magnitude g.

Using **a** = **F**/m, this gives **a** = mg/m = **g**. In other words, the weight of an object (the force of gravity on it) produces an acceleration of **g** if it's the only force acting on the object. This shows that **g** is actually an acceleration, known as the *acceleration due to gravity*. Near the Earth's surface, it has a magnitude of approximately 9.81 m/s^2. Note that the mass m of the object "drops out"—all objects fall with the same acceleration regardless of their mass or size (as long as other forces such as air resistance are negligible compared with gravity).

Another common type of force is a *contact force*, which is the force that an object experiences when it comes into direct physical contact with another object. This occurs, for example, when you push something, when two objects collide, or when two things are pressed together by another force (for example, a book pressing against a table because of its weight). If you are reading a physical copy of this book, lay it on the table. The reason it does not fall through the table is because the latter is exerting an upward contact force that balances the force of gravity on the book.

Another type of contact force is friction, which acts when two objects that are in contact move relative to each other. If you push the book along the table, friction is the force that resists the motion of the book. We'll look at contact forces in Chapter 7.

There are also several examples of forces due to fluids, such as pressure, drag (a type of frictional force), and upthrust. We'll look at these forces in detail in Chapter 7.

Then there are electric and magnetic forces, which can also act together as an electromagnetic force. These forces are exerted and experienced by particles and objects that possess a physical property called electric charge. In fact, apart from gravity, all the everyday forces such as contact forces, fluid forces, and so on originate from the electromagnetic forces that atoms and molecules exert on each other. We'll look at these forces in Chapter 10 and see how they can be used to produce interesting effects.

Combining forces: force diagrams and resultant force

In the equation **F** = m**a**, **F** is the total or resultant force. Because force is a vector quantity, the resultant force due to two or more forces must be obtained by vector addition, as described in Chapter 3.

A vector diagram that shows the forces acting on a body is called a *force diagram*. Force diagrams can be useful tools because they help us to work out the resultant force. The point is that it does not matter if the forces acting on a body are of different types. You can add gravity to friction and drag, for example, as long as you do so using vector addition.

As vectors, forces can be "resolved" or "decomposed" into perpendicular components, as explained in the last chapter. Sometimes it might prove helpful to analyze a problem by resolving forces into their components and combining all the horizontal and vertical components separately.

Figure 4-6 shows an example of a force diagram. It shows the forces acting on an object sliding down an inclined plane. There are three forces acting on this object: its weight **mg**, which acts downward; a frictional force **f** exerted by the surface, which acts opposite to the direction of its motion; and a contact force **R**, which the surface exerts upon it, acting perpendicular to the surface. Note that you don't care about the force that the object exerts on the surface. If you are modeling the motion of an object, you care only about the forces acting on it, not the forces exerted by it.

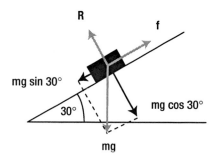

Figure 4-6. Force diagram for a body sliding down an inclined plane

If you were to simulate the motion of an object such as the one shown in Figure 4-6 (perhaps a car going downhill), how would you do it? As always, with a bit of common sense logic, some physics formulas, and some code. We won't go into detail into the physics and coding (we'll save that for Chapter 7, when we look at friction and contact forces in detail), but here is the common sense bit. From experience, you know that the object will slide along the surface while always maintaining contact. So it makes sense to resolve the forces along the plane. Well, **f** is already along the plane; **R** is perpendicular to it and so has no component along it; the component of gravity force (weight) is mg sin 30° down the incline. Hence, the magnitude of the resultant force down the incline is given by

$$F = m\,g\sin(30°) - f$$

Of course, you'll need to know how to calculate the frictional force **f**. We'll tell you that in Chapter 7. Once you know **f**, you can calculate the acceleration **a** = **F**/m, as you must surely know by now.

Forces in equilibrium

Sometimes, with two or more forces acting on an object, it so happens that the vector sum (resultant) of the forces is zero. In that case the forces are said to be in *equilibrium*. In terms of the motion of the body, it's as if no forces were acting on it.

Let's go back once more to the equation $a = F/m$. The equation implies that if the resultant force $F = 0$, then $a = 0$. Therefore, if there is no resultant force acting on a body, the body does not accelerate. In other words, *its velocity does not change, whatever it is*. This means two things. First, if the object is not moving (if it's at rest), it will remain at rest. But also, if the object was already moving at some velocity, it will maintain that velocity and neither accelerate nor decelerate (which is really a negative acceleration). The latter conclusion might come as a surprise to you; we'll pick up on it again when we discuss Newton's laws of motion in the next chapter.

Figure 4-7 shows two examples of an object in equilibrium while under the action of more than one force. In the first example, a book rests motionless on a level table, so it must experience at least two forces that add up to zero. You know that one of them must be the force of gravity, which acts downward. There is another force, a contact force R that the table exerts on the book that acts upward, opposing the force of gravity exactly.

The second, slightly more complicated example, again shows an object at rest. But this time there are three forces acting on it. The object is suspended by means of two strings. So there is a tension force in each string as well as the force of gravity acting on the object. If you add up the three forces, their vector sum must be zero. And if you resolve each force into horizontal and vertical components and then add all the horizontal components together and all the vertical components together, both will add up to zero.

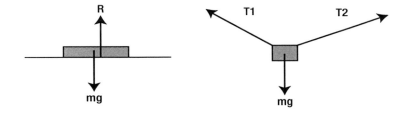

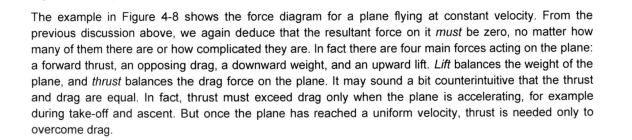

Figure 4-7. Examples of forces in equilibrium

The example in Figure 4-8 shows the force diagram for a plane flying at constant velocity. From the previous discussion above, we again deduce that the resultant force on it *must* be zero, no matter how many of them there are or how complicated they are. In fact there are four main forces acting on the plane: a forward thrust, an opposing drag, a downward weight, and an upward lift. *Lift* balances the weight of the plane, and *thrust* balances the drag force on the plane. It may sound a bit counterintuitive that the thrust and drag are equal. In fact, thrust must exceed drag only when the plane is accelerating, for example during take-off and ascent. But once the plane has reached a uniform velocity, thrust is needed only to overcome drag.

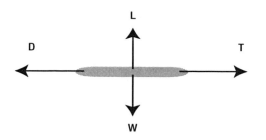

Figure 4-8. Forces on a plane moving at constant velocity are also in equilibrium

An example: object falling under gravity and drag

All this discussion on forces might appear somewhat abstract, and you are probably keen to see how it's all applied in practice. Although we'll have plenty of examples in Part II, let's look at a simple example now to whet your appetite. Don't worry if you don't understand everything immediately: it will all make complete sense after you've seen a few more examples in Part II.

In this example, a ball is dropped in a fluid such as air and, as it falls, it experiences a downward force of gravity W and an upward drag force D (see Figure 4-9). Gravity is, of course, constant and given by this:

$$W = m\,g$$

We'll have more to say about the drag force in Chapter 7; for now we just borrow a formula that says this:

$$D = -k\,v$$

In other words, the drag force is proportional to the velocity of the ball through the fluid (the minus sign indicates that the drag force is opposite in direction to the velocity). Using these two formulas, we can make the following deductions. Initially, the ball is at rest, so the drag force on it is zero. As the ball falls, it accelerates under gravity, so its velocity increases, and so does the drag force D. Eventually (if the ball falls long enough without hitting the ground), the drag force will become equal to the force of gravity, so the two will balance. At that point, we'll have equilibrium, so the acceleration will be zero, as discussed in the previous section. The ball will then continue falling at a constant velocity, known as *terminal velocity*. This is what we expect to happen according to physics theory, but: can we reproduce it in a simulation?

Figure 4-9. A ball falling in air, experiencing forces of gravity W and drag D

To simulate this example, we first create a class, as in the **Projectile** example, that will extend **Mover**. We call this class **Faller**. The job that we want **Faller** to do is to take a **Particle** instance, subject it to the two forces of gravity and drag; calculate their resultant; and then calculate the acceleration, velocity and position of the **Particle** instance. We'd also like to plot graphs of the acceleration and velocity. Here is a piece of code that does all this:

```
package {
        import com.physicscodes.motion.Mover;
        import com.physicscodes.objects.Particle;
        import com.physicscodes.math.Vector2D;
        import com.physicscodes.math.Graph;

        public class Faller extends Mover{
                private var _particle:Particle;
                private var _force:Vector2D;
                private var _acc:Vector2D;
                private var _g:Number=10;
                private var _k:Number=0.5;
                private var _graphAcc:Graph;
                private var _graphVelo:Graph;

                public function Faller(pparticle:Particle):void{
                        _particle = pparticle;
                        setupGraphs();
                        super(pparticle);
                }
                override protected function moveObject():void{
                        super.moveObject();
                        calcForce();
                        updateAccel();
                        updateVelo();
                        plotGraphs();
                }
                private function calcForce():void{
                        _force = new Vector2D(0,_particle.mass*_g-_k*_particle.vy);
                }
                private function updateAccel():void{
                        _acc = _force.multiply(1/_particle.mass);
                }
                private function updateVelo():void{
                        _particle.velo2D = _particle.velo2D.addScaled(_acc,dt);
                }
                private function setupGraphs():void{
                        //_graph= new Graph(xmin,xmax,ymin,ymax,xorig,yorig,xwidth,ywidth);
                        _graphAcc= new Graph(0,30,0,10,150,250,600,200);
                        _graphAcc.drawgrid(5,1,5,1);
                        _graphAcc.drawaxes('time (s)','acceleration (px/s/s)');
                        _particle.stage.addChild(_graphAcc);
                        _graphVelo= new Graph(0,30,0,25,150,550,600,200);
                        _graphVelo.drawgrid(5,1,5,1);
                        _graphVelo.drawaxes('time (s)','velocity (px/s)');
```

```
                        _particle.stage.addChild(_graphVelo)
            }
            private function plotGraphs():void{
                        _graphAcc.plot([time], [_acc.y], 0xff0000, false, true);
                        _graphVelo.plot([time], [_particle.vy], 0xff0000, false, true);
            }
        }
}
```

This is similar to what we did in the **Projectile** class in the last section: extend **Mover**, pass the **Particle** instance via **super()**, and override the **moveObject()** method of **Mover**. The significant additions are the three methods **calcForce()**, **updateAccel()**, and **updateVelo()** that are called within **moveObject()**. If you look at the code within these methods, you will see that they respectively compute the resultant downward force using $F = mg - kv$, the acceleration using $a = F/m$, and the new velocity using $\Delta v = a \, \Delta t$. The rest of the code deals with setting up graphs and plotting the vertical components of acceleration and velocity.

In a separate file, **ForcesExamples.as**, we then create a **Ball** instance, suitably positioned, and feed it to a **Faller** instance whose **startTime()** method is then invoked to start the simulation:

```
package{
        import flash.display.Sprite;
        import com.physicscodes.objects.Ball;
        import com.physicscodes.math.Vector2D;

        public class ForcesExample extends Sprite{
                public function ForcesExample():void{
                        init();
                }
                private function init():void{
                        var ball:Ball;
                        ball = new Ball(15,0x000000,1);
                        ball.pos2D = new Vector2D(75,50);
                        addChild(ball);

                        var faller:Faller=new Faller(ball);
                        faller.startTime();
                }
        }
}
```

Run the code, and you will see something like in Figure 4-10. As the ball falls, it initially accelerates at the value of $g = 10$ (as set in the code) and its velocity starts to increase sharply. But then the drag force starts increasing; this reduces the resultant downward force and therefore the downward acceleration, causing the velocity to increase less rapidly. About 10 seconds into the simulation, the acceleration has fallen to zero because the drag force has now grown enough to exactly balance the downward force of gravity. From then onward, the ball's velocity is constant at the value of 20 px/s. This is all just as described previously, so the simulation really works! In fact, the value of the terminal velocity is exactly as predicted by physics theory.

To see this, we reason that when terminal velocity is reached:

$$\text{drag} = \text{gravity, and so, } k\,v = m\,g$$

This gives v = mg/k. In our simulation, m = 1, g = 10 and k = 0.5. This gives v = 20 px/s, exactly as computed by the simulation. Not bad at all for a first example on forces, don't you agree?

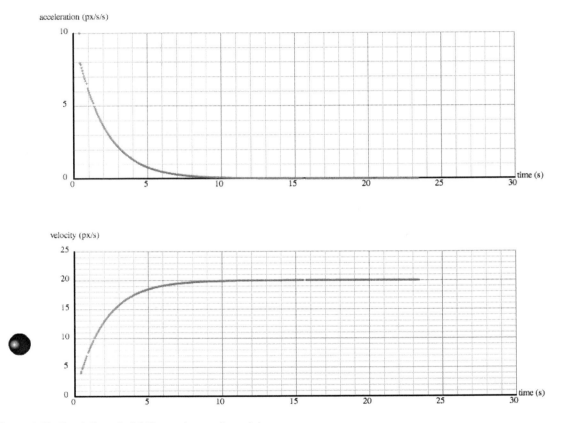

Figure 4-10. Simulating a ball falling under gravity and drag

Energy concepts

We've talked a lot about forces, but there is another physics concept that is perhaps equally important: *energy*. From our point of view, the important thing is that energy concepts sometimes provide an alternative way to solve problems that can prove tricky or even impossible to solve using the approach of forces. Just like momentum, this is because there is a powerful law of conservation of energy (which we'll talk about shortly). In fact, conservation of energy and momentum can be applied together to solve problems involving collisions, as we shall see in Chapter 5 and, in more detail, in Chapter 11.

Unlike momentum, energy is a bit trickier to define. Before we can do so, we need to introduce a closely related concept—that of *work*.

The notion of work in physics

We've often said that force causes motion, but we've also seen that a force can exist in equilibrium with other forces, when motion cannot occur. To distinguish the motion-producing effect of a force from that of merely balancing another force, we introduce the concept of work.

In physics, we say that *work* is done by a force when it produces motion in the direction along which it acts. The amount of work done W is then defined as the product of the force magnitude F and the displacement s in the direction of the force:

$$W = F\,s$$

OK, that may sound a bit abstract. Let's look at an example. Let's say a stone is dropped from a certain height h above the ground (see Figure 4-11).

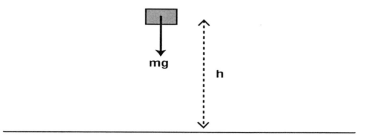

Figure 4-11. An object dropped from rest at a height h above the ground

Then the weight of the stone (the force of gravity on it) does work by displacing it downward. According to the preceding definition, the amount of work done in falling a distance h to the ground is therefore given by the following because here F = mg and s = h:

$$W = F\,s = m\,g\,h$$

Because work is the product of a force and a distance (and recalling that the unit of force is the newton, N), its unit is Nm (newton times meter). This unit also has a special name, the joule (J). So, J = Nm. Work is a scalar quantity.

What if the displacement is not in the same direction as the force? For example, what if the stone is thrown at an angle rather than dropped vertically downward? Then the work done is given as the product of the force and the projection of the displacement in its direction (see Figure 4-12).

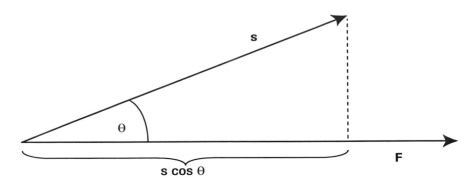

Figure 4-12. Work done is the scalar product of force and displacement

You might recognize this as the dot product between **F** and **s**, where θ is the angle between the force **F** and the displacement **s**:

$$W = \mathbf{F} \bullet \mathbf{s} = F\, s \cos(\theta)$$

Hence, if the angle θ is zero, then W = F s (because cos (0) = 1). But if θ is 90 degrees, cos θ = 0, so W = 0. In other words, the work done by a force is zero if the displacement is perpendicular to the force.

> *Note that the resultant acceleration must always be in the direction of the resultant force. However, the resultant motion (displacement) may or may not be in the direction of the resultant force.*

The capacity to do work: energy

Now that we know what work is, the definition of energy is simple: Energy is the capacity to do work. Take the example of the stone dropped from a height: because it can do work by falling it must possess energy just by being above the ground. This energy is called *potential energy* (usually abbreviated as p.e., with symbol E_p). Similarly, a moving object can do work by colliding with another object, exerting a contact force during the collision and causing it to move under the action of this force. Hence, moving bodies also have energy, known as *kinetic energy* (usually abbreviated as k.e., with symbol E_k).

In fact, *work causes a transfer or conversion of energy*. For example, applying a force to make an object move imparts kinetic energy to it. This causes a decrease in energy for the agent applying the force. This is expressed generally in the *work-energy theorem*:

Energy transferred = work done

In symbols:

$$\Delta E = \Delta W$$

Because we are here equating energy and work, it follows that energy has the same unit as work: the joule (J). Like work, energy is a scalar quantity.

Energy transfer, conversion, and conservation

Just as there are many different types of forces, there are also many different types of energy. Examples include light energy, thermal energy, nuclear energy, and so on. But usually we will be concerned with only two forms of energy: kinetic and potential energy. At a fundamental microscopic level, all forms of energy are manifestations of these two basic forms.

Energy can be transferred from one body to another. Energy can also be converted from one form to another. Whether energy is transferred or converted, total energy is always conserved.

An example of *energy transfer* is the collision of two particles, where one of the particles loses k.e. and the other gains k.e. An *elastic* collision is defined as one in which the total *kinetic* energy is conserved (k.e. is not converted into other forms of energy as a result of the collision); otherwise, the collision is *inelastic*. Therefore, if the collision is elastic, the amount of k.e. gained by one is exactly equal to that lost by the other.

As an example of *energy conversion*, a body released from a certain height loses potential energy but gains kinetic energy as it accelerates downward—its p.e. gets converted to k.e. If the body falls only under the action of the gravitational force, the gain in k.e. is exactly equal to the loss in p.e.—the total energy, kinetic plus potential, remains constant. If there are other forces, such as friction (due to air resistance), a small amount of energy is converted to thermal energy of the body and the surrounding air by doing work against friction. The total energy in all forms still remains the same. This is known as the *principle of conservation of energy*.

This principle is so important, let's state it once more, in a more general way:

> *Energy can be converted from one form to another or transferred from one body to another during interactions, but the total energy of a closed system is constant.*

"Closed system" means a system that has no interaction outside of itself. Within the system, the interactions and exchanges can be as many or as complicated as you want; the principle will still hold. For example, if you have hundreds of particles colliding with each other in a closed system, the principle will hold. If you have zillions of molecules interacting in an isolated gas, the principle still holds.

Potential and kinetic energy

Because potential energy and kinetic energy are so important, let's see how we can calculate them. Let's start with potential energy. When we discussed the concept of work, recall that the work done by an object falling from a height h above ground was shown to be equal to mgh. Now, because work done is equal to energy transferred, the object must have possessed that amount of energy before it fell. Because it was dropped from rest at height h, its velocity was initially zero and so it had no kinetic energy to start with. Hence, its energy was all potential energy to start with. We therefore conclude that an object of mass m at a height h above the ground has an amount of potential energy given by

$$E_p = m\,g\,h$$

This is our formula for potential energy.

Let's now work out a formula for kinetic energy. Consider the same example of the falling stone. Neglecting energy lost by friction, the kinetic energy of the stone just before it hits the ground must equal the potential energy it had initially (because it does not have any p.e. at the ground, so it must all have been converted to k.e.). So the final k.e. is also equal numerically to mgh. Here h is the distance that the stone has fallen. Because k.e. is energy possessed due to motion, we really want a formula for k.e. as a function of the velocity the stone has, not the displacement it has undergone. Remember the formula connecting velocity and displacement? Using $v^2 = u^2 + 2\,\mathbf{a}\,.\,\mathbf{s}$, and noting that u = 0, a = g, and s = h, we get $v^2 = 2gh$.

Using this, all we need to do now is replace gh by ½ v^2 and we end up with this:

$$E_k = \frac{1}{2}m\,v^2$$

This is the formula for the kinetic energy of a body of mass m moving at a velocity v.

Power

The final concept we'll introduce is that of *power*. In talking about energy, we seem to have given up the concept of time. We've talked about work being done and energy being exchanged or transferred, but without reference to how fast it happens. Power introduces time in the energy approach.

Power is defined as the rate of doing work. In calculus notation, the power P is therefore given by the following:

$$P = \frac{dW}{dt}$$

Or, in discrete form:

$$P = \frac{\Delta W}{\Delta t}$$

In words, it is work done divided by time taken. From this definition, the unit of power is therefore J/s. This unit has a special name. It's called the watt (W). Another commonly used unit is the horsepower (HP). Power is a scalar quantity, just like energy.

We can reverse the last formula to obtain the work done in a time interval Δt when power P is deployed:

$$\Delta W = P \Delta t$$

Power is a very useful concept for analyzing the operation of machines, such as vehicles. In this connection, suppose that a machine is doing work by exerting a force F and moving its point of application at a velocity v in the direction of F. Then, the work done is $\Delta W = F\Delta s$. (Note: this is just the formula W = Fs written for small changes ΔW and Δs.)

From the definition of power as rate of doing work, the power output of the machine is therefore this:

$$P = \frac{\Delta W}{\Delta t} = \frac{F \Delta s}{\Delta t}$$

And because $\Delta s/\Delta t$ = v, we end up with this formula:

$$P = F\,v$$

So the power deployed by the machine is equal to the product of the force F it applies and the velocity v it produces.

You usually need to apply power concepts if you are simulating machines engineered by humans, such as cars and boats.

Example: a rudimentary "car" simulation

We conclude this chapter by showing you a simple example of how to apply power and energy concepts to simulate motion, without the explicit use of forces. In this example, you will apply power to a **Ball** object (the car) to accelerate it against frictional and other power losses, in the same manner as you press the gas pedal of your car to keep it moving.

The setup file for this simulation, which is called **EnergyExample.as**, simply creates a **Ball** object, initializes its position and velocity, and then passes it to the constructor of an instance of an **Accelerator** class:

```
package{
        import flash.display.Sprite;
```

```
import com.physicscodes.objects.Ball;
import com.physicscodes.math.Vector2D;

public class EnergyExample extends Sprite{
        public function EnergyExample():void{
                init();
        }

        private function init():void{
                var ball:Ball;
                ball = new Ball(15,0x000000,1);
                ball.pos2D = new Vector2D(50,50);
                ball.velo2D = new Vector2D(20,0);
                addChild(ball);

                var accelerator:Accelerator=new Accelerator(ball);
                accelerator.startTime();
        }
    }
}
```

In the previous code, we have given the ball an initial velocity of 20 px/s in the x-direction. The mass of the ball is 1 unit.

Here is the full code for the **Accelerator** class:

```
package {
        import com.physicscodes.motion.Mover;
        import com.physicscodes.objects.Particle;
        import com.physicscodes.math.Vector2D;
        import com.physicscodes.math.Graph;
        import flash.events.KeyboardEvent;
        import flash.ui.Keyboard;

        public class Accelerator extends Mover{
                private var _particle:Particle;
                private var _powerLossFactor:Number=0.1;
                private var _powerApplied:Number=50;
                private var _ke:Number;
                private var _vmag:Number;
                private var _mass:Number;
                private var _graph:Graph;
                private var _applyThrust:Boolean=false;

                public function Accelerator(pparticle:Particle):void{
                        _particle = pparticle;
                        _mass = _particle.mass;
                        _vmag = _particle.velo2D.length;
                        _ke = 0.5*_mass*_vmag*_vmag;
                        setupGraphs();
                        _particle.stage.addEventListener(KeyboardEvent.KEY_DOWN,startThrust);
                        _particle.stage.addEventListener(KeyboardEvent.KEY_UP,stopThrust);
                        super(pparticle);
                }
```

```
private function startThrust(evt:KeyboardEvent):void{
        if (evt.keyCode==Keyboard.UP){
                _applyThrust = true;
        }
}

private function stopThrust(evt:KeyboardEvent):void{
        _applyThrust = false;
}

override protected function moveObject():void{
        super.moveObject();
        applyPower();
        updateVelo();
        plotGraphs();
}

private function applyPower():void{
        if (_applyThrust){
                _ke += _powerApplied*dt;
        }
        _ke -= _powerLossFactor*_vmag*_vmag*dt;
}

private function updateVelo():void{
        _vmag = Math.sqrt(2*_ke/_mass);
        _particle.vx = _vmag;
}

private function setupGraphs():void{
        //_graph= new Graph(xmin,xmax,ymin,ymax,xorig,yorig,xwidth,ywidth);
        _graph= new Graph(0,60,0,50,100,550,600,400);
        _graph.drawgrid(5,1,5,1);
        _graph.drawaxes('time (s)','velocity (px/s)');
        _particle.stage.addChild(_graph);
}

private function plotGraphs():void{
        _graph.plot([time], [_particle.vx], 0xff0000, false, true);
}

        }

}
```

As in the last example, we are extending **Mover** and adding functionality by overriding its **moveObject()** method as well as adding some other methods. We also have some private properties: **_mass** (the mass of the particle), **_vmag** (its velocity magnitude), **_ke** (its kinetic energy), **_powerApplied** (the applied power), and **_powerLossFactor** (a coefficient we use to calculate the power loss due to friction and other factors). The values of **_vmag** and **_ke** are initialized in the constructor.

The most important parts of the code are the two methods **applyPower()** and **updateVelo()**, which are called at every timestep within the **moveObject()** method.

In **applyPower()**, we are updating the kinetic energy of the ball. The **_applyThrust Boolean** variable tells us if the up arrow key is pressed; if so, the k.e. is updated by multiplying the power by the time interval **dt**. What we are doing here is to apply this formula:

$$\Delta E_k = P \Delta t$$

You might not immediately recognize this formula, but it is obtained by equating the work done $\Delta W = P\Delta t$ with the kinetic energy gained according to the work-energy theorem, as discussed earlier. Conceptually, what is happening is that the applied power is doing mechanical work on the ball, which results in an increase in its kinetic energy.

In **applyPower()**, you will notice that we also *reduce* the kinetic energy of the ball by an amount equal to **_powerLossFactor*_vmag*_vmag*dt**. This is equivalent to applying a power loss given by the following, where k is a constant corresponding to **_powerLossFactor**:

$$P = -k\,v^2$$

This formula comes from applying the formula P = F v we saw in the last section and modeling the total of all resistive forces (such as friction and drag) by F = –k v, as a force proportional to the velocity of the ball (see Chapter 7). This is a crude approximation, but will do for the purpose of our simple example.

The **updateVelo()** method first computes the velocity magnitude from the updated kinetic energy by this formula, which is obtained by reversing the formula for kinetic energy E_k = ½ m v^2:

$$v = \sqrt{2E_k/m}$$

It then updates the ball's velocity accordingly.

There is also code for plotting a graph of the horizontal velocity component of the ball and for applying the power when the user holds down the up arrow key. These pieces of code should be straightforward, so we will not go into them here.

If you run the code, you will find that the ball starts moving, but its velocity is gradually reduced, owing to the effect of the power loss. If you then press and hold down the up arrow key, the applied power will cause an increase in the ball's k.e., making it accelerate. If the power is applied continuously, eventually the velocity will tend to a constant value, but if the up arrow key is released, the velocity will reduce again as shown in Figure 4-13. This behavior mirrors the operation of a car accelerator in a simple way.

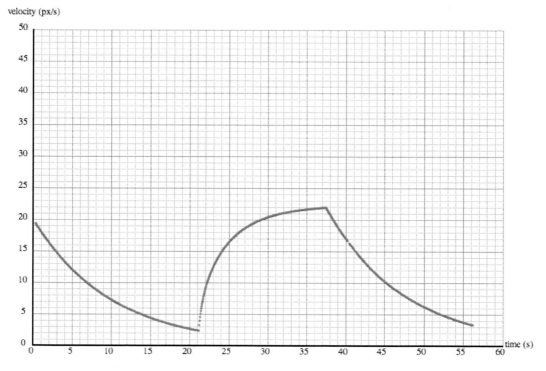

Figure 4-13. A rudimentary car simulation

Summary

That was another long overview chapter, and you've now learned an awful lot of physics concepts. This chapter completes Part I of the book. The next chapter will bring together what you've learned so far to lay out the principles of how to simulate a wide range of forces and motions.

Get ready for the real action!

Part II

Particles, Forces, and Motion

Chapter 5

The Laws Governing Motion

Chapter 4 in Part I of this book provided some of the general conceptual background for describing and analyzing motion. That background included a discussion of motion-related concepts such as velocity, acceleration, and force. In the present chapter, we'll use those concepts to formulate the physics laws that will allow you to calculate the motion of particles under any type of force. The next five chapters will then apply the laws to a number of different forces. We'll illustrate the application of the principles with brief examples, with the aim of building on them in the next few chapters.

We have deliberately kept this chapter brief and focused on the fundamental laws and principles that you will need for applying to the examples in this part of the book and beyond. You can come back to this chapter as needed to refresh your understanding of the underlying physics principles, as you work your way through their applications in the rest of the book.

Topics covered in this chapter include the following:

- Newton's laws of motion: Newton's three laws provide the link between force and motion. These laws allow us to predict the motion of objects under the action of known forces.

- Applying Newton's laws: We build a couple of classes that will help to implement Newton's laws of motion numerically in code and illustrate their use with a couple of examples.

- Newton's second law as a differential equation: In physics textbooks, Newton's second law is sometimes expressed as a differential equation and solved analytically using calculus. We briefly discuss the connection between that formulation and our numerical method, and illustrate it with an example.

- Principle of conservation of energy: We apply the principle of conservation of energy to motion by considering the potential and kinetic energy of moving particles.

- Principle of conservation of momentum: We take a look at conservation of momentum and its application to a simple example involving collisions.

- Laws governing rotational motion: The preceding laws can be extended to objects undergoing rotational motion. We do not discuss rotation here, but will do so in later chapters.

Newton's laws of motion

Newton's three laws of motion, formulated in his classic book *Principia Mathematica* in 1687, provide the link between force and motion. You might recall that we said in the last chapter that the formula **F** = ma provides that link. This formula is actually the second of Newton's three laws of motion. In fact, it is a special form of that law. In this chapter, we'll go a bit deeper, looking at the general form of Newton's second law as well as the two other laws.

Newton's first law of motion (N1)

The first law of motion tells you what happens if there is no force acting on an object (see Figure 5-1). Think of an object that is at rest and not moving. If you don't apply any force on it (in other words, if you leave it alone), what do you think will happen? That's right—nothing. Things don't suddenly start moving on their own. This is basically what the first law says. Common sense? But wait, there is more. Suppose the object is already moving and there is no force on it. What would happen to it? Everyday experience might tempt you into thinking that the object would slow down and finally stop. So you might be surprised to hear that the first law says that the object would carry on moving at its initial velocity as long as there is no force on it!

This proposition seems to run somewhat counter to our everyday experience. For example, a ball rolling on the ground always comes to rest. In fact, it does so because friction with the ground is causing it to slow down. In the absence of friction, the ball would carry on indefinitely. This can be demonstrated by minimizing friction with the underlying surface—for example, by using marbles on a perfectly smooth horizontal surface. The marbles then move in a straight line for long distances without significant decrease in their velocity.

Another way of putting this is that you don't need a force for an object to *continue* moving at constant velocity. You only need a force to make it *change* its velocity—for example, by starting to move, or speeding up or slowing down. In other words, you only need a force to make an object accelerate (or decelerate).

Armed with this insight, we can formulate Newton's first law of motion succinctly in the following form, which covers both the cases of an object at rest and moving at constant velocity:

> *If the resultant force acting on an object is zero, its acceleration is zero.* **F** = **0** *implies* **a** = **0**.

This law is so important, that we'll say it in yet another way. If no resultant force acts on an object, its velocity must be constant (including zero). Conversely, if an object has a constant velocity (which may be zero), you know for certain that the resultant force on it must be zero.

Finally, note that we said that the *resultant force* is zero. We're not saying that no forces are acting on the object. As you saw in the last chapter, two or more forces acting on the same object can be in equilibrium so that their resultant is zero. In such a case, the first law will still hold. It does not distinguish between no resultant force and no force at all.

The Mover class from Chapter 4 implements the first law: it takes a particle and moves it at its velocity forever. It knows nothing about forces.

$$\mathbf{F} = 0 \text{ implies } \mathbf{a} = 0$$

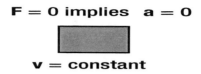

$$\mathbf{v} = \text{constant}$$

Figure 5-1. Schematic illustration of Newton's first law of motion

Newton's second law of motion (N2)

Newton's second law of motion builds upon the first law (see Figure 5-2). The first law tells you what happens when no resultant force acts on an object. The second law tells you what happens when a resultant force does act on an object. It tells you that the object's motion changes. But that's not all. It tells you exactly by what amount it changes—it gives you an exact formula connecting the force applied and the change in motion produced.

Recall from the last chapter that momentum (with the symbol **p** and defined as **p** = m**v**) represents the "quantity of motion" that an object possesses. Newton's second law connects the force applied to the change in momentum it produces. We won't go into how Newton arrived at that formula, but here it is:

> *If a resultant force **F** acts on an object, its momentum changes so that the rate of change of momentum is equal to the force applied.* **F** = d**p**/dt.

This is the general form of Newton's second law, and it may appear somewhat unintuitive, at least until you get used to it! In Calculus-speak, this tells us that the applied force is equal to the time derivative of momentum. Essentially, the time derivative of momentum tells us how fast the momentum is changing on an instantaneous basis. This means that the force being applied at any given time is equal to the change in momentum per unit time.

We have seen similar formulas before. For example, **v** = d**s**/dt and **a** = d**v**/dt. Newton's second law is exactly of the same form: **F** = d**p**/dt. Note that the preceding equations for velocity and acceleration are actually *definitions*, whereas **F** = d**p**/dt is a *law* that tells us how things behave in the real world.

In this general form, the second law might seem quite different from the first law. In the first law, we were talking about acceleration, and now we are talking about rate of momentum change. There is actually a link between the two when we apply the second law to objects whose mass doesn't change, such as particles.

To see the link, recall again that momentum is defined by **p** = m**v**. For a particle, the mass m is constant. In that case, the rules of calculus tell us that d**p**/dt = m d**v**/dt. If you're into calculus, what we've done here is to calculate the (time) derivative of **p**, which must be equal to the derivative of m**v** (because these two things are equal: **p** = m**v**). But m is constant, so the derivative of m**v** is equal to m times the derivative of **v**. You probably recall that d**v**/dt = **a** (the definition of acceleration). Therefore, we conclude that for a particle d**p**/dt = m**a**. Because Newton assures us that **F** = d**p**/dt, we've recovered our old friend **F** = m**a**. So here is the special form of Newton's second law of motion:

> *If a resultant force **F** acts on an object of constant mass m, it produces an acceleration **a** given by the formula* **F** = m**a**.

If you now compare this form of the second law with the statement of the first law given in the last section, you'll see that N1 is really just a special case of N2. Starting with **F** = m**a** and putting **F** = 0 gives m**a** = 0, and hence **a** = 0. In other words, **F** = 0 gives **a** = 0, which is exactly what the first law says. So the first law is "contained" within the second law. Good, that's one fewer law to worry about!

Figure 5-2. Schematic illustration of Newton's second law of motion

You'll use Newton's second law in the form of $F = ma$ most of the time. But do bear in mind that it's not the most general form of the law—it applies only if the mass m does not change. There is a third form of the law that applies when instead of an object of fixed mass m, you have a stream of substance moving at a certain velocity. For example, the exhaust gases from a rocket are pushed out at a constant velocity v relative to the rocket. Because v is now constant, calculus rules tell us that $dp/dt = v\, dm/dt$. Therefore, the force on the gases is given by $F = v\, dm/dt$, where dm/dt is the rate of change of mass (the mass of gas released per second). We'll use this form of Newton's second law to model a rocket in Chapter 6.

> *The force F needed to move any substance at a rate of* dm/dt *at constant velocity* v *is given by* $F = v\, dm/dt$.

Despite its simplicity, Newton's second law is arguably the most important law in Newtonian mechanics. It's almost magical how it connects forces and motion. But it is also utterly useless unless we know how to work out the forces acting on an object. We need *force laws*. We'll look at some examples of force laws shortly. But before we do that, you want to know about Newton's third law, don't you?

Newton's third law of motion (N3)

In the last chapter, we said that force is the cause of changes in motion. As you have just seen, Newton's second law makes that statement much more precise, giving us a formula for calculating the change in motion arising from a given force. But so far, we haven't said much about where forces come from. Many forces arise because of the presence of other objects. Newton's first and second laws tell us how an object's motion responds to an applied force. Newton's third law tells us how two objects interact by exerting forces on each other. Here it goes:

> *If a body A exerts a force F on another body B, body B must in turn exert an equal and opposite force –F on body A.*

Okay, let's clarify things a bit. What this means is that forces between objects always exist as an *action-reaction pair*. Both forces exist *simultaneously*; there is no delay between them. And even if their magnitudes and directions change with time, they remain equal and opposite at all times.

Newton's third law of motion is frequently misunderstood and misquoted. One of the common mistakes is to think that action and reaction forces "balance" each other. In fact, in an action-reaction pair, the forces act on *different* objects. Therefore, it is wrong to think that they "balance" or "cancel" each other. In other words, they are not in equilibrium. Each force acts on a different object and affects its motion individually. Subtleties like these make Newton's third law somewhat difficult to understand deeply at an abstract level. But it helps a lot to see how the law is applied in analyzing specific problems. For example, Newton's third law is applied to analyze the interaction between two particles in the section on "The principle of momentum conservation" that follows. You will also see it applied in the analysis of different examples throughout the book.

Here are some examples of action-reaction pairs of forces:

- Two colliding bodies exert equal and opposite forces on each other, even if they have different masses, as depicted in Figure 5-3.

- The Earth is exerting a force of gravity on you equal to your weight. This implies that you are also exerting an equal and opposite force of gravity on the Earth!

- In a rocket, the engine exerts a downward force on the exhaust gases, which in turn exerts an equal and opposite force on the rocket, propelling it forward.

Figure 5-3. Schematic illustration of Newton's third law of motion

Applying Newton's laws

Practically the whole of the rest of this book is about applying Newton's laws of motion. Here, we'll just establish the method, build a couple of helper classes, and illustrate their application with some simple examples.

General method for applying F = ma

To analyze a problem for applying **F** = **ma**, use the following procedure:

Draw a diagram representing the interacting objects in the problem.

Choose the object whose motion is to be calculated and indicate using arrows all the forces acting *on* it due to other objects. Ignore the forces exerted *by* the object on other objects. This gives you a force diagram, as described in Chapter 4.

Calculate the resultant force **F** on the object (using vector addition, as described in Chapter 3) and apply the second law **F** = **ma** to calculate the acceleration **a**.

In principle, that's all there is to it. You have to do steps 1 and 2 using pen and paper. Let's build a class that will help us do step 3.

The Forcer class

What we need here is a class that allows you to calculate the forces on a particle, find their resultant, and hence compute their acceleration. You can then use the acceleration to update the velocity and position of the particle. Recall the sense in which we are using the term "particle," as discussed in the last chapter: any object whose inner structure is irrelevant from the point of view of the simulation. So, for our purposes, a particle could be a ball as well as a planet.

Let's call the class `Forcer`. Because we are going to move the particle, it makes sense for `Forcer` to extend `Mover`. So we begin with the following code:

```
public class Forcer extends Mover{

        private var _particle:Particle;

        public function Forcer(pparticle:Particle):void{
                _particle = pparticle;
                super(pparticle);
        }

}
```

Next we want to override the `moveObject()` method of `Mover`, so that it not only moves the particle according to its existing velocity but also updates the velocity. To do this, it must first calculate the force and hence the acceleration. So our new `moveObject()` method should look something like this:

```
override protected function moveObject():void{
        super.moveObject();
        calcForce();
        updateAccel();
        updateVelo();
}
```

The job of `calcForce()` is to calculate the resultant force on the particle. We'll look at that last. The `updateAccel()` method updates the acceleration once we know the force. How do we do that? Of course, using $\mathbf{F} = m\mathbf{a}$ to give $\mathbf{a} = \mathbf{F}/m$. So, with `_acc` and `_force` defined as private `Vector2D` objects, `updateAccel()` is just a one-liner:

```
private function updateAccel():void{
        _acc = _force.multiply(1/_particle.mass);
}
```

Recalling from Chapter 4 that $\Delta\mathbf{v} = \mathbf{a}\Delta t$, the `updateVelo()` method is just as simple:

```
private function updateVelo():void{
        _particle.velo2D = _particle.velo2D.addScaled(_acc,dt);

}
```

Finally, the `calcForce()` method should calculate each force acting on the particle and then add them up to give `_force`. Note that the private variable `_force` can be referenced by external code as `force` by the use of getter/setter code. The code that goes into `calcForce()` will depend on the problem and the forces involved. So we create a "dummy" `calcForce()` method, declaring it as `protected` so that it can be overridden by subclasses of `Forcer`:

```
protected function calcForce():void{
        _force = Forces.zeroForce();
}
```

All this method currently does is to set the force to zero. It does this using the `Forces.zeroForce()` method, which produces a `Vector2D` object with zero components. Of course, we haven't talked about the `Forces` class yet, so let's do that now.

The Forces class

Exactly what goes into `calcForce()` is going to depend on the problem at hand, but it will always involve specifying the forces on the particle and then adding them up. So, let's build a new class to help us with these tasks.

The class we'll build will basically just contain static methods for different types of forces. So we'll name the class `Forces`, appropriately enough. In general, the force on a particle could depend on the particle properties (size, position, velocity, mass, charge), as well as on properties of the environment it is in, or on other objects. These properties will need to be specified as arguments in the relevant methods.

Let's look at some examples. First, let's create a zero force. This is a force with a magnitude of zero, and therefore with components equal to zero.

Here is the static function that will make one:

```
static public function zeroForce():Vector2D {
        return (new Vector2D(0,0));
}
```

Next, let's create a gravity force method:

```
static public function constantGravity(m:Number,g:Number):Vector2D {
        return new Vector2D(0,m*g);
}
```

The force of gravity on an object of mass m is given by mg and points downward. Hence, we give the values of m and g as arguments and are given back a vector with the vertical (y) component being mg and the horizontal (x) component being zero. You'll note that we've named the function `constantGravity` instead of simply `gravity`. This is because we are reserving the name *gravity* for the more general form of the force of gravity, which you'll learn about in Chapter 10. The form of gravity given by mg is near-Earth gravity, as experienced by objects near the surface of the Earth. More about this in the next chapter.

As another example, let's look at drag, which is the resistive force experienced by an object moving in a fluid such as air or water. We'll take a much deeper look at drag in Chapter 7, but for now let's just say that at low speeds the drag force is given by −k**v**. That's a constant k times the velocity **v** of an object. The minus sign signifies that the drag force is in the opposite direction to the velocity. Let us create a function for this type of drag force, which we call `linearDrag`.

Here is the static method `linearDrag`:

```
static public function linearDrag(k:Number,vel:Vector2D):Vector2D {
        var force:Vector2D;
        var velMag:Number=vel.length;
        if (velMag>0) {
                force=vel.multiply(-k);
        }else{
                force=new Vector2D(0,0);
        }
        return force;
}
```

As you can see, the linearDrag function takes two arguments: the drag coefficient k and the velocity vel of the object.

Next, we create a static method add() for adding any number of forces:

```
static public function add(arr:Array):Vector2D {
        var forceSum:Vector2D = new Vector2D(0,0);
        for (var i:uint=0; i<arr.length; i++){
                var force:Vector2D = arr[i];
                forceSum.incrementBy(force);
        }
        return forceSum;
}
```

The add() method takes as argument an array of forces. It loops through the array, adding the forces in turn and returning the final vector sum. This is all we need for now. In the next few chapters, we'll be adding lots more force functions as static methods in the Forces class.

A simple example: projectile with drag

To demonstrate how to use the Forcer and Forces class, let's look at a specific example. Suppose we want a particle to move under gravity while experiencing the drag force (such as an object thrown or falling through a fluid such as air or water). Then we would first create a new class that extends Forcer and overrides its calcForce() method. Here is an example of such a class, called TestForcer:

```
package {
        import com.physicscodes.motion.Forcer;
        import com.physicscodes.motion.Forces;
        import com.physicscodes.objects.Particle;
        import com.physicscodes.math.Vector2D;

        public class TestForcer extends Forcer{
                private var _particle:Particle;
                private var _g:Number=10;
                private var _k:Number=0.1;

                public function TestForcer(pparticle:Particle):void{
                        _particle = pparticle;
                        super(pparticle);
                }

                override protected function calcForce():void{
                        var gravity:Vector2D = Forces.constantGravity(_particle.mass,_g);
                        var drag:Vector2D = Forces.linearDrag(_k,_particle.velo2D);
                        force = Forces.add([gravity, drag]);
                }
        }
}
```

The structure of this class is very simple. It takes a Particle reference pparticle in its constructor and passes it to Forcer via super(pparticle). The new thing that it does beyond what Forcer does is to override calcForce() and include the forces of gravity and linear drag by making use of the relevant static methods of the Forces class. So we've invoked Forces.constantGravity(), using g = 10 and the particle mass. We've also invoked `Forces.linearDrag()` using k = 0.1. Then we added the two forces by passing them as an array argument to the `Forces.add()` method and assigned the result to the force variable.

Making a ball move under gravity and drag is now very easy. We do this in `ForcesTest.as`:

```
package{
        import flash.display.Sprite;
        import com.physicscodes.objects.Ball;
        import com.physicscodes.math.Vector2D;

        public class ForcesTest extends Sprite{
                public function ForcesTest():void{
                        init();
                }
                private function init():void{
                        var pos0:Vector2D = new Vector2D(50,400);
                        var velo0:Vector2D = new Vector2D(60,-60);

                        var ball:Ball;
                        ball = new Ball(15,0x0000ff);
                        ball.pos2D = pos0;
                        ball.velo2D = velo0;
                        addChild(ball);

                        var forcer:TestForcer=new TestForcer(ball);
                        forcer.startTime();
                }
        }
}
```

We create a ball with an initial position and velocity and add it to the display list. The code that animates the ball is then just two lines long. We create a `TestForcer` object called `forcer`, passing the `Ball` instance as an argument. Then we invoke the `startTime()` method of `forcer`. That's it.

Run the code and you will see a ball being thrown upward; it is then pulled down by gravity and slowed down by drag.

To appreciate the effect that the additional drag force has on the ball's motion, replace the last two lines in `calcForce()` in `TestForcer.as` with the following line:

```
force = gravity;
```

This makes the ball move under gravity only. If you now run the code, you will see the ball following a parabolic trajectory, as in the projectile simulation of the last chapter.

On the other hand, if you keep the drag force and increase the drag coefficient _k to 0.5, the drag force will have a more extreme effect, quickly killing the horizontal motion of the ball and making it fall almost vertically thereafter—similar to what a balloon might do if you hit it upward.

This simple example demonstrates how easy it is to make use of the `Forcer` and `Forces` classes to build simulations, and how you can get different effects by changing the forces and their parameters in the `calcForce()` method.

Just to give you an idea of how flexible and powerful this approach is, let's look at a relatively more complicated example.

A more complicated example: floating ball

The example we are going to look at involves throwing a ball about in air or water and making it behave as it would do in real life. This example uses more physics than we've covered, so we won't go into the details of the physics or coding involved, leaving a more complete discussion for Chapter 7. At this stage, we just want to whet your appetite by showing you what is possible to be done with a fairly small amount of straightforward coding using the approach outlined in this section.

The source code for this example is in the files FloatingBall.as and Floater.as. FloatingBall.as just sets up the graphic elements (see Figure 5-4) and then creates an instance of Floater, which does all the hard work.

Figure 5-4. The floating ball simulation

Here is the code in Floater.as:

```
package {
        import com.physicscodes.motion.Forcer;
        import com.physicscodes.motion.Forces;
        import com.physicscodes.objects.Particle;
        import com.physicscodes.math.Vector2D;
        import flash.events.MouseEvent;

        public class Floater extends Forcer{
                private var _particle:Particle;
                private var _g:Number=50;
                private var _rho:Number=1.5;
                private var _V:Number=1;
                private var _k:Number=0.01;
                private var _yLevel:Number=200;
                private var _xEdge:Number=300;
                private var _groundLevel:Number=150;
                private var _vfac:Number=-0.8;
                private var _stageWidth:Number=800;

                public function Floater(pparticle:Particle):void{
                        _particle = pparticle;
                        _particle.stage.addEventListener(MouseEvent.MOUSE_DOWN,onDown);
                        super(pparticle);
                }
```

```
override protected function calcForce():void{
        var gravity:Vector2D = Forces.constantGravity(_particle.mass,_g);
        var rball:Number=0.5*_particle.height;
        var xball:Number=_particle.x;
        var yball:Number=_particle.y;
        var dr:Number= (yball-_yLevel)/rball;
        var ratio:Number; // volume fraction of object that is submerged
        if (dr <= -1){ // object completely out of water
                ratio=0;
        }else if (dr < 1){ // object partially in water

                //ratio = 0.5 + 0.5*dr; // for cuboid
                ratio = 0.5 + 0.25*dr*(3-dr*dr); // for sphere
        }else{ // object completely in water
                ratio=1;
        }
        var upthrust:Vector2D = new Vector2D(0,-_rho*_V*ratio*_g);
        var drag:Vector2D = _particle.velo2D.multiply(-
ratio*_k*_particle.velo2D.length);
        force = Forces.add([gravity, upthrust, drag]);
        if (xball < rball){
                _particle.xpos = rball;
                _particle.vx *= _vfac;
        }
        if (xball > _stageWidth - rball){
                _particle.xpos = _stageWidth - rball;
                _particle.vx *= _vfac;
        }
}

private function onDown(e:MouseEvent):void{
        _particle.velo2D = new Vector2D(0,0);
        _particle.stage.addEventListener(MouseEvent.MOUSE_UP,onUp);
        _particle.xpos = _particle.stage.mouseX;
        _particle.ypos = _particle.stage.mouseY;
        stopTime();
}
private function onUp(e:MouseEvent):void{
        _particle.velo2D = new Vector2D(_particle.stage.mouseX-
_particle.xpos,_particle.stage.mouseY-_particle.ypos);
        _particle.stage.removeEventListener(MouseEvent.MOUSE_UP,onUp);
        startTime();
}
        }
    }
}
```

Without going into details, you can see that we have a more complicated `calcForce()` method that includes three forces: gravity, upthrust, and drag. There is also some logic in `calcForce()` that tells the code how to work out the forces on the ball depending on where it is. Additionally, there is some logic to tell the code what to do at the boundaries. Finally, there are a number of parameters to do with the different forces. On the whole, though, this is certainly not an overly complex piece of code, and it should be possible for you to get the gist of what it's doing.

The onDown() and onUp() methods allow the user to interact with the simulation by clicking the mouse. If you click anywhere on the stage, the ball will immediately move there. If you hold down the mouse button, drag the cursor, and then release the mouse, the ball is imparted a velocity numerically equal to the distance between the ball and the point at which the mouse is released.

Run the simulation and play around to see how much it behaves like the real thing, all accomplished with a relatively small amount of code. It's fun!

Newton's second law as a differential equation

This section is especially meant for readers who want to relate what we are doing here with what you would typically find in physics textbooks or on physics web sites or Wikipedia. You can safely skip it if you wish.

If you are a serious physics programmer, it's likely that you'll find yourself digging into physics textbooks or online sources at some point or other. Now, if you are looking for the solution of any problem involving Newton's second law, chances are that you will come across things called differential equations, and pages of math to solve them analytically. How does all that stuff relate to our approach of solving Newton's law numerically as discussed in the last section?

Taking a deeper look at F = ma

A differential equation is an equation that contains derivatives of quantities. Solving differential equations is in general more complicated than solving ordinary algebraic equations because it involves integration (refer to Chapter 3).

Newton's second law, in the form **F** = m**a**, might appear superficially like a simple algebraic equation.

However, it is useful to remember that acceleration is actually the derivative of velocity, **a** = dv/dt, so that we can also write Newton's second law as

$$m\frac{d\mathbf{v}}{dt} = \mathbf{F}$$

This is a so-called first order differential equation with respect to velocity because it involves the first derivative of velocity. Recalling that **v** = ds/dt, we can then write the previous equation as

$$m\frac{d^2\mathbf{s}}{dt^2} = \mathbf{F}$$

This is now a second order differential equation with respect to displacement, because it involves the second derivative of displacement (refer to Chapter 3).

In general, the force **F** can be a function of position and velocity. You will see an example of such a force function shortly.

You will sometimes see Newton's second law expressed in these forms if you look in physics textbooks. In principle, the preceding differential equations can be solved by integrating analytically or numerically to yield the displacement **s** and velocity **v** as a function of time. Most physics textbooks focus on analytical solutions. But an analytical solution is possible only in special cases and it requires application of calculus integration techniques. On the other hand, it is always possible to solve the differential equation numerically. In fact, this is what we are doing in the Mover and Forcer classes. Specifically, we are integrating the first form of the differential equation in the `updateVelo()` method of `Forcer` and then integrating the velocity to give the displacement in the `moveObject()` method of `Mover`.

The next example will illustrate a case in which we can solve Newton's second law both analytically and numerically. We'll use this example to show you what a typical analytical solution of this differential equation might look like. We'll also compare the exact analytical solution with the numerically integrated solution produced by `Forcer` to see how good the latter is.

An example: Fall under gravity and drag revisited

This example builds upon the one described in the last chapter, in which we simulated the fall of a ball under the combined forces of gravity and drag, and showed that it attained terminal velocity as predicted by simple physics theory. Here we'll update the example to compare the detailed analytical solution with the simulation.

The differential equation in this case is as follows (note that this is a 1-D case; hence there is no need to use vector notation):

$$m\frac{d^2s}{dt^2} = mg - kv$$

Or in first-order form in terms of velocity:

$$m\frac{dv}{dt} = mg - kv$$

The analytical solution of this equation is given in many physics textbooks. For an object dropped from rest, it is this:

$$v = \frac{mg}{k}\left[1 - \exp\left(-k\,t/m\right)\right]$$

When the time t is large, the exponential term tends to zero (recall the review of the exponential function in Chapter 3). Therefore, according to this equation, v tends to a limiting value of mg/k, which is of course the terminal velocity. So the solution agrees with what we found in Chapter 4. In addition, it now tells us the velocity at any time t, not just the terminal velocity.

This solution can in turn be integrated to give the displacement s at any time t. The result is this:

$$s = \frac{mg}{k}\left[t + \frac{m}{k}\exp\left(-k\,t/m\right) - \frac{m}{k}\right]$$

These analytical solutions for the displacement s and velocity v may now be compared with the simulated results. In `ForcesExample2.as` and `Faller2.as`, we updated `ForcesExample.as` and `Faller.as` from the last chapter to make this comparison. We have also rewritten the `Faller2` class to extend `Forcer` instead of `Mover`, and overridden the `calcForce()` method as in the last example. In fact, the `calcForce()` method looks identical to that in the last example because the same forces (gravity and drag) are involved.

The relevant piece of code is the function `plotGraphs()` that plots graphs to compare the analytical and numerical values of s and v:

```
private function plotGraphs():void{
        _graphDisp.plot([time], [_particle.ypos-_y0], 0xff0000);
        _graphDisp.plot([time], [_m*_g/_k*(time+_m/_k*Math.exp(-_k/_m*time)-_m/_k)],
0x0000ff);
        _graphVelo.plot([time], [_particle.vy], 0xff0000);
        _graphVelo.plot([time], [_m*_g/_k*(1-Math.exp(-_k/_m*time))], 0x0000ff);
}
```

We are plotting the vertical displacement of the ball, which is `_particle.ypos` minus its initial value `_y0`, as well as its value as given by the analytical solution on the `Graph` instance `_graphDisp`. Similarly, `_graphVelo` displays the vertical velocity as computed by the code and the analytical solution. The simulation is shown in Figure 5-5. The agreement between the two is so good that the respective curves lie on top of each other in both graphs. So we're happy that in this case the simple Euler integration scheme implemented in `Mover` and `Forcer` is actually doing a pretty decent job.

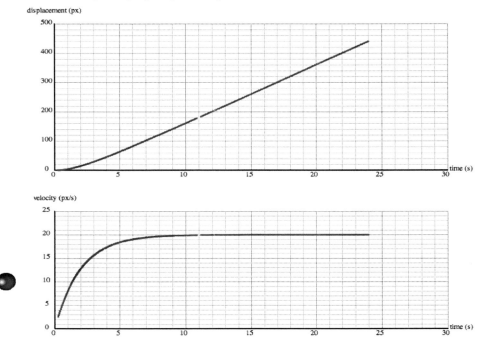

Figure 5-5. Comparing numerical and analytical solutions for a ball falling under gravity and drag

The principle of energy conservation

We introduced energy and its conservation in the last chapter. The key point to reiterate here is that we can apply the principle of conservation of energy to work out how things move and how they interact with other things.

It's also important to remember that the principle can apply to the conversion of energy between different forms, as well as to the transfer of energy between different objects. Here is a statement of the principle once more, in a slightly different form:

In any conversion of energy between different forms, or in transfer of energy between different objects, the total amounts of energy before and after the conversion or transfer are always equal.

A particularly useful form of the principle is when the energy conversion or transfer involves only potential and kinetic energy. We refer to p.e. and k.e. collectively as *mechanical energy.*

Conservation of mechanical energy

Although the principle of conservation of energy in its general form is powerful and is always true, it may be difficult to apply in practice because it is not always easy to calculate all the energy forms involved in an interaction. For example, think of the energy transformations involved when a ball is dropped, falls through air, and bounces off a surface. The ball initially has p.e. and, as it falls through air, the p.e. is gradually converted into k.e. as it accelerates due to gravity. A small amount of energy is also converted into heat due to friction (drag) through the air. When it hits the surface, a large amount of energy may be transferred to the surface. Some more of the energy is usually converted into heat on impact, and some may be converted into sound as well. Now, we'll steer clear of trying to calculate things like heat and sound energy because that can get pretty complicated. But sometimes, if they can be assumed to be small, we only need to deal with p.e. and k.e. In that case, we say that mechanical energy is conserved.

Conservation of mechanical energy is a particularly useful principle because it involves the energy forms associated with motion (k.e.) and position (p.e.). We'll look at two examples of its application in this chapter. One is the elastic collision of two particles, when the total kinetic energy of the particles is conserved. We'll look at this in the next section, "The principle of momentum conservation." The other example is the motion of a projectile neglecting drag due to air resistance. Let's look at this example now.

An example: Energy changes in a projectile

To simplify things, let's assume the projectile is launched vertically upward from ground level with some initial velocity u. Then we have a 1D problem with constant acceleration under gravity, and we can use the 1D version of the analytical equations of motion introduced in the last chapter:

$$v = u + a\,t$$

$$s = u\,t + \frac{1}{2}a\,t^2$$

Here s = h, the height of the projectile above ground, and a = –g, where g is the acceleration due to gravity. So we can write this:

$$v = u - g\,t$$

$$h = u\,t - \frac{1}{2}g\,t^2$$

It is now straightforward to calculate the p.e. and k.e. of the projectile at any time by using the following:

$$E_p = m\,g\,h$$

$$E_k = \frac{1}{2}m\,v^2$$

Here is a code that computes and plots the p.e., k.e., and their sum for 10 seconds, using values of m = 1, g = 10 px/s^2, and u = 50 px/s. Note that the mass of a Ball instance is 1 mass unit by default, so there is no need to set it to 1 in the code. The source code is in ProjectileEnergy.as.

```
package{
        import flash.display.Sprite;
        import flash.utils.Timer;
        import flash.events.TimerEvent;
        import com.physicscodes.math.Graph;
        import com.physicscodes.objects.Ball;

        public class ProjectileEnergy extends Sprite{
                private var u:Number = 50; // initial velocity
                private var g:Number = 10; // gravity
                private var groundLevel:Number=350;
                private var n:int=0;
                private var tA:Array = new Array();
                private var hA:Array=new Array();
                private var peA:Array = new Array();
                private var keA:Array = new Array();
                private var teA:Array = new Array();
                private var ball:Ball;
                private var timer:Timer;
                private var graph:Graph;

                public function ProjectileEnergy(){
                        init();
                }
                private function init():void{
                        setupBall();
                        setupGraph();
                        setupArrays();
                        setupTimer();
                }
                private function setupBall():void{
                        ball = new Ball(10);
                        ball.x = 550;
                        ball.y = groundLevel;
                        addChild(ball);
                }
                private function setupGraph():void{
                        graph = new Graph(0,10,0,1500,50,350,450,300);
                        graph.drawgrid(1,0.5,500,100);
                        graph.drawaxes('t','p.e., k.e., total');
                        addChild(graph);
                }
```

```
private function setupTimer():void{
        timer = new Timer(100);
        timer.addEventListener(TimerEvent.TIMER,animate);
        timer.start();
}
private function setupArrays():void{
        var t:Number;
        var v:Number;
        var m:Number = ball.mass;
        for (var i:uint=0; i<=100; i++){
                tA[i] = i*0.1;
                t = tA[i];
                v = u - g*t;
                hA[i] = u*t - 0.5*g*t*t;
                peA[i] = m*g*hA[i];
                keA[i] = 0.5*m*v*v;
                teA[i] = peA[i] + keA[i];
        }
}
private function animate(evt:TimerEvent):void{
        ball.y = groundLevel-hA[n];
        graph.plot([tA[n]], [peA[n]], 0xff0000, true, false);
        graph.plot([tA[n]], [keA[n]], 0x0000ff, true, false);
        graph.plot([tA[n]], [teA[n]], 0x000000, true, false);
        evt.updateAfterEvent();
        n++;
        if (n==hA.length){
                timer.stop();
                timer.removeEventListener(TimerEvent.TIMER,animate);
        }
    }
  }
}
```

The code should be easy to understand. In Figure 5-6, we show the three plots as a function of time. The series of dots that curves upward is the p.e., the one that curves downward is the k.e. and the one that is horizontal (constant) is the total energy (the sum of p.e. and k.e.). From these plots, we learn that, when the projectile is initially launched at the ground, it has zero p.e. and maximum k.e. Then for the first 5 seconds, as it rises, its p.e. increases at the expense of its k.e. At exactly 5 seconds, its k.e. is zero, signifying that it is momentarily at rest. This happens when it reaches its highest point. It then starts falling down again. As it does so, its p.e. starts falling again, and its k.e. increases as it speeds up toward the ground. Throughout its motion, the sum of the p.e. and k.e. is constant, as indicated by the horizontal series of dots. This demonstrates the conservation of energy. Note that the sum of p.e. and k.e. is only constant because we've neglected drag effects. If you include drag, then you'll find that the sum of p.e. and k.e. decreases slightly with time. If you're extra keen, you can show this by adding a drag term and integrating the equations of motion numerically to give v and h as a function of time.

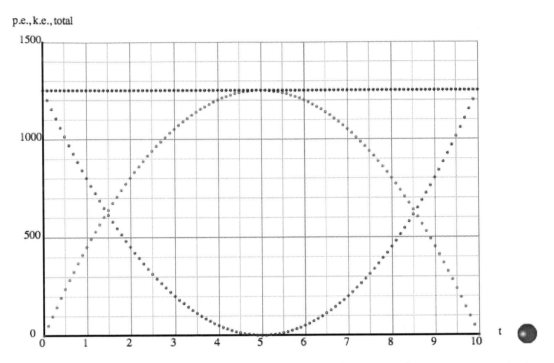

p.e., k.e., total

Figure 5-6. Energy graphs for a projectile—downward curve: k.e.; upward curve: p.e.; constant line: total

The principle of momentum conservation

As mentioned in the last chapter, there is a conservation principle for momentum just like the one for energy. Let's state the principle first and then explain it:

For any system of interacting particles, the total momentum of all the particles remains constant, as long as no external forces act on the system.

"Interacting particles" means that the particles influence each other by exerting forces on each other. The forces can be of any type; for example, gravitational forces between stars in a galaxy. The principle is true regardless of the nature of the forces between the particles. Once you define your system, the particles in that system may be mutually subjected to any number of internal forces between themselves—the total momentum of that system will be conserved as long as there are no forces from external agents.

Conservation of momentum is closely connected with Newton's laws of motion. In fact, under certain conditions, it may be derived from Newton's laws. Let's see how.

The starting point is Newton's second law $F = dp/dt$, which we can write in the discrete form $F = \Delta p/\Delta t$. Multiplying both sides by Δt gives this:

$$\mathbf{F}\,\Delta t = \Delta \mathbf{p}$$

This is, of course, just Newton's second law written in a slightly different form, for a small but finite time interval Δt. What it tells us is that if a force **F** acts on a particle for a small duration Δt, multiplying **F** by Δt gives you the change in momentum Δ**p** of the particle. We call the quantity **F**Δt the *impulse* due to the force. The preceding relationship is called the *impulse-momentum theorem*.

Next, imagine two particles interacting (exerting forces on each other; for example by colliding), as depicted in Figure 5-7. From Newton's third law of motion, they exert equal and opposite forces simultaneously on each other. If they exert forces **F** and –**F** on each other for a time interval of Δt, they experience impulses of –**F** Δt and **F** Δt, respectively. From the impulse-momentum theorem, this implies that they exchange momentum, gaining –Δ**p** and Δ**p**, respectively. The total momentum of both particles is still the same, however, because one gains exactly the negative amount that the other gains; in other words, the momentum lost by one particle is gained by the other. This argument extends to any number of interacting particles, so we have the principle of conservation of momentum.

Figure 5-7. Two interacting particles exchanging momentum

Examples of momentum conservation include the following:

- An apple falling to Earth acquires downward momentum at each instant. Considering the apple-Earth system, the Earth itself must "fall" toward the apple to compensate. But because the mass of the Earth is so large, its velocity toward the apple is tiny.

- The exhaust gases from a rocket and the rocket itself get equal momentum changes in opposite directions.

- In an explosion, the total momentum of all the fragments must equal the momentum of the whole object before the explosion. If the object was initially at rest, the total momentum (as a vector sum of the momenta of all the fragments) after the explosion is still zero.

To give you a feel for how you'll be applying this principle in practice, here is a numerical example. Suppose you fire a bullet of mass 40 g from a rifle of mass 1.6 kg, and the exit velocity of the bullet is 80 m/s. What is the recoil velocity of the rifle?

Let's denote the mass and velocity of the bullet by m and v, respectively. And we'll denote the mass and velocity of the rifle by M and V, respectively. Initially, both are at rest so that the total momentum is zero.

The principle of conservation of momentum therefore implies that the final momentum should be zero, too:

$$M V + m v = 0$$

This equation can be easily rearranged to give this:

$$V = -\frac{m v}{M}$$

Substituting the values of m, v and M give the following:

$$V = -0.04 \times 80 / 1.6 \ \text{m/s} = -2 \ \text{m/s}$$

Therefore, the recoil velocity of the rifle is 2 m/s. The minus sign means that it is in the opposite direction to the velocity of the bullet.

Example: 1D elastic collision between two particles

Conservation of momentum is especially useful in handling collisions between particles. A *collision* is a special type of interaction in which particles exert large forces on each other for a very brief duration.

A whole chapter is dedicated to collisions (see Chapter 11). Here we'll look briefly at the simplest case of elastic collisions between two particles in 1D. *Elastic* in this context means that kinetic energy is conserved. In other words, no energy is converted to other forms (such as heat) during the collision. Momentum is, of course, always conserved.

Let's say the masses of the particles are m1 and m2, their initial velocities before collision are u1 and u2, and their final velocities after collision are v1 and v2 (see Figure 5-8). Applying conservation of momentum then tells us that

$$m1 \cdot v1 + m2 \cdot v2 = m1 \cdot u1 + m2 \cdot u2$$

Applying conservation of kinetic energy gives this:

$$\frac{1}{2}m1 \cdot v1^2 + \frac{1}{2}m2 \cdot v2^2 = \frac{1}{2}m1 \cdot u1^2 + \frac{1}{2}m2 \cdot u2^2$$

Remember that the formula for kinetic energy is ½ m v^2.

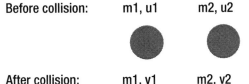

Before collision: m1, u1   m2, u2

After collision: m1, v1   m2, v2

Figure 5-8. Change in particle velocities caused by a collision

What we have here are two equations containing two unknown quantities: the final velocities v1 and v2 of the two colliding particles. Everything else is known. These equations can be solved to give a general formula for v1 and v2 in terms of the known quantities m1, m2, u1, and u2. But we'll save that for Chapter 11.

For now, let's discuss the case where m1 = m2, i.e. the two particles have the same mass. In that case, one can show that v1 = u2 and v2 = u1; in other words, the final velocity of particle 1 is equal to the initial velocity of particle 2, and vice versa. Particles of the same mass that collide elastically simply swap their velocities!

We'll now build an example that implements this special case. First, we'll build a class that implements collisions. Because a collision always involves at least two particles in motion, it makes sense to extend `MultiMover` from Chapter 4. So, let's create a new class called `Collider` that extends `MultiMover` and adds the capability to detect and respond to collisions. Here is a simple way to do that:

```
package {
        import com.physicscodes.motion.MultiMover;
        import         com.physicscodessoBjrticle;
        import com.physicscodes.math.Vector2D;
```

```
public class Collider extends MultiMover{

        private var _particles:Array;

        public function Collider(pparticles:Array):void{
                _particles = pparticles;
                super(pparticles);
        }
        override protected function moveObject():void{
                super.moveObject();
                checkCollision();
        }
        private function checkCollision():void{
                for (var i:uint=0; i<_particles.length; i++){
                        var particle1:Particle = _particles[i];
                        for (var j:Number=i+1; j<_particles.length; j++){
                                var particle2:Particle = _particles[j];
                                if (Vector2D.distance(particle1.pos2D,particle2.pos2D)
                        <= 0.5*(particle1.width+particle2.width)){
                                        var vtemp:Vector2D = particle1.velo2D;
                                        particle1.velo2D = particle2.velo2D;
                                        particle2.velo2D = vtemp;
                                }
                        }
                }
        }
}
```

Like MultiMover, Collider takes an array of particles as an argument in its constructor. The key extra thing it does is to override moveObject() by adding the new method checkCollision(). In checkCollision(), we test for collisions between pairs of particles in the array. We use the Vector2D.distance() static method to do this; note that by using the particle.width property we assume that the particles are circular. If collision is detected, we swap the velocities of the two particles.

The file CollisionsTest.as contains an example of using the Collider class. Here's the full code:

```
package{
        import flash.display.Sprite;
        import com.physicscodes.objects.Ball;
        import com.physicscodes.math.Vector2D;
        import com.physicscodes.motion.Mover;

        public class CollisionsTest extends Sprite{
                private var _ball1:Ball = new Ball(15,0x0000ff);
                private var _ball2:Ball = new Ball(15,0xff0000);
                private var _ball3:Ball = new Ball(15,0x00ff00);

                public function CollisionsTest():void{
                        init();
                }
                private function init():void{
```

```
              setupBall(_ball1,new Vector2D(50,200),new Vector2D(30,0));
              setupBall(_ball2,new Vector2D(500,200),new Vector2D(-20,0));
              setupBall(_ball3,new Vector2D(300,200),new Vector2D(10,0));

              var collider:Collider=new Collider([_ball1,_ball2,_ball3]);
              collider.startTime(10);
       }
       private function setupBall(ball:Ball,pos:Vector2D,velo:Vector2D):void{
              ball.pos2D = pos;
              ball.velo2D = velo;
              addChild(ball);
       }
    }
}
```

To make things a bit more interesting, we created three balls aligned horizontally and given them different horizontal velocities using the private method setupBall(). Then we created an instance of Collider, passing the three Ball instances within an array. We then invoke the startTime() method of the collider to begin the animation.

If you run the code, you'll see that, initially, all three balls get closer together. They then suffer three successive collisions that swap the velocities of each colliding pair. In the end, they all move away from each other.

Laws governing rotational motion

In this chapter, we have focused on translational motion, when the object being considered changes its position. But what if an object rotates about a center or (if it's an extended object) revolves on itself about some axis?

It turns out that analogous principles for rotational kinematics, dynamics, and conservation principles exist. For example, the analog of Newton's laws of motion can be wriiten down for rotational motion. Analogous to momentum, there is a quantity called *angular momentum* and it is also conserved.

We'll look at rotational mechanics in Chapters 9 and 13.

Summary

This chapter laid the foundation for simulating the motion of particles under any type of force. The laws of motion and conservation principles discussed here can be applied in many different scenarios. In the remaining chapters of Part II, we'll apply those laws to simulate the motion of objects under the action of a wide variety of force laws

Chapter 6

Gravity, Orbits, and Rockets

Starting from this chapter, you'll be exploring lots of different forces and the types of motion they produce. Here we focus exclusively on the force of gravity. You'll learn how gravity makes things move both on Earth and in space. And before you know it, you'll be able to code up orbits and rockets!

Topics covered in this chapter include the following:

- **Gravity**: Gravity, or gravitation, is the force that the Earth exerts on all objects near it. But there is a lot more to gravity than we've discussed so far.

- **Orbits**: An example of the effect of gravity is to keep planets in orbits around the Sun. Learn how to easily build simple orbit simulations.

- **Local gravity**: How gravity behaves at the local scale, near the surface of the Earth.

- **Rockets**: Build a simple rocket, launch it, and make it orbit a planet.

Gravity

As inhabitants of a planet, we are aware of *gravity* perhaps more than any other force. Gravity, also known as *gravitation*, will play a part in most of the simulations you'll build in this book. In fact, you've already come across several examples. However, in all the cases you've met so far, we've dealt with gravity as it exists near the surface of the Earth—as a constant force. It's now time to take a deeper look at gravity.

Gravity, weight, and mass

Let's first recap briefly what you already learned about gravity in the previous chapters. If an object has mass m, then Earth exerts a force on it that points vertically downward. The magnitude of this force of gravity is equal to mg, where g is a constant equal to approximately 9.81 m/s^2 near the Earth's surface. This force is also called the weight of the object.

The constant g is equal to the acceleration that any object would experience if it were to move under the sole effect of gravity. We can see this by using Newton's second law F = ma. If the resultant force F is just the force of gravity, then F = mg. Hence, we have this:

$$m\,a = m\,g$$

And dividing both sides by m gives us this:

$$a = g$$

This result tells us that all objects moving under the action of gravity as the only force experience the same acceleration regardless of their mass, or indeed, of any other properties. So, assuming all other forces can be neglected, if you drop a hammer and a house from the same height, both would accelerate at the same rate and therefore fall at the same time!

Of course, if you drop a feather, it will take much longer to fall. That's because there is an upward drag force due to air that opposes its fall. There is also a drag force in the cases of a stone or a house, but in those cases that force is negligibly small compared with their weight, and so has a negligible impact on their motion. If you were to drop a feather and a hammer on the Moon, where there is no air and therefore no drag, they would both fall at the same time. In fact, the astronaut David Scott did exactly that during the Apollo 15 mission. You can even see a video of this feat on NASA's web site or on YouTube (search for "hammer and feather").

Newton's universal law of gravitation

The Earth is not the only object that exerts a force of gravity. Newton taught us that any object exerts a gravitational pull on any other object. So, not only does the Earth exert a gravitational force on us but each of us also exerts a gravitational force on the Earth, and indeed on each other, too!

Newton gave an exact formula for how to calculate the gravitational force between any two objects: the force law for gravity:

$$F = G\,\frac{m_1\,m_2}{r^2}$$

In this formula, m_1 and m_2 are the masses of the objects involved, and r is the distance between their centers. The symbol G is a universal constant with the value of 6.67428 × 10^{-11} Nm^2/kg^2. It is called the *gravitational constant*. By *universal*, we mean that it has the same value irrespective of the properties of the interacting objects. Newton postulated that the same formula, with the same value of G, holds for any two objects—from tiny particles to planets and stars. Hence, we called it *Newton's universal law of gravitation.*

Let's try and understand what this formula is telling us. First of all, the gravitational force F is proportional to the masses m_1 and m_2 of the two objects. Therefore, the larger those masses are, the larger the force will be. Second, the force is inversely proportional to the square of their distance apart—that means we are dividing by r^2. Therefore, the larger the distance between the two objects, the smaller the force will be (because we'll be dividing a number by the square of a very large number). Third, because we are multiplying by a small number G (6.67428×10^{-11} is equal to 0.0000000000667428), the force will be tiny except when very large masses are involved. So, gravity is a very weak force, except when at least one of the objects has a very large mass.

To give you an idea of what we mean, let's calculate the gravitational force between two persons (whom we'll call Joe1 and Joe2) of mass 80 kg each standing a distance of 1m apart, and compare it with the gravitational force that the Earth exerts on each of them.

Using the previous formula, the force between Joe1 and Joe2 is given by F = $6.67428 \times 10^{-11} \times 80 \times 80$ / 1 N = 4.3×10^{-7} N (approximately). That's 0.427 millionth of a newton.

The force that the Earth exerts on each is, of course, equal to their weight mg = 80×9.81 N = 785 N (approximately). That's nearly 2 billion times larger!

We haven't said anything about the direction of the force yet. Newton said that the force always acts along the line joining the centers of the two objects (see Figure 6-1).

Another thing that should be noted is that the forces on Joe1 and Joe2 form an action-reaction pair. So Joe1 exerts a force of 4.3×10^{-7} N on Joe2, and vice-versa, with the two forces being equal and opposite—and similarly for the force between each of the two Joes and the Earth.

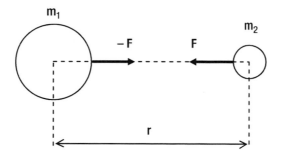

Figure 6-1. Newton's law of universal gravitation

Creating the gravity function

We'll now create a static method of the Forces class that will implement gravity in the form of Newton's law of gravitation. The method will take as input the variables that go into the force law for gravity, namely G, m_1, m_2, and r. It must return a vector force. Therefore, we need a vector form for Newton's law of gravitation that implements the fact that the force points along the line joining the two objects. Let's just give the formula and explain it afterward:

$$F = -G \frac{m_1 m_2}{r^3} r$$

Comparing with the previous formula, what we've done is write the force as a vector; then we multiplied the original equation by −r/r. Recall from Chapter 3 that r/r is a unit vector in the direction of r, where r is here the position vector of one of the objects relative to the location of the other object.

As shown in Figure 6-2, r is the difference in the position vectors of the two objects, and r is its magnitude, which is simply the distance between the two objects. Recall that there are two forces, not one: the force on object 1 due to object 2, and vice-versa. These two forces have the same magnitude but the opposite direction. We always define r to be the position vector of the object on which the force is acting, relative to the object that is exerting the force. We need the minus sign because that force is directed in the opposite direction to r.

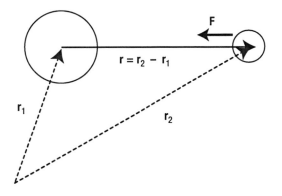

Figure 6-2. Vector form of Newton's law of universal gravitation

Here is the static method to implement the gravity force:

```
static public function gravity(G:Number,m1:Number,m2:Number,r:Vector2D):Vector2D {
        return r.multiply(-G*m1*m2/(r.lengthSquared*r.length));
}
```

We just use the multiply() method of the Vector2D class to return a new vector that multiplies r by (-G m1*m2/r^3). Let's now use this gravity() method in the next few examples.

Before we can apply the gravity function, we have to choose suitable values for G, m1, m2, and r. Remember that we are modeling things on a computer screen. Therefore we have to scale physical values appropriately so that we get the right amount of motion on the screen in a sensible time. For example, if we were simulating the motion of the Earth around the Sun, we really don't want to use the real values of all the variables such as the mass of the Sun and so on. Doing that would mean we'd have to wait for a year to see the Earth go once around the Sun!

In Part IV, we'll show you how to create a scaled computer model properly. For now, we'll simplify things and make some suitable choices just to make things look roughly right on the screen. To do this, we'll choose our own units for all the variables of the model.

Let's start with the distance r. That's an easy one—the natural unit to use here is pixels. This leaves us with mass and G. We can give G any value we like, so let's choose G = 1. Having made these two choices, we now need to choose suitable values for the masses so that the right amount of motion is produced to be noticeable on the screen. Let's look at an example: orbits!

Orbits

With our gravity function, it's very easy to create a realistic-looking orbits simulation. Figure 6-3 shows a screenshot of what we'll create: a planet orbiting a sun, against a background of fixed stars. For simplicity, we assume that the sun remains fixed. In reality, as we saw previously, both the sun and the planet will experience a gravitational force of the same magnitude but in opposite directions (with the force on each one pointing toward the other). So both the planet and the sun will move. But if the mass of the sun is much larger than that of the planet, the motion of the sun will be so small it will hardly be perceivable, anyway. That's because F = ma again, so that the acceleration a = F/m. Thus, if the mass m is very large, the acceleration a will be very small. So to save coding and CPU time, we can neglect the motion of the sun altogether.

Figure 6-3. A planet orbiting a stationary sun

Orbiter class

With this in mind, we can build a class, `Orbiter`, which will make a particle orbit a stationary particle. Here's what `Orbiter` looks like:

```
package {
        import com.physicscodes.motion.Forcer;
        import com.physicscodes.motion.Forces;
        import com.physicscodes.objects.Particle;
        import com.physicscodes.math.Vector2D;

        public class Orbiter extends Forcer{

                private var _orbitingParticle:Particle;
                private var _massOrbiter:Number;
                private var _massAttractor:Number;
                private var _center:Vector2D;
                private var _G:Number = 1;

                public function Orbiter(porbitingParticle:Particle,pattractor:Particle):void{
                        _orbitingParticle = porbitingParticle;
                        _massOrbiter = porbitingParticle.mass;
                        _massAttractor = pattractor.mass;
                        _center = pattractor.pos2D;
                        super(porbitingParticle);
                }

                override protected function calcForce():void{
                        force =
Forces.gravity(_G,_massAttractor,_massOrbiter,_orbitingParticle.pos2D.subtract(_center));
                }
        }
}
```

`Orbiter` extends the `Forcer` class introduced in the last chapter. Remember that `Forcer` extends `Mover` and implements Newton's second law, **F** = m**a**, to make a particle (specified as an argument in its constructor) move under forces specified in its `calcForce()` method. If you look at the `Orbiter()` constructor, you'll see that it takes two arguments, both `Particle` objects. The first particle is the orbiter, which is passed to the constructor of `Forcer` using the `super()` method. The second argument is the fixed attractor. The code stores the masses of the two particles and the position of the attractor particle in private variables.

The last bit of code overrides the `calcForce()` function of `Forcer` by specifying the resultant force as a gravity force. It passes the values of G (set to 1), the masses of the two particles, and the position vector of the orbiter relative to that of the attractor: `_orbiter.pos2D.subtract(_center)`.

Note that the `Forces.gravity()` function has to know the position vector of the orbiter at each timestep, recalculating the gravitational force on the orbiter based on its position vector. Hence, we have supplied `_orbiter.pos2D` within the argument of `Forces.gravity()`. Because the particle masses are constant, we can simply pass the value stored in the private variables `_massOrbiter` instead of referencing `_orbiter.mass` on each timestep.

We'll now use the `Orbiter` class to create the simulation shown in Figure 6-3. Take a look at this listing from `Orbits.as`:

```
package{
        import flash.display.Sprite;
        import com.physicscodes.objects.Ball;
        import com.physicscodes.math.Vector2D;
        import com.physicscodes.objects.Particle;

        public class Orbits extends Sprite{
                public function Orbits():void{
                        init();
                }
                private function init():void{

                        // create 100 stars randomly positioned
                        for (var i:uint=0; i<100; i++){
                                var star:Ball = new Ball(Math.random()*3,0xffff00);
                                star.pos2D = new
Vector2D(Math.random()*stage.stageWidth,Math.random()*stage.stageHeight);
                                addChild(star);
                        }

                        // create a stationary sun
                        var sun:Ball;
                        sun = new Ball(70,0xff9900,1000000);
                        sun.pos2D = new Vector2D(275,200);
                        addChild(sun);

                        // create a moving planet
                        var planet:Ball;
                        planet = new Ball(10,0x0000ff,1);
                        planet.pos2D = new Vector2D(200,50);
                        planet.velo2D = new Vector2D(80,-40);
                        addChild(planet);

                        // make the planet orbit the sun
                        var orbiter:Orbiter=new Orbiter(planet,sun);
                        orbiter.startTime(10);
                }
        }
}
```

The code is very straightforward. First, we create a bunch of 100 stars as `Ball` instances and place them randomly on the stage. This is, of course, purely for aesthetic reasons. If you don't like stars, go ahead and get rid of them. Next we create a sun as another `Ball` instance, setting its radius to 70 pixels and its mass to 1,000,000. We position the sun at (275, 200). By default, the velocity of the sun is zero. Then we create a planet as a `Ball` instance, set its radius to 10, and set its mass to 1. The initial position and velocity of the planet are then set. Finally, the code that makes the planet orbit the sun is as simple as creating an `Orbiter` instance, with planet and sun as its arguments, and invoking its inherited `startTime()` method. Go ahead and run the code—it really works!

Observe that the planet tries to move away at its initial velocity, but is pulled back by the sun's gravity. You might wonder why the planet does not fall into the sun. Well, in fact it is "falling" toward the sun all the time but, because of its initial position and velocity, it "misses" the sun every time. Notice also that the planet travels faster when it's near the sun. This happens because the force of gravity is larger and therefore its acceleration is larger closer to the sun.

This code produces a realistic orbit simulation because it has basically all the physics governing orbital motion under gravity. And the physics really boils down to just four equations:

$$\mathbf{F} = -G\,\frac{M\,m}{r^3}\,\mathbf{r}$$

$$\mathbf{F} = m\,\mathbf{a}$$

$$\mathbf{a} = \frac{d\mathbf{v}}{dt}$$

$$\mathbf{v} = \frac{d\mathbf{s}}{dt}$$

In these equations, m is the mass of the planet, and M is the mass of the sun. The first two equations are laws, and the last two are just definitions. To recap, this is what our code is doing at each timestep: From the first law, you compute the gravitational force. You then use the second law to compute the acceleration. Knowing the acceleration, you integrate the third equation to compute the velocity. Finally, knowing the velocity, you integrate the fourth equation to give the displacement. This tells you where you must move your particle at each timestep.

Have a go at changing the parameters in the code to see their effect. For example, you can change the masses of the planet and the sun, or the initial position and velocity of the planet. We've chosen the mass of the sun to be 1,000,000 times that of the planet. This is a realistic ratio; for example, the mass of the Sun is 330,000 times that of the Earth and 6,100,000 times that of Mercury.

Change the mass of the sun to 2,000,000. The planet is pulled closer to the sun because the force of gravity is proportional to the mass of the sun. So, doubling the sun's mass doubles the force of gravity and therefore the acceleration toward the sun. Conversely, if you decrease the mass of the sun to 900,000, you'll see that the sun's pull on the planet is weaker, so that the planet wanders further away.

Now change the mass of the planet instead. Make it 0.001 and then 1000. You'll see that the mass of the planet has no effect on its motion. What's going on is that you are increasing the force on the planet by increasing its mass, but then you must divide the larger force by its larger mass. Take a look at the first two equations above. In the first one, you multiply by the mass of the planet to calculate the gravitational force. In the second one, you then need to divide that force by the same mass to calculate the acceleration. The net result is that the acceleration is independent of the mass of the planet. This is just as it should be. It's the astronomical equivalent of the hammer-and-feather experiment we mentioned at the beginning of this chapter.

Does this mean that the motion is unchanged even if the planet's mass is comparable to that of the sun? No, not really. Remember the approximation we made at the beginning? We assumed that the mass of the sun was much larger than that of the planet, so that we could neglect the sun's motion under the gravitational force exerted on it by the planet. If the planet's mass is a sizeable fraction of the sun's mass, we'll need to model the motion of the sun too, even if we are just interested in the planet's motion! That's because as the sun moves around, its distance from the planet will change, which will modify the force on the planet. What we've done so far is to model *one-body motion*. To deal with this problem, we'll need to model *two-body motion*. It's not really that much more difficult, and we'll do that later. We'll even look at the motion of a large number of particles under mutual gravitational forces in a later chapter.

Next, experiment with different initial velocities for the planet. For example, changing the velocity vector to (70, −40) gives a more circular orbit, similar to the Earth's orbit. A velocity of (85, −40) gives a highly elongated orbit like that of a comet. Later in the book we'll show you how to work out exactly what velocity you need to produce a circular orbit.

If the velocity of the planet is small, it will get sucked into the sun. For example, change the velocity to (0,0). The planet accelerates toward the sun's center, as it should do, but then something weird happens when it actually gets there. For example, it might bounce back or fly off at high speed. This is an unphysical behavior, and it happens because we have not accounted for the finite size of the objects in the code. Because Newton's law of gravitation is proportional to $1/r^2$, the force becomes larger as the distance r becomes smaller. For example, when r is 10 pixels, $1/r^2$ has the value of 0.01 when r is 1, $1/r^2$ is 1 and when r is 0.1, $1/r^2$ is 100. So, when r approaches zero (when the centers of the two particles nearly coincide), the gravitational force becomes indefinitely large. At the same time, the vector **r**, which is the position vector pointing from the sun to the planet, becomes so small that numerical errors make its direction unpredictable. Therefore, the planet suffers a large acceleration in some apparently random direction at the center of the sun.

This is a general problem that you'll encounter with a force law like Newton's law of gravitation. The way you deal with it depends on precisely what you want to model. If something is falling into the sun, chances are you'd want to make it disappear when it does so—that's simple enough to code up and you don't need any special physics. If something is colliding with a solid planet like the Earth, it will burn up in the Earth's atmosphere, create a crater, or smash up the Earth, depending on its size. Any of this would be rather tricky to model in a precise way, although you could conceivably create some movie-style special effects! If something is falling into one of the gas giants like Jupiter or Saturn, you might want to model how gravity varies *inside* the planet. We'll see an example of how you might be able to do that later in this chapter.

Escape velocity

It turns out that if the velocity magnitude of a planet is less than a certain critical value, it will always be "caught" by the gravitational attraction of the sun, either orbiting or ending up in a collision with the sun. The critical value above which a planet would escape the sun's gravity is called the *escape velocity*. The formula for the escape velocity is given by the following, where M is the mass of the sun and r is the distance from its center:

$$v = \sqrt{\frac{2GM}{r}}$$

So the escape velocity is a function of distance from the center of the attracting body.

Note that whatever we said about a planet orbiting the sun applies more generally to any object orbiting another object under the force of gravity—for example, a satellite (natural or artificial) orbiting a planet. Hence, using the last formula, the escape velocity of any object at the Earth's surface is given by the following, where M_e and r_e are the mass and radius of the Earth, respectively:

$$v = \sqrt{\frac{2GM_e}{r_e}}$$

Putting in the values for G, M_e, and r_e into the above formula gives v = 11.2 km/s. This is the escape velocity at the Earth's surface: if you could throw a projectile with a velocity at least equal to this velocity, it would escape the Earth's gravity. For comparison, the escape velocity from the surface of the Sun is 618 km/s. By contrast, the escape velocity from the surface of Eros (a near-Earth asteroid with dimensions of approximately 34 km × 11 km × 11 km) is a mere 10 m/s. You could drive off the asteroid in a car!

Going back to the Orbits simulation G = 1, the mass of the sun is 1,000,000 and the planet is initially at a distance of $\sqrt{75^2 + 150^2}$ = 167.7 pixels from the sun. So the escape velocity at the initial location of the planet is $\sqrt{(2*1*1000000/167.7)}$ = 109.2 pixels per second. You can check this with the simulation. First, change the initial velocity of the planet to (80, 0), so that its magnitude is 80. The planet will orbit the sun. Now increase the initial velocity magnitude to 100 by changing the velocity to (100, 0). The planet will move further from the Sun, but will still orbit it. Even if you change the velocity to (105, 0) and wait long enough, the planet will disappear from the edge of the stage, but will eventually come back to complete an orbit. But if you increase the velocity magnitude beyond 109.2, it will never come back. We don't advise you to wait!

Two-body motion

So far, we've made a single object move under the gravitational attraction of another object. But we know that gravitational forces come as an action-reaction pair, so the other object must also experience an equal and opposite force. The result is that the other object will also move. We can implement this in a simple way by generalizing the Orbiter class so that the orbiter particle experiences a gravitational force pointing toward a second particle's current position, not just toward a fixed point. We call the new class Gravitator:

```
package {
        import com.physicscodes.motion.Forcer;
        import com.physicscodes.motion.Forces;
        import com.physicscodes.objects.Particle;
        import com.physicscodes.math.Vector2D;

        public class Gravitator extends Forcer{
```

```
                    private var _particleA:Particle;
                    private var _particleB:Particle;
                    private var _G:Number = 100000;
                    private var _massA:Number;
                    private var _massB:Number;
                    private var _r:Vector2D;

                    public function Gravitator(pparticleA:Particle,pparticleB:Particle):void{
                            _particleA = pparticleA;
                            _particleB = pparticleB;
                            _massA = pparticleA.mass;
                            _massB = pparticleB.mass;
                            super(pparticleA);
                    }

                    override protected function calcForce():void{
                            _r = _particleA.pos2D.subtract(_particleB.pos2D);
                            force = Forces.gravity(_G,_massA,_massB,_r);
                    }
            }
    }
```

Comparing `Gravitator` with `Orbiter`, you'll see that it does essentially the same thing as its predecessor, except that in the `calcForce()` method we're now taking the position vector **r** to be in relation to the current position of the second particle. This means that the first particle will be attracted to the second one with the correct gravitational force, even if the latter is moving. The other thing we've done in `Gravitator` is to change the value of G to 100,000. You can give G any value you want if you compensate by using appropriate values for the masses to create the desired effect.

Now look at the code in `TwoMasses.as`:

```
package{
        import flash.display.Sprite;
        import com.physicscodes.objects.Ball;
        import com.physicscodes.math.Vector2D;

        public class TwoMasses extends Sprite{
                public function TwoMasses():void{
                        init();
                }
                private function init():void{

                        var ball1Init:Ball = new Ball(10,0x9999ff,1);
                        ball1Init.pos2D = new Vector2D(150,200);
                        addChild(ball1Init);

                        var ball2Init:Ball = new Ball(40,0xff9999,64);
                        ball2Init.pos2D = new Vector2D(350,200);
                        addChild(ball2Init);

                        var ball1:Ball;
                        ball1 = new Ball(10,0x0000ff,1);
                        ball1.pos2D = ball1Init.pos2D;
```

```
ball1.velo2D = new Vector2D(0,150);
addChild(ball1);

var ball2:Ball;
ball2 = new Ball(40,0xff0000,64);
ball2.pos2D = ball2Init.pos2D;
ball2.velo2D = new Vector2D(0,0);
addChild(ball2);

var gravitator1:Gravitator=new Gravitator(ball1,ball2);
gravitator1.startTime(10);

var gravitator2:Gravitator=new Gravitator(ball2,ball1);
gravitator2.startTime(10);

            }
        }
}
```

What we've done here is pretty simple. We created a couple of `Ball` instances, `ball1` and `ball2`, and then passed them as arguments into a couple of `Gravitator` instances with the order of the arguments reversed. This makes each ball move under the gravity exerted by the other. From the values specified previously, `ball2` has a radius 4 times larger than `ball1` and a mass 64 times larger. Also, `ball1` has an initial velocity of (0, 150), whereas `ball2` is initially stationary.

We also created two more `Ball` instances, `ball1Init` and `ball2Init`, to indicate the initial positions of their respective counterparts in a lighter color.

If you run the code, you'll see that `ball1` orbits `ball2`, while the latter appears to wobble. This makes sense. Both `ball1` and `ball2` experience the same force at any given time, but because `ball2` is 64 times larger than `ball1`, its acceleration is 64 times less (applying a = F/m). Therefore, `ball2` moves much less than `ball1`, as the screenshot in Figure 6-4 suggests.

Now make the mass and size of `ball2` the same as those of `ball1` by modifying the appropriate line so that it reads thus:

```
ball2 = new Ball(10,0x0000ff,1);
```

Then change the initial velocities of the two balls by making the following changes to the code:

```
ball1.velo2D = new Vector2D(0,10);
ball2.velo2D = new Vector2D(0,-10);
```

If you now run the code, you'll find that the two balls orbit each other in a strange sort of dance, alternately coming together and then moving further away. What is happening is that they are orbiting a common center, known as their *center of mass*. In fact, this was also happening when the balls had different masses; but the center of mass then was within the large ball, so that it appeared to wobble.

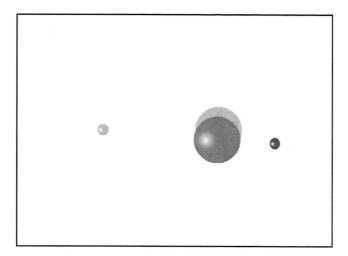

Figure 6-4. Two-body motion (lighter versions show initial positions of respective balls)

Local gravity

We are most familiar with gravity close up. How does local, near-Earth gravity relate to what you've learned so far? In this section, we establish the connection between Newton's universal law of gravitation and the formula F = mg that we previously used for gravity. This will lead us to clarify the significance of the acceleration due to gravity g. We'll then discuss how g varies with distance from the center of the Earth, and how it differs on other celestial bodies.

The force of gravity near the Earth's surface

Time to come back to Earth! At the beginning of this chapter (as well as in previous chapters), we said that the force of gravity near the Earth on an object of mass m is given by F = mg, with g being approximately 9.81 m/s^2. Then, for most of this chapter so far, we've been using Newton's law of universal gravitation, which says that the gravitational force is given by F = Gm$_1$m$_2$/r^2. How do we reconcile those two different formulas?

The answer is that they are both correct. If M is the mass of the Earth (or any other planet or celestial body we're considering), and m is the mass of an object on or near it, the second formula gives this:

$$F = \frac{G\,M\,m}{r^2}$$

This has to give the same force as F = mg. Therefore, this must be true:

$$m\,g = \frac{G\,M\,m}{r^2}$$

Now we can divide both sides of this equation by m to get rid of it. We are then left with this:

$$g = \frac{G\,M}{r^2}$$

This formula shows that g is related to the mass M of the Earth and the distance r from its center. It tells us that g is actually a "nickname" for GM/r^2.

If an object is sitting on the Earth's surface, its distance from the Earth's center is equal to the radius of the Earth. The mass of the Earth is 5.974×10^{24} kg and its radius is 6.375×10^{6} m.

Therefore, using the last formula, the value of g at the Earth's surface is given by this, which is the exact value that was quoted before:

g = $6.67 \times 10^{-11} \times 5.974 \times 10^{24}$ / $(6.374 \times 10^{6})^2$ = 9.81 m/s^2,

Therefore, F = mg is consistent with Newton's law of universal gravitation.

Because it is always pointing toward the Earth's center, gravity acts vertically downward wherever we are on or near the Earth's surface (see Figure 6-5).

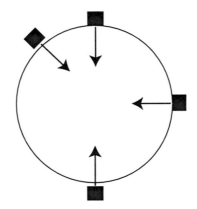

Figure 6-5. Near-Earth gravity

Variation of gravity with height

The formula g = GM/r^2 tells us that we can use F = mg to calculate the force of gravity at any distance from the Earth, provided that we account for the variation of g with distance from the center of the Earth.

If an object is at a height h above the surface of the Earth, its distance from the Earth's center is given by this, where R is the radius of the Earth:

$$r = R + h$$

Therefore, the value of g at a height h above the Earth's surface is given by this:

$$g = \frac{G\,M}{(R+h)^2}$$

Because the value of g at the Earth's surface is 9.81 m/s², a little bit of algebra gives the two equivalent formulas:

$$g = 9.81\,\frac{R^2}{r^2}$$

$$g = 9.81\,\frac{R^2}{(R+h)^2}$$

Using this formula, you can show that the value of g at the height of the International Space Station, which is 350 km above the Earth's surface, is about 8.8 m/s². The value of g at the distance of the Moon (384,000 km away) is approximately 0.0026 m/s². Remember that g gives you the acceleration of an object under gravity, and this acceleration is independent of the mass of the object. So, if the Moon were replaced with a football, it would experience the same acceleration.

You might be curious to know how g varies *within* the Earth. A simple model shows that g decreases approximately linearly from the surface of the Earth down to zero at the Earth's center. The formula is as follows, where R is the radius of the Earth:

$$g = 9.81\,\frac{r}{R}, \quad \text{for } r < R$$

Figure 6-6 shows the variation of g with normalized distance r/R from the Earth's center. As discussed previously, g increases linearly from the center of the Earth up to its surface (where r/R = 1 and g = 9.81). It then decreases rapidly with the inverse square of distance from the Earth's center.

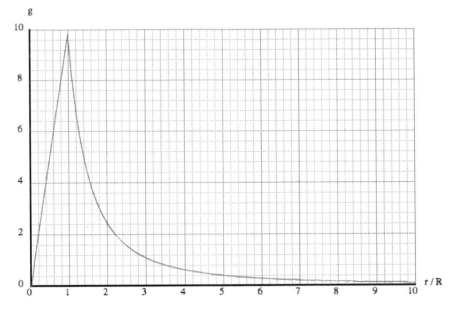

Figure 6-6. Variation of g with distance from the center of the Earth

Gravity on other celestial bodies

The formula $g = GM/r^2$ allows you to calculate the value of g on other celestial bodies such as planets and stars, if you know their mass and radius.

Table 6-1 shows the approximate value of g on the surface of a few celestial bodies. These values show that the Sun's gravity is about 28 times that of Earth, while the Moon's is about one-sixth that of Earth. The value of g on the surface of Jupiter, the largest planet in the solar system, is about 2.5 times that of Earth. Ceres and Eros are asteroids, and their gravity is extremely weak: Earth's gravity is about 36 times that of Ceres and more than 1660 times that of Eros.

Table 6-1. Gravity on Different Celestial Bodies

Celestial Body	Value of g in m/s^2
Earth	9.81
Sun	274
Moon	1.6
Jupiter	25
Ceres	0.27
Eros	0.0059

Rockets

Rockets are used for a variety of purposes, including launching spacecraft and missiles or as fireworks. In all rocket types, the rocket is propelled by exhaust formed from burning propellants within the rocket. In what follows, we give a very simplified account of the physics involved in rocket motion and show you how to put together a simple rocket simulation that can be incorporated in your Flash games.

It *is* rocket science!

Without going into engineering details on the operation of various types of rocket engines, let's just say that hot gases at high pressure are produced and pushed through a nozzle at high velocity. By Newton's third law, the exhaust gases push back upon the rocket, propelling it forward. The forward force generated is called the *thrust*.

Apart from the thrust, there may be other forces on the rocket, depending on where it is and how it's moving. Gravity is one of them. If the rocket is traveling through the Earth's atmosphere, it will also experience a retarding drag force as well as a lift force (see the next chapter). We'll neglect the effects of drag and lift here.

On Earth, there will also be effects due to the variation of pressure with altitude, which will affect the thrust, drag, and lift. We'll neglect those effects, too.

As the rocket rises, the strength of the gravity that it experiences decreases in the manner described earlier in this chapter. We will account for this effect.

Rockets generally carry a substantial proportion of their mass as fuel. Therefore, the mass of a rocket will vary substantially as the fuel gets used up. This decrease in mass will affect the acceleration of the rocket and must therefore be included in the modeling.

Modeling the thrust of a rocket

To model the thrust on a rocket, we make use of the alternate form of Newton's second law given in the last chapter.

Remember that the force needed to move a substance at the rate of dm/dt at a velocity **v** is given by the formula **F** = **v** dm/dt. The exhaust gases from a rocket exit at an *effective exhaust velocity* $\mathbf{v}_e$ and at a mass rate dm/dt that can be controlled. Therefore, the force on the gases is given by

$$\mathbf{F} = \mathbf{v}_e \frac{dm}{dt}$$

Using Newton's third law, the thrust on the rocket is therefore given by this:

$$\mathbf{F} = -\mathbf{v}_e \frac{dm}{dt}$$

The minus sign in the preceding vector equation means that the thrust generated is in the opposite direction to the exhaust velocity.

There may also be side thrusters on a rocket to provide a sideways thrust as needed. These work on the same principle as the main engine.

Building a rocket simulation

Okay, let's built a rocket! But before you jump up and down in glee, please note that we'll just focus on the physics here; we leave it as an exercise for you to come up with the nice graphics and special effects.

To begin with, we'll borrow the `Orbits.as` file, make some modifications, and save the new file as `RocketTest.as`. Here's what it should look like:

```
package{
        import flash.display.Sprite;
        import com.physicscodes.math.Vector2D;
        import com.physicscodes.objects.Ball;

        public class RocketTest extends Sprite{
                public function RocketTest():void{
                        init();
                }
                private function init():void{
                        // create 100 stars randomly positioned
                        for (var i:uint=0; i<100; i++){
                                var star:Ball = new Ball(Math.random()*2,0xffff00);
                                star.pos2D = new
Vector2D(Math.random()*stage.stageWidth,Math.random()*stage.stageHeight);
                                addChild(star);
                        }

                        // create a stationary planet
                        var planet:Ball;
                        planet = new Ball(100,0x0033ff,1000000);
                        planet.pos2D = new Vector2D(400,400);
                        addChild(planet);

                        // create a rocket
                        var rocket:Rocket;
                        rocket = new Rocket(10,15,0xcccccc,10);
                        rocket.pos2D = new Vector2D(400,300);
                        addChild(rocket);

                        // launch the rocket from the planet
                        var rocketer:Rocketer=new Rocketer(rocket,planet);
                        rocketer.startTime(10);
                }
        }
}
```

The setup is pretty similar to that of Orbits, except that we now have a stationary planet in place of the sun and a rocket in place of the planet. Note that the rocket is an instance of the Rocket class, which we will create as a subclass of Particle (as described a little later).

Functionally, the crucial difference from Orbits is that we now invoke a Rocketer instance instead of an Orbiter. So we should create a Rocketer class.

The Rocketer class

The Rocketer class is the "engine" that will drive the rocket, taking into account the planet's gravity. Rocketer takes two arguments: a rocket (as a Rocket object) and a planet (as a Ball object). Like Orbiter, Rocketer will extend the Forcer class and override the calcForce() method. But it will have to do much more work than Orbiter. The full source code is in Rocketer.as, and is fairly long. So we'll dissect it and explain the important bits.

Let's first take a look at the constructor:

```
public function Rocketer(procket:Rocket,pplanet:Ball):void{
        _rocket = procket;
        _massPlanet = pplanet.mass;
        _centerPlanet = pplanet.pos2D;
        _radiusPlanetSquared = pplanet.radius*pplanet.radius;
        pplanet.stage.addEventListener(KeyboardEvent.KEY_DOWN,startSideThrust);
        pplanet.stage.addEventListener(KeyboardEvent.KEY_UP,stopSideThrust);
        super(procket);
}
```

This looks familiar; it's similar to what Orbiter did, except that we also now set up a couple of event listeners that call associated event handlers for detecting when the user presses the right and left arrow keys or releases them:

```
        private function startSideThrust(evt:KeyboardEvent):void{
                if (evt.keyCode==Keyboard.RIGHT){
                        _applySideThrust = true;
                        _orientation = 1;
                }
                if (evt.keyCode==Keyboard.LEFT){
                        _applySideThrust = true;
                        _orientation = -1;
                }
        }

        private function stopSideThrust(evt:KeyboardEvent):void{
                _applySideThrust = false;
        }
```

Whenever the right or left arrow key is pressed and held down, the _applySideThrust Boolean variable is set to true; _applySideThrust reverts to false when the keys are released. This variable will control the thrust applied by the side thrusters. The private variable _orientation is given an integer value of +1 or −1 to distinguish between right and left key presses.

Rocketer overrides the moveObject() method of Forcer (as well as the calcForce() method). After invoking super.moveObject(), it calls a new private method updateMass(). It needs to do this because the mass of the rocket is changing.

```
override protected function moveObject():void{
        super.moveObject();
        updateMass();
        rotateObject();
        monitor();
}
```

The code in updateMass() checks whether there is any fuel left in the main and side thrusters; if so, it increments the mass of fuel used and decrements the mass of the rocket by the same amount. For the side thrusters, it also checks whether _applySideThrust is true:

```
private function updateMass():void{
        if (_fuelUsed < _fuelMass){
                _fuelUsed += _dmdt*dt;
                _rocket.mass += -_dmdt*dt;
        }
        if (_fuelSideUsed < _fuelSideMass && _applySideThrust){
                _fuelSideUsed += _dmdtSide*dt;
                _rocket.mass += -_dmdtSide*dt;
        }
}
```

The rotateObject() method does just what its name suggests. It rotates the rocket so that it always points in the direction in which the rocket is moving:

```
private function rotateObject():void{
        _rocket.rotation = _rocket.velo2D.angle*180/Math.PI + 90;
}
```

We do this by calculating the angle of the velocity vector, using a new angle property that we added to the Vector2D class that returns the angle of a vector:

```
public function get angle():Number{
        return Math.atan2(_y,_x);
}
```

The final method called in moveObject() is monitor(). This method does two things. First, it checks if all the fuel in the main tank has been used up and, if so, it calls the stopExhaust() public method of the rocket so that the exhaust does not show any more. The _showExhaust Boolean variable is used so that it needs to do this only once.

The second thing that `monitor()` does is to check whether the rocket collides with the planet; if so, it simply invokes the `stopTime()` method inherited from `Mover`, which stops the timestepping, freezing all motion:

```
private function monitor():void{
        if (_showExhaust && _fuelUsed >= _fuelMass){
                _rocket.stopExhaust();
                _showExhaust = false;
        }
        if (_rocket.pos2D.subtract(_centerPlanet).lengthSquared <
_radiusPlanetSquared){
                this.stopTime();
        }
}
```

Finally, in `calcForce()`, we specify the forces on the rocket and add them up as usual. The first force is the force of gravity that the planet exerts on it. Then there is the main thrust and side thrust. The main thrust is applied as long as there is fuel; the amount of fuel is set in the variable `_fuelMass`. The side thrust is applied if there is fuel and if `_applySideThrust` is true. In either case, the thrust is calculated using the formula $F = -v_e \, dm/dt$. The amount of fuel, exhaust velocity, and mass rate are set independently for the main thrusters and the side thrusters. (In reality, the exhaust velocity and mass rates can be varied to control the thrust, but for simplicity we've taken them to be fixed here.)

```
override protected function calcForce():void{
        var gravity:Vector2D =
Forces.gravity(_G,_massPlanet,_rocket.mass,_rocket.pos2D.subtract(_centerPlanet));
        var thrust:Vector2D = new Vector2D(0,0);
        var thrustSide:Vector2D = new Vector2D(0,0);
        if (_fuelUsed < _fuelMass){
                thrust = _ve.multiply(-_dmdt);
        }
        if (_fuelSideUsed < _fuelSideMass && _applySideThrust){
                thrustSide = _veSide.multiply(-_dmdtSide*_orientation);
        }
        force = Forces.add([gravity, thrust, thrustSide]);
}
```

If you run the simulation, you'll see that the rocket is launched automatically. It moves very slowly at first; then both its velocity and its acceleration increase until its fuel is used up. It then slows down under the gravitational pull of the planet. If you don't do anything, it will fall back on to the planet. If you press the right or left arrow keys, a side thrust will be applied to the right or left, respectively. If you apply too much or too little side thrust, the rocket will either escape the planet's gravity or be pulled back into a collision course with the planet. See if you can make the rocket orbit the planet! This involves applying the right amount of side thrust at the right time.

Figure 6-7. A rocket orbiting a planet!

The Rocket class

Finally, let's take a quick look at the Rocket class that creates a visible rocket object. Embarrassingly, our "rocket" is simply a rectangle joined to a triangle, with another (transparent) triangle attached at the end to represent gases from the exhaust. But do please go ahead and create a better-looking version if you feel the urge to exercise your artistic skills at this point.

Here is the full source code in Rocket.as:

```
package {
        import flash.display.Sprite;
        import com.physicscodes.objects.Particle;
        import com.physicscodes.objects.Triangle;

        public class Rocket extends Particle{
                private var _width:Number;
                private var _height:Number;
                private var _color:uint;
                private var _particle:Particle;
                private var _exhaust:Triangle;

                public function
Rocket(pwidth:Number=20,pheight:Number=40,pcolor:uint=0x0000ff,pmass:Number=1,pcharge:Number=0
){
                        this.mass=pmass;
                        this.charge=pcharge;
                        _width=pwidth;
                        _height=pheight;
```

```
                    _color=pcolor;
                    _particle = new Particle(pmass,pcharge);
                    drawRocket();
            }
            private function drawRocket():void{
                    drawCapsule();
                    drawTank();
                    drawExhaust();
                    addChild(_particle);
            }
            private function drawCapsule():void{
                    var triangle:Triangle = new Triangle(0,0,_width,1.5*_width,_color);
                    addChild(triangle);
            }
            private function drawTank():void{
                    with (_particle.graphics){
                            beginFill(_color,1);
                            drawRect(0,0,_width,_height);
                            endFill();
                    }
            }
            private function drawExhaust():void{
                    with (_particle.graphics){
                            _exhaust = new
Triangle(0,_height+1.5*_width,_width,2.5*_width,_color,0.4);
                            _particle.addChild(_exhaust);
                    }
            }
            public function stopExhaust():void{
                    _particle.removeChild(_exhaust);
            }
            public function clear():void{
                    _particle.graphics.clear();
                    removeChild(_particle);
            }
            public function dropTank():void{
                    clear();
            }
        }
    }
}
```

Rocket extends Particle and draws a rocket using parameter values for width, height and color, supplied as arguments in the constructor. It does this in three separate stages through three aptly named private methods drawCapsule(), drawTank(), and drawExhaust(). Then there are additional public methods, including the stopExhaust() method mentioned earlier that removes the exhaust when the fuel runs out.

It's easy to see how this simple simulation can be developed into an interesting game. Besides improved graphics and special effects, you could add extra features and controls for greater realism. With this in mind, we need to point out that there are several limitations in the way we implemented some of the operational features of the rocket. For a simple Flash game, these limitations probably won't be a big deal, but they might well matter if you are trying to build a realistic simulator. In any case, it's worth knowing about them.

We already mentioned that we fixed the thrust of the rocket, although in reality it can be controlled by varying the speed of exhaust and the mass rate of the ejected gases. More importantly, the direction of the main and side thrust has been implemented in a way that is, strictly speaking, incorrect. The main thrust of a rocket acts along its axis no matter what the angle of the rocket is, and its side thrust will be at some specified angle relative to the rocket's angle. What we did in this simplified simulation is to fix the main and side thrust to act in the vertical (y) and horizontal (x) directions, regardless of the inclination of the rocket. Another simplification is the way we handled the rotation of the rocket—by simply aligning it with the velocity vector. In reality, rocket rotation and stability is a much more complicated affair. We also neglected the effect of air pressure, drag, and lift when the rocket is moving in an atmosphere.

Another obvious simplification we made is to put the whole rocket into orbit. In reality, space-borne rockets include one or more disposable tanks that are dropped when their fuel gets used up. With this in mind, we created a public `dropTank()` method in the `Rocket` class that basically makes the tank disappear. You might like to use `dropTank()` to create the illusion of the tank being detached from the rocket and falling back to Earth after its fuel is used up. Because the `dropTank()` method just makes the existing tank disappear, you'll have to create a new one and make it fall under the planet's gravity. We leave this as an exercise for you. The `Rocket` class could be enhanced functionally, too. For example, it might make sense to include the amount of fuel, fuel used, exhaust velocity, and mass rate as properties of `Rocket` instead of hard-coding them into `Rocketer`.

Finally, the examples we coded in this chapter are realistic in that they contain the correct physics equations, but the values chosen for the various parameters are not necessarily to scale. For example, in the orbits simulation, the sizes of the planet and the sun are grossly exaggerated in comparison with their distances. This was necessary in order to see both the objects and their motion on a computer screen. Scaling issues are discussed in detail in Chapter 15.

Summary

This chapter showed you the richness and variety that the gravitational force can exhibit, and the different types of motion it can produce. In a fairly short chapter, you've been able to code up orbits, two objects moving in interesting ways under their mutual gravity, and a rocket simulation from launch to orbit.

It's amazing how much fun can be had with a just a few physics formulas and a little bit of code. You now have a taste of what can be done, even with a single force such as gravity. We'll play more with gravity in later chapters. Meanwhile, we'll introduce a whole lot of other forces in the next chapter.

Chapter 7

Contact and Fluid Forces

In the last chapter, we looked in some detail at gravity, which is a force that acts at a distance. Besides gravity, most of the forces that we encounter in our daily lives actually arise due to direct contact with other objects, either solids or fluids. Because on this planet we are usually in contact with a solid floor and are surrounded by fluid, either air or water, it is surely a good thing to know what forces they exert on things. This chapter will look at these forces.

Specifically, these forces include the following:

- **Contact forces**: Contact forces are forces that two solid objects exert on each other when in direct contact. Examples include normal forces, friction, and tension.

- **Pressure**: Fluids exert pressure. Any object in the fluid experiences a force due to this fluid pressure.

- **Upthrust or buoyancy**: Upthrust, also known as buoyancy, is the resultant pressure force experienced by a body that is partially or fully immersed in a fluid.

- **Drag**: An object moving through a fluid experiences a retarding force that tends to oppose its motion. This is the drag force.

- **Lift**: An object moving through a fluid may experience another force perpendicular to the direction of motion, known as the lift force. The lift force is what makes airplanes fly.

- **Wind**: Although wind is not itself a force, it does exert a force on any object over which it blows. Wind also produces turbulence, which can cause an object to move erratically.

As this list indicates, these varieties of forces include interactions between solid objects as well as interactions between a solid object and a fluid, in both cases as a result of direct physical contact. But technically, the term *contact force* is reserved for a force that exists between two solid objects. Only the first section will deal with contact forces in this technical sense. Most of the chapter will then focus on forces exerted by fluids on solid objects. That's partly because the latter are more complex but also manifest in a richer variety, with interesting features and effects. In looking at fluid forces, we'll restrict our attention to forces that solid objects experience in a fluid. We do not consider the forces acting on the fluid and the effect these forces have on the fluid itself. Fluid motion is a more complicated problem and is not treated in this book.

Here are just some of the things you'll be able to simulate after reading this chapter: motion with friction, floating objects, bubbles, balloons, parachutes, lift forces, wind, and turbulence effects. You will also know most of the physics you need to build a submarine simulation (see Chapter 16).

Contact forces

Simply stated, a contact force is a force experienced by a solid object due to contact with another solid object. Pushing and pulling involve contact forces. So does running, or simply standing. Collisions involve large contact forces that operate for a very small duration.

Normal contact forces

Before we do anything else, it must be explained that the word *normal* here is meant in the mathematical sense of the word, which is *perpendicular* rather than the opposite of *abnormal*.

When two solid objects are brought into contact, each of them exerts a normal force on the other that prevents them from merging together. The magnitude of the normal force depends on the force with which the two objects are pushed together.

An example of a normal contact force is the reaction that the floor exerts on you. In fact, that force is why we are aware of our weight. Without the normal reaction from the floor (and therefore without the normal force), we would fall through the floor.

Now, whenever we introduce a new force in this book, we'll give you a way to calculate it. That's how you can simulate it. If you cannot calculate a force, there is no point in talking about it!

How do you calculate the normal force? It depends on the situation. Unlike for gravity, there is no universal formula that will tell you what the normal force is. Usually, you can deduce it from the other forces acting on the object.

Here is an example. Consider a book resting on a flat horizontal table (see Figure 7-1). There are two main forces acting on the book: the force of gravity W = mg exerted by the Earth and acting vertically downward, and the normal contact force N exerted by the table on the book acting vertically upward (the normal contact force is usually denoted by N or R). Because the book does not move, the resultant force on it must be zero (Newton's first law of motion). Therefore, we can deduce that the normal force N in this case is equal in magnitude to the weight W of the book.

The normal force will change if, for example, the table is tilted. You'll see in an example how to calculate the normal force in such a case.

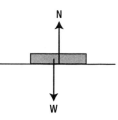

Figure 7-1. The normal contact force acting on a book resting on a table

Tension and compression

Tension in strings is another contact force. If you tie an object with a piece of string and then suspend the object by holding the other end of the string (see Figure 7-2), the string exerts a pull on the object that prevents it from falling down. The string can only do this if it is taut. By Newton's third law of motion, the object exerts an equal and opposite force on the string. The force on the string is called tension. Informally, we also refer to the force that the string exerts on the object as tension. The effect of tension on the string itself is to stretch it slightly. If the object stops moving then the tension must be equal to the weight of the object. If the object is very heavy, the tension may stretch the string to breaking point.

Springs also experience tension. Springs are designed so that large extensions are produced for relatively small tensions. Because a spring will tend to regain its normal length when stretched, it will pull back on the object that is stretching it. The opposite of tension is compression. Springs can also be compressed; they then exert a push on the object compressing them.

Springs are both great fun and extremely useful for producing a variety of effects. In fact, the next chapter is devoted exclusively to springs and spring-like motion.

Figure 7-2. Tension in a string

Friction

Frictional forces are forces that resist the relative movement of two bodies that are in contact or the movement of a body through a fluid. For example, if you push a book along a table, it will slow down and come to a stop. That's because of the frictional force that the table surface exerts on it. The friction between two solid objects is also called *dry friction*. Fluids such as air or water also exert a frictional force, known as *viscous fluid drag*.

We'll discuss fluid drag later in this chapter. In this section, we'll look at dry friction between two solid objects and how we can model it.

As discussed, friction is a force that resists the relative motion of two objects in contact with each other. This implies that the frictional force on an object will act in a direction opposite to its motion. But an object does not necessarily have to move in order to experience friction. If an object is experiencing a force that *tends* to move it against another object, it can also experience friction, even if it does not actually move. In fact, it is friction that stops it from moving. So there are actually two types of friction: friction experienced by a stationary object, and friction experienced by a moving object. We call them *static* and *kinetic* friction, respectively.

Modeling static and kinetic friction

We model both types of friction using the concept of a *coefficient of friction*. Let's start with *kinetic friction* because it is a bit simpler.

Common experience tells us that there will be more friction if we press two surfaces together while trying to slide one over the other. That's because the two objects "stick together" more if pressed together. It's also clear that the amount of friction will depend upon the material making up the object. Rubber, for example, would give more friction than glass. It should therefore come as no surprise to learn that the magnitude of the frictional force F is given by the following, where N is the normal force between the two objects and C_k is a number that depends on the two surfaces, known as the coefficient of kinetic friction:

$$F = C_k N$$

By Newton's third law, a force of the same magnitude acts on both objects; for each object, the force acts in a direction to oppose its motion relative to the other object. Kinetic friction is also sometimes referred to as *dynamic* or *sliding* friction.

Static friction is a bit different. Whereas the kinetic frictional force has just one value for a given pair of surfaces and normal contact force, the static frictional force can take on any value up to a maximum value. The maximum value is given by the following:

$$F_{max} = C_s N$$

This is similar in form to the formula for kinetic friction, but with a different coefficient, known as the *coefficient of static friction*. Its value is usually larger than the corresponding value of C_k for the same two surfaces. Hence, the maximum static frictional force is larger than the kinetic frictional force.

To understand static versus kinetic friction, consider the following thought experiment. Suppose you are pushing an object in contact with a surface. If the force you apply has a magnitude less than F_{max} as given by the preceding formula, the frictional force will be equal to the applied force, so that the resultant force is zero and the object does not move. If you now push harder so that the applied force is larger than the value of F_{max}, the frictional force will be equal to F_{max} (because it cannot exceed that maximum value).

Therefore, the frictional force cannot completely balance the applied force, and the object will begin to accelerate under the resultant force. As soon as it starts moving, the frictional force will reduce to a value equal to the magnitude of the kinetic friction. Hence, the resultant force will suddenly increase, and the object will accelerate faster. If you've ever tried to move a piece of heavy furniture, you will readily appreciate this fact: it is easier to push once it's already moving. That's because kinetic friction is less than the maximum value of static friction.

Coefficients of friction

Some examples of coefficients of friction are given in Table 7-1. The key point is that the values are generally less than 1. It is very rare for the coefficient of friction to be larger than 1 because that would imply a frictional force larger than the normal contact force holding the two objects together.

Note that although the values are representative of the materials cited, actual coefficients of friction may vary due to the nature of the surface of actual objects. For game programming purposes, this does not present a big problem.

It is impossible to give a comprehensive list of friction coefficients; but if what you need is not listed here it should be easy to find it online.

Table 7-1. Static and Kinetic Coefficients of Friction

Materials	C_s	C_k
Wood on wood	0.25–0.5	0.2
Steel on steel	0.74	0.57
Rubber on concrete	1.0	0.8
Glass on glass	0.94	0.4
Ice on ice	0.1	0.03

Example: Sliding down a slope

Time for an example! You can now apply what you learned about normal contact forces and friction to simulate an object sliding down an inclined plane. First, let's apply the physics concepts to this particular example.

The physics

The force diagram for this simulation is shown in Figure 7-3. As indicated on the diagram, there are three forces acting on the object: gravity m**g**, normal contact force **N**, and friction **f**. Because the object moves in a straight line along the surface, the resultant force acts along the surface. There is no resultant force perpendicular to the surface.

Therefore, resolving the forces along the surface gives the magnitude of the resultant force **F** as follows, where θ is the angle of the inclined plane:

$$F = mg\sin(\theta) - f$$

Resolving forces perpendicular to the surface must give a zero resultant, so that the normal contact force **N** is balanced by the component of gravity perpendicular to the surface. Note that friction **f** acts along the surface, so its component perpendicular to the surface is zero. Hence, $N = mg\cos(\theta)$

The magnitude of the frictional force **f** is given by the following when the object is moving:

$$f = C_k N$$

If it is not moving, the resultant force F along the surface must be zero, so f has to balance the component of gravity along the surface. From the preceding equation, setting F = 0 gives this:

$$f = mg\sin(\theta)$$

It will be true up to a maximum value of the following:

$$f = C_s N$$

If the value of the gravity component (mg sin (θ)) exceeds this critical value (C_s N), f will have the latter value, at least momentarily. As soon as the object starts moving, f will have the value C_k N.

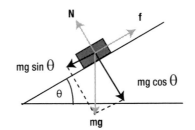

Figure 7-3. Force diagram for an object sliding down an inclined plane

Now that you know the physics and have the relevant formulas, you can start coding. This will be a two-step process, pretty similar to what you did in the last chapter. First, you'll create the visual setup; then you'll put together in a separate class the code that drives the simulation.

Creating the visual setup

The visual setup file is called `Sliding.as`. Here is the code in that file:

```
package{
        import flash.display.Sprite;
        import com.physicscodes.objects.Ball;
```

```
import com.physicscodes.math.Vector2D;
import com.physicscodes.objects.Particle;

public class Sliding extends Sprite{
        public function Sliding():void{
                init();
        }
        private function init():void{

                // create a ball
                var ball:Ball;
                ball = new Ball(20,0x0000ff,1);
                ball.pos2D = new Vector2D(50,130);
                ball.velo2D = new Vector2D(0,0);
                addChild(ball);

                // create an inclined plane
                var xtop:Number=50;
                var ytop:Number=150;
                var xbot:Number=450;
                var ybot:Number=250;

                var surface:Sprite = new Sprite;
                with (surface.graphics) {
                        lineStyle(1,0x333333,1);
                        moveTo(xtop,ytop);
                        lineTo(xbot,ybot);
                }
                addChild(surface);

                // make the ball move
                var angle:Number = Math.atan2(ybot-ytop,xbot-xtop);
                var mover:ObliqueMover = new ObliqueMover(ball,angle);
                mover.startTime(10);
        }
    }
}
```

This code should look very familiar. We create a ball and a line, and place the ball on the line. Then we work out the angle of the line using the end points and the Math.atan2() function. If you are unsure about what is happening here, take a look at the subsection "The inverse trig functions" in Chapter 3 again. Finally, we make the ball move down the inclined line using the yet-to-be-created ObliqueMover class, passing the ball and the angle of the line as parameters in its constructor.

Making things move

The structure of the ObliqueMover class should also look familiar to you. Here is the full code:

```
package {
        import com.physicscodes.motion.Forcer;
        import com.physicscodes.motion.Forces;
        import com.physicscodes.objects.Particle;
        import com.physicscodes.math.Vector2D;
```

```
import flash.display.Sprite;

public class ObliqueMover extends Forcer{
        private var _particle:Particle;
        private var _angle:Number;
        private var _g:Number=10;
        private var _ck:Number=0.2;
        private var _cs:Number=0.25;
        private var _vtol:Number=0.000001;

        public function ObliqueMover(pparticle:Particle,pangle:Number):void{
                _particle = pparticle;
                _angle = pangle;
                super(pparticle);
        }

        override protected function calcForce():void{
                var gravity:Vector2D = Forces.constantGravity(_particle.mass,_g);
                var normal:Vector2D = Vector2D.vector2D(_particle.mass*_g*Math.cos↩
(_angle), 0.5*Math.PI-_angle,false);
                var coeff:Number;
                if (_particle.velo2D.length<_vtol){  // static friction
                        coeff = Math.min(_cs,_particle.mass*_g*Math.sin(_angle));
                }else{  // kinetic friction
                        coeff = _ck;
                }
                var friction:Vector2D = normal.perp(coeff);
                force = Forces.add([gravity, normal, friction]);
        }
    }
}
```

All the code for the simulation is now in place, but if you go ahead and run it you won't see anything moving yet. We'll explain what to do to make that happen shortly. But before doing so, we'll explain what the code is doing.

ObliqueMover extends Forcer, as you expect. The constructor passes the particle and angle parameters to private variables _particle and _angle, respectively and then invokes the constructor of Forcer with the particle as a parameter. ObliqueMover then overrides the calcForce() method as usual, calculating the three relevant forces gravity, normal, and friction at each timestep and then adding them up to get the resultant force by using the Forces.add() method. The calculation of the normal and friction forces requires explanation. For the normal force, we are using a new method of Vector2D called vector2D(), which is defined as follows:

```
static public function vector2D(mag:Number, angle:Number,clockwise:Boolean=true):Vector2D{
        var vec:Vector2D = new Vector2D(0,0);
        vec.x = mag*Math.cos(angle);
        vec.y = mag*Math.sin(angle);
        if (!clockwise){
                vec.y *= -1;
        }
        return vec;
}
```

This method takes two required Number arguments, mag and angle (in radians), and an optional Boolean argument clockwise, and returns a Vector2D object which is a 2D vector with the specified magnitude and angle. It does this by converting from the (magnitude, angle) representation to the component representation of a vector (refer to the section "Resolving vectors," in Chapter 3). The clockwise parameter tells vector2D() whether the angle is taken in a clockwise direction (the default) or in an anticlockwise direction.

Using the previous formulas and Figure 7-3, we know that the magnitude of the normal force is equal to mg cos (θ), and its angle is equal to $\pi/2 - \theta$ (that's 90° $- \theta$, in radians) taken in an anticlockwise sense. Therefore, the normal force is given by this:

```
normal = Vector2D.vector2D(_particle.mass*_g*Math.cos(_angle), 0.5*Math.PI-_angle, false);
```

The friction force is perpendicular to the normal force and has a magnitude of coeff*N, where coeff is the coefficient of friction and N is the magnitude of the normal force. It is therefore given by the following, where perp() is another new method we created in the Vector2D class (which we shall describe shortly) and coeff is equal to C_k N when the object starts moving; and is equal to mg sin (θ), up to a maximum of C_s N, when the object is not moving:

```
var friction:Vector2D = normal.perp(coeff);
```

This is implemented in the following way:

```
if (_particle.velo2D.length<_vtol){  // static friction
      coeff = Math.min(_cs*normal.length,_particle.mass*_g*Math.sin(_angle));
}else{  // kinetic friction
      coeff = _ck*normal.length;
}
```

Note that we make use of the Math.min() function to implement the fact that for static friction, coeff is either equal to mg sin a, or C_k N, whichever is smaller.

The perp() method of Vector2D is defined like this:

```
public function perp(u:Number,anticlockwise:Boolean=true):Vector2D{
      var vec:Vector2D = new Vector2D(_y, -_x);
      if (length > 0) {
            if (anticlockwise){
                  vec.scaleBy(u/length);
            }else{
                  vec.scaleBy(-u/length);
            }
      }else{
            vec=new Vector2D(0,0);
      }
      return vec;
}
```

This definition implies that if vec is a Vector2D object, and k is a number, vec.perp(k) returns a Vector2D object that is perpendicular to vec and of length k, with an anticlockwise orientation to vec (in the Flash coordinate system). Refering to Figure 7-4, which shows a screenshot of the setup, `normal.perp(coeff)`therefore gives a vector of magnitude `coeff` directed up the slope, just as the frictional force should be.

Figure 7-4. An object sliding down a slope

When checking to see if the object is not moving, we don't actually check that its velocity is zero but that it's smaller than some small value `_vtol` (set at 0.000001 in the code). The value of `_g` is set at 10 and, taking both the sliding object and the surface to be made of wood, we choose `_ck` = 0.2 and `_cs` = 0.25.

If you run the code with the given choice of values for the parameters, you'll see that nothing happens. The object just stays there. How can this be? To understand this, take a look again at Figure 7-3. It is clear that the object can slide only if the component of gravity along the slope exceeds the maximum static friction. In other words, it will slide if the following condition is true:

$$mg\sin(\theta) > C_s N$$

Because N = mg cos (θ), this is equivalent to the following:

$$mg\sin(\theta) > C_s \, mg\cos(\theta)$$

Dividing both sides of this inequality by mg cos (θ) gives you this:

$$\tan(\theta) > C_s$$

So the object will slide only if the tangent of the slope angle is greater than the coefficient of static friction.

Now you can calculate tan (θ) from the values of xtop, ytop, xbot, and ybot as follows:

$$\tan(\theta) = \frac{\text{ybot} - \text{ytop}}{\text{xbot} - \text{xtop}} = \frac{250 - 150}{450 - 50} = 0.25$$

This is exactly equal to the value of C_s specified in the code. Therefore, gravity is not sufficient to overcome the force of friction, and the object does not slide. If you increase the angle of the slope slightly, the object will slide. For example, if you change the value of ybot to 260, this will give tan (θ) = 110/400 = 0.275, which is larger than the value of C_s.

In this example, the object slides along a surface without rolling. Rolling involves rotational motion of a rigid body (it will be discussed in Chapter 13).

Pressure

The rest of this chapter will deal with forces that originate from pressure, more specifically fluid pressure. Technically, pressure is associated with solids as well as liquids and gases. But the concept is especially useful in relation to fluids, so it tends to be associated more with liquids and gases.

The meaning of pressure

So what is *pressure*? It is the normal (perpendicular) force per unit area exerted on the surface of an object. The origin of that perpendicular force can be different in different cases. Pressure due to solids and liquids is usually due to the force of gravity. Pressure in gases is due to collisions by gas molecules.

The key question is this: how can we calculate pressure and thus the forces on an object in a fluid? Once we can do that, we can try to simulate the motion of an object in a fluid.

Based on this definition of pressure, if a force F acts normally to a surface with area A, the average pressure P on the surface is given by the following:

$$P = \frac{F}{A}$$

Because pressure is force divided by area, its unit is N/m^2. This unit has a special name: the pascal, Pa.

What if F acts at an angle to the normal? Then you need to resolve F to find the component along the normal, and that normal component is what you use in the preceding formula. This gives us a method for calculating the pressure if we know the force, and vice versa.

Pressure is not restricted to fluids (although fluid pressure will be our main concern in this chapter), and it is actually easier to introduce the method of calculating pressure using a simple illustrative example of a solid object.

Suppose that a cuboid (box) of length l, width w, height h, and mass m sits on a table (see Figure 7-5). What is the pressure it exerts on the table?

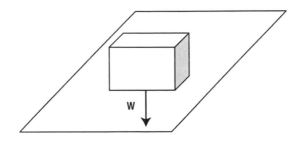

Figure 7-5. A box sitting on a table

The force it exerts on the table is equal to its weight, and that force is perpendicular to the table surface, so we have F = mg. The area A = lw. Hence, the pressure P is given by this:

$$P = \frac{mg}{A} = \frac{mg}{lw}$$

Density

We can make some more progress by introducing the concept of density.

Density is defined as mass per unit volume. Density gives you a way of comparing the relative "heaviness" of different substances—take the same volume of each substance and compare how much each weighs.

We use the Greek symbol ρ ("rho") for density. So, based on the definition, we can write:

$$\rho = \frac{m}{V}$$

Because density is a mass divided by a volume, its unit is kg/m^3. Because things expand when heated, especially liquids and gases, the density of a fluid varies with temperature (and also with pressure). At 20°C and standard atmospheric pressure, the density of water is approximately 1000 kg/m^3, and that of air is approximately 1.2 kg/m^3. That means a box measuring 1m x 1m x 1m (of volume $1m^3$) would hold 1000 kg (1 ton) of water and 1.2 kg of air.

Manipulating the above formula gives this:

$$m = \rho V$$

It also gives this:

$$V = \frac{m}{\rho}$$

We'll use these formulas frequently in the rest of this chapter.

Just like pressure, the concept of density applies to solids as well as liquids. Going back to the preceding illustrative example of the cuboid, we can replace the mass m in the formula for pressure by using m = ρV = ρlwh because the volume of the cuboid is V = lwh:

$$P = \frac{mg}{lw} = \frac{\rho lwhg}{lw} = \rho gh$$

This is a very useful formula. It gives the pressure exerted by a regular object (in this case, a cuboid) on a surface in terms of three known quantities: the density of the object, the acceleration due to gravity, and the height of the object. Note that we could have used another shape other than a box, as long as it had regular cross-section A. The area A would cancel out in the same way, leaving the same formula: P = ρgh.

In the next section, we'll find that this formula is actually even more general, and also applies to the pressure exerted by fluids, provided that we reinterpret h.

Variation of pressure with depth in a fluid

Instead of a solid, now consider a column of liquid of the same shape as the solid in the last section.

Exactly the same math applies, and we again end up with the following, where P is the pressure underneath the column of fluid, ρ is the density of the fluid, and h is the height of the fluid column:

$$P = \rho g h$$

Now mentally transport yourself to the ocean.

At a depth h beneath the sea surface, there is a column of water of height h above. Hence, the pressure at depth h below the surface is given by the same formula:

$$P = \rho g h$$

Note that this is the pressure due to the water only. There is also an additional pressure due to the air above the water surface. This is atmospheric pressure, which we can denote by A. Then the total pressure at a depth h in the ocean is A + ρgh, assuming the density of water is constant with depth. This formula shows that pressure in a fluid increases with depth, which makes perfect sense because there is more fluid above that is "weighing down."

The same is true in the atmosphere, too. The air pressure we feel at the surface of the Earth is due to the column of air above our heads. Standard atmospheric pressure is approximately 100 kPa, or 100,000 Pa. This is sometimes simply called 1 atmosphere (atm).

Because the density of water is 1000 kg/m^3, and g is approximately 10 m/s^2, using the formula P = ρgh tells us that 10 m of water will exert approximately the same pressure as 1 atm. So, at an ocean depth of 10 m, the pressure will be 2 atm, including the pressure of the air above.

Static and dynamic pressure

So far, when we talked about pressure in a fluid, we've been referring to *static pressure*. The formula P = ρgh applies to static pressure. Static pressure is defined at any point in a flow, and it is isotropic; that is, it has the same value in any direction. It exists even in static fluids (fluids that are at rest).

In a moving fluid, there is another kind of pressure, known as *dynamic pressure*. Dynamic pressure is due to the flow of fluid. For example, the flow of water from a tap gives rise to dynamic pressure. When the water hits the sink, it exerts a force on the sink. Similarly, the wind exerts a force due to the dynamic pressure associated with it. The formula for the dynamic pressure at any point in a fluid is the following, where v is the velocity of the fluid at that point:

$$P = \frac{1}{2}\rho v^2$$

The same is true for an object moving with velocity v in a fluid; it's the relative velocity between the object and the fluid that matters.

The total pressure in a moving fluid is the sum of the static and the dynamic pressure.

Upthrust (buoyancy)

After this background on pressure and density, we are now ready to introduce the forces due to fluids. So let's start with upthrust, also known as buoyancy.

Here is a simple experiment for you to do in the bath. Try pushing a hollow ball under water. What do you feel? You should feel a force trying to push the ball back upward. This is the upthrust force. Now let go of the ball. What happens? It pops back up and oscillates at the water surface before settling down. You will create such an effect soon.

Upthrust is also responsible for making us feel lighter in the swimming pool or bath. It acts upward, opposing the force of gravity.

What causes upthrust? The physical origin of upthrust is the difference in pressure that exists at different heights in a fluid. To see what we mean, take a look at Figure 7-6a, which shows an object partially immersed in a fluid such as water. The pressure on the top face of the object is equal to atmospheric pressure A and pushes the object downward, while the pressure on the bottom surface is equal to A + ρgh, where ρ is the density of the fluid, and h is the depth to which the object is submerged. This pressure acts upward, so that there is a net upward pressure equal to ρgh. Hence, because force = pressure x surface area, there is a resultant upward force U due to this pressure difference given by the following (where S is the area of the top and bottom faces of the object—taken to be equal here for simplicity):

$$U = \rho g h S$$

This is the upthrust or buoyancy force.

Note that because pressure is isotropic, it also acts on the sides of the object. But the pressures on opposite sides are equal and opposite at each height, so their effects are cancelled. Similar conclusions hold if the object is completely immersed in a fluid (see Figure 7-6b), including objects in air. That's basically because pressure increases with depth in a fluid, so the pressure at the base of a submerged object will always be greater than that at its top. So there will be a net upward pressure on the object due to the fluid.

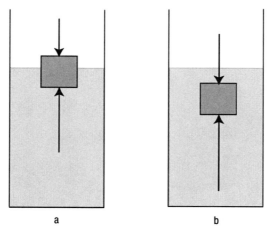

a   b

Figure 7-6. An object immersed in a fluid experiences upthrust due to a pressure difference

Archimedes's Principle

Let's revisit the last formula we derived in the last section. The magnitude of the upthrust U was found to be given by U = ρghS. Now h is the height of the submerged portion of the object and S is its cross-sectional area (which we assume to be constant for simplicity). Hence, hS is equal to the volume V of the submerged portion of the object. So we can write this:

$$U = \rho g h S = \rho g V$$

But then ρV = m, the mass of the *fluid* whose place has been taken by the submerged portion of the object, so we can now write this:

$$U = m_{\text{fluid}}\, g$$

This is just the weight of the displaced fluid. Hence, we have derived Archimedes's principle:

> ***Archimedes's principle****: The upthrust on an object immersed in a fluid is equal to the weight of fluid it displaces.*

Archimedes was an ancient Greek scientist, mathematician, and all-round genius. According to legend, upon discovering this principle, he jumped out of his bath shouting "Eureka!", which means "Found it!"

Apparent weight

Upthrust leads to the phenomenon of *apparent weight*. Figure 7-7 illustrates the concept. Any object that is partially or completely immersed in a fluid will experience an upward upthrust force U that opposes the downward force of gravity W on it.

Hence, the apparent weight of the object is given by

$$W_{apparent} = W - U .$$

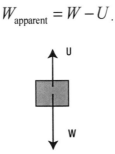

Figure 7-7. Upthrust reduces the apparent weight of an object to W – U

The phenomenon of apparent weight is responsible for why we feel lighter in the bath or a swimming pool. Exploiting the apparent weight effect, astronauts train while submerged in a giant water tank to simulate reduced or zero gravity.

Submerged objects

Objects that are completely immersed (submerged) in a fluid obviously displace their own volume of fluid.

The apparent weight of a completely immersed object can therefore be written as follows because both the object and the displaced fluid have the same volume V:

$$W_{apparent} = W - U = m_{object}\, g - m_{fluid}\, g = \rho_{object}\, V g - \rho_{fluid}\, V g$$

It can therefore be written in the following form:

$$W_{apparent} = \left(\rho_{object} - \rho_{fluid} \right) V g$$

This is a very useful formula that gives the resultant downward force, or apparent weight, of an object submerged in a fluid in terms of their densities and the volume of the submerged object.

From this formula, we can deduce:

- If the density of the object is greater than that of the fluid, the apparent weight will be positive (i.e. downward) but less than the real weight. You can experience this lower apparent weight in the bath or a swimming pool.

- If the density of the object is *much* larger than that of the fluid, the apparent weight is nearly equal to the real weight because the upthrust is negligible compared to the weight of the object. For example, the upthrust on a stone in air can usually be neglected.

- If the density of the object is exactly equal to that of the fluid, the apparent weight will be zero, and so the object will float in the fluid.

- If the density of the object is less than that of the fluid, the apparent weight is negative (it acts upward) and so the object will rise. For example, air bubbles in water have a very large upthrust compared with their weight due to the density of air being much lower than that of water, hence they rise quickly.

Floating objects

A special form of Archimedes's principle applies for floating bodies. This is the so-called law of flotation.

> *Law of flotation*: A floating object displaces its own weight of fluid.

Here's the logic. A floating body has no *net* force acting on it; otherwise, it would either rise or sink. Because the only two forces acting on it are its weight and upthrust, they must balance. Hence, the upthrust on a floating body must equal the weight of the body. By Archimedes's principle, this implies that the weight of fluid displaced is equal to the weight of the body. So the apparent weight of a floating object is zero—it "feels weightless."

As discussed previously, this is also the situation when a body is submerged in a fluid with a density equal to the body's own density. In fact, an object that is floating on the surface of a liquid, such as a ship on water, has an "effective density" that is the same as that of the water, even though it may be made of metal with a higher density than that of water. That's because the part of the ship below the water surface also includes air enclosed within the ship's interior, which lowers its average density.

Example: Balloon

We've had a fair bit of theory, so let's look at an example. This example (shown in Figure 7-8) simulates a simple hot-air balloon. Hot-air balloons work, well, by heating air. The heated air has a density less than that of the ambient air, so it rises. By controlling the temperature of the air in the balloon, you can control its density and therefore the upthrust on it.

The setup code for this simulation is found in `Balloon.as`, and is very simple:

```
package{
        import flash.display.Sprite;
        import com.physicscodes.objects.Ball;
        import com.physicscodes.math.Vector2D;
        import com.physicscodes.objects.Particle;

        public class Balloon extends Sprite{
                public function Balloon():void{
                        init();
```

```
        }
        private function init():void{

                // create a balloon
                var balloon:Ball;
                balloon = new Ball(20,0x0000ff,1);
                balloon.pos2D = new Vector2D(400,500);
                balloon.velo2D = new Vector2D(0,0);
                addChild(balloon);

                // make the balloon rise
                var riser:Riser=new Riser(balloon);
                riser.startTime(10);
        }
    }
}
```

We simply create a balloon as a `Ball` object, we make it rise using the `Riser` class, passing the balloon object as a parameter.

You could probably write the code for `Riser` without too much help by now. Here is a basic code that subjects the balloon to gravity and upthrust:

```
package {
        import com.physicscodes.motion.Forcer;
        import com.physicscodes.motion.Forces;
        import com.physicscodes.objects.Particle;
        import com.physicscodes.math.Vector2D;

        public class Riser extends Forcer{
                private var _particle:Particle;
                private var _g:Number=10;
                private var _rho:Number=1.2;
                private var _rhoP:Number=1.1;
                private var _V:Number;

                public function Riser(pparticle:Particle):void{
                        _particle = pparticle;
                        super(pparticle);
                }

                override protected function calcForce():void{
                        var gravity:Vector2D = Forces.constantGravity(_particle.mass,_g);
                        _V = _particle.mass/_rhoP;
                        var upthrust:Vector2D = Forces.upthrust(_rho,_V,_g);
                        force = Forces.add([gravity, upthrust]);
                }
        }
}
```

Nothing new here in terms of the code structure. Riser extends Forcer and overrides the `calcForce()` method, specifying two forces (gravity and upthrust) and then adds them up. The upthrust is calculated using the newly created `Forces.upthrust()` static function that basically uses the formula $U = \rho g V$, where ρ (variable _rho) in the code is the density of the fluid and V (variable _V in the code) is the volume of air displaced. This is the volume of the balloon because it is completely immersed in air. So _V is calculated using the mass of the balloon and its effective density _rhoP, using the formula volume = mass/density. The effective density _rhoP is the density of the whole balloon, including any load it carries (not just the density of the air in it).

The critical parameter in the simulation is the ratio of the balloon density to ambient air density _rhoP/_rho. If the effective balloon density _rhoP is smaller than the air density _rho (that ratio is smaller than 1), the balloon will rise. If _rhoP is larger than _rho, it will sink.

Figure 7-8. Simulating a hot-air balloon

To make the simulation more interactive, we've also included some code in Riser.as so that you can increase and decrease the density _rhoP of the balloon by pressing the up and down arrow keys, respectively. The code traces out the value of the ratio (_rhoP/_rho) whenever _rhoP is changed. See if you can make the balloon rise and then remain stationary at some height.

There is something missing in this simulation. The balloon rises too fast; it basically accelerates under the effect of the excess upthrust force, so its upward velocity keeps on rising. In reality, it will be slowed down by drag. So let's take a look at how we can include drag effects.

Drag

Trying to model drag can prove somewhat confusing for someone who is not familiar with fluid dynamics. One reason is because there is not just one, but several types of drag. Depending on the object and flow you are simulating, you might need to consider different types of drag.

Another source of difficulty is that a lot of what we know about drag is based on empirical work. The laws of drag were discovered by doing lots of experiments, and not as part of a beautiful universal theory like gravity.

The bottom line is that you will bump into formulas that were developed from experimental results that you just have to accept without argument.

For most of what we'll do in this book, we'll use one of two drag laws: one that holds for low velocities (or so-called *laminar flow*) and another (more common) one that holds for higher velocities (or so-called *turbulent flow*).

Drag law for low velocities

For an object moving through a fluid at very low velocities, the flow around the object is *laminar*, or streamlined. This generates relatively low drag. The drag force then obeys Stokes's law, which says that the drag force is proportional to the velocity of the object. For a spherical object, the Stokes's drag formula is the following, where r is the radius of the sphere and the Greek letter η denotes a property of the fluid known as *viscosity* (more precisely, *dynamic viscosity*):

$$\mathbf{F} = -6\,\pi\,\eta\,r\,\mathbf{v}$$

Note that dynamic viscosity is also denoted by the Greek letter μ. The viscosity of a fluid is a measure of the resistance it offers to objects moving through it. Intuitively, it represents the "thickness" of the fluid. So the viscosity of water is higher than that of air, and the viscosity of oil is higher than that of water. Therefore, an object moving at the same velocity through water experiences a larger drag force than through air. The formula also tells us that a larger object experiences more drag because the parameter r is greater for a larger object.

To use this formula in an accurate simulation, you need to know the viscosity of the fluid in which your object is moving. Like density, viscosity depends on temperature. At 20°C, the dynamic viscosity of water is 1.0×10^{-3} kg/(ms), and that of air is 1.8×10^{-5} kg/(ms)—about 55 times smaller.

In coding up this drag force, we will lump together all the factors multiplying the velocity into a single factor denoted by k, so that the linear drag law becomes the following, where k = 6πηr for a sphere:

$$\mathbf{F} = -k\,\mathbf{v}$$

Writing the linear drag law in this form is in fact more general because it then also applies to other, non-spherical objects, for which k is not given by this formula. By choosing suitable values for k, we can model the linear drag force on objects of any shape.

This is basically the form of drag that we coded up into the Forces.linearDrag() function back in Chapter 5:

```
static public function linearDrag(k:Number,vel:Vector2D):Vector2D {
        var force:Vector2D;
        var velMag:Number=vel.length;
        if (velMag>0) {
                force=vel.multiply(-k);
        }else {
                force=new Vector2D(0,0);
        }
        return force;
}
```

Drag law for high velocities

Stokes's drag law holds only for low velocities. At higher velocities, the flow around the immersed object becomes *turbulent*, generating eddies that disturb the flow and make it chaotic. The drag force law is then different from that of laminar flow and is proportional to the square of the velocity of the object. The drag formula is given by the following, where ρ is the density of the fluid; A is the area of the frontal area of the object (the area on which the fluid impacts as the object moves through it); and C_d is a parameter called the *drag coefficient*, which depends on characteristics of the object such as its shape, surface properties, and characteristics of the flow:

$$\mathbf{F} = -\frac{1}{2} \rho A C_d v \mathbf{v}$$

Note that the formula involves the product of the velocity $\mathbf{v}$ with its magnitude v. This gives a vector of magnitude v^2 in the direction of $\mathbf{v}$. Hence, the drag force law is quadratic in the velocity, with a magnitude given by this:

$$F = \frac{1}{2} \rho A C_d v^2$$

In this form, it is clear that quadratic drag depends on dynamic pressure P = ½ ρv^2, and indeed we can write this:

$$F = P A C_d$$

As mentioned previously, the drag coefficient C_d can depend on a large number of factors. Its value is found by experiment for particular objects and setups. For example, the drag coefficient of a sphere can range from 0.07 to 0.5. Similarly, you can find the drag coefficients for a large number of object shapes (both in 2D and in 3D) in physics or engineering textbooks or websites.

As for the laminar drag formula, we'll simplify the previous formula by defining a drag constant k for high velocities as the following:

$$k = \frac{1}{2} \rho A C_d$$

So the drag law for high velocities can be written in this form:

$$\mathbf{F} = -k v \mathbf{v}$$

We now define a second drag force function in the Forces class called drag(), which looks as follows:

```
static public function drag(k:Number,vel:Vector2D):Vector2D {
        var force:Vector2D;
        var velMag:Number=vel.length;
```

```
    if (velMag>0) {
            force=vel.multiply(-k*velMag);
    }else {
            force=new Vector2D(0,0);
    }
    return force;
}
```

Which drag law should I use?

We have described two drag laws, linear and quadratic, saying the former applies at low velocities and the latter at high velocities. But so far we've been rather vague about what "low" and "high" mean. What is the "critical velocity" that distinguishes between low and high?

To answer this question, we introduce the concept of *Reynolds number* of a flow. In simple terms, the Reynolds number tells us whether a flow is laminar or turbulent. Therefore it tells us, among other things, whether a linear or a quadratic drag law applies. The Reynolds number, denoted by the symbol Re, is defined by the following equation, where u is a characteristic velocity associated with the flow, d is a characteristic length scale, and the Greek symbol v ("nu") is the so-called *kinematic viscosity* of the fluid:

$$\mathrm{Re} = \frac{u\,d}{v}$$

The kinematic viscosity is defined as the ratio of the dynamic viscosity and the density of the fluid:

$$v = \frac{\mu}{\rho}$$

Using the values of dynamic viscosity and density given before, we can deduce that at 20°C the kinematic viscosity of water is 1.0×10^{-6} m²/s and that of air is 1.5×10^{-5} m²/s.

The choice of what velocity u and what length scale d to use to calculate the Reynolds number depends on the problem. For an object such as a sphere moving in a fluid, u is just the velocity of the object and d is a linear dimension (the diameter for a sphere).

Now it is found experimentally that laminar flow dominates and therefore Stokes's law for linear drag holds when the Reynolds number is much less than 1. Using the formula for the Reynolds number and setting Re = 1, this implies that the critical velocity that determines which drag law applies is given by

$$u_c \approx \frac{v}{d}$$

If the velocity of the object is much less than this critical value v_c, the drag law is linear; if it is much larger than v_c, the drag law is quadratic. If the velocity is intermediate between those two limits, a combination of both laws can be used.

As an example, the diameter of a soccer ball is 22 cm, or 0.22 m. Using the values of the kinematic viscosity of water and air given previously, we deduce that the critical velocity for such a ball is 0.1 mm/s in water and 1.5 mm/s in air (yes, those are in millimeters per second). These are tiny velocities, so for all practical purposes you can assume that a ball this size moving in water or air will always obey a quadratic drag law. This also applies to most everyday objects moving at normal velocities in air or water.

On the other hand, a ball bearing of diameter 1 mm falling in glycerin (which has a kinematic viscosity of 1.2×10^{-3} m^2/s at 20°C) has a critical velocity of 1.2 m/s. That's a much larger critical velocity. The maximum velocity that the ball bearing reaches (its terminal velocity) is much less than this. Therefore, the linear drag law applies in this case.

Adding drag to the balloon simulation

As shown in the last section, the drag law that is appropriate for most everyday objects moving in air or water is the quadratic drag law, as coded up in the Forces.drag() function. It is a very simple matter to add drag to the last example of the balloon simulation. We simply update calcForce() as follows:

```
override protected function calcForce():void{
        var gravity:Vector2D = Forces.constantGravity(_particle.mass,_g);
        _V = _particle.mass/_rhoP;
        var upthrust:Vector2D = Forces.upthrust(_rho,_V,_g);
        var drag:Vector2D = Forces.drag(_k,_particle.velo2D);
        force = Forces.add([gravity, upthrust, drag]);
}
```

The new private variable _k is the drag constant k. In the sample code provided, we give it the value of 0.01. If you run the simulation with these modifications, you'll see that the balloon no longer rises at an accelerating rate. The addition of the drag force slows down its ascent, and the effect is more realistic.

Example: Floating ball

Let's build another simulation from scratch to illustrate the effect of drag, together with upthrust and gravity. We'll simulate the motion of a ball that is thrown, dropped, or released in water.

The main code is in the file FloatingBall.as and should once again look familiar to you:

```
package{
        import flash.display.Sprite;
        import com.physicscodes.objects.Ball;
        import com.physicscodes.math.Vector2D;
        import com.physicscodes.objects.Particle;

        public class FloatingBall extends Sprite{
                public function FloatingBall():void{
                        init();
                }
                private function init():void{

                        // create a ball
                        var ball:Ball;
                        ball = new Ball(20,0x0000ff,1);
```

```
                    ball.pos2D = new Vector2D(50,50);
                    ball.velo2D = new Vector2D(40,-20);
                    addChild(ball);

                    // create water
                    var water:Sprite = new Sprite;
                    with (water.graphics) {
                            beginFill(0x00ffff,0.5);
                            drawRect(0,100,stage.stageWidth,stage.stageHeight-100);
                            endFill();
                    }
                    addChild(water);

                    // make the ball move
                    var floater:Floater=new Floater(ball);
                    floater.startTime(10);
            }
        }
}
```

First, we create a Ball instance and set its position and velocity. Then we create a bluish filled rectangle to represent water, setting its alpha property to 0.5, so that you can see the ball through it. The rectangle is positioned so that its upper edge, representing the water level, is at y = 100. Finally, the ball is moved by instantiating a Floater class and calling its startTime() method.

This is what the Floater class looks like:

```
package {
        import com.physicscodes.motion.Forcer;
        import com.physicscodes.motion.Forces;
        import com.physicscodes.objects.Particle;
        import com.physicscodes.math.Vector2D;
        import flash.events.MouseEvent;

        public class Floater extends Forcer{
                private var _particle:Particle;
                private var _g:Number=10;
                private var _rho:Number=1.5;
                private var _V:Number=1;
                private var _k:Number=0.01;
                private var _yLevel:Number=100;

                public function Floater(pparticle:Particle):void{
                        _particle = pparticle;
                        _particle.addEventListener(MouseEvent.MOUSE_DOWN,onDown);
                        super(pparticle);
                }

                override protected function calcForce():void{
                        var rball:Number=0.5*_particle.height;
                        var yball:Number=_particle.y;
                        var dr:Number= (yball-_yLevel)/rball;
                        var ratio:Number; // volume fraction of object that is submerged
                        if (dr <= -1){ // object completely out of water
```

```
                    ratio=0;
            }else if (dr < 1){ // object partially in water
                    //ratio = 0.5 + 0.5*dr; // for cuboid
                    ratio = 0.5 + 0.25*dr*(3-dr*dr); // for sphere
            }else{ // object completely in water
                    ratio=1;
            }
            var gravity:Vector2D = Forces.constantGravity(_particle.mass,_g);
            var upthrust:Vector2D = Forces.upthrust(_rho,_V*ratio,_g);
            var drag:Vector2D = Forces.drag(_k*ratio,_particle.velo2D);
            force = Forces.add([gravity, upthrust, drag]);
    }

    private function onDown(e:MouseEvent):void{
            _particle.velo2D = new Vector2D(0,0);
            _particle.stage.addEventListener(MouseEvent.MOUSE_UP,onUp);
            _particle.startDrag(true);
            stopTime();
    }
    private function onUp(e:MouseEvent):void{
            _particle.pos2D = new Vector2D(_particle.x,_particle.y);
            _particle.stage.removeEventListener(MouseEvent.MOUSE_UP,onUp);
            _particle.stopDrag();
            startTime(10);
    }
  }
}
```

As you expect, `Floater` extends `Forcer` and overrides its `calcForce()` method. We also added code that allows dragging and dropping the ball, which should be self-explanatory. Of course, the user won't be able to drag the ball when it's completely immersed in water.

Let us focus on the code within the `calcForce()` method. The last four lines of the code should be evident: we are calculating the three forces (gravity, upthrust, and drag) that act on the ball and then adding them up to obtain the resultant force. The new thing here is the inclusion of a factor called `ratio`, which is the fraction by volume of the ball that is submerged in the water. This is used to compute the upthrust in the water (according to Archimedes's principle), and the drag in the water (assuming that this is also proportional to the volume fraction that is submerged—it is actually a fairly crude approximation, but will help keep things much simpler). For simplicity, we neglect the upthrust and drag forces that the ball might experience in air. It is not difficult to see how they could be included too, if needed. All this should be easy to follow; the subtlety is in the piece of code that calculates `ratio`.

To calculate `ratio`, you need to do some geometrical thinking. Take a look at Figure 7-9, which represents a cuboid and a sphere partially immersed in water. In our Flash movie, assuming that the registration point of the corresponding objects is at the center of the objects, we need a formula that gives `ratio` in terms of the position of the object and the position of the water level.

Figure 7-9. Objects partially immersed in water

To do this, it turns out to be convenient to first define a parameter dr that tells you how much the center of the object is above or below the water level, as a fraction of the radius of the ball (or half-height of the cuboid). So, dr is defined as the following, where r is the half-height of the object (and is equal to the radius for the ball):

$$dr = \frac{\text{position of object - water level}}{\text{half-height of object}} = \frac{d}{r}$$

A little bit of thinking should convince you that dr = −1 means that the object (whether ball or cuboid) is just completely out of the water, and that dr = 1 means that it is just completely inside the water. Therefore, if dr <= −1, ratio is zero, and if dr >= 1, ratio is 1. The trickier bit is when the object is partially submerged. In the case of a cuboid, simple geometry tells us that (yes, you can work it out yourself)

$$\text{ratio} = 0.5 + 0.5\,dr$$

In the case of a sphere, it's a bit more complicated to work out (you need to do a bit of calculus), but here is the formula:

$$\text{ratio} = 0.5 + 0.25\,dr\left(3 - dr^2\right)$$

That's all we need.

In the code, the volume _V of the ball is set to 1, and its mass is also 1. Therefore, its density (= mass/volume) is 1. The density of the water is set to 1.5. Therefore, because the density of the ball is less than that of the water, it will float.

In FloatingBall.as, the initial position and velocity of the ball are given as follows:

```
ball.pos2D = new Vector2D(50,50);
ball.velo2D = new Vector2D(40,-20);
```

This puts the ball initially above the water and imparts a velocity with an upward component and a component to the right. If you run the code, you'll see that the ball then follows a curved (parabolic) path in the air until it hits the water. It then slows down suddenly because of the drag and upthrust in the water, sinking a bit and then rising again to the surface and oscillating on the water surface until it stops. A screenshot of the simulation is shown in Figure 7-10.

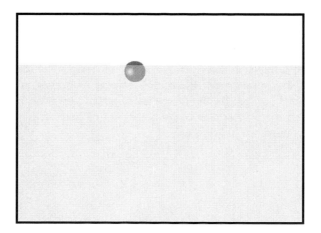

Figure 7-10. A floating ball

The simulation is so realistic that you can experiment with it to learn about the physics involved! While the ball floats, drag it by clicking on any part that is above the water. Then release it above the water. It will fall into the water, decelerate, rise, and again oscillate on the water surface a few times before stopping. The higher you drop it, the further it will sink. Now drag it and release it underwater. It will rise to the surface and again oscillate a few times before stopping.

You can also play around by changing the initial conditions or the values of the parameters. For example, change the mass of the ball to 2 or the volume to 0.5, so that the density is 2. The ball will then sink instead of floating because its density is greater than the density of the water, which is 1.5.

Want to try something different? What would happen if the ball were very light? Try it. Reduce the density to 0.5 by increasing the volume to 2. What happens when you release the ball under water? It shoots out into the air, before falling back into the water. If you've ever tried doing this with a real ball, you'll know that it's a real effect. Our simulation is so realistic it can be used to perform "virtual experiments". And we haven't even paid any attention to numerical accuracy (which we'll look at in Part Four of the book).

This example is particularly instructive in that it shows how a simulation that includes the relevant physics can behave pretty much like the real thing would do in real life. The simulation knows how to deal with any change in initial conditions or parameters, without the need for you to tell it anything more! This is the power of real physics simulation. It gives you a lot for your money, perhaps more than you'd expect—and it's much easier than faking it!

Terminal velocity

As you discovered in the last examples, the presence of the drag force means that the velocity of a rising or falling object cannot increase indefinitely. To understand why, consider the case of an object released from a height (far from the ground) and falling under gravity. This example was discussed in Chapter 4 and elaborated upon in Chapter 5, but it is worth having a recap here to gain a deeper understanding, now that we know more about the drag force. In particular, the previous discussions were in terms of the linear drag formula; it is useful to know how the results generalize to quadratic drag, and also when upthrust is taken into account.

In Figure 7-11, there is a downward gravity force W = mg acting on the object, and an upward drag force D. The drag force has a magnitude given by kv at very low velocities but more usually by kv². Now initially the velocity of the object is zero, so that the drag force is zero. As it accelerates under gravity, its velocity increases and therefore the drag force increases, too. This reduces the resultant downward force to W – D, and therefore reduces the acceleration. Because the force of gravity is constant, as the velocity increases, there will be a point at which the drag force will be equal to gravity; in other words, the resultant force W – D will be zero, so the acceleration of the object will be zero. In other words, it will eventually move at a constant velocity: the terminal velocity.

Figure 7-11. Force balance giving rise to terminal velocity

As shown in Chapter 4, it is easy to work out the magnitude of the terminal velocity. It is the value of v at which W – D = 0. Because W = mg, if we use D = kv, we get this:

$$m\,g = k\,v$$

So that

$$v = \frac{m\,g}{k}$$

This is the terminal velocity for laminar flow. It holds for an object moving in a fluid with high viscosity (such as oil).

If we use the drag law for higher velocities, D = kv², we instead get

$$m\,g = k\,v^2$$

It then implies that

$$v = \sqrt{\frac{m\,g}{k}}$$

We can also generalize these formulas to include upthrust (see Figure 7-12) by replacing the weight W = mg by the absolute value of the apparent weight $W_{apparent} = (\rho_{object} - \rho_{fluid})\,V\,g$.

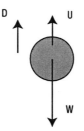

Figure 7-12. Force balance with upthrust

If you are doing a simulation in which the object attains terminal velocity very quickly, you may get away with just giving the object a constant velocity equal to the terminal velocity by making use of the preceding formulas. This will preserve the physical realism of the simulation (if the initial acceleration is not important) while cutting down the computing time significantly. For example, bubbles rising in water attain terminal velocity very rapidly and can be simulated in this way if there are no other forces apart from gravity, upthrust, and drag.

As discussed in Chapter 5, the motion of an object under gravity, upthrust, and drag can be solved analytically using calculus to give not only the terminal velocity but also the velocity at any time. For example, for an object dropped from rest in a fluid, the analytical solution assuming linear drag and neglecting upthrust is given by

$$v = \frac{mg}{k}\left[1 - \exp\left(-k\,t/m\right)\right]$$

This gives the velocity of the object at time t after being dropped. The solutions with quadratic drag and including upthrust look a bit more complicated, and you can find them in physics textbooks.

Example: Parachute

Parachutes work by exploiting the fact that the drag force is proportional to the area of an object. Going back to the formula for quadratic drag $\mathbf{F} = -k\mathbf{v}v$, with the drag constant k given by $k = \frac{1}{2}\,\rho A C_d$, we can see that the larger the area of an object, the greater the drag force will be. Opening a parachute suddenly increases the surface area exposed to the air, thereby increasing the value of k. This greatly increases the drag force and therefore slows down a parachutist.

Our present example is an educational exercise to illustrate this principle. Take a look at ParachuteTest.as:

```
package{
        import flash.display.Sprite;
        import com.physicscodes.objects.Ball;
        import com.physicscodes.math.Vector2D;
        import com.physicscodes.objects.Particle;

        public class ParachuteTest extends Sprite{
                public function ParachuteTest():void{
                        init();
```

```
        }
        private function init():void{

                // create a sky diver
                var skydiver:Ball;
                skydiver = new Ball(20,0x0000ff,1);
                skydiver.pos2D = new Vector2D(650,50);
                addChild(skydiver);

                // make the skydiver fall
                var parachute:Parachute=new Parachute(skydiver);
                parachute.startTime(10);
        }
    }
}
```

This simply creates a skydiver as a Ball instance (!) and then sends him into a parachute fall using the Parachute class, which looks like this:

```
package {
        import com.physicscodes.motion.Forcer;
        import com.physicscodes.motion.Forces;
        import com.physicscodes.objects.Ball;
        import com.physicscodes.math.Vector2D;
        import com.physicscodes.math.Graph;
        import flash.events.MouseEvent;

        public class Parachute extends Forcer{

                private var _particle:Ball;
                private var _g:Number=10;
                private var _rho:Number=0.1;
                private var _V:Number=1;
                private var _k:Number=0.01;
                private var _linearFactor:Number=3;
                private var _graph:Graph;

                public function Parachute(pparticle:Ball):void{
                        _particle = pparticle;
                        _particle.stage.addEventListener(MouseEvent.MOUSE_DOWN,
openParachute);
                        setupGraph();
                        super(pparticle);
                }
                override protected function moveObject():void{
                        super.moveObject();
                        plotGraph();
                }
                override protected function calcForce():void{
                        var gravity:Vector2D = Forces.constantGravity(_particle.mass,_g);
                        var upthrust:Vector2D = Forces.upthrust(_rho,_V,_g);
                        var drag:Vector2D = Forces.drag(_k,_particle.velo2D);
                        force = Forces.add([gravity, upthrust, drag]);
                }
```

```
            private function openParachute(evt:MouseEvent):void{
                    _k *= _linearFactor*_linearFactor;
                    _particle.radius *= _linearFactor;
                    _particle.stage.removeEventListener(MouseEvent.MOUSE_DOWN,
openParachute);
            }
            private function setupGraph():void{
                    _graph = new Graph(0,100,0,50,50,350,450,300);
                    _graph.drawgrid(10,5,10,5);
                    _graph.drawaxes('t','vy');
                    _particle.stage.addChild(_graph);
            }
            private function plotGraph():void{
                    _graph.plot([time], [_particle.vy], 0xff0000, false, true);
            }
        }
    }
```

Parachute extends `Forcer` and overrides `calcForce()`, adding gravity, upthrust, and drag in the usual way. In addition, an event listener is set up in the constructor for a `MOUSE_DOWN` event. In the corresponding event handler `openParachute()`, the radius of the parachute is increased by a factor equal to `_linearFactor` (which is given the value of 3 in the code), and the value of the drag constant `_k` is increased by a factor equal to the square of `_linearFactor` (by 9). The event listener is then removed. This means that the parachute is made three times bigger (by radius) and the drag constant is made nine times larger the first time the user clicks the mouse. Finally, a `Graph` object is set up in `setupGraph()`, which is called in the constructor, and used to plot the vy component of the parachute's velocity at each time by calling the `plotGraph()` method within the `moveObject()` method.

If you now run the code (without opening the parachute) you'll find that the parachute accelerates quickly at first, more slowly until it reaches a constant velocity (terminal velocity) about 10 seconds into the fall. The value of the terminal velocity is approximately 30 pixels per second. If you then click to "open the parachute," it will become bigger and immediately slow down, reaching a new lower terminal velocity of approximately 10 pixels per second in a few seconds. The terminal velocity is the same whenever you open the parachute: it's independent of time, only depending on the mass m of the parachute, the acceleration due to gravity g, and the drag constant k through the formula $v = \sqrt{mg/k}$. Figure 7-13 shows a typical shape of the velocity-time graph.

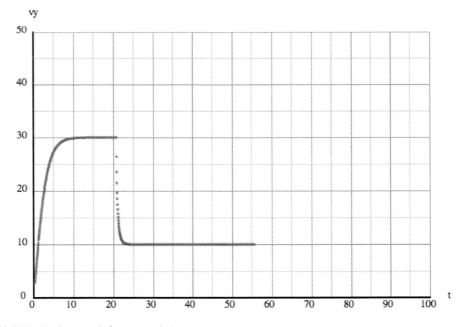

Figure 7-13. Velocity-time graph for a parachute

Lift

You saw that the drag force depends upon the dynamic pressure. There is another force that also depends on the dynamic pressure: it's called lift. More precisely, it is the difference in dynamic pressure on opposite sides of an object that is responsible for these forces. Whereas the drag force on an object acts opposite to the velocity of the object, the lift force acts perpendicular to the velocity (see Figure 7-14). Now, because there is always a difference in the dynamic pressure between the front and back of a moving object, there is always a drag force on a moving object. However, if an object is perfectly symmetrical along an axis in the direction of motion, the flow (and therefore the dynamic pressure) on either side of the object will be exactly the same). In that case, there is no lift force. But any asymmetry in the flow—for example, caused by an asymmetrical wing shape (for aircraft) or angle of attack, will give rise to a lift force perpendicular to the direction of motion.

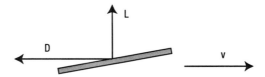

Figure 7-14. Drag and lift force on an object moving in a fluid

The lift force is what enables airplanes to fly. In that case, the direction of motion is usually horizontal, so the lift force acts vertically upward and balances the weight of the plane. But lift does not always have to act vertically upward. Depending on the direction of motion, it can act in any direction.

Lift is sometimes confused with upthrust. In fact, upthrust is sometimes mistakenly referred to as lift. Like upthrust, lift arises because of a difference in pressure. Upthrust is due to the difference in static pressure between the top and bottom of an object that is due to the weight of the displaced fluid (buoyancy); but lift is due to the difference in dynamic pressure between opposite sides of an object that lie along the direction of its motion. This causes a difference in the static pressure between the opposite sides mentioned earlier. Thus, whereas upthrust is always upward (as its name suggests), this is not necessarily so for lift. More crucially, the physics laws and therefore the formulas that govern these two forces are completely different. Consider this: lift is the force that makes an airplane fly; upthrust is the force that makes a balloon float; the mechanisms are different in the two cases.

Lift coefficients

The lift force is modeled in terms of a lift coefficient, in exactly the same way as quadratic drag. Hence the magnitude of the lift force can be written as follows, where C_L is the *lift coefficient* and A is the area of the object along the direction of motion (rather than perpendicular to it as for drag):

$$F = \frac{1}{2} \rho A C_L v^2$$

Like the drag coefficient C_d, the lift coefficient C_L depends on a variety of factors. For aircraft, the important variables are wing shape and angle of attack.

As we did for the drag force, we can define a lift constant $k = \frac{1}{2} \rho A C_L$, which then enables us to write the magnitude of the lift force as $F = kv^2$.

The direction of the lift force is perpendicular to the direction of the velocity. Taking this into account, we can define a Forces.lift() function as follows:

```
static public function lift(k:Number,vel:Vector2D):Vector2D {
        var force:Vector2D;
        var velMag:Number=vel.length;
        if (velMag>0) {
                force=vel.perp(k*velMag);
        }else {
                force=new Vector2D(0,0);
        }
        return force;
}
```

Example: An airplane

Let's now demonstrate how the lift force can make an airplane fly. The file Airplane.as contains the setup code for a basic flight demonstration:

```
package{
        import flash.display.Sprite;
        import com.physicscodes.objects.Ball;
        import com.physicscodes.math.Vector2D;
```

```
            import com.physicscodes.objects.Particle;

    public class Airplane extends Sprite{
            public function Airplane():void{
                    init();
            }
            private function init():void{

                    // create a plane
                    var plane:Plane = new Plane();
                    plane.width *= 0.3;
                    plane.height *= 0.3;
                    plane.pos2D = new Vector2D(100,750);
                    plane.velo2D = new Vector2D(0,0);
                    addChild(plane);

                    // make the plane fly
                    var flyer:Flyer=new Flyer(plane);
                    flyer.startTime(10);
            }
    }
}
```

A plane object is created (in the Flash version, from a Plane symbol in the library) and placed on the "runway" with an initial velocity of zero. Then the plane is made to move by instantiating a Flyer class. Here is the code in Flyer.as:

```
package {
        import com.physicscodes.motion.Forcer;
        import com.physicscodes.motion.Forces;
        import com.physicscodes.objects.Particle;
        import com.physicscodes.math.Vector2D;

        public class Flyer extends Forcer{

                private var _particle:Particle;
                private var _g:Number=10;
                private var _kDrag:Number=0.01;
                private var _kLift:Number=0.5;
                private var _magThrust:Number=5;
                private var _groundLevel:Number=750;

                public function Flyer(pparticle:Particle):void{
                        _particle = pparticle;
                        super(pparticle);
                }

                override protected function calcForce():void{
                        var gravity:Vector2D = Forces.constantGravity(_particle.mass,_g);
                        var velX:Vector2D = new Vector2D(_particle.vx,0);
                        var drag:Vector2D = Forces.drag(_kDrag,velX);
                        var lift:Vector2D = Forces.lift(_kLift,velX);
                        var thrust:Vector2D = new Vector2D(_magThrust,0);
                        var normal:Vector2D;
```

```
            if (_particle.y >= _groundLevel){
                    normal = gravity.multiply(-1);
            }else{
                    normal = new Vector2D(0,0);
            }
            force = Forces.add([gravity, drag, lift, thrust, normal]);
        }
    }
}
```

As depicted in Figure 7-15, there are four main forces on an airplane in flight: gravity (W), thrust (T), drag (D), and lift (L). When the airplane is on the ground, there is also the normal contact force due to the ground. Hence, the calcForce() method of Flyer computes these forces and adds them up. Gravity is straightforward as usual. The drag and lift forces are computed in a simplified way, by only considering the horizontal component of the airplane's velocity. Also, the airplane is assumed to be horizontal at all times, with an angle of attack that is zero. The thrust is modeled as a constant force. Finally, the normal force is set to be equal and opposite to gravity when the plane is on the ground, and zero otherwise.

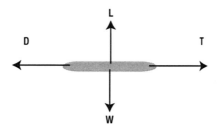

Figure 7-15. The four forces on a airplane in flight

When you run the simulation, you'll see that the plane takes off only when it has attained a high enough velocity to create sufficient lift to overcome its weight (see Figure 7-16). If you reduce the magnitude of the thrust _magThrust to 3 or 4, the plane moves along the runway, but never takes off. Under the horizontal thrust and drag forces, it attains a maximum horizontal velocity (similar to terminal velocity) that is insufficient to generate enough lift to overcome its weight.

Figure 7-16. Plane flying due to the lift force

To reiterate, we've made a lot of simplifications in this example. We'll build a much more complete and realistic flight simulator in the final chapter, in which we'll also look at the drag, lift, and thrust forces on an airplane in more detail.

Wind and turbulence

Wind is not itself a force, but it can generate forces. Wind is the movement of air, and has an associated velocity at each point in space and time. It can be quite complicated, but fairly realistic effects can be achieved even with simple models of the wind. A constant wind blowing over a stationary object can be viewed in a similar way to an object moving through air, with the direction reversed. It generates drag and lift forces in a similar way.

Force due to the wind

As we saw at the beginning of the chapter, moving fluids have an associated dynamic pressure. Wind is nothing but moving air. When wind blows on an object or surface, it therefore exerts a force due to the dynamic pressure.

How do we calculate this force? According to what we said, only the relative velocity matters. So, the force exerted by the wind is just the drag force in reverse, where **w** is the wind velocity:

$$F = \frac{1}{2}\rho A C_d\, w\, \mathbf{w}$$

Hence, we can use the drag force function to model wind, using the wind velocity and a negative drag constant k.

Wind and drag

An object moving in air will, of course, still experience drag, even in the presence of wind. Therefore, the net force due to the motion of the object and that of the air (wind) will be the drag force taking as reference the relative velocity between the object and the air. Therefore, the combined force due to wind and drag is given by the following, where $|\mathbf{w} - \mathbf{v}|$ denotes the magnitude of the vector $(\mathbf{w} - \mathbf{v})$:

$$F = \frac{1}{2}\rho A C_d \left|\mathbf{w} - \mathbf{v}\right|\left(\mathbf{w} - \mathbf{v}\right)$$

Note that $|\mathbf{w} - \mathbf{v}|$ is *not* usually equal to the difference $(w - v)$ in the magnitudes of $\mathbf{w}$ and $\mathbf{v}$.

We can use the drag force function to compute the combined effect of wind and drag by using the relative velocity between an object and the air.

Steady and turbulent flow

We now know how to calculate the force on an object in the presence of wind given the wind velocity. But how do we model the wind velocity $\mathbf{w}$ itself?

The answer is that it depends on the situation we are modeling. The behavior of the wind is rather complicated because it varies both in space and in time. Wind depends on complex atmospheric conditions as well as obstacles such as buildings and trees. However, for most purposes, you'd probably want to keep things as simple as you can get away with. So we'll discuss only some simple ways of modeling the wind velocity.

The simplest model of the wind is to assume that the velocity $\mathbf{w}$ is constant both in space and time. This corresponds to what is called a uniform and steady flow. A slightly more complicated model is to assume a steady flow (still constant in time) that is constant horizontally but varies with height. This model would account for the fact that the wind speed is lower near the ground and becomes higher farther up.

Most of the time, the wind is not steady, but consists of gusts that blow apparently randomly. The gusts produce what is called turbulent flow, which can make things move in complex ways.

Example: Air bubbles in a steady wind

In this example, we'll model a steady and uniform wind blowing some bubbles in air. `BubblesWind.as` contains the setup code:

```
package{
        import flash.display.Sprite;
        import com.physicscodes.objects.Ball;
        import com.physicscodes.math.Vector2D;
        import com.physicscodes.objects.Particle;

        public class BubblesWind extends Sprite{
                public function BubblesWind():void{
                        init();
                }
```

```
private function init():void{

        // create bubbles
        var bubbles:Array = new Array();
        var color:uint = 0x00ffff;
        var numBubbles:Number = 20;
        var rho:Number = 0.99;
        for (var i:uint=1; i<=numBubbles; i++){
                var radius:Number = Math.random()*20+5;
                var V:Number = 4*Math.PI*Math.pow(radius,3)/3;
                var mass:Number = rho*V;
                var bubble:Ball = new Ball(radius,color,mass);
                bubble.pos2D=newVector2D(Math.random()*stage.stageWidth, ↪
Math.random()*stage.stageHeight);
                bubble.velo2D=new Vector2D((Math.random()-0.5)*20,0);
                addChild(bubble);
                bubbles.push(bubble);
        }

        // make the bubbles move
        var mover:BubbleWindMover=new BubbleWindMover(bubbles);
        mover.startTime(10);
    }
  }
}
```

We're creating a bunch of bubbles as `Ball` objects and giving them a random radius. Their volume and mass are then calculated using the formula for the volume of a sphere and the density of the bubbles, which is specified as 0.99. The bubbles are given a random position and a small random horizontal velocity. Then they are collected into an array, which is then passed as a parameter into the constructor of the class that contains the simulation "engine" `BubbleWindMover`.

Here is the code in `BubbleWindMover.as`:

```
package {
        import com.physicscodes.motion.MultiForcer;
        import com.physicscodes.motion.Forces;
        import com.physicscodes.objects.Particle;
        import com.physicscodes.math.Vector2D;

        public class BubbleWindMover extends MultiForcer{

                private var _particles:Array;
                private var _g:Number=10;
                private var _rho:Number=1;
                private var _rhoP:Number=0.99;
                private var _kfac:Number=0.01;
                private var _windvel:Vector2D = new Vector2D(40,0);

                public function BubbleWindMover(pparticles:Array):void{
                        _particles = pparticles;
                        super(pparticles);
                }
```

```
override protected function calcForce(pparticle:Particle):void{
        var V:Number = pparticle.mass/_rhoP;
        var k:Number = pparticle.width*pparticle.width*_kfac;
        var gravity:Vector2D = Forces.constantGravity(pparticle.mass,_g);
        var upthrust:Vector2D = Forces.upthrust(_rho,V,_g);
        var relwind:Vector2D = _windvel.subtract(pparticle.velo2D);
        var wind:Vector2D = Forces.drag(-k,relwind);
        force = Forces.add([gravity, upthrust, wind]);
    }
  }
}
```

BubbleWindMover extends MultiForcer, overriding its calcForce() method. Three forces are calculated and added: gravity, upthrust, and the wind (drag) force. The upthrust is calculated using the volume of each bubble, worked out using the formula volume = mass/density. To compute the force due to wind, the relative velocity is computed by subtracting the bubble's current velocity from the velocity of the wind _windvel, which is given as a constant horizontal vector. The wind/drag force is then calculated by using Forces.drag() with a negative drag coefficient –k and the relative velocity as arguments. Note that k includes a factor equal to the square of the bubble's width. That's to take into account the fact that the drag force is proportional to the area of the bubble, which is itself proportional to the square of its diameter.

If you run the simulation, you'll see that the bubbles drift in the direction of the wind while rising slowly, as you'd expect (see Figure 7-17). Play with the wind velocity and other parameters to see how the motion is modified.

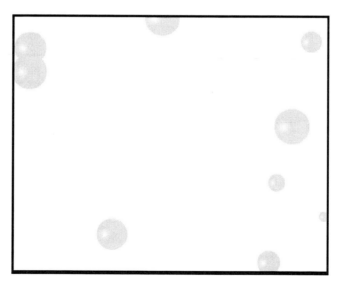

Figure 7-17. Bubbles in a steady wind

Modeling turbulence

Turbulence is a complex phenomenon. In fact, it is so complex that you need huge supercomputers with hundreds of processors to accurately compute turbulent flows even for simple configurations. On the other hand, there are numerous approaches for modeling turbulence in an approximate way. One simple approach is to use random numbers.

You can produce effects that look like turbulence by superimposing random noise on an otherwise steady wind field. This exploits the statistical properties of turbulence, which can usually be represented by decomposing the wind velocity at any time in the following way, where $\mathbf{w}_{steady}$ is a steady part and $\mathbf{w}_{fluctuating}$ is a time-varying part that captures the turbulent fluctuations:

$$\mathbf{w} = \mathbf{w}_{steady} + \mathbf{w}_{fluctuating}$$

The steady part $\mathbf{w}_{steady}$ is just a constant vector, as we modeled in the previous bubbles simulation. We can model $\mathbf{w}_{fluctuating}$ by a vector whose components are random numbers that are updated at each timestep. To do this in the bubbles simulation, just add the following line of code at the beginning of calcForce() in BubbleWindMover.as:

```
_windvel = new Vector2D(20 + (Math.random()-0.5)*1000,(Math.random()-0.5)*1000);
```

We did this and saved the new file as BubbleTurbulenceMover.as, together with a modified setup file BubblesTurbulence.as. We also added some code to indicate the variation of the wind vector **w**. The code produces a line in the middle of the stage directed along the instantaneous wind direction and with length proportional to the magnitude of the wind velocity.

The preceding line of code specifies the wind velocity **w** as the sum of a steady wind vector (20, 0) that blows to the right at 20 pixels per second, and a random wind vector (Math.random()-0.5)*1000,(Math.random()-0.5)*1000) with x and y components that range from −500 to 500 pixels per second. The wind velocity is the same at all locations on the stage.

Experiment by changing these values to whatever you like. The magnitude of the steady wind (here set by the value of 20) gives the bubbles a steady drift. The magnitude of the fluctuations (here set by the factor of 1000), controls the gustiness of the wind and makes the bubbles fluctuate. You can produce a fairly convincing turbulence effect in this way.

Summary

This chapter introduced a number of forces that act on solid objects in contact with other solid objects or with fluids. If you are simulating nearly anything on Earth, chances are you'll need to model these forces. What you learned in this chapter has given you a solid foundation upon which you can build to create more complex effects and simulations. In the final chapter, you will have the opportunity to develop more complete simulations using the physics explained here.

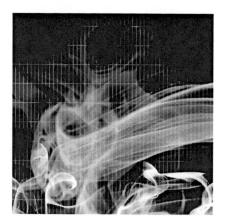

Chapter 8

Restoring Forces: Springs and Oscillations

Springs are among the most useful tools you'll come across, especially when it comes to creating interesting physics effects. A great many systems can be modeled using springs and spring-like motion. Therefore, learning the basics of spring motion is time well spent. But beware: springs are strangely addictive!

Topics covered in this chapter include the following:

- **Free oscillations**: An object will oscillate under the action of a spring force, also known as a *restoring force*.

- **Damped oscillations**: Damping dissipates the energy of oscillations so that they die out with time.

- **Forced oscillations**: Oscillations can be driven by external forces that sustain them against damping forces.

- **Coupled oscillators**: Interesting effects can be produced by using multiple springs and objects coupled together.

Springs and oscillations: Basic concepts

We introduced oscillations back in Chapter 3, while discussing sinusoidal waves and their combinations (refer to the section "Using trig functions for animation"). An *oscillation* is a repeating motion around some central position. Simple examples of oscillating systems include a pendulum and a swing.

Oscillations abound in natural systems, too: trees oscillate under a blowing wind, and floating objects oscillate on the water surface due to passing waves. Man-made mechanisms that include springs involve oscillations. Hence, there is an intuitive association between oscillations and springs; in fact, we will use the terms *oscillations* and *spring-like motion* interchangeably. This association is more than verbal: oscillating systems can usually be modeled using virtual "springs."

What causes oscillations and why are they so common? Let's answer these questions before we begin to model springs and spring-like behavior.

Spring-like motion

You've already met spring-like motion in this book, probably without realizing it. The floating ball simulation of the last chapter provided an example in which the ball oscillated on the water surface in a spring-like fashion. Lots of other things undergo spring-like motion: the suspension mechanism of a car; and the swaying of a tree, its branches, and their leaves in the wind. Other things, although they don't necessarily appear to be spring-like, can nevertheless be modeled using springs: deformable bodies such as ropes, clothes, and hair. Surely then, there must be common characteristics that these systems exhibit that make them amenable to modeling using springs. So, what are the general characteristics of oscillating systems?

Restoring force, damping, and forcing

An oscillating system will usually involve the following ingredients:

- An *equilibrium position* in which an object would remain if it were not moving.

- A *restoring force* that pulls the object back toward the equilibrium position if it is displaced.

- A *damping force* that reduces the oscillations with time.

- A *driving force* that displaces the object from its equilibrium position.

Of those, the first two are essential to generate oscillations, whereas the last two may or may not be present, depending on the system. Although more complex systems may not appear to show these characteristics, they can be composed of (or be modeled by) component parts that do—such as a rope that can be represented as a chain of springs.

In understanding the roles of the restoring force, damping and forcing, a relevant concept is that of *amplitude*. The amplitude of an oscillation is the maximum displacement from the equilibrium position. If you pull a swing away from its equilibrium position and then let go, the initial displacement will be the amplitude of the oscillation.

The restoring force changes the displacement with time, but it does not change the amplitude (maximum displacement). The amplitude depends on the amount of energy in the system. A damping force takes away energy from the system and therefore reduces the amplitude with time. This is what would happen if, after initially displacing it, you left the swing to oscillate on its own. A driving force puts energy into the system and therefore tends to increase the amplitude of the oscillations. With both damping and forcing being present, it is possible for the energy put into the system to compensate exactly for the energy lost by damping. In that case, the amplitude remains constant with time, as if only a restoring force were present. In the swing example, this is achieved by pushing the swing periodically with the right amount of force.

Hooke's law

In most oscillating systems, the force law that governs the restoring force is Hooke's law (because a gentleman name Robert Hooke discovered it at some point in history).

Hooke's law is quite simple. Let's explain it for springs first because that's the original form of the law. Take a look at Figure 8-1, which shows a spring of natural length l, fixed at one end, that is then stretched by an amount x, so that its length becomes l + x.

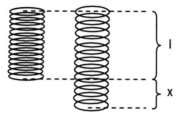

Figure 8-1. A stretched spring experiences a restoring force proportional to the extension x.

Hooke's law then says that the spring will be pulled back by a force of magnitude F given by

$$F = -k\,x$$

In other words, the restoring force is proportional to the extension x. The constant of proportionality k is known as the *spring constant*, and it is a measure of the stiffness of the spring. The larger the value of k is, the larger the force will be for a given extension, so that the spring will be pulled back more strongly when stretched.

The minus sign indicates that the force is in the opposite direction to the extension. So if the spring is compressed instead, the force will push back to increase its length.

The vector form of the equation is this, where now **r** is interpreted as the displacement vector of the free endpoint of the spring:

$$\mathbf{F} = -k\,\mathbf{r}$$

For most of what we'll do in this chapter (and probably for what you'll want to do, too, we won't care much about the actual spring. What we'll be more interested in is the motion of a particle attached to the end of a spring. How would such an object move? As every kid knows, it will oscillate about the equilibrium position.

In fact, we could get rid of the spring altogether and just consider the effect of the restoring force on the particle. This is what we'll do in many examples. In such a case, the displacement vector **r** in Hooke's law is interpreted as the displacement from the equilibrium position about which the particle is oscillating, as shown in Figure 8-2.

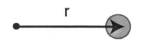

Figure 8-2. A particle oscillating about an equilibrium position

A word of warning before we end this section: it should not be assumed that all oscillations obey Hooke's law; many don't. However, a great many types of moving systems follow Hooke's law, at least approximately. So we'll stick with Hooke's law in this chapter.

Free oscillations

Let's start by modeling *free oscillations*. What that means is that the system oscillates purely under the action of the restoring force, without any other force. Of course, for an object to oscillate, something (an applied force) must have moved it away from its equilibrium position in the first place. But what we are interested in here is what happens after that initial forcing is removed and the oscillating system is left to itself.

The spring force function

To begin with, we need to create a new force function in the Forces class for the restoring force. Let's call it spring(). It is a very simple function:

```
static public function spring(k:Number,r:Vector2D):Vector2D {
        return r.multiply(-k);
}
```

The function spring() takes two arguments, which are the spring constant k and the displacement vector r (this is just the vector r in the previous formulas). It returns the restoring force F = –k r.

Let's now use that function to create a basic oscillator.

Creating a basic oscillator

You know what's coming next, don't you? Here is some code that creates the object that we want to oscillate as a Ball object called object. We don't actually create a spring (in the visual sense) but instead another Ball object that we call attractor, whose position will be the equilibrium position. We then pass both object and attractor to the constructor of a BasicOscillator object, which is what will create the oscillations. Both are given an initial velocity of zero and are placed some distance apart by giving them different position vectors pos2D:

```
package{
        import flash.display.Sprite;
        import com.physicscodes.objects.Ball;
        import com.physicscodes.math.Vector2D;
        import com.physicscodes.objects.Particle;

        public class BasicOscillations extends Sprite{
```

```
                public function BasicOscillations():void{
                        init();
                }

                private function init():void{
                        // create an object
                        var object:Ball;
                        object = new Ball(15,0x0000cc,1);
                        object.pos2D = new Vector2D(100,50);
                        object.velo2D=new Vector2D(0,0);
                        addChild(object);

                        // create a spring
                        var attractor:Ball;
                        attractor=new Ball(2,0x000000);
                        attractor.pos2D=new Vector2D(275,200);
                        attractor.velo2D=new Vector2D(0,0);
                        addChild(attractor)

                        // make the object-spring system move
                        var oscillator:BasicOscillator=new BasicOscillator(object,attractor);
                        oscillator.startTime(10);
                }
        }
}
```

And here is the code for `BasicOscillator`:

```
package {
        import com.physicscodes.motion.Forcer;
        import com.physicscodes.motion.Forces;
        import com.physicscodes.objects.Ball;
        import com.physicscodes.math.Vector2D;

        public class BasicOscillator extends Forcer{
                private var _object:Ball;
                private var _center:Vector2D;
                private var _displ:Vector2D;
                private var _kSpring:Number=1;

                public function BasicOscillator(pobject:Ball,pattractor:Ball):void{
                        _object = pobject;
                        _center = pattractor.pos2D;
                        super(_object);
                }
                override protected function calcForce():void{
                        _displ=_object.pos2D.subtract(_center);
                        force = Forces.spring(_kSpring,_displ);
                }
        }
}
```

Pretty standard stuff, with the overridden `calcForce()` method first calculating the displacement vector `_displ` of the object relative to the attractor and then using it to calculate the spring force that the attractor exerts on the object. The parameter `_kSpring` is the spring constant k.

Run the code and you'll see the ball oscillate about the attractor, as expected. Now change the spring constant value from 1 to 10. This gives you a stiff spring. If you now run the code, you'll see the ball oscillate faster. If you want it to oscillate at a different amplitude, just change the initial position in `BasicOscillations.as`.

Next change the value of k back to 1, then change the initial velocity of the ball to (200,0):

```
object.velo2D=new Vector2D(200,0);
```

When you run the code, you should now see the ball "orbit" the attractor in some sort of oval trajectory. It's a bit like what you saw with gravity in Chapter 6. Both gravity and springs are attractive forces that always act toward a point. But gravity *decreases* with distance, whereas the spring force *increases* with distance. That's because gravity is proportional to $1/r^2$, whereas the spring force is proportional to r, where r is the distance from the center of attraction.

Simple harmonic motion

The type of oscillatory motion you've just seen is technically called *simple harmonic motion* (SHM). An object undergoes SHM if the only force acting on it is the spring force, as was the case in the previous example.

Because the only force in SHM is the restoring force **F** = –kr, and Newton's second law says that **F** = ma, these two equations together tell us that for SHM:

$$m\,\mathbf{a} = -k\,\mathbf{r}$$

Dividing both sides of this equation by m gives this:

$$\mathbf{a} = -\frac{k}{m}\mathbf{r}$$

Here m is the mass of the oscillating particle, and k is the spring constant, so the ratio k/m is a constant. This equation therefore tells us that the acceleration of the oscillating particle is proportional to its displacement vector from the center. The constant of proportionality is negative, meaning that the acceleration is always opposite to the displacement vector (it always points toward the center because the displacement vector always points away from the center by definition). See Figure 8-3.

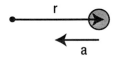

Figure 8-3. The acceleration in SHM always points toward the center, opposite to displacement

Remember back in Chapter 3 where we talked about derivatives and said that acceleration is the second derivative of displacement? This means the following:

$$\mathbf{a} = \frac{d^2\mathbf{r}}{dt^2}$$

Therefore we can write the SHM equation $\mathbf{a} = -(k/m)\mathbf{r}$ in the equivalent form:

$$\frac{d^2\mathbf{r}}{dt^2} = -\frac{k}{m}\mathbf{r}$$

This makes it clear that the equation that governs SHM is a second–order differential equation, as described in Chapter 5. What `BasicOscillator` has been doing is to solve this second–order differential equation numerically using the Euler scheme (again as described in Chapter 5). As a reminder, `BasicOscillator` extends `Forcer`, which itself extends `Mover`; and `Forcer` integrates the acceleration to give the velocity (in the `updateVelo()` method), whereas `Mover` integrates the velocity to give the displacement (in `moveObject()`), both using Euler.

In fact the preceding differential equation can also be solved analytically to give a formula for the displacement as a function of time. This is an exercise in college-level calculus, and here is the solution, where **A** and **B** are constant vectors that depend on the initial conditions, and ω is the angular velocity of the oscillation (see Chapter 3):

$$\mathbf{r} = \mathbf{A}\cos(\omega t) + \mathbf{B}\sin(\omega t)$$

Hence, SHM consists of the sum of a sine and a cosine function. This is not surprising because SHM is basically an oscillatory motion and, as you know from Chapter 3, sin and cos are oscillatory functions. The value of ω sets the frequency and therefore the period of oscillation, whereas the values of **A** and **B** set the amplitude of the oscillations (the maximum displacement of the object from its equilibrium position).

Anyone with a little knowledge of calculus can immediately write down the velocity vector **v** by differentiating the preceding expression for **r** because $\mathbf{v} = d\mathbf{r}/dt$. The result is this:

$$\mathbf{v} = -\omega\mathbf{A}\sin(\omega t) + \omega\mathbf{B}\cos(\omega t)$$

What are the values of **A**, **B**, and ω? **A** and **B** are set by the initial conditions that you specify for the displacement and velocity of the object at the start (the values of **r** and **v** at time t = 0). Let's call the initial displacement vector $\mathbf{r}_0$ and the initial velocity vector $\mathbf{v}_0$. If we now put t = 0 into the preceding equations for **r** and **v** because cos(0) = 1 and sin(0) = 0, we get this:

$$\mathbf{r}_0 = \mathbf{A}$$

We also get the following:

$$\mathbf{v}_0 = \omega\,\mathbf{B}$$

This tells us right away that $\mathbf{A} = \mathbf{r}_0$ and $\mathbf{B} = \mathbf{v}_0/\omega$.

If you were to solve that differential equation, you would also find that the angular velocity ω is actually given by this formula:

$$\omega = \sqrt{\frac{k}{m}}$$

This is called the *natural frequency* of the system. If the oscillating system is given an initial perturbation (to move the object away from its equilibrium position), but is thereafter left on its own, it will oscillate at that frequency and only at that frequency in the absence of other influences such as damping.

Now, if you remember (again from Chapter 3) that $\omega = 2\pi f$ and $f = 1/T$, where f is the frequency (the number of oscillations per second) and T is the period of oscillation (the time to do one oscillation), you can use the preceding formula to obtain both the frequency and period of the oscillation in terms of the parameters k and m:

$$f = \frac{1}{2\pi}\sqrt{\frac{k}{m}}$$

$$T = 2\pi\sqrt{\frac{m}{k}}$$

These formulas tell you that if you increase the spring stiffness k, the frequency of the oscillations will increase and its period will decrease (it will oscillate faster). If you increase the mass of the oscillating particle instead, the reverse will happen, and it will oscillate more slowly. Go ahead and try it!

These are the only two parameters that affect the frequency and period; the initial position and velocity of the object do not. You might think that if the object is initially farther away from the center it will take longer to complete one oscillation. But not with SHM. What happens is that if the object is farther away, it experiences a larger acceleration at the start so that on average it acquires a larger velocity, which compensates for the longer distance it has to travel to complete one oscillation. Skeptical? Try it by timing the oscillations with a stopwatch or tracing the time.

In fact, we can do better than that. Let's plot a graph.

Oscillations and numerical accuracy

We modify `BasicOscillations.as` by changing the initial position of the oscillating object as follows:

```
object.pos2D = new Vector2D(100,50);
```

Then we modify this line:

```
var oscillator:BasicOscillator=new BasicOscillator(object,attractor);
```

to the following:

```
var oscillator:FreeOscillator=new FreeOscillator(object,attractor);
```

After changing the class and constructor names from `BasicOscillations` to `FreeOscillations`, we then save the file as `FreeOscillations.as`.

Now it's time to create `FreeOscillator.as` by modifying `BasicOscillator.as`. The modifications we need to do are to enable a graph to be plotted showing the displacement of the object against time as it moves.

Here is the full code for `FreeOscillator.as` with the changes in bold text:

```
package {
        import com.physicscodes.motion.Forcer;
        import com.physicscodes.motion.Forces;
        import com.physicscodes.objects.Ball;
        import com.physicscodes.math.Vector2D;
        import com.physicscodes.math.Graph;

        public class FreeOscillator extends Forcer{
                private var _object:Ball;
                private var _center:Vector2D;
                private var _displ:Vector2D;
                private var _kSpring:Number=1;
                private var _graph:Graph;

                public function FreeOscillator(pobject:Ball,pattractor:Ball):void{
                        _object = pobject;
                        _center = pattractor.pos2D;
                        setupGraph();
                        super(_object);
                }

                override protected function moveObject():void{
                        super.moveObject();
                        plotGraph();
                }

                override protected function calcForce():void{
                        _displ=_object.pos2D.subtract(_center);
                        force = Forces.spring(_kSpring,_displ);
                }
```

```
            // create a displacement-time graph
            private function setupGraph():void {
                    _graph= new Graph(0,20,-250,250,50,250,450,200);
                    _graph.drawgrid(5,1,50,50);
                    _graph.drawaxes('time (s)','displacement (px)');
                    _object.stage.addChild(_graph);
            }
            private function plotGraph():void{
                    _graph.plot([time], [_displ.x], 0xff0000, false, true);
                    _graph.plot([time], [_displ.y], 0x0000ff, false, true);
            }
        }
    }
```

So we import the Graph class, declare a new private variable _graph as a Graph object, call the new private method setupGraph() from within the constructor, and override the moveObject() method to call the new private method plotGraph() at each timestep.

The setupGraph() method does exactly what its name suggests: it sets up the Graph object _graph with appropriate parameters and adds it to the stage.

The plotGraph() method, which is called at each timestep, invokes the plot() public method of Graph to plot the x and y coordinates of the displacement of the object relative to the attractor.

If you now run the code, you'll see something like Figure 8-4. Sure enough, the horizontal displacement (x) of the object with time is a sinusoidal wave, as we said in the last section. The vertical displacement is always zero because of the initial condition we chose. But it's easy to change it by giving the object an initial vertical component of velocity or a different initial vertical position. Then the y displacement would also vary sinusoidally. You can also change the values of k, m, and the initial position of the object to verify the statements we made at the end of the last section on how the frequency and period of oscillations vary (or not) with these parameters.

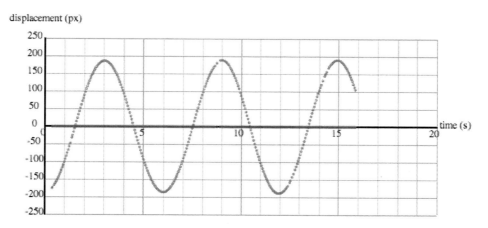

Figure 8-4. Plotting the displacement of an oscillating object as a function of time

Let's now see how accurate our simulation is by comparing the trajectory of the oscillating object with what the analytical solution given in the last section predicts.

To do this, we modify `FreeOscillations.as` to `FreeOscillations2.as` by changing the initial velocity of the oscillating object as follows:

```
object.velo2D=new Vector2D(0,50);
```

Then we modify this line:

```
var oscillator:FreeOscillator=new FreeOscillator(object,attractor);
```

to the following:

```
var oscillator:FreeOscillator2=new FreeOscillator2(object,attractor);
```

The `FreeOscillator2` class is just a modified version of `FreeOscillator`, with the addition of code that calculates the values of **A**, **B**, and ω (defined as private variables `_A`, `_B` and `_omega` in the code) using the previously given equations ω = √(k/m), **A** = r_0 , and **B** = v_0/ω. This is done in the constructor of `FreeOscillator2`, which therefore contains the additional lines:

```
_omega = Math.sqrt(_kSpring/_object.mass);
_A = _object.pos2D.subtract(_center);
_B = _object.velo2D.multiply(1/_omega);
```

In the `plotGraph()` method, we then insert the following additional lines to plot the x and y components of the analytical solution **v** = −ω**A** sin (ωt) + ω**B** cos (ωt):

```
var r:Vector2D = _A.multiply(Math.cos(_omega*time)).add(_B.multiply(Math.sin(_omega*time)));
_graphX.plot([time], [r.x], 0x00ff00, false, true);
_graphY.plot([time], [r.y], 0xff00ff, false, true);
```

Another modification compared to `FreeOscillator2` is that we now have two `Graph` objects `_graphX` and `_graphY` (set up in a suitably modified `setupGraph()` method), on which we plot the x and y displacements, respectively, in `plotGraph()`.

If you now run the code, you'll see the object orbiting the attractor in an elongated orbit, and you'll see a pair of graphs for each of the horizontal and vertical displacements of the object. In each pair of graphs, one corresponds to the analytical solution computed by the specified formulas, whereas the other corresponds to the numerical solution as computed by the simulation. You can see that they are quite close to each other, practically overlapping (see Figure 8-5). Euler integration is not doing such a bad job in this case.

However, if you now change the value of `_kSpring` to 10, for example, so that the "spring" is stiffer and the object moves faster, you'll see that the difference between the two is more significant, signaling that Euler is losing accuracy. If you try a value for `_kSpring` of 100, then Euler gives you complete rubbish, and the object ends up in completely the wrong place at the wrong time. So here you begin to see that you can get the wrong physics if you are not careful with your integrator, especially in the case of springs. You'll see how to overcome this problem in Chapter 14. Meanwhile, for the rest of this chapter we'll avoid very high values of the spring constant.

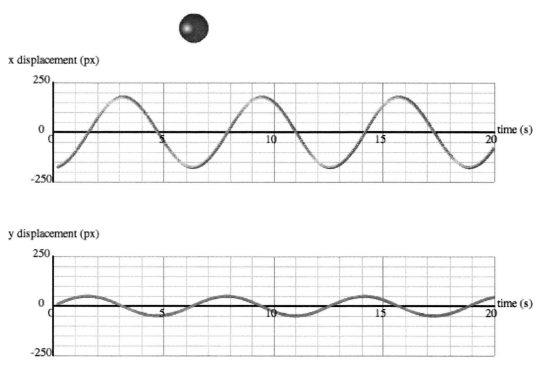

Figure 8-5. Comparing the numerical and analytical solutions for the oscillator

Damped oscillations

In the previous examples, the oscillations just go on forever. In practice, this rarely happens. Oscillating systems are usually *damped*. That means the oscillations are reduced and die out in time due to energy being removed from the system. This is similar to the drag force, which dissipates kinetic energy of a moving object and makes it slow down. To implement damping in our springs, we need a damping force.

Damping force

The *damping force* is usually modeled as being proportional to the velocity of the moving object. This means that, at any instant in time, it is given by this equation, where c is a constant known as the damping coefficient, and the minus sign indicates that the force is in the opposite direction to the velocity:

$$\mathbf{F} = -c\,\mathbf{v}$$

Notice that this is of exactly the same form as the force law for linear drag. We could, therefore, use the linearDrag() function to implement damping in spring motion. However, although drag is certainly a form of damping, it is not physically the only form of damping, although the two terms are sometimes used

233

interchangeably. Drag is the resistive force exerted by a fluid on a moving object immersed in it. Spring damping, on the other hand can be due to external factors such as fluid drag or external friction, or to internal factors such as internal friction, which arise from the molecular material properties of springs. In fact, you could have both internal damping due to spring resistance and drag due to fluid resistance side by side (with different coefficients, of course). For example, a mass suspended on a spring and oscillating in a fluid such as air or water experiences both internal friction and fluid drag. For these reasons, we prefer to create a separate function for damping. The form of this function is identical to that for `linearDrag()`, as shown in this listing:

```
static public function damping(c:Number,vel:Vector2D):Vector2D {
        var force:Vector2D;
        var velMag:Number=vel.length;
        if (velMag>0) {
                force=vel.multiply(-c);
        }else {
                force=new Vector2D(0,0);
        }
        return force;
}
```

The effect of damping on oscillations

We'll now modify `FreeOscillations.as` and `FreeOscillator.as` to create classes that handle damping in addition to the spring force. The new files are called `DampedOscillations.as` and `DampedOscillator.as`, respectively. `DampedOscillations.as` differs from `FreeOscillations.as` only in the name of the class and constructor and in that it instantiates a `DampedOscillator` class. `DampedOscillator.as` basically introduces a new force: damping. So one difference from `FreeOscillator` is that it declares a damping coefficient `_cDamping` and assigns it a value:

```
private var _cDamping:Number=0.5;
```

The other difference is that it includes a damping force in `calcForce()` and adds it to the spring force to work out the resultant force:

```
override protected function calcForce():void{
        _displ=_object.pos2D.subtract(_center);
        var restoring:Vector2D = Forces.spring(_kSpring,_displ);
        var damping:Vector2D = Forces.damping(_cDamping,_object.velo2D);
        force = Forces.add([restoring, damping]);
}
```

That's it. If you run the code with `_kSpring = 10` and `_cDamping = 0.5`, you'll see something like what's shown in Figure 8-6. The oscillations die out in time, and the object eventually settles at the equilibrium position, as you'd expect.

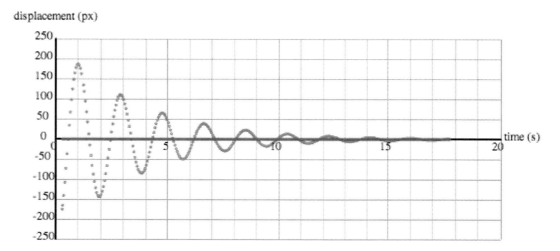

Figure 8-6. Damped oscillations

At this point, you should play with the damping constant _cDamping to see what you get. Choose a lower value, and you'll see the oscillations persist longer, whereas a higher value will kill them off sooner. You might think that the larger the value of c, the quicker the object will stop. In fact, there is a critical value of c for which the oscillations die in the minimum time. In fact, there are no oscillations at all. The object simply moves smoothly to the equilibrium position without oscillating beyond it. This is called *critical damping*, and an example is shown in Figure 8-7. For _kSpring = 10 in our simulation, the critical value of _cDamping is about 5.5, and the object reaches its equilibrium position in about 1 second. If you increase _cDamping beyond this critical value, for example to 10 or 20, you'll see that the object actually takes longer to reach its equilibrium location. This is because the increased damping slows it down so much that, although it does not go beyond the equilibrium position, it takes longer to get there. Critical damping is a very useful thing that's applied in things like damping mechanisms in doors.

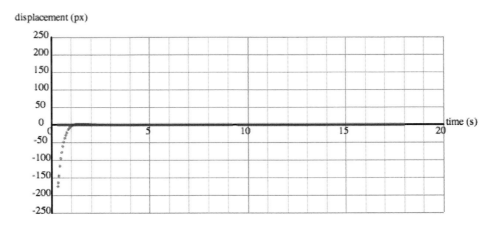

Figure 8-7. Critical damping

Analytical solutions for oscillations with damping

This brief section is for enthusiasts. You may safely skip it if complicated formulas are not your thing. The point of this section is to show you how the analytical solution quoted previously for free oscillations changes in the presence of damping, and how well our simulation does at reproducing it. Thus, it is more educational than practical.

Newton's second law for oscillations under a spring force **F** = –k**r**, together with a damping force **F** = –c**v** is the following:

$$m\,\mathbf{a} = -k\,\mathbf{r} - c\,\mathbf{v}$$

This can be written in terms of derivatives as (after dividing both sides by m):

$$\frac{d^2\mathbf{r}}{dt^2} = -\frac{k}{m}\mathbf{r} - \frac{c}{m}\frac{d\mathbf{r}}{dt}$$

The analytical solution of this differential equation is given by the following:

$$\mathbf{r} = \left[\mathbf{A}\cos(\omega_d t) + \mathbf{B}\sin(\omega_d t)\right]\exp(-\gamma\omega_0 t)$$

where the constants γ, ω_0, ω_d, **A** and **B** are given by the following:

$$\gamma = \frac{c}{2\sqrt{mk}}$$

$$\omega_0 = \sqrt{\frac{k}{m}}$$

$$\omega_d = \omega_0\sqrt{1-\gamma^2}$$

$$\mathbf{A} = \mathbf{r}_0$$

$$\mathbf{B} = \frac{\left(\mathbf{v}_0 + \gamma\,\omega_0\,\mathbf{r}_0\right)}{\omega_d}$$

Comparing with the previous solution without damping, you'll notice that there is an additional exponential factor in the expression for **r**, which is responsible for the decay in the sinusoidal oscillations (see Chapter 3). The new parameter γ is due to the damping. In the absence of damping, $c = 0$ and so $\gamma = 0$; the solution then reduces to that without damping. Note also that the angular frequency of the oscillations is now ω_d (because it appears in the sine and cosine), which is less than the natural frequency ω_0 in the absence of damping (which was previously denoted by ω).

We coded up these equations in a modified version of FreeOscillator2.as that we call DampedOscillator2.as. Take a look at the code if you wish. If you run the corresponding code DampedOscillations2.as, you'll find that there is again some discrepancy between this analytical solution and the numerical solution computed by the simulation. In fact, sometimes you might find that the oscillating object goes seemingly wild, ending up in places it shouldn't be. The important take-away message from all this is that Euler simply does not cut it when it comes to simulations like this, except for the simplest motions. In Chapter 14, we shall discuss alternative integration schemes that overcome this problem.

Forced oscillations

In the presence of damping, the oscillations of a system will die out in time. Therefore, a force is needed to sustain oscillations or to initiate them in the first place. That's called a driving force, or forcing.

Driving forces

Driving forces can be of any form, so let's denote them simply by **f** (t). This simply means that the force is a function of time without specifying the form of the force law at all.

For example, we could have a periodic force of the form **F** = **A** cos (ωt) + **B** sin (ωt), where **A** and **B** are constant vectors that give the amplitude (maximum magnitude) and direction of the force, and ω is the angular frequency of the forcing. This could, for example, represent an oscillator interacting with and driving another, such as a periodic wind blowing over a suspension bridge and causing it to vibrate.

Let's start with an example.

Example: A periodic driving force

We'll start by modifying `DampedOscillator2.as`. We do not want to plot the analytical solutions here, so we get rid of the relevant lines in `plotGraph()`, but keep the three lines that compute `_gamma`, `_omega0`, and `_omegad` in the constructor. These are the variables corresponding to the constants γ, ω_0, and ω_d. After deleting any unnecessary variable declarations, we rename the class and constructor to `ForcedOscillator` and save the file as `ForcedOscillator.as`. We also create a `ForcedOscillations.as` file to go with it.

Remember that `_omega0` (ω_0) is the natural angular frequency of the undamped system, and `_omegad` (ω_d) is the angular frequency with damping. Let's begin by adding the following lines to `calcForce()`:

```
var forcing:Vector2D = new Vector2D(200*Math.cos(2*_omegad*time)+200*Math.sin↩
(2*_omegad*time), 0);
force = Forces.add([restoring, damping, forcing]);
```

This adds a driving force of the form **F** = **A** cos (ωt) + **B** sin (ωt), with **A** and **B** both of magnitude 200 and in the x direction (we need fairly large values to see a noticeable difference of the forcing on the oscillations), and ω = 2 ω_d. So we are forcing the system with a driving force that varies sinusoidally with time at an angular frequency that is twice the frequency of the damped system.

Run the code, and you'll see that the oscillations start to die out as they did before without the forcing. Then, after awhile, the object starts to oscillate at around twice the frequency it did before, but with at a much smaller amplitude. This carries on indefinitely. So, the effect of the sinusoidal driving force is to eventually make the system oscillate at the driving frequency (albeit at reduced amplitude), rather than the frequency that the system would prefer to oscillate at on its own. You can try this with different forcing frequencies. For example, if you use ω_d/2, half the damped system's frequency, the oscillations will eventually have a frequency of half the initial, unforced frequency. The conclusion is that if you force a system to oscillate at a frequency other than its natural frequency, it will still oscillate but at a reduced amplitude.

Now make the forcing frequency exactly equal to ω_d by modifying the forcing vector to this:

```
var forcing:Vector2D = new Vector2D(200*Math.cos(_omegad*time)+200*Math.sin(_omegad*time), 0);
```

When you run the code, you'll now see that the oscillations quickly settle into equilibrium at the original frequency ω_d and maintain a large, constant amplitude without decaying. The system is now "happy" because it is forced at exactly the frequency it likes to oscillate. Hence, it settles down quickly and oscillates with a large amplitude. So, although damping reduces the energy of the system, forcing puts energy back into the system and sustains the oscillations.

When the forcing frequency is equal to the natural frequency of the oscillating system, we have what is called *resonance*. It happens in lots of situations, from pushing a child's swing to the tuning of radio circuits. Resonance can have bad effects, too, such as unwanted vibrations in bridges due to periodic wind gusts. In fact, resonance due to wind gusts was infamously responsible for the collapse of the Tacoma Narrows Bridge in Washington in 1940.

Example: A random driving force

Next, let's try a random forcing. This is as easy as replacing one line of code. Let's try this first:

```
var forcing:Vector2D = new Vector2D(1000*Math.random(),0);
```

This applies a random force of up to 1,000 units in the positive x direction (to the right). If this were the only force, it would send the object flying off to the right, never to be seen again. But the presence of the restoring force (as its name suggests) pulls the object back toward the attractor. In fact, because the restoring force is proportional to the displacement from the attractor, the farther away the object moves, the stronger it gets pulled back. This creates an interesting effect that you'll surely want to experiment with. Because we made the force act only to the right, the object will spend most of its time on the right side of the attractor, although it occasionally gets pulled slightly to the left.

To make the oscillations more symmetrical around the attractor, simply change that line of code to this:

```
var forcing:Vector2D = new Vector2D(1000*(Math.random()-0.5),0);
```

This produces a random force with an x component between −500 and +500, where the minus sign means that the force is directed to the left instead of to the right. Run the code, and you'll get a non-periodic oscillator (the object oscillates without regularity).

Finally, let's make the object oscillate under a random force in 2D by modifying the same line of code to the following:

```
var forcing:Vector2D = new Vector2D(1000*(Math.random()-0.5),1000*(Math.random()-0.5));
```

If you run the code, you'll see that the system quickly goes into a state where the oscillations in the x and y directions are of comparable magnitude, with the object hovering around the attractor (see Figure 8-8). The object is kicked in different directions at every timestep, but it is also pulled back toward the attractor. It's not allowed to get away, no matter how large the forcing is because the farther it goes the more strongly it gets pulled back. That's an interesting effect. It's some kind of crazy random orbiting motion. Or maybe even like a bee buzzing around a flower. Play with that one for sure!

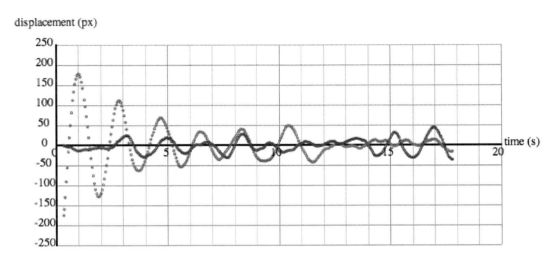

Figure 8-8. Oscillator with random forcing

Gravity as a driving force: bungee jumping

Let's now move on to something a little different: bungee jumping! Someone jumps off a bridge or similar structure tied to an elastic cord whose other end is tied to a fixed support on the structure. The elastic cord has a natural unstretched length, say cordLength. So if the distance of the jumper from the fixed support is less than cordLength, gravity and drag are the only forces on the jumper. But once that distance exceeds cordLength, the elastic (spring) force will come into effect, and pull the jumper back.

So here gravity is acting as the driving force, so that f(t) = mg, where m is the mass of the jumper. It's a constant forcing, unlike the types of forcing discussed before. The main damping mechanism is provided by drag through the air, so can be implemented using the Forces.drag() method. Finally, the spring force is applied only if the jumper's distance from the fixed support exceeds the natural unstretched length of the cord, cordLength. This distance may be less than cordLength initially (before the jumper jumps off some supporting structure), but also whenever the jumper bounces back high enough.

Because this example is a little different from the last few, we'll list the full source code and then go through the main points. Let's start with the setup file, which is called simply Bungee.as:

```
package{
        import flash.display.Sprite;
        import com.physicscodes.objects.Ball;
        import com.physicscodes.math.Vector2D;
```

```
import com.physicscodes.objects.Particle;

public class Bungee extends Sprite{

        public function Bungee():void{
                init();
        }

        private function init():void{
                // create a spring
                var spring:Sprite=new Sprite();
                addChild(spring);

                // create a fixed support
                var fixedPoint:Ball;
                fixedPoint=new Ball(2,0x000000);
                fixedPoint.pos2D=new Vector2D(275,50);
                addChild(fixedPoint);

                // create the bungee jumper
                var jumper = new Jumper();
                jumper.pos2D = new Vector2D(275,50);
                jumper.mass = 90;
                addChild(jumper);

                // get things moving
                var oscillator:BungeeOscillator = new BungeeOscillator↬
(jumper,fixedPoint, spring);
                oscillator.startTime();
        }
    }
}
```

Notice that we are creating three objects here: a spring, a fixed point, and a jumper. The spring object is just an empty sprite; we'll actually draw something on it in the BungeeOscillator class that makes the whole thing work. The jumper is an instance of Jumper, a drawn MovieClip with the base class of Particle. The three objects are passed into the constructor of BungeeOscillator, which looks like this:

```
package {
        import com.physicscodes.motion.Forcer;
        import com.physicscodes.motion.Forces;
        import com.physicscodes.objects.Particle;
        import com.physicscodes.objects.Ball;
        import com.physicscodes.math.Vector2D;
        import flash.display.Sprite;

        public class BungeeOscillator extends Forcer{
                private var _object:Particle;
                private var _center:Vector2D;
                private var _displ:Vector2D;
                private var _g:Number=20;
                private var _kDamping=0.1;
                private var _kSpring=25;
```

```
            private var _cordLength:Number=100;
            private var _spring:Sprite;

            public function BungeeOscillator(pobject:Particle,pfixedSupport:Ball,↪
pspring:Sprite):void{
                    _object = pobject;
                    _center = pfixedSupport.pos2D;
                    _spring = pspring;
                    super(_object);
            }

            override protected function moveObject():void{
                    super.moveObject();
                    drawSpring();
            }

            private function drawSpring():void{
                    with (_spring.graphics){
                            clear();
                            if (_displ.length > _cordLength){
                                    lineStyle(2,0x999999);
                            }else{
                                    lineStyle(1,0xcccccc);
                            }
                            moveTo(_center.x,_center.y);
                            lineTo(_object.x,_object.y)
                    }
            }

            override protected function calcForce():void{
                    _displ=_object.pos2D.subtract(_center);
                    var gravity:Vector2D = Forces.constantGravity(_object.mass,_g);
                    var damping:Vector2D = Forces.drag(_kDamping,_object.velo2D);
                    var extension:Vector2D = _displ.subtract(_displ.unit().multiply↪
(_cordLength));
                    var restoring:Vector2D;
                            if (_displ.length > _cordLength) {
                            restoring = Forces.spring(_kSpring,extension);
                    }else{
                            restoring = new Vector2D(0,0);
                    }
                    force = Forces.add([gravity, damping, restoring]);
            }
        }
}
```

First, note the large value we used for the spring constant _kSpring (25). That's because we've specified the mass of the jumper as 90 in Bungee.as, instead of 1 as in all the previous simulations. This mirrors the fact that, if you want to make a big guy oscillate at the end of an elastic cord, the cord had better be pretty stiff!

Looking next at the calcForce() method, we see that we are including gravity, damping, and restoring forces, as discussed previously. The first two are implemented in a straightforward way as usual. There are two differences in how we calculate the restoring force compared with earlier examples. First, the displacement vector that must be used to calculate the restoring force is now the displacement vector of the end point of the elastic cord (the extension), as explained at the beginning of this chapter, not the displacement of the object from the fixed support. Therefore, we first calculate that extension as a vector in the line:

```
var extension:Vector2D = _displ.subtract(_displ.unit().multiply(_cordLength));
```

We then supply `extension` as the second argument in `Forces.spring()`.

Secondly, the restoring force is non-zero only if the object is farther from the support than the length of the cord. That's the same as saying that `_displ.length > _cordLength`. This explains the code within the if block.

The other new thing is that we've included a `drawSpring()` method, called within an overridden `moveObject()` method, that draws a line to represent the elastic cord at each timestep. The line is drawn thinner and fainter when the cord is unstretched. As usual, run the code and feel free to play with the parameters. The initial position of the object is the same as that of the fixed support. This makes the object oscillate in a vertical straight line (it makes the oscillations 1D). To make it 2D, simply change the initial x-coordinate of the object in `Bungee.as`; for example:

```
object.pos2D = new Vector2D(300,50);
```

A screenshot of the demo is shown in Figure 8-9.

Figure 8-9. A bungee jump simulation

Example: Driving force by user interaction

User interaction can also be viewed as some kind of forcing. In this example, we will build a simulation in which the user can click and drag the object and release it in any location. This will disturb the system, setting it to oscillate.

It is fairly straightforward to modify the bungee simulation to do what we want here. We'll call the new classes `DraggingOscillations.as` and `DraggingOscillator.as`. `DraggingOscillations.as` is actually pretty similar to `Bungee.as`, so we won't bother discussing it here, other than mention that we've changed the mass of the object back to 1. In `DraggingOscillator.as`, the main changes are that we've added code to enable dragging and modified the `calcForce()` method. Here is the modified code:

```
package {
        import com.physicscodes.motion.Forcer;
        import com.physicscodes.motion.Forces;
        import com.physicscodes.objects.Ball;
        import com.physicscodes.math.Vector2D;
        import flash.display.Sprite;
        import flash.events.MouseEvent;

        public class DraggingOscillator extends Forcer{
                private var _object:Ball;
                private var _center:Vector2D;
                private var _displ:Vector2D;
                private var _g:Number=20;
                private var _kDamping=0.5;
                private var _kSpring=1;
                private var _springLength:Number=200;
                private var _spring:Sprite;

                public function DraggingOscillator(pobject:Ball, pfixedSupport:Ball,↪
 pspring:Sprite):void{
                        _object = pobject;
                        _center = pfixedSupport.pos2D;
                        _spring = pspring;
                        _object.addEventListener(MouseEvent.MOUSE_DOWN,onDown);
                        super(_object);
                }
                override protected function moveObject():void{
                        super.moveObject();
                        drawSpring();
                }
                private function drawSpring():void{
                        with (_spring.graphics){
                                clear();
                                lineStyle(2,0x999999);
                                moveTo(_center.x,_center.y);
                                lineTo(_object.x,_object.y)
                        }
                }
                override protected function calcForce():void{
                        _displ=_object.pos2D.subtract(_center);
                        var gravity:Vector2D = Forces.constantGravity(_object.mass,_g);
                        var damping:Vector2D = Forces.damping(_kDamping,_object.velo2D);
                        var extension:Vector2D = _displ.subtract(_displ.unit().multiply↪
(_springLength));
                        var restoring:Vector2D = Forces.spring(_kSpring,extension);
                        force = Forces.add([gravity, damping, restoring]);
                }
                private function onDown(e:MouseEvent):void{
                        _object.velo2D = new Vector2D(0,0);
                        _object.stage.addEventListener(MouseEvent.MOUSE_UP,onUp);
```

```
                        _object.startDrag(true);
                        _spring.graphics.clear();
                        stopTime();
                }
                private function onUp(e:MouseEvent):void{
                        _object.pos2D = new Vector2D(_object.x,_object.y);
                        _object.stage.removeEventListener(MouseEvent.MOUSE_UP,onUp);
                        _object.stopDrag();
                        startTime();
                }
        }
}
```

In calcForce(), we include gravity as before, while damping is included using the Forces.damping() function. We then calculate the extension of the spring and feed it into the restoring force as before. However, because this is a spring that can also be compressed and is not an elastic cord, we apply the restoring force even if the extension is negative, so we got rid of the if statement we had before.

There is also an event listener in the constructor, listening out for MOUSE_DOWN events and triggering the onDown() event handler when the object is clicked. The onDown() method sets the velocity of the object to zero, sets up an event listener that listens to MOUSE_UP events, allows dragging, clears the spring, and stops the timer. The onUp() event handler is invoked when the object is released, and it updates the position vector of the object, removes the event listener, stops dragging, and restarts the timer.

All that is fairly straightforward. Run the code and you'll see the object fall down under gravity and be pulled back again by the spring, oscillating with reducing amplitude due to the damping. If you drag the object and release it, it oscillates again due to the forcing.

Coupled oscillators: Multiple springs and objects

In all the examples so far, we've considered only a single object and spring system. Things get even more interesting when you couple more than one object and spring system together. In fact, you can create extended systems based on objects with masses connected by springs. In the next subsection, you'll see an example of what can be done. Then we'll look at more complicated examples in Chapter 13 when we model deformable bodies.

Example: A chain of objects connected by springs

What you'll create is shown in Figure 8-10: a number of balls connected by springs, with the first ball connected to a support. The support will then be moved around, causing the chain of suspended balls to move around, too.

Figure 8-10. A chain of objects held together by springs

The forces that will be modeled include gravity, damping, and restoring force. The springs will have a natural length, as in the last couple of examples. Each ball will therefore experience gravity, damping, a restoring force due to a spring above, and another restoring force due to a spring below (except for the last ball). The springs themselves will be assumed to be massless.

Here is the code in the setup file, called `CoupledOscillations.as`:

```
package{
        import flash.display.Sprite;
        import com.physicscodes.objects.Ball;
        import com.physicscodes.math.Vector2D;
        import com.physicscodes.objects.Particle;

        public class CoupledOscillations extends Sprite{
                public function CoupledOscillations():void{
                        init();
                }

                private function init():void{
                        // create a spring
                        var spring:Sprite=new Sprite();
                        addChild(spring);

                        // create a fixed support
                        var fixedPoint:Ball;
                        fixedPoint=new Ball(2,0x000000);
                        fixedPoint.pos2D=new Vector2D(275,50);
                        addChild(fixedPoint);

                        // create the oscillating objects
```

```
                        var objects:Array = new Array();
                        var numObjects:Number = 6;
                        for (var i:uint=0; i<numObjects; i++){
                                var object:Ball= new Ball(15,0x0000ff,1);
                                //object.pos2D = new Vector2D(275+60*i,100+60*i);
                                object.pos2D = new Vector2D(275,100+60*i);
                                addChild(object);
                                objects.push(object);
                        }

                        // get things moving
                        var oscillator:CoupledOscillator = new CoupledOscillator↪
(objects,fixedPoint,spring);
                        oscillator.startTime();
                }
        }
}
```

As in the last two examples, we first create a spring sprite on which the "springs" will be drawn. We then create a Ball object to act as a "fixed" support (in reality, we'll make it move, too). Then we create a whole bunch of Ball objects and put them in an array called objects. Finally, we create an instance of a CoupledOscillator class, pass it the relevant objects, and fire the startTime() method.

Before we look at CoupledOscillator.as, we need to modify MultiForcer slightly. We call the modified version MultiForcer2, and here is the full code of that class:

```
package com.physicscodes.motion {
        import com.physicscodes.motion.Mover;
        import com.physicscodes.objects.Particle;
        import com.physicscodes.math.Vector2D;

        public class MultiForcer2 extends Mover{

                private var _particles:Array;
                private var _force:Vector2D;
                private var _acc:Vector2D;

                public function MultiForcer2(pparticles:Array):void{
                        _particles = pparticles;
                        super(null);
                }

                public function get force():Vector2D {
                        return _force;
                }
                public function set force(pforce):void {
                        _force = pforce;
                }
                override protected function moveObject():void{
                        for (var i:uint=0; i<_particles.length; i++){
                                var particle:Particle = _particles[i];
                                particle.pos2D = particle.pos2D.addScaled(particle.velo2D,dt);
```

```
                    calcForce(particle,i);
                    _acc = _force.multiply(1/particle.mass);
                    particle.velo2D = particle.velo2D.addScaled(_acc,dt);
                }
            }
            protected function calcForce(pparticle:Particle,pnum:uint):void{
                    _force = Forces.zeroForce();
                }
        }
}
```

If you compare this with the code for MultiForcer, you'll notice that the only differences between the two are in the two lines set in bold. We have modified the method calcForce() by including another argument, which is of type uint. In moveObject(), when we call calcForce(), we then include an additional parameter i, which is the index number of the relevant particle in the array. Why do we need to do this? For each ball, we need to calculate the spring force exerted by the springs connected to it from the previous and the next balls. Therefore, it would be handy if we knew exactly which ball we're dealing with, and therefore which balls are before and after it. That's what the extra parameter achieves.

By extending MultiForcer2, CoupledOscillator will automatically have this capability, too. So, it will be able to work out each ball's nearest neighbors and hence apply the spring force linked with each one. Here is the code in CoupledOscillator.as:

```
package {
        import com.physicscodes.motion.MultiForcer2;
        import com.physicscodes.motion.Forces;
        import com.physicscodes.objects.Ball;
        import com.physicscodes.objects.Particle;
        import com.physicscodes.math.Vector2D;
        import flash.display.Sprite;

        public class CoupledOscillator extends MultiForcer2{
                private var _objects:Array;
                private var _support:Ball;
                private var _center:Vector2D;
                private var _displ:Vector2D;
                private var _g:Number=20;
                private var _kDamping=0.5;
                private var _kSpring=10;
                private var _springLength:Number=50;
                private var _spring:Sprite;

                public function CoupledOscillator(pobjects:Array,psupport↪
:Ball,pspring:Sprite):void{
                        _objects = pobjects;
                        _support = psupport;
                        _center = _support.pos2D;
                        _spring = pspring;
                        super(_objects);
                }
                override protected function moveObject():void{
                        super.moveObject();
```

```
                  drawSpring();
          }

      override protected function calcForce(pparticle:Particle,pnum:uint):void{
              var centerPrev:Vector2D;
              var centerNext:Vector2D;
              if (pnum > 0){
                      centerPrev = _objects[pnum-1].pos2D;
              }else{
                      centerPrev = _center;
              }
              if (pnum < _objects.length-1){
                      centerNext = _objects[pnum+1].pos2D;
              }else{
                      centerNext = pparticle.pos2D;
              }
              var displPrev:Vector2D = pparticle.pos2D.subtract(centerPrev);
              var displNext:Vector2D = pparticle.pos2D.subtract(centerNext);
              var extensionPrev:Vector2D = displPrev.subtract(displPrev.unit().↵
multiply(_springLength));
              var extensionNext:Vector2D = displNext.subtract(displNext.unit().↵
multiply(_springLength));
              var gravity:Vector2D = Forces.constantGravity(pparticle.mass,_g);
              var damping:Vector2D = Forces.damping(_kDamping,pparticle.velo2D);
              var restoringPrev:Vector2D = Forces.spring(_kSpring,extensionPrev);
              var restoringNext:Vector2D = Forces.spring(_kSpring,extensionNext);
              force = Forces.add([gravity, damping, restoringPrev, restoringNext]);
      }

      private function drawSpring():void{
              with (_spring.graphics){
                      clear();
                      lineStyle(2,0x999999);
                      moveTo(_center.x,_center.y);
                      for (var i:uint=0; i<_objects.length; i++){
                              var X:Number = _objects[i].xpos;
                              var Y:Number = _objects[i].ypos;
                              lineTo(X,Y);
                      }
              }
      }

  }
}
```

Most of the code should be familiar to you by now. The new features are the bits of code that deal with the fact that we have multiple moving objects and springs, and each object experiences a restoring force due to its nearest neighbors. In calcForce(), we take this into account by first defining variables centerPrev and centerNext that are given the positions of the balls just before and just after the current ball, by using the array index pnum that is now passed as a parameter in calcForce(). For the first ball, centerPrev is given the position of the fixed support; for the last ball, centerNext is given the position of the current ball. The values of centerPrev and centerNext are then used to calculate the displacement vectors of the ball from the previous and the next balls in the usual way. Then the spring extension from the natural length of the spring _springLength is worked out for each spring as in the last two examples. Finally, the spring force due to each spring is calculated using Forces.spring() and added to the gravity and damping forces.

The drawSpring() method, which is called from the moveObject() method, now draws a line starting from the fixed support through each ball.

The initial positions of the objects are set in CoupledOscillations.as. Run the code with different initial positions to see how the balls move under the gravity and the spring forces to rearrange themselves in their equilibrium positions.

Again, don't be afraid to experiment. For example, add the following code in moveObject() to make the support oscillate sinusoidally, dragging the chain along with it:

```
_support.xpos = 100*Math.sin(1.0*time)+275;
_center = _support.pos2D;
```

This gives you something like what's pictured in Figure 8-10.

How about trying different masses and different spring constants? Or allowing the balls to be dragged? Or see if you can figure out how to make closed chains? We'll leave you to it.

Summary

We hope you had a lot of fun playing with the examples in this chapter. As we said at the beginning of the chapter, springs are not only fun but also extremely useful. Springs can be used creatively in many ways—for example, you could apply them to velocity, so that an object accelerates and decelerates smoothly to attain a given "equilibrium" velocity. Hopefully you'll be able to find many uses for them. Your imagination is the limit. We'll certainly bump into springs again later in this book.

Chapter 9

Centripetal Forces: Rotational Motion

Circular and rotational motions are widespread both in nature and in man-made machines, from merry-go-rounds to the orbits and spins of planets. To analyze and model such types of motion, we need some special tools: the linear kinematics and dynamics presented in Chapter 5 need to be extended to rotational motion. In a nutshell, this is what the present chapter will begin to look into.

Topics covered in this chapter include the following:

- **Kinematics of uniform circular motion**: The kinematics of rotational motion can be developed in analogy with linear kinematics.

- **Centripetal acceleration and centripetal force**: An object in uniform circular motion still experiences acceleration and therefore a force directed toward the center of rotation.

- **Non-uniform circular motion**: This happens if there is a tangential component of force in addition to a centripetal component.

The material covered in this chapter will also be relevant for handling rigid body motion in Chapter 13.

Kinematics of uniform circular motion

In Chapter 4, we laid out the framework for describing motion using concepts such as displacement, velocity, and acceleration. As we said there, this framework is technically called *kinematics*. Those concepts sufficed to describe so-called linear or translational motion. But for analyzing circular or rotational motion, we need additional concepts.

In fact, the concepts of rotational kinematics can be developed in complete analogy with those of linear kinematics. For starters, we have rotational analogs of displacement, velocity, and acceleration that are called *angular displacement*, *angular velocity*, and *angular acceleration*, respectively. So let's start by looking at them.

Angular displacement

Recall that displacement was defined back in Chapter 4 as distance moved in a specified direction. What is the equivalent definition for angular displacement?

First, we need to figure out what concepts are equivalent to distance and direction in rotational motion. Take a look at Figure 9-1, which compares translational motion with rotational motion. On the left, an object moves along a distance d in a given direction. On the right, an object rotates through an angle θ about some center, in a given sense (clockwise in this case). So, it's clear that in rotational kinematics, angle takes the place of distance, and rotation sense (clockwise or anticlockwise) takes the place of direction.

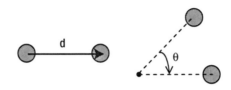

Figure 9-1. Translation and rotation compared for particle motion

Another context in which angular displacement arises is when a rigid body rotates about a fixed axis, as shown in Figure 9-2. In this case, each point on the rigid body moves through the same angle θ about the axis of rotation.

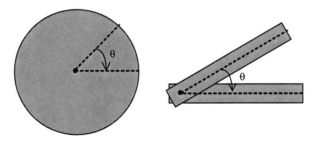

Figure 9-2. Rotation of a rigid body about an axis

In either case (particle rotation about a center or rigid body rotation about an axis), the idea is therefore the same. Hence, we define *angular displacement* as the angle through which an object moves about a specified center and in a specified sense.

This definition implies that the magnitude of angular displacement is an angle. The usual convention is to use radians for the angle, so we'll do that here.

Angular velocity

In analogy with linear velocity, *angular velocity* is defined as the rate of change of angular displacement with time. The usual symbol for angular velocity is ω (the Greek letter omega), so its defining equation in calculus notation is this:

$$\omega = \frac{d\theta}{dt}$$

For a small time interval Δt and angle change Δθ, it can be expressed in this discrete form:

$$\omega = \frac{\Delta\theta}{\Delta t}$$

The latter equation can also be written in the following form:

$$\Delta\theta = \omega\,\Delta t$$

This last form of the equation is what we'll use most frequently in code, to calculate the angular displacement due to an angular velocity ω in a time interval Δt.

Angular velocity is measured in radians per second (rad/s) because we divide angle by time to calculate it.

You'll frequently deal with situations where the angular velocity is constant. For example, a particle in uniform circular motion has a constant angular velocity, although its linear velocity is not constant (because its direction of motion changes). Another example is that of an object spinning at a constant rate, such as the Earth.

Angular acceleration

Angular acceleration is the rate of change of angular velocity. It is denoted by the Greek letter α (alpha), and its defining equation is this:

$$\alpha = \frac{d\omega}{dt}$$

The definition of angular acceleration implies that it is zero if the angular velocity is constant. Therefore, an object in uniform circular motion has zero angular acceleration. That does not mean that its linear acceleration is zero. In fact, the linear acceleration cannot be zero because the direction of motion (and therefore the linear velocity) is constantly changing. We'll come back to this point a little later in the chapter.

Period, frequency, and angular velocity

Uniform circular motion or rotation is a type of periodic motion (see "Basic Trigonometry" in Chapter 3) because the object returns to the same position at regular intervals. In fact, as discussed in Chapter 3, circular motion is related to oscillatory, sinusoidal motion. Back then, we defined the angular frequency, frequency, and period of an oscillation and showed that they were related by these equations:

$$f = \frac{1}{T}$$

$$\omega = 2\pi f = \frac{2\pi}{T}$$

The same relationships hold for circular motion, as should be evident by considering Figure 3-16. For circular motion ω is now the angular velocity; it's the same as the angular frequency of the corresponding sinusoidal oscillation. Similarly, f is the frequency of rotation (the number of revolutions per second). Finally, T is the period of revolution (the time it takes to perform one complete revolution).

As an example, let's calculate the angular velocity of the Earth as it orbits the Sun using the formula $\omega = 2\pi/T$. We know that the period T is approximately 365 days. In seconds, it has the following value:

T = 365 × 24 × 60 × 60 s ≈ 3.15×10^7 s

Therefore the angular velocity has the following value:

$\omega = 2\pi/T = 2\pi/(3.15 \times 10^7) \approx 2.0 \times 10^{-7}$ rad/s

This is the angle, in radians, through which the Earth moves around the Sun every second.

Let's now calculate the angular velocity of the Earth as it revolves around its axis using the same formula. In this case, the period of revolution is 24 hours, and so T has the following value:

T = 24 × 60 × 60 s = 86400 s

Therefore, the angular velocity is the following:

$\omega = 2\pi/T = 2\pi/86400 = 7.3 \times 10^{-5}$ rad/s

Note that this is the angular velocity of every point on the Earth, both on its surface and within it. That's because the Earth is a rigid body so that, as it revolves about its axis, every point rotates through the same angle in the same time. However, different points have different *linear velocities*. How is the angular velocity related to the linear velocity? Time to find out!

Relation between angular velocity and linear velocity

There is a simple relationship between the linear velocity and angular velocity for an object moving in uniform circular motion. To arrive at this relationship, we first note that the displacement Δs of an object moving through an angle Δθ around a circle of radius r is the length of arc that subtends that angle at the center of rotation. It is therefore given by the following:

$$\Delta s = r \, \Delta \theta$$

This follows from the definition of the radian given in Chapter 3: one radian is the angle subtended at the center of a circle by an arc of length equal to the radius of the circle. So, by proportion, an arc that makes an angle of Δθ radians at the center must be of length r Δθ (see Figure 9-3).

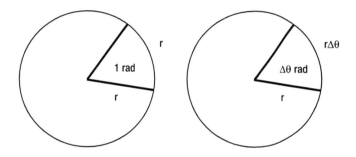

Figure 9-3. Relationship between length of arc and angle at center

Now we can divide this equation on both sides by the time interval Δt for the object to move through that angle:

$$\frac{\Delta s}{\Delta t} = r \, \frac{\Delta \theta}{\Delta t}$$

But Δs/Δt = v and Δθ/Δt = ω, by definition. Hence, we have the following:

$$v = r \, \omega$$

This formula gives us the linear velocity of an object moving in a circle of radius r at angular velocity ω.

It also applies to a rigid body undergoing rotation about an axis. In that case, it gives the linear velocity at a distance r from the axis of rotation. For a given angular velocity ω, the formula then tells us that the velocity is proportional to the distance from the axis (the farther away you are, the faster is the linear velocity).

Let's apply this formula to the examples discussed in the last section. First, we'll calculate the linear velocity of the Earth in its orbit around the Sun. To work this out, we need to know the radius of Earth's orbit (the distance of the Earth from the Sun): 1.5×10^{11} m. We've already worked out the angular velocity of the Earth in its orbit. It is 2.0×10^{-7} rad/s.

Therefore, the orbital velocity of the Earth is given by the following:

$v = r\,\omega = 1.5 \times 10^{11} \times 2.0 \times 10^{-7} = 3 \times 10^{4}$ m/s

This is 30 km/s, or 100 000 km/hr. That's about 100 times the typical speed of an airplane!

As a second example, because the Earth's radius is 6.4×10^{6} m, and its angular velocity about its own axis is 7.3×10^{-5} rad/s (as we worked out in the last section) the speed of any point on the Earth's surface at the equator due to Earth's rotation has the following value:

$v = r\,\omega = 6.4 \times 10^{6} \times 7.3 \times 10^{-5}$ m/s ≈ 470 m/s

This is about 1500 km/hr, or about one and a half times the typical speed of an airplane.

Example: A rolling wheel

We now know enough to be able to put together some simple examples. Our first example will be to create rolling wheels. In contrast with most of the examples in the last few chapters, this example will not involve any dynamics, but only kinematics. So we will not compute motion using forces, but will just tell the objects how to move by specifying the velocity directly.

Another difference is that we will code this example up as a standalone piece of code without using the physics library we've been developing. This is partly because we haven't included rotational motion in our physics engine yet and partly as an exercise to make sure we remember the basics.

To begin with, let's create a wheel. We'd like the wheel to look like that shown in Figure 9-4, with an inner and outer rim, and a number of equally spaced spokes (so that we can see it rotating).

Figure 9-4. A rolling wheel

Here is a Wheel class that does the job:

```
package{
        import flash.display.Sprite;
        import flash.display.Graphics;

        public class Wheel extends Sprite{

                private var _innerRadius:Number;
                private var _outerRadius:Number;
                private var _numSpokes:Number;
```

```
        public function Wheel(pIR:Number,pOR:Number, pnumS:Number):void{
                _innerRadius = pIR;
                _outerRadius = pOR;
                _numSpokes = pnumS;
                drawWheel();
        }

        private function drawWheel():void{
                with (graphics){
                        beginFill(0);
                        drawCircle(0,0,_outerRadius);
                        endFill();
                        beginFill(0xffffff);
                        drawCircle(0,0,_innerRadius);
                        endFill();
                        lineStyle(4);
                }
                for (var n:uint=0; n<_numSpokes; n++){
                        with (graphics){
                                moveTo(0,0);
                                lineTo(_innerRadius*Math.cos↵
(2*Math.PI*n/_numSpokes), _innerRadius*Math.sin(2*Math.PI*n/_numSpokes));
                        }
                }
        }
    }
}
```

The constructor of Wheel takes three arguments: the inner radius, the outer radius, and the number of spokes.

Now we'll create a Wheel instance and make it roll. Take a look at the code in WheelDemo.as:

```
package{
        import flash.display.Sprite;
        import flash.events.Event;

    public class WheelDemo extends Sprite{

            private var _innerRadius:Number=40;
            private var _outerRadius:Number=50;
            private var _numSpokes:Number=10;
            private var _v:Number;
            private var _w:Number=1;           // angular velocity in radians per second
            private var _dt:Number=0.025;      // timestep = 1/FPS
            private var _fac:Number=1;         // slipping/sliding factor

            private var _wheel:Wheel;

            public function WheelDemo():void{
                    init();
            }

            private function init():void{
```

```
        _v = _fac*_w*_outerRadius;        // v = r w
        _wheel = new Wheel(_innerRadius,_outerRadius,_numSpokes);
        _wheel.x = 100;
        _wheel.y = 200;
        addChild(_wheel);
        addEventListener(Event.ENTER_FRAME,onEachTimestep);
    }

    private function onEachTimestep(evt:Event):void{
        _wheel.rotation += _w*_dt*180/Math.PI; // convert w to deg/s
        _wheel.x += _v*_dt;
    }

  }
}
```

We created a Wheel instance and then set up an ENTER_FRAME event listener with an event handler onEachTimestep() that increments the rotation and x properties of the wheel at each timestep. This is done using the angular velocity _w and the linear velocity _v by using these formulas:

```
_wheel.rotation += _w*_dt*180/Math.PI;
_wheel.x += _v*_dt;
```

The first formula indicates that we are specifying the angular velocity in radians per second; hence the need for the factor 180/Math.PI. The second formula uses the value of velocity _v that is precalculated in the constructor using this formula:

```
_v = _fac*_w*_outerRadius;
```

This is basically the formula v = rω, but with an additional factor _fac included to model the effect of slipping or sliding (skidding), with pure rolling if _fac = 1.

Finally, _dt is the timestep that is given the value of 0.025. You may be wondering where that value comes from. This is an estimate of the time interval between successive calls of onEachTimestep(). We expect _dt to be approximately equal to the 1/FPS, where FPS is the frame rate of the movie, which we set at 40. We reiterate that this is just approximate, but is good enough for this simple demo. Recall that in Mover we used the getTimer() function to compute _dt much more accurately.

Run the code with _fac = 1, and you'll see the wheel move so that its translational velocity is consistent with its rotation rate. This gives the appearance of pure rolling without slipping or skidding. If you change the value of _fac to less than 1, say 0.2, the wheel does not move forward fast enough in relation to its rotation; it looks like it's stuck in the mud and is slipping. If you give _fac a value greater than 1, say 5, the wheel moves forward faster than it would do purely as a result of its rotation: it appears to be skidding on ice.

Particles with spin

Before we proceed further, let's update the Particle and Mover classes to allow particles to spin about their center. This is quite straightforward.

In Particle, we create a new property _omega with an associated getter get angVelo() and setter set angVelo() to represent angular velocity:

```
// angular velocity in radians per second
private var _omega:Number=0;

public function get angVelo():Number{
        return _omega;
}
public function set angVelo(pomega:Number):void{
        _omega = pomega;
}
```

In Mover, we include an additional protected method spinObject() in the onTimer() function:

```
private function onTimer(pEvent:TimerEvent):void {
        _dt = 0.001 * (getTimer() - _t0);
        _time += _dt;
        _t0  =getTimer();
        moveObject();
        spinObject();
        pEvent.updateAfterEvent();
}
```

with spinObject() looking as follows:

```
protected function spinObject():void{
        if (_particle.angVelo !=0){
        _particle.rotation += _particle.angVelo*_dt*180/Math.PI;
        }
}
```

This code will make the Particle instance spin on its axis if its angular velocity is non-zero. Note the factor of 180/Math.PI, which converts angles to degrees (because the rotation property deals with degrees rather than radians). A positive value of angVelo will result in a clockwise rotation, and a negative value will result in a counterclockwise rotation.

Any Particle instance animated by a Mover instance will automatically spin if its angular velocity is non-zero. Let's look at a specific example now.

Example: Satellite around a rotating Earth

What we want to achieve in this example is in essence quite simple: an animation of a satellite in a circular orbit around a rotating Earth. The twist is that we want the satellite to orbit so that it is always over the same spot on Earth. This is called a *geostationary orbit*; as you might guess, it's very useful for telecommunications as well as spying.

Once again, this example will involve only kinematics and no dynamics (no forces). Later on in the chapter, we'll add in the forces.

Let's dive right in and create the setup. We borrow the orbits simulation from Chapter 6 and come up with the following code, in the file SatelliteDemo.as:

```
package{
        import flash.display.Sprite;
        import com.physicscodes.objects.Ball;
        import com.physicscodes.math.Vector2D;
        import com.physicscodes.objects.Particle;

        public class SatelliteDemo extends Sprite{
                public function SatelliteDemo():void{
                        init();
                }
                private function init():void{
                        // create 100 stars randomly positioned
                        for (var i:uint=0; i<100; i++){
                                var star:Ball = new Ball(Math.random()*3,0xffff00);
                                star.pos2D = new Vector2D(Math.random()*stage.↵
stageWidth,Math.random()*stage.stageHeight);
                                addChild(star);
                        }

                        // create a spinning Earth
                        var earth:Ball;
                        earth = new Ball(70,0x0099ff,1000000);
                        earth.pos2D = new Vector2D(400,300);
                        earth.angVelo = 0.4;
                        addChild(earth);

                        // create a moving satellite
                        var satellite:Ball;
                        satellite = new Ball(8,0x999999,1);
                        satellite.pos2D = new Vector2D(600,300);
                        //satellite.angVelo = earth.angVelo;
                        // draw antennae
                        with (satellite.graphics){
                                lineStyle(2,0xffffff);
                                moveTo(0,0);
                                lineTo(-20,-10);
                                moveTo(0,0);
                                lineTo(-20,10);
                                moveTo(0,0);
                                lineTo(-15,0);
                        }
                        addChild(satellite);

                        // make the satellite orbit the Earth
                        var orbiter:SatelliteOrbiter=new SatelliteOrbiter(satellite,earth);
                        orbiter.startTime(10);
```

```
                                // make the Earth spin
                                earth.move();
                        }
                }
        }
```

Most of the code will look familiar. We create some stars, an Earth and a satellite, all as Ball instances. The masses that are given to the various objects are irrelevant here as there is no dynamics. You can put any value you want and the animation will behave in exactly the same way.

In addition, we give the Earth a non-zero angular velocity. We also draw three lines on the satellite to give it a nice old-fashioned, Sputnik-like appearance. Then we make the satellite move with the help of the SatelliteOrbiter class, to be described shortly. Finally we make the Earth spin by the move() method.

The SatelliteOrbiter class is simpler than you might expect. Here is the full code:

```
package {
        import com.physicscodes.motion.Mover;
        import com.physicscodes.objects.Particle;
        import com.physicscodes.math.Vector2D;

        public class SatelliteOrbiter extends Mover{
                private var _orbiter:Particle;
                private var _omega:Number;
                private var _r:Number;
                private var _x0:Number;
                private var _y0:Number;

                public function SatelliteOrbiter(porbiter:Particle,pattractor:Particle):void{
                        _orbiter = porbiter;
                        _r = _orbiter.pos2D.subtract(pattractor.pos2D).length;
                        _omega = pattractor.angVelo;
                        _x0 = pattractor.xpos;
                        _y0 = pattractor.ypos;
                        super(porbiter);
                }

                override protected function moveObject():void {
                        _orbiter.pos2D = new
Vector2D(_r*Math.cos(_omega*time)+_x0,_r*Math.sin(_omega*time)+_y0);
                }

        }
}
```

The first thing to note is that SatelliteOrbiter extends Mover instead of Forcer (as we've been doing most of the time). That's because we are not going to have any forces here. The SatelliteOrbiter constructor takes as arguments an orbiter particle (the satellite) and an attractor particle (the Earth). Although we are using the words *orbiter* and *attractor*, we will not model any actual gravitational forces between the particles. Hence, the nature of the animation is different from that of the orbits simulation of Chapter 6. In the constructor, the satellite particle is assigned to a private variable _orbiter, and the distance of the satellite from the Earth is computed and stored in the variable _r. This distance does not change because the orbit will be circular. Then the angular velocity, and x and y position of the Earth are stored in the private variables _omega, _x0 and _y0, respectively.

The action takes place in the overridden moveObject() method, with a single line of code. All we are doing here is telling the satellite where it must be at any time, using these formulas:

$$x = r\cos(\omega t) + x0$$

$$x = r\sin(\omega t) + y0$$

You might recall from Chapter 3 that using cos and sin in this way produces circular motion with angular frequency ω at a radius r. Adding x0 and y0 (the coordinates of the center of the Earth) makes the satellite orbit the Earth. The other important thing is that ω is chosen to be equal to the angular velocity of the Earth. This makes the satellite orbit the Earth at exactly the same rate as the Earth spins on its axis. Run the simulation, and you'll see that this is indeed the case.

We can improve the animation by adding the following line of code to SatelliteDemo.as to make the satellite's antennae always point toward the Earth (see Figure 9.5):

```
satellite.angVelo = earth.angVelo;
```

All this line does is to assign the Earth's angular velocity to the satellite's angVelo property, so that it spins in sync with the Earth.

Figure 9-5. A spy satellite orbiting the Earth

The alert reader will have noticed that we've called this example an *animation* rather than a *simulation*. That's because we basically told the satellite how to move, rather than prescribing the forces that act on it and letting them determine the motion of the satellite. Although the animation does have some physics realism, it is not totally realistic. One reason is that we have forced the satellite to orbit the Earth at the same rate (the same angular velocity) as the Earth spins around its axis. You can change the distance of the satellite from the Earth's center and it will still orbit at the same rate. In reality, satellites can only do so at a specific distance from the Earth's center; in other words, all geostationary satellites must be at the same distance from the Earth! It is not obvious why that should be so, but the next section will help clarify that and help you to build this feature into the animation.

Centripetal acceleration and centripetal force

Now that we've covered the basics, it's time to move on to some slightly more difficult concepts: centripetal acceleration and centripetal force. Actually they are not really difficult, but they are frequently misunderstood. Hence, we'll try and clear some of the possible confusion as we go along.

Centripetal acceleration

As we pointed out in the section on angular velocity, an object moving in a circle (or in a curved path in general) has a linear velocity that is changing with time because its direction is changing all the time. Therefore, from the definition of acceleration as rate of change of velocity, that means it has a non-zero acceleration—we never said that acceleration means just a change in the magnitude of velocity (speed); it could mean a change in direction as well.

It may not be obvious at all, but for an object moving in a circle, this acceleration actually points toward the center of the circle. Therefore, it is called *centripetal acceleration* (from the Latin: *centr* = "center," and *petere* = "to seek"). One way to appreciate this is to think of the center as pulling the object, thereby changing its direction constantly (see Figure 9-6). We'll see in a moment how to calculate the centripetal acceleration.

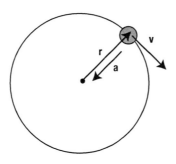

Figure 9-6. Centripetal acceleration

Centripetal acceleration must not be confused with angular acceleration. As explained earlier in this chapter, angular acceleration refers to the rate of change of angular velocity. In the case of uniform circular motion, the angular acceleration is zero because the angular velocity is constant (that's what "uniform" means), but the centripetal acceleration is not zero. The centripetal acceleration is a measure of the rate of change of linear velocity, when the latter is only changing in direction while its magnitude remains constant.

Centripetal acceleration, velocity and angular velocity

How do we calculate the centripetal acceleration? Well, there is a simple formula for it. It's not easy to prove, so the best thing is just to believe us! Here is one form of the formula:

$$a = \frac{v^2}{r}$$

Referring to Figure 9-6, this formula tells us the centripetal acceleration for an object moving with velocity v in a circle or arc of radius r. From this we deduce that if the velocity is large, the acceleration is large (for the same radius); and if the radius is small, the acceleration is large (for the same velocity magnitude).

Remembering that $v = r\omega$, you can replace v in the preceding formula to come up with an alternative form for the formula in terms of r and ω:

$$a = r\,\omega^2$$

This formula now tells us that the centripetal acceleration is larger when the angular velocity is larger (for the same radius). But it also tells us that the centripetal acceleration is larger when the radius is larger, *for the same angular velocity*. This does not contradict what we said previous in relation to the other form of the formula, but can seem confusing at first! The key point is that here the linear velocity magnitude is not assumed to be constant for different radiuses. In fact, if the angular velocity is constant, then the linear velocity magnitude must increase with radius because $v = r\omega$.

One consequence of the last formula is that for a rigid body spinning about its axis, points farther away from the axis have a larger acceleration (because all points on the rigid body have the same angular velocity) as well as a larger velocity (because $v = r\omega$).

Centripetal force

We've just seen that any object in uniform circular motion must experience an acceleration toward the center of the circular trajectory. Therefore, by Newton's second law, there must be a *resultant force* on it that is also directed toward the center. This is known as the *centripetal force*.

The centripetal force is the force that is needed to keep an object in circular motion. It needs to be provided continuously by some physical agent; otherwise, the object cannot maintain circular motion.

As an example, an object whirled around by a string gets its centripetal force from the tension in the string. A car moving around a circular track gets centripetal force from friction exerted by the ground on the tires. Planets orbiting the Sun experience a centripetal force due to the Sun's gravitational attraction.

It's very easy to work out the formula for centripetal force. Because F = ma, you just need to multiply the formulas for centripetal acceleration by m (the mass of the moving object) to obtain this:

$$F = \frac{m\,v^2}{r}$$

And to get this:

$$F = m\,r\,\omega^2$$

In vector form, the first formula can be written as follows:

$$\mathbf{F} = -\frac{m\,v^2}{r^2}\,\mathbf{r}$$

Or it can be written like this, where $\mathbf{r}_u$ is a unit vector in the direction of the position vector $\mathbf{r}$ of the moving object with respect to the center:

$$\mathbf{F} = -\frac{m\,v^2}{r}\,\mathbf{r}_u$$

The minus sign arises because the force points toward the center (opposite to the vector $\mathbf{r}$). Similar vector forms also hold for the formula $F = mr\omega^2$.

Common misconceptions about centripetal force

Centripetal force is probably one of the most misunderstood concepts in physics. Let's try and clear some of the confusion.

- Centripetal force is not a new "type" of force in the same sense that gravity and friction are types of forces. It is simply the force that must be present to make an object move in a circle. Different forces can act as centripetal forces, including gravity and friction.

- Sometimes people mistakenly talk about the need to "balance" the centripetal force. For example, a common misunderstanding is that the gravitational force on a planet in orbit around the Sun balances the centripetal force. That does not make sense for several reasons. First, the centripetal force must point toward the Sun, and so does the gravitational force, so they are both in the same direction. Second, *if* the two forces *did* balance, the resultant force on the planet would be zero; its acceleration would therefore be zero and so it would have to move in a straight line at constant velocity (by Newton's first law of motion). Third, centripetal force is not even a "type" of force. The correct thinking is that the gravitational force *provides* the centripetal force necessary for the planet to orbit the Sun.

- You may also hear about something called *centrifugal force*, which has the same magnitude as the centripetal force but acts in the opposite direction (away from the center of rotation). Centrifugal force is not a real force but a so-called pseudo force. It arises out of the attempt to analyze motion within the framework of Newton's laws but from the point of view of a rotating frame of reference. An example is the description of atmospheric motion from a reference frame on the Earth (which is, of course, rotating). Although centrifugal force certainly has its place in physics in analyzing problems like this, it can cause a lot of confusion, too. Our recommendation is therefore to avoid thinking in terms of centrifugal forces.

Example: Revisiting the satellite animation

As a first example of the application of the centripetal force concept, let's go back to the satellite animation and inject some more realism into it as promised.

Here the centripetal force is provided by the force of gravity on the satellite. Therefore we can equate the expression for centripetal force with that for the gravitational force to obtain the following equation, where m is the satellite mass, M is the Earth mass, r is the distance of the satellite from the Earth's center and ω is the angular velocity of the satellite:

$$m\, r\, \omega^2 = \frac{G\,M\,m}{r^2}$$

It is easy to rearrange this equation to give the following:

$$r = \sqrt[3]{\frac{G\,M}{\omega^2}}$$

This formula tells us the radius at which the satellite must be in order to orbit at an angular velocity ω. In other words, the satellite cannot have just any angular velocity at any distance; the centripetal force dictates that it has to rotate at a fixed angular velocity for any given distance from the Earth! In particular, we can use the formula to calculate the distance at which it must be to rotate at the same angular velocity as the Earth's spin. If you substitute the values for G, M (the mass of the Earth), and ω (the Earth's angular velocity as we worked out before), you'll find that the radius of a geostationary orbit is 42,400 km, or approximately 6.6 times the radius of the Earth.

Going back to our animation, we need to make the satellite aware of the constraint between its distance from the Earth and its angular velocity around the Earth, as expressed by the previous equation. In fact, in the animation we'll specify the position of the satellite, and therefore the distance r from the Earth, and want to work out its resulting angular velocity ω instead of setting it to be equal to that of the Earth.

Therefore, we want a formula for ω in terms of r. It's easy enough to manipulate the previous equation to give the following:

$$\omega = \sqrt{\frac{GM}{r^3}}$$

That's all we need. We copied SatelliteDemo.as to SatelliteDemo2.as, and SatelliteOrbiter.as to SatelliteOrbiter2.as. If you look at the latter file, you'll see that practically the only change we've made is to replace this line:

```
_omega = pattractor.angVelo;
```

by the following line:

```
_omega = Math.sqrt(_G*pattractor.mass/(_r*_r*_r));
```

with the value of the gravitational constant _G being set to 1.

If you now run the code with the previous positions and masses of the satellite and Earth and angular velocity of the Earth, you'll see that the satellite is no longer in a geostationary orbit. In fact, by the time it completes one orbit, its antennae are already pointing the wrong way. If you use the previous formula to calculate the value of r for a geostationary orbit with the given values of G = 1, M = 1000000, and ω = 0.4, you will get r = 184.2. This is the distance that the satellite should be from the Earth's center. Given that the Earth is located at (400,300), you just need to change the position of the satellite to (584.2,300) in SatelliteDemo2.as:

```
satellite.pos2D = new Vector2D(584.2,300);
```

Do this and then run the code. You'll see that the satellite does orbit at the same angular velocity as the Earth.

Example: Circular orbits with gravitational force

In this example, we go back to a full dynamical simulation. In fact, we already did that in the orbits simulation in Chapter 6, in which we simulated the motion of a planet round the Sun. The simulation already "knows" that gravity is a centripetal force, so there is nothing else to add. But if we want circular orbits, we can use the centripetal force formula to work out exactly what velocity we need to give the planet.

Again, this is simply a matter of equating the expressions for centripetal force and gravitational force. This time, we use the form F = mv²/r for the centripetal force:

$$\frac{m\,v^2}{r} = \frac{G\,M\,m}{r^2}$$

A little bit of algebra then gives us the following, which is the velocity magnitude that the planet must have in order to have a circular orbit around the Sun at a distance r from its center:

$$v = \sqrt{\frac{G\,M}{r}}$$

Let's code this up into a modified version of the orbits simulation. The new source files are called CircularOrbits.as and Orbiter.as. Let's look at what Orbiter looks like first:

```
package {
        import com.physicscodes.motion.Forcer;
        import com.physicscodes.motion.Forces;
        import com.physicscodes.objects.Particle;
        import com.physicscodes.math.Vector2D;

        public class Orbiter extends Forcer{

                private var _orbiter:Particle;
                private var _massOrbiter:Number;
                private var _massAttractor:Number;
                private var _center:Vector2D;
                private var _G:Number;

                public function Orbiter(porbiter:Particle,pattractor:Particle,pG:Number):void{
                        _orbiter = porbiter;
                        _massOrbiter = porbiter.mass;
                        _massAttractor = pattractor.mass;
                        _center = pattractor.pos2D;
                        _G = pG;
                        super(porbiter);
                }

                override protected function calcForce():void{
                        force = Forces.gravity(_G,_massAttractor,_massOrbiter,↪
_orbiter.pos2D.subtract(_center));
                }
        }
}
```

This is very similar to its previous incarnation in Chapter 6. We calculate the gravitational force using Newton's formula in the calcForce() method using the masses of the planet and the Sun and their distance apart. One difference is that the constructor now takes three arguments: the orbiter particle, the attractor particle, and the value of the gravitational constant G.

Next, let's take a look at the code in `CircularOrbits.as`:

```
package{
        import flash.display.Sprite;
        import com.physicscodes.objects.Ball;
        import com.physicscodes.math.Vector2D;
        import com.physicscodes.objects.Particle;

        public class CircularOrbits extends Sprite{
                public function CircularOrbits():void{
                        init();
                }
                private function init():void{
                        var G:Number = 1; // Gravitational constant
                        var sunMass:Number = 1000000;
                        var planetMass:Number = 1;
                        var distance:Number;
                        var vMag:Number;

                        // create 100 stars randomly positioned
                        for (var i:uint=0; i<100; i++){
                                var star:Ball = new Ball(Math.random()*3,0xffff00);
                                star.pos2D = new Vector2D(Math.random()*stage.↪
stageWidth,Math.random()*stage.stageHeight);
                                addChild(star);
                        }

                        // create a stationary sun
                        var sun:Ball;
                        sun = new Ball(60,0xff9900,sunMass);
                        sun.pos2D = new Vector2D(400,300);
                        addChild(sun);

                        // create a moving planet
                        var planet:Ball;
                        planet = new Ball(10,0x0000ff,planetMass);
                        planet.pos2D = new Vector2D(400,50);

                        distance = planet.pos2D.subtract(sun.pos2D).length;
                        vMag = Math.sqrt(G*sunMass/distance);
                        planet.velo2D = new Vector2D(vMag,0);
                        addChild(planet);

                        // make the planet orbit the sun
                        var orbiter:Orbiter=new Orbiter(planet,sun,G);
                        orbiter.startTime();
                }
        }
}
```

Most of the code should be very familiar. We have not given the Sun and planet any spin because that is not what we are demonstrating here. The new thing in this simulation is that we give the planet exactly the initial velocity it needs to move in a circular orbit. This is done in the two lines highlighted in bold, using the formula v = √(GM/r) that we just derived.

Run the simulation with the initial values as given in the previous code listing, and you'll find that the planet indeed describes a circular orbit around the Sun. To convince yourself that this works at any distance from the Sun, change the initial position of the planet to the following:

```
planet.pos2D = new Vector2D(400,150);
```

This positions the planet closer to the Sun. If you now run the code, you'll see that the planet orbits the Sun at a faster rate, but the orbit is still circular.

Note that the velocity must be tangential with no radial component (see Figure 9-7). If there is any radial velocity component, the planet will either approach or recede from the Sun (its orbit won't be circular). For example, with the initial position of the planet at (400, 50), try the following:

```
planet.velo2D = new Vector2D(vMag/Math.sqrt(2), vMag/Math.sqrt(2));
```

This gives the planet an initial velocity of the same magnitude vMag as before, but in a different direction, so that it has a radial component toward the Sun as well as a tangential component. You will find that the planet's orbit is now highly elliptical, with the planet getting very close to the Sun and then receding away from it.

You are encouraged to try different initial positions and velocities to see the types of orbits you get. You should find that, without using the formula v = √(GM/r), it is rather hard to get the initial conditions just right to produce even approximately circular orbits by simple trial and error!

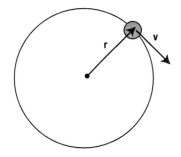

Figure 9-7. Tangential velocity

Example: Car moving around a bend

In the next example, we simulate the motion of a car round a circular track and use it to demonstrate skidding if the car goes too fast.

The basic physics here is that when a car moves round a curve or bend, the centripetal force it needs to do so is provided by the frictional force on the tires in contact with the road surface (see Figure 9-8).

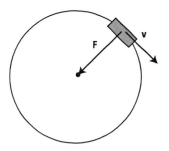

Figure 9-8. Friction provides the centripetal force for a car to negotiate a bend

Going back to the formula for centripetal force, the faster the car moves, the larger the centripetal force needed to keep it moving around the bend:

$$F = \frac{m\,v^2}{r}$$

Incidentally, the formula also shows that the centripetal force is larger for sharper bends, which curve with a *smaller* radius.

The frictional force is the static frictional force and, as discussed in Chapter 7, it has a maximum value given by $f = C_s N$, where N is the normal force (which is here equal to the car's weight mg), and C_s is the coefficient of static friction between the tires and the road surface. Therefore, if the centripetal force needed to negotiate a bend exceeds the maximum static friction, the car won't be able to follow the curvature of the bend—it will skid.

We now build a simulation that can handle this scenario in a natural way. The file CarDemo.as creates the setup shown in Figure 9-9.

Figure 9-9. The skidding car simulation

Here is the code that does it:

```
package{
        import flash.display.Sprite;
        import com.physicscodes.objects.Ball;
        import com.physicscodes.objects.Box;
        import com.physicscodes.math.Vector2D;
        import com.physicscodes.objects.Particle;
        import flash.display.Graphics;

        public class CarDemo extends Sprite{

                public function CarDemo():void{
                        init();
                }

                private function init():void{

                        // create a circular track, e.g. a roundabout
                        with (graphics){
                                beginFill(0xcccccc);
                                drawCircle(275,200,100);
                                drawCircle(275,200,50);
                                endFill();
                        }

                        var center:Ball;
                        center=new Ball(5,0x000000);
                        center.pos2D=new Vector2D(275,200);
                        addChild(center);

                        // create a car
                        var car:Box;
                        car = new Box(10,20,0x0000ff,90);
                        car.pos2D = new Vector2D(350,200);
                        car.velo2D=new Vector2D(0,-20);
                        car.angVelo = -car.velo2D.length/(car.pos2D.subtract➥
(center.pos2D).length);
                        addChild(car);

                        // make the car move
                        var mover:CarMover=new CarMover(car,center.pos2D);
                        mover.startTime(10);
                }
        }
}
```

As shown in the figure, we begin by drawing a circular track and then create a Ball instance representing the center of the track. The next step introduces a bit of artistic novelty.

Because we are dealing with a car, a `Ball` instance simply won't do. Instead, our car is a Box instance. Box is a class that is essentially similar to `Ball` except that it draws a filled rectangle instead of a circle with a gradient fill. Box takes five parameters (width, height, color, mass, and charge), all of which have default values and are therefore optional:

```
Box(pboxWidth:Number=20,pboxHeight:Number=20,pcolor:uint=0x0000ff,pmass:Number=1,↪
pcharge:Number=0)
```

After creating the car as a Box instance, we position it on the track and give it an initial tangential velocity. The next line then gives the car a spin angular velocity equal to its "orbital" angular velocity by using the formula $\omega = v/r$, where v is the car's speed, and r is its distance from the center.

Finally, a CarMover instance drives the action. CarMover takes the car instance and the position vector of the center as arguments. This is what CarMover looks like:

```
package{
        import com.physicscodes.motion.Forcer;
        import com.physicscodes.motion.Forces;
        import com.physicscodes.objects.Box;
        import com.physicscodes.math.Vector2D;

        public class CarMover extends Forcer{
                private var _car:Box;
                private var _center:Vector2D;
                private var _dist:Vector2D;
                private var _velo:Number;
                private var _g:Number=10;
                private var _Cs:Number=1;

                public function CarMover(pcar:Box,pcenter:Vector2D):void{
                        _car = pcar;
                        _center = pcenter;
                        _velo = pcar.velo2D.length;
                        super(_car);
                }

                override protected function calcForce():void{
                        _dist=_car.pos2D.subtract(_center);
                        var centripetalForce:Vector2D = _dist.unit().multiply↪
(-_car.mass*_velo*_velo/_dist.length);
                        var radialFriction:Vector2D = _dist.unit().multiply↪
(-_Cs*_car.mass*_g);
                        if(radialFriction.length > centripetalForce.length) {
                                force = centripetalForce;
                        }
                        else{
                                force = radialFriction;
                        }
                }
        }
}
```

The code should be easy to follow. In calcForce(), we calculate the centripetal force using the formula F = mv^2/r in vector form and the maximum frictional force on the car using the formula F = C_smg (see Chapter 7), where m is the mass of the car. For simplicity, we assume that static and dynamic friction are the same. Also, we assume that the resultant force on the car is friction in the radial direction. The if block checks whether the maximum friction is sufficient to provide the centripetal force. If so, the resultant force is taken to be equal to the centripetal force; if not, the resultant force is equal to the maximum friction.

If you run the simulation with an initial velocity of 10 or 20 px/s, you'll find that the car moves around the track without problem. However, if you increase the velocity beyond about 30, the car will skid!

Non-uniform circular motion

So far in this chapter we've dealt only with uniform circular motion. How do we handle rotations when the angular velocity is not constant? In this last section, we'll begin to look at this problem and illustrate it with an example. A fuller treatment of non-uniform rotation will involve delving into concepts such as angular momentum and torque. For that, you'll have to await Chapter 13.

Tangential force and acceleration

The underlying difference between uniform and non-uniform circular motion is that in the former, centripetal force is the only force, whereas in the latter there is a tangential as well as a centripetal force (see Figure 9-10). *Tangential* literally means "along a tangent" to the circle. The centripetal force in non-uniform circular motion is given by the same formulas as for the uniform case. As with centripetal force, the tangential force can be due to any number of factors such as gravity or friction.

Note that centripetal force changes only the direction of motion, which is why uniform circular motion is uniform. But because tangential forces act in the direction of the velocity vector, they cause a change in the speed of the rotating object. This also means there is a non-zero angular acceleration when a tangential force is present.

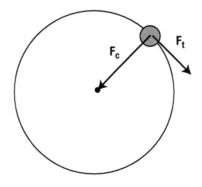

Figure 9-10. Tangential (**F**t) and centripetal (**F**c) forces

The bottom line: to simulate non-uniform circular motion, we need forces that will provide both centripetal and tangential force components, as demonstrated in our next and final example.

Example: A simple pendulum

A so-called *simple pendulum* consists of a heavy bob suspended by a cord to a fixed pivot. The pendulum is set into oscillation by displacing the bob slightly and releasing it. Simulating a simple pendulum is not totally straightforward and does require a bit of thinking to get the physics right.

Figure 9-11 shows the force diagram for a simple pendulum. The cord will usually be inclined at some angle θ to the vertical. We assume that the cord has negligible mass and that there is no friction or drag. Let m denote the mass of the bob. There are then two forces acting on the bob: gravity acting vertically downward with magnitude mg; and the tension in the cord acting toward the fixed pivot with magnitude T.

Obviously, the bob moves in a circular arc with the pivot as its center. But the angular velocity of the bob is non-uniform. In fact, it is zero when the bob is in its uppermost position and maximum when the bob is at its lowest point. Therefore, there is an angular acceleration because of a tangential force component. Because the tension is in the radial direction (which is perpendicular to the tangential direction), it has no tangential component. But the force of gravity in general does have a tangential component given by mg sin(θ). This is the force that causes the angular acceleration. Note that because the angle θ changes with time, the tangential force and therefore the angular acceleration are not constant.

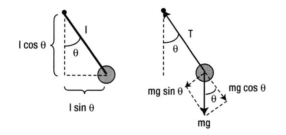

Figure 9-11. Geometrical and force diagram for a pendulum

What is the radial force component that provides the centripetal force? From Figure 9-11, it's clear that gravity has a component mg cos(θ) that acts away from the pivot. Hence, the net radial force component is T − mg cos(θ), and this must be equal to the centripetal force:

$$T - mg\cos(\theta) = \frac{m v^2}{r}$$

Therefore, this implies that the magnitude of the tension T is given by the following:

$$T = mg\cos(\theta) + \frac{m v^2}{r}$$

As is clear from Figure 9-11, the direction of the tension force is opposite to the position vector **r** of the bob relative to the pivot.

Now comes the clever bit. All we need to do is to specify the forces of gravity mg and tension T, as given by the last equation. Then, once we give it an initial position, the bob ought to know how to move under those two forces. Let's go ahead and code it up.

PendulumDemo.as contains the code that sets up the objects:

```
package{
        import flash.display.Sprite;
        import com.physicscodes.objects.Ball;
        import com.physicscodes.math.Vector2D;
        import com.physicscodes.objects.Particle;

        public class PendulumDemo extends Sprite{

                public function PendulumDemo():void{
                        init();
                }

                private function init():void{
                        // create a cord
                        var cord:Sprite=new Sprite();
                        addChild(cord);

                        // pendulum length
                        var lengthP:Number=100;

                        // create a pivot
                        var pivot:Ball;
                        pivot=new Ball(2,0x000000);
                        pivot.pos2D=new Vector2D(275,150);
                        addChild(pivot)

                        // create a pendulum bob
                        var bob:Ball;
                        bob = new Ball(10,0x333333,1);
                        var initAngle:Number = 30;
                        var relativePos:Vector2D = new Vector2D(lengthP*Math.↵
sin(initAngle*Math.PI/180), lengthP*Math.cos(initAngle*Math.PI/180));
                        bob.pos2D = pivot.pos2D.add(relativePos);
                        addChild(bob);

                        // make the pendulum move
                        var pendulum:Pendulum=new Pendulum(bob,cord,pivot.pos2D);
                        pendulum.startTime(10);
                }
        }
}
```

We begin by creating a cord (a blank Sprite that we'll draw a line on during the simulation), a pivot, and a pendulum bob. The bob is positioned so the cord makes an initial angle of 30 degrees with the vertical.

To see this, refer to Figure 9-11, which shows that the x and y coordinates of the bob relative to the pivot are given by the following, where l is the "length" of the pendulum, defined as the distance of the center of the bob to the fixed pivot:

$$x = l \sin(\theta)$$

$$y = l \cos(\theta)$$

Physically, l is equal to the sum of the length of the cord and the radius of the bob. In the code, we denote this by the variable `lengthP`. This relative position vector is calculated and stored in the variable `relativePos`, which is then added to the pivot's `pos2D` property to set the position of the bob. The initial inclination angle (in degrees) is set by the parameter `initAngle`.

The pendulum is set in motion by instantiating the class Pendulum and passing the bob, the cord, and the position of the pivot as parameters. This is what `Pendulum.as` looks like:

```
package {
        import com.physicscodes.motion.Forcer;
        import com.physicscodes.motion.Forces;
        import com.physicscodes.objects.Ball;
        import com.physicscodes.math.Vector2D;
        import com.physicscodes.objects.Particle;
        import flash.display.Sprite;

        public class Pendulum extends Forcer{
                private var _bob:Ball;
                private var _cord:Sprite;
                private var _center:Vector2D;
                private var _dist:Vector2D;
                private var _bobMass:Number;
                private var _lengthP:Number;
                private var _g:Number=100;

                public function Pendulum(pbob:Ball,pcord:Sprite,ppivotPos:Vector2D):void{
                        _bob = pbob;
                        _bobMass = pbob.mass;
                        _center = ppivotPos;
                        _cord = pcord;
                        _lengthP = _bob.pos2D.subtract(_center).length;
                        super(pbob);
                }

                override protected function moveObject():void{
                        super.moveObject();
                        drawSpring();
                }

                private function drawSpring():void{
                        with (_cord.graphics){
                                clear();
```

```
                               lineStyle(2,0x999999);
                               moveTo(_center.x,_center.y);
                               lineTo(_bob.x,_bob.y)
                      }
              }

              override protected function calcForce():void{
                      _dist=_bob.pos2D.subtract(_center);
                      var gravity:Vector2D = Forces.constantGravity(_bobMass,_g);
                      var tension:Vector2D;
                      if(_dist.length >= _lengthP) {
                              tension = _dist.unit().multiply(-(gravity.projection(_dist)+↵
_bobMass*_bob.velo2D.lengthSquared/_lengthP));
                      }else{
                              tension = new Vector2D(0,0);
                      }
                      force = Forces.add([gravity, tension]);
              }
      }
}
```

You've seen this type of code enough times now, so we'll just concentrate on explaining the bits that are different. That's basically what's in the calcForce() method. We calculate gravity in the usual way. The if block of code checks to see if the distance of the bob from the pivot is greater or equal to the cord length. If so, that means the cord is taut and therefore the tension is non-zero, being calculated using the formula $T = mg \cos(\theta) + mv^2/r$; otherwise, the cord is not taut, so the tension is zero. In the current setup, it is not strictly necessary to check if the cord is taut because the simulation starts with a taut cord and it remains so all the time. But implementing this check makes the code more robust to possible future modifications. Note that the radial component of gravity $mg \cos(\theta)$ is computed using the nifty projection() method, which we introduced into the Vector2D class so that vec1.projection(vec2) gives the projection of vector vec1 in the direction of vector vec2. Here is the definition of projection():

```
public function projection(vec:Vector2D):Number {
      var proj:Number;
      if( (length == 0) || ( vec.length == 0) ){
              proj = 0;
      }else {
              proj = (_x*vec.x + _y*vec.y)/vec.length;
      }
      return proj;
}
```

If you run the code and play with the parameters, you'll see that the pendulum oscillates faster if the cord length is shorter and if the value of g is larger. This is just as it should be in reality. In fact you can test how good your simulated pendulum is by comparing the period of the oscillations with the theoretical value.

Physics theory says that for oscillations of small amplitude, the period of a simple pendulum is given approximately by the following, where l is the length of the pendulum:

$$T = 2\pi \sqrt{\frac{l}{g}}$$

The values we used in the simulation are l = 100 and g = 100. This gives you T = 2π, which is approximately 6.3 seconds. Check if the simulation gives this value by tracing the time and timing to ten oscillations, for example, and then dividing the total time by ten. You should get a value very close to 6.3 s. It works almost like the real thing! See Figure 9-12.

Figure 9-12. The pendulum simulation

Summary

This chapter introduced some of the physics needed to handle circular and rotational motion, focusing on particle and simple rigid body rotation. This chapter has laid the foundations for a more detailed look at rigid body rotation, which we'll present in Chapter 13. Some of the concepts introduced here will also be applied and developed further in the next chapter on long-range forces.

Chapter 10

Long-Range Forces

In this last chapter of Part II, we'll introduce yet more force laws. However, the approach and purpose here will be more playful than in previous chapters. You'll learn things that you may not necessarily use for making realistic simulations, but more for producing fun animations and effects.

Topics covered in this chapter include:

- **Particle interactions and force fields:** There are two ways of viewing forces that act at a distance: in terms of direct interactions between particles or in terms of force fields.

- **Gravitational force:** We revisit gravity as an example of a long-range force, giving further examples and building a black hole game!

- **Electrostatic force:** This relates to the force between electrically charged particles at rest, which can be attractive or repulsive. Interesting effects can be produced with electric forces.

- **Electromagnetic force:** Moving charges experience a magnetic force as well as an electric force. Together, they constitute an electromagnetic force, which can be used to produce more complicated types of motion.

- **Other force laws:** There is no reason why you can't invent your own force laws to produce cool effects. We'll take a look at some examples, including so-called central forces of different types.

Particle interactions and force fields

Whenever we've talked about forces so far in this book, we've thought of them as being exerted by particles on other particles. But there is another way to think of forces that are exerted at a distance—we can think of them as being due to *force fields*. This is a fairly subtle concept, so we'll take some time to explain things in the next couple of sections.

Interaction at a distance

In this chapter, we'll deal exclusively with forces that are exerted and felt at a distance; the interacting objects don't need to be in contact. Actually, at a fundamental level, all forces are like that, even contact forces. The difference is that contact forces are felt when two objects are very close together. Collisions are similar; they occur when two objects are so close together that their constituent molecules exert electrical forces on each other. So the real distinction is really between short-range and long-range forces. Contact forces and collisions involve short-range forces. Gravity is a long-range force. In general, both short-range and long-range forces can be attractive or repulsive.

From particle interactions to force fields

Historically, physicists were not very happy about the fact that forces like gravity appear to be exerted across empty space, with two remote objects being apparently able to influence each other instantly. This was the so-called *action-at-a-distance* problem. So they came up with the concept of a *force field* to replace the action-at-a-distance concept.

The idea of a force field, though seemingly esoteric, is actually quite simple. A *field of force* is simply a region of space where a force is felt. If you have two objects with mass, such as a star and a planet, the usual way to think of gravity is that they each exert a gravitational force on each other. In the field conception, you say that the star sets up a gravitational field that permeates the space around it. Any other object, such as a planet, then experiences a force due to the field at the point where it is located. The key idea is that the field mediates the interaction between the star and the planet. There is then no action-at-a-distance any more; the force felt by the planet is a local one, due to the force field that exists locally. In fact, the force field exists whether or not there is a planet there to experience a force.

Note that in the previous example, the planet also sets up its own gravitational field, which then causes the star to experience a force equal and opposite to that experienced by the planet, in accordance with Newton's third law of motion.

As we know, the force felt by the planet depends on its distance from the star. In the field concept, the variation of the force with distance is encapsulated in the concept of *field strength*. In the case of gravity, the field strength decreases with distance from the source of the field (in this case, a star). In the next section we'll see the precise form of the field strength due to the star. It is also customary to refer to the field strength simply as the *field*.

Similar ideas apply to other long-range forces, such as electric forces. Particles create force fields. Other particles then experience forces in the presence of that field. The amount of force they experience depends on the field strength.

Why do you have to care about force fields? One important practical advantage is that force fields free us from the need to have particles just so they can exert forces. As you'll see later in the chapter, we can produce a force field without worrying about how it can be produced by particles. This gives us great flexibility in the type of forces we can subject particles to. The concepts of force field and field strength are especially useful in connection with electric and magnetic forces, but let's take a closer look at them in the context of gravity. They will then be easier to appreciate when we talk about the rather more abstract electric and magnetic fields.

Newtonian gravitation

Gravity is an archetypal example of a long-range force. The field strength in this case is defined as the force per unit mass that acts on a particle at any given point in the field. This is a sensible definition: It tells us how strong the gravity force field is by telling us the force that it exerts on an object of unit mass.

Gravitational field strength is a vector denoted by the symbol **g**. So, the definition tells us that

$$\mathbf{g} = \frac{\mathbf{F}}{m}$$

You will recognize this as being equivalent to the familiar formula for the gravitational force on an object of mass m:

$$\mathbf{F} = m\,\mathbf{g}$$

So, the gravitational field strength is a vector with magnitude equal to the acceleration due to gravity g. In particular, that means it has the same value for all objects, regardless of their mass or other characteristics. In general, the gravitational field strength vector **g** can change with position, just like the (non-bolded) scalar g. In a uniform gravitational field, such as close to the surface of the Earth, both **g** and g are constant.

To reiterate an important point, the key thing with the definition of the gravitational field strength is that it is a property only of the field, as it exists independently of any object that may experience a force due to it. Whereas the gravitational *force on* an object will depend on its mass, the gravitational field strength **g** itself tells us the force per unit mass at any point in the field. From this, we can work out the force **F** on any mass m by multiplying by m.

Gravitational field due to a particle

As an example, the gravitational field strength due to a particle of mass M, such as a star, can be computed starting from Newton's law of gravitation:

$$\mathbf{F} = -\frac{G\,M\,m}{r^3}\,\mathbf{r}$$

Here, m is the mass of any other particle in the field generated by the mass M, and **r** is its position vector relative to the source of the field.

Because the gravitational field strength is defined by **g** = **F**/m, we just have to divide the preceding formula by m to give this:

$$\mathbf{g} = -\frac{G\,M}{r^{3}}\,\mathbf{r}$$

As you can see explicitly in the previous formula, the gravitational field **g** depends only on the mass M of the particle that is producing it and the position vector from the particle, but not on any other particles that may be present. We can also deduce that the magnitude of **g** is given by g = GM/r^2, consistent with the variation of acceleration due to gravity derived in Chapter 6.

In general, **g** could be much more complicated than this simple formula. In a galaxy, for example, **g** is the vector sum of all the fields produced by the individual stars (all of which are, of course, moving). But simulating the motion of stars in a galaxy can be done much more efficiently using the field concept than by directly calculating all the forces between every pair of stars, as you'll see in Chapter 12. Meanwhile, it's time to start playing with some simpler examples of gravity as a long-range force.

Gravity with multiple orbiters

Our first example will involve a single gravitational attractor, which will be held fixed. We borrow the Orbits simulation from Chapter 6, but we'll add more orbiting planets to make it more interesting and to illustrate the fact that each planet experiences a different gravitational field strength at any given time, and therefore moves along a different trajectory. Here is the modified code that does this in `Orbits.as`:

```
package{
        import flash.display.Sprite;
        import com.physicscodes.objects.Ball;
        import com.physicscodes.math.Vector2D;
        import com.physicscodes.objects.Particle;

        public class Orbits extends Sprite{
                public function Orbits():void{
                        init();
                }
                private function init():void{
                        // create 100 stars randomly positioned
                        for (var i:uint=0; i<100; i++){
                                var star:Ball = new Ball(Math.random()*2,0xffff00);
                                star.pos2D = new Vector2D(Math.random()*stage.stageWidth,↵
Math.random()*stage.stageHeight);
                                addChild(star);
                        }

                        // create a stationary sun
                        var sun:Ball;
                        sun = new Ball(50,0xff9900,1000000);
                        sun.pos2D = new Vector2D(400,300);
                        addChild(sun);

                        // create a moving planet
```

```
                        var planet:Ball;
                        planet = new Ball(10,0x0000ff,1);
                        planet.pos2D = new Vector2D(400,50);
                        planet.velo2D = new Vector2D(65,0);
                        addChild(planet);

                        // create another moving planet
                        var planet2:Ball;
                        planet2 = new Ball(6,0xcccccc,1);
                        planet2.pos2D = new Vector2D(500,300);
                        planet2.velo2D = new Vector2D(0,100);
                        addChild(planet2);

                        // create another moving planet
                        var planet3:Ball;
                        planet3 = new Ball(12,0x996633,1);
                        planet3.pos2D = new Vector2D(200,300);
                        planet3.velo2D = new Vector2D(0,-70);
                        addChild(planet3);

                        // make the planet orbit the sun
                        var orbiter:Orbiter=new Orbiter([planet, planet2, planet3],sun);
                        orbiter.startTime(10);
                }
        }
}
```

The main thing here is that we are creating three planets and then initializing their positions and velocities so that they end up orbiting the sun. The planets are placed at different distances from the sun and then given an initial tangential velocity. The magnitudes of the velocities are chosen essentially by trial and error; or you can use the method given in Chapter 9 to choose the velocities that will give a roughly circular orbit.

Orbiter.as is based on the version coded up in Chapter 6, with some suitable modifications to allow multiple orbiters:

```
package {
        import com.physicscodes.motion.MultiForcer;
        import com.physicscodes.motion.Forces;
        import com.physicscodes.objects.Particle;
        import com.physicscodes.math.Vector2D;

        public class Orbiter extends MultiForcer{
                private var _massAttractor:Number;
                private var _center:Vector2D;
                private var _G:Number = 1;

                public function Orbiter(porbiters:Array,pattractor:Particle):void{
                        _massAttractor = pattractor.mass;
                        _center = pattractor.pos2D;
                        super(porbiters);
                }
                override protected function calcForce(porbiter:Particle):void{
```

```
                          force = Forces.gravity(_G,_massAttractor,porbiter.mass,↪
porbiter.pos2D.subtract(_center));
                    }
            }
}
```

Notably, `Orbiter` now extends `MultiForcer` and the force of gravity is calculated for each orbiter in `calcForce()` using the `Forces.gravity()` function.

If you run the code, you'll get a nice solar system toy simulation (see Figure 10-1). The basic physics is there. For example, the nearer a planet is to the sun, the faster it orbits. But this simulation is not completely accurate. As you saw in earlier examples, the Euler integration scheme quickly accumulates errors. If you are looking to do an accurate Solar System simulation, you'll need a better integrator. We'll do that in Chapter 16, where we'll also account for the forces between the planets as well as input accurate data on the masses, sizes, positions, and velocities of the planets.

Figure 10-1. Multiple orbiting planets around a sun

Gravity with multiple attractors

Let's complicate things a little by adding another attractor. As in the previous example, we'll keep the attractors fixed. It's not difficult to make them move; that would produce some interesting overall motion. But we'd have to be more careful with our numerical integration scheme. We'll come back to this issue in Chapter 14.

The new setup code is called `Attractors.as` and looks as follows:

```
package{
        import flash.display.Sprite;
        import com.physicscodes.objects.Ball;
        import com.physicscodes.math.Vector2D;
        import com.physicscodes.objects.Particle;

        public class Attractors extends Sprite{
                public function Attractors():void{
                        init();
                }
                private function init():void{
```

```
                        var G:Number = 1; // Gravitational constant

                        // create a fixed attractor
                        var center:Ball;
                        center = new Ball(20,0x0099ff,1000000);
                        center.pos2D = new Vector2D(300,300);
                        addChild(center);

                        // create another fixed attractor
                        var center2:Ball;
                        center2 = new Ball(20,0x0099ff,1000000);
                        center2.pos2D = new Vector2D(500,300);
                        addChild(center2);

                        // create an orbiter
                        var orbiter:Ball;
                        orbiter = new Ball(8,0x999999,1);
                        orbiter.pos2D = new Vector2D(400,300);
                        orbiter.velo2D = new Vector2D(0,60);

                        // make the orbiter move
                        var attractor:Attractor=new Attractor(orbiter,[center, center2],G);
                        attractor.startTime(10);
                }
        }
}
```

The code is basically self-explanatory: We create two attractors called center and center2 and an orbiter, all as Ball instances. The attractors are given the same radius and mass. The initial position and velocity of the orbiter are then set. As we shall see, completely different trajectories can be produced just by changing those initial conditions.

The orbiter is moved by an instance of the Attractor class. As can be seen from the code, Attractor takes three arguments: the orbiter object, an array of attractors, and the value of the gravitational constant G (set to 1 here). Here is the code in Attractor.as:

```
package {
        import com.physicscodes.motion.Forcer;
        import com.physicscodes.motion.Forces;
        import com.physicscodes.objects.Particle;
        import com.physicscodes.math.Vector2D;

        public class Attractor extends Forcer{
                private var _orbiter:Particle;
                private var _attractors:Array;
                private var _massOrbiter:Number;
                private var _G:Number;

                public function Attractor(porbiter:Particle,pattractors:Array,pG:Number):void{
                        _orbiter = porbiter;
                        _attractors = pattractors;
                        _massOrbiter = porbiter.mass;
                        _G = pG;
```

```
                        super(porbiter);
                }

        override protected function calcForce():void{
                var gravity:Vector2D;
                force = Forces.zeroForce();
                for (var i:uint=0; i<_attractors.length; i++){
                        var attractor:Particle=_attractors[i];
                        gravity = Forces.gravity(_G,attractor.mass,_massOrbiter, ↪
_orbiter.pos2D.subtract(attractor.pos2D));
                        force = Forces.add([force, gravity]);
                }
        }
    }
}
```

Again, the code structure is familiar. The new bit is the loop within calcForce(), where we calculate and then sum the forces acting on the orbiter due to all the attractors. The code can handle any number of attractors.

Run the code with the following initial conditions specified in Attractors.as:

```
orbiter.pos2D = new Vector2D(400,300);
orbiter.velo2D = new Vector2D(0,60);
```

This positions the orbiter exactly in the middle of the two attractors and gives it a downward velocity of 60 px/s. You'll see that the orbiter oscillates up and down, so that it is at the same distance from each attractor, so none of the attractors "wins."

Now change the initial conditions to the following and rerun the code:

```
orbiter.pos2D = new Vector2D(400,400);
orbiter.velo2D = new Vector2D(10,60);
```

You'll find that the orbiter moves in an interesting way: orbiting each attractor alternately, but doing a twist in between so that it orbits both of them in a clockwise sense.

If you now keep the same initial position but change the initial velocity to the following, you'll see that the orbiter orbits both attractors:

```
orbiter.velo2D = new Vector2D(120,0);
```

In general, you could have a distribution of different attractors and it would still be possible for an object to orbit the whole bunch.

Next change the initial conditions to the following:

```
orbiter.pos2D = new Vector2D(300,400);
orbiter.velo2D = new Vector2D(90,0);
```

This time, the orbiter orbits each attractor alternately, but does so in the opposite sense by following a figure-eight trajectory.

The key lesson learned from these experiments (see Figure 10-2) is that although the gravitational field is fixed by the attractors, the actual trajectories of particles in that field will also depend on their positions and velocities.

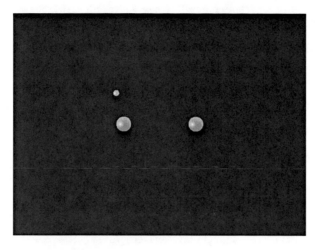

Figure 10-2. An orbiter moving under the gravitational influence of two attractors

Needless to say, there are lots of ways you can experiment with this simulation. As an exercise, why don't you add another attractor and see what kind of motion you get?

Particle trajectories in a gravity field

In this example, we have a number of attractors, giving rise to a complicated gravity field. The resulting trajectories of particles in such a field can be quite complex and sometimes difficult to predict. To make things even more interesting, we assume that our attractors are black holes. Let's first take a look at the code that sets up the objects (the relevant file is GravityField.as):

```
package {
    import flash.display.Sprite;
    import com.physicscodes.objects.Ball;
    import com.physicscodes.math.Vector2D;
    import com.physicscodes.objects.Particle;

    public class GravityField extends Sprite{
        public function GravityField():void{
            init();
        }
        private function init():void{
            var timeStep:Number = 10; // simulation timestep in milliseconds
            var G:Number = 1; // Gravitational constant
            var c:Number = 300; // Speed of light
            var numCenters = 10;

            // create black holes
            var centers:Array = new Array();
```

```
                   for (var i:uint=0; i<numCenters; i++){
                           var radius:Number=20*(Math.random()+0.5);
                           var mass:Number=(0.5*c*c/G)*radius; // mass of black hole
                           var center:Ball = new Ball(radius,0x000000,mass,0,false);
                           center.pos2D = new Vector2D(Math.random()* stage.stageWidth,↪
    Math.random()*stage.stageHeight);
                           addChild(center);
                           centers[i] = center;
                   }

                   // create a moving object
                   var orbiter:Ball = new Ball(5,0xff0000,1);
                   orbiter.pos2D = new Vector2D(Math.random()*stage.stageWidth,↪
    Math.random()*stage.stageHeight);
                   orbiter.velo2D = new Vector2D((Math.random()-0.5)*100,↪
    (Math.random()-0.5)*100);
                   addChild(orbiter);

                   // make the object move
                   var attractor:GravityAttractor=new GravityAttractor↪
    (orbiter,centers,G);
                   attractor.startTime(timeStep);
               }
           }
    }
```

In this code, we create a bunch of black holes as ball instances, place them at random positions on the stage and put references to them in an array called centers. We then create a moving Ball object called orbiter and assign it a random position and a random velocity. The action is initiated by a GravityAttractor instance, which we'll describe shortly. But before we do that, we need to explain how we've set the masses of the black holes.

As you can see from the code, we've used the formula M = $(0.5c^2/G)$ R, where M is the mass and R is the radius of the black hole (which is given a random value between 10 and 30 pixels in the code). What is c, and where does this formula come from? This is the formula for the mass of a black hole in terms of its radius. The constant c is the speed of light. Our black holes are actually hypothetical Newtonian black holes; real (Einsteinian) black holes do not obey Newton's law of gravitation, but require Einstein's General Relativity (a much more complicated theory that we have no intention of simulating in this book!). The value of c will determine the range of masses of the black holes. It's a case of playing with that value to make the black holes produce sufficient, but not too much, attraction so that the particles have a chance to do something interesting before being swallowed up by a black hole. The value we chose is 300.

The main job of the GravityAttractor class is to move the "orbiter" in the combined gravitational field of the black holes, which it does in calcForce() by looping over all the attractors and summing their gravity forces as in the last example. But it does a few other things as well, which are worth explaining here. First, if the orbiter collides with any black hole it disappears and is "recycled" by calling the recycleOrbiter() method, as shown in the highlighted code within calcForce():

```
override protected function calcForce():void{
        var gravity:Vector2D = Forces.zeroForce();
        force = Forces.zeroForce();
```

```
        for (var i:uint=0; i<_attractors.length; i++){
            var attractor:Ball=_attractors[i];
            var dist:Vector2D = _orbiter.pos2D.subtract(attractor.pos2D);
            if (dist.lengthSquared > Math.pow(attractor.radius+_orbiter.radius,2)){
                gravity = Forces.gravity(_G,attractor.mass,_massOrbiter,dist);
                force = Forces.add([force, gravity]);
            }else{
                recycleOrbiter();
            }
        }
    }
```

The recycleOrbiter() method simply changes the color of the orbiter and reinitializes its position and velocity:

```
private function recycleOrbiter():void{
    _orbiter.color=Math.random()*0xffffff;
    _orbiter.pos2D=new Vector2D(Math.random()*_stageWidth, Math.random()*_stageHeight);
    _orbiter.velo2D=new Vector2D((Math.random()-0.5)*100, (Math.random()-0.5)*100);
}
```

The orbiter is also "recycled," if it goes outside of the visible stage area, by a piece of "if" logic in the moveObject() method:

```
override protected function moveObject():void{
    super.moveObject();
    plotGraph();
    if (_orbiter.xpos < 0 || _orbiter.xpos > _stageWidth || _orbiter.ypos < 0 ||↪
_orbiter.ypos > _stageHeight){
        recycleOrbiter();
    }
}
```

You'll notice that we also call a plotGraph() method. What's this about? Well, we are not really plotting a graph, but the trajectory of the orbiter. But we can do this using a Graph instance that has the same range as the stage. This is done in the setupGraph() method, which is called within the constructor of GravityAttractor. The plotGraph() method then plots the y position of the orbiter against its x position. Because plotGraph() is called within moveObject(), it executes on each timestep, so the code effectively traces out the trajectory of the orbiter:

```
private function setupGraph():void {
    _graph= new Graph(0,_stageWidth,0,_stageHeight,0,0,_stageWidth,_stageHeight);
    _orbiter.stage.addChild(_graph);
}
private function plotGraph():void{
    _graph.plot([_orbiter.xpos], [-_orbiter.ypos], _orbiter.color, false, true);
}
```

Take a look at the file GravityAttractor.as if you want to see how all this code fits together. Run the code, and you'll be treated to some interesting trajectories as the orbiter moves through the complex gravity field and eventually ends up into a black hole. Each time this happens, it reappears somewhere else in a different color and traces out another trajectory that either ends into a black hole or just outside of the stage area. Figure 10-3 shows the type of thing you'll be able to see. The randomness in the initial conditions of the particles has the consequence that different patterns emerge over time, so you might want to leave the simulation running for a long time to see this. Moreover, each time you run the simulation you will get a different configuration of black holes that will also give different patterns of particle trajectories.

Figure 10-3. Particle trajectories in the gravity field of black holes

Building a simple black hole game

In our next project, we'll be a bit more adventurous and actually build a simple game by modifying the last simulation. Figure 10-4 shows a screenshot of what the game will look like. The objective of the game is to navigate a spaceship (the triangle) through a black hole field. The spaceship starts off near the lower end of the stage, and you win if you can pass the winning line at the top. Each time you win, a new black hole is added. The positions of the black holes are initialized randomly so that their centers all lie between the winning line and another horizontal line lower down. You lose a life each time a black hole captures the spaceship. If you go off the stage, the spaceship is repositioned at its initial location.

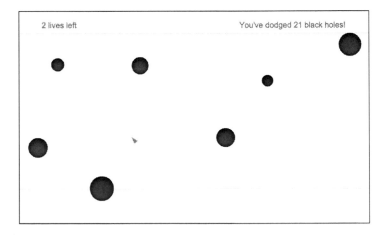

Figure10-4. The black hole game

Creating the visual setup

The setup file for the game is called BlackHoles.as, and the code is as follows:

```
package{
        import flash.display.Sprite;
        import com.physicscodes.objects.Ball;
        import com.physicscodes.math.Vector2D;
        import com.physicscodes.objects.Particle;
        import flash.display.Graphics;

        public class BlackHoles extends Sprite{
                public function BlackHoles():void{
                        init();
                }
                private function init():void{
                        var timeStep:Number = 10; // simulation timestep in milliseconds
                        var G:Number = 1; // Gravitational constant
                        var c:Number = 200; // Speed of light
                        var numCenters = 1;

                        // create a winning line and a bounding line
                        var yposWinning:Number=50;
                        var yposEdge:Number=400;
                        with (graphics){
                                lineStyle(2,0xccffcc);
                                moveTo(0,yposWinning);
                                lineTo(stage.stageWidth,yposWinning);
                                lineStyle(1,0xccccff);
                                moveTo(0,yposEdge);
                                lineTo(stage.stageWidth,yposEdge);
                        }

                        // create a spaceship
                        var ship:Spaceship = new Spaceship(10,15,0xff0000,1);
                        ship.pos2D = new Vector2D(stage.stageWidth/2,stage.stageHeight-50);
                        addChild(ship);

                        // create black holes
                        var centers:Array = new Array();
                        for (var i:uint=0; i<numCenters; i++){
                                var radius:Number=20*(Math.random()+0.5);
                                var mass:Number=(0.5*c*c/G)*radius; // mass of black hole
                                var center:Ball = new Ball(radius,0x000000,mass,0,false);
                                center.pos2D = new Vector2D(Math.random()*stage.stageWidth, ↵
Math.random()*(yposEdge-yposWinning)+yposWinning);
                                addChild(center);
                                centers[i] = center;
                        }
```

```
                         // make the spaceship move
                         var attractor:BlackHoleAttractor=new BlackHoleAttractor(ship,↪
centers,G,c,yposWinning,yposEdge);
                         attractor.startTime(timeStep);
                   }
            }
      }
```

The code that creates the black holes and assigns their properties is similar to that in the last example, with the modification that we're positioning them between the two vertical levels yposWinning and yposEdge, which set the locations of the two horizontal lines. Note that we reduced the speed of light to 200 px/s so that the attraction is not too strong, making it actually possible to avoid the black holes!

Then there is a straightforward piece of code that draws the two lines mentioned previously, followed by another simple piece of code that creates a spaceship and initializes its position. This code instantiates a Spaceship class, which looks as follows:

```
package {
        import flash.display.Sprite;
        import com.physicscodes.objects.Particle;
        import com.physicscodes.objects.Triangle;

        public class Spaceship extends Particle{
                private var _width:Number;
                private var _height:Number;
                private var _color:uint;

                public function Spaceship(pwidth:Number=20,pheight:Number=40,↪
pcolor:uint=0x0000ff,pmass:Number=1,pcharge:Number=0){
                        this.mass=pmass;
                        this.charge=pcharge;
                        _width=pwidth;
                        _height=pheight;
                        _color=pcolor;
                        drawSpaceship();
                }
                private function drawSpaceship():void{
                        var triangle:Triangle = new Triangle(0,0,_width,_height,_color);
                        addChild(triangle);
                }
        }
}
```

As you can see, Spaceship extends Particle and simply draws a triangle based on parameters that specify the width, height, and color of the triangle, in addition to parameters that specify its mass and charge as a Particle subclass.

The final piece of code in BlackHoles.as instantiates a BlackHoleAttractor class, passing it references to the spaceship, the black hole objects and the relevant parameters. This class contains the code that implements the functionality of the game, and is described next.

Programming the game functionality

The BlackHoleAttractor class contains a fair bit of code, so let's dissect it into smaller chunks. To start with, here is the class definition and constructor:

```
public class BlackHoleAttractor extends Forcer{
        private var _orbiter:Spaceship;
        private var _attractors:Array;
        private var _massOrbiter:Number;
        private var _G:Number;
        private var _c:Number;
        private var _stageWidth:Number;
        private var _stageHeight:Number;
        private var _yposEdge:Number;
        private var _yposWinning:Number;
        private var txtLives:TextField = new TextField();
        private var txtScore:TextField = new TextField();
        private var txtFormat:TextFormat = new TextFormat();
        private var _applyThrust:Boolean=false;
        private var _direction:String="";
        private var _dir:Vector2D=new Vector2D(0,1);
        private var _vedmdt:Number=10; // ve*dm/dt
        private var _numLives:uint=10;
        private var _score:uint=0;

        public function BlackHoleAttractor(porbiter:Spaceship, pattractors:Array,↵
pG:Number, pc:Number, pyposW:Number, pyposE:Number):void{
                _orbiter = porbiter;
                _attractors = pattractors;
                _massOrbiter = porbiter.mass;
                _G = pG;
                _c = pc;
                _yposEdge = pyposE;
                _yposWinning = pyposW;
                _stageWidth = _orbiter.stage.stageWidth;
                _stageHeight = _orbiter.stage.stageHeight;
                setupEventListeners();
                setupText();
                super(porbiter);
        }
}
```

It should be obvious what most of the variable names refer to, so we'll just describe the few that are perhaps less obvious (the last six). The four variables _applyThrust, _direction, _dir, and _vedmdt work together in that they are needed to specify the thrust on the spaceship.

- The first variable, _applyThrust, is a Boolean with a value of true if thrust is applied.

- The second variable, _direction, is a string that tells us which direction the thrust is applied in.

- The third, _dir, is a unit vector pointing downward; it will be used to work out the thrust vector.

- The fourth, _vedmdt, is the value of ve*dm/dt, which gives the magnitude of the thrust on the rocket (refer to Chapter 6).

- The last two variables, _numLives and _score, are uint variables that store the current number of lives and score, respectively.

Apart from assigning relevant variable values, the constructor calls the two private methods setupEventListeners() and setupText(). The latter simply adds the text fields that will hold the text displaying the lives and score, and sets their size, position, and formats. So it won't be shown here, but you can take a look in the file BlackHoleAttractor.as. The setupEventListeners() method looks as follows:

```
private function setupEventListeners():void{
        _orbiter.stage.addEventListener(KeyboardEvent.KEY_DOWN,startThrust);
        _orbiter.stage.addEventListener(KeyboardEvent.KEY_UP,stopThrust);
        _orbiter.stage.addEventListener(MouseEvent.DOUBLE_CLICK,changeSetup);
        _orbiter.stage.doubleClickEnabled = true;
}
```

So, the event handler startThrust() will be invoked if a key is pressed, stopThrust() is invoked if the key is released, and changeSetup() is invoked if we double-click. Here is what startThrust() and stopThrust() look like:

```
private function startThrust(evt:KeyboardEvent):void{
        _applyThrust = true;
        if (evt.keyCode==Keyboard.UP){
                _direction = "UP";
        }
        if (evt.keyCode==Keyboard.DOWN){
                _direction = "DOWN";
        }
        if (evt.keyCode==Keyboard.RIGHT){
                _direction = "RIGHT";
        }
        if (evt.keyCode==Keyboard.LEFT){
                _direction = "LEFT";
        }
}
private function stopThrust(evt:KeyboardEvent):void{
        _applyThrust = false;
        _direction = "";
}
```

Hence, startThrust() sets _applyThrust to true and gives values of "UP", "DOWN", "RIGHT", or "LEFT" to _direction based on which of the direction keys is pressed. For its part, stopThrust() resets _applyThrust to false and assigns a blank string to _direction.

The changeSetup() event handler that is invoked by double-clicking anywhere on the stage looks like this:

```
private function changeSetup(evt:MouseEvent):void{
        repositionAttractors();
        recycleOrbiter();
}
```

The two private methods repositionAttractors() and recycleOrbiter() do exactly what their names suggest:

```
private function repositionAttractors():void{
        for (var i:uint=0; i<_attractors.length; i++){
                var attractor:Ball=_attractors[i];
                attractor.pos2D = new Vector2D(Math.random()*_stageWidth,↪
 Math.random()*(_yposEdge-_yposWinning)+_yposWinning);
        }
}
private function recycleOrbiter():void{
        _orbiter.pos2D = new Vector2D(_stageWidth/2,_stageHeight-50);
        _orbiter.velo2D = new Vector2D(0,0);
        _orbiter.rotation = 0;
}
```

So you can reset the positions of the black holes and the spaceship at any time by double-clicking anywhere on the stage.

Let's now look at what calcForce() looks like:

```
override protected function calcForce():void{
        force = Forces.zeroForce();
        // calculate and add gravity due to all black holes
        var gravity:Vector2D = Forces.zeroForce();
        for (var i:uint=0; i<_attractors.length; i++){
                var attractor:Ball=_attractors[i];
                var dist:Vector2D = _orbiter.pos2D.subtract(attractor.pos2D);
                if (dist.lengthSquared > Math.pow(attractor.radius,2)){
                        gravity = Forces.gravity(_G,attractor.mass,_massOrbiter,dist);
                        force = Forces.add([force, gravity]);
                }else{ // if a black hole eats the ship
                        updateLives();
                        recycleOrbiter();
                }
        }
        // calculate and add thrust
        var thrust:Vector2D = Forces.zeroForce();
        if (_applyThrust){
                if (_direction=="UP"){
                        thrust = _dir.para(-_vedmdt);
                }else if (_direction=="DOWN"){
                        thrust = _dir.para(_vedmdt);
                }else if (_direction=="RIGHT"){
                        thrust = _dir.perp(_vedmdt);
                }else if (_direction=="LEFT"){
                        thrust = _dir.perp(-_vedmdt);
                }else{
                        thrust = new Vector2D(0,0);
                }
                force = Forces.add([force, thrust]);
        }
}
```

The force of gravity due to each black hole is calculated in a `for` loop and then added to the total force. A collision detection test checks that the spaceship is not within the current black hole; if it is, the method `updateLives()` is called, and the spaceship is recycled. The thrust on the spaceship is then calculated depending on which arrow key is pressed, as determined by the string stored in the `_direction` variable. For example, if `_direction=="UP"`, the thrust is applied opposite to the unit vector `_dir` (which points downward) by using the `para()` public method of `Vector2D`, scaling `_dir` by `-_vedmdt`. If the right or left arrow key is pressed, the `perp()` method is used instead, to give a horizontal vector of length `_vedmdt`. The thrust is then added to the total force.

The `updateLives()` method mentioned before decrements the number of lives variable `_numLives` and then calls the `showLives()` method to display the remaining number of lives:

```
private function updateLives():void{
        _numLives--;
        showLives();
}
private function showLives():void{
        txtLives.text = String(_numLives) + " lives left";
        if (_numLives==0){
                txtLives.text = "Game over";
                stopTime();
        }
        txtLives.setTextFormat(txtFormat);
}
```

Next we'll take a look at the `moveObject()` method:

```
override protected function moveObject():void{
        super.moveObject();
        if (_orbiter.xpos < 0 || _orbiter.xpos > _stageWidth || _orbiter.ypos > _stageHeight){
                recycleOrbiter();
        }
        if (_orbiter.ypos < _yposWinning){
                updateScore();
                recycleOrbiter();
                addAttractor();
                repositionAttractors();
        }
        rotateOrbiter();
}
```

The new bits in here are `if` blocks of code and the `rotateOrbiter()` method. The first `if` block recycles the ship if it is outside of the stage area. The second `if` block checks to see whether the ship has passed the winning line. If it has, it updates the score, recycles the orbiter, adds a new black hole, and repositions all the black holes. The `recycleOrbiter()` and `repositionAttractors()` methods were described previously. The `updateScore()` method increments the current score variable `_score` by the current number of black holes (and so `_score` has a value equal to the total number of black holes evaded) and then calls the `showScore()` method to display the score:

```
private function updateScore():void{
        _score += _attractors.length;
```

```
        showScore();
}
private function showScore():void{
        if (_score==1){
                txtScore.text = "You've just dodged a black hole!"
        }else{
                txtScore.text = "You've dodged " + _score + " black holes!"
        }
                txtScore.setTextFormat(txtFormat);
        }
```

And here is the `addAttractor()` method, which adds a new black hole:

```
private function addAttractor():void{
        var radius:Number=20*(Math.random()+0.5);
        var mass:Number=(0.5*_c*_c/_G)*radius; // formula for mass of black hole
        var attractor:Ball = new Ball(radius,0x000000,mass,0,false);
        _orbiter.stage.addChild(attractor);
        _attractors.push(attractor);
}
```

Finally, the `rotateOrbiter()` method rotates the spaceship so that it always points in the direction of its velocity:

```
private function rotateOrbiter():void{
        _orbiter.rotation = _orbiter.velo2D.angle*180/Math.PI + 90;
}
```

This completes the description of the game. Take a look at the source files and have fun playing around! Feel free to develop the game further. It could certainly do with enhanced graphics and perhaps some sound effects, too. In terms of functionality, see if you can improve the controls: for example, allow the user to move the spaceship diagonally by pressing an up or down key together with a left or right key.

Electrostatic force

The next long-range force we'll look at is one that exists between electrically charged particles. This is called an electric or electrostatic force. But before we get to the force law, we need to explain a few facts about electric charges.

Electric charge

Electric charge is a physical property of particles just like mass is. Elementary particles, the fundamental building blocks of matter, are frequently charged. For example, electrons are particles that orbit the nuclei of atoms, and they have negative charge. The nuclei of atoms include protons, which have positive charge, and neutrons, which have zero charge. What we call an *electric current* is actually a flow of free electrons in a metal—moving charges (whether electrons or not) constitute an electric current.

A particle with mass creates a gravitational field that exerts a force on other particles with mass. Similarly, a charged particle creates an electric field that exerts a force on other charged particles. The interesting thing is that there are two types of charges: positive and negative.

Like charges repel; unlike charges attract.

So a positive charge will attract a negative charge, and vice versa. But the positive charge will repel another positive charge; similarly, a negative charge will repel another negative charge. This is different from mass, which is always positive and always leads to an attractive gravitational force.

Coulomb's law of electrostatics

The force law for the electric force between two particles is called *Coulomb's law*. It is virtually identical in form with Newton's law of gravitation, being given by the following, where Q_1 and Q_2 are the charges on the two particles, r is the distance between them, and k is a constant analogous to G:

$$F = k\frac{Q_1 Q_2}{r^2}$$

Don't worry about the value of k; we are not going to model real electrical charges but we'll just play around with the force law to see what kind of motion it produces. So, we can give k any value we like.

The forces exerted on each particle by the other have the same magnitude but opposite direction, in accordance with Newton's third law. Like gravity, the force is directed along the line joining the two particles, so Coulomb's law can be written in vector form in the following two ways, where $\mathbf{r}_u$ is a unit vector in the direction of **r**:

$$\mathbf{F} = k\frac{Q_1 Q_2}{r^2}\mathbf{r}_u$$

or

$$\mathbf{F} = k\frac{Q_1 Q_2}{r^3}\mathbf{r}$$

Here **r** is the position vector of the object experiencing the force relative to the object that is exerting the force, just like gravity (refer to Chapter 6).

Note the absence of a negative sign in the preceding formula (recall that the equivalent vector formula for gravity had a negative sign). That's because like charges repel, whereas masses always attract. So if Q_1 and Q_2 are both positive or both negative, their product is positive, and the force **F** is a positive number times **r**. **F** then is oriented in the direction of **r** (it is repulsive). But if one of the charges is positive and the other is negative, **F** is a negative number times **r** and directed opposite to **r** (it is attractive).

Let's create an electric force function similar to the gravity function in the Forces class:

```
static public function electric(k:Number,q1:Number,q2:Number,r:Vector2D):Vector2D {
        return r.multiply(k*q1*q2/(r.lengthSquared*r.length));
}
```

This is similar in form to the gravity force function, but without the minus sign. As explained previously, the sign of the product q1*q2 determines whether we get an attractive or repulsive force. Just by allowing two different signs for charges, we get a "richer" force than gravity, although the formula is nearly identical in form.

Charged particle attraction and repulsion

To see the electric force in action, let's build a simulation similar to GravityField.as, but with electrically charged particles instead of black holes. The new files are ElectricField.as and ElectricInteractor.as, and they are similar to GravityField.as and GravityAttractor.as, respectively. Let's take a look first at ElectricField.as:

```
package{
        import flash.display.Sprite;
        import com.physicscodes.objects.Ball;
        import com.physicscodes.math.Vector2D;
        import com.physicscodes.objects.Particle;

        public class ElectricField extends Sprite{
                public function ElectricField():void{
                        init();
                }
                private function init():void{
                        var timeStep:Number = 10;
                        var k:Number = 1;
                        var numCenters = 20;

                        var centers:Array = new Array();
                        for (var i:uint=0; i<numCenters; i++){
                                var center:Ball;
                                var charge:Number = (Math.random()-0.5)*1000000;
                                var color:uint;
                                if (charge < 0){
                                        color = 0xff0000;
                                }else if (charge > 0){
                                        color = 0x0000ff;
                                }else{ // neutral
                                        color = 0x000000;
                                }
                                center = new Ball(20*(Math.random()+0.5),color,1,charge,true);
                                center.pos2D = new Vector2D(Math.random()*stage.stageWidth,↵
Math.random()*stage.stageHeight);
                                addChild(center);
                                centers[i] = center;
                        }

                        var orbiter:Ball;
                        orbiter = new Ball(5,0xff0000,1,1);
                        orbiter.pos2D = new Vector2D(Math.random()*stage.stageWidth,↵
Math.random()*stage.stageHeight);
                        orbiter.velo2D = new Vector2D((Math.random()-0.5)*100,↵
(Math.random()-0.5)*100);
```

```
                           addChild(orbiter);

                           var electric:ElectricInteractor=new ElectricInteractor(orbiter,↪
centers,k);
                           electric.startTime(timeStep);
                    }
              }
       }
```

The main difference is that we are giving the centers random positive and negative charges, and coloring them blue if their charge is positive and red if their charge is negative (and black if they turn out to have zero charge, which would be a rare occurrence because Math.random() would have to return exactly 0.5 for that to be true). The moving particle, still called orbiter, is given a positive charge of 1. So it will be attracted by the red centers and repelled by the blue ones.

The code for ElectricInteractor.as is very similar to GravityAttractor.as, with the Forces.electric() replacing Forces.gravity() in calcForce(), and charges being used instead of masses. So let's just show the calcForce() function:

```
override protected function calcForce():void{
       var electric:Vector2D = Forces.zeroForce();
       force = Forces.zeroForce();
       for (var i:uint=0; i<_centers.length; i++){
              var center:Ball=_centers[i];
              var dist:Vector2D = _orbiter.pos2D.subtract(center.pos2D);
              if (dist.lengthSquared > Math.pow(center.radius+_orbiter.radius,2)){
                     electric = Forces.electric(_k,center.charge,_chargeOrbiter,dist);
                     force = Forces.add([force, electric]);
              }else{
                     recycleOrbiter();
              }
       }
}
```

Figure 10-5 shows an example of what you should see when you run the code.

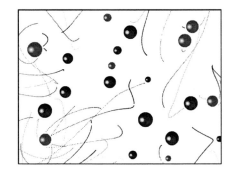

Figure 10-5. Trajectories in the electric field of multiple charged particles

Electric fields

As with gravity, we can invoke the concept of a force field in electrostatics. Recall that the gravitational field strength **g** was defined as the force exerted per unit mass, **g** = F/m. Similarly, electric field strength **E** is defined as the force exerted per unit *charge*:

$$\mathbf{E} = \mathbf{F} / q$$

Therefore, if we know the electric field strength, we can easily calculate the electric force the field exerts on a particle by multiplying by its charge:

$$\mathbf{F} = q\,\mathbf{E}$$

Compare this with the equivalent formula for gravity:

$$\mathbf{F} = m\,\mathbf{g}$$

Because we want to use the formula **F** = qE, why not create a force function for it? Let's call it Forces.forceField:

```
static public function forceField(q:Number, E:Vector2D):Vector2D {
        return E.multiply(q);
}
```

Note that nothing stops us from using the same function to calculate **F** = mg, too, if we use m for the parameter q and **g** for **E**.

Electric field due to a charged particle

As an example, using Coulomb's law, we can calculate the electric field due to a charged particle. Let the particle have charge Q. Then the force it exerts on a particle of charge q a distance r away is this:

$$F = \frac{k\,Q\,q}{r^2}$$

Therefore, the force per unit charge is this:

$$E = \frac{k\,Q}{r^2}$$

In vector form, it can be written as follows:

$$\mathbf{E} = \frac{kQ}{r^3}\mathbf{r}$$

This is the formula for the electric field produced by a charged particle. But we can also play around with any form for **E** that we want, without worrying about how it is actually produced. Let's look at a couple of examples.

Time-varying electric fields

The electric field of a stationary charge is constant in time, even though it varies in space, as described in the previous section. This is similar to the gravitational field of a stationary mass. But if a charged particle moves, the electric field it sets up will vary in time. For example, an oscillating charge will produce an oscillating electric field.

A simple example is an electric field that varies in time like a sine or cosine wave. Wave concepts such as frequency and amplitude can then be applied to such a sinusoidally varying field, as discussed in Chapters 3 and 8. Moreover, because an electric field is a vector, its components can vary independently of each other. If all this sounds a bit abstract, that's because an electric field *is* an abstract concept! You can't visualize an oscillating electric field with two or more components as you can visualize an oscillating mass-spring system. Nevertheless, the same math can be applied to both.

Interesting effects can be produced with electric fields that vary in time. In the files `ElectricFieldExamples.as` and `Electro.as`, we take a look at the types of motion that different electric fields produce. `ElectricFieldExamples.as` is very simple, creating a particle instance and making it move using an instance of the `Electro` class:

```
package{
        import flash.display.Sprite;
        import com.physicscodes.math.Vector2D;
        import com.physicscodes.objects.Ball;

        public class ElectricFieldExamples extends Sprite{
                public function ElectricFieldExamples():void{
                        init();
                }
                private function init():void{
                        var particle:Ball;
                        particle = new Ball(5,0xff0000,1,1);
                        particle.pos2D = new Vector2D(100,300);
                        addChild(particle);

                        var timeStep:Number = 10;
                        var electro:Electro=new Electro(particle);
                        electro.startTime(timeStep);
                }
        }
}
```

Electro.as is simple, too; it basically calculates the force in calcForce() and plots its trajectory using the plotGraph() method to draw on a Graph instance previously set up in setupGraph():

```
package {
        import com.physicscodes.motion.Forcer;
        import com.physicscodes.motion.Forces;
        import com.physicscodes.objects.Ball;
        import com.physicscodes.math.Vector2D;
        import com.physicscodes.math.Graph;

        public class Electro extends Forcer{
                private var _particle:Ball;
                private var _particleCharge:Number;
                private var _E:Vector2D;
                private var _graph:Graph;
                private var _stageWidth;
                private var _stageHeight;

                public function Electro(pparticle:Ball):void{
                        _particle = pparticle;
                        _particleCharge = pparticle.charge;
                        _stageWidth = _particle.stage.stageWidth;
                        _stageHeight = _particle.stage.stageHeight;
                        setupGraph();
                        super(pparticle);
                }
                override protected function calcForce():void{
                        _E = new Vector2D(20*Math.sin(1*time),20*Math.cos(1*time));
                        force = Forces.forceField(_particleCharge,_E);
                }
                override protected function moveObject():void{
                        super.moveObject();
                        plotGraph();
                }
                private function setupGraph():void {
                        _graph= new Graph(0, _stageWidth, 0, _stageHeight, 0, 0,↪
_stageWidth, _stageHeight);
                        _particle.stage.addChild(_graph);
                }
                private function plotGraph():void{
                        _graph.plot([_particle.xpos], [-_particle.ypos],0x666666, false,↪
true);
                }

        }
}
```

Now it's play time! In the source file, Electro.as, we included a number of different sinusoidally varying functions (as commented-out code) for _E in calcForce() that you can try. Try the following function to start with:

```
_E = new Vector2D(0, 50*Math.cos(1*time));
```

What we're doing is to apply an electric field with a vertical component that varies sinusoidally in time with an amplitude (maximum magnitude) of 50 and a frequency of 1 cycle per second. When you run the code, you'll see that the particle oscillates up and down in response to the applied electric field.

What happens if we change the amplitude or frequency of the oscillation? If we increase the amplitude, we'll be applying a larger force, so it's no surprise that the particle will oscillate with larger amplitude. But the effect of increasing the frequency of the applied electric field might not be so obvious. Try changing the frequency to 3, so that _E becomes this:

```
_E = new Vector2D(0, 50*Math.cos(3*time));
```

If you now run the code, you'll find that the particle oscillates with a much smaller amplitude. What's happening here is that the particle, because it has inertia (mass), cannot keep up with the speed of variation of the electric field.

The following function gives a more interesting pattern, by applying an electric field with a constant component of magnitude 1 in the horizontal and a sinusoidally varying vertical component with an amplitude given by 2*time:

```
_E = new Vector2D(1, 2*time*Math.cos(1*time));
```

This makes the particle accelerate in the horizontal and oscillate with an increasing amplitude in the vertical (see Figure 10-6).

We'll let you play with the other example functions given in the file, as well as try your own. Of course, there is no reason to restrict yourself to sinusoidally varying functions: feel free to experiment with any function you like.

Figure 10-6. Example of the effect of a time-varying electric field on a charged particle

Electromagnetic force

The electric (electrostatic) force is but one aspect of charged particles. *Moving* charged particles experience and exert another force—a *magnetic force*—in addition to the electric force. Therefore, accounting for the magnetic force will change the way that charged particles move. In this section, you'll see how to compute the magnetic force and how combining it with the electric force affects the motion of charged particles.

Magnetic fields and forces

We've all experienced the fascination of magnets as kids. Part of their appeal is that you can actually feel the force acting between two magnets without them actually touching. Because of this action-at-a-distance characteristic, magnetism fits neatly into the force field concept: a magnet generates a magnetic field around it, which then exerts a force on other magnets and magnetic materials.

What is not obvious at all is that the magnetic field actually has a close connection with the electric field. Magnetic fields are generated by moving charges or by electric fields that vary in time. So, an electric current in a wire will create a magnetic field. A sinusoidally varying electric field will produce a sinusoidally varying magnetic field. The relationship between electric and magnetic fields and the precise way in which they are generated are complex; they are described mathematically by a set of vector differential equations called *Maxwell's equations*. To keep things simple, we'll simply assume given electric and magnetic fields without worrying about how they are produced or how they interact with each other, and focus on how they affect the motion of charged particles.

We already know that the force due to an electric field of strength **E** on a particle of charge q is given by **F** = qE. What is the equivalent force law for a magnetic field?

First we need to introduce a magnetic field strength analogous to the electric field strength. There is no need to go into the actual definition; suffice it to say that it exists and is given the symbol **B**, and that it is a vector like the electric field strength **E**.

The force on a charge q due to a magnetic field **B** is then given by the following, where **v** is the velocity vector of the charged particle and x denotes the cross (vector) product (refer to Chapter 3):

$$\mathbf{F} = q\,\mathbf{v} \times \mathbf{B}$$

As explained in Chapter 3, the cross product **v** x **B** gives a vector that is perpendicular to both **v** and **B** (it points in a direction perpendicular to the plane containing the vectors **v** and **B**). Multiplying this by q gives a vector in the same direction but with q times its magnitude. From Chapter 3, the magnetic force can also be written thus, where θ is the angle between the **v** and **B** vectors and **n** is the unit vector perpendicular to **v** and **B** vectors and oriented according to the right hand rule (refer to Chapter 3):

$$\mathbf{F} = q\,v\,B\sin(\theta)\,\mathbf{n}$$

Note that because the magnetic force is always perpendicular to the particle velocity, it therefore acts as a centripetal force, causing rotation (refer to Chapter 9). Therefore, we can equate the magnetic force law with the centripetal force formula:

$$q\,v\,B\sin(\theta) = \frac{m\,v^2}{r}$$

Rearranging this equation gives this:

$$r = \frac{m\,v}{q\,B\sin(\theta)}$$

This gives the radius of the trajectory that the charged particle follows. The formula tells us that the radius of the circle increases if the mass or velocity increases, and it decreases if either the charge q or the magnetic field magnitude B increases.

The Lorentz force law

You can combine the electric and magnetic forces on a charged particle to give a single formula for the *electromagnetic force* on the particle:

$$\mathbf{F} = q\left(\mathbf{E} + \mathbf{v} \times \mathbf{B}\right)$$

This is called the *Lorentz force equation.*

We'll now create a static force function called `lorentz()` in the `Forces` class to implement this force law. The only problem is that the vector product is only defined in 3D, whereas our forces are currently only in 2D. But we can implement the magnetic force qv x **B** in a restricted way if we assume that the magnetic field **B** is always pointing either into or out of the screen. The magnetic force is given by qv x **B** = qvB sin (θ) **n** (refer to the last section), where θ is the angle between **v** and **B**, and in 2D **v** is always perpendicular to **B** if the latter is pointing into or out of the screen. Because sin (90°) = 1, this gives, in that special case, the following, where **n** is perpendicular to **v**:

$$q\,\mathbf{v} \times \mathbf{B} = q\,v\,B\,\mathbf{n}$$

This means that in ActionScript the magnetic force is given by the following, where `vel` is the velocity vector **v** and B is the magnitude of the magnetic field:

```
vel.perp(q*B*vel.length)
```

The complete Lorentz force function is then as follows:

```
static public function lorentz(q:Number, E:Vector2D, B:Number, vel:Vector2D):Vector2D{
        return E.multiply(q).add(vel.perp(q*B*vel.length));
}
```

Let's now play with the Lorentz force function. The file `LorentzForce.as` sets up a particle and a `Lorentz` class to make it move:

```
package{
        import flash.display.Sprite;
        import com.physicscodes.math.Vector2D;
        import com.physicscodes.objects.Ball;

        public class LorentzForce extends Sprite{
```

```
        public function LorentzForce():void{
                init();
        }
        private function init():void{
                var particle:Ball;
                particle = new Ball(5,0xff0000,1,1);
                particle.pos2D = new Vector2D(400,500);
                particle.velo2D = new Vector2D(40,0);
                addChild(particle);

                var timeStep:Number = 10;
                var lorentz:Lorentz=new Lorentz(particle);
                lorentz.startTime(timeStep);
        }
    }
}
```

We initialized the velocity of the particle to be 40 px/s in the x direction; different results will be obtained for different choices of initial velocity.

The Lorentz class is nearly identical with the Electro class, save for an extra variable _B to represent the magnitude of the magnetic field, and a different force function in calcForce():

```
override protected function calcForce():void{
        _E = new Vector2D(0,0);
        _B = 0.2;
        force = Forces.lorentz(_particleCharge,_E,_B,_particle.velo2D);
}
```

Let's try using different values and math functions for _E and _B to see what we get. To begin with, let _E be a zero vector and let _B = 0.2 as in the previous code snippet—in other words, we have a constant magnetic field. Run the code and you'll see that the particle traces out a circular path, as discussed in the last section. You can verify what we said at the end of the last section by increasing the value of _B to 0.5 and noting that the radius of the circular path decreases.

You can reduce the velocity of the particle on each timestep by adding the following line in calcForce() or updateObject():

```
_particle.velo2D = _particle.velo2D.multiply(0.999);
```

This will give you the spiral pattern shown in Figure 10-7.

Figure 10-7. A spiral traced by a particle with decreasing velocity in a constant magnetic field

Now add in a non-zero electric field; for example:

```
_E = new Vector2D(1,0);
_B = 0.5;
```

This will produce a helical trajectory. You can also make the electric field and/or the magnetic field time-varying functions; for example:

```
_E = new Vector2D(0,50*Math.cos(1*time));
_B = 0.5;
```

This will produce interesting trajectories that are not always what you might expect. Have fun experimenting!

Other force laws

So far in this chapter, we have discussed physical forces that actually exist in nature. But there is no reason why we cannot invent our own. Because our main purpose is to play around with forces and their effects, we don't have to be limited by reality. In the next few sections, we'll introduce different force laws and see what they can do. Feel free to create your own!

Central forces

A *central force* is one that satisfies the following two conditions:

- The magnitude of the force depends only on the distance from a given point.
- The direction of the force is always toward that point.

Newtonian gravity, electrostatic forces, and spring forces are all examples of central forces. Mathematically, the above two conditions can be combined to give the force vector at any point P as follows, where r_u is a unit vector of the point P from the force center, r is its distance from that center, and f(r) is a function of r:

$$\mathbf{F} = f(r)\, \mathbf{r}_u$$

As you already know, for gravity and electrostatic forces, f(r) is proportional to $1/r^2$:

$$f(r) \propto \frac{1}{r^2}$$

This is usually referred to as an *inverse square law*. Ever wondered what things would be like if gravity obeyed a different law—for example, an inverse $1/r$ or an inverse cube $1/r^3$ law? Well we can easily find out by creating a modified force function for gravity. But rather than create special functions for these different cases, let's create a general central force function that varies according to the following, where both k and n can be positive or negative:

$$f(r) = k\, r^n$$

This gives the following vector form:

$$\mathbf{F} = k\, r^n\, \mathbf{r}_u$$

Or equivalently:

$$\mathbf{F} = k\, r^{n-1}\, \mathbf{r}$$

If k is positive, the force is repulsive (because it is in the direction of **r**); if k is negative, the force is attractive (because it is in the opposite direction from **r**). If n is positive, the force increases with distance; if n is negative, the force decreases with distance.

Examples include the spring force law, for which k is negative and n is 1; and gravity, for which k is negative and n is –2. The constant k is usually related to some property of the particle (for example, mass or charge).

Let's add a central force function to the `Forces` class:

```
static public function central(k:Number,n:Number,r:Vector2D):Vector2D {
        return r.multiply(k*Math.pow(r.length,n-1));
}
```

The following code, `CentralForces.as`, sets up a particle that will be subjected to a central force through the `CentralForcer()` class:

```
package{
        import flash.display.Sprite;
        import com.physicscodes.math.Vector2D;
        import com.physicscodes.objects.Ball;

        public class CentralForces extends Sprite{
                public function CentralForces():void{
                        init();
                }
                private function init():void{
                        var center:Ball;
                        center = new Ball(2,0x000000);
                        center.pos2D = new Vector2D(400,300);
                        addChild(center);

                        var particle:Ball;
```

```
                        particle = new Ball(5,0xff0000,1);
                        particle.pos2D = new Vector2D(300,300);
                        particle.velo2D = new Vector2D(0,-20);
                        addChild(particle);

                        var timeStep:Number = 10;
                        var forcer:CentralForcer=new CentralForcer(particle,center);
                        forcer.startTime(timeStep);
                }
        }
}
```

And here is the code for `CentralForcer.as`:

```
package {
        import com.physicscodes.motion.Forcer;
        import com.physicscodes.motion.Forces;
        import com.physicscodes.objects.Ball;
        import com.physicscodes.math.Vector2D;
        import com.physicscodes.math.Graph;

        public class CentralForcer extends Forcer{

                private var _particle:Ball;
                private var _center:Vector2D;
                private var _graph:Graph;
                private var _stageWidth;
                private var _stageHeight;
                private var _k:Number=-10;
                private var _n:Number=0.5;

                public function CentralForcer(pparticle:Ball,pcenter:Ball):void{
                        _particle = pparticle;
                        _center = pcenter.pos2D;
                        _stageWidth = _particle.stage.stageWidth;
                        _stageHeight = _particle.stage.stageHeight;
                        setupGraph();
                        super(pparticle);
                }

                override protected function calcForce():void{
                        var r:Vector2D = _particle.pos2D.subtract(_center);
                        force = Forces.central(_k,_n,r);
                }

                override protected function moveObject():void{
                        super.moveObject();
                        plotGraph();
                }

                private function setupGraph():void {
                        _graph= new Graph(0, _stageWidth, 0, _stageHeight, 0, 0,↪
 _stageWidth, _stageHeight);
                        _particle.stage.addChild(_graph);
```

```
                }
                private function plotGraph():void{
                        _graph.plot([_particle.xpos], [-_particle.ypos],0x666666,↪
   false, true);
                }

         }
}
```

Nothing exceptional here. We are applying a central force to the particle in calcForce() and then plotting its resulting trajectory as before. You can experiment with different values for k and n, as well as different initial positions and velocities for the particle.

Can you always make a particle follow a closed orbit with an attractive central force (negative k)? We already know this is possible for a $f(r) = k/r^2$ law (for example, gravity) and a $f(r) = kr$ law (springs). But what about other force laws, such as $f(r) = k/r$ or $f(r) = r^3$? Try it out and see for yourself!

As an example, with the following initial conditions, and with (k = −1, n = 1), a spring-like force, you get an elongated closed orbit:

```
center.pos2D = new Vector2D(400,300);
particle.pos2D = new Vector2D(200,300);
particle.velo2D = new Vector2D(0,-20);
```

With (k = −100000, n = −2), a gravity-like law, you also get a closed elliptical orbit. But with (k = −1000, n = −1), a 1/r law, you get a flower-like trajectory that does not close on itself (see Figure 10-8); it is a bound orbit, but not a closed one. And with a $1/r^3$ law you get trajectories that either spiral in or spiral out, but do not close: they are neither closed nor bound. Note that the magnitude of k needs to be adjusted depending on the value of n to produce displacements of the right magnitude to fit on the stage.

There is actually a mathematical theorem called *Bertrand's theorem* that says the only central force laws that give closed orbits are $f(r) = k/r^2$ and $f(r) = kr$ laws. Lucky for Earth (and us!) that gravity is a $1/r^2$ law!

In spite of the last statement, it turns out that closed circular orbits exist, as a special case, for all attractive central forces if you have just the correct tangential velocity. It's easy to work out the velocity needed for that: just equate the force law with the formula for centripetal force, where m is the mass of the particle:

$$\frac{m\,v^2}{r} = -k\,r^n$$

Solving for v gives this:

$$v = \sqrt{\frac{-k\,r^{n+1}}{m}}$$

You can test this formula with the simulation. It should work for any value of n, provided that k is negative.

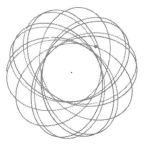

Figure 10-8. Trajectory traced by a particle in a 1/r force field

Gravity with a spring force law?

Can you imagine what the universe would be like if gravity obeyed a different force law, for instance a spring force law? Well, let's find out!

SpringGravity.as sets up a bunch of particles with random positions and velocities and puts them in an array called particles. It then creates a Ball object called center that will act as a gravitational attractor and gives it a mass of 1 and a charge of 1. Both particles and center are then passed to a SpringGravityForcer instance:

```
package{
        import flash.display.Sprite;
        import com.physicscodes.math.Vector2D;
        import com.physicscodes.objects.Ball;

        public class SpringGravity extends Sprite{
                public function SpringGravity():void{
                        init();
                }
                private function init():void{
                        var numParticles:Number=100;
                        var vmax:Number=100;
                        var particles:Array = new Array();
                        for (var i:uint=0; i<numParticles; i++){
                                var particle:Ball;
                                particle = new Ball(4,0x000000,1);
                                particle.pos2D = new Vector2D(Math.random()*
stage.stageWidth, Math.random()*stage.stageHeight);
                                particle.velo2D = new Vector2D((Math.random()-0.5)*vmax,
 (Math.random()-0.5)*vmax);
                                addChild(particle);
                                particles.push(particle);
                        }

                        // spring force kr
                        var center:Ball;
                        center = new Ball(20,0xff0000,1,1);
                        center.pos2D = new Vector2D(400,300);
                        addChild(center);
```

```
                              var timeStep:Number = 10;
                              var forcer:SpringGravityForcer=new SpringGravityForcer(particles,↪
          center);
                              forcer.startTime(timeStep);
                    }
          }
}
```

SpringGravityForcer.as is pretty simple. It extends MultiForcer because there's a bunch of particles to move. The calcForce() method basically computes a central force, using k = –GMm, where the gravitational constant G = 1, M is the mass of the center; and m is the mass of the relevant particle (all 1 here). Note that we've stored the value of n in the charge property of center. There's no reason why we can't do that because we won't use charge here. Now because k is negative and n = 1, we have a spring force. We've created spring-force gravity!

```
package {
          import com.physicscodes.motion.MultiForcer;
          import com.physicscodes.motion.Forces;
          import com.physicscodes.objects.Particle;
          import com.physicscodes.objects.Ball;
          import com.physicscodes.math.Vector2D;

          public class SpringGravityForcer extends MultiForcer{

                    private var _center:Ball;
                    private var _G:Number=1;

                    public function SpringGravityForcer(pparticles:Array,pcenter:Ball):void{
                              _center = pcenter;
                              super(pparticles);
                    }

                    override protected function calcForce(pparticle:Particle):void{
                              var k:Number = -_G*_center.mass*pparticle.mass;
                              var n:Number = _center.charge;
                              var r:Vector2D = pparticle.pos2D.subtract(_center.pos2D);
                              force = Forces.central(k,n,r);
                    }
          }
}
```

Run the code to get an interesting insight into what life might be like with gravity obeying the spring force law. You'll see that all the particles are pulled toward the center undergoing some kind of oscillation (see Figure 10-9). If you increase the value of the velocity coefficient vmax, say to 1000, the particles will move about more, but will still be pulled into this oscillatory motion.

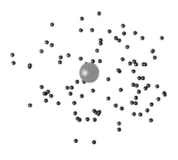

Figure 10-9. Modeling gravity with a spring force

Multiple attractors with different laws of gravity

In our final example, `FieldForcer.as`, we'll combine central forces with different values of k and n to produce a complex force field. This is a universe in which different attractors exert gravity according to different force laws.

Here is the code in `FieldForcer.as`:

```
package{
        import flash.display.Sprite;
        import com.physicscodes.math.Vector2D;
        import com.physicscodes.objects.Ball;

        public class ForceFields extends Sprite{
                public function ForceFields():void{
                        init();
                }
                private function init():void{
                        var numParticles:Number=100;
                        var vmax:Number=20;
                        var particles:Array = new Array();
                        for (var i:uint=0; i<numParticles; i++){
                                var particle:Ball = new Ball(4,0x000000,1);
                                particle.pos2D = new Vector2D(Math.random()➥
*stage.stageWidth, Math.random()*stage.stageHeight);
                                particle.velo2D = new Vector2D((Math.random()-0.5)*vmax,➥
 (Math.random()-0.5)*vmax);

                                addChild(particle);
                                particles.push(particle);
                        }

                        // k/r force
                        var center1:Ball = new Ball(20,0xff0000,1000,-1);
                        center1.pos2D = new Vector2D(200,500);
                        center1.velo2D = new Vector2D(10,-10);
                        addChild(center1);
                        center1.move();
```

```
                    // k/r2 force
                    var center2:Ball = new Ball(20,0x00ff00,100000,-2);
                    center2.pos2D = new Vector2D(500,100);
                    addChild(center2);

                    // k/r3 force
                    var center3:Ball = new Ball(20,0x0000ff,10000000,-3);
                    center3.pos2D = new Vector2D(600,300);
                    addChild(center3);

                    var timeStep:Number = 10;
                    var forcer:FieldForcer=new FieldForcer(particles, [center1, center2,↪
 center3]);

                    forcer.startTime(timeStep);
            }
        }
}
```

As in SpringGravity.as, we set up a bunch of particles and give them random positions and velocities. Then we set up three attractors called center1, center2, and center3 and give them masses of 1000, 100000, and 10000000; and charges of –1, –2, and –3, respectively. As in the last example, the values of the charges are used to store the values of n, the central force law index. This means that the attractors will exert $1/r$, $1/r^2$, and $1/r^3$ force laws, respectively. We also give center1 a non-zero velocity and make it move by invoking the move() method.

The simulation is driven by a FieldForcer class instance, which looks as follows:

```
package {
        import com.physicscodes.motion.MultiForcer;
        import com.physicscodes.motion.Forces;
        import com.physicscodes.objects.Particle;
        import com.physicscodes.objects.Ball;
        import com.physicscodes.math.Vector2D;

        public class FieldForcer extends MultiForcer{

                private var _centers:Array=new Array();
                private var _G:Number=1;

                public function FieldForcer(pparticles:Array,pcenters:Array):void{
                        _centers = pcenters;
                        super(pparticles);
                }

                override protected function calcForce(pparticle:Particle):void{
                        var central:Vector2D;
                        force = Forces.zeroForce();
                        for (var i:uint=0; i<_centers.length; i++){
                                var center:Ball=_centers[i];
                                var k:Number = -_G*center.mass*pparticle.mass;
                                var n:Number = center.charge;
                                var r:Vector2D = pparticle.pos2D.subtract(center.pos2D);
                                if (r.lengthSquared > Math.pow(center.radius,2)){
```

```
                              central = Forces.central(k,n,r);
                    }else{
                              central = Forces.zeroForce();
                    }
                    force = Forces.add([force, central]);
          }
     }

   }
}
```

This is similar to the last example, except that we now have an array of attracting centers (see Figure 10-10), so we sum the central force that each exerts in a for loop in calcForce(). Note that we are setting the force to be zero if a particle happens to be within a center. This is to improve the visual effect. After all, it's a universe of our own creation, so we can do whatever we want, can't we?

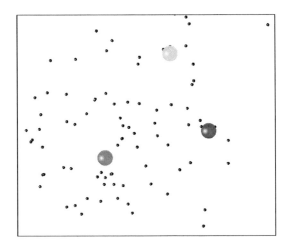

Figure 10-10. Particles moving in a field composed of different central forces

If you run the code, you'll see that most of the particles gravitate around the center that exerts the 1/r force. As it moves along, it captures more particles. The gravity of this attractor dominates because a 1/r force is a longer-range force than a $1/r^2$ or a $1/r^3$ force: it decays less rapidly with distance. The attractor that exerts the $1/r^3$ force holds onto very few particles: its influence decays very rapidly with distance.

There are tons of other things you could try; for example, make the attractors move in more complicated ways (for example, orbit a center or move around and bounce). You could add more attractors or include antigravity. Your imagination is the limit.

Summary

You now have plenty of tools with a whole lot of forces for creating interesting types of motion. This concludes Part II of the book. In Part III, you will apply what you learned in Part II to build more complex systems consisting of interacting particles or extended objects. Things will get more complicated, but also more fun!

Part III

Multi-particle and Extended Systems

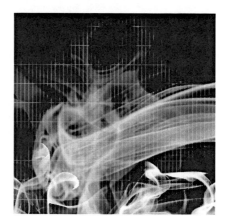

Chapter 11

Collisions

This chapter deals with an important subject that is bound to crop up in any animation or simulation: collisions. More precisely, it focuses primarily on *collision resolution*—how to respond to collision events—as opposed to *collision detection*, which was discussed to some extent in Chapter 2. Both collision detection and collision resolution are vast subjects in their own right. The intricacies of collision detection for general objects are outside the scope of this book (because we focus on the physics), but things are much simpler for collisions between particles, which is the main subject of this chapter. Similarly, it is impossible to cover all aspects of collision resolution in a single chapter. We shall, therefore, concentrate on some of the basics that are most commonly encountered. Specifically, we shall restrict attention to collisions of particles with fixed walls (bouncing) and with other particles.

Topics covered in this chapter include the following:

- **Collisions and their modeling:** This brief introductory section explains what collisions are and outlines the approach we will take to model them.

- **Bouncing off horizontal or vertical walls:** By *wall*, we mean any fixed flat surface that a particle can bounce off of. We start with the example of a ball bouncing off a horizontal or vertical wall. The collision resolution in this case is simple. The effects of energy loss by bouncing or wall friction can also be implemented in a straightforward way.

- **Bouncing off inclined walls:** Things get a lot more complicated if the wall is inclined. A general method will be given to resolve collisions with walls of any inclination.

- **Collisions between particles in 1D:** When particles move along the line joining them, collisions are one-dimensional and can be resolved in a straightforward way by applying the laws of conservation of momentum and energy.

- **Collisions between particles in 2D:** We discuss a general method for resolving more complicated two-dimensional collisions between particles that occur at an angle to the line joining them.

Collisions and their modeling

Let's begin by defining what we mean by collisions in the context of this book. A *collision* between two objects is a brief interaction during which they come into contact and exchange forces that then modify their motion. The task of collision resolution is to determine the motion of the two colliding objects immediately after the collision has taken place.

In Part II of the book, you have been used to solving motion problems using forces. This is not how collisions are usually treated. It is very difficult to model the large and brief forces that are exerted during collisions. The way collisions are normally handled is through their effect. We know from Newton's second law of motion that forces produce changes in momentum. In Chapter 5, this relationship was expressed in the following way through the concept of an impulse $F\Delta t$, where Δp is the change in momentum produced by an impulse:

$$F\Delta t = \Delta p$$

For a particle with constant mass m:

$$\Delta p = m\Delta v$$

so that:

$$F\Delta t = m\Delta v$$

So the effect of a large and brief collision force, in other words an impulse $F\Delta t$, is to produce a change of velocity given by the preceding formula.

The way to handle collisions is to directly work out that change in velocity. If you look back to Chapter 5, you will recall that this is what the principle of momentum conservation is all about. But momentum conservation on its own is not enough for collision resolution. We also have to make assumptions about what happens to the kinetic energy of the colliding objects. Hence, the physics involved in collisions consist of those two conservation principles taken together. We will apply them either explicitly or tacitly in what follows.

Broadly speaking, we will simulate two types of collisions: particle-particle collisions and particle-wall collisions. A *wall* here means an immovable object, whose motion is not itself being simulated. Specifically, we'll use the word *wall* to refer to any fixed flat surface from which particles can bounce. Therefore, our walls can be horizontal or vertical or oblique; they can also be bounding barriers or barriers placed anywhere else in the simulation space.

Bouncing off horizontal or vertical walls

In the first application of collision physics, we will look at how to make a ball bounce off a straight wall that is either horizontal or vertical in a 2D simulation space such as a floor, ceiling, or room wall. For illustration, we use a vertical wall, but similar principles will apply to horizontal walls as well.

We'll look at elastic and inelastic bouncing in turn (bouncing in which the kinetic energy of the ball is or is not conserved).

Elastic bouncing

If the ball bounces elastically off a wall, its kinetic energy just after bouncing must equal its kinetic energy just before bouncing. Because k.e. = ½ mv^2, this implies that its velocity magnitude is unchanged by the collision.

Consider first a special case in which the ball hits the wall perpendicularly with velocity **v** (see Figure 11-1). In that case, the ball will bounce back at right angles as well. Therefore, because its velocity magnitude is unchanged, its velocity just after bouncing will be –**v**.

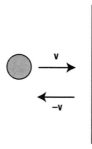

Figure 11-1. A ball bouncing off a wall at right angles

This is very easy to implement in code: you just reverse the velocity direction after the collision detection. However, there is something else to consider. When collision is detected, the ball may have passed the edge of the wall, penetrating it slightly. Therefore, before you reverse the ball's velocity, you need to reposition the ball just at the edge of the wall (see Figure 11-2). This is necessary not just to avoid the visual effect of the ball penetrating into the wall but also avoids the potential problem of the ball "getting stuck" into the wall. The latter situation might arise if the reversed velocity of the ball is not sufficient for it to get out of the wall (especially if the velocity is also reduced to account for energy loss—see the next section). In that case, the velocity of the ball would be reversed again on the next timestep, sending it back into the wall.

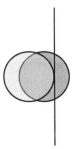

Figure11-2. Repositioning the ball after collision detection

Here is a piece of code to illustrate these steps for the scenario shown in Figure 11-2, for a `Ball` instance named _ball and a wall `Sprite` object named _wall:

```
if (_ball.x > _wall.x - _ball.radius){ // collision detection
        _ball.x = _wall.x - _ball.radius;  // reposition ball at wall edge
        _ball.vx *= -1; // reverse ball's velocity
}
```

This simple three-line piece of code encapsulates the whole process of how to handle the bouncing of a ball colliding perpendicularly with a horizontal or vertical wall:

1. Collision detection: simple in this case.

2. Reposition the particle at the point of collision: in this case, just shift it horizontally or vertically so that it just touches the wall.

3. Calculate the particle's new velocity just after the collision: here, for elastic collisions normal (perpendicular) to the wall, just reverse the velocity.

Note that in steps 1 and 2 in the preceding code we have assumed that the ball's registration point is at its center. If, for instance, the registration point is in the upper-left corner of the ball's bounding box, then the ball's diameter should be subtracted instead in the corresponding lines of code. Also, this code only covers the situation where the ball is moving from left to right, but it is not difficult to see how it can be modified if the ball were moving from right to left instead.

This is all nice and simple, but what if the ball hits the wall at an oblique angle, instead of at right angles (see Figure 11-3). In that case, in implementing step 3, we need to consider the components of velocity perpendicular and parallel to the wall separately. In the case of a vertical wall shown in Figure 11-3, the perpendicular component is _ball.vx, and the parallel component is _ball.vy. What we need to do is to reverse the perpendicular component as before and leave the parallel component unchanged. This is just what the previous piece of code does, so it should work fine for an oblique impact as well. This technique of decomposing the velocity vector into a normal (perpendicular) and a parallel (tangential) component with respect to the wall seems entirely natural in this context. But its application is more general: you'll see in the next section that a variant of it applies to the collision between two particles.

If you need to be extra accurate, there is something else you need to worry about, this time in relation to step 2. Take a look again at Figure 11-3. In the previous code, we are repositioning the ball by moving it along the x-direction so that it just touches the wall. But when the collision is oblique, its real position at the point of collision is along the line of collision. So the ball also needs to be moved a little along the y-direction. We'll devise a general method to do this in the next section. For this simple example, let's just adjust the x-position only. This should work fine and produce a smooth bouncing effect in most common situations except perhaps if you have a slow machine, in which case you might find that the ball occasionally sticks to the wall.

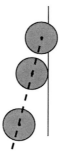

Figure 11-3. Ball bouncing off a wall at an oblique angle

The files `WallBouncing.as` and `WallBouncer.as` demonstrate this simple example. Here is the code in `WallBouncing.as`:

```
package{
        import flash.display.Sprite;
        import com.physicscodes.objects.Ball;
        import com.physicscodes.math.Vector2D;
        import com.physicscodes.objects.Wall;

        public class WallBouncing extends Sprite{
                public function WallBouncing():void{
                        init();
                }
                private function init():void{
                        var ball:Ball = new Ball(15,0x000000,1);
                        ball.pos2D = new Vector2D(100,100);
                        ball.velo2D = new Vector2D(500,100);
                        addChild(ball);

                        var wall:Sprite = new Sprite();
                        with (wall.graphics){
                                lineStyle(1);
                                moveTo(0,50);
                                lineTo(0,350);
                        }
                        wall.x = 400;
                        addChild(wall);

                        var bouncer:WallBouncer=new WallBouncer(ball,wall);
                        bouncer.startTime();
                }
        }
}
```

As you can see, this code simply creates a ball as a Ball object and creates a wall as a Sprite on which a straight line is drawn. The ball and wall are then made to interact through an instance of WallBouncer, which looks like this:

```
package {
        import com.physicscodes.motion.Mover;
        import com.physicscodes.objects.Ball;
        import com.physicscodes.objects.Wall;
        import com.physicscodes.math.Vector2D;
        import flash.display.Sprite;

        public class WallBouncer extends Mover{
                private var _ball:Ball;
                private var _wall:Sprite;

                public function WallBouncer(pball:Ball,pwall:Sprite):void{
                        _ball = pball;
                        _wall = pwall;
                        super(pball);
                }

                override protected function moveObject():void{
                        super.moveObject();
                        checkBounce();
                }

                private function checkBounce():void{
                        if (_ball.x > _wall.x - _ball.radius){
                                _ball.x = _wall.x - _ball.radius;
                                _ball.vx *= -1;
                        }
                }
        }
}
```

The code is very straightforward: WallBouncer extends Mover rather than Forcer because here we are not imposing any forces. Therefore, the velocity of the ball is constant, except when it collides with the wall. The key functionality is provided by the checkBounce() method, which contains a piece of conditional code identical to the one given previously for a ball colliding perpendicularly with the wall. Note that this piece of code would have to be modified slightly if the wall is on the left side or if it is horizontal. And if the wall is neither horizontal nor vertical, but at some angle, you need a lot more code than just those three lines in the checkBounce() method, as you'll soon find out!

Implementing energy loss due to bouncing

In the previous example, we assumed that there is no loss of kinetic energy, in other words that the collision is elastic. Doing this means that the ball bounces back with the same velocity magnitude. It is very easy to include the effect of loss of kinetic energy due to bouncing. All you have to do is multiply the velocity of the ball normal to the wall by a factor of less that 1 when reversing it.

Hence, in the above example, the following line:

```
_ball.vx *= -1;
```

would be replaced by something like this, where _vfac is a number between 0 and 1:

```
_ball.vx *= -_vfac; // energy loss on bouncing
```

A value of 1 corresponds to an elastic collision while a value of 0 corresponds to a completely inelastic collision (discussed in more detail a little later), in which the ball just sticks to the wall. You can experiment with different values of _vfac to see what you get.

The reason for multiplying the velocity by this constant factor will become clear further on, when we discuss one-dimensional collisions.

Similarly, you can model the effect of wall friction in a simple way by multiplying the tangential velocity of the ball (the velocity component parallel to the wall) by a factor between 0 and 1:

```
_ball.vy *= _vfac2; // wall friction
```

Note the absence of a minus sign in this case, as friction reduces but does not reverse the tangential velocity.

Bouncing off inclined walls

Things get significantly more complicated if the wall on which the ball bounces is inclined at some angle to the horizontal or vertical. The same steps apply as in the case of a horizontal or vertical wall, but they are now a bit more complex to implement. Different approaches could be taken here. One common approach, described in Keith Peters's book, *Foundation ActionScript 3.0 Animation*, is to perform a coordinate rotation to make the wall horizontal, do the bouncing, and then rotate the coordinate system back. This is a perfectly good way to do it, and we refer you to that book for more details of the procedure. For our present purposes, because we are using vectors, we have devised an alternative method that exploits the vector formulation and avoids doing the two coordinate rotations. We explain the steps in the new method in detail before giving an example of how to implement it.

Collision detection

Collision detection is much less straightforward in this case because it is not simply a case of checking the x or y position of the ball in relation to that of the wall. But thinking in terms of vectors helps a lot. Take a look at Figure 11-4, which shows a particle approaching collision with a wall. There are basically two conditions that must be met for a collision to occur:

- The perpendicular distance of the particle from the wall must be smaller than its radius.

- The particle must be located between the end points of the wall.

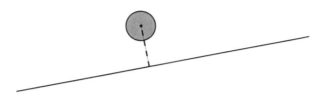

Figure 11-4. A ball approaching a wall

There are a number of ways of implementing either condition. We describe one possible approach here. See Figure 11-5, which shows a diagram of the position and displacement vectors corresponding to the setup in Figure 11-4. In this diagram, **p1** and **p2** are the position vectors of the end points of the wall with respect to the origin O; **w** is a vector from the end point marked A (with position vector **p1**) to the other end point. Similarly, **p** is the position vector of the ball with respect to the origin, **b1** and **b2** are vectors from the ball to the end points of the wall, and **d** is a perpendicular vector from the ball to the wall (so that **d** is equal to the distance PQ of the ball from the wall). (Note that we are taking the position of a particle to be at its center.) In the code implementation, we also assume that the registration point of any particle is located at its center. This is true of any `Ball` instance created from the `Ball` class.

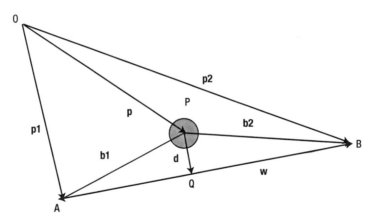

Figure 11-5. Vector diagram for analyzing collision of a ball with an inclined wall

In terms of these vectors, the first condition is simply the following, where r is the radius of the ball:

$$d < r$$

The second condition can be phrased in terms of the projections QA and QB of the vectors **b1** and **b2** in the direction of the wall vector **w**. If the length of both of those projections is smaller than the length of **w**, it means that the ball is between the end points of the wall. Otherwise, if either projection exceeds the length of **w**, the ball must be outside of that range and won't hit the wall.

It remains now to work out the length of the projections and the distance d from the known vectors **p1**, **p2**, and **p**. By using the rules of vector addition:

$$\mathbf{w} = \mathbf{p2} - \mathbf{p1}$$

In pseudocode, this is the following:

```
wallVec = _wall.p2.subtract(_wall.p1);
```

By a similar reasoning, the vectors **b1** and **b2** are given by this:

$$\mathbf{b1} = \mathbf{p1} - \mathbf{p}$$

$$\mathbf{b2} = \mathbf{p2} - \mathbf{p}$$

In pseudocode, this can be written as follows:

```
ballToWall1 = _wall.p1.subtract(_ball.pos2D);
ballToWall2 = _wall.p2.subtract(_ball.pos2D);
```

Then the projection of the vectors `ballToWall1` and `ballToWall2` onto **w** are given by this:

```
proj1 = ballToWall1.projection(wallVec);
proj2 = ballToWall2.projection(wallVec);
```

The vector **d**, which we'll call `dist` in pseudocode, can then be obtained by subtracting from **b1** the projection vector of **b1** onto **w**. In pseudocode it can be written like this:

```
dist = ballToWall1.subtract(ballToWall1.project(wallVec));
```

You can probably express these quantities in a number of different but equivalent ways. Feel free to do so.

Repositioning the particle

The formula we gave in the last section for repositioning the particle at collision detection is specific to a vertical wall on the right side in relation to the location of the ball. Its form will look slightly different for the walls on the left, top, or bottom. And it's no good if the wall is inclined. We need something better. That's where vectors come to the rescue again. With vector methods, it is possible to come up with a formula that works for any particle velocity and any wall orientation.

Figure 11-6 shows a ball hitting an inclined wall, the collision being detected after the ball has gone a small distance into the wall. As the diagram indicates, the ball must be moved a distance $\Delta s = h$ back along its line of approach (opposite to its velocity vector). Here we are assuming that the direction of the velocity vector is constant during that small interval. If a force such as gravity is present, this is not strictly true, but because the time interval is so small, the velocity direction can be taken as constant to a very good approximation.

Simple trigonometry then shows that the magnitude of Δs is given by this, where **d** is a perpendicular vector from the particle's center at the point of collision *detection* to the wall (so that its magnitude d is the distance of the particle from the wall), **n** is a unit vector perpendicular to the wall and pointing into the side where the particle normally resides, and θ is the angle between the line of approach of the particle (and therefore its velocity just before collision) and the wall:

$$\Delta s = \frac{r + \mathbf{d} \bullet \mathbf{n}}{\sin(\theta)}$$

Note that if the ball's center at the point of collision detection lies in front of the wall, then **d** is opposite to **n**, and therefore **d** • **n** = –d; if it lies behind the wall, then **d** points along **n**, and so **d** • **n** = d. Using the dot product automatically handles both cases.

In pseudocode, the displacement vector to reposition the particle is then given by this:

```
displ = _particle.velo2D.para(deltaS);
```

Therefore, the particle's position needs to be updated as follows:

```
_particle.pos2D = _particle.pos2D.subtract(displ);
```

This all looks nice and simple in comparison to the use of special non-vector code for each wall.

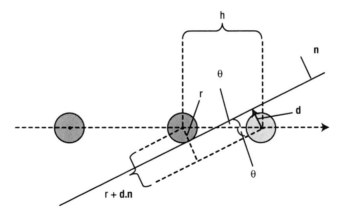

Figure 11-6. Repositioning a particle after collision detection with an inclined wall

Calculating the new velocity

Just as for a horizontal or vertical wall, the new velocity after bouncing is calculated by first decomposing the velocity before bouncing into components parallel and normal to the wall, and then reversing the normal component. But because the wall is now oblique, those components are not just the vx and vy properties of the particle. Instead, we have to specify them as Vector2D objects in their own right.

See Figure 11-7 for an illustration of how to do this. If **d** is a vector from the particle center normal to the wall at the point of collision, the normal velocity is given as a vector with magnitude equal to the projection of the particle's velocity onto **d** and in the same direction as **d**.

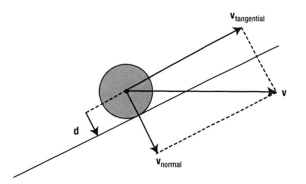

Figure 11-7. Decomposing the velocity vector

In pseudocode, if we calculate the perpendicular vector from the particle to the wall as dist and denote the particle as _particle, the normal velocity is given by the following using the projection() and para() methods of the Vector2D class:

```
normal_velo = dist.para(_particle.velo2D.projection(dist));
```

Recall that vec1.projection(vec2) gives the length of the projection of vector vec1 in the direction of vec2, and that vec.para(mag) gives a vector parallel to vector vec and of length mag.

We can make things even simpler by creating the following project() method in the Vector2D class:

```
public function project(vec:Vector2D):Vector2D {
        return vec.para(this.projection(vec));
}
```

So, vec1.project(vec2) gives a vector in the direction of vector vec2, and with magnitude equal to the projection of vec1 in the direction of vec2. With this newly defined method, we can write the normal velocity simply as follows:

```
normalVelo = _particle.velo2D.project(dist);
```

The tangential velocity can then be obtained simply by subtracting the normal velocity from the particle velocity (see Figure 11-7):

```
tangentVelo = _particle.velo2D.subtract(normalVelo);
```

These are the precollision velocities. Assuming there is no energy loss, the collision will reverse the normal velocity while leaving the tangential velocity unchanged. Therefore, the new velocity of the particle as a result of the collision is given by this:

```
_particle.velo2D = tangent_velo.addScaled(normalVelo,-1);
```

If there is energy loss due to bouncing, simply replace the –1 in the previous code by the fraction _fac discussed in the last section.

Velocity correction just before collision

If the simulation involved a force, such as gravity, there is something else to worry about. Whenever there is a force involved, it means that the particle is accelerating (its velocity is changing all the time). In that case, when the particle is repositioned at the edge of the wall, its velocity must also be adjusted to what it was at that point. Although this may seem like a small correction, failure to do so could in some cases have serious consequences. This applies equally to horizontal or vertical walls if the velocity is changing with time.

As an example, consider a simple example: a ball dropped from a certain height onto a horizontal floor. Suppose that collision is detected when the ball has gone slightly past the floor level. If you simply follow the procedure given so far, you would move the ball to the level of the floor and then reverse its velocity (if you assume no energy loss due to bouncing). The trouble is that because the ball is accelerating under gravity, its velocity at the point of *collision detection* is higher than what it should be at the actual point of collision. By simply reversing this velocity, you are sending it off with higher kinetic energy than it's supposed to have as a result of having lost potential energy by falling from its initial height. The consequence is that the ball will end up reaching higher than the point it fell from! After a few bounces, things could go completely haywire. Of course, if you implement energy loss on bouncing, you may not even notice the problem—if accuracy is not important, that may be a simple trick to solve the problem. But if you want to be as accurate as possible, or if the nature of the simulation does not permit you to include energy loss, then here is the way to do it.

The aim is to compute the velocity of the particle at the point of collision given that it is accelerating. We know the velocity, acceleration, and displacement at the point of collision detection. To proceed, let's start with the calculus definition of acceleration:

$$a = \frac{dv}{dt}$$

For a reason that will become apparent shortly, we can write it as this (you can think of the two ds factors as "cancelling out"):

$$a = \frac{dv}{ds}\frac{ds}{dt}$$

Now, because v = ds/dt, we can write it as follows:

$$a = v\frac{dv}{ds}$$

This gives us a differential equation connecting the quantities that we were just talking about. Because we are doing a discrete simulation, let's write this:

$$\frac{dv}{ds} \approx \frac{\Delta v}{\Delta s}$$

Substituting into the above equation gives this:

$$a \approx v\frac{\Delta v}{\Delta s}$$

And so:

$$\Delta v \approx \frac{a\,\Delta s}{v}$$

This formula gives the change in velocity Δv that results from a displacement Δs under an acceleration a. Let v be the velocity at collision detection and v' be the velocity at collision, so that:

$$\Delta v = v - v'$$

Simple algebra gives this:

$$\frac{v'}{v} \approx 1 - \frac{a\,\Delta s}{v^2}$$

This gives the ratio of the magnitude of the velocity at the point of collision to that at the point of collision detection in terms of the acceleration (which is constant in the case of gravity), the velocity at the point of collision detection and the displacement of the particle from the point of collision to the position where collision is detected. The latter quantity was worked out in the section on "Repositioning the particle." Therefore, the adjustment factor for the velocity can be calculated from these known quantities as given by the preceding formula. The preceding formula was derived for a 1D case because we didn't use vectors, but it applies equally to 2D, when the acceleration a and the displacement Δs are vectors that may not be in the same direction (for example, for a ball moving under gravity). In that case, we take the acceleration resolved in the direction of the displacement, so that in effect we need to replace the product $a\Delta s$ by the dot product $a.\Delta s$; and v is the magnitude of the velocity vector.

Let's denote the code variable corresponding to the velocity correction factor v'/v as vcor. Then, assuming that the direction of the velocity does not change much between the point of collision and the point of collision detection, we can write in pseudocode:

```
veloAtCollision = veloAtCollisionDetection.multiply(vcor);
```

An example of a ball bouncing off an inclined wall

All that vector algebra is probably beginning to sound a bit heavy. So it's time to pull together all that we have learned in this section to build a full example. Because we are going to do a lot of bouncing around walls, it would make sense to create a reusable Wall class. Let's do that first.

Creating a Wall class

The Wall class is a simple class that draws a line between two specified end points to represent a wall. The end points are taken to be Vector2D objects. Here is the full code of the Wall class:

```
package com.physicscodes.objects {
        import flash.display.Sprite;
        import com.physicscodes.math.Vector2D;

        public class Wall extends Sprite{
                private var _p1:Vector2D;
                private var _p2:Vector2D;
                private var _sprite:Sprite;

                public function Wall(p1:Vector2D,p2:Vector2D){
                        _p1 = p1;
                        _p2 = p2;
                        _sprite = new Sprite();
                        drawWall();
                }

                public function get p1():Vector2D{
                        return _p1;
                }
                public function set p1(pvec:Vector2D):void{
                        _p1 = pvec;
                        clear();
                        drawWall();
                }
                public function get p2():Vector2D{
                        return _p2;
                }
                public function set p2(pvec:Vector2D):void{
                        _p2 = pvec;
                        clear();
                        drawWall();
                }
                public function get dir():Vector2D{
                        return _p2.subtract(_p1);
                }
                public function get normal():Vector2D{
                        return this.dir.perp(1);
                }
                private function drawWall():void{
                        with (_sprite.graphics){
                                lineStyle(1);
                                moveTo(_p1.x,_p1.y);
```

```
                              lineTo(_p2.x,_p2.y);
                      }
                      addChild(_sprite);
              }
              public function clear():void{
                      _sprite.graphics.clear();
                      removeChild(_sprite);
              }
      }
}
```

The end points, denoted by p1 and p2, can be changed via setters that clear and redraw the line between the updated end points. Properties wall.dir and wall.normal are defined via getters that return the vector from p1 to p2 (the vector along the wall) and the unit vector normal to the wall, respectively. The usefulness of these properties will soon become apparent.

Creating a Wall instance

In the file BouncingOffInclinedWall.as, we create a Wall instance that is at an oblique angle to the horizontal by the following piece of code:

```
var wall:Wall;
wall=new Wall(new Vector2D(50,200), new Vector2D(700,500));
addChild(wall);
```

So the end point vectors p1 and p2 are [50, 200] and [700, 500], respectively. The rest of the code in BouncingOffInclinedWall.as creates a Ball instance, sets its position above the wall, and then passes the ball and wall objects to an instance of an InclinedWallBouncer class that makes the ball move and handles the bouncing.

Getting a ball to bounce off an inclined wall

The InclinedWallBouncer class extends Forcer and overrides moveObject() and calcForce(). In the latter, it implements the Forces.constantGravity force, so that the ball will be moving under gravity. The overridden moveObject() method adds a new private method, checkBounce(), that looks as follows:

```
private function checkBounce():void{
// vector along wall
        var wdir:Vector2D = _wall.dir;
// vectors from ball to end points of wall
        var ballp1:Vector2D = _wall.p1.subtract(_ball.pos2D);
        var ballp2:Vector2D = _wall.p2.subtract(_ball.pos2D);
// projection of above vectors onto wall vector
        var proj1:Number = ballp1.projection(wdir);
        var proj2:Number = ballp2.projection(wdir);
// perpendicular distance vector from the object to the wall
        var dist:Vector2D = ballp1.addScaled(wdir.unit(), proj1*(-1));
// collision detection
        var test:Boolean = ((Math.abs(proj1) < wdir.length) && (Math.abs(proj2) <↵
wdir.length));
```

```
        if ((dist.length < _ball.radius) && test){
// angle between velocity and wall
            var angle:Number = Vector2D.angleBetween(_ball.velo2D, wdir);
// reposition object
            var normal:Vector2D = _wall.normal;
            if (normal.dotProduct(_ball.velo2D) > 0){
                normal.scaleBy(-1);
            }
            var deltaS:Number = (_ball.radius+dist.dotProduct(normal))/Math.sin(angle);
            var displ:Vector2D = _ball.velo2D.para(deltaS);
            _ball.pos2D = _ball.pos2D.subtract(displ);
// velocity correction factor
            var vcor:Number = 1-acc.dotProduct(displ)/_ball.velo2D.lengthSquared;
// corrected velocity vector just before impact
            var Velo:Vector2D = _ball.velo2D.multiply(vcor);
// velocity vector component perpendicular to wall just before impact
            var normalVelo:Vector2D = dist.para(Velo.projection(dist));
// velocity vector component parallel to wall; unchanged by impact
            var tangentVelo:Vector2D = Velo.subtract(normalVelo);
// velocity vector component perpendicular to wall just after impact
            _ball.velo2D = tangentVelo.addScaled(normalVelo,-_vfac);
        }
// collision at the wall boundaries
    else if (Math.abs(ballp1.length) < _ball.radius){
        bounceOffEnd point(_wall.p1);
    }
    else if (Math.abs(ballp2.length) < _ball.radius){
        bounceOffEnd point(_wall.p2);
    }
}
```

This code closely mirrors the description given in the previous sections. Most of it should therefore be straightforward (and we've left the comments in so you can follow the logic more easily). Let's therefore focus on just a couple of features that were not covered in the preceding discussion.

First, in the code that repositions the ball after collision detection, note that we check whether the wall normal vector has a positive dot product with the ball's velocity vector; if so, we reverse the wall normal vector. To understand why this is done, refer to the section on "Repositioning the particle," in which we said that the normal must point to the side where the particle resides. The latter condition is equivalent to saying that the normal vector should point so that it has a normal component in the opposite direction to the ball's velocity and so should have a negative dot product with it (see Figure 11-8). The if code enforces that condition. But why do we need to check this every timestep; can't we fix the normal once and for all? The reason is that by doing so we allow for the possibility that the ball could bounce on the bottom surface as well as on the top surface of the wall.

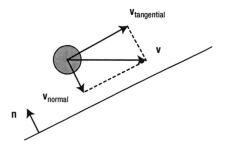

Figure 11-8. The unit normal vector to the wall should be oriented opposite to the velocity vector.

The second thing to point out is the presence of the two `else if` blocks of code at the end of the `checkBounce()` function. They are there to handle the case where the ball is within a radius of either of the end points of the wall. In that case, they call a private method: `bounceOffEndpoint()`. The idea is that bouncing off the edge of the wall should give rise to a different type of motion and should therefore be handled differently. The approach we take is to handle such a collision in a similar way to that between two particles, with the additional feature that here one of the "particles," the wall end point, is fixed and has zero radius. The code within the `bounceOffEndpoint()` method probably won't make too much sense now, but should do so once you've covered the material on collisions between particles later in the chapter.

To make the simulation more interactive and fun, there is also code that allows you to click and drag anywhere on the stage to change the position and size of the ball. On releasing the mouse, the simulation resumes with the new ball.

Spend some time experimenting with the simulation. Click and drag to create balls of different sizes and see how they fall and bounce onto the inclined wall in a natural way. Avoid overlapping the ball with the wall when you are dragging as this will result in erratic behavior. Release the ball onto the end points of the wall and notice the difference in the way it bounces. Change `gravity _g` and the energy loss factor `_vfac`. See Figure 11-9.

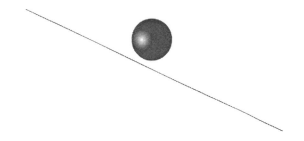

Figure 11-9. A ball bouncing off an inclined wall

Next release the ball just above the line and see how it slides down the wall smoothly. This is strongly reminiscent of the simulation of a ball sliding down an inclined plane that we did back in Chapter 7 using normal contact forces. So, interestingly, our procedure for collision resolution has an unexpected side benefit: we also have *contact resolution* for free. In fact, this is a common approach to handle contact resolution: using impulses produced by "micro-collisions" rather than by explicitly including a normal contact force.

Dealing with a potential "tunneling" problem

The method of collision detection we described in the last section and implemented in this simulation should work well under most normal circumstances. But in some cases, especially if the simulation is run on a slow machine and the ball is small and moving fast, it may be possible for the ball to cross the wall completely in a single timestep. In that case, collision detection will fail. This is known as *tunneling*. You can probably see this effect if you make the ball very small, (1 px) and release it a long way above the wall so that it achieves a high velocity by the time it hits the wall. The ball might then pass straight through the wall.

The collision detection algorithm outlined in the last section fails because the first condition (that the particle is closer to the wall than its radius) is never satisfied. We need to modify the algorithm to include the new possible scenario. A simple solution is to test whether the ball's center has moved from one side of the wall to the other. If so, that means it has "tunneled" and that in itself provides the collision detection.

We have implemented this collision detection mechanism in a modified version of the simulation with source files BouncingOffInclinedWall2.as and InclinedWallBouncer2.as. If you compare this modified code with the original, you will find that a key change is the inclusion of the following code in the checkBounce() and onUp() methods in the InclinedBouncer2 class, as well as in the setup file BouncingOffInclinedWall2.as:

```
if (dist.dotProduct(_wall.normal) < 0){
        _wall.side = -1;
}else{
        _wall.side = 1;
}
```

This piece of code provides a way of keeping track of which side of each wall the ball is at any moment. To do this, it checks the sign of the dot product between the perpendicular vector dist from the particle to the wall and the wall normal vector. If the sign is negative, it sets the side property of the wall to −1; otherwise, it sets it to 1. The side property of the Wall class has been created specifically for this purpose.

Another important piece of code is the following, which checks to see whether the sign of the dot product has reversed (which means that the ball has tunneled); if so, it sets the testTunneling Boolean variable to true:

```
var testTunneling:Boolean;
if (_wall.side*dist.dotProduct(_wall.normal) < 0){
        testTunneling = true;
}else{
        testTunneling = false;
}
```

This sets up the basic collision detection in the case of tunneling. The rest of the changes in the code should be easy to follow.

If you test `BouncingOffInclinedWall2.as` you should find that the tunneling problem is fixed.

Example of ball bouncing off multiple inclined walls

`BouncingOffMultipleInclinedWalls.as` and `MultipleInclinedWallsBouncer.as` generalize the last simulation to include several walls (see Figure 11-10). Take a look at the source files; the codes generalize the last ones in a straightforward way. In `BouncingOffMutipleInclinedWalls.as`, you just add more walls in the same way - four inclined walls, plus four bounding walls to form a box that encloses the other walls and the ball. The walls are then put into an array that is passed, together with the ball, to a `MultipleInclinedWallsBouncer` instance.

The code in `MultipleInclinedWallsBouncer.as` is pretty similar to that in `InclinedWallBouncer.as`, with the `checkBounce()` method now looping over each wall. It also includes a new `hasHitAWall` Boolean variable that is used to stop the looping once a collision with one of the walls is detected.

Experiment with the simulation, remembering that you can click and drag to reposition and resize the ball. As before, avoid positioning the ball so that it overlaps with any of the walls. Doing so will introduce an unphysical initial condition (a ball cannot physically overlap with a wall) that will cause some of the equations to give nonsensical results, resulting in erratic and unpredictable behavior.

See how the simulation handles different scenarios properly. For example, try balls of different sizes and release them at different locations: above the walls, so that they bounce off; just on the walls, so that they slide down; or just above a gap between the walls too small for them, so that they get trapped. You will see that collisions under the walls are also handled properly. Note that the four confining walls are treated in exactly the same way as the others. You can also click and drag *above* the top wall to make the ball bounce off it!

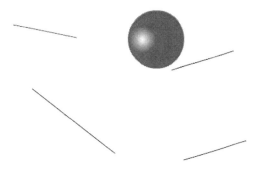

Figure 11-10. Ball bouncing off multiple walls

As in the previous simulation, you may encounter the tunneling problem on a slower machine. To fix this, we have modified the simulation in exactly the same way as described in the previous subsection. The modified source code is in the files `BouncingOffMultipleInclinedWalls2.as` and `MultipleInclinedWallsBouncer2.as`. You might find that tunneling still sometimes happens at very high velocities (for example, try initializing the ball's velocity with a magnitude in excess of 1000 px/s). The problem there is that we are at the limit of the time resolution of the simulation. In principle, you could overcome this by reducing the simulation timestep, but you will at some point be limited by how fast your machine can run the simulation.

Collisions between particles in 1D

In this section, we will show you how to handle collisions between particles when the approach direction of the particles lies along the line joining them. This situation can be described as a 1D collision because the motion of the particles takes place in a straight line, both before and after the collision. In general, two particles may collide at any angle, changing their direction as they do so. Therefore, the case discussed in this section may seem like a very special case. So why study it? The reason is that the methods and formulas that hold in this special case can be readily generalized to the more general case where the particles may collide at any angle. In fact, this will be done in the next section.

The steps for handling 1D particle collisions are the following (mirroring the steps for resolving the bouncing of a particle moving perpendicular to a wall):

1. Collision detection

2. Repositioning the particles at the moment of collision

3. Calculating the new velocities just after the collision

In the case of spherical particles (or circular in 2D), the first step, collision detection is very simple. As discussed in Chapter 2, you just see whether the distance d between the centers of the two particles is less than the sum of their radii, where d is calculated from the position coordinates (x_1, y_1) and (x_2, y_2) using Pythagoras's theorem:

$$d < r_1 + r_2$$

In 2-D:

$$d = \sqrt{\left(x_2 - x_1\right)^2 + \left(y_2 - y_1\right)^2}$$

Let's now look at how to reposition the particles when a collision is detected.

Repositioning the particles

Just as a particle may sink some distance into a wall by the time a collision is detected, two particles may similarly overlap. The complication in this case is that in general both particles may be moving, so both need to be moved back to their position at the actual point of contact. But how do we know how much to move each particle?

Let's begin by considering the case when the two particles are moving toward each other, as shown in Figure 11-11.

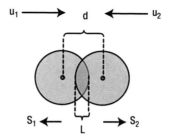

Figure 11-11. Separating overlapping particles moving toward each other

The amount of overlap L is given by the following, where r_1 and r_2 are the radii of the two particles, and d is the distance between their centers, as given by the Pythagoras formula discussed in the last section:

$$L = r_1 + r_2 - d$$

Let s_1 and s_2 be the magnitudes of the displacements by which the particles must be moved, in opposite directions, so that they are just touching. These displacements must add up to give the overlap distance L:

$$s_1 + s_2 = L$$

This gives one equation relating s_1 and s_2 in terms of a known variable L. In order to be able to work out s_1 and s_2, we need a second equation connecting them. We can come up with such an equation by recalling that, in a small time interval t:

$$s_1 = u_1 t$$

And

$$s_2 = u_2 t$$

where u_1 and u_2 are the velocities of the respective particles just before the collision. That's just using the fact that displacement = velocity x time (see Chapter 4).

Dividing the first equation by the second gives this:

$$\frac{s_1}{s_2} = \frac{u_1}{u_2}$$

This is our second equation. It is now a matter of simple algebra to solve for s_1 and s_2 to give this:

$$s_1 = \frac{u_1}{u_1 + u_2} L$$

$$s_2 = \frac{u_2}{u_1 + u_2} L$$

What this result tells us is that the particles must be displaced in proportion to their velocities just before the impact.

This is great, but what if we have the other possible situation, in which the two particles are moving in the same direction (rather than toward each other) with the one behind moving faster (so that a collision actually happens), as shown in Figure 11-12.

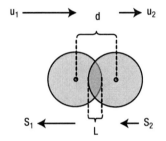

Figure 11-12. Overlapping particles moving in the same direction

In that case, the first equation connecting the displacement magnitudes s_1 and s_2 becomes the following, while the second equation is unchanged:

$$s_1 - s_2 = L$$

Solving them simultaneously then gives this:

$$s_1 = \frac{u_1}{u_1 - u_2} L$$

and this:

$$s_2 = \frac{u_2}{u_1 - u_2} L$$

This is a bit messy because we have different equations depending on whether the particles are moving toward each other or not. Luckily, it is possible to incorporate both cases in a single solution by thinking in terms of vector displacements. The reasoning is slightly less intuitive, but here is the final result, where the symbol $|\mathbf{v}|$ signifies the magnitude of vector $\mathbf{v}$:

$$\mathbf{s}_1 = -\frac{\mathbf{u}_1}{|\mathbf{u}_1 - \mathbf{u}_2|} L$$

$$\mathbf{s}_2 = -\frac{\mathbf{u}_2}{|\mathbf{u}_1 - \mathbf{u}_2|} L$$

Note that we always divide by the magnitude of the *relative velocity* ($\mathbf{u}_1 - \mathbf{u}_2$). When the particles are approaching each other, this is ($u_1 + u_2$); otherwise, it is ($u_1 - u_2$). Hence, these equations indeed reduce to the corresponding equations for the displacement magnitudes in the two cases discussed previously. The other good thing is that here the direction of the displacements is also explicit in the formulas: the minus sign tells us that $\mathbf{s}_1$ is opposite to $\mathbf{u}_1$, and $\mathbf{s}_2$ is opposite to $\mathbf{u}_2$.

You now know how to reposition the particles once the collision is detected. The final thing to do is to calculate the new velocities of the colliding particles just after the collision. We'll do this separately for elastic and inelastic collisions.

Elastic collisions

Recall from Chapter 4 that an elastic collision is one in which kinetic energy is conserved. This means that we can apply conservation of kinetic energy in addition to conservation of momentum (which is always conserved in any collision, elastic or not). For example, the collisions between billiard balls are usually modeled as elastic collisions.

Let the two colliding particles (which we can call particle1 and particle2) have masses m_1 and m_2, initial velocities u_1 and u_2, and final velocities v_1 and v_2, respectively. Note that we need only one component of velocity because the motion is 1D. Then we can write momentum conservation and energy conservation as follows:

$$m_1 v_1 + m_2 v_2 = m_1 u_1 + m_2 u_2$$

$$m_1 v_1^2 + m_2 v_2^2 = m_1 u_1^2 + m_2 u_2^2$$

Here the masses m_1 and m_2 of the particles are known, and so are the initial velocities u_1 and u_2. The aim is to calculate the final velocities v_1 and v_2 in terms of these known variables. This is a matter of solving these two equations simultaneously. The easiest method to do so involves deriving an important intermediate result involving the relative velocities of the particles before and after the collision. So let's do that now.

Relative velocity of colliding particles

The first step is to rearrange the previous two equations by combining the terms for each particle on each side of the equation (put all the terms with a 1 subscript on one side and the terms with a 2 subscript on the other side of the equation):

$$m_1\left(v_1 - u_1\right) = m_2\left(u_2 - v_2\right)$$

$$m_1\left(v_1^2 - u_1^2\right) = m_2\left(u_2^2 - v_2^2\right)$$

Now recall the following identity from your school algebra:

$$a^2 - b^2 = \left(a - b\right)\left(a + b\right)$$

This allows you to write the second equation as follows:

$$m_1\left(v_1 - u_1\right)\left(v_1 + u_1\right) = m_2\left(u_2 - v_2\right)\left(u_2 + v_2\right)$$

You can now see that each side of this equation contains the corresponding side of the first equation as a factor. So you can divide this equation by the first equation to get rid of those factors, leaving us with this:

$$\left(v_1 + u_1\right) = \left(u_2 + v_2\right)$$

This can be rearranged by combining the initial velocities (the u variables) on one side and the final velocities (the v variables) on the other side of the equation to give this:

$$v_1 - v_2 = u_2 - u_1$$

Or, equivalently, this:

$$v_1 - v_2 = -\left(u_1 - u_2\right)$$

This is our result. Note that ($u_1 - u_2$) is the initial relative velocity of particle1 from the point of view of particle2. Similarly, ($v_1 - v_2$) is the final relative velocity of particle1 from the point of view of particle2. Therefore, the preceding result tells us that the relative velocity of separation of the two particles is the negative of their relative velocity of approach. This result does not depend on the masses of the particles because m_1 and m_2 were cancelled out. But note that it holds only for elastic collisions. We shall see in the next section how it is modified for inelastic collisions.

As an immediate application of this result, consider the case when one of the particles, say particle2, is immovable (such as a wall). This is the same as saying that $u_2 = v_2 = 0$. Putting these values into the last equation gives us this:

$$v_1 = -u_1$$

This is elastic bouncing off an immovable object, and is the condition that we applied in the first example of a ball bouncing elastically off a wall.

Calculating velocities after an elastic collision

Using the result derived in the last section, it is now easy to work out the velocities after an elastic collision. The logic is that energy conservation is incorporated into the equation for relative velocities:

$$v_1 - v_2 = u_2 - u_1$$

So we need to solve this equation simultaneously with the equation expressing momentum conservation:

$$m_1 v_1 + m_2 v_2 = m_1 u_1 + m_2 u_2$$

The goal is to find the final velocities, v_1 and v_2, in terms of the other variables (the initial velocities and the masses). This can be done by eliminating either v_1 or v_2 between the two equations and then rearranging the resulting equation to find the other one. For example, we first multiply the first equation by m_2 to give this:

$$m_2 v_1 - m_2 v_2 = m_2 u_2 - m_2 u_1$$

Adding this to the second equation then gets rid of v_2, giving this:

$$\left(m_1 + m_2\right) v_1 = \left(m_1 - m_2\right) u_1 + 2 m_2 u_2$$

Dividing by (m_1+m_2) then gives the final result for the velocity of particle1:

$$v_1 = \frac{\left(m_1 - m_2\right) u_1 + 2 m_2 u_2}{\left(m_1 + m_2\right)}$$

You could go through a similar algebraic manipulation to calculate v_2, but there is no need to: you can just swap the 1 and 2 indices on the last equation to give this:

$$v_2 = \frac{\left(m_2 - m_1\right) u_2 + 2 m_1 u_1}{\left(m_1 + m_2\right)}$$

This is the result you are after: you can now calculate the velocities of the two particles just after the impact, from the velocities just before the impact (and the masses of the particles).

Finally, note that you don't have to calculate v_2 from the second equation. Once you know v_1, you can just work out v_2 by rearranging the equation for relative velocities to give the following, which saves on cpu time:

$$v_2 = v_1 + u_1 - u_2$$

A special case: particles of equal masses

In the special case when the particles have the same mass, the formulas take a particularly simple form. To see this, simply replacing $m_1 = m_2 = m$ into the above equations gives this:

$$v_1 = u_2$$

and this:

$$v_2 = u_1$$

In other words, the particles simply exchange velocities after the collision! This applies regardless of the initial velocities of the particles, as long as they have the same mass and the collision is elastic. This is a very useful result. If your simulation will only ever involve elastic collisions between particles of the same mass, there is no need to code in the complicated general formula given previously, saving on valuable cpu time. You might recall that we made use of this result in the simple collision example in Chapter 5.

As a special case of this special case, if one of the particles is initially at rest ($u_2 = 0$), we get $v_1 = 0$ and $v_2 = u_1$; the other particle then stops dead in its track after the collision, while the initially stationary particle moves off at the velocity that the other one had before the collision.

Another special case: collision with a particle of much larger mass

On the other hand, if the mass of one of the particles is much larger than the other (for example, $m_2 \gg m_1$), the formulas for the final velocities reduce to this:

$$v_1 \approx -u_1 + 2u_2$$

and this:

$$v_2 = u_2 + 2\left(\frac{m_1}{m_2}\right)u_1$$

In particular, if the particle with large mass (particle2) is initially stationary, $u_2 = 0$, so

$$v_1 \approx -u_1$$

and

$$v_2 = 2\left(\frac{m_1}{m_2}\right)u_1$$

Hence, the lighter particle bounces off the heavier one, almost reversing its velocity. Noting that (m_1/m_2) is a small number much less that 1, we conclude that $v_2 \ll u_1$; hence, the heavier particle moves off at a much smaller velocity than the velocity at which the first particle hit it. This is all common sense.

Inelastic collisions

Although it is common to model collisions as elastic, most collisions in real life are rarely elastic—they usually involve a loss of kinetic energy and are therefore inelastic.

To model inelastic collisions, a useful starting point is again the relative velocity of the colliding particles—through the introduction of a concept known as the *coefficient of restitution*.

Coefficient of restitution

The coefficient of restitution (denoted by the symbol C_R) is defined as the ratio between the relative velocity after a collision to the relative velocity before the collision:

$$C_R = \frac{v_1 - v_2}{u_2 - u_1}$$

This equation can be rewritten as follows:

$$v_1 - v_2 = C_R\left(u_2 - u_1\right)$$

For an elastic collision, the relative velocities before and after the collision are related by the equation $v_1 - v_2 = u_2 - u_1$, so the preceding equation tells us that $C_R = 1$ for an elastic collision.

Conceptually, the coefficient of restitution is a measure of the departure from perfectly elastic collisions. Generally, the value of C_R will be less than 1. Collisions for which $C_R > 1$ are also possible; they correspond to collisions that generate explosive forces, so that the total kinetic energy of the particles after the collision is larger than their initial kinetic energy. Such collisions are called *superelastic*.

The special case when $C_R = 0$ refers to so-called *completely inelastic* collisions. In that case, the relative velocity equation reduces to this:

$$v_1 - v_2 = 0$$

So that:

$$v_1 = v_2$$

In other words, the final velocities of the particles are the same: they stick together. In a completely inelastic collision, the loss of kinetic energy is maximum, but not complete (if it were complete, the particles would just stop; this would violate momentum conservation).

As another special case, suppose that one of the particles is immovable (such as a wall). For example, if particle2 is immovable, $u_2 = v_2 = 0$, so that the relative velocity equation gives this:

$$v_1 = -C_R u_1$$

This is exactly how we modeled wall collisions involving energy loss earlier in this chapter, with C_R representing the "bounce" factor.

Calculating velocities after an inelastic collision

Starting from the relative velocity equation for inelastic collisions and using a similar method to that used to derive the corresponding elastic collision equations, it is easy to show that the final velocities due to an inelastic collision are given by this:

$$v_1 = \frac{(m_1 - C_R m_2)u_1 + (m_2 + C_R m_2)u_2}{(m_1 + m_2)}$$

and this:

$$v_2 = \frac{(m_2 - C_R m_1)u_2 + (m_1 + C_R m_1)u_1}{(m_1 + m_2)}$$

This is the most general formula for collisions, as it also includes the elastic formula as a special case (set $C_R = 1$ in the above formulas and verify that they reduce to the corresponding formulas for elastic collisions).

Completely inelastic collisions

If the collision is completely inelastic (with $C_R = 0$), the last equations reduce to this:

$$v_1 = v_2 = \frac{m_1 u_1 + m_2 u_2}{\left(m_1 + m_2\right)}$$

So the two particles stick together and move at the same velocity after the collision. Examples in which you might want to model completely inelastic collisions include hitting a character with a snowball or firing a bullet that sticks into its target.

This completes our discussion of particle collisions in 1D. You are no doubt keen to see all that math applied in a demo. You'll get to see a code example very soon, but before we do that, let's quickly discuss how this extends to 2D. Once we've covered that, we will then be able to build simulations that can handle both 1D and 2D collisions.

Collisions between particles in 2D

We are now ready to look at general 2D collisions, in which the direction of approach of the particles is not necessarily along the line joining their centers. The way to handle such collisions is to resort to a trick similar to that used for a ball colliding with a wall: at the point of collision (when the particles are just touching), resolve the velocity of each particle into a normal component along the line joining them, and a tangential component perpendicular to that line (see Figure 11-13). The revelation is that, just like in a collision with a wall, only the normal velocity components are affected by the collision; the tangential components remain the same after the collision (provided it is frictionless). What's more, the normal velocity components are changed in exactly the same way as if the collision were in 1D (as if the tangential components were zero). That's great; it means that we can treat any 2D collision as a 1D collision in terms of the normal velocity components.

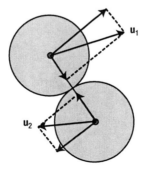

Figure 11-13. Resolving velocity normal and parallel to line joining particles

So the steps for handling 2D particle collisions are the following:

4. Detecting the collision

5. Decomposing the initial velocities in normal and tangential components

6. Repositioning the particles at the moment of collision

7. Calculating the new normal velocities just after the collision

8. Adding the new normal velocity components back to the tangential components

Compared with the procedure for handling 1D collisions, the extra steps are steps 2 and 5. Note also that, in step 3, the particles are repositioned using the same formula we derived for 1D collisions (see the section on "Repositioning the particles"), but using the normal velocities.

As mentioned in the section on oblique walls, the usual method we found that people in the Flash community use to handle 2D collisions is to rotate the coordinate system, perform a 1D collision, and then rotate back the coordinate system. But armed with vectors, the method we suggest actually proves simpler: in place of coordinate rotations, we simply resolve vectors and later add them up again. Let's see the method in action!

An example: 2D collisions between two particles

This example will pull together everything we have covered on collisions between particles. We will create a simulation that can handle a general 2D collision between two particles. Obviously, it will also be able to handle 1D collisions simply by choosing appropriate initial positions and velocities for the particles.

Creating a two-particle collision simulator

First we create a setup file, BallCollision.as, that will create the two particles as Ball instances and set their initial sizes, masses, positions and velocities. Here is the source code that does this:

```
package{
        import flash.display.Sprite;
        import com.physicscodes.objects.Ball;
        import com.physicscodes.math.Vector2D;

        public class BallCollision extends Sprite{
                public function BallCollision():void{
                        init();
                }

                private function init():void{
                        var ball1:Ball = new Ball(15,0xff0000,1);
                        ball1.pos2D = new Vector2D(0,200);
                        ball1.velo2D=new Vector2D(250,0);
                        addChild(ball1);

                        var ball2:Ball = new Ball(75,0x0000ff,125);
                        ball2.pos2D = new Vector2D(300,200);
                        ball2.velo2D = new Vector2D(50,0);
```

```
                    addChild(ball2);

                    var collider:BallCollider=new BallCollider(ball1,ball2);
                    collider.startTime();
                }
            }
    }
```

In this source code example, we are creating a small ball of radius 15 pixels and 1 mass unit and a large ball of radius 75 pixels and 125 mass units. Note that we've scaled masses on the cube of the radius, based on 3D geometry (recall that volume of a sphere = $4\pi r^3/3$), and assuming that the two balls have the same density (recall that mass = density x volume). On this basis, because the large ball has a radius 5 times that of the smaller one, its mass should be 125 times larger.

The balls are made to move and interact with an instance of the BallCollider class, which looks like this:

```
package {
        import com.physicscodes.motion.MultiMover;
        import com.physicscodes.objects.Ball;
        import com.physicscodes.math.Vector2D;

        public class BallCollider extends MultiMover{
                private var _ball1:Ball;
                private var _ball2:Ball;

                public function BallCollider(pball1:Ball,pball2:Ball) :void{
                        _ball1 = pball1;
                        _ball2 = pball2;
                        super([_ball1,_ball2]);
                }

                override protected function moveObject():void{
                        super.moveObject();
                        checkCollision();
                }

                private function checkCollision():void{
                        var dist:Vector2D = _ball1.pos2D.subtract(_ball2.pos2D);
                        if (dist.length < (_ball1.radius +_ball2.radius) ) {
                                // normal velocity vectors just before the impact
                                var normalVelo1:Vector2D = _ball1.velo2D.project(dist);
                                var normalVelo2:Vector2D = _ball2.velo2D.project(dist);
                                // tangential velocity vectors
                                var tangentVelo1:Vector2D =↪
_ball1.velo2D.subtract(normalVelo1);
                                var tangentVelo2:Vector2D =↪
_ball2.velo2D.subtract(normalVelo2);

                                // move particles so that they just touch
                                var L:Number = _ball1.radius + _ball2.radius-dist.length;
                                var vrel:Number =normalVelo1.subtract(normalVelo2).length;
                                ball1.pos2D = _ball1.pos2D.addScaled(normalVelo1,-L/vrel);
```

```
                                ball2.pos2D = _ball2.pos2D.addScaled(normalVelo2,-L/vrel);
                                // normal velocity components after the impact
                                var m1:Number = _ball1.mass;
                                var m2:Number = _ball2.mass;
                                var u1:Number = normalVelo1.projection(dist);
                                var u2:Number = normalVelo2.projection(dist);
                                var v1:Number = ((m1-m2)*u1+2*m2*u2)/(m1+m2);
                                var v2:Number = ((m2-m1)*u2+2*m1*u1)/(m1+m2);

                                // normal velocity vectors after collision
                                normalVelo1 = dist.para(v1);
                                normalVelo2 = dist.para(v2);

                                // final velocity vectors after collision
                                _ball1.velo2D = normalVelo1.add(tangentVelo1);
                                _ball2.velo2D = normalVelo2.add(tangentVelo2);
                        }
                }

        }
}
```

The code follows the explanations given in the previous subsections closely, and the comments in the code should make it clear what is going on at each step. In fact, the code is substantially simpler than the corresponding code for bouncing off an oblique wall. Notice also the symmetry with respect to the two balls. The simplicity and relative brevity of the code provide what we think is an attractive alternative to the usual method of rotating the coordinate system to resolve oblique collisions.

Finally, the formula for calculating the final velocities assumes elastic collisions, but it is a simple matter to replace it with the alternative (and more general) formula for inelastic collisions. We leave this as an exercise for you.

Experimenting with the particle collision simulation

If you run the simulation, you'll see the small ball in a 1D collision with the larger one (see Figure 11-14). Let's start by verifying some of the things we said before when discussing special cases in 1D elastic collisions.

First, set the initial velocity of the large one to zero, simply by commenting out the line that sets its velocity in BallCollision.as. You will see that the small ball almost reverses its velocity after the collision, while the larger one moves off with a very small velocity, just as we said before.

Next, make the second ball the same size and mass as the first by replacing the line that instantiates it with the following modified line:

```
var ball2:Ball = new Ball(15,0x0000ff,1);
```

Keep the second ball's velocity at zero and run the code. You will see that, upon collision, the first ball stops right in its track, while the second ball moves off at the initial velocity of the first ball. Again this confirms the deductions we made previously on the basis of the governing collision equations.

Figure 11-14. A two-particle collision simulator

This is a full 2D collision simulator, so why not get the balls to collide at an angle? For example, while keeping the masses and the sizes of the two particles the same, try the following:

```
ball1.velo2D=new Vector2D(100,-30);
ball2.velo2D = new Vector2D(-50,-30);
```

This shows that our basic 2D particle collision simulator can handle both 1D and 2D collisions properly. So let's now add a bit more complexity.

Example: multiple particle collisions

Extending the last simulation to handle lots of particles is simply a matter of creating more ball instances and then checking for collisions between each pair of particles. In MultipleBallCollision.as, we create nine particles of the same size and mass, put them in an array and then pass that array to an instance of a MultiBallCollider class. The latter is very similar to the two-particle version BallCollider class, the main difference being a double for loop in the checkCollision() method:

```
private function checkCollision():void{
        for (var i:uint=0; i< _balls.length; i++){
                var ball1:Ball = _balls[i];
                for(var j:uint=i+1; j< _balls.length; j++){
                        var ball2: Ball = _balls[j];

                        // code in here is similar to BallCollider.as
                }
        }
}
```

The key things with the for loops is to pick all possible pairs of particles without double-counting. So the first loop iterates over all the elements of the _balls array, picking the first ball, ball1, from it. The second loop then iterates over the elements of _balls again to pick ball2, but this time starting from the next element from ball1. This avoids checking for collisions between ball1 and ball2, and then again between ball2 and ball1.

The nine balls are initially positioned randomly on the stage. They are given velocities toward the center of the stage, with a velocity magnitude proportional to their distance from the center. When you run the simulation, the balls move to the center, where they collide a number of times in quick succession, as a result of which they bounce outward. Feel free to experiment with different configurations and initial velocities.

Example: multiple particle collisions with bouncing

The last example was interesting, but the particles only collided briefly before separating and disappearing outside of the stage area. It would be much more fun to confine them so that they collide over and over again. To do this, we need to introduce confining walls. So, let's combine everything we have learned in this chapter and build one final example involving multiple particles colliding with each other and with walls. The particles will also have different sizes and masses.

We call the new class Molecules because the result will look like gas molecules bouncing about. Here is the setup code in Molecules.as:

```
package{
        import flash.display.Sprite;
        import com.physicscodes.objects.Ball;
        import com.physicscodes.objects.Wall;
        import com.physicscodes.math.Vector2D;

        public class Molecules extends Sprite{

                private var _numBalls:uint = 20;

                public function Molecules():void{
                        init();
                }

                private function init():void{
                        var balls:Array=new Array();
                        for(var i:uint = 0; i < _numBalls; i++){
                                var radius:Number = Math.random()*20 + 5;
                                var mass:Number = 0.01*Math.pow(radius,3);
                                var ball:Ball = new Ball(radius,0x666600,mass);
                                ball.pos2D = new Vector2D( Math.random()*➥
(stage.stageWidth-2*radius)+radius, Math.random()*(stage.stageHeight-2*radius)+radius);
                                ball.velo2D = new Vector2D((Math.random()-0.5)*80,➥
(Math.random()-0.5)*80);
                                addChild(ball);
                                balls.push(ball);
                        }

                        var walls:Array=new Array();
                        var wall1:Wall=new Wall(new Vector2D(stage.stageWidth,0),new➥
Vector2D(0,0));
                        addChild(wall1);
                        walls.push(wall1);
                        var wall2:Wall=new Wall(new Vector2D(stage.stageWidth,stage.➥
stageHeight), new Vector2D(stage.stageWidth,0));
                        addChild(wall2);
                        walls.push(wall2);
                        var wall3:Wall=new Wall(new Vector2D(0,stage.stageHeight), new➥
Vector2D(stage.stageWidth,stage.stageHeight));
                        addChild(wall3);
                        walls.push(wall3);
```

```
                        var wall4:Wall=new Wall(new Vector2D(0,0), new Vector2D(0,stage.↪
stageHeight));
                        addChild(wall4);
                        walls.push(wall4);

                        var collider:MoleculesCollider = new MoleculesCollider(balls,walls);
                        collider.startTime(10);
                }
        }
}
```

A bunch of 20 balls is created with random radius ranging from 5 px to 25 px, and with masses proportional to the cube of the radius. The balls are positioned randomly on the stage and given random velocities with a maximum magnitude of 40 px/s. Then four walls are created at the edges of the stage. All the objects are then passed to an instance of MoleculesCollider.

MoleculesCollider is basically a hybrid of the codes for multiple colliding particles and bouncing off multiple walls. Hence, there is nothing substantially new, except in the way that they are combined. Here is the general structure of the code:

```
package {
        import com.physicscodes.motion.MultiMover;
        import com.physicscodes.objects.Ball;
        import com.physicscodes.objects.Wall;
        import com.physicscodes.math.Vector2D;

        public class MoleculesCollider extends MultiMover{
                private var _balls:Array;
                private var _walls:Array;
                private var _vfac:Number=1;

                public function MoleculesCollider(pballs:Array,pwalls) :void{
                        _balls = pballs;
                        _walls=pwalls;
                        super(_balls);
                }

                override protected function moveObject():void{
                        super.moveObject();
                        checkCollision()
                }

                ...

        }
}
```

The checkCollision() method is almost identical with that of the last example, except for the addition of one line in the outer for loop:

```
private function checkCollision():void{
        for (var i:uint=0; i<_balls.length; i++){
                var ball1:Ball = _balls[i];
```

```
                    for(var j:uint=i+1; j<_balls.length; j++){
                        var ball2: Ball = _balls[j];
                        var dist:Vector2D = ball1.pos2D.subtract(ball2.pos2D);
                        if (dist.length < (ball1.radius +ball2.radius) ) {
                        // normal velocity vectors just before the impact
                        var normalVelo1:Vector2D = ball1.velo2D.project(dist);
                        var normalVelo2:Vector2D = ball2.velo2D.project(dist);
                        // tangential velocity vectors
                        var tangentVelo1:Vector2D = ball1.velo2D.subtract(normalVelo1);
                        var tangentVelo2:Vector2D = ball2.velo2D.subtract(normalVelo2);
                        // move particles so that they just touch
                        var L:Number = ball1.radius +ball2.radius-dist.length;
                        var vrel:Number = normalVelo1.subtract(normalVelo2).length;
                        ball1.pos2D = ball1.pos2D.addScaled(normalVelo1,-L/vrel);
                        ball2.pos2D = ball2.pos2D.addScaled(normalVelo2,-L/vrel);
                        // perpendicular velocity components after the impact
                        var m1:Number = ball1.mass;
                        var m2:Number = ball2.mass;
                        var u1:Number = normalVelo1.projection(dist);
                        var u2:Number = normalVelo2.projection(dist);
                        var v1:Number = ((m1-m2)*u1+2*m2*u2)/(m1+m2);
                        var v2:Number = ((m2-m1)*u2+2*m1*u1)/(m1+m2);
                        // normal velocity vectors after collision
                        normalVelo1 = dist.para(v1);
                        normalVelo2 = dist.para(v2);
                        // final velocity vectors after collision
                        ball1.velo2D = normalVelo1.add(tangentVelo1);
                        ball2.velo2D = normalVelo2.add(tangentVelo2);
                        }
                    }
                checkWallBounce(ball1);
            }
    }
}
```

The extra line tells the code to see whether `ball1` is in collision with any wall. The `checkWallBounce()` method is given here for completeness, but it is essentially the same as in `MultipleInclinedWallsBouncer.as`, except that we got rid of the pieces of code that handle bouncing off the wall end points because there are no free wall end points to bounce off in this example:

```
private function checkWallBounce(pball:Ball):void{
    var hasHitAWall:Boolean = false;
    for (var i:int=0; (i<_walls.length && hasHitAWall==false); i++){
        var wall:Wall = _walls[i];
        var wdir:Vector2D = wall.dir;
        var ballp1:Vector2D = wall.p1.subtract(pball.pos2D);
        var ballp2:Vector2D = wall.p2.subtract(pball.pos2D);
        var proj1:Number = ballp1.projection(wdir);
        var proj2:Number = ballp2.projection(wdir);
        var dist:Vector2D = ballp1.addScaled(wdir.unit(), proj1*(-1));
        var test:Boolean=((Math.abs(proj1) < wdir.length) && (Math.abs(proj2) <↪
 wdir.length));
        if ((dist.length < pball.radius) &&  test){
            var angle:Number = Vector2D.angleBetween(pball.velo2D, wdir);
```

```
                    var normal:Vector2D = wall.normal;
                    if (normal.dotProduct(pball.velo2D) > 0){
                            normal.scaleBy(-1);
                    }
                    var deltaS:Number =↪
(pball.radius+dist.dotProduct(normal))/Math.sin(angle);
                    var displ:Vector2D = pball.velo2D.para(deltaS);
                    pball.pos2D = pball.pos2D.subtract(displ);
                    var normalVelo:Vector2D = pball.velo2D.project(dist);
                    var tangentVelo:Vector2D = pball.velo2D.subtract(normalVelo);
                    pball.velo2D = tangentVelo.addScaled(normalVelo,-_vfac);
                    hasHitAWall = true;
            }
        }
}
```

Figure 11-15 shows a screenshot of what you will see when you run the code: gas molecules bouncing about! Notice that the little molecules generally end up moving faster than the bigger ones because they can pick up a lot of momentum when a large one collides with them. A lot of time can be wasted playing with this simulation or simply watching it! To make things even more fun, in the source code we have also included a modified version of the simulation that allows you to add your own particles by clicking and dragging. The relevant files are `Molecules2.as` and `MoleculesCollider2.as`. With a lot of particles, you might find that some of them, especially the smaller ones, will occasionally tunnel out of the confining walls. You can fix this by using the method described in the section on bouncing off inclined walls.

You may also find that some particles will be overlapping when they are initially created because of the random positioning. This will result in some initial erratic behavior that should mostly sort itself out in a few timesteps. Other problems could also occur with lots of particles (apart from the obvious one of your computer not being able to cope), especially if they are crammed into a small space or if they are moving at high speed. You could, for example, have a particle colliding with two other particles in the same timestep. Or you could have a particle that is repositioned and ends up overlapping with another particle close by. We could go into elaborate methods for dealing with scenarios like these, but we've already covered a lot of ground in this chapter and need to stop somewhere!

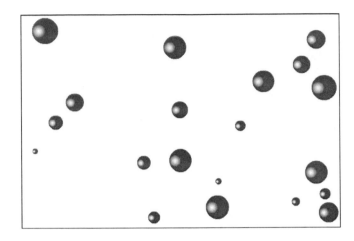

Figure 11-15. "Molecules" bouncing off each other and off walls

Summary

In this chapter, we have gone from a simple demonstration of a ball bouncing off a vertical wall to creating complex simulations involving particles bouncing off multiple inclined walls and particles colliding with other particles. We have covered the underlying physics in considerable detail, discussing the equations that govern different types of collisions in 1D and 2D. In implementing collision resolution, both with walls and between particles, we introduced a novel method using vector algebra that avoids the usual need for performing coordinate rotations to resolve collisions in 2D.

Chapter 12

Particle Systems

In a nutshell, this chapter will show you how to create animated effects and simulations using systems of multiple particles. Particle systems are very popular, and a lot of creative work has been done in the Flash community over the years using them. We can only really scratch the surface of what is possible in a single chapter. Therefore, we shall content ourselves with giving you a few ideas and examples to play with and build upon.

Topics covered in this chapter include these:

- **Introduction to particle system modeling**: This brief section will explain what we mean by a particle system and what is needed to set one up.

- **Creating animated effects using particles**: It is possible to produce some interesting animated effects such as smoke and fire using a bunch of particles and some simple physics. We'll walk you through some examples in this section.

- **Particle animations with long-range forces**: Particle animations don't have to look realistic; they can be just for fun! We look at a couple of wacky examples using long-range forces such as gravity.

- **Interacting particle systems**: More complex particle systems include interactions between the particles. But this can get pretty computationally expensive with large numbers of particles. We give a couple of examples, discussing tricks to overcome this problem.

The approach in this chapter is to create animations that use some physics, but without necessarily being accurate simulations. Above all, this is a subject where experimentation and creativity pay dividends. Therefore, don't be afraid to tinker and invent, even if that means breaking a few laws of physics!

Introduction to particle system modeling

Although a precise definition of a particle system probably does not exist, it helps to explain what we have in mind before we do anything else. In the sense in which we use the term, a *particle system* consists of the following ingredients:

- A group of particles

- Rules by which they move and change

- Rules by which they interact (if any)

This definition is very general: the said "rules" could be based on physics, artificial intelligence, biology, or anything else. It won't come as a surprise that we'll limit ourselves to particles moving and interacting under physical laws (with perhaps the odd tweak here and there). Therefore, the particle systems we'll consider will animate particles according to Newton's laws of motion under the action of a subset of the forces that we discussed in Part II of the book. The different categories of interaction between the particles can include the following:

- **No mutual interaction**: In this case, the particles are unaware of each other and move independently under the action of globally prescribed forces (such as external gravity). Even though this is the simplest case, quite impressive effects can be generated using non-interacting particles. We will look at several examples in the next two sections.

- **Interaction by collision**: Here the particles do not interact except very briefly when they collide. The collisions can be resolved using the methods given in Chapter 11. In fact, the last example in Chapter 11 showed just such a system of particles interacting via collisions.

- **Short-range interactions**: In this case, the particles interact only when they are close together but not necessarily touching. They can be modeled using short-range forces of a type that exists between molecules. Using such forces it is possible to model fluid effects such as the formation and fall of a liquid drop. But these simulations require more advanced methods and will not be covered in this book.

- **Long-range interactions**: This category involves mutual interactions between the particles at any distance, such as gravitational or electric forces between the particles. Typically, every particle experiences a force due to every other particle. Clearly the number of computations that need to be performed gets very large pretty quickly as you increase the number of particles in the system. We look at some examples in the last section of this chapter.

- **Local interactions**: These are intermediate interactions between short-range and long-range interactions; particles within a certain local neighborhood are linked and interact. Such interactions can give rise to organized systems and connected structures. Examples include mass-spring systems, which can be used to simulate deformable bodies like ropes and clothes. These particle systems are explored in Chapter 13.

So what do we need, in terms of physics and coding, to create a particle system? The answer might surprise you: not a lot beyond what we've already covered in the previous chapters. So there won't be much theory in this chapter, but more on the application of principles that have already been discussed with a few extra tricks added in. That means you get to see code much sooner!

Creating animated effects using particles

One of the most common uses of particle systems is to create animated visual effects such as smoke and fire. In this section, we show you simple ways of producing some of these effects using physics-based animation. We start with a very simple example and then create a particle emitter that will allow us to create some more elaborate effects. The approach in this section is that we wish to produce animations that *look* realistic, but that don't have to be completely accurate.

A simple example: splash effect with particles

In this example, we will drop objects in water and then create a splash effect using particles. The objects will be balls of different sizes and will be dropped one at a time from the same height. The splash will be made from a group of Ball objects of smaller size. Let's dive straight into the code that creates these objects. The file is called Splash.as. Here is a full listing of the code:

```
package{
        import flash.display.Sprite;
        import com.physicscodes.objects.Ball;
        import com.physicscodes.math.Vector2D;

        public class Splash extends Sprite{
                public function Splash():void{
                        init();
                }
                private function init():void{

                        var water:Sprite = new Sprite();
                        with (water.graphics) {
                                beginFill(0x00ffff,0.5);
                                drawRect(0,500,stage.stageWidth,stage.stageHeight-500);
                                endFill();
                        }
                        addChild(water);

                        var drop:Ball = new Ball(8,0x399ff);
                        drop.pos2D = new Vector2D(400,100);
                        drop.velo2D = new Vector2D(0,100);
                        addChild(drop);

                        var numSplashDrops:uint = 20;
                        var splash:Array = new Array();
                        for (var i:uint=0; i<numSplashDrops; i++){
                                var radius:Number = Math.random()*2+1;
                                var splashDrop:Ball = new Ball(radius,0x3399ff);
                                splashDrop.visible = false;
```

```
                    addChild(splashDrop);
                    splash.push(splashDrop);
            }

            var mover:SplashMover=new SplashMover(drop,splash);
            mover.startTime();
            drop.move();
        }
    }
}
```

As you can see, we first create a filled rectangle with a transparency of 0.5 to represent water and position it at the bottom of the stage. We then create a Ball object named drop (think raindrop) with a radius of 8 pixels and position it above the water surface, at y = 100. The drop is then given a velocity of 100 px/s vertically downward. Next, 20 Ball objects are created with random radiuses between 1 and 3 pixels. These will be the splash droplets, and their visibility is initially set to false. They are put into an array called splash.

The drop and the splash array are then passed to a SplashMover instance (to be described shortly) to start the animation. The drop is animated independently by invoking its move() method. This makes it move at the constant downward velocity of 100 px/s specified earlier in the code. You may be wondering why we make the object fall at a constant velocity instead of making it accelerate under gravity. The answer is that if it is a raindrop, it would probably have reached terminal velocity anyway.

We'll now take a look at the SplashMover class. The full code is not too long, so here it is:

```
package {
        import flash.display.Sprite;
        import com.physicscodes.motion.MultiForcer;
        import com.physicscodes.motion.Forces;
        import com.physicscodes.objects.Particle;
        import com.physicscodes.objects.Ball;
        import com.physicscodes.math.Vector2D;

        public class SplashMover extends MultiForcer{

                private var _drop:Ball;
                private var _particles:Array = new Array();
                private var _g:Number = 20;
                private var _vx:Number = 20;
                private var _vy:Number = -15;
                private var _wlevel:Number = 510;
                private var _fac:Number = 1;

                public function SplashMover(pdrop:Ball,psplash:Array):void{
                        _drop = pdrop;
                        _particles = psplash;
                        super(_particles);
                }

                override protected function moveObject():void{
                        super.moveObject();
                        checkDrop();
```

```
                }

                private function checkDrop():void{
                        if (_drop.ypos > _wlevel){
                                for (var i:uint=0; i<_particles.length; i++){
                                        var splashDrop:Ball = _particles[i];
                                        var posx:Number = _drop.xpos+↪
(Math.random()-0.5)*_drop.width;

                                        var posy:Number = _wlevel-10+↪
Math.random()*_drop.height;

                                        var velx:Number = (Math.random()-0.5)*_vx*_fac;
                                        var vely:Number = (Math.random()+0.5)*_vy*_fac;
                                        splashDrop.pos2D = new Vector2D(posx,posy);
                                        splashDrop.velo2D = new Vector2D(velx,vely);
                                }
                                _drop.xpos = Math.random()*600+100;
                                _drop.ypos = 100;
                                _drop.radius = 4 + 8*Math.random();
                                _fac = Math.pow(_drop.radius/8,1.5);;
                        }
                }

                override protected function calcForce(pparticle:Particle):void{
                        force = Forces.constantGravity(pparticle.mass,_g);
                        if (pparticle.ypos > _wlevel){
                                pparticle.visible = false;
                        }else{
                                pparticle.visible = true;
                        }
                }

        }
}
```

The first thing to note is that SplashMover extends MultiForcer. That's because we have a whole bunch of particles to move (the splash droplets) and they will be moving under a force (gravity). The splash array is assigned to a private variable called _particles.

The main action takes place in the checkDrop() method, which is executed at every timestep, being called from an overriding moveObject() method. This code checks if the drop has fallen below the water level (set at 10px below the top edge of the blue rectangle representing the body of water to give a fake 3D effect). If that happens, the splash droplets are repositioned around the region of impact and given random velocities with an upward vertical component. The magnitude of the velocities depends on parameters _vx and _vy that are set initially in the code as well as on a factor _fac, which is updated every time a splash occurs, as will be described shortly. The droplets are then made to fall under gravity by using the Forces.constantGravity() method in calcForce(). There is an if-else condition that makes them invisible if they are below the water level; otherwise they are made visible.

Back in the checkDrop() method, the falling drop is repositioned at the initial height and at a new random horizontal location as soon as it hits the water level. Its radius is then changed to a random value between 4 and 12 pixels.

Then the velocity factor _fac is updated according to the following formula, in which r_m is the mean radius of the drop (8 pixels):

$$fac = \left(\frac{r}{r_m}\right)^{3/2}$$

What is happening here? The idea is that the larger the drop is, the heavier its mass will be (its mass is proportional to its volume, or the cube of its radius, r^3). Because the drop always has the same velocity, its kinetic energy ($E_k = \frac{1}{2} mv^2$) will be proportional to its mass, and therefore to r^3. A fraction of that energy will be imparted to the splash droplets, and one can therefore expect the average kinetic energy of those droplets to be proportional to r^3. Because the masses of the droplets are constant, their kinetic energy is proportional to the square of their velocity. So we have the following:

$$E_k \propto v^2 \propto r^3$$

Therefore, we can write the following:

$$v \propto r^{3/2}$$

This shows that we expect the droplets to have a mean velocity proportional to the radius of the falling drop raised to the power of 1.5. The previous formula for _fac implements this fact, with the value of _fac being set to 1 when the radius is equal to the mean radius of 8 px.

If you run the simulation, you will find that the larger the drop is, the higher the droplets will splash because of their larger initial velocities. A screenshot is shown in Figure 12-1. As usual, feel free to experiment with different parameters. Of course, the visual aspects of the animation can be enhanced in many ways according to your imagination and artistic skills. We have focused on the physics and coding aspects; feel free to season the appearance to taste.

Figure 12-1. Producing a splash!

Creating a particle emitter

Many applications of particle systems require a continuous source of particles. This can be achieved using *particle emitters*. Creating a particle emitter is not difficult; essentially what you need is to create new particles over time. But it is also important to somehow limit the total number of particles to avoid crashing your computer! This may mean fixing the total number of particles or recycling/removing them.

There are several approaches you could take to do these things. We can only give an example here, without attempting to cover all the different approaches.

An example is given in the ParticleEmitterExample.as and ParticleEmitter.as files. The ParticleEmitterExample class is very simple, and looks like this:

```
package{
        import flash.display.Sprite;

        public class ParticleEmitterExample extends Sprite{
                public function ParticleEmitterExample():void{
                        init();
                }
                private function init():void{
                        var sprite:Sprite = new Sprite();
                        addChild(sprite);

                        var mover:ParticleEmitter = new ParticleEmitter(sprite);
                        mover.startTime();
                }
        }
}
```

As you can see, there is not much to it. ParticleEmitterExample simply creates a sprite and passes it to a ParticleEmitter instance. Everything is happening within the ParticleEmitter class, which looks like this:

```
package {
        import flash.display.Sprite;
        import com.physicscodes.motion.MultiForcer;
        import com.physicscodes.motion.Forces;
        import com.physicscodes.objects.Particle;
        import com.physicscodes.objects.Ball;
        import com.physicscodes.math.Vector2D;

        public class ParticleEmitter extends MultiForcer{
                private var _sprite:Sprite;
                private var _particles:Array = new Array();
                private var _maxParticles:uint = 120;
                private var _g:Number = 20;
                private var _k:Number = 0.003;
                private var _vx:Number = 60;
                private var _vy:Number = -80;

                public function ParticleEmitter(psprite:Sprite):void{
                        _sprite = psprite;
                        super(_particles);
                }

                override protected function calcForce(pparticle:Particle):void{
```

```
                        var gravity:Vector2D = Forces.constantGravity(pparticle.mass,_g);
                        var drag:Vector2D = Forces.drag(_k,pparticle.velo2D);
                        force = Forces.add([gravity, drag]);
            }

            override protected function moveObject():void{
                    super.moveObject();
                    createNewParticles(new Vector2D(_sprite.mouseX,_sprite.mouseY));
                    limitParticles();
            }

            private function createNewParticles(ppos:Vector2D):void{
                    var newBall:Ball = new Ball(2);
                    newBall.pos2D = ppos;
                    newBall.velo2D = new Vector2D((Math.random()-0.5)*_vx, ➥
(Math.random()+0.5)*_vy);
                    _sprite.addChild(newBall);
                    _particles.push(newBall);
            }

            private function limitParticles():void{
                    if (_particles.length > _maxParticles){
                            _sprite.removeChild(_particles[0]);
                            _particles.shift();
                    }
            }

        }
}
```

As in the previous example, ParticleEmitter extends MultiForcer. The particles are stored in an array named _particles. In this example, the calcForce() method includes gravity and drag force. The really new stuff appears in the two methods createNewParticles() and limitParticles(), which are called from within the moveObject() method.

The createNewParticles() method does exactly what its name suggests, creating new particles as Ball objects at a location specified as a Vector2D input parameter. In this case, the particles are given a random velocity, added to the stage of the sprite object, and then pushed into the _particles array. This happens once per timestep, so that a new particle is created at each timestep. You might alternatively specify a rate at which new particles are created per second; we leave this as an exercise.

Without the limitParticles() method your animation would quickly fill up with particles until your computer couldn't cope any more. In this example, limitParticles() checks to see if the number of particles exceeds the maximum allowed number _maxParticles. If it does, the first (and oldest) particle is removed. You don't want to set _maxParticles too high. In the example file, a value of 120 is chosen.

Run the simulation and you'll have a particle emitter! Little balls projected upward and falling back under gravity and drag, looking a bit like a spray. We have specified the position of the emitter as the location of the mouse cursor, so that you can move the mouse around and watch the fun.

You can produce some interesting effects by changing the parameters and initial conditions. For example, instead of giving the particles a random velocity, you can introduce the following lines of code into `createNewParticles()`:

```
var n:int;
n = _i%7;
var angle:Number = -(60+10*n)*Math.PI/180;
var mag:Number = 100;
newBall.velo2D = Vector2D.vector2D(mag,angle);
_i++;
```

Here, `_i` is a private `int` variable initially given the value of 0. This produces a fountain-like pattern, as shown in Figure 12-2.

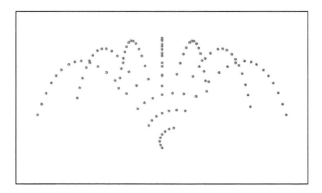

Figure 12-2. Creating a particle emitter

Creating a smoke effect

Let us now use our particle emitter to create a smoke effect. This is easier than you might think; in fact, you've already done most of the work. Let us start with a setup file, `Smoke.as`, that is essentially the same as that in the previous example, except for the relevant class names:

```
package{
        import flash.display.Sprite;

        public class Smoke extends Sprite{
                public function Smoke():void{
                        init();
                }
                private function init():void{
                        var sprite:Sprite = new Sprite();
                        addChild(sprite);

                        var mover:SmokeMover=new SmokeMover(sprite);
                        mover.startTime();
                }
        }
}
```

The corresponding mover class SmokeMover is built on top of the ParticleEmitter class of the previous example, and looks like this, with the new or modified bits highlighted in bold:

```
package {
        import flash.display.Sprite;
        import com.physicscodes.motion.MultiForcer;
        import com.physicscodes.motion.Forces;
        import com.physicscodes.objects.Particle;
        import com.physicscodes.objects.Ball;
        import com.physicscodes.math.Vector2D;

        public class SmokeMover extends MultiForcer{
                private var _sprite:Sprite;
                private var _particles:Array = new Array();
                private var _maxParticles:uint = 120;
                private var _g:Number = -5;
                private var _k:Number = 0.005;
                private var _vx:Number = 60;
                private var _vy:Number = -80;

                public function SmokeMover(psprite:Sprite):void{
                        _sprite = psprite;
                        super(_particles);
                }

                override protected function calcForce(pparticle:Particle):void{
                        var gravity:Vector2D = Forces.constantGravity(pparticle.mass,_g);
                        var drag:Vector2D = Forces.drag(_k,pparticle.velo2D);
                        force = Forces.add([gravity, drag]);
                }

                override protected function moveObject():void{
                        super.moveObject();
                        createNewParticles(new Vector2D(_sprite.mouseX,_sprite.mouseY));
                        limitParticles();
                        modifyParticles();
                }

                private function createNewParticles(ppos:Vector2D):void{
                        var radius:Number = 1 + 3*Math.random();
                        var newBall:Ball = new Ball(radius,0xffffff);
                        newBall.pos2D = ppos;
                        newBall.velo2D = new Vector2D((Math.random()-0.5)*_vx,↵
        (Math.random()+0.5)*_vy);
                        _sprite.addChild(newBall);
                        _particles.push(newBall);
                }

                private function limitParticles():void{
                        if (_particles.length > _maxParticles){
                                _sprite.removeChild(_particles[0]);
                                _particles.shift();
                        }
```

```
        }

        private function modifyParticles():void{
                for (var i:uint=0; i<_particles.length; i++){
                        var particle:Ball = _particles[i];
                        particle.scaleX *= 1.01;
                        particle.scaleY *= 1.01;
                        particle.alpha += -0.01;
                }
        }

    }
}
```

Compared with ParticleEmitter there are two modifications plus the addition of a new method: modifyParticles(). The first modification is that we are randomizing the radiuses of the particles between the values of 1 and 4 pixels in createNewParticles(). The second modification might appear a bit weird: we are giving the gravity constant g a negative value (–5)! What's going on here? The thing is that smoke will tend to rise rather than fall because forces such as buoyancy (upthrust) will overcome the force of gravity. But instead of modeling buoyancy, it makes more sense here to simply modify gravity so that it acts upward because we are interested only in reproducing the visual effect of smoke approximately.

The new method, modifyParticles(), is called from moveObject() and is therefore executed at each timestep. All we are doing here is to increase the size of the particles by a constant factor and reduce their transparency by a fixed amount at each timestep.

The result of the previous additions and modifications is that the particles grow and fade as they rise, before disappearing altogether and being removed and replaced by new particles. If you were to run the code as shown previously, you would get an interesting effect, but you couldn't really call it smoke—see Figure 12-3.

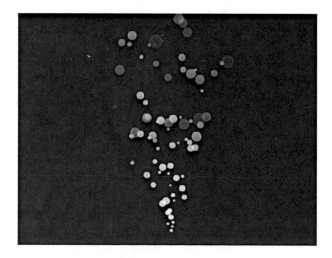

Figure 12-3. An interesting effect, but not quite smoke yet!

Time to introduce filters! If you are not familiar with ActionScript filters, we encourage you to spend some time reading about them and playing around with them. Check out Adobe's online AS3.0 documentation or pick up a copy of *Foundation ActionScript 3.0 Image Effects* by Todd Yard.

We'll use one of the simplest filters, the `BlurFilter`, applying it to the Smoke class, which now looks like this:

```
package{
        import flash.display.Sprite;
        import flash.filters.BlurFilter;

        public class Smoke extends Sprite{
                public function Smoke():void{
                        init();
                }
                private function init():void{
                        var sprite:Sprite = new Sprite();
                        addChild(sprite);

                        var mover:SmokeMover=new SmokeMover(sprite);
                        mover.startTime();

                        filters = [new BlurFilter(8,8,2)];
                }
        }
}
```

As you can see, the changes (highlighted in bold) are minimal: just one line of code plus the appropriate import statement. The `BlurFilter()` function takes three optional arguments:

```
BlurFilter(blurX:Number = 4.0, blurY:Number = 4.0, quality:int = 1)
```

The first two arguments specify the amount of blur to apply in the x and y directions. The third argument specifies the number of times to apply the filter and therefore indicates the quality of the blur. A value of 1 is a low quality blur, 2 is medium quality, and 3 is high quality. We have specified a medium quality blur with blur amounts of eight units in each direction; feel free to experiment with different values of these parameters.

If you now run the code, you will see something that looks much more like smoke, as depicted in the screenshot in Figure 12-4.

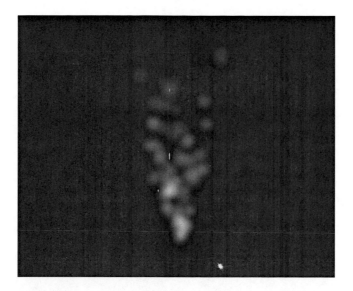

Figure 12-4. The smoke effect at last

This is a basic smoke effect that can be tweaked and enhanced in endless ways. Think of it as a starting point for further experimentation rather than as a final result. Moreover, there are lots of other ways to produce a smoke effect like this. The preceding method has been adapted from a tutorial by Seb Lee-Delisle that appeared in *Computer Arts* magazine (March 2008). It's nice because of its simplicity and the fact that it can be done with pure code alone.

Creating a fire effect

It is extremely easy to modify the smoke animation to produce something that looks like fire. In fact, we changed only one line of code in the SmokeMover class, just to make the particles slightly bigger:

```
var radius:Number = 3 + 3*Math.random();
```

This makes particles with radiuses between 3 and 6 pixels. We saved the new file as FireMover.as. We then modify the Smoke class by adding a new filter GradientGlowFilter and after appropriate class and constructor name changes, save the new file as Fire.as:

```
package{
        import flash.display.Sprite;
        import flash.filters.BlurFilter;
        import flash.filters.GradientGlowFilter;

        public class Fire extends Sprite{
                public function Fire():void{
                        init();
                }
                private function init():void{
                        var sprite:Sprite = new Sprite();
                        addChild(sprite);
```

```
                         var mover:FireMover=new FireMover(sprite);
                         mover.startTime();

                         var blurFilter:BlurFilter = new BlurFilter(8,8,2);
                         var gradientGlowFilter:GradientGlowFilter = new GradientGlowFilter⤳
(0,45,[0xff0000,0xffff00],[1,1],[50,255],15,15);
                         filters = [blurFilter, gradientGlowFilter];
              }
          }
}
```

The relevant changes are highlighted in bold. The GradientGlowFilter is a more complicated filter than the BlurFilter, with no fewer than 11 optional parameters, of which we've specified 7. We refer you to Adobe's online AS3.0 reference for what these parameters mean and leave you to play with their values to see their effects. If you run the code with the values shown in the previous listing, you'll see something like Figure 12-5. Of course, you need to see the actual animation to appreciate the effect and colors.

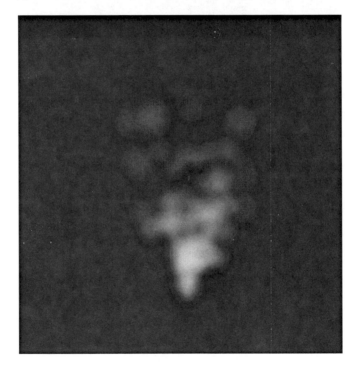

Figure 12-5. Creating a fire effect

Now that you have the basic tools at your fingertips, you can create more elaborate effects by applying the methods to different setups and by combining different techniques. For example, by attaching emitters to objects, you can create the illusion of the objects being on fire. You can also add wind, combine smoke with the fire, add sparks, and so on. Talking of sparks, let's go create some now.

Creating fireworks

The end result we want to achieve in this section is an animation that looks like fireworks: a series of little explosions each generating colorful sparks that fall under gravity with drag. In order to get there, we will first modify the `Particle` class and then create a sparks animation using the updated `Particle` class before finally adding extra features to make the fireworks.

Modifying the Particle class

Something like a spark exists for only a certain duration, after which it will need to be removed or recycled. It makes sense therefore to introduce a couple of new properties in the `Particle` class to represent the lifetime and age of a `Particle` instance. To do this, we add the following code to the `Particle` class:

```
// lifetime and age in seconds
private var _lifetime:Number = 1e8;
private var _age:Number = 0;

public function get lifetime():Number{
        return _lifetime;
}
public function set lifetime(plifetime:Number):void{
        _lifetime = plifetime;
}
public function get age():Number{
        return _age;
}
public function set age(page:Number):void{
        _age = page;
}
```

This creates the two properties, `lifetime` and `age`, with default values of 10^8 and 0, respectively. These represent the lifetime and age of a `Particle` instance in seconds. The value of 10^8 seconds is equal to approximately three years: so as long as your Flash movie does not run for longer than three years, a particle with the default lifetime value should never be destroyed. Of course, we could have specified any other value that is large enough. The age is the current time in seconds since the `Particle` instance was created.

It is up to your external code that creates the `Particle` instance to update its age as time progresses and to check and take the appropriate action if its age exceeds its lifetime.

Making sparks

Let us now apply the newly created `lifetime` and `age` properties to create sparks that exist for a specified duration. The new setup file is called `Sparks.as` and looks like this:

```
package{
        import flash.display.Sprite;
        import flash.filters.GlowFilter;

        public class Sparks extends Sprite{
                public function Sparks():void{
```

```
                              init();
                     }
             private function init():void{
                              var sprite:Sprite = new Sprite();
                              addChild(sprite);

                              var mover:SparksMover=new SparksMover(sprite);
                              mover.startTime();

                              filters = [new GlowFilter()];
                     }
             }
     }
```

This is very similar to the setup files in the previous examples, except that we are now using a different filter, a GlowFilter() with default parameters. (Again, see the Adobe online AS3.0 reference to learn more about this filter and its parameters.) The SparksMover class is a modified version of the FireMover class, with the modifyParticles() method replaced by a new ageParticles() method (which calls a new removeParticle() method) as well a few small changes, as highlighted in bold in the following code:

```
package {
        import flash.display.Sprite;
        import com.physicscodes.motion.MultiForcer;
        import com.physicscodes.motion.Forces;
        import com.physicscodes.objects.Particle;
        import com.physicscodes.objects.Ball;
        import com.physicscodes.math.Vector2D;

        public class SparksMover extends MultiForcer{

                private var _sprite:Sprite;
                private var _particles:Array = new Array();
                private var _maxParticles:uint = 200;
                private var _g:Number = 10;
                private var _k:Number = 0.005;
                private var _vx:Number = 100;
                private var _vy:Number = -100;

                public function SparksMover(psprite:Sprite):void{
                        _sprite = psprite;
                        super(_particles);
                }

                override protected function calcForce(pparticle:Particle):void{
                        var gravity:Vector2D = Forces.constantGravity(pparticle.mass,_g);
                        var drag:Vector2D = Forces.drag(_k,pparticle.velo2D);
                        force = Forces.add([gravity, drag]);
                }

                override protected function moveObject():void{
                        super.moveObject();
                        createNewParticles(new Vector2D(_sprite.mouseX,_sprite.mouseY));
                        limitParticles();
```

```
                        ageParticles();
        }

        private function createNewParticles(ppos:Vector2D):void{
                var newBall:Ball = new Ball(2,0xffff00,1,0,false);
                newBall.pos2D = ppos;
                newBall.velo2D = new Vector2D((Math.random()-0.5)*_vx, ↪
(Math.random()-0.5)*_vy);
                newBall.lifetime = 2 + 2*Math.random();
                _sprite.addChild(newBall);
                _particles.push(newBall);
        }

        private function limitParticles():void{
                if (_particles.length > _maxParticles){
                        _sprite.removeChild(_particles[0]);
                        _particles.shift();
                }
        }

        private function ageParticles():void{
                for (var i:uint=0; i<_particles.length; i++){
                        var particle:Ball = _particles[i];
                        particle.age += dt;
                        particle.alpha += -0.005;
                        if (particle.age > particle.lifetime){
                                removeParticle(particle,i);
                        }
                }
        }

        private function removeParticle(pparticle:Particle,pnum:uint):void{
                _sprite.removeChild(pparticle);
                _particles.splice(pnum,1);
        }

    }
}
```

So we now have 200 particles and give them values of _g, _k, _vx, and _vy of 10, 0.005, 100, and −100, respectively (which you can change if you want). In createNewParticles(), each particle is given the same radius of 2 pixels. Because sparks can fly in any direction, the particles are given random velocities in any direction. Then their lifetime is set to a random value between two and four seconds.

The new ageParticles() method loops over all the particles in the _particles array, updating their age every timestep and decreasing their alpha value. This makes them fade with time. The particle's age is then checked against its lifetime: if it exceeds the lifetime, the removeParticle() method is called, which removes the particle from the stage and from the _particles array.

Run the simulation and you'll get to see some nice sparks following the mouse (see Figure 12-6).

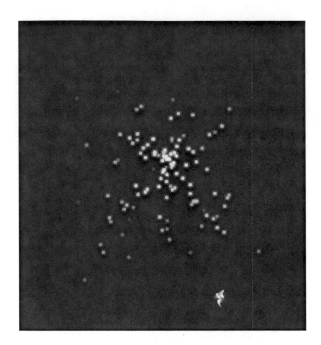

Figure 12-6. Making sparks

Making the fireworks animation

Now that we have sparks, we can use them to produce fireworks. Instead of producing the sparks continuously, we want to do that in a series of little explosions. We'll have an initial explosion that will create a bunch of sparks with random velocities; these sparks will then fall under gravity with drag, fading with time. When each spark reaches the end of its lifetime, it will explode, producing further sparks. Obviously, we want to stop this process at some point. The easiest way to do this is to limit the duration of the animation by imposing a global cutoff time.

To get started, we produce a setup file named `Fireworks.as` that is practically identical with the `Sparks.as` file except for the relevant class names. We also need a corresponding `FireworksMover` class. This is modified from the `SparksMover` class and looks like the following, with modified bits highlighted in bold:

```
package {
        import flash.display.Sprite;
        import com.physicscodes.motion.MultiForcer;
        import com.physicscodes.motion.Forces;
        import com.physicscodes.objects.Particle;
        import com.physicscodes.objects.Ball;
        import com.physicscodes.math.Vector2D;

        public class FireworksMover extends MultiForcer{

                private var _sprite:Sprite;
                private var _particles:Array = new Array();
```

```
            private var _maxParticles:uint = 200;
            private var _g:Number = 10;
            private var _k:Number = 0.005;
            private var _vx:Number = 150;
            private var _vy:Number = -100;
            // number of sparks per explosion
            private var _numSparks:uint = 10;
            //minimum and maximum lifetime of sparks in seconds
            private var _minLife:Number = 2;
            private var _maxLife:Number = 4;
            //maximum duration of fireworks in seconds
            private var _duration:Number = 6;

            public function FireworksMover(psprite:Sprite):void{
                    _sprite = psprite;
                    super(_particles);
                    createNewParticles(new Vector2D(400,200),0xffff00);
            }

            override protected function calcForce(pparticle:Particle):void{
                    var gravity:Vector2D = Forces.constantGravity(pparticle.mass,_g);
                    var drag:Vector2D = Forces.drag(_k,pparticle.velo2D);
                    force = Forces.add([gravity, drag]);
            }

            override protected function moveObject():void{
                    super.moveObject();
                    limitParticles();
                    ageParticles();
            }

            private function createNewParticles(ppos:Vector2D,pcol:uint):void{
                    for (var i:uint=0; i<_numSparks; i++){
                            var newBall:Ball = new Ball(2,pcol,1,0,false);
                            newBall.pos2D = ppos;
                            newBall.velo2D = new Vector2D((Math.random()-0.5)*_vx, ↪
(Math.random()-0.5)*_vy);

                            newBall.lifetime = _minLife + (_maxLife-_minLife)↪
*Math.random();

                            _sprite.addChild(newBall);
                            _particles.push(newBall);
                    }
            }

            private function limitParticles():void{
                    if (_particles.length > _maxParticles){
                            _sprite.removeChild(_particles[0]);
                            _particles.shift();
                    }
            }

            private function ageParticles():void{
                    for (var i:uint=0; i<_particles.length; i++){
                            var particle:Ball = _particles[i];
```

```
                                 particle.age += dt;
                                 particle.alpha += -0.005;
                                 if (particle.age > particle.lifetime){
                                         if (time<_duration){
                                                 explode(particle);
                                         }
                                         removeParticle(particle,i);
                                 }
                         }
                 }

        private function explode(pparticle:Particle){
                createNewParticles(pparticle.pos2D,0x00ff00);
        }

        private function removeParticle(pparticle:Particle,pnum:uint):void{
                _sprite.removeChild(pparticle);
                _particles.splice(pnum,1);
        }

        }
}
```

First note that we changed the value of _vx from 100 to 150. This is just so that the sparks spread horizontally more than vertically. We added four new private variables: _numSparks, _minLife, _maxLife, and _duration to store the number of sparks, their minimum and maximum lifetimes, and the duration of the animation, respectively. The next change is that the createNewParticles() method is now called from within the constructor, not within the moveObject() method. This means that the particles are created initially, not at every timestep. The createNewParticles() method is modified to accept a new argument that specifies the color of the sparks, to create a number _numSparks of particles at a time instead of just one, and to assign to those particles a random lifetime between _minLife and _maxLife.

The ageParticles() method is modified so that, as long as _duration has not been exceeded, any particle that exceeds its lifetime explodes before being removed. The explosion is handled by the explode() method, which simply calls the createNewParticles() method and specifies the position of the dying particle as the location for the explosion and gives a new color for the next generation of sparks.

Run the code and you will be treated to a fireworks display (see Figure 12-7). Needless to say, you can tweak the animation endlessly to improve the appearance and add further effects such as trailing sparks, smoke, and even sound effects. We've done our job of showing you how to implement the basic physics. Now go for it!

In the source code, we have also included a modified version of the simulation in files named Fireworks2.as and FireworksMover2.as. This is an interactive version where you click and hold down the mouse anywhere on the stage. The number of sparks _numSparks will be set to equal the duration in seconds for which you hold down the mouse, so the longer you press the mouse the greater the number of sparks that will be produced per explosion. When you release the mouse, the initial explosion will take place at the location of the mouse. The colors of the sparks are also randomized in this version. Try it out!

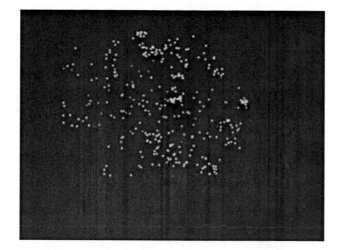

Figure 12-7. Fireworks!

Particle animations with long-range forces

It's now time to transcend reality and start playing around with particles and physics. In this section, we'll be moving lots of particles around under the action of long-range forces and create some interesting patterns and animations.

In this section and the next, we'll generally be dealing with large numbers of particles and lots of calculations. To reduce any unnecessary overheads, we shall therefore make use of a slightly lighter version of the Ball class that we'll call Star. The Star class is similar to the Ball class, but does not draw a gradient fill and so does away with the extra code needed to do that. The remaining examples in this chapter will make use of the Star class.

Particle paths in a force field

Particle trajectories are commonly used in generative art projects. We'll now set up a simple example using multiple particles that can be used as a basis for further explorations.

The idea of this animation is very simple. We set up a number of stars randomly around a central attractor and give them small random velocities. The stars are subjected to a gravitational force toward the attractor and move around it, tracing trajectories.

The setup file is called LongRange.as and contains the following code:

```
package{
        import flash.display.Sprite;
        import com.physicscodes.objects.Star;
        import com.physicscodes.math.Vector2D;
        import com.physicscodes.objects.Particle;

        public class LongRange extends Sprite{
```

```
          public function LongRange():void{
                  init();
          }
          private function init():void{

                  // create a stationary attracting nucleus
                  var massNucleus:Number = 10000;
                  var nucleus:Star = new Star(20,0x333333,massNucleus);
                  nucleus.pos2D = new Vector2D(400,400);
                  addChild(nucleus);

                  // initial distribution of stars
                  var stars:Array=new Array();
                  var numStars:Number = 50;
                  for (var i:Number=0;i<numStars; i++){
                          var star:Star = new Star(5,0xffff00,1000);
                          star.pos2D = new Vector2D(Math.random()*stage.stageWidth,⮑
Math.random()*stage.stageHeight);
                          star.velo2D = new Vector2D(50*(Math.random()-0.5),⮑
50*(Math.random()-0.5));
                          addChild(star);
                          stars.push(star);
                  }

                  // make the stars move
                  var mover:LongRangeMover=new LongRangeMover(stars,nucleus);
                  mover.startTime();
          }
      }
}
```

This code should be very easy to follow and requires no explanation. The only significantly new thing is that we are creating Star instances instead of Ball instances. The mover class LongRangeMover contains the following code:

```
package {
        import com.physicscodes.motion.MultiForcer2;
        import com.physicscodes.motion.Forces;
        import com.physicscodes.objects.Particle;
        import com.physicscodes.objects.Star;
        import com.physicscodes.math.Vector2D;
        import com.physicscodes.math.Graph;

        public class LongRangeMover extends MultiForcer2{
                private var _particles:Array;
                private var _attractor:Star;
                private var _massAttractor:Number;
                private var _center:Vector2D;
                private var _G:Number = 10;
                private var _graph:Graph;
                private var _stageWidth;
                private var _stageHeight;
                private var _cols:Array = new Array();
```

```
public function LongRangeMover(pparticles:Array,pattractor:Star):void{
        _massAttractor = pattractor.mass;
        _center = pattractor.pos2D;
        _particles = pparticles;
        _attractor = pattractor;
        _stageWidth = pattractor.stage.stageWidth;
        _stageHeight = pattractor.stage.stageHeight;
        setupCols();
        setupGraph();
        super(pparticles);
}

override protected function calcForce(pparticle:Particle,pnum:uint):void{
        var radius:Vector2D=pparticle.pos2D.subtract(_center);
        var gravityCentral:Vector2D;
        if (radius.length < _attractor.radius) {
                gravityCentral = new Vector2D(0,0);
        }
        else{
                gravityCentral = Forces.gravity(_G, _massAttractor,↩
pparticle.mass, radius);
        }
        force = gravityCentral;
        plotGraph(pparticle,_cols[pnum]);
}

private function setupCols():void{
        for (var i:uint=0; i<_particles.length; i++){
                _cols.push(0xffffff*Math.random());
        }
}

private function setupGraph():void {
        _graph = new Graph(0, _stageWidth, 0, _stageHeight, 0, 0,↩
_stageWidth, _stageHeight);
        _attractor.stage.addChild(_graph);
}
private function plotGraph(pparticle:Particle,pcol:uint):void{
        _graph.plot([pparticle.xpos], [-pparticle.ypos], pcol, false, true);
}
    }
}
```

Again, there is little that you have not seen before in this code, and we'll focus on the few new bits. In calcForce(), we are subjecting the stars to the gravitational force due to the attractor using the Forces.gravity() function, but note that we are setting that force to zero if the stars happen to be within the attractor. The setupCols() method sets up an array with random uint values to represent colors, and they are used at the end of calcForce() to plot the trajectory of each star in a different random color.

Run the simulation and play around by changing the parameters and modifying it in any way you can think of. If you have a slow machine, you might want to reduce the number of particles. You can come up with some interesting patterns (see, for example, Figure 12-8).

Figure 12-8. An example of particle trajectories under a central gravitational force

Building a wormhole

In this wacky example we are going to create something that does not reflect any real physics but is nevertheless interesting to watch!

A *wormhole* is a hypothetical object in which you enter a black hole and emerge at some other location in space. In our animation, we'll have a wormhole made up of a black hole that sucks in stars and a white hole that spews them out again. To make the animation more visually interesting, the stars coming out of the black hole will be increased in size and given a randomized velocity back toward the black hole, creating a cycling system. What do you expect to happen eventually? Let's find out. Here is the code in the setup class, Wormhole.as:

```
package{
        import flash.display.Sprite;
        import com.physicscodes.objects.Star;
        import com.physicscodes.math.Vector2D;
        import com.physicscodes.objects.Particle;

        public class Wormhole extends Sprite{
                public function Wormhole():void{
                        init();
                }
                private function init():void{
                        // create a stationary black hole
                        var blackHole:Star = new Star(20,0x222222,10000);
                        blackHole.pos2D = new Vector2D(400,400);
```

```
                    addChild(blackHole);

                    // create a stationary white hole
                    var whiteHole:Star = new Star(10,0xffffff);
                    whiteHole.pos2D = new Vector2D(400,100);
                    addChild(whiteHole);

                    // create an initial distribution of stars
                    var numStars:uint = 1000;
                    var stars:Array=new Array();
                    for (var i:Number=0;i<numStars; i++){
                            var star:Star = new Star(2,0xffff00);
                            star.pos2D = new Vector2D(Math.random()*stage.stageWidth,↪
Math.random()*stage.stageHeight);
                            addChild(star);
                            stars.push(star);
                    }

                    // make the stars move
                    var mover:WormholeMover=new WormholeMover(stars,blackHole,whiteHole);
                    mover.startTime();
            }
        }
}
```

We create a black hole in the middle of the stage and a white hole some distance away. We next create 1000 stars and place them randomly on the stage. The stars are animated using an instance of the WormholeMover class. The code in this class is shown below:

```
package {
        import com.physicscodes.motion.MultiForcer2;
        import com.physicscodes.motion.Forces;
        import com.physicscodes.objects.Particle;
        import com.physicscodes.objects.Star;
        import com.physicscodes.math.Vector2D;
        import com.physicscodes.math.Graph;

        public class WormholeMover extends MultiForcer2{
                private var _particles:Array;
                private var _attractor:Star;
                private var _massAttractor:Number;
                private var _radiusAttractor:Number;
                private var _center:Vector2D;
                private var _emitterPos:Vector2D;
                private var _G:Number = 10;

                public function WormholeMover(pparticles:Array, pattractor:Star,↪
pemitter:Star):void{
                        _massAttractor = pattractor.mass;
                        _radiusAttractor = pattractor.radius;
                        _center = pattractor.pos2D;
                        _emitterPos = pemitter.pos2D
                        _particles = pparticles;
                        _attractor = pattractor;
```

```
                        super(pparticles);
                }

        override protected function calcForce(pparticle:Particle,pnum:uint):void{
                var radius:Vector2D=pparticle.pos2D.subtract(_center);
                var gravityCentral:Vector2D;
                if (radius.length < _attractor.radius) {
                        gravityCentral = new Vector2D(0,0);
                }
                else{
                        gravityCentral = Forces.gravity(_G,_massAttractor,↪
pparticle.mass,radius);
                }
                force = gravityCentral;
        }

        override protected function moveObject():void{
                super.moveObject();
                recycleParticles();
        }

        private function recycleParticles():void{
                for (var i:uint=0; i< _particles.length; i++){
                        var star:Star = _particles[i];
                        var radius:Vector2D = star.pos2D.subtract(_center);
                        if (radius.length<_radiusAttractor){
                                star.pos2D =_emitterPos;
                                star.velo2D = new Vector2D((Math.random()-0.5)*50,↪
Math.random()*10);

                                star.radius *= 1.5;
                        }
                }
        }
    }
}
```

The constructor and `calcForce()` method are nearly the same as those in the previous example. The main novelty is that we have a new `recycleParticles()` method that is called from an overriding `moveObject()` method. The `recycleParticles()` method moves particles that enter the black hole to the location of the white hole, gives them a random downward velocity, and increases their radius by 50 percent.

If you run the code, you'll find that the stars are sucked into the black hole, emerging larger out of the white hole. Because they are spewed around the black hole again, some of the stars are attracted back into it, while others end up in an orbit around it. Some stars might manage to escape, depending on what maximum magnitude of velocity you set. A few stars go through the wormhole a few times, growing bigger and bigger. Eventually you end up with stars of different sizes trapped in perpetual orbit around the black hole, as shown in Figure 12-9. Because those stars are in a closed orbit around the black hole and having originated from the white hole, their orbits close back on the white hole, giving the impression that the latter is also attracting them!

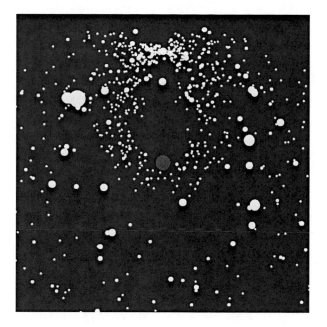

Figure 12-9. Stars circulating through a wormhole!

Interacting particle systems

So far, the particle systems we have looked at have not involved any mutual interactions between the particles. For example, you could let the particles exert a gravitational force on each other. This would create some interesting effects. The trouble is that the number of calculations then becomes very large as the number of particles is increased. For N particles, there are on the order of N^2 interactions because every particle interacts with every other particle. Even with only 100 particles, that's 10,000 extra gravity calculations per timestep! The next two examples will illustrate different ways in which we may be able to handle this.

Multiple particles under mutual gravity

In this example, we will modify the gravity animations in the previous two examples by including mutual gravitational forces between the stars. In physics jargon, this will be a direct N-body calculation.

The following listing is the code in the setup file MultiGravity.as:

```
package{
        import flash.display.Sprite;
        import com.physicscodes.math.Vector2D;
        import com.physicscodes.objects.Particle;
        import com.physicscodes.objects.Star;

        public class MultiGravity extends Sprite{
                public function MultiGravity():void{
```

```
                        init();
                  }
            private function init():void{
                  // create a stationary attracting nucleus
                  var massNucleus:Number = 1000;
                  var nucleus:Star = new Star(20,0x333333,massNucleus);
                  nucleus.pos2D = new Vector2D(stage.stageWidth/2, stage.stageHeight/2);
                  addChild(nucleus);

                  // initial distribution of stars
                  var stars:Array=new Array();
                  var numStars:uint = 200;
                  var massStar:Number = 100;
                  var vmag:Number = 10;
                  for (var i:Number=0;i<numStars; i++){
                        var star:Star = new Star(2,0xffff00,massStar*➥
(Math.random()+0.1));
                        star.pos2D = new Vector2D(Math.random()*stage.stageWidth, ➥
Math.random()*stage.stageHeight);
                        star.velo2D = new Vector2D(vmag*(Math.random()-0.5), vmag*➥
(Math.random()-0.5));
                        addChild(star);
                        stars.push(star);
                  }

                  // make the stars move
                  var mover:MultiGravitator=new MultiGravitator(stars,nucleus);
                  mover.startTime();
            }
      }
}
```

Here we are creating a central attracting nucleus as well as 200 stars randomly positioned around it and with small random velocities. The mass of the nucleus is made 10 times larger than that of the stars, but those are parameters that you can change to see their effect. To move the stars, we have a MultiGravitator class that looks like this:

```
package {
      import com.physicscodes.motion.MultiForcer2;
      import com.physicscodes.motion.Forces;
      import com.physicscodes.objects.Particle;
      import com.physicscodes.math.Vector2D;

      public class MultiGravitator extends MultiForcer2{

            private var _particles:Array;
            private var _massAttractor:Number;
            private var _center:Vector2D;
            private var _G:Number = 1;
            private var _eps:Number = 1;
            private var _rmin:Number = 100;

            public function MultiGravitator(pparticles:Array,pattractor:Particle):void{
```

```
                    _massAttractor = pattractor.mass;
                    _center = pattractor.pos2D;
                    _particles = pparticles;
                    super(pparticles);
            }

        override protected function calcForce(pparticle:Particle,pnum:uint):void{
                    var radius:Vector2D=pparticle.pos2D.subtract(_center);
                    var gravityCentral:Vector2D;
                    if (radius.length < 20) {
                            gravityCentral = new Vector2D(0,0);
                    }
                    else{
                            gravityCentral = Forces.gravity(_G,_massAttractor,↵
pparticle.mass,radius);
                    }
                    var gravityMutual:Vector2D = new Vector2D(0,0);
                    for (var i:uint=0; i<_particles.length; i++){
                            if (i != pnum){
                                    var particle:Particle = _particles[i];
                                    var radiusP:Vector2D = pparticle.pos2D.subtract↵
(particle.pos2D);

                                    if (radiusP.length < _rmin){
                                            var gravityP:Vector2D =↵
 Forces.gravityModified(_G, particle.mass, pparticle.mass, radiusP, _eps);
                                            gravityMutual.incrementBy(gravityP);
                                    }
                            }
                    }
                    force = Forces.add([gravityCentral, gravityMutual]);
            }

        }
}
```

The structure of MultiGravitator is quite simple: it consists of just the constructor and calcForce(). You are already familiar with the first half of the code in calcForce(), which computes the force gravityCentral on the stars due to the central nucleus. The second half of the code calculates the total force gravityMutual on a star because of all the other stars (excluding itself, hence the if (i != pnum){} condition) and adds it to the gravityCentral force to get the total force on each star.

There are two new features in this code, in another if statement nested within the first:

```
if (radiusP.length < _rmin){
        var gravityP:Vector2D - Forces.gravityModified(_G, particle.mass, pparticle.mass,↵
 radiusP, _eps);
        gravityMutual.incrementBy(gravityP);
}
```

The first new feature is the if condition, which checks to see whether the distance of the current star from any other star is less than a certain minimum distance _rmin. The gravity force due to the latter star is included only if the condition is satisfied. This is called the *local interaction approximation*. The idea is that because gravity is an inverse square law, its magnitude falls off rapidly with distance. So if the other star is very far away, including the force it exerts won't make much difference to the total force and is just a waste of resources. So you include only the influence of the nearest neighbors. In an accurate simulation, you would have to be careful to implement this approximation properly, as there are some subtleties. But because we are just playing around, so to speak, there is no need to go into those finer points. The value of _rmin chosen in the code is 100 pixels, but you can experiment with other values. Giving _rmin the value of 0 would effectively exclude all mutual interactions between the stars. Giving _rmin a value larger than 800 would include interactions between all 200 stars: that's about 400,000 extra gravity calculations, and will certainly slow down your animation!

The second new feature is that we are using a modified version of the gravity function called Forces.gravityModified() to compute the interactions between the stars. The new function is defined like this:

```
static public function gravityModified(G:Number, m1:Number, m2:Number, r:Vector2D,↪
  eps:Number):Vector2D {
        return r.multiply(-G*m1*m2/((r.lengthSquared+eps*eps)*r.length));
}
```

Comparing this with the Forces.gravity() function, you will find that we have introduced a new parameter eps, whose square gets added to the r^2 term in the denominator of the function. The corresponding mathematical formula is this:

$$F = G\,\frac{m_1\,m_2}{r^2 + \varepsilon^2}$$

The ε symbol stands for the eps parameter. Why do we modify the gravity function in this way? When two objects exerting gravitational forces on each other get very close, the forces become very large or even infinite (because r goes to zero, and we end up dividing by a small number or zero). This, as you will recall, causes the two objects to accelerate enormously and be sent flying off in random directions. The ε factor is a common "fudge" to bring that under control. Because ε^2 is always positive (being the square of a real number), the denominator will never be zero. And as long as ε is small, it will not alter the force calculation much for most values of r except the very smallest. In the example, eps has a value of 1 pixel. You can also experiment with different values to see what effect it produces.

Run the simulation and experiment with different values of the parameters. For example, you can change the masses of the central nucleus and the stars to change the relative importance of the central force versus the mutual forces between the stars. Running the code with the default values of the parameters will make the stars tend to lump together in different locations, with a few lingering around the central attractor. A screenshot is shown in Figure 12-10. Again, you may wish to reduce the number of particles if the simulation runs slow on your machine.

Figure 12-10. Lots of stars exerting gravitational forces on one another

A simple galaxy simulation

What would you need to do to simulate the motion of stars in a galaxy? Well, that is not a trivial job to do properly, typically requiring some serious hardware and lots of physics and code. But it is possible to cheat and come up with a very simplified approach. While the result certainly won't look like that in more sophisticated approaches, it will give you something interesting to play and experiment further with.

The most obvious problem that we hit when attempting to model a system like this is how to handle the large number of particles you'd need. We are talking at least thousands here, and possibly tens of thousands. A direct N-body calculation is impractical with such large numbers of particles, especially for an animation that's going to run in a web browser!

An alternative approach is to consider the motion of each star in the effective gravitational force field due to all the other stars taken together. This is the so-called *mean field approach*. The star system is then effectively considered as a non-interacting collisionless system with each star moving independently in that mean field. The mean field can of course evolve over time as the positions of the stars change, and this evolution needs to be incorporated in such a simulation.

There are numerical methods for calculating the mean field due to a general distribution of point masses, but they are beyond the scope of this book. However, if we make the assumption that the stars are distributed in a spherically symmetric way around the galactic center, things become much simpler thanks to a neat mathematical principle. The principle says that for any spherically symmetric mass distribution, the gravitational force at any distance r from the center is the same force exerted by the total mass enclosed within a sphere of radius r, with that mass taken to be at the center. Any mass outside that radius does not have any effect. That makes things pretty easy. If you start a simulation with a spherically symmetric distribution of stars, it should remain spherically symmetric at all times. So you can apply this principle at each timestep.

The stars in a galaxy are not the only source of mass. Many galaxies have a central nucleus that may be a supermassive black hole. So the mass of this galactic nucleus needs to be taken into account. But that's easy; we just use the Forces.gravity() function with a specified mass for the nucleus.

There is also something more exotic that lurks in galaxies: dark matter. In fact, it is estimated that most of the mass in a galaxy exists in a dark matter halo around the galaxy. Again, assuming spherical symmetry, the contribution of this dark matter to the gravitational force can be calculated in the same way as that of the stars.

With these basic ingredients, let's put together a quick and dirty galaxy simulation. The setup code is in the file Galaxy.as, which looks like this:

```
package{
        import flash.display.Sprite;
        import com.physicscodes.math.Vector2D;
        import com.physicscodes.objects.Star;

        public class Galaxy extends Sprite{
                public function Galaxy():void{
                        init();
                }
                private function init():void{
                        // create a stationary galaxy center
                        var nucleus:Star;
                        //var massNucleus:Number = 0;
                        var massNucleus:Number = 100000;
                        nucleus = new Star(20,0x333333,massNucleus);
                        nucleus.pos2D = new Vector2D(stage.stageWidth/2, stage.stageHeight/2);
                                addChild(nucleus);

                        // initial distribution of stars
                        var stars:Array = new Array();
                        var numStars:uint = 10000;
                        var massStar:Number = 10;
                        var veloMag:Number = 20;
                        var maxRadius:Number = 400;
                        for (var i:Number=0; i<numStars; i++){
                                var star:Star = new Star(1,0xffff00,massStar);
                                var radius:Number = nucleus.radius +↪
(maxRadius-nucleus.radius)*Math.random();
                                var angle:Number = 2*Math.PI*Math.random();
                                star.pos2D = new Vector2D(radius*Math.cos(angle),↪
radius*Math.sin(angle)).add(nucleus.pos2D);
                                var rvec:Vector2D = nucleus.pos2D.subtract(star.pos2D);
                                star.velo2D = rvec.perp(veloMag);
                                addChild(star);
                                stars.push(star);
                        }
```

```
                        // make the stars move
                        var mover:GalaxyMover=new GalaxyMover(stars,nucleus);
                        mover.startTime();
                }
        }
}
```

We first create a galactic nucleus of mass 100,000 units and radius 20 pixels and place it in the middle of the stage. Then we create 10,000 stars (depending on your computer's speed, you might want to reduce this number), each with mass 10 units, and place them in a random circular distribution around the galactic center (that's what the bit of trig code achieves). Note that each "star" here really represents lots of stars; there are typically billions of stars in a galaxy, not thousands! The stars are then given an initial tangential velocity around the galactic center. Note that the velocity magnitude for each star has the same value veloMag; that's because observed galactic rotation curves show that the velocity in a galaxy is approximately independent of the distance from the galactic center. There are already a lot of parameters to play with here, such as the mass of the galactic center, the mass of each star, the rotational velocity, and so on. You can also try out different initial positions and velocities for the stars. In the file Galaxy.as there are some commented lines with different options for these initial conditions. Do try them out to see how they lead to different evolutions of the galaxy.

Here is the full source code for the GalaxyMover class that drives the simulation:

```
package {
        import com.physicscodes.motion.MultiForcer;
        import com.physicscodes.motion.Forces;
        import com.physicscodes.math.Vector2D;
        import com.physicscodes.objects.Particle;
        import com.physicscodes.objects.Star;

        public class GalaxyMover extends MultiForcer{
                private var _massAttractor:Number;
                private var _radiusAttractor:Number;
                private var _center:Vector2D;
                private var _orbiters:Array;
                private var _massStars:Array=new Array(); // total mass of stars↪
within radius r
                private var _massDark:Array=new Array(); // total mass of dark matter↪
within radius r
                private var _G:Number = 1;
                private var _rmax:Number = 500;
                private var _constDark:Number=1000;
                private var _A:Number=1;
                private var _alpha:Number=0.5;

                public function GalaxyMover(porbiters:Array,pattractor:Star):void{
                        _massAttractor = pattractor.mass;
                        _radiusAttractor = pattractor.radius;
                        _center = pattractor.pos2D;
                        _orbiters = porbiters;
                        super(porbiters);
                }
```

```
        override protected function moveObject():void{
                calcMass();
                super.moveObject();
        }

        override protected function calcForce(porbiter:Particle):void{
                var radius:Vector2D = porbiter.pos2D.subtract(_center);
                if (radius.length < _radiusAttractor) {
                        force=new Vector2D(0,0);
                }
                else{
                        force = Forces.gravity(_G,_massAttractor+_massStars↦
[Math.ceil(radius.length)]+_massDark[Math.ceil(radius.length)], porbiter.mass,radius);
                }
        }

        private function calcMass():void{
                var distanceToCenter:Number;
                var orbiter:Particle;
                var massStarRing:Array = new Array();
                var massDarkRing:Array = new Array();
                for (var l:uint=0; l<_rmax; l++){
                        massStarRing[l] = 0;
                        massDarkRing[l] = _constDark*l*l*Math.exp↦
(-_A*Math.pow(l,_alpha));
                }
                for (var k:uint=0; k<_orbiters.length-1; k++){
                        orbiter = _orbiters[k];
                        distanceToCenter = orbiter.pos2D.subtract(_center).length;
                        massStarRing[Math.ceil(distanceToCenter)] += orbiter.mass;
                }
                _massStars[0] = massStarRing[0];
                _massDark[0] = massDarkRing[0];
                for(var j:uint=1; j<_orbiters.length-1; j++){
                        _massStars[j] = _massStars[j-1] + massStarRing[j];
                        _massDark[j] = _massDark[j-1] + massDarkRing[j];
                }
                //trace(_massAttractor,_massStars[_rmax-1],_massDark[_rmax-1]);
        }
    }
}
```

Let's start with the calcForce() method. As you can see from the code, we are calculating the total gravitational force on each star at its distance from the center (radius) by using the Forces.gravity() function, with a mass that is the sum of the galactic nucleus mass and the masses of the stars and dark matter within that radius, as stored in the arrays _massStars and _massDark. These arrays are updated at each timestep by summing the mass at different distances from the center in the calcMass() method. A commented out line at the end of calcMass() traces the three total masses.

The mass of the stars is computed simply by locating the stars. For the dark matter, things are different because it is not included in the simulation as an object. Therefore, we prescribe a mass distribution based on the so-called Einasto profile, which is commonly used in computer simulations of dark matter. The mathematical form of that distribution is the following:

$$\rho(r) = \rho_0 \exp\left(-A r^{\alpha}\right)$$

Here ρ_0, A and r are constants that must be specified. This formula gives the mass density (mass per unit volume). To get the mass at a distance r, one must multiply this mass density by the volume of a thin spherical shell of thickness dr. This introduces an extra factor of $4\pi r^2 dr$ (surface area of sphere times the thickness of the spherical shell). This gives the formula that is coded up in calcMass(). Don't worry if this dark matter stuff seems a bit difficult to follow. We included it because it can change the dynamics of the interacting stars in a significant way, making for a "richer" simulation. But even if you don't fully understand everything here you can still play with the relevant parameters to explore the range of possible effects you get with this additional physics included.

If you run the code with the default parameter values, you should find that after successive initial contractions and expansions, the star distribution settles into a quasi steady state. Figure 12-11 shows a screenshot of what you might be able to see. One can even discern a hint of a spiral arm structure at times (see Figure 12-11), although it would take a more careful simulation to achieve that properly. Again, you can change the parameters in GalaxyMover, especially those of the dark matter distribution. It would be instructive to see how the simulation changes when you change the relative magnitudes of the galactic nucleus mass, the total star mass, and the total dark matter mass. Have fun!

Figure 12-11. A simple galaxy simulation

Summary

This chapter has provided a taste of what can be achieved with particles and some simple physics. In just a short chapter it is impossible to fully cover the subject. We therefore encourage you to search the Web and explore what has been achieved within the Flash community and beyond. There is also an open source AS3.0 particle engine called Flint, developed by Richard Lord. Take a look here: `http://flintparticles.org`.

Many examples of inspiring creations by talented individuals exist, too numerous to mention here, but we've included relevant links on our web site: `http://www.physicscodes.com`. We're also encouraging readers to share their creations on our website, so you can find more code, ideas, inspiration, and above all, you'll be able to show off your own masterpieces!

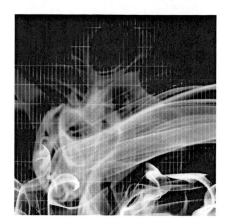

Chapter 13

Extended Objects

In much of this book, we have focused on the motion of particles. In this chapter, we will explore the physics governing the motion of extended objects. This topic is important for obvious reasons: objects in everyday life are extended in space and have all sorts of shapes, sizes and behavior. To model the motion of extended objects, we need to cover some additional physics and methods. This is a big subject that could easily have filled several chapters, or even a whole book. We have therefore been selective in our coverage, focusing on two topics that we can cover in sufficient depth to provide a good introduction, instead of giving a wider but more superficial presentation.

Topics covered in this chapter include these:

- **Rigid bodies**: A *rigid body* is an extended object with a fixed shape and size. In addition to changing its position, such an object can also rotate to change its orientation. We will cover rigid body dynamics, rolling, and rigid body collisions, and illustrate them with a number of different examples.

- **Deformable bodies**: Objects such as ropes and clothes can change their shapes. We can model such *deformable bodies* by means of mass-spring systems, building upon the principles discussed in Chapter 8.

Most of the chapter is devoted to rigid bodies, with a much shorter section on deformable bodies.

Rigid bodies

A *rigid body* is defined as an object that maintains its shape and size when a force is applied to it. In other words, rigid bodies do not deform under the action of forces. The rigid body concept is an idealization because in reality nearly all objects suffer some deformation when subjected to forces, even if it is by a minute amount. However, when modeling the motion of many objects, it is frequently possible to ignore any such deformation and still obtain good results. This is the approach we'll adopt in this section.

Basic concepts of rigid body modeling

Before we can model the motion of rigid bodies, we need to review some relevant concepts from earlier chapters and introduce some new ones. These concepts will then be brought together in the next section to formulate the laws governing rigid body rotational motion.

Rigid body motion versus particle motion

The key difference in the motion of rigid bodies compared to that of particles is that they can undergo rotation as well as translation. The translational motion of a rigid body obeys the same laws as that of particles (as described in Chapter 5). We must now discuss how the rotational motion can be analyzed.

Rotational kinematics

In Chapter 9, we looked at the kinematics of rotational motion, introducing concepts such as angular displacement θ, angular velocity ω, and angular acceleration α. As a brief recap, here are the defining equations for some of these quantities:

Angular velocity:

$$\omega = \frac{d\theta}{dt}$$

Angular acceleration:

$$\alpha = \frac{d\omega}{dt}$$

These rotational kinematics variables are related to the corresponding linear variables, for example:

Linear and angular displacements:

$$s = r\,\theta$$

Linear and angular velocities:

$$v = r\,\omega$$

Linear (tangential) and angular accelerations:

$$a = r\,\alpha$$

In the context of rigid body rotation, these formulas give the displacement, velocity, and tangential acceleration of a point on a rigid body at a distance r from the center of rotation in the absence of translational motion—or in addition to those due to translational motion.

In addition to the tangential acceleration, there is a centripetal (radial) acceleration given by this formula:

$$a = v^2 / r = r\,\omega^2$$

Note that all points on a rigid body must have the same angular displacement, angular velocity, and angular acceleration, whereas the linear counterparts of these quantities depend on the distance r from the center of rotation.

We shall also use vector equivalents of the preceding quantities and formulas. For example, the angular velocity is really a vector ω with a direction perpendicular to the plane of rotation and with an orientation as shown in Figure 13-1. The angular acceleration, as the derivative of the angular velocity, is therefore also a vector α.

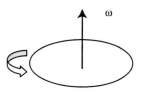

Figure 13-1. Angular velocity as a vector

Rotational kinematics with the Particle and Mover classes

Although this section is about rigid body motion, with the eventual aim of simulating rotational dynamics, there are many occasions when you might need a particle or ball to rotate without necessarily dealing with full rigid body dynamics. Therefore, it is useful to have functionality that will enable Particle instances to exhibit rotational kinematics.

We accomplished this to some extent in Chapter 9 by introducing the angVelo property into the Particle class and the spinObject() method into the Mover class. Let's now complete the task by including a corresponding property for angular displacement that we'll call angDispl.

Internally this property is stored in a private variable named _theta, with a corresponding getter/setter pair:

```
private var _theta:Number=0; //angular displacement in radians

public function get angDispl():Number{
        return _theta;
}
public function set angDispl(ptheta:Number):void{
        _theta = ptheta;
        this.rotation = ptheta*180/Math.PI;
}
```

Notice that angDispl is in radians and that the setter modifies the rotation property of the Particle instance by first converting it into radians.

Next we update the spinObject() method of the Mover class to make use of the newly created angDispl property:

```
protected function spinObject():void{
        if (_particle.angVelo !=0){
                _particle.angDispl += _particle.angVelo*_dt;
                _particle.rotation = _particle.angDispl*180/Math.PI;
        }
}
```

These changes will not only enable particles to exhibit rotational kinematics (but not dynamics) but also make it automatically available for the rigid body object and mover classes that we will build later by extending the Particle and Mover classes.

Turning effect of a force: torque

Suppose a rigid body is at rest and we want to translate it (give it some linear velocity). How do we do that? We need to apply a force. But what must we do if we want to rotate it about a given axis? Again we need to apply a force. But the line of action of the force must not pass through the axis. The *turning effect* of a force is known as a *moment* or *torque*, and is defined as the product of the force and the perpendicular distance of its line of action from the axis (see Figure 13-2):

$$T = F\,d = F\,r\sin(\theta)$$

Here, θ is the angle between the force **F** and the vector **r** from the center of rotation to the point of application of the force.

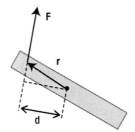

Figure 13-2. Definition of torque due to a force

In vector form, it is the following:

$$\mathbf{T} = \mathbf{r} \times \mathbf{F}$$

Note that the vector product is not commutative, so the order in which the product is performed matters. Because the vector product of two vectors gives a vector that is perpendicular to both, if **r** and **F** are in the plane of the paper, the torque will point either into or out of the paper (see the section on the vector product in Chapter 3 for how to work out the direction of the resulting vector).

From this definition, it is clear that the torque is zero if the line of action of the force passes through the axis. In general, a force will produce both a linear acceleration and a turning effect.

Center of mass

From what we have said in the last section, if an object is free to move (without any constraints) and you apply a force on it, it will undergo both a translation and a rotation. An exception arises if the line of action of the force passes through a special point known as the *center of mass* of the object. In that case, the applied force produces only translation, but no rotation.

Center of mass is a general concept that applies to collections of point particles as well as to extended objects. In both cases, it represents the location at which the overall mass of the system appears to act. For a collection of point particles of mass m_1, m_2, ... located at positions r_1, r_2, ..., the position vector of the center of mass is given by the following formula:

$$\mathbf{r} = \frac{m_1\mathbf{r}_1 + m_2\mathbf{r}_2 + \dots}{m_1 + m_2 + \dots}$$

So we add the products mr of the particles vectorally and divide the sum by their total mass. Using the symbol Σ, which stands for sum, we can write this formula in the following shorthand form:

$$\mathbf{r} = \frac{\sum m_i\mathbf{r}_i}{\sum m_i}$$

For a rigid body, a generalization of this formula is used by considering the body as being composed of a continuous distribution of particles. The center of mass of a rigid body can then be computed using the calculus formula:

$$\mathbf{r} = \frac{\int \mathbf{r}\, dm}{\int dm}$$

The denominator of this formula is simply equal to the total mass of the rigid body. The location of the center of mass will depend on the shape of the body as well as on how its mass is distributed. For objects that are symmetrical and with a uniform mass distribution, the center of mass is located at their geometrical center. For example, the center of mass of a sphere is located at its center. It is similar for other objects such as a cuboids, discs, and rectangles.

The center of mass is important for a number of reasons. First, it provides a connection between particle dynamics and rigid body dynamics: in terms of its translational motion, a rigid body can be thought of as a particle located at its center of mass. Second, the analysis of rigid body motion is much simpler if expressed in terms of a coordinate system with the center of mass as the origin.

Moment of inertia

We said that torque is the analogue of force for rotational motion: torque is the cause of angular acceleration. What is the rotational analogue of mass (inertia)? This may not be obvious, but, as will be demonstrated in the next section, it is a quantity known as the *moment of inertia*. The moment of inertia is defined as the sum of mr^2 for all the particles comprising the particle system or rigid body, where m is the mass of the particle and r is its distance from the axis of rotation. For a discrete system of particles, the definition of the moment of inertia (denoted by the symbol I) is therefore the following:

$$I = \sum m_i r_i^2$$

This formula tells us that the larger the mass of the particles or the greater their distance from the axis, the larger the moment of inertia.

For a continuous distribution of mass such as a rigid body, the corresponding calculus definition is the following:

$$I = \int r^2 \, dm$$

Both these formulas tell us that the moment of inertia is a property that quantifies the mass distribution in a rigid body. Using the calculus formula, one can work out the moment of inertia of a variety of regular rigid bodies in both 2D and 3D. The result is a formula in terms of the total mass and some linear dimensions of the rigid body.

For example, the moment of inertia of a hollow sphere of mass m and radius r about an axis through its center is given by the following formula:

$$I = \frac{2}{3} m r^2$$

Because moment of inertia depends on the mass distribution, a solid sphere of the same mass m and radius r has a different moment of inertia, being given by this formula:

$$I = \frac{2}{5} m r^2$$

So a hollow sphere has a larger moment of inertia (and is therefore harder to rotate) than a solid sphere of the same mass and radius.

The moment of inertia also depends on the axis around which the rotation takes place. For example, the solid cylinder shown in Figure 13-3 has a moment of inertia about the x-axis and y-axis given by the following formula (where m is its mass, r is the radius of its circular cross-section and h is its height):

$$I = \frac{1}{12} m \left(3r^2 + 4h^2 \right)$$

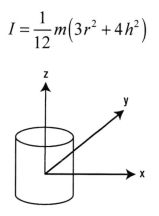

Figure 13-3. Rotation of a solid cylinder about different axes

The corresponding moment of inertia of the same cylinder about the z-axis is given by a different formula:

$$I = \frac{1}{2} m r^2$$

You can find the moments of inertia of a wide variety of 2D and 3D objects in physics or engineering textbooks and web sites.

Angular momentum

Another important concept is that of *angular momentum*, which is the rotational analogue of linear momentum. For a particle rotating about a center at a distance r from it, the angular momentum (denoted by the symbol L) is defined as the product of its linear momentum and the distance r:

$$L = pr = mvr$$

In vector form, the angular momentum vector is the vector product of the position and momentum vectors:

$$\mathbf{L} = \mathbf{r} \times \mathbf{p}$$

Using the relationship between linear and angular velocity v = rω, gives this:

$$L = mr^2 \omega$$

Therefore, for a collection of particles all rotating with the same angular velocity ω, the total angular momentum is given by the following:

$$L = \sum m_i r_i^2 \,\omega$$

Using the definition of moment of inertia, this gives the following result:

$$L = I\,\omega$$

In vector form, it is this:

$$\mathbf{L} = I\,\boldsymbol{\omega}$$

This result also applies to rigid bodies, with the appropriate calculus definition of moment of inertia.

Modeling rigid bodies

Armed with our knowledge of rigid body concepts, we may now build some basic classes that will help us create rigid body objects.

Creating a RigidBody class

The first class we'll create is the RigidBody class. Because a rigid body has all the properties of a particle plus more, it makes sense to extend the Particle class. In fact, our RigidBody class will add only two new properties to those already included in the Particle class: center of mass and moment of inertia. So here is the RigidBody class code:

```
package com.physicscodes.objects {
        import com.physicscodes.math.Vector2D;

        public class RigidBody extends Particle{
                private var _cm:Vector2D; // center of mass
                private var _im:Number; // moment of inertia

                public function RigidBody(pcm:Vector2D, pim:Number=1, pmass:Number=1,➥
    pcharge:Number=0){
                        this.mass = pmass;
                        this.charge = pcharge;
                        this.pos2D = pcm; // define position of rigid body as its center➥
    of mass
                        _cm = pcm;
                        _im = pim;
                }

                public function get momentOfInertia():Number{
                        return _im;
                }
                public function set momentOfInertia(pim:Number):void{
                        _im = pim;
```

```
                }
                public function get centerOfMass():Vector2D{
                        return _cm;
                }
                public function set centerOfMass(pcm:Vector2D):void{
                        _cm = pcm;
                        this.pos2D = pcm;
                }
        }
}
```

The public names of the two new properties are momentOfInertia and centerOfMass. The former is a Number; the latter is of Vector2D type. Note that the pos2D property of a RigidBody object is defined as its centerOfMass via an assignment in the constructor. That means whenever a RigidBody object is instantiated, it will be placed at the location specified by its center of mass.

Extending the RigidBody class

Like Particle, the RigidBody class has no graphics. To do anything with it in practice, you need to extend it and include some graphics. Let's create some examples that will be used later in this chapter.

The BallRB class

First, let's modify the Ball class by extending RigidBody instead of Particle. We'll call the new class BallRB. If you look at the code you'll find that it's very similar to that of Ball. BallRB takes two more parameters than Ball; as you'd expect, these are the center of mass and the moment of inertia, specified as parameters pcm and pim, respectively:

```
public function BallRB(pcm:Vector2D, pradius:Number=20, pcolor:uint=0x000000, pim:Number=1,↪
pmass:Number=1, pcharge:Number=0, pgradient:Boolean=true){}
```

Except for pcm, all the parameters are optional.

The PolygonRB class

Next we create a PolygonRB class in a similar way to the BallRB class. The parameters in the constructor of this class are as follows:

```
public function PolygonRB(pvertices:Array, pcm:Vector2D, pcolor:uint=0x000000, pim:Number=1,↪
pmass:Number=1, pcharge:Number=0){
```

In addition to the new parameters pcm and pim (similar to the BallRB class), the PolygonRB class has a pvertices parameter. This is an array of Vector2D values that corresponds to the locations of the vertices *relative to the center of mass*.

The PolygonRB class draws a Polygon with a fill of the specified color. The order in which the vertices are specified is important. The code draws the Polygon by joining the vertices in the specified order, so that different shapes result from different orderings of the vertices.

The RectangleRB class

The RectangleRB class extends the PolygonRB class, drawing a filled rectangle of specified width and height, with the center of mass located at its geometrical center:

```
public function RectangleRB(prwidth:Number, prheight:Number, pcm:Vector2D,↪
 pcolor:uint=0x000000, pim:Number=1, pmass:Number=1, pcharge:Number=0){
```

You can, of course, use the PolygonRB class to create a rectangular rigid body, but this class makes the task easier.

Using the rigid body classes

The file RigidBodyTest.as contains code that demonstrates the use of these rigid body classes. This code produces a stationary rectangular rigid body rotated by 45°, a stationary ball rotated by 90°, and a rotating square rigid body:

```
package{
        import flash.display.Sprite;
        import com.physicscodes.math.Vector2D;
        import com.physicscodes.objects.RigidBody;
        import com.physicscodes.objects.PolygonRB;
        import com.physicscodes.objects.RectangleRB;
        import com.physicscodes.objects.BallRB;

        public class RigidBodyTest extends Sprite{
                public function RigidBodyTest():void{
                        init();
                }
                private function init():void{
                        var cmR:Vector2D = new Vector2D(100,100);
                        var rectangle:RectangleRB = new RectangleRB(60,30,cmR,0xff0000);
                        rectangle.angDispl = Math.PI/4;
                        addChild(rectangle);

                        var cmB:Vector2D = new Vector2D(100,300);
                        var ball:BallRB = new BallRB(cmB,40,0x0000ff);
                        ball.angDispl = Math.PI/2;
                        addChild(ball);

                        var cm:Vector2D = new Vector2D(275,200);
                        var vertices:Array = new Array();
                        var vertex:Vector2D;
                        vertex = new Vector2D(50,50);
                        vertices.push(vertex);
                        vertex = new Vector2D(50,-50);
                        vertices.push(vertex);
                        vertex = new Vector2D(-50,-50);
                        vertices.push(vertex);
                        vertex = new Vector2D(-50,50);
                        vertices.push(vertex);
                        var polygon:PolygonRB = new PolygonRB(vertices,cm);
                        addChild(polygon);
```

```
                    polygon.velo2D = new Vector2D(10,0);
                    polygon.angVelo = 1;
                    polygon.move();
            }
        }
    }
```

By extending `Particle`, these rigid body classes can already exhibit rotational as well as linear kinematics when used with `Mover`, as demonstrated by assigning a non-zero angular velocity (as well as a non-zero linear velocity) and invoking the `move()` method on the last object, `polygon`:

```
polygon.velo2D = new Vector2D(10,0);
polygon.angVelo = 1;
polygon.move();
```

This makes the polygon (a rectangle) rotate clockwise while moving slowly to the right.

This is all good, but there are much more interesting things we can do if we implement rotational dynamics into our simulations. But before we can do that we need a bit more theory.

Rotational dynamics of rigid bodies

Having developed relevant rotational motion concepts in analogy with their linear counterparts, we are now in a position to formulate the laws of rotational dynamics. Let's start with the most important one: the rotational equivalent of Newton's second law of motion.

Newton's second law for rotational motion

Consider a rigid body that is rotating about an axis under the action of a force F (which produces a torque T), as shown in Figure 13-4.

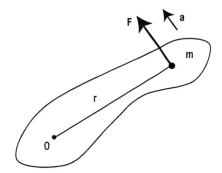

Figure 13-4. A rotating rigid body

405

Let's think of the rigid body as being composed of little particles, each of mass m, each undergoing a tangential acceleration a (ignore any radial acceleration, which does not contribute to rotation). Then, applying Newton's second law to such a particle gives the following:

$$F = m\,a$$

Recalling the formula relating the tangential acceleration to the angular acceleration, a = rα, we can write the previous formula as follows:

$$F = m\,r\,\alpha$$

Therefore, the torque T = Fr on the particle is obtained by multiplying the previous formula by r to give this:

$$T = m\,r^2\,\alpha$$

To get the total torque on the rigid body, we sum the torques on each particle to give the following formula:

$$T = \sum m\,r^2\,\alpha$$

Strictly speaking, we should use an integral rather than a discrete sum for a rigid body, but the reasoning and final answer are the same: because an integral is nothing but a continuous sum. So we'll use the simpler discrete summation notation here.

Because all points on a rigid body have the same angular acceleration, α is a constant, and we can take it out of the sum. Recognizing Σ mr² as the moment of inertia I, we then obtain the following final result:

$$T = I\,\alpha$$

In vector form, it is this:

$$\mathbf{T} = I\,\boldsymbol{\alpha}$$

This formula is the equivalent of Newton's second law **F** = m**a** for rotational motion, with torque, moment of inertia, and angular acceleration replacing force, mass, and linear acceleration, respectively. The formula enables us to calculate the angular acceleration of a rigid body from the torque exerted on it. It will be implemented in the same way that **F** = m**a** was implemented in Forcer.

As a special case, if the torque T is zero, the formula implies that the angular acceleration is also zero. This is the analogue of Newton's first law of motion.

Just as in linear motion, you can have retarding torques as well as accelerating torques. For example, you apply an accelerating torque to make a merry-go-round spin. It then slows down and stops because of the action of a retarding torque applied by friction.

Rigid bodies in equilibrium

In Chapter 4, we discussed the situation of an object in equilibrium under the action of multiple forces. For example, an airplane moving at constant velocity is in equilibrium under the action of four main forces (gravity, thrust, drag, and lift). The condition for equilibrium is that the forces balance (the resultant force is zero). But for an extended object, such as a rigid body, this condition is not enough. The resultant torque must also be zero; otherwise, the object will undergo rotational acceleration.

This concept of rotational equilibrium is well illustrated with the example of a balance (see Figure 13-5).

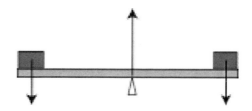

Figure 13-5. Rotational equilibrium illustrated by a balance

Assuming that the balance is in equilibrium, the downward force exerted by the combined weights on either side of the pivot is balanced by the upward contact force exerted by the pivot. Also, the clockwise torque or moment generated by one weight is balanced by the counterclockwise torque generated by the other weight: this is known as the *principle of moments*. In vector terms, one of the torques points out of the paper and the other points into the paper.

An example of a situation in which the resultant force may be zero and the resultant torque is not is when you turn a knob (see Figure 13-6). In that case, there are two opposite forces applied to either side of the knob. If their magnitudes are equal, they will give a zero resultant force. However, their torques will be in the same direction (into the paper) because they both generate clockwise rotations. This is an example of a *couple*: a pair of equal and opposite forces that have parallel non-coincident lines of action that therefore generate a resultant torque.

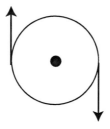

Figure 13-6. A couple

Conservation of angular momentum

Just as there is a rotational analogue of Newton's second law, rotational analogues of other laws exist, too. We shall now state these laws without proof, starting with the principle of conservation of angular momentum.

This principle states that the angular momentum of a rigid body or a system of particles is conserved if no external torque acts on it. For example, if an object is spinning at constant angular velocity, it will carry on doing so unless an external torque is applied to it. That's the reason the Earth continues to spin on its axis. On the other hand, a spinning top soon stops spinning because of opposing frictional torque.

Angular impulse-momentum theorem

The conservation of angular momentum is a special case of the angular impulse-momentum theorem. Recall the linear impulse-momentum theorem from Chapter 5. The formula expressing that theorem looks like this:

$$\mathbf{F} \, \Delta t = \Delta \mathbf{p}$$

This formula tells us that the impulse applied to an object is equal to the change in momentum produced.

The rotational analogue of the previous equation is obtained by taking the vector product of $\mathbf{r}$ with each side of the equation to give the following (because $\mathbf{T} = \mathbf{r} \times \mathbf{F}$ and $\mathbf{L} = \mathbf{r} \times \mathbf{p}$):

$$\mathbf{T} \, \Delta t = \Delta \mathbf{L}$$

In other words, the angular impulse applied to an object is equal to the change in angular momentum it produces. Recall that, for a rigid body, angular momentum $\mathbf{L} = I\omega$. This result will be useful when we consider collisions between rigid bodies.

If the torque $\mathbf{T} = 0$, the theorem gives $\Delta \mathbf{L} = 0$, angular momentum conservation. Therefore, the principle of angular momentum conservation is a special case of the angular impulse-momentum theorem as stated earlier.

Rotational kinetic energy

Because a rigid body can rotate as well as translate, there is kinetic energy associated with rotational motion in addition to the kinetic energy associated with linear motion. Recall that the linear kinetic energy is given by the following formula:

$$E_k = \frac{1}{2} m v^2$$

We said that moment of inertia is analogous to mass, and angular velocity is analogous to linear velocity. Therefore, you might not be surprised to learn that rotational kinetic energy is given by the following formula:

$$E_k = \frac{1}{2} I \omega^2$$

Therefore, the total kinetic energy of a rigid body is the sum of these two kinetic energies.

Work-energy theorem for rotational motion

In an analogy of the work done by a force, the work done by a torque is equal to the product of the torque and the angular displacement it produces:

$$W = T\theta$$

We can then apply the work-energy theorem (see Chapter 4) to the case of rotational motion, concluding that the work done by a torque is equal to the change in rotational kinetic energy that it produces:

$$\Delta W = \Delta E_k$$

In that case, the kinetic energy is given by $E_k = \frac{1}{2} I\omega^2$.

Simulating rigid body dynamics

We are now ready to implement rigid body dynamics. To do this, we will need to modify the `Forcer` and `MultiForcer` classes.

Modifying Forcer and MultiForcer to include rotation

The `ForcerRB` class modifies `Forcer` in a straightforward way to include torque and angular acceleration, in an exact analogy to force and linear acceleration. The code listing is shown in full with the added bits in bold:

```
package com.physicscodes.motion{
        import com.physicscodes.motion.Mover;
        import com.physicscodes.motion.Forces;
        import com.physicscodes.objects.RigidBody;
        import com.physicscodes.math.Vector2D;

        public class ForcerRB extends Mover{
                private var _rigidBody:RigidBody;
                private var _force:Vector2D;
                private var _acc:Vector2D;
                private var _torque:Number;
                private var _alp:Number;

                public function ForcerRB(prigidBody:RigidBody):void{
                        _rigidBody = prigidBody;
                        super(prigidBody);
                }

                public function get force():Vector2D {
                        return _force;
                }

                public function set force(pforce):void {
                        _force = pforce;
                }
```

```
            public function get torque():Number {
                    return _torque;
            }

            public function set torque(ptorque):void {
                    _torque = ptorque;
            }

            override protected function moveObject():void{
                    super.moveObject();
                    calcForce();
                    updateAccel();
                    updateVelo();
            }

            protected function calcForce():void{
                    _force = Forces.zeroForce();
                    _torque = 0;
            }

            private function updateAccel():void{
                    _acc = _force.multiply(1/_rigidBody.mass);
                    _alp = _torque/_rigidBody.momentOfInertia;
            }

            private function updateVelo():void{
                    _rigidBody.velo2D = _rigidBody.velo2D.addScaled(_acc,dt);
                    _rigidBody.angVelo += _alp*dt;
            }
        }
}
```

In this code, _torque represents the *magnitude* of the torque and _alp represents the *magnitude* of the angular acceleration. Hence, they are both numbers rather than Vector2D objects like the corresponding _force and _acc variables. The reason we only represent the magnitudes of the torque and angular acceleration is that in the 2D examples that we'll consider the rotation can only take place in the x–y plane (there *is* only one plane), so the direction of any associated angular velocity, angular acceleration, and torque will always be in a hypothetical third dimension that sticks either into or out of that plane. The sign of the relevant quantity will determine which way it points.

The MultiForcerRB class modifies the MultiForcer2 class in a similar way to allow multiple rigid bodies to be subjected to a torque and to experience a resulting angular acceleration.

A simple test

Let's test the new rotational dynamics code with a simple example. In RigidBodyDynamics.as, we create a square rigid body and then subject it to an imposed torque. The setup code looks like this:

```
package{
        import flash.display.Sprite;
        import com.physicscodes.math.Vector2D;
```

```
        import com.physicscodes.objects.RectangleRB;

        public class RigidBodyDynamics extends Sprite{
                public function RigidBodyDynamics():void{
                        init();
                }
                private function init():void{
                        var cm:Vector2D = new Vector2D(100,200);
                        var rectangle:RectangleRB = new RectangleRB(100,100,cm);
                        rectangle.mass = 1;
                        rectangle.momentOfInertia = 5;
                        rectangle.velo2D = new Vector2D(10,0);
                        rectangle.angVelo = 1;
                        addChild(rectangle);

                        var mover:RigidBodyMover = new RigidBodyMover(rectangle);
                        mover.startTime();
                }
        }
}
```

The body's mass and moment of inertia are set and its velocity and angular velocity are initialized. The RigidBodyMover class that drives the simulation extends ForcerRB and looks like this:

```
package {
        import com.physicscodes.motion.ForcerRB;
        import com.physicscodes.motion.Forces;
        import com.physicscodes.objects.RigidBody;

        public class RigidBodyMover extends ForcerRB{
                private var _body:RigidBody;
                private var _kLin:Number=0.1; // linear damping factor
                private var _kAng:Number=0.5; // angular damping factor

                public function RigidBodyMover(pbody:RigidBody):void{
                        _body = pbody;
                        super(pbody);
                }

                override protected function calcForce():void{
                        force = Forces.zeroForce();
                        force = force.addScaled(_body.velo2D,-_kLin); // linear damping
                        torque = 1;
                        torque += -_kAng*_body.angVelo; // angular damping
                }
        }
}
```

As you can see in the calcForce() method, a torque of magnitude 1 unit is applied at each timestep. If that was all that was done, the square would undergo continuous angular acceleration, rotating faster and faster. Therefore, an angular damping term proportional to the angular velocity is also applied to limit its angular velocity. A linear damping term is also added to the force.

If you run the simulation, you will find that the square translates to the right while rotating in a clockwise sense. As time progresses, its linear velocity decreases until it stops (because there is no driving force but a retarding force proportional to its velocity), whereas its angular velocity increases to a constant value (you can check this by tracing the angular velocity at each timestep). The latter happens because the applied torque of 1 unit tends to increase the angular velocity whereas the angular damping term grows as the angular velocity increases. Therefore, at some point the damping term balances the applied torque and rotational equilibrium is achieved (as well as linear equilibrium). It's the equivalent of terminal velocity for rotational motion. You can calculate the "terminal angular velocity" in the following way.

Start with the equation of angular motion relating torque and angular acceleration:

$$T = I\alpha$$

In the present simulation, because there is a driving torque of 1 unit and a retarding torque proportional to the angular velocity, the resultant torque T is given by this:

$$T = 1 - k\omega$$

Using the previous equation of motion then gives the following:

$$I\alpha = 1 - k\omega$$

At equilibrium, the angular acceleration α is zero. Therefore, the left hand side of this equation is zero. Rearranging gives the following result:

$$\omega = 1/k$$

This is the "terminal" angular velocity. Using the value of k = 0.5 in the code gives a value of 2 for this angular velocity. If you trace the body's angular velocity at each timestep in the simulation you will find that it indeed converges to this value.

Experiment by changing the mass and moment of inertia of the body. You will find that they affect the time it takes to achieve linear and rotational equilibrium respectively, but do not affect the final linear velocity (0) or final angular velocity (2).

We can now simulate rotational dynamics! Let's build some more interesting examples then.

Example: a simple wind turbine simulation

In this example we'll extend MultiForcerRB to simulate the motion of more than one rigid body. The objects we'll simulate are wind turbines. So we start by creating a TurbineRB class that extends PolygonRB, drawing a filled polygon consisting of six vertices. Three of the vertices lie equidistant along the circumference of an inner circle, and the other three lie on an outer circle. The vertices on the inner and outer circle alternate so that the resulting Polygon looks like a wind turbine. The TurbineRB takes parameters as shown here:

```
public function TurbineRB(pri:Number, pro:Number, pcm:Vector2D, pcolor:uint=0x000000,↪
pim:Number=1, pmass:Number=1, pcharge:Number=0){}
```

The new parameters are the first two, `pri` and `pro`, representing the inner and outer radius, respectively. The code then positions the vertices at the right place and draws the resulting filled polygon.

The file `WindTurbines.as` creates three turbines of different sizes, as shown in Figure 13-7.

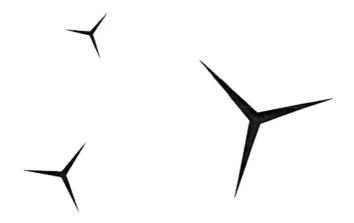

Figure 13-7. Creating wind turbines!

The code in `WindTurbines.as` assigns different masses and moments of inertia to the turbines. The masses are assigned in proportion to the square of the outer radius of the turbines (treating them as two-dimensional), while the moments of inertia are in proportion to the fourth power of the outer radius (because I is proportional to mr^2, and m is itself proportional to r^2). The masses themselves are really irrelevant because the turbines will only rotate. Changing their values to anything else won't make any difference to the rotation. But we set appropriate values for physical consistency. Here is the code that does all this:

```
package{
        import flash.display.Sprite;
        import com.physicscodes.math.Vector2D;
        import com.physicscodes.objects.TurbineRB;

        public class WindTurbines extends Sprite{
                public function WindTurbines():void{
                        init();
                }
                private function init():void{
                        var turbines:Array = new Array();
                        var cm:Vector2D;

                        cm = new Vector2D(200,150);
                        var turbine1:TurbineRB = new TurbineRB(4,50,cm);
                        turbine1.mass = 1;
                        turbine1.momentOfInertia = 1;
                        addChild(turbine1);
```

```
                    turbines.push(turbine1);

                    cm = new Vector2D(150,400);
                    var turbine2:TurbineRB = new TurbineRB(6,75,cm);
                    turbine2.mass = 2.25;
                    turbine2.momentOfInertia = 5;
                    addChild(turbine2);
                    turbines.push(turbine2);

                    cm = new Vector2D(500,300);
                    var turbine3:TurbineRB = new TurbineRB(12,150,cm);
                    turbine3.mass = 9;
                    turbine3.momentOfInertia = 81;
                    addChild(turbine3);
                    turbines.push(turbine3);

                    var mover:TurbinesMover = new TurbinesMover(turbines);
                    mover.startTime();
                }
        }
}
```

The mover class is TurbinesMover, which extends MultiForcer2 and looks like this:

```
package {
        import com.physicscodes.motion.MultiForcerRB;
        import com.physicscodes.motion.Forces;
        import com.physicscodes.objects.RigidBody;
        import com.physicscodes.math.Vector2D;
        import flash.events.MouseEvent;

        public class TurbinesMover extends MultiForcerRB{
                private var _bodies:Array;
                private var _k:Number=0.5; // angular damping factor
                private var _tqMax:Number=2;
                private var _tq:Number=0;

                public function TurbinesMover(pbodies:Array):void{
                        _bodies = pbodies;
                        _bodies[0].stage.addEventListener(MouseEvent.MOUSE_DOWN, onDown);
                        super(pbodies);
                }

                override protected function calcForce(pbody:RigidBody,pnum:uint):void{
                        force = Forces.zeroForce();
                        torque = _tq;
                        torque += -_k*pbody.angVelo; // angular damping
                }

                private function onDown(e:MouseEvent):void{
                        _bodies[0].stage.addEventListener(MouseEvent.MOUSE_UP,onUp);
                        _tq = _tqMax;
                }
                private function onUp(e:MouseEvent):void{
```

```
                         _bodies[0].stage.removeEventListener(MouseEvent.MOUSE_UP, onUp);
                         _tq = 0;
                    }
              }
      }
```

This code should look familiar from the last example. In the calcForce() method, we specify a zero resultant force and a driving torque of magnitude _tq as well as an angular damping term proportional to the angular velocity. The value of the torque magnitude _tq is controlled by mouse-click event handlers: if the mouse is pressed, _tq is given a value _tqMax (which is 2 by default); if not, it has a value of 0. This means any time the mouse is clicked, a constant driving torque is applied to each turbine; otherwise, the driving torque is zero.

Run the simulation and click anywhere on the stage. What do you see? The smallest turbine starts turning almost immediately while the largest one only starts turning slowly. This illustrates the concept of rotational inertia: a rigid body with a larger moment of inertia will accelerate less than one with a smaller moment of inertia for the same torque. This is, of course, nothing but the consequence of $T = I\alpha$. Similarly, if you stop pressing the mouse, the smallest turbine will stop quickly; the largest one will stop only after a long time.

While this simulation captures the basic dynamics of a rotating turbine, more work is needed to make a more realistic simulation of how it operates in practice with wind forcing. For example, the torque and damping coefficient for each turbine will depend on characteristics such as its surface area. Wind modeling is another subject in its own right. We won't dwell on these complicating factors; instead we'll move to another example!

Example: Rolling down an inclined plane

Rolling involves an interesting and particularly instructive application of rotational dynamics, but can be fairly complex to understand. Therefore we'll approach the subject through a specific example.

In Chapter 7, we simulated the motion of a ball sliding down an inclined plane. One of the things noted there was that the ball would slide only if the incline were steeper than a certain critical angle that depends on the coefficient of static friction. The simulation worked well, but there was a major defect: the ball would not move if the angle was not high enough. This is hardly realistic; in reality balls *roll* down inclined planes whatever their angle of inclination!

From a particle to a rigid body simulation

We are now in a position to incorporate rolling into that simulation. But first we need to treat the ball as a rigid body instead of a particle. So let's dig out that old code and modify it to make use of our new rigid body classes BallRB and ForcerRB. The new setup file, Rolling.as, initially looks like this:

```
package{
        import flash.display.Sprite;
        import com.physicscodes.objects.BallRB;
        import com.physicscodes.math.Vector2D;

        public class Rolling extends Sprite{
                public function Rolling():void{
                        init();
```

```
                }
                private function init():void{
                        // create an inclined plane
                        var xtop:Number=50;
                        var ytop:Number=150;
                        var xbot:Number=450;
                        var ybot:Number=250;

                        var surface:Sprite = new Sprite;
                        with (surface.graphics) {
                                lineStyle(1,0x333333,1);
                                moveTo(xtop,ytop);
                                lineTo(xbot,ybot);
                        }
                        addChild(surface);
                        var angle:Number = Math.atan2(ybot-ytop,xbot-xtop);

                        // create a rigid ball
                        var radius:Number = 20;
                        var cm:Vector2D = new Vector2D(xtop+radius*Math.sin(angle),↪
ytop-radius*Math.cos(angle));
                        var ball:BallRB = new BallRB(cm,radius,0x0000ff);
                        ball.mass = 20;
                        ball.momentOfInertia = 0.4*ball.mass*ball.radius*ball.radius;
                        addChild(ball);

                        // make the ball move
                        var mover:RollingMover=new RollingMover(ball,angle);
                        mover.startTime();
                }
        }
}
```

This is similar to the code we had before in Chapter 7, and it produces the setup shown in Figure 13-8. In addition, we have specified the mass and moment of inertia of the ball. For the latter, we are using the formula for the moment of inertia of a solid sphere ($I = 2mr^2/5$), assuming we are simulating a solid spherical ball.

Figure 13-8. A ball rolling down an inclined plane

The new mover class is `RollingMover.as`, and here is what it looks like initially (we will soon modify it):

```
package {
        import com.physicscodes.motion.ForcerRB;
        import com.physicscodes.motion.Forces;
        import com.physicscodes.objects.RigidBody;
        import com.physicscodes.objects.BallRB;
        import com.physicscodes.math.Vector2D;

        public class RollingMover extends ForcerRB{
                private var _body:BallRB;
                private var _angle:Number;
                private var _g:Number=10;
                private var _ck:Number=0.2;
                private var _cs:Number=0.25;
                private var _vtol:Number=0.000001;

                public function RollingMover(pbody:BallRB,pangle:Number):void{
                        _body = pbody;
                        _angle = pangle;
                        super(pbody);
                }

                override protected function calcForce():void{
                        var gravity:Vector2D = Forces.constantGravity(_body.mass,_g);
                        var normal:Vector2D = Vector2D.vector2D(_body.mass*_g*Math.cos⤷
(_angle),0.5*Math.PI-_angle,false);
                        var coeff:Number;

                        if (_body.velo2D.length < _vtol){  // static friction
                                coeff = Math.min(_cs*normal.length,_body.mass*_g*Math.sin⤷
(_angle));
                        }else{  // kinetic friction
                                coeff = _ck*normal.length;
                        }
                        var friction:Vector2D = normal.perp(coeff);
                        force = Forces.add([gravity, normal, friction]);
                }
        }
}
```

If you compare this class with the corresponding mover class `ObliqueMover` from Chapter 7, you'll find that it does the same thing, with identical forces and parameter values. All that we've done so far is to replace `Ball` with `BallRB` and `Forcer` with `ForcerRB` so that we can introduce rigid body dynamics. If you were to run the code in its current form, the ball would not move, just as in Chapter 7, unless you made the incline steeper (for example, by changing the value of ybot in the setup file to 260 or more). We know that in real life the ball would roll down the slope even if it can't slide. So what's missing?

Simulating rolling without slipping

You might be tempted to just add a torque to `calcForce()` and see whether that makes the ball roll. As you can see from the last line of code, there are three forces included in the simulation: gravity, the normal force, and friction (see the force diagram in Figure 13-9). Because both gravity and the normal force act through the center of mass, they do not have any associated torque about the center of mass. Only the frictional force has a torque about the center of mass of the ball, and the magnitude of that torque is fr, where f is the magnitude of the friction force, and r is the radius of the ball.

Add the following line of code after the last line in `calcForce()`:

```
torque = _body.radius*friction.length;
```

Now run the code. What do you find? Sure the ball rotates faster and faster under the action of the torque generated by the frictional force, but it does not go anywhere! We are still missing something. Leave the torque code because it is correct. But we need to do a bit more thinking.

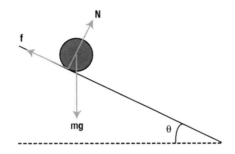

Figure 13-9. Force diagram for a ball rolling down an inclined plane

Let's take another look at Figure 13-9. What else needs to change apart from accounting for the torque due to friction? The only other thing is whether the three forces are still the same with rolling. Now gravity is a fixed force that depends only on the mass of the object, so it will remain exactly the same, with magnitude mg and acting vertically downward. So will the normal force because it must still be equal and opposite to the component of gravity normal to the plane (there is no motion in that direction). Therefore, the normal force still has magnitude mg cos(θ) and acts normal to the plane, as implemented in the code.

But what needs to change is the frictional force. Rolling friction is generally smaller than static or kinetic friction (that's what makes the wheel such a useful invention!). At the moment, the frictional force is generally too large. So the problem really boils down to one thing: to specify the correct frictional force that will give rolling without slipping.

The point is that the condition for rolling without slipping constrains the linear and rotational motion to "work together," and this in turn constrains the magnitude of the frictional force. By formulating the constraint from first principles and working out its implications using the equations of linear and rotational motion, it is possible to deduce what the frictional force must be. Let's do that now.

To make things easier to visualize (but without loss of generality) think of a ball or wheel of radius r that is rolling on flat ground with an angular velocity ω, as shown in Figure 13-10.

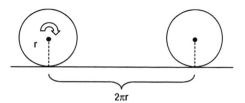

Figure 13-10. A ball or wheel rolling without slipping.

If the ball or wheel rolls without slipping (let's call this *pure rolling*), when it completes one revolution it has moved forward a distance equal to 2πr. It does that in a time equal to its period T, which is equal to 2π/ω (see Chapter 9). The velocity of its center of mass is given by the ratio of the distance moved to the time taken, which is therefore given by the following:

$$v = r\omega$$

You will recall that this is just the formula for the linear velocity of any point on the circumference of a circle; in pure rolling it also gives the velocity with which the whole object moves forward. This formula holds at any time, even if the angular velocity (and therefore the linear center of mass velocity) is changing. Differentiating with respect to time then gives the equivalent formula relating the linear center of mass acceleration to the angular acceleration:

$$a = r\alpha$$

This is the crucial constraint that will help us to calculate the pure rolling frictional force (denoted by **f**). The way that force comes into play is of course through the equations of motion. Applying the linear equation of motion **F** = m**a** along the slope gives (see Figure 13-9):

$$mg\sin(\theta) - f = ma$$

Applying the angular equation of motion T = Iα gives the following:

$$fr = I\alpha$$

We need to solve for the frictional force f, but we don't know the acceleration a or the angular acceleration α. But we do have the constraint a = rα that relates them, so we can use that together with the previous equation to eliminate α and obtain the following relationship between the acceleration a and the frictional force f:

$$a = fr^2/I$$

We can now substitute this into the previous equation that arose from the linear equation of motion and, after rearranging, obtain the following final result:

$$f = \frac{mg\sin(\theta)}{1 + mr^2/I}$$

We can also then use the previous equation connecting a and f to deduce the following formula for the acceleration of the rolling object:

$$a = \frac{g\sin(\theta)}{1 + I/(mr^2)}$$

Comparing this with the acceleration of a freely falling object, g, we find that the acceleration of a rolling object is reduced by a factor that depends on the ratio I/mr^2 for the body, as well as on the angle of inclination of the plane (the latter is just because we are looking at the acceleration component down the slope, rather than vertically downward).

Now that we have the formula for the frictional force for pure rolling, it's a simple matter to include it in the code. Remove the `if` block of code that computes the magnitude of the friction `coeff` in `calcForce()` and replace it by the following code, which is exactly the formula for f:

```
coeff = _body.mass*_g*Math.sin(_angle) / (1 + _body.mass*_body.radius*_body.radius /↪
 _body.momentOfInertia);
```

Now run the code, and you'll have the ball rolling down the slope without slipping!

Allowing both slipping and rolling

Now increase the slope by changing the value of ybot to 850 and rerun the simulation. The slope is now very steep, but the ball will still roll down without slipping. Now we have the opposite problem: the ball does not know how to slip!

To make the simulation more realistic, we need to implement the possibility of both rolling and slipping in a simple way just by adding the following `if` block just after the line that computes `coeff`:

```
if (coeff > _cs*normal.length){
        coeff = _ck*normal.length;
}
```

This imposes a limit on the maximum magnitude that the rolling friction can have; it resets the magnitude of the computed friction to the kinetic friction if it exceeds the static friction. Run the code and you'll see that the ball now slips as it rolls down. If you change ybot back to 250 you will find that the ball undergoes pure rolling as before. In fact, you can add a `trace("slipping")` line inside the `if` block and run the code for different values of ybot. This will tell you unequivocally when the ball is slipping. With the given parameter values, you should find that pure rolling occurs up to the value of ybot = 500, corresponding to a slope angle of approximately 41.2°. We leave it as an exercise for you to figure out why. (Hint: equate the expression for the rolling friction given in the last subsection with that for the limiting static friction $\mu N = \mu mg \cos(\theta)$).

More experiments with the simulation

A classic college physics problem is the following: suppose you release two solid cylinders, a light one and a heavy one, at the same height on a slope. Assuming that they both roll down the slope without slipping, which one will reach the bottom first? Well, you can use your simulation to find out!

First, change the value of `ybot` in `Rolling.as` back to 250, so that you have pure rolling. Then change the moment of inertia formula to the following:

```
ball.momentOfInertia = 0.5*ball.mass*ball.radius*ball.radius;
```

This differs from the previous formula for a sphere only in the factor of 0.5; the moment of inertia of a cylinder is $I = mr^2/2$. Finally, add the following code at the end of the `calcForce()` method in `RollingMover.as`:

```
if (_body.y > 250-_body.radius){
        trace(time);
        stopTime();
}
```

This will tell you when the cylinder has reached the bottom and will stop the simulation when that happens. Experiment with the simulation using different values for the mass and the radius of the cylinder and make a note of the time it takes for it to reach the bottom. What do you notice?

Well, counterintuitive as it may seem, you should find that the cylinder always takes the same time to reach the bottom of the slope, regardless of its mass or its radius. To see why that is so, refer to the formula for the acceleration derived in the last subsection. Because the moment of inertia of a cylinder is given by $I = mr^2/2$, the ratio I/mr^2 that appears in that formula has the value of 0.5, giving the acceleration of a solid cylinder down the slope as

$$a = \frac{2}{3}g\sin(\theta)$$

This interesting result tells us that the acceleration is completely independent of the properties of the cylinder such as mass and radius or moment of inertia: they've all cancelled out! So, as long as two cylinders are both solid, they should always roll down a slope at the same rate!

However, a hollow cylindrical tube has a moment of inertia given by approximately $I = mr^2$. Going through the same calculation then gives the following acceleration:

$$a = \frac{1}{2}g\sin(\theta)$$

So a hollow cylindrical tube would accelerate more slowly and therefore take longer to reach the bottom of the slope.

Rigid body collisions and bouncing

In Chapter 11, we spent a considerable amount of time discussing particle collisions and bouncing. You might perhaps have felt that the math got a bit complicated then. Well, with rigid bodies, things get even more complicated! With rigid bodies you have to take into account both the linear motion and the rotation of the objects involved in the collision. Particles, spheres, and circular objects don't rotate as a result of collisions (at least if we assume the collisions are frictionless). That's because for such objects the line of collision is always through their center of mass (see Figure 13-11), so the impulsive force due to collision does not generate a torque.

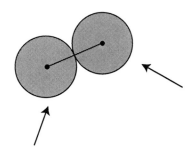

Figure 13-11. Colliding spheres

For an object with a more complicated shape, this won't be true in general. As with a sphere, the line of collision is normal to the surface of an object, but it may not pass through the center of mass of the object (see Figure 13-12). Hence, a torque about the center of each of the colliding objects is generated in this case, causing them to rotate.

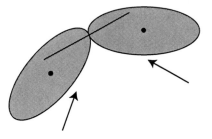

Figure 13-12. Collision between two rigid bodies of arbitrary shape

The task of collision resolution in this more general case is therefore to calculate the final linear velocities v_1^f and v_2^f *and* angular velocities ω_1^f and ω_2^f of the two objects, given their initial linear velocities v_1^i and v_2^i and angular velocities ω_1^i and ω_2^i (the objects could already be rotating before the collision) just before the impact. This is what we shall do in this section.

Linear impulse due to collision

The linear velocities v_1^i, v_2^i, v_1^f, and v_2^f are the initial and final linear velocities of the center of mass of the two colliding rigid bodies (denoted by the subscript 1 and 2, respectively). The angular velocities ω_1^i, ω_2^i,

$\omega_1{}^f$, and $\omega_2{}^f$ are the corresponding angular velocities about the respective center of mass of each rigid body.

The starting point is to apply the impulse-momentum theorem:

$$\mathbf{F}\,\Delta t = \Delta\mathbf{p} = m\,\Delta\mathbf{v}$$

Let's denote the impulse $\mathbf{F}\Delta t$ by the symbol $\mathbf{J}$. Then, applying the impulse-momentum theorem to each rigid body and remembering that they experience equal and opposite impulse, we can write the following equations:

$$\mathbf{J} = m_1\left(\mathbf{v}_1^f - \mathbf{v}_1^i\right)$$

$$-\mathbf{J} = m_2\left(\mathbf{v}_2^f - \mathbf{v}_2^i\right)$$

We note in passing that together these two equations imply the following equation:

$$m_1\mathbf{v}_1^i + m_2\mathbf{v}_2^i = m_1\mathbf{v}_1^f + m_2\mathbf{v}_2^f$$

This is nothing but conservation of momentum, as we saw in Chapter 11. We used this equation together with the one for the coefficient of restitution C_R to obtain the final velocities $\mathbf{v}_1{}^f$ and $\mathbf{v}_2{}^f$ (denoted therein by $\mathbf{v}_1$ and $\mathbf{v}_2$) in terms of the initial velocities (denoted therein by $\mathbf{u}_1$ and $\mathbf{u}_2$). Refer to the section "Calculating velocities after an inelastic collision" in Chapter 11. Here things are more complicated because we also have the angular velocities to worry about, and we need to proceed via a slightly different route.

The approach we'll adopt is to express the final velocities in terms of the impulse $\mathbf{J}$ and then to work out what $\mathbf{J}$ is. For the linear velocities, this is simply a matter of rearranging the previous equations involving $\mathbf{J}$ to obtain the following:

$$\mathbf{v}_1^f = \mathbf{v}_1^i + \mathbf{J}/m_1$$

$$\mathbf{v}_2^f = \mathbf{v}_2^i - \mathbf{J}/m_2$$

As with particle collisions, we can supplement these equations by one involving a coefficient of restitution. In the particle case, the coefficient of restitution was equal to the negative ratio of the relative normal velocities of the colliding particles before and after the collision. One might be tempted to assume the same here, using the linear velocities of the center of mass of each particle. But, in fact, the relevant velocities in this case are the linear velocities of the points of contact on each body normal to the contact surfaces. Referring again to Figure 13-12, these are the velocities at the point P where the two rigid bodies make contact. Let's denote these velocities by $\mathbf{v}_{p1}$ and $\mathbf{v}_{p2}$. They are each given by the vector sum of the center of mass velocity and the velocity at the point P due to rotation about the center of mass.

So we have the following equations:

$$\mathbf{v}_{p1} = \mathbf{v}_1 + \boldsymbol{\omega}_1 \times \mathbf{r}_{p1}$$

$$\mathbf{v}_{p2} = \mathbf{v}_2 + \boldsymbol{\omega}_2 \times \mathbf{r}_{p2}$$

These equations are valid at any time and, in particular, just before and just after the collision. Hence, they can be written with the "i" and "f" superscripts we have used before. The vectors $\mathbf{r}_{p1}$ and $\mathbf{r}_{p2}$, which are the position vectors of the point P relative to the center of mass of each body, are the same during that brief interval, so they do not require these superscripts.

The relative velocities before and after the collision are given by the following:

$$\mathbf{v}_r^i = \mathbf{v}_{p1}^i - \mathbf{v}_{p2}^i$$

$$\mathbf{v}_r^f = \mathbf{v}_{p1}^f - \mathbf{v}_{p2}^f$$

The coefficient of restitution is then given by the negative ratio of the normal components of these relative velocities (where **n** is the unit normal vector):

$$C_R = -\frac{\mathbf{v}_r^f \bullet \mathbf{n}}{\mathbf{v}_r^i \bullet \mathbf{n}}$$

The problem is that this involves the final angular velocities as well, which we don't know. So we need to solve for the angular velocities simultaneously. That means we need more equations. This comes from applying the angular impulse-momentum theorem.

Angular impulse due to collision

Let's now apply the angular impulse-momentum theorem:

$$\mathbf{T}\,\Delta t = \Delta \mathbf{L}$$

Because **T** = **r** x **F** and **L** = I**ω**, this is equivalent to the following:

$$\mathbf{r} \times \mathbf{J} = I\,\Delta\boldsymbol{\omega}$$

Applying this to each body and again remembering that they experience equal and opposite impulses gives us the following equations:

$$\mathbf{r}_{p1} \times \mathbf{J} = I_1\left(\boldsymbol{\omega}_1^f - \boldsymbol{\omega}_1^i\right)$$

$$-\mathbf{r}_{p1} \times \mathbf{J} = I_2\left(\boldsymbol{\omega}_2^f - \boldsymbol{\omega}_2^i\right)$$

These equations can be rearranged to give the final angular velocities in terms of the initial angular velocities and the impulse:

$$\boldsymbol{\omega}_1^f = \boldsymbol{\omega}_1^i + \mathbf{r}_{p1} \times \mathbf{J}/I_1$$

$$\boldsymbol{\omega}_2^f = \boldsymbol{\omega}_2^i - \mathbf{r}_{p2} \times \mathbf{J}/I_2$$

The only thing we need now is the impulse **J**, and we can then obtain both the linear and angular velocities.

The final result

It is possible to solve all these equations together to obtain an expression for the impulse **J**. We'll spare you the detailed algebra and just give the final answer. Writing **J** = J**n**, where J is the magnitude of the impulse, and **n** is the unit normal vector as before (because the impulse is along the direction of the normal), we obtain the following expression for the magnitude of the impulse:

$$J = -\frac{\left(1 + C_R\right)\mathbf{v}_r^i \bullet \mathbf{n}}{1/m_1 + 1/m_2 + \left(\mathbf{r}_{p1} \times \mathbf{n}\right)^2/I_1 + \left(\mathbf{r}_{p2} \times \mathbf{n}\right)^2/I_2}$$

In the preceding equation, the square of each of the cross product terms (which are vector quantities) refers to taking the dot product with itself.

In the case in which the second rigid body is an immovable object, such as a wall, we can make m_2 and I_2 infinite in the previous equation (which eliminates the terms involving them). Note that the relative velocity $\mathbf{v}_r^i$ in that case is just the velocity $\mathbf{v}_{p1}^i$ of point P on body 1. We then end up with the following:

$$J = -\frac{\left(1 + C_R\right)\mathbf{v}_{p1}^i \bullet \mathbf{n}}{1/m_1 + \left(\mathbf{r}_{p1} \times \mathbf{n}\right)^2/I_1}$$

For easy reference, let's repeat the equations that allow you to then calculate the final linear and angular velocities:

$$\mathbf{v}_1^f = \mathbf{v}_1^i + \mathbf{J}/m_1$$

$$\mathbf{v}_2^f = \mathbf{v}_2^i - \mathbf{J}/m_2$$

$$\boldsymbol{\omega}_1^f = \boldsymbol{\omega}_1^i + \mathbf{r}_{p1} \times \mathbf{J}/I_1$$

$$\boldsymbol{\omega}_2^f = \boldsymbol{\omega}_2^i - \mathbf{r}_{p2} \times \mathbf{J}/I_2$$

In the case of the second object being an immovable wall, $\mathbf{v}_2^f$ and $\boldsymbol{\omega}_2^f$ are zero.

Having been through that complex-looking math, you'll be glad to know that the previous formulas are not actually very hard to code up. In coding terms, the trickier aspects of simulating rigid body collisions are probably those of collision detection and repositioning, which are equally important and require careful consideration when creating realistic simulations.

Note that these equations are valid for collisions between rigid bodies of any shape. In the examples we will put together shortly, we are going to consider polygons. In that case, the most common collision event is the collision of a vertex of one polygon with an edge of another. The line of collision is then the normal to the relevant edge. But collisions between the vertices of two polygons are also quite common, and it is important to have a method to handle them. Other less-common collision scenarios include two vertices of an object hitting two different objects at the same time.

To avoid complications associated with these different collision scenarios and the collision detection and handling methods needed to deal with them, we will start with a simple example of a single polygon bouncing off a floor. This will allow us to focus on implementing the collision resolution method that was developed in the preceding sections. Afterward we will build a more complex simulation involving multiple colliding and bouncing objects, which will require us to confront some of the trickier issues mentioned here.

Example: Simulating a single bouncing block

We will now build a simple simulation of a rectangular block bouncing off a floor, so that we have a single movable object. The setup file for this simulation, `RigidBodyBouncing.as`, looks like this:

```
package{
        import flash.display.Sprite;
        import com.physicscodes.objects.RectangleRB;
        import com.physicscodes.objects.Wall;
        import com.physicscodes.math.Vector2D;

        public class RigidBodyBouncing extends Sprite{
                public function RigidBodyBouncing():void{
                        init();
                }
```

```
                private function init():void{
                        // create a rectangular block
                        var cm:Vector2D = new Vector2D(275,100);
                        var body:RectangleRB = new RectangleRB(100,50,cm,0x0000ff);
                        body.mass = 1;
                        body.momentOfInertia = 5000;
                        body.angDispl = Math.PI/4;
                        addChild(body);

                        // create the floor
                        var wall:Wall;
                        wall=new Wall(new Vector2D(30,350),new Vector2D(520,350));
                        addChild(wall);

                        // get things moving
                        var mover:RigidBodyBouncer =new RigidBodyBouncer(body,wall);
                        mover.startTime();
                }
        }
}
```

We create a rectangular block as a RectangleRB instance and a floor object using the Wall class of Chapter 11. The block is given a moment of inertia of 5000 and an initial orientation of π/4 radians (45°). The simulation is driven by the RigidBodyBouncer class, which looks like this:

```
package {
        import com.physicscodes.motion.ForcerRB;
        import com.physicscodes.motion.Forces;
        import com.physicscodes.objects.PolygonRB;
        import com.physicscodes.objects.Wall;
        import com.physicscodes.math.Vector2D;

        public class RigidBodyBouncer extends ForcerRB{
                private var _body:PolygonRB;
                private var _wall:Wall;
                private var _g:Number=20;
                private var _cr:Number=0.4; // coefficient of restitution
                private var _k:Number=1; // angular damping factor

                public function RigidBodyBouncer(pbody:PolygonRB,pwall:Wall):void{
                        _body = pbody;
                        _wall = pwall;
                        super(pbody);
                }

                override protected function calcForce():void{
                        // external forces and torques
                        force = Forces.constantGravity(_body.mass,_g);
                        torque = 0; // no external torque since gravity is the only force
                        torque += -_k*_body.angVelo; // damping

                        // collision detection
                        var testCollision:Boolean = false;
                        var j:uint;
```

```
                        for (var i:uint=0; i<_body.vertices.length;i++){
                        if (_body.pos2D.add(_body.vertices[i].rotate(_body.angDispl)).y >=↪
 _wall.p1.y){
                                if (testCollision==false){
                                        testCollision = true;
                                        j = i;
                                }else{ // that means one vertex is already touching
                                        stopTime(); // block is lying flat on floor, so stop
                                }
                        }
                        }

                        // collision resolution
                        if (testCollision == true){
                                _body.ypos += _body.pos2D.add(_body.vertices[j].rotate↪
 (_body.angDispl)).y*(-1) + _wall.p1.y;
                                var normal:Vector2D = _wall.normal;
                                var rp1:Vector2D = _body.vertices[j].rotate(_body.angDispl);
                                var vp1:Vector2D = _body.velo2D.add(rp1.perp↪
 (-_body.angVelo*rp1.length));
                                var rp1Xnormal:Number = rp1.crossProduct(normal);
                                var impulse:Number = -(1+_cr)*vp1.dotProduct(normal) /↪
 (1/_body.mass + rp1Xnormal*rp1Xnormal/_body.momentOfInertia);
                                _body.velo2D = _body.velo2D.add(normal.multiply↪
 (impulse / _body.mass));
                                _body.angVelo += rp1.crossProduct(normal)*impulse↪
 /_body.momentOfInertia;
                                testCollision = false;
                        }
                }
            }
    }
}
```

As you can see, the code looks surprisingly short given the apparent complexity of the preceding discussion of the theory. The code in calcForce() is split into three parts, specifying the external forces and torques, collision detection, and collision resolution. The first part prescribes gravity as the only force on the block and specifies a zero external torque because gravity does not generate torque about its center of mass. We do include a damping torque, though, the magnitude of which is controlled by the damping parameter _k (which you can set to zero if you wish).

The collision detection code loops over the vertices of the block and tests to see whether any of them is lower than the floor using the following condition:

```
if (_body.pos2D.add(_body.vertices[i].rotate(_body.angDispl)).y >= _wall.p1.y){}
```

This line might look a bit complicated, so let's break it down. First the easy bit: `_wall.p1.y` just gives the y position of the wall. Next `_body.vertices[i]` is the position vector of the vertex currently being tested relative to the center of mass of the block. The `rotate()` method is a newly created method of the `Vector2D` class that rotates a vector through the angle specified as its argument (in radians). It is defined as follows:

```
public function rotate(angle:Number):Vector2D{
        return new Vector2D(_x*Math.cos(angle)-_y*Math.sin(angle), _x*Math.sin(angle)↪
 +_y*Math.cos(angle));
}
```

It uses some trigonometry to do that, which you may try to figure out as an exercise. We are therefore rotating the position vector of the current vertex through an angle equal to the angular displacement `_body.angDispl` of the block to account for the block's orientation. Then we add this to the block's (center of mass) position. We do this because we need the position vector of the vertex in the Flash coordinate system, not in the center of mass coordinate system. Finally, we test whether the y component of this vector is greater than the y location of the wall. If it is, a collision is detected, and the Boolean parameter `testCollision` (with an obvious name) is set to `true` and the index of the vertex is stored in the `uint` variable j. But this is only done provided `testCollision` is currently `false` (another collision has not already been detected in the same timestep). If `testCollision` was already `true`, that means another vertex is already in collision with the floor. Physically, it means that the block is now lying flat on the floor. The reasonable thing to do then is to stop the simulation. We do this using the `stopTime()` public method inherited from `Mover`.

The collision resolution code executes if a collision is detected (if `testCollision` is true). The first line repositions the block by simply moving it up by the amount that it fell below the wall. The next few lines of code simply implement the equations given at the end of the last section and should be straightforward to follow. The only subtlety is the use of the `crossProduct()` method, which is another newly created public method of the `Vector2D` class defined as follows:

```
public function crossProduct(vec:Vector2D):Number {
        return _x*vec.y - _y*vec.x;
}
```

This might confuse you if you recall that the cross product of two vectors is only supposed to exist in 3D and to be itself a vector. Because our simulation is in 2D, we've defined the analogue of the cross product, but can only give its magnitude because the cross product of two vectors should be perpendicular to both and should therefore need a third dimension to exist. The bottom line is that this trick enables us to use the formulas involving vector products in the last section pretty much as they are, as long as we keep in mind that it will only give us the magnitude of the cross product (which, in fact, is all that we need in those formulas).

There is not much more to say about this simulation. Run it and enjoy! See Figure 13-13 for a screenshot. As usual, see the effect of changing the parameters like the moment of inertia, the coefficient of restitution, and the angular damping factor. As an additional exercise, why not replace the rectangle with another polygon, such as a triangle or a pentagon?

Figure 13-13. A falling block bouncing off a floor

Example: Colliding blocks

As discussed earlier, with multiple blocks colliding together, a large part of the effort is involved with detecting collisions between the objects and then keeping them apart. So let's spend some time discussing how they are applied in a specific example. The example will involve a group of polygons with different sizes and orientations dropped from a height so that they fall onto and bounce off a floor, colliding with one another as they do so.

Referring to Figure 13-14, consider first the most common scenario when a vertex P of one block (object 1) collides with an edge of another (object 2). At the moment of collision detection, P is inside the second polygon. If you consider the position vectors of the vertices of the second polygon relative to P, they should all have positive dot products with the normal from P to the side adjacent to them (by convention, we'll consider the side that is in an counterclockwise direction from the relevant vertex). So if you test all these dot products and any one of them is negative, you know that no collision has taken place. You could also do a weaker test first by seeing whether the distance between the centers of mass of the two objects is larger than the distance to their farthest vertices. If so, you don't have to bother doing the more detailed collision detection test.

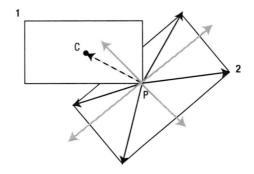

Figure 13-14. Vertex-edge collision between two polygons

To reposition an object after a vertex-edge collision, you simply move it back along the normal to the edge where the collision took place by an amount equal to the perpendicular distance from the point P to the relevant edge. The correct normal is determined by checking which one has the minimum angle with the position vector of P relative to the center of mass of object 1 (refer to Figure 13-14).

Another scenario is when a vertex of one object collides with a vertex of another. You might think that would be a rare event, but it tends to happen more often than you'd think. For example, a vertex of one polygon can slide along an edge of another until it hits the vertex at the end. In the case of vertex-vertex collisions, a simple method is to check for the distance between two vertices; if it's smaller than a certain amount (let's say 1 px), that's counted as a collision.

We apply these methods in our example simulation. The setup code for the simulation is in the file RigidBodyCollisions.as. This code produces a number of polygons of different sizes and orientations and assigns them masses proportional to their areas and moments of inertia based on their masses and dimensions. A Wall object is also produced to represent the floor. The mover class is called RigidBodyCollider and it builds upon the RigidBodyBouncer class of the last example. We won't list all the code here, but only show the calcForce() method so you get an idea of the main logic:

```
override protected function calcForce(pbody:PolygonRB,pnum:uint):void{
        force = Forces.constantGravity(pbody.mass,_g);
        torque=0;
        checkWallBounce(pbody);
        for (var i=0;i<_objects.length;i++){
                if(i!==pnum){
                        checkObjectCollision(pbody,_objects[i]);
                }
        }
}
```

There is only gravity as an external force on each object and no external torque. At each timestep, the checkWallBounce() method checks if the current object is colliding with a wall and handles the collision if necessary. This method is in essence very similar to the code we saw in the previous example for detecting and resolving wall collisions. Then the checkObjectCollision() method sees whether the current object is colliding with any other object and resolves the collision if it takes place. The collision resolution code is along the same lines as that of the wall collision, but of course using the corresponding formulas for two-body collisions. The rest of the code in checkObjectCollision() detects any vertex-side or vertex-vertex collisions between two objects and repositions them according to the methods described previously. See the source code for the detailed implementation.

If you run the code you will find that the simulation generally works well, correctly handling the collision scenarios it is designed to detect. But because we kept the simulation simple, you may notice some problems every now and then, especially when things get crowded and multiple collisions are involved. The problems can get worse if higher velocities are involved; for example, if g is increased. You could improve the simulation by devising methods to handle more of these possible collision scenarios. You could also introduce friction to make it look more realistic at the moment the blocks slide along the floor once they have settled due to the lack of friction. A screenshot of the simulation is shown in Figure 13-15.

Figure 13-15. The multiple colliding blocks simulation

Deformable bodies

You now know how to simulate rigid body motion, but how do you simulate the motion of deformable bodies such as ropes and clothes, whose shapes can change? There are various approaches to do that, but we'll introduce one particular approach based on the spring physics that we covered in Chapter 8. Let's begin by a brief recap of the main principles and formulas of spring physics and discussion of how they can be applied to model deformable bodies.

Mass-spring systems

The basic modeling approach is to represent a deformable extended object as a series of particles with mass joined together by virtual springs. Hence we generally refer to such models as mass-spring systems. As an illustration of the method, consider the simple one-dimensional chain of particles and springs shown in Figure 13-16.

Figure 13-16. A 1D chain of particles connected by springs

Each particle experiences a spring force that depends on its distance from the adjacent particles. We can impose a certain equilibrium distance L between the particles. If two particles are closer together than the distance L, they repel; if they are farther apart than L, they attract. The length can be thought of as the natural unstretched length of the virtual spring connecting the two particles.

As described in Chapter 8, the spring force between any two particles is given by the following equation, in which k is the spring constant and **x** is the extension:

$$\mathbf{F} = -k\,\mathbf{x}$$

The magnitude of the extension x is the amount by which the spring is stretched beyond its unstretched length L. In the case of two adjacent particles connected by a spring, it is therefore equal to the distance d between the particles minus L:

$$x = d - L$$

In vector form, it is this:

$$\mathbf{x} = (d - L)\frac{\mathbf{d}}{d}$$

Here $\mathbf{d}$ is the distance vector between the two particles. For example, the ith particle in the preceding 1D chain experiences a force due to the $(i+1)^{th}$ particle given by this, where $\mathbf{r}$ is the position vector of the respective particle:

$$\mathbf{F} = -k\left(\left|\mathbf{r}_i - \mathbf{r}_{i+1}\right| - L\right)\frac{\mathbf{r}_i - \mathbf{r}_{i+1}}{\left|\mathbf{r}_i - \mathbf{r}_{i+1}\right|}$$

Similarly, the ith particle experiences a force due to the $(i-1)^{th}$ particle given by the following:

$$\mathbf{F} = -k\left(\left|\mathbf{r}_i - \mathbf{r}_{i-1}\right| - L\right)\frac{\mathbf{r}_i - \mathbf{r}_{i-1}}{\left|\mathbf{r}_i - \mathbf{r}_{i-1}\right|}$$

This 1D model can be extended to 2D or 3D, and each particle can then be subjected to a spring force due to more neighbors according to the previous formulas.

You also want to have damping in your mass-spring system; otherwise, the particles would just oscillate forever. The damping term is usually linear in the relative velocity with a constant coefficient c (which can be chosen to minimize the time it takes to reach equilibrium), as we discussed in Chapter 8:

$$\mathbf{F} = -c\mathbf{v}_r$$

In the specific context of our connected mass-spring system, the velocity $\mathbf{v}_r$ is the velocity of the relevant particle relative to the particle exerting the force on it. Therefore, the damping force on the ith particle relative to the $(i+1)^{th}$ particle is given by this:

$$\mathbf{F} = -c\left(\mathbf{v}_i - \mathbf{v}_{i+1}\right)$$

Similarly, the damping force on the ith particle relative to the $(i+1)^{th}$ particle is given by the following:

$$\mathbf{F} = -c\left(\mathbf{v}_i - \mathbf{v}_{i-1}\right)$$

To get a mass-spring system to work properly, it is frequently necessary to adjust the mass, stiffness, and damping coefficient. Generally you'll want the stiffness k to be high to reduce the stretchiness of your object. The problem is that the resulting spring system becomes more unstable, and it is not unusual to see a simulation explode before your very eyes! Let's put together an example, and you'll soon get to see what we mean!

Rope simulation

This example builds upon the last example in Chapter 8, where we simulated a chain of particles connected together by springs (see the "Coupled Oscillations" code). We will now make some small but significant changes to that simulation to make it behave more like a rope. The modified code is Rope.as and RopeMover.as. Rope.as sets up the visual elements and looks like this:

```
package{
        import flash.display.Sprite;
        import com.physicscodes.objects.Ball;
        import com.physicscodes.math.Vector2D;

        public class Rope extends Sprite{
                public function Rope():void{
                        init();
                }
                private function init():void{
                        // create a sprite to draw the springs on
                        var spring:Sprite=new Sprite();
                        addChild(spring);

                        // create a fixed support
                        var fixedPoint:Ball;
                        fixedPoint=new Ball(2,0x000000);
                        fixedPoint.pos2D=new Vector2D(100,100);
                        addChild(fixedPoint);

                        // create the masses
                        var objects:Array = new Array();
                        var numObjects:Number = 15;
                        var spacing:Number = 20; // make close to spring length
                        for (var i:uint=0; i<numObjects; i++){
                                var object:Ball= new Ball(2,0x000000,10);
                                object.pos2D = new Vector2D(fixedPoint.x+spacing*(i+1),➥
fixedPoint.y);

                                addChild(object);
                                objects.push(object);
                        }

                        // get things moving
                        var mover:RopeMover=new RopeMover(objects,fixedPoint,spring);
                        mover.startTime();
                }
        }
}
```

In this code, we are creating 16 Ball objects of radius 2 pixels and placing them initially 20 pixels apart on a horizontal straight line. The first ball will remain fixed in the simulation. A Sprite object named *spring* is also created. This will hold lines that will connect the balls together, giving the appearance of a rope.

The system is set into motion by a RopeMover instance. RopeMover is a modification of the CoupledOscillator class of Chapter 8 and looks like this, with the changes in bold:

```
package {
        import com.physicscodes.motion.MultiForcer2;
        import com.physicscodes.motion.Forces;
        import com.physicscodes.objects.Ball;
        import com.physicscodes.objects.Particle;
        import com.physicscodes.math.Vector2D;
        import flash.display.Sprite;
        import flash.events.MouseEvent;

        public class RopeMover extends MultiForcer2{
                private var _objects:Array;
                private var _support:Ball;
                private var _center:Vector2D;
                private var _displ:Vector2D;
                private var _g:Number=10;
                private var _kDamping:Number=20;
                private var _kSpring:Number=500;
                private var _springLength:Number=20;
                private var _spring:Sprite;
                private var _drop:Boolean=false;

                public function RopeMover(pobjects:Array,psupport:Ball,pspring:Sprite):void{
                        _objects = pobjects;
                        _support = psupport;
                        _center = _support.pos2D;
                        _spring = pspring;
                        _spring.stage.addEventListener(MouseEvent.MOUSE_DOWN, onDown);
                        super(_objects);
                }

                override protected function moveObject():void{
                        super.moveObject();
                        drawSpring();
                        _center = _support.pos2D;
                }

                override protected function calcForce(pparticle:Particle,pnum:uint):void{
                        var centerPrev:Vector2D;
                        var centerNext:Vector2D;
                        var veloPrev:Vector2D;
                        var veloNext:Vector2D;
                        if (pnum > 0){
                                centerPrev = _objects[pnum-1].pos2D;
                                veloPrev = _objects[pnum-1].velo2D;
                        }else{
                                centerPrev = _center;
                                veloPrev = new Vector2D(0,0);
                        }
                        if (pnum < _objects.length-1){
                                centerNext = _objects[pnum+1].pos2D;
                                veloNext = _objects[pnum+1].velo2D;
                        }else{
                                centerNext = pparticle.pos2D;
                                veloNext = pparticle.velo2D;
```

```
                        }
                        var gravity:Vector2D = Forces.constantGravity(pparticle.mass,_g);
                        var velo:Vector2D = pparticle.velo2D.multiply(2).subtract↪
(veloPrev).subtract(veloNext);
                        var damping:Vector2D = Forces.damping(_kDamping,velo);
                        var displPrev:Vector2D = pparticle.pos2D.subtract(centerPrev);
                        var displNext:Vector2D = pparticle.pos2D.subtract(centerNext);
                        var extensionPrev:Vector2D = displPrev.subtract↪
(displPrev.unit().multiply(_springLength));
                        var extensionNext:Vector2D = displNext.subtract↪
(displNext.unit().multiply(_springLength));
                        var restoringPrev:Vector2D = Forces.spring(_kSpring,extensionPrev);
                        var restoringNext:Vector2D = Forces.spring(_kSpring,extensionNext);
                        force = Forces.add([gravity, damping, restoringPrev, restoringNext]);
                        if (pnum==_objects.length-1 && !_drop){
                                force = new Vector2D(0,0);
                                pparticle.velo2D = new Vector2D(0,0);
                        }
                }

                private function drawSpring():void{
                        with (_spring.graphics){
                                clear();
                                lineStyle(2,0x009999);
                                moveTo(_center.x,_center.y);
                                for (var i:uint=0; i<_objects.length; i++){
                                        var X:Number = _objects[i].xpos;
                                        var Y:Number = _objects[i].ypos;
                                        lineTo(X,Y);
                                }
                        }
                }

                private function onDown(e:MouseEvent):void{
                        _spring.stage.addEventListener(MouseEvent.MOUSE_UP, onUp);
                        _drop = true;
                }
                private function onUp(e:MouseEvent):void{
                        _spring.stage.removeEventListener(MouseEvent.MOUSE_UP, onUp);
                        _drop = false;
                }

        }
}
```

Most of the code is unchanged from that in CoupledOscillations.as, and we therefore refer you to the relevant discussion in Chapter 8 if it is not completely obvious and you need a refresher of how it works. We'll instead focus on the key changes.

First, notice that we are storing the velocities of the particles before and after the current one in variables veloPrev and veloNext. They are then combined with the velocity of the current particle to give the parameter velo, which is used to compute the damping force using the Forces.damping() function. You might be wondering why we are combining the velocities in that way. Referring to the formulas for the damping force given in the last subsection, we are adding up the damping force on the current particle relative to the two neighboring particles to give this:

$$\mathbf{F} = -c\left(\mathbf{v}_i - \mathbf{v}_{i+1}\right) + -c\left(\mathbf{v}_i - \mathbf{v}_{i-1}\right) = -c\left(2\mathbf{v}_i - \mathbf{v}_{i+1} - \mathbf{v}_{i-1}\right)$$

The variable velo is just the combined effective velocity that results from that sum. Note that in CoupledOscillator.as we used the absolute velocity of the current particle (not the velocities relative to its neighbors) to compute the damping force on it. You might want to experiment by comparing the behavior of the simulation if you do the same here.

Another change is that we are fixing the last particle in the chain by setting the force on it and its velocity to zero, unless the Boolean parameter _drop is true:

```
if (pnum==_objects.length-1 && !_drop){
        force = new Vector2D(0,0);
        pparticle.velo2D = new Vector2D(0,0);
}
```

The parameter _drop, initially set to false, is controlled by user interaction through the event handlers onDown() and onUp() that respond to a MOUSE_DOWN and MOUSE_UP event, respectively. As long as the user holds the mouse down, _drop is true, and the last particle can move under the action of forces like the rest of the particles (except the first). If the mouse is released, the last particle stops wherever it is. There is a slightly modified version of the simulation with the source files Rope2.as and RopeMover2.as that responds in a different way to mouse clicks: when the mouse is held down, a force is applied toward the mouse with a magnitude proportional to the distance from the mouse to the last particle; the force is removed when the mouse is released. Although we refer to the first version of the simulation in the following discussion, much of it applies equally well to the modified version.

Note the values of the parameters that we specify in RopeMover.as and Rope.as: gravity is 10 units, spring length is 20 pixels, and the mass of the particles is 10 units. Most importantly, note the high values used for the spring damping coefficient (20) and the spring constant (500) compared to what they were in the coupled oscillations simulation of Chapter 8, where these parameters had values of 0.5 and 10, respectively. As you experiment with this simulation, do try different values for these parameters to see how they change its behavior.

Run the simulation with the default values of these parameters. See how the particles fall from their initial positions under the effect of gravity, but are held together by the spring force. After some brief oscillations and slight stretching, they settle down into a curved shape that hangs down like a rope (see Figure 13-17). This is a characteristic mathematical curve known as a *catenary*: it's the shape that a chain fixed at both ends naturally takes under the effect of its own weight. After it has settled down, click and hold down the mouse so that the end of the string falls down: see how the "rope" can readjust itself. Now release the mouse and notice that the rope again settles into a characteristic curve: this is a different section of the catenary.

Figure 13-17. A rope simulation

Experiment by changing the values of the parameters. First, let's increase the value of the spring constant _kSpring to 1000. See how the rope now stretches less. You might be tempted to try a much larger value to see whether you can get an even tighter rope. Fine, go ahead and increase _kSpring to 5000 (just don't say we didn't warn you) and rerun the simulation. Whoops! Your rope just blew up! Welcome to numerical instability. Unfortunately, this is a common problem with mass-spring systems: they are prone to blow up, especially for high values of the spring constant. This arises because of an underlying issue with integration schemes known as numerical instability, which we'll discuss in more detail in the next chapter.

You can similarly play with the damping coefficient _kDamping and note that its value affects how quickly the oscillations stop. Things can get nasty here, too. For example, keep _kSpring at its initial value of 500 and decrease the value of _kDamping to 1. The simulation seems to be well-behaved initially, apparently settling down as before. But wait a little longer and you soon start seeing little fluctuations growing and distorting the rope into something that you can't call a rope any more. And before you know it, it all explodes again!

To conclude: mass-spring systems are easy to create and fun to watch, but they can prove highly unstable in certain parameter regimes. Some things can be done to improve their stability, for example by using an improved integration scheme (see the next chapter), but they should be used with care.

Cloth simulation

It is fairly straightforward to extend our rope simulation to 2D to create a simple cloth simulation. Of course, to create a realistic simulation of a cloth that can bend we really need a 3D simulation, even if the cloth itself is 2D, to allow for movement and bending of the cloth in the third dimension. But we can quickly make a 2D version that will reproduce at least some elements of the behavior of a moving cloth. So let's make some quick modifications to the rope simulation and create a 2D version of it. The new setup file is called Cloth.as and contains the following code:

```
package{
        import flash.display.Sprite;
        import com.physicscodes.objects.Ball;
        import com.physicscodes.math.Vector2D;

        public class Cloth extends Sprite{
                public function Cloth():void{
                        init();
                }

                private function init():void{
```

```
                        // create a sprite to draw the springs on
                        var spring:Sprite=new Sprite();
                        addChild(spring);

                        // create the masses
                        var rows:uint=10;
                        var cols:uint=15;
                        var refPoint:Vector2D = new Vector2D(120,50);
                        var objects:Array = new Array();
                        for (var i:uint=0; i<cols*rows; i++){
                                var object:Ball= new Ball(2,0x000000,10);
                                var ncol:Number=Math.floor(i/rows);
                                var spacing:Number = 20; // make close to spring length
                                object.pos2D = new Vector2D(refPoint.x+ncol*spacing,➥
refPoint.y+(i-ncol*rows-1)*spacing);
                                addChild(object);
                                objects.push(object);
                        }

                        // fixed points
                        var fixedPoints:Array = new Array(0,70,140);

                        // get things moving
                        var mover:ClothMover = new ClothMover(objects, fixedPoints, cols,➥
rows, spring);
                        mover.startTime();
                }
        }
}
```

Apart from the obvious generalization of the setup to 2D, note that we have also specified an array of points on the cloth that we want to remain fixed. In the listing, we are holding the cloth fixed at three points, giving the appearance of a piece of cloth that is hung on a line.

The ClothMover class that drives the simulation is fairly long, but it is an obvious generalization of the RopeMover class and so we won't list it here. Take a look at the code in the source files, though. Arguably some of the coding in that class could be done more concisely and elegantly by using arrays instead of different variables (such as extensionUp, extensionDown, and so on) that do the same thing in different directions. But the code is probably easier to understand in the current inelegant form, and the comments should also help. The main idea is that now each particle is experiencing a force due its four nearest neighbors to the left, right, up, and down, respectively. If a particle is on the edge of the cloth, it obviously does not have one or more of these forces. All the particles are subject to gravity. The other change is in terms of user interaction; clicking and holding down the mouse now applies a steady wind blowing to the right.

Run the simulation and you'll have a hanging piece of cloth that you can blow the wind over by clicking the mouse (see Figure 13-18). Experiment with the parameters of the simulation to see what they do. For example, you can try and increase the number of particles, reduce their spacing, and so on. You might also want to increase the spring constant and see how far you can go before you tear the cloth to pieces!

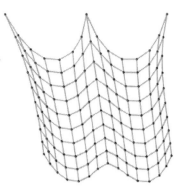

Figure 13-18. A simple cloth simulation

Needless to say, this is a very basic cloth simulation that can be enhanced in endless ways. Functionally, the most important improvement is probably to make the cloth move in 3D. You could also connect each particle to more neighbors; for example, the four nearest diagonal neighbors and the next nearest neighbors up, down, left, and right. That would improve the way the cloth behaves. Visually, you could fill up the areas between the particles, add texture, lighting and so on. Over to you!

Summary

This chapter introduced rigid body dynamics and collisions, and showed you how to model deformable bodies using mass-spring systems. Needless to say, what we have covered in this chapter is only the tip of the iceberg. There are many more topics on the general subject of extended systems that we can only briefly mention here: constrained systems, forward and inverse kinematics, and Verlet systems. Some of them can provide alternative approaches to simulating both rigid bodies and deformable bodies, but we do not have the space to include a discussion of them in this book.

This chapter completes Part III. In the first two chapters of Part IV, we will look at advanced numerical schemes and some other technical issues involved in creating more complex simulations, and then conclude with some simulation projects in the final chapter.

Part IV

Building More Complex Simulations

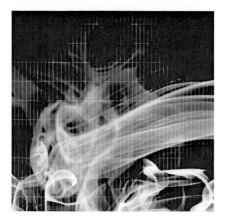

Chapter 14

Numerical Integration Schemes

In the previous two parts of this book we have covered a lot of physics. In the process we have managed to largely avoid getting into complex numerical issues. In this fourth and last part of the book we will discuss, over the next two chapters, some technical and numerical issues that you'll need to consider if you are building more complex simulations, and illustrate their application with some examples in the final chapter. In this chapter we will focus exclusively on the important subject of *numerical integration schemes*. Because no new physics will be presented, there won't be any new simulations in this chapter, but just some simple codes to test the different schemes.

Numerical integration is a branch of numerical analysis that deals with the solution of differential equations. An *integration scheme* is a particular method for doing numerical integration in a form that you can readily write into code. We need an integration scheme to simulate motion because it involves solving Newton's second law of motion (which is a differential equation; see Chapter 5).

Topics covered in this chapter include the following:

- **General principles**: We begin by stating the general problem to be solved and explain the different types of integration schemes available and their characteristics.

- **Euler integration**: This is the simplest integration method and is the one we have been using throughout the book so far. It is fast and very easy to code up, but it is inaccurate and can be unstable, which can lead to problems with some types of simulations.

- **Runge-Kutta integration**: This method is much more accurate than the Euler scheme, but it involves a lot of calculations and can therefore slow down your simulation. It is particularly suited to highly accurate simulations.

- **Verlet integration**: This method is not as accurate as Runge-Kutta, but is generally better than the Euler scheme. It is well suited to a number of game programming and animation applications.

443

General principles

Before we look at specific integration schemes, it is useful to start by posing the problem of numerical simulation in a general way and then looking at how numerical integration approaches its solution. We then discuss the general characteristics of integration schemes and review some terminology associated with different types of schemes.

Statement of the problem

Numerical integration is a method of solution of a problem. So what is the problem we are trying to solve?

Motion of a particle as an initial value problem

To simplify the discussion, consider the problem of simulating the motion of a single particle under the action of forces. Suppose the particle starts out at a location given by its initial position vector **x**(0) with respect to an origin O and with an initial velocity **v**(0) (see Figure 14-1). The problem is then to determine the trajectory as a function of time. Mathematically, this is equivalent to determining the position and velocity vectors **x**(t) and **v**(t) as a function of time. This is called an *initial value problem*.

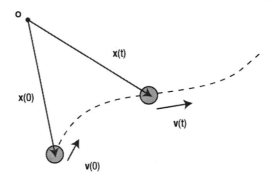

Figure 14-1. The initial value problem for particle motion simulation

In the preceding problem, the velocity of the particle **v** could itself be changing in time (in other words, the particle could be accelerating). That is why we need Newton's second law:

$$\mathbf{a} = \frac{\mathbf{F}}{m}$$

Knowing the acceleration at any time then allows us to calculate the velocity **v** by integrating the equation defining acceleration:

$$\frac{d\mathbf{v}}{dt} = \mathbf{a}$$

Similarly, applying the definition of velocity, the position can be obtained by integrating the velocity in time:

$$\frac{d\mathbf{x}}{dt} = \mathbf{v}$$

As discussed in Chapter 5, these differential equations can sometimes be solved analytically to give closed-form expressions for $\mathbf{x}(t)$ and $\mathbf{v}(t)$ as functions of time. In computer simulation, the integration needs to be done numerically.

Numerical integration means that the position and velocity of the particle can be calculated and updated only in small discrete steps. This is done by first *discretizing* the previous equations of motion.

Numerical discretization and difference schemes

We gave an example of the discretization procedure back in Chapter 3 when discussing the numerical calculation of gradient functions in general mathematical terms. You may want to refer to the section on calculus in Chapter 3 for a refresher.

In the current context, you can apply numerical discretization to the last two equations to convert them into a form that can be put into code and solved on a computer.

This is done by approximating the derivatives in those equations by algebraic fractions. For example, we can approximate the acceleration dv/dt using small changes $\Delta \mathbf{v}$ and Δt in $\mathbf{v}$ and t like this:

$$\mathbf{a} = \frac{d\mathbf{v}}{dt} \approx \frac{\Delta \mathbf{v}}{\Delta t}$$

The next step is then to represent the discrete step changes $\Delta \mathbf{v}$ and Δt in terms of values at definite times because that is what you know (or rather what your computer knows). This can be done in different ways, known as *difference schemes*.

As an example, you can take Δt to be the time at the next timestep minus the current time, and similarly for the velocity interval $\Delta \mathbf{v}$. This gives a forward difference scheme, as discussed in Chapter 3 (n here denotes the timestep number):

$$\mathbf{a}(n) = \frac{\mathbf{v}(n+1) - \mathbf{v}(n)}{t(n+1) - t(n)}$$

Similarly, the velocity can be approximated by a forward difference scheme in the following way:

$$\mathbf{v}(n) = \frac{\mathbf{x}(n+1) - \mathbf{x}(n)}{t(n+1) - t(n)}$$

Now you've converted the differential equations into algebraic equations that you can understand and manipulate easily. More importantly, it's in a form that a computer can calculate. This is the role of discretization.

But before you can put anything into code, there is one more step you need to do: convert the preceding difference scheme to an integration scheme.

Numerical integration and integration schemes

Numerical integration was also introduced in general terms in Chapter 3. The key idea is that we need to find the velocity and position at the new time in terms of those at the old time. So, just as we did in Chapter 3, we manipulate the previous equations to give the following expressions for v(n+1) and x(n+1), in which we have written the time difference t(n+1) – t(n) as Δt (the timestep):

$$\mathbf{v}(n+1) = \mathbf{v}(n) + \mathbf{a}(n) \cdot \Delta t$$

$$\mathbf{x}(n+1) = \mathbf{x}(n) + \mathbf{v}(n) \cdot \Delta t$$

This gives a forward integration scheme known as the Euler scheme, as you know. With these equations, you can obtain the new velocity and position of your particle in terms of its velocity and position at the previous timestep. You can now put these equations directly into code and simulate the motion of the particle by repeating that calculation at each timestep. This will give you a discrete approximation to the true trajectory of the particle, as shown schematically in Figure 14-2. A good simulation means that this approximated trajectory is as close to the real one as needed for your particular purpose. How good the approximation turns out to be will depend on a number of factors, including the following:

- **Physics of the problem**: Effectively, this is captured by how the acceleration **a** varies with time. Some physical problems are easier to simulate accurately than others, especially if the acceleration does not vary too much with time.

- **Simulation timestep**: Generally, the smaller the timestep the better the approximation will be. But reducing the timestep comes at a cost because your simulation may run more slowly. Referring to Figure 14-2, smaller timesteps mean that the distance between the dots is reduced and that the approximated curve is closer to the true one.

- **Integration scheme**: The choice of integration scheme generally has a significant effect on the accuracy, stability, and speed of execution of your simulation. But there is often a trade-off between these desirable characteristics.

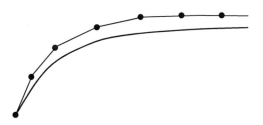

Figure 14-2. Numerical integration gives an approximation to the true trajectory.

Characteristics of numerical schemes

When deciding which integration scheme to use there is a set of characteristics that you need to bear in mind, which determine how "good" that scheme is and how well suited it is to the application you have in mind. We'll briefly discuss some of these characteristics separately, but remember that they are connected.

Consistency

Consistency of a numerical scheme is the property that the numerical scheme is consistent with the original differential equation in the sense that it approximates the differential equation. Formally, in the limit of indefinitely small timesteps, the numerical solution should be identical to the true solution of the differential equation. This can be viewed as a necessary condition for any numerical scheme. If it's not true, the scheme will give the wrong physics and is essentially useless.

Stability

In the last chapter you saw a spectacular example of numerical instability with the rope simulation "blowing up" when the spring stiffness was too high. Formally, the *stability* of a numerical scheme is its capability to reduce errors (or "perturbations," as they are usually called) over time. A scheme is stable if an error or perturbation at any time decays with time; it is unstable if the error grows with time. A scheme can be conditionally stable (meaning that it is stable under certain conditions) or unconditionally stable (it is always stable, regardless of the conditions).

Convergence

Convergence is the requirement that as we reduce the timestep, the resulting numerical solution should approach the true solution. Consistency is a necessary condition for convergence, but not a sufficient condition. Again, clearly a numerical scheme is of no use if it is not convergent. For convergence, a scheme must also be stable.

Accuracy

Replacing a differential equation by finite differences inevitably introduces errors (known as *discretization errors*). Needless to say, it is desirable to keep these errors as small as possible. The *accuracy* of a numerical scheme determines how small or how large these errors will be. The timestep also has an important effect on the numerical errors; errors are generally smaller the smaller the timestep (if the scheme is convergent). The *order* of a numerical scheme determines how quickly the errors diminish as you reduce the timestep. A *first-order* scheme has an error that is proportional to the timestep Δt, a second-order scheme has an error proportional to $(\Delta t)^2$, and so on. Therefore, as the timestep Δt is reduced, a second-order scheme will converge faster to the real solution, making it more accurate.

Efficiency

The *efficiency* of a numerical scheme quantifies how quickly (in wall clock time) it can compute a solution per unit simulation time. For the same timestep, the more complex a numerical scheme is, the lower is its efficiency because it has to perform a greater number of calculations and associated operations to produce a given solution per timestep. More accurate schemes are usually more complex and therefore less efficient. There is, therefore, usually a trade-off to achieve between accuracy and efficiency. However, in an actual implementation, the overall efficiency of a numerical method depends on the size of timestep that it can allow while preserving stability and accuracy. It could turn out that a simple scheme requires a much larger timestep to remain stable than a more complicated one, making it effectively less efficient in terms of overall computing time per simulation time.

Types of integration schemes

The terminology of numerical analysis can sound confusing because of the plethora of schemes, their associated names, and the different ways to classify them. The following list contains very brief descriptions of some of the terminology associated with the classification of integration schemes. Note that the categories mentioned here are not mutually exclusive; they overlap.

- **Forward/backward schemes**: You may come across scheme names such as *forward Euler* and *backward Euler*. These names show that the scheme is derived from a corresponding forward or backward difference scheme.

- **Implicit/explicit schemes**: An *explicit scheme* is one in which the values of the state variables at the new timestep are computed in terms of only the variables at the previous timestep; this makes an explicit scheme straightforward to apply. In an *implicit scheme*, an equation involving variables at both the old and the new timestep must be solved to calculate the variables at the new timestep; this makes such schemes less efficient.

- **Single-step/multistep methods**: A *single-step method* uses information from a single previous timestep to calculate variables at the new timestep. A *multistep method* uses information from more than one previous timesteps.

- **Predictor-corrector methods:** As its name suggests, a predictor-corrector method involves two stages: a step that predicts a value at the new timestep, followed by another step that applies a correction to the estimated value.

- **Runge-Kutta methods**: This refers to a class of higher-order methods that proceed by employing intermediate stages and can be explicit as well as implicit. We will consider two examples of such methods, including the fourth-order Runge-Kutta (RK4) method, which is often referred to as *the* Runge-Kutta method.

Modifying Forcer to allow for different integration schemes

In the next sections we discuss a number of different schemes and then write code that will implement them. It would be helpful to be able to switch between different schemes easily, which would be convenient for comparing different schemes and for choosing an appropriate scheme for each problem.

So let's modify `Forcer` to allow that. The new version is called `ForcerIntegrator`, and the code looks like this to start with:

```
package com.physicscodes.motion{
        import com.physicscodes.motion.Mover;
        import com.physicscodes.objects.Particle;
        import com.physicscodes.math.Vector2D;
        import com.physicscodes.motion.Forces;

        public class ForcerIntegrator extends Mover{
                private var _particle:Particle;
                private var _force:Vector2D;
                private var _acc:Vector2D;

                public function ForcerIntegrator(pparticle:Particle):void{
                        _particle = pparticle;
                        _oldpos = _particle.pos2D; // initialize old position
                        super(pparticle);
                }

                public function get force():Vector2D {
                        return _force;
                }

                public function set force(pforce):void {
                        _force = pforce;
                }

                protected function calcForce(ppos:Vector2D,pvel:Vector2D):void{
                        _force = Forces.zeroForce();
                }
```

```
        private function getAcc(ppos:Vector2D,pvel:Vector2D):Vector2D{
                calcForce(ppos,pvel);
                return _force.multiply(1/_particle.mass);
        }

        override protected function moveObject():void{
                myFavoriteScheme();
        }

        private function myFavoriteScheme():void{
                // scheme-specific code goes in here
        }

    }
}
```

We have made some changes to the code (indicated with bold type). The calcForce() method now takes two arguments, ppos and pvel, which reference position and velocity vectors. This will be needed because some schemes require the evaluation of the acceleration (and hence the force) at different times. They will do that by calling the private getAcc() method that calculates the acceleration, also with position and velocity vectors as arguments. The moveObject() method overrides the default one in Mover. This is where you will call the method that implements the integration scheme. All the scheme-specific code will be in its own method. In this way it will be easy to implement new schemes and to switch between schemes. Note that we are only applying the changes to the linear motion because we will only use the new integration schemes for particle motion; you could also implement them on the rotational motion along the same lines.

Euler integration

We have talked about and used the Euler integration scheme a lot in this book, so you are therefore very familiar with it by now. But what you might not know is that there are several different versions of the Euler scheme. Let's take a look at some of them and their properties.

Explicit Euler

The Euler integration scheme that we derived earlier in this section from the forward difference scheme is called (appropriately enough) the *forward Euler scheme*. Also, because it is an explicit scheme, it is also known as the *explicit Euler scheme*. Here are the equations again:

$$\mathbf{v}(n+1) = \mathbf{v}(n) + \mathbf{a}(n) \cdot \Delta t$$

$$\mathbf{x}(n+1) = \mathbf{x}(n) + \mathbf{v}(n) \cdot \Delta t$$

Because it is simple, the explicit Euler scheme is fast, but it is only first-order accurate and is often unstable.

Note that when implementing this scheme in code, we update the position based on the current velocity before updating the velocity based on the current acceleration, to be consistent with the previous equations.

In our new class ForcerIntegrator, the relevant code is in the EulerExplicit() method, which looks like this:

```
private function EulerExplicit():void{
        _acc = getAcc(_particle.pos2D,_particle.velo2D);
        _particle.pos2D = _particle.pos2D.addScaled(_particle.velo2D,dt);
        _particle.velo2D = _particle.velo2D.addScaled(_acc,dt);
}
```

Implicit Euler

The explicit Euler scheme was obtained by starting from a forward difference approximation to the derivative. You can instead start from a backward difference scheme:

$$\mathbf{a}(n+1) = \frac{\mathbf{v}(n+1) - \mathbf{v}(n)}{t(n+1) - t(n)}$$

$$\mathbf{v}(n+1) = \frac{\mathbf{x}(n+1) - \mathbf{x}(n)}{t(n+1) - t(n)}$$

Rearranging these difference equations then gives the following:

$$\mathbf{v}(n+1) = \mathbf{v}(n) + \mathbf{a}(n+1) \cdot \Delta t$$

$$\mathbf{x}(n+1) = \mathbf{x}(n) + \mathbf{v}(n+1) \cdot \Delta t$$

This looks similar to the corresponding equation for the explicit Euler scheme, except for one crucial difference: the right sides of those equations contain the acceleration as well as the velocity at the new timestep. We therefore have an implicit equation that needs to be solved first before we can obtain the velocity at the new timestep. This involves further calculations, which make implicit schemes less efficient (as well as a pain to code up!). A major advantage of the implicit scheme is that it is unconditionally stable. If you want to make sure that your simulation will never blow up, it's worth considering using an implicit scheme. But because we don't use the implicit Euler scheme in this book, we won't bother coding it up.

Semi-implicit Euler

The *semi-implict Euler scheme*, as its name suggests, is somewhere between the explicit and implicit Euler schemes. In one common variant, the velocity is advanced based on the acceleration at the previous timestep, as in the explicit scheme, but the position is advanced based on the updated velocity at the new timestep, as in the implicit scheme:

$$\mathbf{v}(n+1) = \mathbf{v}(n) + \mathbf{a}(n) \cdot \Delta t$$

$$\mathbf{x}(n+1) = \mathbf{x}(n) + \mathbf{v}(n+1) \cdot \Delta t$$

The advantage of the semi-implicit scheme is that it is more stable than the explicit scheme and also conserves energy. This energy-conserving property makes it more accurate than the explicit scheme, although it is still first order.

The semi-implicit scheme is simple to implement. Compared with the implementation of the explicit scheme, you just reverse the order in which you update the position and velocity. Here is the corresponding function EulerSemiImplicit() in ForcerIntegrator:

```
private function EulerSemiImplicit():void{
        _acc = getAcc(_particle.pos2D,_particle.velo2D);
        _particle.velo2D = _particle.velo2D.addScaled(_acc,dt);
        _particle.pos2D = _particle.pos2D.addScaled(_particle.velo2D,dt);
}
```

There is another variant of the semi-implicit Euler scheme (with similar properties to the other version), in which the position is advanced based on the current velocity instead of the updated velocity, and the velocity is advanced based on the updated acceleration (and therefore at the updated position):

$$\mathbf{x}(n+1) = \mathbf{x}(n) + \mathbf{v}(n) \cdot \Delta t$$

$$\mathbf{v}(n+1) = \mathbf{v}(n) + \mathbf{a}(n+1) \cdot \Delta t$$

Note that because the acceleration potentially depends on the position and it must be evaluated at the new time, the position must be updated first in code. This version of the semi-implicit Euler scheme is the one that we have been using throughout most of the book, and it has mostly worked quite well, at least from the perspective of creating simple demos of various types of physics effects.

We've coded this up in the function EulerSemiImplicit2() in ForcerIntegrator:

```
private function EulerSemiImplicit2():void{
        _particle.pos2D = _particle.pos2D.addScaled(_particle.velo2D,dt);
        _acc = getAcc(_particle.pos2D,_particle.velo2D);
        _particle.velo2D = _particle.velo2D.addScaled(_acc,dt);
}
```

Comparing the explicit and semi-implicit Euler schemes

To compare the explicit and semi-implicit Euler schemes, let's put together a very simple simulation of a particle oscillating under the effect of a spring force. The file Spring.as sets up a particle and a center toward which a spring force acts, and creates two other particles at the points where its trajectory should theoretically end. The Oscillator class then applies the spring force and simulates the motion of the moving particle, tracing out its trajectory. There is nothing new in terms of physics or coding in those files, so we won't list any code here. But the key thing is that Oscillator extends ForceIntegrator, and you can change the integration scheme in the moveObject() method of the latter.

For the purpose of comparing the different schemes, let's set the timestep at 50 milliseconds in all the tests that we'll be doing. In the present example, we do this by specifying 50 as an argument within the startTime() method of the mover class in Spring.as as follows:

```
var oscillator:Oscillator=new Oscillator(particle,center);
oscillator.startTime(50);
```

Run the simulation in turn with the EulerExplicit(), EulerSemiImplicit() and EulerSemiImplicit2() methods, keeping the same timestep in all three cases. You can choose an integration scheme by uncommenting the relevant line of code in the moveObject() method in ForcerIntegrator.as and commenting out the other lines. You will find that the particle oscillates as expected and remains nicely within the bounds of the endpoints with either of the two semi-implicit schemes. The semi-implicit Euler method nearly conserves energy; it's a so-called *symplectic method*. However, the explicit Euler scheme behaves very badly: the oscillations grow larger and larger (see Figure 14-3). The simulation blows up:

explicit Euler creates energy! Things get much better if you introduce some physics that can remove energy, such as drag or friction. However, the scheme can't simulate pure periodic oscillatory motion.

Figure 14-3. The explicit Euler scheme is too unstable to properly simulate spring motion

As another test of the stability of these schemes, try running the rope simulation of the last chapter with the explicit Euler scheme by changing the order of the position and velocity updates in `MultiForcer2`: it's not a pretty sight! The explicit Euler scheme can't simulate the rope even at a much lower stiffness. Interestingly, even the first version of the semi-implicit scheme does not do as well as the second version, becoming unstable for much smaller values of the stiffness. By comparison, the second version of the semi-implicit scheme is quite robust, although it also eventually fails, as you saw in the last chapter.

Why use Euler and why not?

Many programmers use nothing but Euler integration, whereas others keep as far away from Euler as they can. So should you use Euler or not?

To answer this question wisely, it is important to distinguish between the different versions of the Euler method. People often talk of the Euler scheme as if there were only one. But we've just seen that different versions of Euler have very different properties, which can lead to vastly different performance depending on the nature of your simulation. There is bad Euler and there is better Euler. You should definitely avoid the bad, explicit Euler. Semi-implicit Euler is actually not that bad (after all, we've survived for most of the book with it!). It is as easy to code up as the explicit Euler scheme, but has much nicer properties. In code, the difference between the explicit and semi-implicit Euler schemes simply amounts to swapping the order in which you compute things (so be careful!). So there really is no reason to use the explicit Euler scheme. The semi-implicit Euler scheme is widely used in rigid body physics engines.

If you need absolute stability, the fully implicit Euler scheme is worth considering, although we haven't really shown you how to solve an implicit equation. But now that you have a better insight into numerical schemes, it shouldn't be hard to figure it out from books or online sources. The extra computational cost involved in solving the resulting implicit equation makes the implicit Euler scheme seem less attractive in terms of efficiency. But you can use large timesteps without worrying about numerical instability, which would improve the efficiency. However, large timesteps would then result in poor accuracy, especially given that Euler is only first order. That's probably fine if accuracy is not important compared with stability (for example, if you just want your simulation not to blow up, without worrying about its accuracy).

However, if you really need accuracy, the first-order Euler schemes we have discussed won't serve you well. What you probably need then is something like a Runge-Kutta scheme.

Runge-Kutta integration

Runge-Kutta schemes are more complex than the Euler scheme, but they pay off in terms of considerably greater accuracy. If accuracy is critical for your simulation, you should seriously consider Runge-Kutta. It does come at a performance price, though, especially if you opt for the higher-order schemes. We'll describe two of the most popular Runge-Kutta schemes.

Second-order Runge-Kutta scheme (RK2)

The second-order Runge-Kutta method (RK2) is also known as Heun's method or the improved Euler method. It is a two-stage predictor-corrector method that uses the explicit Euler's method as predictor and a so-called trapezoidal method as corrector. Here are the equations defining the method:

$$\mathbf{p}_1 = \mathbf{x}(n)$$

$$\mathbf{v}_1 = \mathbf{v}(n)$$

$$\mathbf{a}_1 = \mathbf{a}(\mathbf{p}_1, \mathbf{v}_1)$$

$$\mathbf{p}_2 = \mathbf{p}_1 + \mathbf{v}_1 \cdot \Delta t$$

$$\mathbf{v}_2 = \mathbf{v}_1 + \mathbf{a}_1 \cdot \Delta t$$

$$\mathbf{a}_2 = \mathbf{a}(\mathbf{p}_2, \mathbf{v}_2)$$

$$\mathbf{x}(n+1) = \mathbf{x}(n) + \frac{(\mathbf{v}_1 + \mathbf{v}_2)}{2} \cdot \Delta t$$

$$\mathbf{v}(n+1) = \mathbf{v}(n) + \frac{(\mathbf{a}_1 + \mathbf{a}_2)}{2} \cdot \Delta t$$

The temporary variables $\mathbf{p}_1$, $\mathbf{v}_1$, and $\mathbf{a}_1$ are the initial position, velocity, and acceleration vectors; similarly, $\mathbf{p}_2$, $\mathbf{v}_2$, and $\mathbf{a}_2$ are the corresponding variables at the end of the timestep as computed by the forward Euler scheme. That's the predictor part. The last two equations apply the corrector by updating the position and velocity using (respectively) the average velocity and average acceleration over the timestep interval.

RK2 is more accurate than Euler because the Euler scheme uses only the velocity and acceleration at the old timestep to work out the new velocity and position of the particle. That would be fine if there were no acceleration, so that the velocity remained constant during a timestep, but both the velocity and the acceleration could be changing. For example, for a projectile the velocity changes both in magnitude and in direction. The Euler scheme takes into account the velocity only at the beginning of a timestep, but the RK2 scheme takes the average of the velocities at the beginning and the end of the timestep. So the position at the end of the timestep as predicted by RK2 ends up being closer to the real position.

The accuracy of this method is second order, so it is significantly more accurate than the Euler method. Here is the relevant RK2() function in ForcerIntegrator:

```
private function RK2():void{
        var pos1:Vector2D = _particle.pos2D;
        var vel1:Vector2D = _particle.velo2D;
        var acc1:Vector2D = getAcc(pos1,vel1);
        var pos2:Vector2D = pos1.addScaled(vel1,dt);
        var vel2:Vector2D = vel1.addScaled(acc1,dt);
        var acc2:Vector2D = getAcc(pos2,vel2);
        _particle.pos2D = pos1.addScaled(vel1.add(vel2),dt/2);
        _particle.velo2D = vel1.addScaled(acc1.add(acc2),dt/2);
{
```

The RK2() function involves a few more lines of code than the semi-implicit Euler schemes. For the same timestep an increase in accuracy is therefore achieved at the expense of reduced speed.

Fourth-order Runge-Kutta scheme (RK4)

This is the most well-known Runge-Kutta scheme, and is often called *the* Runge-Kutta scheme. As its name suggests, it is fourth-order accurate. So if you halve the timestep, the error should be reduced by a factor of one-sixteenth! The idea is similar to that of RK2, but there are more intermediate steps, and the intermediate variables and their averages are computed differently. Here is the full set of equations:

$$\mathbf{p}_1 = \mathbf{x}(n)$$

$$\mathbf{v}_1 = \mathbf{v}(n)$$

$$\mathbf{a}_1 = \mathbf{a}(\mathbf{p}_1, \mathbf{v}_1)$$

$$\mathbf{p}_2 = \mathbf{p}_1 + \mathbf{v}_1 \cdot \Delta t/2$$

$$\mathbf{v}_2 = \mathbf{v}_1 + \mathbf{a}_1 \cdot \Delta t/2$$

$$\mathbf{a}_2 = \mathbf{a}(\mathbf{p}_2, \mathbf{v}_2)$$

$$\mathbf{p}_3 = \mathbf{p}_1 + \mathbf{v}_2 \cdot \Delta t/2$$

$$\mathbf{v}_3 = \mathbf{v}_1 + \mathbf{a}_2 \cdot \Delta t/2$$

$$\mathbf{a}_3 = \mathbf{a}(\mathbf{p}_3, \mathbf{v}_3)$$

$$\mathbf{p}_4 = \mathbf{p}_1 + \mathbf{v}_3 \cdot \Delta t$$

$$\mathbf{v}_4 = \mathbf{v}_1 + \mathbf{a}_3 \cdot \Delta t$$

$$\mathbf{a}_4 = \mathbf{a}(\mathbf{p}_4, \mathbf{v}_4)$$

$$\mathbf{x}(n+1) = \mathbf{x}(n) + \frac{(\mathbf{v}_1 + 2\mathbf{v}_2 + 2\mathbf{v}_3 + \mathbf{v}_4)}{6} \cdot \Delta t$$

$$\mathbf{v}(n+1) = \mathbf{v}(n) + \frac{(\mathbf{a}_1 + 2\mathbf{a}_2 + 2\mathbf{a}_3 + \mathbf{a}_4)}{6} \cdot \Delta t$$

Following is the corresponding RK4() method:

```
private function RK4():void{
        var pos1:Vector2D = _particle.pos2D;
        var vel1:Vector2D = _particle.velo2D;
```

```
        var acc1:Vector2D = getAcc(pos1,vel1);
        var pos2:Vector2D = pos1.addScaled(vel1,dt/2);
        var vel2:Vector2D = vel1.addScaled(acc1,dt/2);
        var acc2:Vector2D = getAcc(pos2,vel2);
        var pos3:Vector2D = pos1.addScaled(vel2,dt/2);
        var vel3:Vector2D = vel1.addScaled(acc2,dt/2);
        var acc3:Vector2D = getAcc(pos3,vel3);
        var pos4:Vector2D = pos1.addScaled(vel3,dt);
        var vel4:Vector2D = vel1.addScaled(acc3,dt);
        var acc4:Vector2D = getAcc(pos4,vel4);
        var velsum:Vector2D = vel1.addScaled(vel2,2).addScaled(vel3,2).add(vel4);
        var accsum:Vector2D = acc1.addScaled(acc2,2).addScaled(acc3,2).add(acc4);
        _particle.pos2D = pos1.addScaled(velsum,dt/6);
        _particle.velo2D = vel1.addScaled(accsum,dt/6);
}
```

That's a lot of calculations to do in a single timestep! So let's see what RK4 can do for us. We'll compare the Euler, RK2, and RK4 methods for three different problems.

Stability and accuracy of RK2 and RK4 compared with Euler

To check the stability of RK2 and RK4, you can repeat the Springs test, using the RK2() and RK4() methods. You'll find that the oscillatory motion is perfectly simulated by both: there isn't even a slight decrease or increase in the amplitude of oscillation (and therefore of energy) as far as the eye can tell (if you want, you can perform more quantitative tests by plotting a graph).

To test the accuracy of the schemes and compare it with that of the previous schemes in a simple way, let's put together a simple orbits simulation. The files are called Orbits.as and Orbiter.as. Again there is nothing that you haven't seen in those files, and we won't list any code from them here. The test is that the orbits should close on themselves; if they don't, the scheme is introducing significant errors.

Run the code with different integration schemes in ForcerIntegrator as before. With the explicit Euler integrator, the orbit will end up all over the place: it never closes on itself (see Figure 14-4). That should be enough to convince you never to use the explicit Euler scheme!

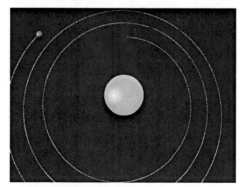

Figure 14-4. The explicit Euler scheme is too inaccurate to produce a closed orbit

All the other schemes do a pretty decent job. But if you run the simulation for a long time, you will find that even the semi-implicit Euler schemes start losing accuracy and tracing slightly non-overlapping circles (see Figure 14-5) because they are only first-order accurate. By comparison, we ran the RK4 scheme for a much longer duration, but could not notice any loss of accuracy. The RK2 scheme is intermediate in accuracy between the semi-implicit Euler scheme and the RK4 scheme. For this simple example you will hardly notice any difference between RK2 and RK4.

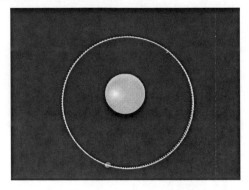

Figure 14-5. The semi-implicit Euler scheme accumulates errors after a few orbits

Verlet integration

The third and final class of integration schemes that we'll discuss is called *Verlet integration*. Originally developed for handling complex and variable molecular dynamics simulations because of its stability properties, the approach is now widely used in game programming and animation.

Verlet integration is employed in so-called *Verlet systems* to simulate the motion of particles subject to constraints. This technique can be applied to connected structures as in ragdoll physics, forward and inverse kinematics, and even rigid body systems. We do not have space to explore this approach, but we refer you to a very good introduction to the subject in the book *Advanced ActionScript 3.0 Animation*, by Keith Peters. We mention Verlet systems merely to distinguish them from the Verlet integration scheme because they are sometimes confused: Verlet systems are named as such because they use the Verlet integration scheme. But the scheme itself is completely independent of that modeling approach; in fact, it can be used with any other approach, such as the rigid body dynamics discussed in Chapter 13.

Verlet integration schemes are generally not as accurate as RK4 but, on the other hand, are very efficient in comparison. Let's take a look at two common variants of the method: Position Verlet and Velocity Verlet.

Position Verlet

In the *Position Verlet method*, also known as the *Standard Verlet method*, the velocity of a particle is not stored. Instead, the last position of the particle is stored, and its velocity can then be computed as needed by subtracting the last position from the current position and dividing by the timestep.

Just as the explicit Euler scheme can be derived starting from the forward difference approximation of the first derivative, the standard Verlet scheme can be derived from the central difference approximation to the second derivative (see Chapter 3). We won't show the derivation here but only quote the final result:

$$\mathbf{x}(n+1) = 2\,\mathbf{x}(n) - \mathbf{x}(n-1) + \mathbf{a}(n)\cdot(\Delta t)^2$$

This equation gives the position at the new timestep in terms of the positions at the previous two timesteps without using the velocity.

If desired, the velocity can be computed from the positions—for example, using backward differencing:

$$\mathbf{v}(n+1) = \frac{\mathbf{x}(n+1) - \mathbf{x}(n)}{\Delta t}$$

Alternatively you can use the central differencing scheme, because the previous position is also known, to give a more accurate estimate of the velocity:

$$\mathbf{v}(n+1) = \frac{\mathbf{x}(n+1) - \mathbf{x}(n-1)}{2\Delta t}$$

One problem with the Position Verlet equation as given previously is that it assumes that the timestep is constant. But in general the timesteps in your simulation could be variable. In fact, if you are using Timer or EnterFrame, the timesteps will usually vary slightly. To allow for variable timesteps a modified version of the equation is used:

$$\mathbf{x}(n+1) = 2\,\mathbf{x}(n) - \mathbf{x}(n-1)\Delta t(n)\big/\Delta t(n-1) + \mathbf{a}(n)\cdot\big(\Delta t(n)\big)^2$$

In this equation, $\Delta t(n)$ denotes the current timestep, and $\Delta t(n-1)$ denotes the previous timestep. This form can be called the time-corrected or time-adjusted Position Verlet scheme.

Another potential problem that arises in the implementation of the Position Verlet scheme is the specification of the initial conditions. Because the scheme does not use velocity but the position at the previous timestep, you cannot directly specify the initial velocity together with the initial position as you would normally do. Instead, you need to specify the initial position $\mathbf{x}(0)$ as well as the previous position $\mathbf{x}(-1)$ *before* the initial position! That might sound like nonsense, but you can actually infer the value of that hypothetical position from the initial velocity by applying the backward difference formula for the velocity given previously. Setting n = −1 in that formula gives the following:

$$\mathbf{v}(0) = \frac{\mathbf{x}(0) - \mathbf{x}(-1)}{\Delta t}$$

Solving this equation for $\mathbf{x}(-1)$ then gives this:

$$\mathbf{x}(-1) = \mathbf{x}(0) - \mathbf{v}(0)\Delta t$$

We can now code up a PositionVerlet() function in ForcerIntegrator as follows:

```
private function PositionVerlet():void{
        var temp:Vector2D = _particle.pos2D;
        if (_n==0){
                _acc = getAcc(_particle.pos2D,_particle.velo2D);
                _oldpos = _particle.pos2D.addScaled(_particle.velo2D,-dt).addScaled(_acc,↪
dt*dt/2);
                _olddt = dt;
        }
        _acc = getAcc(_particle.pos2D,_particle.velo2D);
        _particle.pos2D = _particle.pos2D.addScaled(_particle.pos2D.subtract(_oldpos),↪
dt/_olddt).addScaled(_acc,dt*dt);
        _particle.velo2D = (_particle.pos2D.subtract(_oldpos)).multiply(0.5/dt);
        _oldpos = temp;
        _olddt = dt;
        _n++;
}
```

Note that we have new private variables _oldpos and _olddt for storing the previous position and the previous timestep. There is also a private uint variable _n that represents the number of timesteps that have elapsed since the last call to that function. As you can see from the code, the first time the function is called, the position **x**(−1) is set.

Velocity Verlet

One of the problems with the Position Verlet method is that the velocity estimation is not very accurate. The *Velocity Verlet method* fixes this, albeit at some cost in efficiency. The Velocity Verlet is the more commonly used version of the two. The scheme equations are these:

$$\mathbf{x}(n+1) = \mathbf{x}(n) + \mathbf{v}(n)\cdot \Delta t + \frac{1}{2}\mathbf{a}(n)\cdot(\Delta t)^2$$

$$\mathbf{v}(n+1) = \mathbf{v}(n) + \frac{1}{2}\big[\mathbf{a}(n) + \mathbf{a}(n+1)\big]\Delta t$$

Comparing the first equation with the corresponding equation in the Euler scheme shows that we now have an additional term that includes the acceleration. The Euler scheme therefore assumes that the acceleration is zero in the interval of one timestep, whereas the Velocity Verlet method takes into account the acceleration but assumes it is constant during that interval. Perhaps you recall the equation **s** = ut + ½ at² from Chapter 4. The equation for the position update in the Velocity Verlet is exactly of that form (the displacement is **s** = **x**(n+1) − **x**(n)).

Also note that the velocity update equation uses the average of the acceleration at the old and the new timestep rather than the acceleration just at the old timestep. Hence, it is a better approximation of the velocity. For these reasons the Velocity Verlet scheme is more accurate than the Euler scheme, as well as having other nice properties such as greater stability and conservation of energy.

Here is the VelocityVerlet() method in ForcerIntegrator:

```
private function VelocityVerlet():void{
        _acc = getAcc(_particle.pos2D,_particle.velo2D);
        var accPrev:Vector2D = _acc;
        _particle.pos2D=_particle.pos2D.addScaled(_particle.velo2D,dt).addScaled(_acc,dt*dt/2)
;
        _acc = getAcc(_particle.pos2D,_particle.velo2D);
        _particle.velo2D = _particle.velo2D.addScaled(_acc.add(accPrev),dt/2);
}
```

Testing the stability and accuracy of the Verlet schemes

You can now run the spring and orbit simulations using the Verlet schemes. You should find that they do quite a good job in both cases. Verlet schemes are stable, but they are less accurate than RK4.

A simple test to illustrate the differences in the accuracy of all the different schemes can be done by performing a simulation for a problem with a known analytical solution, against which the numerical solutions can then be compared. You might recall that we did such a test for the Euler scheme for a projectile simulation back in Chapter 4. Let's do something similar now for all the different schemes.

The files Projectile.as and Projector.as contain the setup code and the simulation code, respectively. Once again we won't show any code listings because you've seen those sorts of things tons of times by now. The main thing is that the Projectile class creates a ball and initializes its position and velocity such that the ball is thrown upward at an angle, and the `Projector` class extends `ForcerIntegrator` and subjects the ball to gravity. We have set the timestep at 50 milliseconds, as in the other test simulations.

Run the simulation with different integrators specified in `ForcerIntegrator`. The code in `Projector` plots the analytical trajectory as well as the numerically computed trajectory (which, of course, the ball follows). You will find that the time-corrected Position Verlet and all the Euler integrators give a trajectory that deviates slightly from the analytical trajectory (see Figure 14-6). On the other hand, the trajectories predicted using the Velocity Verlet, RK2, and RK4 schemes are so close to the analytical trajectory that they cannot be distinguished. Like RK2, the Velocity Verlet scheme is a second-order scheme. Note that these comparisons are for a specific problem, involving constant acceleration. Different schemes might be more or less accurate with different problems.

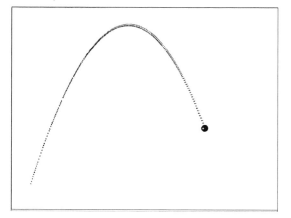

Figure 14-6. Projectile trajectory simulated with Position Verlet scheme (lower curve)

Finally, you might want to check how well the standard Position Verlet does without the time correction. To do this, replace the line of code that updates the position in `PositionVerlet()` with the following one:

```
_particle.pos2D =↩
_particle.pos2D.add(_particle.pos2D).subtract(_oldpos).addScaled(_acc,dt*dt);
```

If you then run the code you will find that the simulation gets it completely wrong! The message is that time correction is essential if you have variable timesteps in your simulation.

Summary

If you plan to get into physics simulation seriously, sooner or later you need to worry about the accuracy and stability of your integration scheme. This chapter has presented some of the most common options at your disposal. The choice of a particular scheme depends on the problem as well as on other practical factors. In the previous chapters of the book we used the Euler scheme exclusively. In Chapter 16 you'll see an example in which you need a more accurate integration scheme.

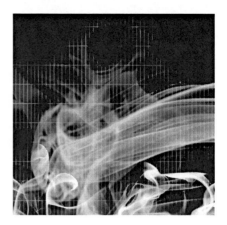

Chapter 15

Other Technical Issues

This penultimate chapter brings together a few topics that you may need to consider if you are going to build more complex simulations. When building such simulations there are likely to be other considerations besides just the physics. Specifically, this chapter focuses on issues that crop up in the following common scenarios: if you are building simulations in 3D, if you want your simulation to be a "scale model" of a real system, or if accuracy is particularly important.

Topics covered in this chapter include these:

- **Doing physics in 3D**: This section discusses how to extend our framework to create 3D simulations. In the process we'll cover some 3D vector and matrix math and associated ActionScript 3.0 classes that will help to handle rigid body rotations in 3D.

- **Building scale models**: This section discusses how to choose units and parameter values to create a scale model of the system you are trying to simulate.

- **Building accurate simulations**: This section reviews some of the factors you need to take into account if you want to create a simulation that needs to be highly accurate.

Because 3D physics is probably what you are likely to be most interested in, we devote the major part of the chapter to doing that. Please note that the focus will be very much on *doing physics in 3D*, rather than on 3D programming in general. Thus, although we'll inevitably have to discuss some aspects of 3D coding in Flash, this chapter is *not* about the latest cutting-edge 3D technology. Flash 3D is a huge subject in itself; there are now a multitude of 3D engines in ActionScript that can do very powerful things, and Adobe's upcoming Stage3D will revolutionize the way we do 3D in Flash. But these topics are really outside the scope of this book. We'll take a much more "primitive" approach here, giving you a good basic understanding of how to program physics in 3D that will help you, regardless of whether you use one of the more advanced frameworks or not.

Doing physics in 3D

With the exception of some simple examples in the earlier chapters, the coded examples in this book have all been in 2D. What does it take to do physics in 3D? How do the physics and coding in 3D differ from that in 2D?

3D versus 2D physics

Let's first discuss 3D physics. Most of the physics we've discussed is essentially unchanged in going from 2D to 3D. The fundamental laws of motion for linear and rotational motion remain the same in their vector forms. Particle motion is treated in a similar way, with the difference that in 3D particles can move in an extra dimension (that's obvious, isn't it?). Later on in this section we'll extend the motion classes to 3D, which will allow you to simulate the motion of any number of particles under the action of different types of forces in 3D space.

Collisions are more complicated because you have to consider the 3D geometry of the colliding objects. Rigid body dynamics is also more complicated because rotation in 3D is more complex and requires some more advanced math. So the next section mainly concentrates on presenting the math background needed to handle 3D rotations.

3D math

There are two pieces of math you need in 3D: vectors in 3D, which are needed to analyze motion just like in 2D; and matrices, which you need to handle rotations.

Vector math in 3D

Vectors in 3D are straightforward extensions of their 2D counterparts. In Chapter 3, we reviewed vector algebra in 2D and in 3D side by side. You may wish to read that section again if you need a refresher. The most important difference between vector algebra in 2D and 3D, apart from the fact that there are three components instead of two, is that you can do cross products in 3D.

The Vector3D class

Back in Chapter 3, we built a **Vector2D** class that we have then steadily been enhancing with new methods. In Flash Player 10 there is now a built-in **Vector3D** class with methods that permit all the basic vector algebra operations that we would expect, such as **add()**, **subtract()**, **scaleBy()**, **dotProduct()**, **crossProduct()**, and so on. However, note that there are no corresponding methods equivalent to our **Vector2D** methods such as **multiply()** and **addScaled()**.

In addition to the three vector components x, y, and z, the **Vector3D** class also allows for a fourth component, w, which can be used to provide additional information such as rotation. If a value for w is not specified, then a default value of 0 is assumed, like for the other components:

```
public function Vector3D(x:Number = 0, y:Number = 0, z:Number = 0, w:Number = 0)
```

Do take the time to have a look at the different properties and methods of **Vector3D** in the online AS3.0 documentation.

Extending Vector3D: the Vector3DX class

The additional methods of the **Vector2D** class such as **multiply()** and **addScaled()** have proven to be quite useful. The difference between the **multiply()** and **scaleBy()** methods is that the former returns a new vector whereas the latter updates the current vector. This is similar to the difference between the `add()` and `incrementBy()` methods. As pointed out in the last section, the `Vector3D` class has an `add()` method but no corresponding `multiply()` method. We have therefore created a `Vector3DX` class in the `com.physicscodes.math` package that extends the `Vector3D` class, augmenting it with additional methods such as `multiply()`, `addScaled()`, and `unit()` that work in analogy with their `Vector2D` counterparts. There is also a public static `convert()` method for converting a `Vector3D` object into a `Vector3DX` object. All these methods leave the `w` property unchanged.

You don't have to use the `Vector3DX` class, but it can save a few lines of code, especially if your code is long and complex. We'll make use of the `Vector3DX` class in the next chapter.

Matrices and rotation in 2D

We've done a good job of avoiding matrices so far, even when discussing rigid body rotation in Chapter 13. While it was fine to do so in 2D, it is more difficult to ignore matrices in 3D. But before we discuss matrix algebra and rotations in 3D, it would help a lot to do so first in the simpler 2D context.

A matrix is essentially an array of numbers, pretty much like a vector. But although a vector is a one-dimensional array, a matrix can be higher dimensional. We'll only ever need to worry about two-dimensional matrices, which look something like this:

$$\begin{pmatrix} 1 & 3 & 4 & 5 \\ 3 & 2 & 5 & 2 \\ 0 & -2 & 7 & 2 \end{pmatrix}$$

This matrix has 3 rows and 4 columns; it's a 3 x 4 matrix. Let's call it A. Then we can identify particular matrix elements by the row and column number. For example, A(3,2) = −2.

Just like arrays, matrices are useful when you have to deal with similar quantities and you have to perform the same operations on them. They provide a compact way to perform calculations; for example, when you have to do rotations and other transformations. But, just as a math vector is more than an array in the sense that it has definite rules for vector algebra (such as vector addition or multiplication), so is a matrix. Let's look at the rules of matrix algebra.

Matrix algebra in 2D

You can add and subtract matrices by adding and subtracting the corresponding elements. This means that you can only add or subtract matrices with the same size, for example for 2 x 2 matrices:

$$\begin{pmatrix} a_1 & b_1 \\ c_1 & d_1 \end{pmatrix} + \begin{pmatrix} a_2 & b_2 \\ c_2 & d_2 \end{pmatrix} = \begin{pmatrix} a_1 + a_2 & b_1 + b_2 \\ c_1 + c_2 & d_1 + d_2 \end{pmatrix}$$

Matrix addition can be applied to represent translations, or displacements, where the position of an object is shifted in space; for example, the following shifts the position of a point by an amount dx and dy along the x and y directions, respectively. This can be represented using 2 x 1 matrices as follows:

$$\begin{pmatrix} x \\ y \end{pmatrix} + \begin{pmatrix} dx \\ dy \end{pmatrix} = \begin{pmatrix} x + dx \\ y + dy \end{pmatrix}$$

Matrix multiplication is a bit more complicated. When you multiply two matrices A and B, you multiply each row of A by each column of B, element by element, and add the results. Here's an example for 2 x 2 matrices:

$$\begin{pmatrix} a_1 & b_1 \\ c_1 & d_1 \end{pmatrix}\begin{pmatrix} a_2 & b_2 \\ c_2 & d_2 \end{pmatrix} = \begin{pmatrix} a_1 a_2 + b_1 c_2 & a_1 b_2 + b_1 d_2 \\ c_1 a_2 + d_1 c_2 & c_1 b_2 + d_1 d_2 \end{pmatrix}$$

This means that you can only multiply matrix A by matrix B if A has the same number of columns as B has rows. In other words, you can multiply an M x N matrix only by an N x P matrix.

Note that multiplying the mth row by the nth column gives you the (m,n) matrix element in the product. Also, the result of multiplying an M x N matrix by an N x P matrix is an M x P matrix.

Matrix multiplication can transform objects in all sorts of ways, depending on the form of the matrix we're multiplying with. Let's begin with rotation matrices.

Rotation matrices in 2D

Matrices are especially useful for doing rotations. To see this, let's say you have an object that you want to rotate through an angle θ about an axis perpendicular to the xy plane through the origin (see Figure 15-1). For now let's use the math coordinate system so that the y-axis points upward, and angles are measured in a counterclockwise sense.

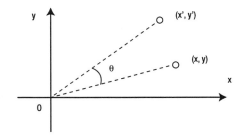

Figure 15-1. Rotating an object in 2D

Using trigonometry, you can show that each point on the object with coordinates (x, y) will be moved to a new position with coordinates (x', y') given by the following equations:

$$x' = x\cos(\theta) - y\sin(\theta)$$
$$y' = x\sin(\theta) + y\cos(\theta)$$

By the way, this is the math behind the **rotate()** method of the **Vector2D** class that we introduced in Chapter 13. You can represent this relationship between the new and old coordinates as a single matrix equation:

$$\begin{pmatrix} x' \\ y' \end{pmatrix} = \begin{pmatrix} \cos(\theta) & -\sin(\theta) \\ \sin(\theta) & \cos(\theta) \end{pmatrix}\begin{pmatrix} x \\ y \end{pmatrix}$$

What we have done here is to represent each of the position vectors **r** and **r'** of points (x, y) and (x', y') as a matrix with a single column (called a *column matrix* or *column vector*). If you multiply out the matrices on the right side and equate the elements of the resulting column vector with those on the left side of the equation, you will recover the previous two equations.

We can write this matrix equation in a convenient shorthand form as follows:

$$\mathbf{r'} = \mathbf{R}\,\mathbf{r}$$

The matrix **R** is called the *rotation matrix*, and is given by the following:

$$\mathbf{R} = \begin{pmatrix} \cos(\theta) & -\sin(\theta) \\ \sin(\theta) & \cos(\theta) \end{pmatrix}$$

Instead of rotating the object, you could also rotate the coordinate system (axes):

$$\mathbf{R} = \begin{pmatrix} \cos(\theta) & \sin(\theta) \\ -\sin(\theta) & \cos(\theta) \end{pmatrix}$$

What's happening here is that rotating the coordinate axes by angle θ is the same as rotating the object by angle –θ. So, if you replace θ by –θ in the original matrix and use the fact that sin (–θ) = – sin (θ), and cos (–θ) = cos (θ), you end up with the second matrix. So, the rule for swapping between object and coordinate system rotations is to "reverse the signs of the sines."

Doing other transformations with matrices

You can do all sorts of other transformations with matrices, not just rotation. Here are the matrices for some common transformations in 2D:

Reflection in x-axis: $\begin{pmatrix} 1 & 0 \\ 0 & -1 \end{pmatrix}$

Reflection in y-axis: $\begin{pmatrix} -1 & 0 \\ 0 & 1 \end{pmatrix}$

Scaling: $\begin{pmatrix} sx & 0 \\ 0 & sy \end{pmatrix}$

Skewing (shearing) parallel to x-axis: $\begin{pmatrix} 1 & k \\ 0 & 1 \end{pmatrix}$

Skewing (shearing) parallel to y-axis:
$$\begin{pmatrix} 1 & 0 \\ k & 1 \end{pmatrix}$$

Using the Matrix class

AS3.0 includes a **Matrix** class, which is basically a transformation matrix that combines four major types: translation, scaling, rotation and skewing.

The **Matrix** class takes six numbers (a, b, c, d, tx, and ty) as input and produces a matrix with this form:

$$\begin{pmatrix} a & c & tx \\ b & d & ty \\ 0 & 0 & 1 \end{pmatrix}$$

The resulting transformation properties of the matrix depend on the values of these inputs. The two translation parameters tx and ty specify the distance by which an object is shifted along the x and y direction, respectively.

If b and c are zero, then we have a scaling with a = sx and d = sy, the scaling factors in the x and y directions respectively.

If a and d are zero, we can set b and c to skew an object along the y- and x-axis, respectively.

Finally, we can set a, b, c, and d in the form of a rotation matrix that (no surprise) will rotate an object through an angle θ:

$$\begin{pmatrix} \cos(\theta) & -\sin(\theta) \\ \sin(\theta) & \cos(\theta) \end{pmatrix}$$

Note that the AS3.0 **Matrix** class is not endowed with ordinary matrix algebra. You cannot, for example, perform matrix multiplication on two **Matrix** objects in the math sense. Instead you apply the transformations using built-in methods of the **Matrix** class; for example, **rotate()**, **scale()**, **translate()**. Much more detailed explanations can be found in the AS3.0 online documentation.

Matrices and rotation in 3D

In 3D, the situation is complicated by the fact that you have three components and also three independent directions about which you can perform rotations. The rotation matrix is a 3 x 3 matrix, and for rotation about the z-axis it is given by this:

$$\begin{pmatrix} \cos(\theta) & -\sin(\theta) & 0 \\ \sin(\theta) & \cos(\theta) & 0 \\ 0 & 0 & 1 \end{pmatrix}$$

The rotation matrix about the x-axis is given by this:

$$\begin{pmatrix} 1 & 0 & 0 \\ 0 & \cos(\theta) & -\sin(\theta) \\ 0 & \sin(\theta) & \cos(\theta) \end{pmatrix}$$

A rotation about the y-axis is given by this matrix:

$$\begin{pmatrix} \cos(\theta) & 0 & \sin(\theta) \\ 0 & 1 & 0 \\ -\sin(\theta) & 0 & \cos(\theta) \end{pmatrix}$$

As in the 2D case, the signs of the sines are reversed if the coordinate axes are rotated instead.

Rotation matrices can be combined by multiplying them together. So a rotation with matrix $\mathbf{R}_1$ followed by a rotation with matrix $\mathbf{R}_2$ is equivalent to a rotation with matrix $\mathbf{R}_2 \mathbf{R}_1$. Note that the order of the rotation matters in 3D. For example, rotating a cuboid by 90° clockwise about the x-axis and then 90° clockwise about the z-axis will have the cuboid end up in a different orientation than a corresponding rotation about the z-axis followed by a rotation about the x-axis. Try it with a book! Mathematically, this corresponds to the fact that matrix multiplication is not commutative. In other words:

$$\mathbf{R}_1 \mathbf{R}_2 \neq \mathbf{R}_2 \mathbf{R}_1$$

On the other hand, very small incremental (infinitesimal) rotations *are* commutative, so it does not matter in what order infinitesimal rotations about different axes are performed. This has important implications for how we can represent angular orientation and angular velocity in 3D. The noncommutativity of rotations about the x-, y-, and z-axis means that there is no unambiguous meaning to angular orientation as a vector with three components. So you cannot form a true vector from angular rotation θ in 3D. However, you *can* form a vector for small angular increments $\Delta\theta$ and therefore for angular velocity $\omega = d\theta/dt$. This point may sound like it's of mere academic interest, but you'll soon see how it will help us to build relevant classes and generate rotations for rigid bodies in 3D.

Matrix3D class

Flash Player 10 has a `Matrix3D` class that, like the 2D `Matrix` class, avoids the need to perform any matrix multiplications to apply transformations such as rotations. Instead it performs transformations using built-in methods. The transformations it can handle are rotations, scaling, and translation.

A `Matrix3D` instance is assigned automatically to any display object if its `z` property or any scaling or rotation property (such as `rotationX`) is set. The `Matrix3D` object can then be accessed through the display object's `transform.matrix3D` property as follows:

`obj.transform.matrix3D`

An example of a `Matrix3D` method is the `appendRotation()` method:

`public function appendRotation(degrees:Number, axis:Vector3D, pivotPoint:Vector3D = null):void`

This method performs an incremental rotation of an object about a specified axis after other transformations have been applied. It takes three arguments, the third being optional. The first argument is the angle in degrees through which the object is to be rotated; the second argument is the axis about which the rotation takes place. Any **Vector3D** instance can be specified, and there are also **Vector3D** constants to denote the coordinate axes: **X_AXIS** (Vector3D(1,0,0)), **Y_AXIS** (Vector3D(0,1,0)), and **Z_AXIS** (Vector3D(0,0,1)).

We will not go into all the various methods but instead explain each method that we use when we introduce them. Refer to the AS3.0 online documentation for details.

Creating classes for 3D objects and motion

After all that theory, we are now in a position to modify some of the base classes in our framework to include 3D properties and methods.

First, let's modify the **Particle** class. This class already had some 3D properties—**xpos**, **ypos**, **zpos**; and **vx**, **vy**, **vz** (and their associated **Vector3D** properties **pos** and **velo**)—but we'll modify it and create a separate **Particle3D** class so as not to clutter **Particle** with extra code that won't be needed. Also, there is code in **Particle** that we won't need in **Particle3D**: code associated with the **angDispl()** property. We do not need angular displacement because it does not generalize to 3D. This follows from the fact that there is no unambiguous meaning to an angular orientation vector in 3D due to the noncommutativity of rotations about different axes, as discussed in the previous section on "Matrices and rotation in 3D." Therefore, we'll get rid of it. But because angular velocity does generalize to a vector, the **angVelo()** **Number** property is now replaced by a **Vector3D** property with the same name. This is to allow for the fact that these quantities can have any direction in 3D space because an object in 3D can rotate about any axis (whereas rotation in 2D is restricted to be around the z-axis because objects are constrained to remain within the 2D plane). We've also added corresponding components of these vectors with public names **omegax**, **omegay**, and **omegaz** (for the angular velocity components about the x-, y-, and z-axis).

Next, we modify the **RigidBody** class, calling the new class **RigidBody3D**, by extending the **Particle3D** class (instead of **Particle**) and replacing all **Vector2D** variables by corresponding **Vector3D** variables. A significant change in **RigidBody3D** is to replace the **momentOfInertia** property (a **Number**) by a moment of inertia vector **Im** consisting of three components **Ixx**, **Iyy**, and **Izz**, so that the constructor of **RigidBody3D** takes a total of four arguments:

```
RigidBody3D(pcm:Vector3D, pim:Vector3D, pmass:Number=1, pcharge:Number=0)
```

Strictly speaking, the moment of inertia I in 3D is a 3 x 3 matrix and is not given by just three numbers. But for some shapes, such as cuboids, only the three diagonal elements of that matrix **Ixx**, **Iyy**, and **Izz** are non-zero. Assuming that we will be dealing only with such objects, we can then simplify the math and coding considerably by working with those three components that we can put into a **Vector3D** object rather than with a 3 x 3 matrix.

Now it's time to modify the relevant motion classes. We'll modify three of them for now (**Mover**, **ForcerRB**, and **Forces**), calling the new classes **Mover3D**, **ForcerRB3D**, and **Forces3D**, respectively. In **Mover3D**, we replace all **Particle** and **Vector2D** objects by **Particle3D** and **Vector3D**, respectively. In using **Vector3D** we have to remember that some methods that we used for **Vector2D**, such as **addScaled()**, are not available for **Vector3D**. So we need to modify the code accordingly. For example, this is the updated **moveObject()** method:

```
protected function moveObject():void {
        var vec:Vector3D = _particle.velo;
        vec.scaleBy(_dt);
        _particle.pos = _particle.pos.add(vec);
}
```

Because there is now no **angDispl** property, we get rid of the **spinObject()** method used to update the angular displacement. So although **Mover3D** will make a 3D object translate, it won't make it rotate. We'll apply rotations in a different way, as you'll see in the example toward the end of this section.

ForcerRB3D, which extends **Mover3D**, takes a **RigidBody3D** object in its constructor:

```
public function ForcerRB3D(prigidBody:RigidBody3D):void{
        _rigidBody = prigidBody;
        super(prigidBody);
}
```

The main modification is then to take into account the **Vector3D** nature of the torque, angular acceleration, and angular velocity vectors. The important changes are the following methods:

```
protected function calcForce():void{
        _force = new Vector3D(0,0,0);
        _torque = new Vector3D(0,0,0);
}

private function updateAccel():void{
        var vec:Vector3D = _force;
        vec.scaleBy(1/_rigidBody.mass);
        _acc = vec; // linear acceleration update

        // (note that a diagonal moment of inertia matrix is assumed here)
        vec=_torque;
        vec.x*=1/_rigidBody.Im.x;
        vec.y*=1/_rigidBody.Im.y;
        vec.z*=1/_rigidBody.Im.z;
        _alp=vec; // angular acceleration update
}

private function updateVelo():void{
        var vec:Vector3D = _acc;
        vec.scaleBy(dt);
        _rigidBody.velo = _rigidBody.velo.add(vec);      // linear velocity update

        vec=_alp;
        vec.scaleBy(dt);
        _rigidBody.angVelo = _rigidBody.angVelo.add(vec); // angular velocity update
}
```

As you can see, in **updateAccel()** we are assuming that the inertia matrix of the rigid body is diagonal (as discussed earlier in this section), so that we can deal with the diagonal components **Ixx**, **Iyy**, and **Izz** instead of a matrix. This approach will suffice for the simple example that we'll build in this chapter.

Finally, we update the **Forces** class to **Forces3D.as** simply by replacing **Vector2D** objects by **Vector3D** objects, taking care to use only methods that are defined for **Vector3D**.

We are now almost ready to go 3D. The only thing we are missing is a 3D object that we can actually see (remember that **Particle3D** and **RigidBody3D**, like their 2D counterparts, don't have any graphics). We need a 3D model.

Creating 3D models

There are a variety of ways to create 3D models. We refer you to the growing number of books on 3D in Flash—or perhaps you are a 3D expert yourself! We'll keep things very simple here and use the drawing application programming interface (API) to create a polyhedron (the 3D equivalent of a polygon) just like we created the **Polygon** class in Chapter 13.

Applying perspective distortion

The method we will use here is based on a 3D tutorial by Barbara Kaskosz on the Flash & Math web site (**www.flashandmath.com**), which is a highly recommended web site. The method consists of applying perspective projection to a polyhedron object defined by vertices and faces, sorting the faces by their average z distance (so-called z-sorting), and then drawing the edges and faces of the resulting polyhedron using the drawing API. The following perspective formula is used to rescale the coordinates of the vertices:

$$\lambda = \frac{f}{f+z}$$

Here λ is the scaling factor, z is the z-coordinate of the vertex, and f is a perspective parameter analogous to the focal length of a camera. The scaling factor is the factor by which the dimensions of an object are modified due to perspective. This formula shows that the scaling factor depends on the distance z. If z is large, the scaling factor λ is much less than 1, so we have a large amount of perspective distortion. But if z is zero, the scale factor λ is 1, so there is no distortion.

The formula also shows that the scaling factor to perspective depends on the value of f due. If f is large, adding z to it does not change it much (unless z is very large), so the ratio f/(f+z) is nearly unity. Therefore, larger values of f produce less perspective distortion. You need to choose a value for f that will produce the desired perspective effect.

PolyhedronRB class

The **PolyhedronRB** class implements the method described in the previous section. The constructor of **PolyhedronRB** takes no fewer than 11 arguments, the last five of which are optional:

```
PolyhedronRB(pfl:Number, pcm:Vector3D, pim:Vector3D, pvertices:Vector.<Vector3D>,↰
pfaces:Vector.<Array>, pfacesColors:Array, pedgesColor:uint=0x000000, pfacesAlpha:Number=0.8,↰
pedgesThickness:uint=2, pmass:Number=1, pcharge:Number=0)
```

The first parameter is the "focal length," the next two are **Vector3D** parameters that specify the center of mass and moment of inertia components (**Ixx**, **Iyy**, **Izz**), respectively. The **pvertices** parameter is a **Vector** (typed array) consisting of **Vector3D** instances that each specifies the position of a vertex in 3D space. The **pfaces** parameter is a **Vector** of arrays, each of which specifies a group of vertices (identified by the index number in the **pvertices Vector**). An example will soon make all this clearer.

The next parameter is an array that gives the colors of each face. The next five parameters are optional and specify the color of the edges (as a single color, with a default of black), the transparency of the faces (with a default value of 0.8), the thickness of the edges (default value 2), and the mass (default value 1) and charge (default value 0) of the object.

The key piece of code in the **PolyhedronRB** class that we need to focus on is the **updatePolyhedron()** public method:

```
public function updatePolyhedron(rotx:Number,roty:Number,rotz:Number):void{
        _sprite.transform.matrix3D.appendRotation(rotx,Vector3D.X_AXIS);
```

```
            _sprite.transform.matrix3D.appendRotation(roty,Vector3D.Y_AXIS);
            _sprite.transform.matrix3D.appendRotation(rotz,Vector3D.Z_AXIS);
            drawPolyhedron();
}
```

The method adds incremental rotations (specified as arguments) to the **matrix3D** property of a **Sprite** object named **_sprite** using the **appendRotation()** method of the **Matrix3D** class described previously. The **drawPolyhedron()** method is then called. This is a private method that transforms the polyhedron by applying the **Matrix3D** transform just updated and then doing the perspective projection, z-sorting, and drawing as described in the previous section. We do not need to go over the details, except to show how the first step (applying the **Matrix3D** transform) is done:

```
for (i=0; i<_numVertices; i++){
        newVertices[i] = _sprite.transform.matrix3D.deltaTransformVector(_vertices[i]);
}
```

Here we are applying the **Matrix3D** instance that we updated in **updatePolyhedron()** to each vertex using the **deltaTransformVector()** method of **Matrix3D**. This method applies the transformation matrix without using its translation coefficients. In other words, it applies only rotations and scalings. This is exactly what we want because we'll be doing translations using **Mover3D**, anyway. An alternative **Matrix3D** method is the **transformVector()** method, which does apply translations as well.

In a simulation, we would typically call the **updatePolyhedron()** public method at each timestep to apply the **Matrix3D** transform to the vertices of the polyhedron and redraw the polyhedron, making it rotate dynamically. The physics comes in specifying the angular increments **rotx**, **roty**, and **rotz** as arguments in the **updatePolyhedron()** method at each timestep. Let's look at a simple example now.

Example: A rotating cube

This example will be a 3D extension of the **RigidBodyDynamics** and **WindTurbines** simulations of Chapter 13. We will create a cube in 3D and apply a torque about a given axis through its center of mass by clicking and holding the mouse, causing the cube to rotate about that axis in 3D.

The setup file is called **RotatingRBCube.as** and contains the following code:

```
package{
        import flash.display.Sprite;
        import flash.geom.Vector3D;
        import com.physicscodes.objects.PolyhedronRB;

        public class RotatingRBCube extends Sprite{
                private var _cube:PolyhedronRB;
                private var _vertices:Vector.<Vector3D>=new Vector.<Vector3D>();
                private var _faces:Vector.<Array>=new Vector.<Array>();
                private var _facesColors:Array;
                private var _radius:Number = 60; // half-height of cube
                private var _fl:Number = 500; // focal length
                private var _cm:Vector3D = new Vector3D(0,0,0);
                private var _im:Vector3D = new Vector3D(1,1,1);

                public function RotatingRBCube():void{
                        init();
                }
                private function init():void{
```

```
                        // define the cube's vertices relative to its center of mass
                        _vertices[0] = new Vector3D(-_radius,-_radius,-_radius);
                        _vertices[1] = new Vector3D(_radius,-_radius,-_radius);
                        _vertices[2] = new Vector3D(_radius,-_radius,_radius);
                        _vertices[3] = new Vector3D(-_radius,-_radius,_radius);
                        _vertices[4] = new Vector3D(-_radius,_radius,-_radius);
                        _vertices[5] = new Vector3D(_radius,_radius,-_radius);
                        _vertices[6] = new Vector3D(_radius,_radius,_radius);
                        _vertices[7] = new Vector3D(-_radius,_radius,_radius);

                        // define the cube's faces
                        _faces[0] = [0,4,5,1];
                        _faces[1] = [1,5,6,2];
                        _faces[2] = [2,6,7,3];
                        _faces[3] = [3,7,4,0];
                        _faces[4] = [4,5,6,7];
                        _faces[5] = [0,1,2,3];

                        // define the faces' colors
                        _facesColors = ↵
[0xff0000,0x00ff00,0x0000ff,0x00ffff,0xff00ff,0xffff00];
                        // create the cube as a PolyhedronRB instance
                        _cube = new PolyhedronRB(_fl, _cm, _im, _vertices, _faces,↵
_facesColors);

                        addChild(_cube);

                        // make the cube move
                        var mover:RotatingRBCubeMover = new RotatingRBCubeMover(_cube);
                        mover.startTime();
                }
        }
}
```

This code should be quite straightforward to follow. The cube (a **PolyhedronRB** instance) is assigned to a private variable **_cube**, and the private variables **_vertices** and **_faces** are **Vector** objects that hold the vertices (as **Vector3D** instances) and faces (as arrays of integers), respectively. The colors of the faces are stored in an array called **_facesColors**. The focal length is set to 500, although you can adjust its value as desired. The **_cm** variable is the location of the center of mass (set to **Vector3D(0,0,0)**) by default here, although that will be changed in the **Mover** class). The moment of inertia vector is set to **Vector3D(1,1,1)**; because it's a cube I_{xx}, I_{yy}, and I_{zz} need to be equal, but you can change the actual value if you wish.

In the **init()** private method the vertices are specified relative to the center of mass of the cube. The faces are then defined by specifying the array indices of the vertices on each face. The colors of the faces are then specified as an array, and the cube is instantiated and added to the display list. Finally, the cube is animated through the **startTime()** method of a **RotatingRBCubeMover** instance.

The **RotatingRBCubeMover** class, as you'd expect, extends the **ForcerRB3D** class. Here is the full code:

```
package {
        import com.physicscodes.motion.ForcerRB3D;
        import com.physicscodes.motion.Forces3D;
        import com.physicscodes.objects.PolyhedronRB;
        import flash.geom.Vector3D;
        import flash.events.MouseEvent;
```

```
public class RotatingRBCubeMover extends ForcerRB3D {
        private var _object:PolyhedronRB;
        private var _mass:Number;
        private var _g:Number = 0;
        private var _k:Number = 0.2; // angular damping factor
        private var _tq:Vector3D = new Vector3D(0,0,0);
        private var _tqMax:Vector3D = new Vector3D(10,10,10);

        public function RotatingRBCubeMover(pobject:PolyhedronRB):void {
                _object = pobject;
                _mass = _object.mass;
                _object.pos = new Vector3D(275,200,0);
                _object.stage.addEventListener(MouseEvent.MOUSE_DOWN, onDown);
                super(_object);
        }
        override protected function calcForce():void {
                force = Forces3D.constantGravity(_mass,_g);
                torque = _tq;
                var vec:Vector3D = _object.angVelo;
                vec.scaleBy(-_k);
                torque = torque.add(vec);
        }

        override protected function moveObject():void{
                super.moveObject();
                updateObject();
        }

        private function updateObject():void{
                var vec:Vector3D = _object.angVelo;
                vec.scaleBy(dt);
                _object.updatePolyhedron(vec.x,vec.y,vec.z);
        }

        private function onDown(e:MouseEvent):void{
                _object.stage.addEventListener(MouseEvent.MOUSE_UP,onUp);
                _tq = _tqMax;
        }
        private function onUp(e:MouseEvent):void{
                _object.stage.removeEventListener(MouseEvent.MOUSE_UP,onUp);
                _tq = new Vector3D(0,0,0);
        }

    }
}
```

Again, this is not a difficult piece of code by any means, and you should be able to figure out most of it. In the **calcForce()** method we have a gravity force (but note that g is set to zero by default, so gravity will be zero unless you change the value of g) and a constant torque set by the **_tq Vector3D** variable that is controlled by user interaction. If the mouse is held down, the value of **_tq** is set (through the **_tqMax** variable) to **Vector3D(10,10,10)**; otherwise, it is **Vector3D(0,0,0)**. In **calcForce()** we also apply a damping torque proportional to the angular velocity of the cube.

We override `moveObject()` to add a new private method named `updateObject()`, whose task is to calculate the angular increment that needs to be applied and to call the public `updatePolyhedron()` method of the cube, passing the components of the angular increment as arguments. The angular increment is calculated by multiplying the current angular velocity of the cube by the timestep (using the definition of angular velocity):

$$\Delta\boldsymbol{\theta} = \boldsymbol{\omega}\,\Delta t$$

This ties in with our earlier discussion on matrices in 3D: we can treat a small incremental change in angular orientation as a vector.

Run the simulation and click anywhere on the screen to apply a torque that causes the cube to start rotating (see Figure 15-2). Because of the included angular damping torque, the angular velocity does not increase indefinitely under the applied torque, but reaches a steady value just like in the 2D wind turbine simulation. Experiment by changing the different parameters such as the moment of inertia, the magnitude of the applied torque, and the value of g. For example, changing the value of `_tqMax` to `Vector3D(10,0,0)` applies a torque about the x-axis and therefore generates rotation about that axis. Change the value of g to a non-zero value such as 10, and you can make the cube fall as it rotates.

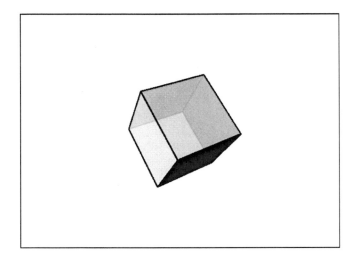

Figure 15-2. A cube rotating under the action of an applied torque

In the source code for this chapter you will also find a slightly modified (and more interactive) version of the simulation in the files `RotatingRBCube2.as` and `RotatingRBCubeMover2.as`. In that version the magnitude of the applied torque is proportional to the distance of the mouse from the cube's center, and its direction is along the axis joining the mouse to the cube's center.

Integrating with 3D engines

That last example was fun, but a lot more can be done with the right tools. The native 3D capabilities of Flash Player 10 are rather limited, but there are a number of third-party 3D engines that are vastly more powerful. Examples include Away3D, Papervision3D, and Sandy3D. Flash 3D is a whole subject in its own right, and a deeper exploration of it is beyond the scope of this book. If you are interested in doing physics in 3D, we encourage you to pick up one of the many books on 3D in Flash that have appeared in recent years. We look forward to seeing what you create by combining those 3D engines with the physics you learn in this book!

Looking ahead to Stage3D

The 3D capabilities of Flash Player 10 that we have explored could more precisely be described as 2.5D. They allow 2D objects to be rendered to the screen using perspective projection to create the illusion of 3D content. A major new development in the upcoming Flash Player 11 release is the Stage3D APIs (formerly known by the code name Molehill). This is a set of low-level, shader-based APIs that will have many advanced 3D features, allow GPU hardware acceleration for significant performance improvements, and allow both 2D and 3D content to be delivered across multiple devices.

It is expected that most of the existing Flash 3D engines will be enabled to use Stage3D by the time it is available in a future release of Flash Player.

Building scale models

Let's begin this section by clarifying the meaning of the title. By *scale model* we do not mean a physical scale model like that of an airplane. We mean a computer model in which all the relevant physical parameters are in appropriate proportion relative to the real system it is meant to simulate. In this sense, a scale model may include representing physical objects to scale, but it goes well beyond this simple visual aspect; it must also, in some sense that we'll make more precise soon, scale the physics correctly.

Scaling for realism

Why is scale modeling important? Correct scale modeling is necessary for a simulation to replicate realistically the behavior of a system that is being modeled. Having the correct physics equations and appropriate visual representations as well as added effects like 3D are obviously important for realism in your games and simulations. Perhaps less obvious is the need to choose appropriate parameter values consistently so that all the aspects of your simulation work together with the right length and time scales to produce a realistic model of the real world.

How do we do this? First, we'll illustrate the process of scale modeling with a very simple example; then at the end of this section we'll give you a general formal method for dealing with more complex simulations.

A simple example

Suppose you want to create a 2D game of volleyball: characters will be tossing the ball around and for much of the time it will therefore be moving under gravity, like a projectile. There will be scenery and buildings around, and you want your game to be a scale model visually and functionally. To proceed, let's consider a simple hypothetical scene where the ball is at the height of a building and is falling down under gravity. You want the ball to fall down at a rate that is consistent with the length scales in the surrounding scenery; in this case, the building height. Assuming that the only force is pure gravity without drag or friction or wind effects, and considering only the vertical motion for simplicity (but without loss of generality), the underlying physics can be described by a single equation. Applying Newton's second law, F = ma, with the force F given by mg, we arrive at this equation:

$$a = g$$

This equation, of course, merely expresses the fact that all objects fall with the same vertical acceleration of g, regardless of their mass or other characteristics. As you know, your simulation will integrate this equation twice: the first time to obtain the velocity of the ball and the second time to obtain its displacement. The whole problem is controlled by a single parameter: the acceleration due to gravity g. The question therefore boils down to this: what value of g must you use in your simulation so that the ball falls at a realistic rate, consistent with the sizes and distances in the game? The actual value of g is 9.8 m/s^2, or approximately 10 m/s^2. But this is not the value you can use in your simulation because you are not using the same units in your simulation. See Figure 15-3.

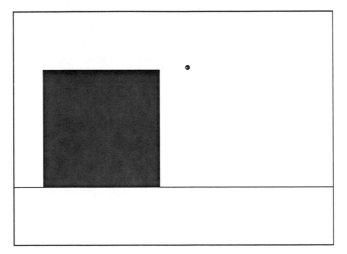

Figure 15-3. Simulating a falling ball to scale

Choosing units

First you need to choose the units for relevant physical quantities in your simulation. The most important units you need are those for time, length, and mass. They are called *base quantities* in physics. Other quantities such as velocity and acceleration depend on these base quantities and their units can be derived from those of the base quantities by using their defining equations: they are therefore called *derived quantities*.

In this case, because mass drops out of the equations, it's completely irrelevant what unit or indeed what value you use for the mass of the ball. So that leaves two base quantities that we need to worry about: time and length (or distance).

Let's assume that you want *real-time simulation*: in other words, the simulation should proceed at the same rate as real "wall-clock" time. (Sometimes you might not want this: for example, if you are simulating the solar system, you may not want to wait a year for the Earth to go round the Sun once!) In Figure 15-3, the ball in your simulation would then take exactly the same time to fall as it would if falling from the height of a real building. Therefore, you choose to measure time in seconds, as in real life. Not only that, but you want 1 second of simulation time to be equal to 1 second of real time: your scaling factor for time is 1.

The natural unit of distance to use for a screen-based visual simulation is the pixel (px). You also need to decide on an appropriate scaling factor to convert actual distances to pixels.

Scaling factors and parameter values

Suppose that the building in your scene would be 5 m tall in real life, and that you represent it by a rectangle of height 200 px. That means your scaling factor is 0.025 m/px; each pixel represents 0.025 m or

2.5 cm. You can use this length scale factor to scale other objects accordingly. So if your ball is a volleyball of radius 10 cm, its radius in the simulation would be 4 pixels.

Going back to our original question: what value should you give to g? The way you figure this out is as follows. Being an acceleration, g is measured in m/s^2. Now, each second is an actual second in the simulation, but each meter is 40 px in the simulation. Therefore, scaling the approximate value of g = 10 m/s^2 would give g = 400 in the simulation!

The files ScaleModel.as and ScaleModelMover.as implement these values in this simple simulation. In the code, the ball is made to stop when it falls the 200 px (equivalent to 5 m in reality) to the ground. The time since the beginning of the simulation is then traced. Run the simulation and you'll find that the ball takes approximately 1 second to fall to the ground. Is this realistic? It's easy to find out using the old formula you met in Chapter 4:

$$s = ut + \frac{1}{2}at^2$$

Here the displacement s is the height fallen (5 m); u is the initial velocity magnitude (zero) and a is the acceleration due to gravity g (10 m/s^2). Substituting these values indeed gives t = 1 s. We have a real-time scale model! The value traced in the simulation is not exactly 1, but it is close enough. One of the reasons it's not exactly 1 is because the ball is detected to be past the ground level slightly later because it's moving so fast. When you run the simulation, you'll see that it stops slightly below the "ground".

Suppose you naively gave g the value of 10 in the simulation. What would be the consequence? Do this now, and you should find that the ball takes more than 6 seconds to reach the ground – hardly realistic!

Of course, you may not always need to be as careful as this in fixing the parameters of your simulation. You may not care about having a scale model at all; perhaps you are just interested in creating an animation that looks roughly right. But it's useful to know how to do this when realism is really important. In more complex simulations it helps to have a systematic method to work out the values of your parameters.

Rescaling equations

The method of *rescaling* is a formal procedure that can help to do just this. It is especially useful when you have more than one parameter whose value you need to work out or if there are multiple scale factors, but we'll demonstrate the method for the simple example we've just looked at.

Rescaling involves scaling the variables in a system, re-expressing the equations in terms of the new scaled variables and then comparing the scaled equation with the original one. The procedure is as follows.

First, write down the governing equation or equations (algebraic or differential), identifying all the variables. In our example, the equation is a = g, but this is really the following differential equation:

$$\frac{d^2s}{dt^2} = g$$

Next, define scaling factors for each of the variables as follows:

$$s = \lambda \hat{s} \qquad t = \tau \hat{t}$$

Here, the variables with hats are the new scaled variables, and the Greek letters are the corresponding scaling factors.

Next, substitute the old variables into the original equation. In the preceding differential equation, note that the second derivative means that we are dividing a displacement increment by a time increment twice. Making the substitution, we therefore arrive at this:

$$\frac{\lambda}{\tau^2}\frac{d^2\hat{s}}{d\hat{t}^2}=g$$

We can rewrite this transformed equation as the following:

$$\frac{d^2\hat{s}}{d\hat{t}^2}=\frac{\tau^2 g}{\lambda}$$

Comparing this with the original equation, we deduce that the equation in terms of the scaled variables will be exactly the same form as the original equation, provided that the right side is equal to the rescaled value of g:

$$\hat{g}=\frac{\tau^2 g}{\lambda}$$

This equation gives a constraint between the scaling factors and the rescaled value of the parameter g. So if we choose two of them, we can obtain the third. In this example, we chose the scaling factors for distance and time. So we can get the rescaled value of g by substituting the values of the scaling factors τ and λ. The scaling factor τ for time t is 1, as discussed previously, while the scaling factor λ for distance s is 5/200 or 0.025 m/px, as seen in the last subsection. Therefore, the scaled value of g that we need for the simulation is given by the following:

$$\hat{g}=\tau^2 g/\lambda=10/0.025=400$$

This is just as we reasoned earlier.

Note that we could alternatively fix the rescaled value of g together with the scaling factor of one of the variables (either time or length). The previous constraint would then give us the scaling factor for the remaining variable.

For this simple example, the formal procedure just outlined is certainly overkill, but add in more variables and a more complex system of equations, and it will come in handy indeed.

Building accurate simulations

If you want to build really accurate simulations, there are a number of things that you need to consider carefully. We discussed most of them at various times through the book, but it is useful to briefly review them here.

Using Number for calculations

As we pointed out in Chapter 4, you should avoid using pixel-based properties such as **x** and **y** for performing calculations. That's because Flash stores them in units of twips, which are 1/20th of a pixel, or 0.05 px. Hence, variables that use pixel-based quantities are never more accurate than 0.05, and errors may quickly accumulate, making visible differences in simulations.

Instead you should use **Number** variables for performing calculations and then assign the result to an object's **x**, **y**, or **z** properties to update their position as necessary. This is why we defined position variables such as **xpos** as **Number** variables in classes such as **Particle** to use in calculations. The resulting increase in accuracy can be considerable.

Choosing an appropriate integration scheme

The previous chapter was wholly devoted to numerical integration schemes and their characteristics such as accuracy and stability. Therefore, there is not much more to be said here. Just to reiterate briefly, the usual Euler scheme is not very accurate, being only a first-order scheme; The fourth-order Runge-Kutta scheme, RK4, is generally a good choice for simulations where accuracy is important, although this comes at the price of reduced efficiency. The RK2 and Velocity Verlet schemes offer a good compromise between accuracy and speed, being second order (and therefore more accurate than the Euler scheme) and at the same time being substantially simpler than RK4.

Using an appropriate timestep

Together with the integration scheme, you need to choose an appropriate timestep for your simulation. Numerical schemes are more accurate with smaller timesteps. Higher-order schemes such as RK4 converge faster than lower-order schemes such as Euler. This implies that RK4 is more accurate for a given timestep. You can control the timestep by setting the rate at which a **Timer** instance fires. However, there is a limit to how small the timestep can be because the actual time interval between **Timer** events includes the time it takes to execute all the code within the event handler. Therefore, if your simulation is complex and involves lots of calculations or animation, the actual timestep may be substantially larger than what you specify in the timer.

Some simulations are so complex that the calculations cannot be done within a reasonably small timestep, and it may not therefore be possible to perform them in real time. One possible solution is to precompute and then animate afterward. In this way, you can "decouple" the simulation timestep from the animation timestep. An example of this method will be applied in the solar system simulation in Chapter 16.

Using accurate initial conditions

Some simulations are sensitive to the values for the position and velocity of the simulated object that you start with. A small change in these initial conditions could produce a large change in the subsequent motion. For example, in simulations involving orbits, the trajectory of a satellite can change substantially, or it may even crash into a planet with the wrong choice of initial conditions. Initial conditions are part of the specification of a simulation: the more accurately they are specified, the closer the resulting trajectory will be to the expected trajectory.

Dealing with boundaries carefully

Simulations that involve boundaries are particularly prone to inaccuracy. Such interactions must be dealt with using special methods to detect and handle collisions at specific instants, and they introduce additional sources of error that can be even more important than those associated with numerical integration over time. In Chapter 11, we described how to deal with some of those problems in special cases, including repositioning and velocity correction at a boundary. Another source of inaccuracy arises from uncertainities about the time of collision. In the example of the last section, the ball was detected and stopped after it had gone "through" the ground. The time for it to fall to the ground was therefore slightly over-estimated. This error can get larger at higher velocities. For extra accuracy, they need to be accounted for and corrected.

Summary

Well done for making it this far into the book! You now know how to make physics simulations in 3D as well as how to create simulations that are accurate scale models of real systems. These are just some of the technical issues involved in building more complex simulations. The example simulations we'll create in the final chapter will bring together what you learned in this chapter as well as in the rest of the book.

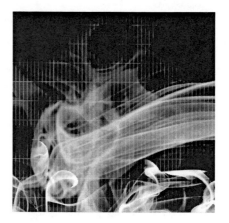

Chapter 16

Simulation Projects

This final chapter consists of three simulation projects that will illustrate how the physics and methods you've learned in this book can be used for different types of applications. The examples are quite different from one another, reflecting differences not only in the underlying physics but also in the purpose for which they are built.

The three examples are the following:

- **Build a submarine**: The aim here is to show how easily you can modify some of the existing code you've already come across to create a submarine that you could incorporate in a 2D game.

- **Build a flight simulator**: In this example we'll create a 3D flight simulator that could be further developed in many interesting ways just for pure fun!

- **Create an accurate solar system model**: This project is to create an accurate 3D model of the solar system that could be used as an e-learning tool. We will then compare the simulation with data generated from a simulation by NASA.

The idea is that these are *your* projects, so we give the relevant physics and help you build a basic version, but then leave it to you to develop and enhance them in any ways you might want. Have fun!

Build a submarine

In Chapter 7 we had a simple but interesting example of a ball floating in water. It is actually quite easy to modify that example and turn it into an interactive submarine of a type that can be used in simple 2D games. Let's first quickly review the main physics involved.

Brief review of the physics

In the floating ball example, we identified three main forces that acted on the ball: gravity, upthrust, and drag, which are given respectively by the following formulas:

$$\mathbf{W} = m\,\mathbf{g}$$

$$\mathbf{U} = -\rho V\,\mathbf{g}$$

$$\mathbf{F} = -k\,v\,\mathbf{v}$$

Note that we have written the upthrust formula in vector form: the minus sign is because upthrust acts upward, opposing the gravity vector $\mathbf{g}$. Just as a reminder, in that formula ρ is the density of water and V is the volume of water displaced by the object.

With a submarine you have a fourth force: the thrust $\mathbf{T}$ that pushes the sub, allowing it to move horizontally through the water. This will be modeled as a horizontal force of constant magnitude when power is applied.

Another relevant piece of physics (as discussed in Chapter 7), is that an object will float if its density (mass per unit volume) is less than or equal to that of water, and it will sink otherwise. A submarine functions on the principle that its effective density can be varied by filling ballast tanks with sea water or pressurized air: its density (mass/volume ratio) varies because its mass thus changes while its volume remains the same.

The visual setup

The graphics for this simulation was produced using the Flash IDE. The visual background is quite simple, consisting of a rectangle with a gradient fill to represent the sky and another one to represent the sea. A screenshot of the simulation is shown in Figure 16-1. There is also some text on the screen that displays the ratio of the density of the submarine to that of the water.

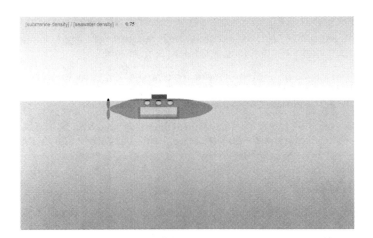

Figure 16-1. Screenshot of the submarine simulation

The submarine was also created using the Flash drawing tools. Figure 16-2 takes a closer look at it. There are a few things to be noted about this object. The first is that its registration point is at the bottom of the sub, along its middle horizontally. Secondly, the blue rectangle within the sub represents water in the ballast tanks. It is an embedded movie clip named **water**, and its registration point is at its lower-left corner.

By controlling its height, the illusion of changing the water level will be created, with the mass of the submarine being adjusted accordingly. Finally the propeller is also a separate embedded movie clip; its rotation will be flipped alternately by 180°, giving the impression of rotation when a thrust will be applied.

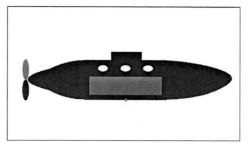

Figure 16-2. A closer look at the submarine

The setup code

The setup code is in a file called **Submarine.as**. The full code listing is as follows:

```
package{
        import flash.display.Sprite;
        import flash.text.TextField;
        import com.physicscodes.math.Vector2D;
        import com.physicscodes.objects.Particle;

        public class Submarine extends Sprite{
                public function Submarine():void{
                        init();
                }
                private function init():void{
                        var sub:Particle = new Sub();
                        sub.pos2D = new Vector2D(250,300);
                        addChild(sub);

                        var sea:Sea = new Sea();
                        sea.x = 0;
                        sea.y = 200;
                        sea.alpha = 0.6;
                        addChild(sea);

                        var txt:TextField = new TextField();
                        txt.x = 250;
                        txt.y = 10;
                        txt.width = 30;
                        addChild(txt);

                        var mover:SubmarineMover=new SubmarineMover(sub,txt);
                        mover.startTime();
                }
        }
}
```

The sub's class is set as "**Sub**", and its base class is set to **com.physicscodes.objects.Particle** by setting its properties in the library. Similarly, the "sea" movie clip is a symbol in the library with a class name of

483

Sea. An instance is created and positioned appropriately on the stage, and its transparency is set to 0.6 so that we can see the sub through it. A `TextField` instance named **txt** is created. This will be used to display the current ratio of the sub's density to that of the water. Finally, the sub is made to move using an instance of the `SubmarineMover` class.

The basic motion code

The `SubmarineMover` class is a modification of the `Floater` class that we created back in Chapter 7. The main changes have to do with the visual effects and controls (they are described in the next section). The basic motion code, as implemented in the **calcForce()** method, is not actually that different from that in `Floater`. Here is the **calcForce()** method:

```
override protected function calcForce():void{
        var dr:Number = (_sub.y-_yLevel)/_sub.height;
        var ratio:Number; // volume fraction of object that is submerged
        if (dr <= -1){ // object completely out of water
                ratio=0;
        }else if (dr < 1){ // object partially in water
                ratio = dr; // for cuboid
        }else{ // object completely in water
                ratio = 1;
        }
        var gravity:Vector2D = Forces.constantGravity(_sub.mass,_g);
        var upthrust:Vector2D = Forces.upthrust(_rho,_V*ratio,_g);
        var drag:Vector2D = Forces.drag(_k*ratio,_sub.velo2D);
        force = Forces.add([gravity, upthrust, drag, _thrust]);
}
```

The variable **dr** is the fraction of the height of the sub that is submerged under the water level. The variable **ratio** is the volume fraction that is submerged (which determines the upthrust and drag on the sub) and depends on the shape of the sub in a complex way. Because this simulation is meant for a simple game, it makes sense to deal with it in an approximate way. So we simply treat the sub like a cuboid, in which case the volume ratio is simply equal to **dr** as long as the value of **dr** is between 0 and 1. If **dr** is negative (in which case the sub is completely outside the water), **ratio** is set to zero. If **dr** is greater than 1 (in which case the sub is fully immersed), **ratio** is set to 1.

The variable **ratio** is used to adjust the upthrust and drag, and they are then added to the weight of the sub. There is a fourth force, **_thrust**, that is added and that was obviously not in the floating ball example of Chapter 7. This is a private **Vector2D** variable whose value is set according to user interaction. So let's take a look at how the user controls the simulation.

Adding controls and visual effects

The aim is to control the submarine by means of the arrow keys on the keyboard. The right arrow will apply a forward thrust; the left arrow will apply a backward thrust; the down arrow will introduce water in the ballast tanks; and the up arrow will remove water from the ballast tanks and fill them with air. This is done via the following two event handlers, which respond to the **KEY_DOWN** and **KEY_UP** keyboard events, respectively:

```
private function keyDownListener(e:KeyboardEvent):void {
        if (e.keyCode == Keyboard.RIGHT) {
                _thrust = new Vector2D(_thrustMag,0);
                _rotate = true;
        } else if (e.keyCode == Keyboard.LEFT) {
                _thrust = new Vector2D(-_thrustMag,0);
```

```
            _rotate = true;
        }
        if (e.keyCode == Keyboard.DOWN) {
                _ballastInc = _incMag;
        } else if (e.keyCode == Keyboard.UP) {
                _ballastInc = -_incMag;
        }
}

private function keyUpListener(e:KeyboardEvent):void {
        _thrust = new Vector2D(0,0);
        _ballastInc = 0;
        _rotate = false;
}
```

The private variables **_thrustMag** and **_incMag** control the amount of thrust and the amount by which the water level is to be increased or decreased (per timestep). The default values in the code are 20 and 0.01, respectively. The current value of thrust and water level increment are stored in the private variables **_thrust** and **_ballastInc**, respectively. The thrust and water level increment are both reset to zero when the keys are up again. Finally, the private **Boolean** variable **_rotate** determines whether the propeller will rotate or not. It is **true** when the thrust is non-zero and **false** otherwise.

The necessary visual changes are controlled by individual methods that are called at each timestep from an overriding **moveObject()** method:

```
override protected function moveObject():void{
        super.moveObject();
        rotatePropeller();
        adjustBallast();
        updateInfo();
}
```

First the **rotatePropeller()** method flips the rotation of the propeller at each timestep whenever a thrust is applied:

```
private function rotatePropeller():void{
        if (_rotate){
                _sub.propeller.rotation += 180;
        }
}
```

Next, the **adjustBallast()** method increments the **_waterFraction** private variable, which keeps track of the amount of water in the ballast tank as a fraction of the amount when it is full. Obviously that fraction cannot be made less than 0 or more than 1, hence the code also makes sure that never happens:

```
private function adjustBallast():void{
        if (_ballastInc != 0){
                _waterFraction += _ballastInc;
                if (_waterFraction < 0){
                        _waterFraction = 0;
                }
                if (_waterFraction > 1){
                        _waterFraction = 1;
                }
                setWater();
        }
}
```

The final line of code in **adjustBallast()** calls a **setWater()** method, whose task it is to adjust the height of the water level and the mass of the sub as a result of the change in the mass of the water in the tank:

```
private function setWater():void{
        _sub.water.height = _waterHeight*_waterFraction;
        _sub.mass = _emptySubMass + _waterMass*_waterFraction;
}
```

The final method called from **moveObject()** is the **updateInfo()** method, which computes and displays the updated ratio of the density of the submarine to that of water:

```
private function updateInfo():void{
        var ratio:Number = _sub.mass/_V/_rho; // ratio of submarine density to water density
        ratio = Math.round(ratio*100)/100; // round to 2 d.p.
        _txt.text = String(ratio);
}
```

The full mover code

This is now the full code in the **SubmarineMover** class:

```
package {
        import com.physicscodes.motion.Forcer;
        import com.physicscodes.motion.Forces;
        import com.physicscodes.objects.Particle;
        import com.physicscodes.math.Vector2D;
        import flash.text.TextField;
        import flash.events.KeyboardEvent;
        import flash.ui.Keyboard;

        public class SubmarineMover extends Forcer{
                private var _sub:Particle;
                private var _g:Number=10;
                private var _rho:Number=1; // water density
                private var _V:Number=1;
                private var _k:Number=0.05;
                private var _yLevel:Number=200;
                private var _thrustMag:Number=20;
                private var _thrust:Vector2D = new Vector2D(0,0);
                private var _txt:TextField;
                private var _rotate:Boolean = false;
                private var _waterHeight:Number;
                private var _waterMass:Number = 1;
                private var _emptySubMass:Number = 0.5;
                private var _waterFraction:Number = 0.4; // must be between 0 and 1
                private var _ballastInc:Number=0; // ballast increment
                private var _incMag:Number = 0.01; // magnitude of the ballast increment

                public function SubmarineMover(pparticle:Particle,ptxt:TextField):void{
                        _sub = pparticle;
                        _txt = ptxt;
                        super(pparticle);
                        initSetup();
                }

                private function initSetup():void{
                        _waterHeight = _sub.water.height;
```

```
                setWater();
                _sub.stage.addEventListener(KeyboardEvent.KEY_DOWN, keyDownListener);
                _sub.stage.addEventListener(KeyboardEvent.KEY_UP, keyUpListener);

        }

        private function keyDownListener(e:KeyboardEvent):void {
                if (e.keyCode == Keyboard.RIGHT) {
                        _thrust = new Vector2D(_thrustMag,0);
                        _rotate = true;
                } else if (e.keyCode == Keyboard.LEFT) {
                        _thrust = new Vector2D(-_thrustMag,0);
                        _rotate = true;
                }
                if (e.keyCode == Keyboard.DOWN) {
                        _ballastInc = _incMag;
                } else if (e.keyCode == Keyboard.UP) {
                        _ballastInc = -_incMag;
                }
        }

        private function keyUpListener(e:KeyboardEvent):void {
                _thrust = new Vector2D(0,0);
                _ballastInc = 0;
                _rotate = false;
        }

        override protected function moveObject():void{
                super.moveObject();
                rotatePropeller();
                adjustBallast();
                updateInfo();
        }

        private function rotatePropeller():void{
                if (_rotate){
                        _sub.propeller.rotation += 180;
                }
        }

        private function adjustBallast():void{
                if (_ballastInc != 0){
                        _waterFraction += _ballastInc;
                        if (_waterFraction < 0){
                                _waterFraction = 0;
                        }
                        if (_waterFraction > 1){
                                _waterFraction = 1;
                        }
                        setWater();
                }
        }

        private function setWater():void{
                _sub.water.height = _waterHeight*_waterFraction;
                _sub.mass = _emptySubMass + _waterMass*_waterFraction;
```

```
        }
        private function updateInfo():void{
                var ratio:Number = _sub.mass/_V/_rho;
                ratio = Math.round(ratio*100)/100; // round to 2 d.p.
                _txt.text = String(ratio);
        }

        override protected function calcForce():void{
                var dr:Number = (_sub.y-_yLevel)/_sub.height;
                var ratio:Number;
                if (dr <= -1){
                        ratio=0;
                }else if (dr < 1){
                        ratio = dr;
                }else{ // object completely in water
                        ratio = 1;
                }
                var gravity:Vector2D = Forces.constantGravity(_sub.mass,_g);
                var upthrust:Vector2D = Forces.upthrust(_rho,_V*ratio,_g);
                var drag:Vector2D = Forces.drag(_k*ratio,_sub.velo2D);
                force = Forces.add([gravity, upthrust, drag, _thrust]);
        }
    }
  }
}
```

The submarine is now ready for a test drive! Have fun playing around and experimenting with the parameter values as usual.

Further ideas

That wasn't too bad, was it? You now have a basic but functional submarine that you can add in a game. Now that it's in your hands, you can further develop it as you see fit. You can enhance the visual appearance of the sub, add scenery such as a nice background with aquatic creatures and plants, add bubbles, and so on. You could add a sea floor and handle contact with it using a normal force. It should also not be very difficult to convert this simulation to 3D. If you do that, you would, of course, also need to add rotation.

Build a flight simulator

This project is quite a bit more complicated than the last example because we'll be working in 3D, and also because the physics and operation of aircraft are fairly complex. Therefore we'll need to spend a bit more time on theory before we can get to the coding.

Physics and control mechanisms of aircraft

There are two aspects of theory to understand in order to model aircraft. The first is the underlying physics, which includes an understanding of the forces and torques acting on the aircraft and how they affect the aircraft's motion. The second aspect is the mechanism by which aircraft control these forces and torques; this requires an understanding of the relevant parts of the aircraft and their associated maneuvers.

Forces on an aircraft

We discussed the forces on an airplane in Chapter 7: gravity, thrust, drag, and lift. Figure 16-3 shows a force diagram for a plane at an angle to the horizontal. This is a generalization of the force diagram shown in Figure 7-15, which was for the special case of an airplane in horizontal flight. Therefore the directions of the thrust and drag are not necessarily horizontal, and the lift is not necessarily vertical. As a result, the force balance is a little more complex in this case. It is clearly important to get the magnitudes as well as the directions of these different forces right at all times (during ascent and descent, and not just during horizontal flight), so we need robust equations for computing them in general.

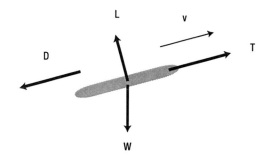

Figure 16-3. The four forces on an airplane during flight

The force of gravity **W** = mg still acts downward and is constant, of course; so that one is easy. The thrust **T**, whether generated by a propeller or by a jet engine, will usually act along the axis of the plane in the forward direction (unless you are considering an aircraft model such as the Harrier, in which the direction of the thrust can be varied). The magnitude of the thrust depends on many factors such as engine type, engine efficiency, and altitude effects. In our simulation, we'll simplify things by disregarding all these effects, simply prescribing a value that can be changed by the user.

The drag and lift forces are more subtle. Strictly speaking, they are defined relative to the direction of the airflow over the relevant aircraft part such as the wing. Assuming there is no wind, we can approximate this as the direction of the aircraft's velocity. The drag force can then be defined as the component of the aerodynamic force (force exerted as a result of the airflow) that acts opposite to the aircraft's velocity. The lift force is the component perpendicular to the aircraft's velocity.

The drag formula is the same as that given in Chapter 7, in which **v** is now interpreted as the velocity of the aircraft:

$$\mathbf{F} = -\frac{1}{2} \rho \, A \, C_d \, v \, \mathbf{v}$$

The lift formula that we gave in Chapter 7 is generalized to the following formula, in which **k** is a unit vector perpendicular to the plane's velocity and oriented to point upward from the plane's wings:

$$\mathbf{F} = \frac{1}{2} \rho \, A \, C_L \, v^2 \, \mathbf{k}$$

These are general fomulas that need to be adapted once we look at the aircraft parts in more detail. In particular, the relevant areas for use in those equations should be defined. We also need to specify the drag and lift coefficients, which can vary depending on several factors.

Torques on an aircraft: rotation

The forces on an aircraft are not sufficient to compute its motion. As you know, the resultant force determines the translational motion, but these forces can also exert torques if their lines of action do not pass through the center of mass. The weight of an object acts through a point known as its *center of gravity*. In uniform gravitational fields such as near the surface of the Earth (and an airplane is near enough the Earth's surface for that purpose) the center of gravity coincides with the center of mass. Therefore, the weight of an airplane never generates a torque. However, the drag and lift forces act through a point known as the *center of pressure*. This is a similar concept to that of center of gravity, but it depends on the shape and inclination of the airplane, and does not in general coincide with its center of mass. So it can produce a torque that can send the aircraft spinning if unbalanced. An aircraft therefore needs to have stability mechanisms in place to balance this torque.

Of course, you do sometimes want an airplane to rotate. Figure 16-4 shows three ways in which an airplane can rotate about its center of mass and the axes about which it does so. It can *pitch* by moving its nose and tail up and down; it can *roll* by moving its wing tips up and down; and it can *yaw* by moving its nose and tail sideways. The axes are defined relative to the shape of the aircraft and they all pass through its center of gravity. The *pitch axis* is oriented in a direction parallel to the wingspan, the *roll axis* is along the length of the aircraft, and the *yaw axis* is perpendicular to the other two axes. An aircraft is designed so that it has special parts that can produce these types of motion by controlling the lift and drag forces. Let's look at those now.

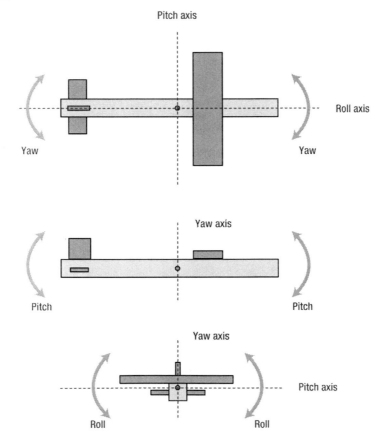

Figure 16-4. Pitch, roll, and yaw

Aircraft parts and controls

Aircraft can control their motion by modifying the thrust, drag, and lift forces acting on them. We briefly describe the parts of an aircraft that do this and how they do it. The thrust is controlled by the engine (which can be of different types, such as propeller or jet) and will propel the plane forward. Figure 16-5 shows a schematic of an airplane emphasizing those parts that are relevant to the drag and lift and their control.

Fixed "main" parts include these:

- **Fuselage**: This is the main body of the aircraft. It is responsible for much of the drag. It also creates lift and pitching torque, but only for large inclination angles, and they can usually be neglected. It can also create yawing torque for large lateral inclination; again this can usually be neglected.

- **Wings**: The two wings of an aircraft contribute the most of the lift and drag forces on it. Without wings, an airplane just wouldn't fly. The center of pressure of the lift and drag forces on the main wings is close to the center of mass, so one can assume that they contribute no torque, just like the fuselage. However, they have movable parts called flaps and ailerons that can be maneuvered to modify the lift and drag force and generate rolling torque.

- **Tails**: The tails consist of two parts: a horizontal and a vertical tail, which help in maintaining horizontal and vertical stability of the airplane. They also have movable parts called elevators and rudders that generate pitching and yawing torques.

Movable "control" parts include the following:

- **Flaps**: Flaps are attached to the rear of the wings and are rotated downward during takeoff and landing to increase the lift force (and also the drag force during landing to slow down the fast-moving aircraft).

- **Ailerons**: Ailerons are also attached to the rear of the wing, but farther along toward the wing tips. Rotating an aileron downward increases the lift, and rotating it upward decreases the lift. The two ailerons are rotated in opposite directions to produce a rolling torque (couple). Because the ailerons are far from the center of mass, large torques can be produced by relatively small changes in lift on either side of the wings (recall that moment = force x distance). Ailerons are usually controlled by a control stick; moving the stick to the right or left causes the aircraft to roll to the right or left.

- **Elevators**: Elevators are hinged to the rear side of the horizontal tail. Unlike ailerons, the elevators move together (both upward or both downward), thereby generating a pitching torque. Elevators are controlled by moving a stick forward to raise the nose of the aircraft and moving the stick backward to cause the aircraft nose to dip.

- **Rudder**: The rudder is attached to the rear of the vertical tail fin. It can rotate to either side, causing a yawing torque. The rudder is controlled by two foot pedals so that depressing the left or right pedal moves the aircraft's nose to the left or right, respectively.

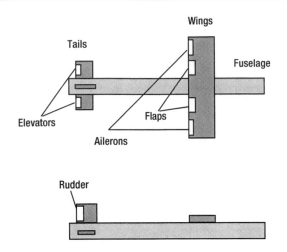

Figure 16-5. Aircraft parts

Airfoil geometry and angle of attack

The shape and inclination of aircraft wings are important factors that determine the magnitude of lift. Figure 16-6 shows the shape of a cross-section of a wing, called an *airfoil*. The shape of an airfoil is usually rounded at the front and sharp at the rear. The line joining the centers of curvature of the front and rear edges is called the *chord line*.

The angle between the chord line and the incident air flow (which is generally along the velocity of the plane) is called the *angle of attack*, usually denoted the Greek letter α. The drag and lift coefficients of an airfoil depend on the angle of attack, and flight models generally use experimental data or a simple function to evaluate those coefficients as a function of angle of attack.

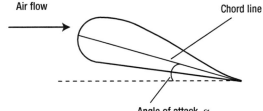

Figure 16-6. Flow over an aircraft wing (airfoil)

Takeoff and landing

An airplane can take off only if its velocity exceeds a certain threshold. That threshold value corresponds to the point at which the lift force balances the weight of the plane. In that case, you can equate the expressions for the lift force and the weight:

$$\frac{1}{2}\rho A C_L v^2 = mg$$

You can then rearrange this formula to give a formula for the velocity, which is the threshold velocity for takeoff:

$$v = \sqrt{\frac{2mg}{\rho \, A \, C_L}}$$

During landing you have the opposite problem. You don't want the velocity with which the plane touches the ground to be too high; otherwise, the plane will crash. You can set a reasonable threshold velocity in your game or simulation. Another consideration during landing is that the pitch angle must be zero or slightly positive; otherwise, the nose of the plane will hit the ground.

Turning

Turning is achieved by banking to give a horizontal *unbalanced* component of the lift force that, because it is always perpendicular to the velocity, generates a centripetal force that makes the plane move in a circle (see Figure 16-7). Banking is achieved by rolling the plane using the ailerons. The yawing motion produced by a rudder is not used for turning, but for aligning the plane in the direction of the velocity.

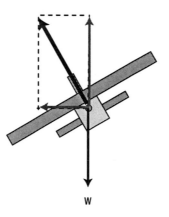

W

Figure 16-7. Force diagram for a banked plane

What we will create

The simulation we will create will include the essential physics needed to make an airplane fly, with the ability to undergo the different types of motion (straight flight, pitch, roll, and yaw) and maneuvers (takeoff, landing, and turning) discussed. The user will be able to control a very simple airplane model using the keyboard, in a similar way to a pilot controlling an airplane. The operation of the elevators, ailerons, and rudder in creating pitching, rolling, and yawing torque will be simulated. The user can also adjust the amount of thrust.

Creating the visual setup

The visual setup is minimalist, consisting of a sky background (produced using the Flash drawing tools, although it could certainly be done using ActionScript), a runway (produced by a **Road** class that makes use of the drawing API) and a very simple airplane model that is an instance of the **PolyhedronRB** class introduced in the last chapter.

The visual setup code is in the file **Airplane.as** and it looks like this:

```
package{
        import flash.display.Shape;
        import flash.display.Sprite;
        import flash.geom.Vector3D;
        import com.physicscodes.objects.PolyhedronRB;

        public class Airplane extends Sprite{
                private var _airplane:PolyhedronRB;
                private var _vertices:Vector.<Vector3D>=new Vector.<Vector3D>();
                private var _faces:Vector.<Array>=new Vector.<Array>();
                private var _facesColors:Array;
                private var _h:Number = 90;
                private var _fl:Number = 200;
                private var _cm:Vector3D = new Vector3D(400,600,0);
                private var _im:Vector3D = new Vector3D(300000,100000,200000);

                public function Airplane():void{
                        makeRunway();
                        init();
                }
                private function init():void{
                        var h:Number = _h;
                        _vertices[0] = new Vector3D(h,0,0);
                        _vertices[1] = new Vector3D(-h/2,0,-h/2);
                        _vertices[2] = new Vector3D(-h/2,0,h/2);
                        _vertices[3] = new Vector3D(2*h/3,0,0);
                        _vertices[4] = new Vector3D(-h/2,0,h/4);
                        _vertices[5] = new Vector3D(-h/2,0,-h/4);
                        _vertices[6] = new Vector3D(-h/2,-h/3,0);
                        _faces[0] = [0,1,2];
                        _faces[1] = [3,4,6];
                        _faces[2] = [3,5,6];
                        _faces[3] = [6,5,4];
                        _facesColors = [0xFFFFCC,0x00FF66,0x00FF66,0x990000];
                        _airplane = new PolyhedronRB(_fl, _cm, _im, _vertices, _faces,
_facesColors);

                        _airplane.mass = 30000;
                        _airplane.pos = _airplane.centerOfMass;
                        _airplane.velo = new Vector3D(0,0,0);
                        addChild(_airplane);

                        var mover:AirplaneMover = new AirplaneMover(_airplane);
                        mover.startTime();
                }
                private function makeRunway():void{
                        var road:Road = new Road(400,2000,0xcccccc,1);
                        road.x = 400;
                        road.y = 600;
                        road.z = 0;
                        road.rotationX = -90;
                        addChild(road);
                }
        }
}
```

The airplane is created as an instance of the **PolyhedronRB** class and is given a mass of 30000 units and a moment of inertia vector of (30000, 10000, 20000). As discussed in the last chapter, this is a simplification in which we consider the inertia matrix to consist of only three diagonal components: **Ixx**, **Iyy**, and **Izz**. Doing it properly would involve some matrix math and extra computational overhead that seems unnecessary for a simple simulation like this one. The "runway" is a **Road** instance: we won't show the code for the **Road** class, but you can take a look in the source files. The airplane is driven by an instance of the **AirplaneMover** class. This is a rather lengthy piece of code, so we'll discuss different parts of it separately.

Coding up the physics

The guts of the **AirplaneMover** class is the calculation of the forces and torques on the airplane, which is done in the **calcForce()** method. This looks quite complicated at first sight, but will make sense when you go through it step by step. We have also included plenty of comments in the actual source file; some of them are included in the following listings.

The first three lines of calcForce() set up **Vector3D** variables **ix**, **iy**, and **iz** to store the airplane's three axes:

```
// update plane axes
var ix:Vector3D = _airplane.ix;// unit vector of x axis of airplane;
var iy:Vector3D = _airplane.iy;// unit vector of y axis of airplane;
var iz:Vector3D = _airplane.iz;// unit vector of z axis of airplane;
```

Referring to Figure 16-4, these axes correspond to the roll, yaw and pitch axes respectively. They are defined relative to the airplane, and will therefore change in so-called "world space" and need to be updated as the plane moves. This is done in the **updatePolyhedron()** public method of the **PolyhedronRB** class, which has been modified to read as follows:

```
public function updatePolyhedron(rotx:Number,roty:Number,rotz:Number):void{
        // add incremental rotations to matrix3D property of _sprite
        _sprite.transform.matrix3D.appendRotation(rotx,Vector3D.X_AXIS);
        _sprite.transform.matrix3D.appendRotation(roty,Vector3D.Y_AXIS);
        _sprite.transform.matrix3D.appendRotation(rotz,Vector3D.Z_AXIS);

        var clMat:Matrix3D = _sprite.transform.matrix3D.clone();
        // unit vectors of the coordinate systems linked with the object
        _ix= clMat.deltaTransformVector(Vector3D.X_AXIS);
        _iy= clMat.deltaTransformVector(Vector3D.Y_AXIS);
        _iz= clMat.deltaTransformVector(Vector3D.Z_AXIS);

        drawPolyhedron();
}
```

The private variables **_ix**, **_iy**, and **_iz** refer to the airplane's axes, which are accessible publicly as **ix**, **iy**, **iz** via appropriate getters. Note that the **deltaTransformVector()** method of the **Matrix3D** class is used to transform the axes using the current transformation matrix. The **updatePolyhedron** method is called every timestep from the **updateObject()** method in **AirplaneMover** (which is itself called in **moveObject()** every timestep):

```
private function updateObject():void{
        var vec:Vector3D = _airplane.angVelo;
        vec.scaleBy(dt);
        _airplane.clear();
        _airplane.updatePolyhedron(vec.x,vec.y,vec.z);
}
```

This passes the current angular displacement increment to **updatePolyhedron**, which is used to update the transformation matrix and thereafter the airplane's axes and orientation. The key thing is then the update of the angular velocity, which takes place in **ForcerRB3D** (which **AirplaneMover** extends) based on the applied torques. As in the rotating cube example of the last chapter, the update in the translational motion is applied separately by **Mover3D**.

Going back to **calcForce()**, the next section of code prescribes the forces on the airplane as a whole. This includes gravity, a normal force if the plane is on the ground, a drag force, and a thrust. The drag force is computed assuming a constant drag coefficient. This is a simplification; generally the drag coefficient will depend on the angle of attack, but this dependence is not modeled here for simplicity. The thrust is applied in the direction of the plane's ix (roll) axis, and its magnitude is controlled by the user by updating the _thrustMag variable (as will be described later). The net torque due to these forces is assumed to be zero so that the plane maintains rotational equilibrium. A rotational damping term is also applied to help stabilize the airplane whenever it does rotate:

```
// *** forces on whole plane ***
if(_airplane.ypos < _groundLevel){
        force = Forces3D.constantGravity(_massAirplane,_g);      // gravity
}else{
        force= new Vector3D(0,0,0); // reaction from ground cancels gravity
}
force=force.add(Forces3D.drag(_kDrag,_airplane.velo)); // add drag

var thrust:Vector3D;
if (_thrustMag > 0){
        thrust = ix.clone();
        thrust.scaleBy(_thrustMag);
}else{
        thrust = new Vector3D(0,0,0);
}
force = force.add(thrust); // add thrust

// *** torques on whole plane ***
torque = new Vector3D(0,0,0); // gravity, drag and thrust don't have torques

// but let's add angular damping for stability
var vec:Vector3D = _airplane.angVelo;
vec.scaleBy(-_kAng);
torque = torque.add(vec);
```

The remaining code deals exclusively with the forces and torques generated by lift. Because the lift force is zero if the plane is not moving, the whole calculation is only done if the plane's velocity is non-zero. The lift forces consist of vertical lift on the wings, elevators and ailerons and of horizontal lift on the rudder. They depend on the velocities in the xy and xz planes relative to the airplane. These velocities are therefore calculated first. Then they are used to compute the angle of attack α and lateral angle β (the angle between the x and z component of the plane's velocity). Note that we are here assuming that there is no wind. It would be straightforward to add in the effect of the wind, but that would only complicate the code further.

Next, the lift force on the wings is calculated. The cross product is used because the lift force on the wings is perpendicular to the velocity in the xy plane and the wing axis (the pitch axis). The lift coefficient is calculated assuming a linear dependence on the angle of attack, with a constant gradient dC_L/dα:

$$C_L = \left(\frac{dC_L}{d\alpha} \right) \alpha$$

Note that we add the inclination of the wing relative to the plane's roll axis (_alphWing) to the value of α calculated previously to obtain the actual angle of attack. We also impose a limiting value on the lift force because in reality the lift force does not increase indefinitely with the angle of attack, but reaches a maximum value. The lift force on the main wings is also assumed to generate no torque when the plane is in equilibrium, just like drag and thrust (or, more accurately, the combined torques of these forces are made to cancel out in practice).

The remaining blocks of code then go on to compute the lift forces on the movable control surfaces (elevators, ailerons, and rudder) and the torques they generate. The lift calculation is done in the same way as for the main wings. Note that, for simplicity, we consider the whole horizontal tail and vertical tail as movable when considering the lift forces and torques on the elevators and rudder. The torques are calculated as usual by taking the cross product of the distance vector of the lift force from the center of mass and the lift force:

$$\mathbf{T} = \mathbf{r} \times \mathbf{F}$$

The appropriate distance vector needs to be specified for each control surface.

And here is the block of code that calculates the forces and torques due to lift on the airplane wings and control surfaces as just described.

```
// *** Now we consider the lift forces and torques on wings and control surfaces
if (_airplane.velo.length > 0){ // no lift if velocity is zero
// velocity of airplane along its x, y and z axes
        var viX:Number = _airplane.velo.dotProduct(ix);
        var viY:Number = _airplane.velo.dotProduct(iy
        var viZ:Number = _airplane.velo.dotProduct(iz);

        var vecX:Vector3D = ix.clone();
        var vecY:Vector3D = iy.clone();
        vecY.scaleBy(viY);
        vecX.scaleBy(viX);
        var viXY:Vector3D = vecX.add(vecY); // airplane's velo in its xy plane

        vecX = ix.clone();
        var vecZ:Vector3D = iz.clone();
        vecX.scaleBy(viX);
        vecZ.scaleBy(viZ);
        var viZX:Vector3D = vecX.add(vecZ); // airplane's velo in its xz plane

        // calculate angle of attack and lateral angle
        _alph = Math.atan2(viY,viX); // so, the angle of attack
        if ((viY==0) && (viX==0)){
                _alph = 0;
        }
        _beta = Math.atan2(viZ,viX);// lateral angle
        if ((viZ==0) && (viX==0)){
                _beta = 0;
        }

        // force: lift on the Wing
        var veloXY:Vector3D = viXY.clone();
        veloXY = veloXY.crossProduct(iz);
        if (Math.abs(_alph+_alphWing) > 20*Math.PI/180){
                _cLift = 1.2*_alph/Math.abs(_alph);  // impose limit on _cLift
        }else{
```

497

```
                        _cLift = _dcLdalpha*(_alph+_alphWing);
        }

        veloXY.scaleBy(0.5*_rho*viXY.length*_areaWing*_cLift);
        var liftW:Vector3D = veloXY.clone();
        force = force.add(liftW);

        // assume no overall torque generated by lift on main wings

        // *** lift forces and torques on control surfaces ***

        // force: ailerons; form a couple, so no net force
        // torque: ailerons
        veloXY = viXY.clone();
        veloXY = veloXY.crossProduct(iz);
        veloXY.scaleBy(0.5*_rho*viXY.length*_areaAileron*_dcLdalpha *(_alphAl));
        var liftAl:Vector3D = veloXY.clone(); // lift on one aileron only
        var ptorque:Vector3D = iz.crossProduct(liftAl); // T = r x F
        ptorque.scaleBy(_distAlToCM*2); // factor of 2 because two ailerons
        torque = torque.add(ptorque);

        // force: horizontal tail (elevators); same formula as for the wing
        veloXY = viXY.clone();
        veloXY = veloXY.crossProduct(iz);
        if(Math.abs(_alphEl+_alph) > 20*Math.PI/180){
                _cLift = 1.2*(_alphEl+_alph)/Math.abs(_alphEl+_alph);
        }else{
                _cLift = _dcLdalpha*(_alphEl+_alph);
        }
        veloXY.scaleBy(0.5*_rho*viXY.length*_areaHorizontalTail*_cLift);
        var liftHt:Vector3D = veloXY.clone();
        force = force.add(liftHt);
        // torque: horizontal tail
        ptorque = ix.crossProduct(liftHt); // T = r x liftHt
        ptorque.scaleBy((-1)*_distVtToCM); // note negative distance along ix
        torque = torque.add(ptorque);

        // force: vertical tail (rudder); same formula as for the wing;
        var veloZX:Vector3D = viZX.clone();
        veloZX = veloZX.crossProduct(iy); // note axis is along iy.
        if (Math.abs(_alphRd+_beta) > 20*Math.PI/180){
                _cLift = 1.2*(_alphRd+_beta)/Math.abs(_alphRd+_beta);
        }else{
                _cLift = _dcLdalpha*(_alphRd+_beta);
        }
        veloZX.scaleBy(-0.5*_rho*viZX.length*_areaVerticalTail*_cLift);
        var _liftVt:Vector3D = veloZX.clone();
        force = force.add(_liftVt);
        // torque: vertical tail
        ptorque = ix.crossProduct(_liftVt); // T = r x liftVt
        ptorque.scaleBy(-_distVtToCM);
        torque = torque.add(ptorque);
    }
```

Implementing the controls

The airplane is controlled by using the arrow, Shift and Control (Command on the Mac) keys to control the elevators, ailerons, and rudder; and the spacebar together with the caps lock key to control the thrust. This is done in the `startControl()` method. (We won't list the code here because it's quite straightforward.) The down arrow key increases the pitch raising the airplane's nose upward, and the up key lowers it. The left and right arrow keys make the plane roll to the left and right, respectively. These movements are similar to the way the control stick is used by a pilot to control the elevators and ailerons. The rudder is controlled using the Shift and Control keys. The maximum angles and increments for these movable parts are set at the beginning of the program. The thrust magnitude is increased and decreased by pressing the spacebar with the caps lock off and on, respectively. Again, the maximum magnitude of the thrust and its increment are set at the beginning of the code, with the default values being 300,000 and 10,000, respectively.

Displaying flight information

Information about the airplane's position and velocity as well as currently applied controls is displayed on screen when the simulation runs. The relevant text fields are set up in the `setupDisplay()` method (which is called from the constructor) and the information is updated at each timestep in the `updateDisplay()` method (called from the `moveObject()` method).

The displayed information includes the altitude of the airplane, its vertical velocity (vy), its horizontal (x, z) location and its horizontal (vx, vz) velocity. The first two pieces of information are important to bear in mind when you are trying to keep the plane in flight without crashing it. A negative vertical velocity means that the airplane is rising; if the vertical velocity is positive, it is losing altitude, so you'd better be on your guard. The other two pieces of information are useful to know if you are trying to go somewhere.

Test flying the simulator

The airplane is now ready to fly! Run it with the default parameter values. When the simulation starts, the plane will just sit there on the runway because its initial velocity is zero and there is no applied thrust. Increase the thrust to the maximum value by pressing and holding down the spacebar until the value of 300,000 is displayed. Then increase the elevators' angle to -5 by pressing the down arrow key. You will see the plane gradually rising as it moves along the runway. Then decrease the pitch angle by pressing the up arrow key, which will reduce the lift and decrease the ascent of the plane, or even make it descend. See if you can make the airplane rise up to a given altitude and remain there. To do that you need to play with the thrust and/or the pitch angle, and you need to make the vertical velocity reach close to zero at your desired altitude. Once you've achieved that, you can sit back and relax; the plane will take care of itself.

Restart the simulation and try out the aileron and rudder controls. Note that the plane turns when the plane rolls, just as described in the "Turning" section. Too much rolling or yawing might make the airplane behave somewhat unpredictably, though. See also the detailed comments included in the source code. Figure 16-8 shows a screenshot of the simulation with the plane in flight.

Figure 16-8. The airplane in flight

Further things to do

You probably already have a lot of ideas about how to improve this simulator. Creating a much more impressive 3D model airplane is probably one of them, and possibly more visually appealing scenery, too. If you use a 3D engine with this flight simulator model, you could go much further with the 3D effects, such as switching between different camera views and following the airplane or watching the scenery from the plane cockpit. You could also incorporate a more extensive terrain, which could be either generated or based on real aerial information. Or add crash scenarios, and so on. You probably have even better ideas of your own!

Create an accurate solar system model

This project will be somewhat different from most of the examples in the book. The aim here is to create an accurate computer model of the solar system that could be used as an e-learning tool for students. The key word here is *accurate*: the visual and animation effects are of lesser importance compared with the correctness of the physics and the accuracy of the simulation. Consequently we will depart from our usual Mover/Forcer framework and adopt a somewhat different coding approach from the outset that will reflect the simulation rather than the animation aspect of the project.

What we will create

Our aim is to create a scale model of the solar system that includes the Sun and the planets. In the supplied source code we include the innermost four planets (Mercury, Venus, Earth, and Mars)—the so-called *terrestrial planets*. We leave it as an exercise for you to add the other four (Jupiter, Saturn, Uranus and Neptune)—the so-called *gas giants*. This should be easy to do, but will give you a valuable hands-on experience with the code.

Note that Pluto is no longer classified as a planet. In the simulation we'll pretend that smaller celestial bodies like these do not exist, including asteroids and moons. We can neglect them because their effects on the motion of the planets are pretty negligible.

The project will proceed in different stages. First, we'll set up a simulation loop using the fourth-order Runge-Kutta scheme (RK4) in 3D, which we'll test with a simple example. The source code for this is in **RK4Test3D.as**. Second, we'll use that simulation loop to model the motion of a single planet in a simple idealized way. The source code for that step is in the file **SinglePlanet.as**. Third, we will include the four inner planets and set their properties and initial conditions based on mean astronomical data, so that we'll end up with a reasonably realistic solar system model (or rather half of it). We'll also need to set up appropriate scales carefully. The corresponding file is named **SolarSystemBasic.as**. Fourth, in the file **SolarSystem.as**, we will include accurate initial conditions, run the simulation for a year, and compare the results with corresponding simulation data from NASA to see how good our simulation is.

The physics

The simulation will involve modeling the motion of each planet under the action of the combined gravitational force exerted on it by the Sun and the other planets. The effect of the Sun will, of course, be much larger because of its very large mass compared with those of any of the planets. We'll adopt a coordinate system in which the Sun is fixed, so that we don't have to model the motion of the Sun itself. The planets will be able to move in 3D space under the action of those forces.

Let m be the mass of a planet, r_i its position vector relative to each of the other planets and the Sun (with r_i^u being the corresponding unit vector), and m_i the mass of each of the other planets and the Sun. Then the total force on each planet is given by the following formula:

$$\mathbf{F} = \sum_i -G \frac{m_i\, m}{r_i^2}\, \mathbf{r}_i^u$$

Dividing by the mass, we obtain the acceleration of each planet:

$$\mathbf{a} = \sum_i -G \frac{m_i}{r_i^2}\, \mathbf{r}_i^u$$

This is the equation that the numerical integration code will solve. That's it. The physics of this problem is pretty simple! But there are other issues that make the simulation non-trivial: implementing an accurate numerical integration scheme, scaling the model properly, and incorporating accurate initial conditions. We'll handle each of these requirements one step at a time.

Coding up an appropriate integration scheme

Because accuracy is our prime concern, it makes complete sense to use RK4. To implement RK4, we'll first create a simple "simulation loop" that will do the timestepping, but we'll do that independently of the "animation loop" like that generated by **Timer** that we've been using so far. It's easier to do this than to explain it, so let's just do it and we'll explain afterward.

We borrow the RK4 code from the **ForcerIntegrator** class of Chapter 14 and modify it to come up with the following code, which is in the file **RK4Test3D.as**:

```
package{
        import flash.display.Sprite;
        import com.physicscodes.math.Vector3DX;

        public class RK4Test3D extends Sprite{
                private var _dt:Number = 0.05;
                private var _numSteps:Number = 20;
                private var _t:Number = 0;
                private var _g:Number = 10;
                private var _v:Vector3DX = new Vector3DX(0,0,0);
                private var _s:Vector3DX = new Vector3DX(0,0,0);

                public function RK4Test3D():void{
                        init();
                }

                private function init():void{
                        simulate();
                }
                private function simulate():void{
                        trace(_t,_s.y);
                        for (var i:uint=0; i<_numSteps; i++){
                                _t += _dt;
                                RK4();
                                trace(_t,_s.y);
                        }
                }
                private function RK4():void{
                        // step 1
                        var pos1:Vector3DX = _s;
                        var vel1:Vector3DX = _v;
                        var acc1:Vector3DX = getAcc(pos1,vel1);
                        // step 2
                        var pos2:Vector3DX = pos1.addScaled(vel1,_dt/2);
                        var vel2:Vector3DX = vel1.addScaled(acc1,_dt/2);
                        var acc2:Vector3DX = getAcc(pos2,vel2);
                        // step 3
                        var pos3:Vector3DX = pos1.addScaled(vel2,_dt/2);
                        var vel3:Vector3DX = vel1.addScaled(acc2,_dt/2);
                        var acc3:Vector3DX = getAcc(pos3,vel3);
                        // step 4
                        var pos4:Vector3DX = pos1.addScaled(vel3,_dt);
                        var vel4:Vector3DX = vel1.addScaled(acc3,_dt);
                        var acc4:Vector3DX = getAcc(pos4,vel4);
                        // sum vel and acc
                        var velsum:Vector3DX =↪
vel1.addScaled(vel2,2).addScaled(vel3,2).addScaled(vel4,1);
                        var accsum:Vector3DX =↪
acc1.addScaled(acc2,2).addScaled(acc3,2).addScaled(acc4,1);
                        // update pos and velo
                        _s = pos1.addScaled(velsum,_dt/6);
                        _v = vel1.addScaled(accsum,_dt/6);
                }
```

```
private function getAcc(ppos:Vector3DX,pvel:Vector3DX):Vector3DX{
        return new Vector3DX(0,_g,0);
    }
}
}
```

Okay, let's start with the familiar. The RK4() method is a modification of the RK4() method in the ForcerIntegrator class that we first saw in Chapter 14. If you compare the two versions you will notice one crucial difference: the code deals with the current position and velocity through abstract private variables _s and _v, instead of actual particle position and velocity properties. This is the first sign of the separation of the animation aspect from the simulation. The other obvious difference is that Vector2D has been replaced by Vector3DX. As mentioned in Chapter 15, Vector3DX is a homemade subclass of the native Vector3D class that augments it with additional methods such as multiply() and addScaled() that we've got attached to using (and that simplify resulting code substantially). You can view the Vector3DX code in the package com.physicscodes.math. It also has a static method called convert() that converts a Vector3D instance into a Vector3DX one.

Let's look at the rest of the code in RK4Test3D.as. The getAcc() method that previously invoked calcForce() has been simplified here to simply return a constant acceleration vector pointing downward in the y direction. That means we are here specializing to a simple gravity problem. The other remaining piece of code is the simulate() method, which is called once upon initialization. The core of the code is incredibly simple. It is the following for loop, which does all the timestepping, incrementing the current time, and calling the RK4() method, which updates the position and velocity vectors _s and _v at each timestep:

```
for (var i:uint=0; i<_numSteps; i++){
        _t += _dt;
        RK4();
}
```

From an animation perspective, this code and the associated timestepping will execute all in one go: effectively we'll be pre-computing the motion before doing any animation of existing display objects. There isn't even a display object in this code. The advantage of doing this is that it "decouples" the simulation loop from the animation loop (if there's going to be one), so that either can do their job unhindered by any time delays introduced by the other. However, this doesn't work if your simulation needs to be interactive.

Looking at how the variables are initialized, we can see that we are simulating the fall of an object from rest (_v is initially zero) under gravity for one time unit (because _dt * _numSteps = 0.05*20 = 1). For example, choosing units of seconds for _dt and m/s^2 for g, this corresponds to letting an object fall from rest for 1 second under gravity with g equal to 10 m/s^2. Using the formula s = ut + ½ at^2 then tells us that the object falls a distance of 5 m in that time. In the code, we have traced the pair of values _t and _s.y at each timestep, which tells us how far the object has fallen at each time. Run the code and you'll find that the final distance is indeed 5. You can try different timesteps (adjusting the number of steps accordingly) and you'll find that RK4 is doing a pretty good job, pretty much whatever the timestep. For example, even with a timestep of 0.5 and with 2 steps (so that the duration is still 1 time unit), it still gives exactly 5!

Now that we've got a good integrator and a basic simulation loop set up, we're ready to move on and create something closer to a planetary system.

Building an idealized single-planet simulation

It is straightforward to modify the basic RK4 simulator we just created to simulate a planetary orbit: you essentially have to modify the getAcc() method according to Newton's $1/r^2$ formula for gravitational force and choose appropriate initial conditions for _s and _v. But we also want to see something on the stage! So we also add a sun and a planet as Ball objects, and include some code that will show us how their positions change with time. We come up with the following code, saved as SinglePlanet.as:

```
package{
        import flash.display.Sprite;
        import com.physicscodes.math.Vector3DX;
        import com.physicscodes.objects.Ball;

        public class SinglePlanet extends Sprite{
                private var _dt:Number = 0.05;
                private var _numSteps:Number = 2500;
                private var _animFreq:Number = 40;
                private var _t:Number = 0;
                private var _v:Vector3DX = new Vector3DX(5,0,14);
                private var _s:Vector3DX = new Vector3DX(400,150,0);
                private var _center:Vector3DX = new Vector3DX(400,400,0);
                private var _G:Number = 10;
                private var _massSun:Number = 5000;
                private var _planet:Ball;
                private var _sun:Ball;

                public function SinglePlanet():void{
                        init();
                }

                private function init():void{
                        setup();
                        simulate();
                }
                private function setup():void{
                        _sun = new Ball(30,0xffff00);
                        _sun.pos = _center;
                        addChild(_sun);

                        _planet = new Ball(5);
                        _planet.pos = _s;
                        addChild(_planet);
                }
                private function simulate():void{
                        for (var i:uint=0; i<_numSteps; i++){
                                _t += _dt;
                                RK4();
                                if (i%_animFreq==0){
                                        animate();
                                }
                        }
                }

                private function animate():void{
                        _planet.pos = _s;
                        clonePlanet();
                }

                private function clonePlanet():void{
                        var pcopy:Ball = _planet.clone();
                        pcopy.pos = _planet.pos;
                        addChild(pcopy);
                }
```

```
        private function getAcc(ppos:Vector3DX,pvel:Vector3DX):Vector3DX{
                var r:Vector3DX = Vector3DX.convert(ppos.subtract(_center));
                return r.multiply(-_G*_massSun/(r.lengthSquared*r.length));
        }

        private function RK4():void{
                // code as in previous example
        }

    }
}
```

The **getAcc()** method does what we just said: it applies an acceleration due to the sun's attraction on the planet. We have added an **if** block of code in the **simulate()** function that calls an **animate()** method at intervals of _animFreq. The **animate()** method moves the planet to the current position and then calls the **clonePlanet()** method, which creates a copy of the planet at that position. The net result is a series of cloned planets at locations where it has been after equal amounts of time (see Figure 16-9). Not quite "animation" because if you run the code you will see everything displayed at once, but it does convey some sense of stepping through time. This is a planetary trajectory in 3D; you can see the perspective effect causing the planet to appear smaller when its z-coordinate is larger.

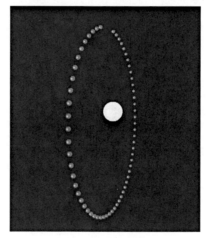

Figure 16-9. A planetary trajectory in 3D

Choosing appropriate scaling factors

Now that we have an accurate orbits simulator, it's time to represent the real solar system to scale as the next step toward a realistic simulation. To do this, we need to go back to the governing equation. For the purpose of choosing appropriate scaling factors, it is the form of the equation that matters instead of the details of the various terms. So it will be fine to consider only the portion of the equation reflecting the effect of the sun. Also, it's the magnitude of the relevant quantities that matters, not their direction. The last equation therefore leads to the following approximate equation for the acceleration of each planet, in which M_s is the mass of the Sun and r is the distance of the planet from it:

$$\frac{d^2s}{dt^2} = G\,\frac{M_s}{r^2}$$

We now define scaling factors for time, distance, and mass in a similar way to the example in the last chapter:

$$s = \lambda \hat{s} \qquad t = \tau \hat{t} \qquad m = \mu \hat{m}$$

Substituting them into the previous equation and rearranging gives the following corresponding equation in terms of the rescaled variables:

$$\frac{d^2\hat{s}}{d\hat{t}^2} = \left(\frac{G\mu\tau^2}{\lambda^3} \right) \frac{\hat{M}_s}{\hat{r}^2}$$

Comparing the two equations then tells us that the value of the gravitational constant G in the rescaled system is given by this:

$$\hat{G} = \frac{G\mu\tau^2}{\lambda^3}$$

We now need to choose appropriate scaling factors μ, τ, and λ for the base units for converting quantities from the usual SI units to corresponding simulation units. In any given problem a sensible choice for the scaling factors should reflect scales relevant to the physics. In this case for example, it makes no sense to think of mass values in terms of kg but instead in terms of the mass of the Sun or the mass of the Earth. Let's choose the latter. Similarly, it makes little sense to stick with the second as a unit of time because we will be interested in seeing the planets complete at least one revolution around the Sun (the duration of the simulation will be on the order of years). Therefore, we'll choose 1 day as the unit of time. Finally, we could choose the mean distance of the Earth from the Sun (known as an *astronomical unit*: au) as the distance unit. That's about 150 million km, or 150 x 10^9 m. This would make the distance between the Earth and the Sun 1 unit in the simulation by definition. However, because we are building a visual simulation, we'll be thinking of distance in terms of pixels and want to see the Earth a decent number of pixels away from the Sun. A more suitable choice of scaling factor in that case is 1 million km (10^9 m) per pixel, which would make the Earth-Sun distance around 150 pixels. Table 16-1 summarizes these choices of scaling factors.

Table 16-1. Scaling Factors for Base Units

Scaling factor	Value
μ (mass)	Earth mass = 5.9736 x 10^{24} kg
τ (time)	Earth day = 86400 s
λ (length)	1 million km = 10^9 m

Scaling factors for derived quantities such as velocity can be worked out from those of the base quantities. For example, the scale factor for velocity is given by λ/τ.

Obtaining planetary data and initial conditions

The next thing to do is to obtain some planetary data such as the masses of the planets and some suitable values for the initial conditions (planets' positions and velocities). This web page from NASA's web site has all the required information: **http://nssdc.gsfc.nasa.gov/planetary/planetfact.html**.

For easy access, we have saved some of the data that we'll be using as public static constants in the class **Astro** in package **com.physicscodes.constants**. This includes, for example, the constants **EARTH_MASS**, **EARTH_RADIUS**, **EARTH_ORBITAL_RADIUS**, and **EARTH_ORBITAL_VELOCITY** and similar constants for other planets. Take a look at the file **Astro.as**. There is a related class called **Phys** in the same package, which contains values of a few physical constants such as the gravitational constant G (**GRAVITATIONAL_CONSTANT**) and the standard value of the acceleration due to gravity on Earth (**STANDARD_GRAVITY**). These values were obtained from the following web page on the NIST web site: **http://physics.nist.gov/cuu/Constants/**.

The values of the mean orbital radius and the orbital velocity of the planets in the **Astro** class will be used as approximate initial conditions in the basic version of the solar system model that we will construct next.

Basic solar system model

We are now ready to put together a basic solar system model that will include all the essential aspects of the simulation. The relevant file, **SolarSystemBasic.as**, contains a fair amount of code. So we'll break things down a bit. Let's begin by listing the private variables and the **init()** method:

```
package{
        import flash.display.Sprite;
        import flash.geom.Vector3D;
        import com.physicscodes.math.Vector3DX;
        import com.physicscodes.motion.Forces3DX;
        import com.physicscodes.objects.Ball;
        import flash.events.Event;
        import com.physicscodes.constants.*;
        import flash.geom.Matrix3D;

        public class SolarSystemBasic extends Sprite{
                // time-keeping variables
                private var _dt:Number = 1/24; // simulation time unit is 1 day; time-step is
1 hr
                private var _numSteps:Number = 8760; // 1 year; 365*24
                private var _animFreq:Number = 168; // once per week; 24*7
                private var _t:Number = 0;

                // gravitational constant
                private var _G:Number;

                // sun variables
                private var _center:Vector3DX;
                private var _massSun:Number;
                private var _radiusSun:Number=30;

                // velocity and position vectors for all planets
                private var _v:Vector.<Vector3DX>;
                private var _s:Vector.<Vector3DX>;

                // visual objects
                private var _sprite:Sprite;
                private var _sun:Ball;
                private var _planets:Vector.<Ball>;
                private var _numPlanets:uint=4;

                // planets' properties
```

```
        private var _colors:Array;
        private var _radiuses:Array;
        private var _masses:Array;
        private var _distances:Array;
        private var _velos:Array;

        // scaling factors
        private var _scaleTime:Number;
        private var _scaleDist:Number;
        private var _scaleMass:Number;
        private var _scaleVelo:Number;

        public function SolarSystemBasic():void{
                init();
        }

        private function init():void{
                _sprite = new Sprite();
                addChild(_sprite);
                setupScaling();
                setupPlanetData();
                setInitialConditions();
                setupObjects();
                simulate();
        }
    }
}
```

First, take a look at the private variable definitions. Note in particular that _s and _v are now **Vector** variables consisting of **Vector3DX** objects: they will contain the position and velocity vectors of all the planets. Note also the arrays **_colors**, **_radiuses, and so on** that will hold the properties of the planets. Next take a look at the **init()** function. A **Sprite** instance called **_sprite** is created; the Sun and planets will be placed on that sprite. Then the following methods are called in succession: **setupScaling()**, **setupPlanetData()**, **setInitialConditions()**, **setupObjects()**, and **simulate()**. Let's briefly discuss each one in turn.

The **setupScaling()** method does exactly what its name suggests: it defines the scale factors and then uses them to rescale the mass of the sun and the gravitational constant to their simulation values:

```
private function setupScaling():void{
        scaleMass = Astro.EARTH_MASS;
        scaleTime = Astro.EARTH_DAY;
        scaleDist = 1e9; // 1 million km or 1 billion meters
        scaleVelo = _scaleDist/_scaleTime; // million km per day

        massSun = Astro.SUN_MASS/_scaleMass;

        var G:Number = Phys.GRAVITATIONAL_CONSTANT;
        G = _scaleMass*_scaleTime*_scaleTime*G / (_scaleDist*_scaleDist*_scaleDist);
}
```

The **setupPlanetData()** method puts the appropriate values for the planets' properties in the five arrays **_radiuses**, **_colors**, **_masses**, **_distances**, and **_velos**. The values we chose for **_radiuses** are in proportion to the four planets' real radiuses. But please note that they are not in proportion to the radius of the Sun (which in reality would be much larger compared with those of the planets). Moreover, neither the radiuses of the planets nor the radius of the Sun are in proportion to the distances between them. If we did that, the planets would all be tiny dots in the space available on the stage. The masses, distances, and velocities are scaled values of those read in from the **Astro** class for each planet.

```
private function setupPlanetData():void{
        _radiuses = [1.9, 4.7, 5, 2.7];
        _colors = [0xffffcc, 0xffcc00, 0x0099ff, 0xff6600];

        _masses = new Array();
        _distances = new Array();
        _velos = new Array();

        _masses[0] = Astro.MERCURY_MASS/_scaleMass;
        _masses[1] = Astro.VENUS_MASS/_scaleMass;
        _masses[2] = Astro.EARTH_MASS/_scaleMass;
        _masses[3] = Astro.MARS_MASS/_scaleMass;

        _distances[0] = Astro.MERCURY_ORBITAL_RADIUS/_scaleDist;
        _distances[1] = Astro.VENUS_ORBITAL_RADIUS/_scaleDist;
        _distances[2] = Astro.EARTH_ORBITAL_RADIUS/_scaleDist;
        _distances[3] = Astro.MARS_ORBITAL_RADIUS/_scaleDist;

        _velos[0] = Astro.MERCURY_ORBITAL_VELOCITY/_scaleVelo;
        _velos[1] = Astro.VENUS_ORBITAL_VELOCITY/_scaleVelo;
        _velos[2] = Astro.EARTH_ORBITAL_VELOCITY/_scaleVelo;
        _velos[3] = Astro.MARS_ORBITAL_VELOCITY/_scaleVelo;
}
```

The `setInitialConditions()` method uses the distances and velocities set up in `setupPlanetData()` to set the initial values of the position and velocity vectors _s and _v for each planet relative to the Sun.

```
private function setInitialConditions():void{
        _center = new Vector3DX(400,300,0);

        _s = new Vector.<Vector3DX>();
        _s[0] = new Vector3DX(400+_distances[0],300,0);
        _s[1] = new Vector3DX(400+_distances[1],300,0);
        _s[2] = new Vector3DX(400+_distances[2],300,0);
        _s[3] = new Vector3DX(400+_distances[3],300,0);

        _v = new Vector.<Vector3DX>();
        _v[0] = new Vector3DX(0,_velos[0],0);
        _v[1] = new Vector3DX(0,_velos[1],0);
        _v[2] = new Vector3DX(0,_velos[2],0);
        _v[3] = new Vector3DX(0,_velos[3],0);
}
```

The setupObjects() method then creates Ball instances for the Sun and each planet, giving each one the appropriate radius, color, and mass and setting the initial positions and velocities.

```
private function setupObjects():void{
        // sun
        _sun = new Ball(_radiusSun,0xffff00);
        _sun.pos = _center;
        _sprite.addChild(_sun);

        // planets
```

```
        _planets = new Vector.<Ball>();
        for (var n:uint=0; n<_numPlanets; n++){
                var planet:Ball = new Ball(_radiuses[n], _colors[n], _masses[n]);
                planet.pos = _s[n];
                planet.velo = _v[n];
                _sprite.addChild(planet);
                _planets.push(planet);
        }
}
```

Finally we have the **simulate()** method, together with the associated methods **animate()** and **clonePlanet()** that we had in the previous version of the code. These are all natural generalizations of their previous counterparts to multiple planets, effected with the addition of a **uint** parameter n that represents the array index of the relevant planet. The **RK4()** and **getAccc()** methods are also updated to include this planet index parameter n, so that they know which planet they are calculating for. Note that **getAcc()** now includes the gravitational force exerted by each of the other planets in addition to that exerted by the Sun in calculating the resultant force and acceleration of each planet.

```
private function simulate():void{
        for (var i:uint=0; i<_numSteps; i++){
                _t += _dt;
                for (var n:uint=0; n<_numPlanets; n++){
                        RK4(n);
                        if (i%_animFreq==0){
                                animate(n);
                        }
                }
        }
}

private function animate(n:uint):void{
        _planets[n].pos = _s[n];
        clonePlanet(n);
}

private function clonePlanet(n:uint):void{
        var pcopy:Ball = _planets[n].clone();
        pcopy.pos = _planets[n].pos;
        _sprite.addChild(pcopy);
}

private function getAcc(ppos:Vector3DX,pvel:Vector3DX,pn:uint):Vector3DX{
        var massPlanet:Number = _planets[pn].mass;
        var r:Vector3DX = Vector3DX.convert(ppos.subtract(_center));
        // force exerted by sun
        var force:Vector3DX = Forces3DX.gravity(_G, _massSun, massPlanet,r);
        // forces exerted by other planets
        for (var n:uint=0; n<_numPlanets; n++){
                if (n!=pn){ // exclude the current planet itself!
                        r = Vector3DX.convert(ppos.subtract(_s[n]));
                        var gravity:Vector3DX = Forces3DX.gravity(_G, _masses[n],↪
massPlanet,r);
                        force = Forces3DX.add([force, gravity]);
                }
        }
        // acceleration
```

```
        return force.multiply(1/massPlanet);
}

private function RK4(n:uint):void{
        // step 1
        var pos1:Vector3DX = _s[n];
        var vel1:Vector3DX = _v[n];
        var acc1:Vector3DX = getAcc(pos1,vel1,n);
        // step 2
        var pos2:Vector3DX = pos1.addScaled(vel1,_dt/2);
        var vel2:Vector3DX = vel1.addScaled(acc1,_dt/2);
        var acc2:Vector3DX = getAcc(pos2,vel2,n);
        // step 3
        var pos3:Vector3DX = pos1.addScaled(vel2,_dt/2);
        var vel3:Vector3DX = vel1.addScaled(acc2,_dt/2);
        var acc3:Vector3DX = getAcc(pos3,vel3,n);
        // step 4
        var pos4:Vector3DX = pos1.addScaled(vel3,_dt);
        var vel4:Vector3DX = vel1.addScaled(acc3,_dt);
        var acc4:Vector3DX = getAcc(pos4,vel4,n);
        // sum vel and acc
        var velsum:Vector3DX=vel1.addScaled(vel2,2).addScaled(vel3,2).addScaled(vel4,1);
        var accsum:Vector3DX=acc1.addScaled(acc2,2).addScaled(acc3,2).addScaled(acc4,1);
        // update pos and velo
        _s[n] = pos1.addScaled(velsum,_dt/6);
        _v[n] = vel1.addScaled(accsum,_dt/6);
}
}
```

Run the simulation. Note that it will take a few seconds to run; nothing will seem to happen for a few seconds while it's calculating. That's because it goes through the whole timestepping loop before doing any rendering. The default values in the code for the timekeeping variables are _dt = 1/24, _numSteps = 8760, and _animFreq = 168. Recalling that in the simulation the unit of time is 1 day, _dt = 1/24 corresponds to a timestep of 1 hr. Making it larger will mean that the simulation can run the simulation for longer in the same wall clock time or can run for the same simulated time in half the wall clock time.

You can experiment with the timestep to see how large you can make it without losing accuracy significantly. The value of 8760 for _numSteps equals 365 x 24; so we are doing an Earth year's worth of simulation. The _animFreq value of 168 is equal to 7 x 24, and so the planets' positions are visually updated once per week. Running the simulation with the default values will produce the trajectories shown in Figure 16-10. Earth is, of course, the third planet from the Sun, and it completes a full orbit in the 1 year of simulation time, which is reassuring! On the other hand, Mars completes only slightly more than half an orbit. If you reduce the simulation time to 8500 timesteps (about 354 days), you will find that Earth just fails to complete one orbit, as expected. This is a good indication that we got the simulation at least approximately right.

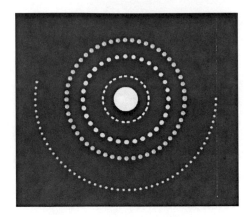

Figure 16-10. A basic solar system model that looks a bit artificial

This is a fully functional and physically quite realistic scale model of the solar system. Apart from the minor fact that the sizes of the planets and Sun are not visually represented in proportion to the distances between them, the real limitation of the model is that the initial conditions chosen for the planets are not actual instantaneous values; they are based on mean values of their distances from the Sun and their mean orbital velocities. Also the planets are all aligned in a straight line to start with, which is a bit artificial. Let's fix these limitations now.

Incorporating accurate initial conditions

We're almost there, but to create a truly realistic solar system simulation you need to use accurate data as initial conditions. The only thing that needs to change in the code is really the **setInitialConditions()** method. You need to put some real data in there; you can get that data from NASA's HORIZONS system here: **http://ssd.jpl.nasa.gov/horizons.cgi**.

This system generates highly accurate trajectory data (known as *ephemerides*) for a large number of objects in the solar system. The data is generated by NASA's own simulation to extremely high accuracy (typically 16 significant figures!). You can choose the data type, coordinate origin, time span, and other settings. The file **intial_conditions.txt** contains some data that we downloaded for the positions and velocities of the eight planets at the time of 00:00 on 1 January 2012. Next to the name of each planet there are six fields that contain values of x, y, z, vx, vy, and vz, respectively. The positions are in km and the velocities in km/s, both relative to the Sun. We have used this data as initial conditions for the four planets we are simulating in the version of the code with the filename **SolarSystem.as**.

Because we have access to NASA's simulation data, why not compare our simulation with theirs? So let's do a bit more work before we show you the results.

Comparing the model results with NASA data

We have also downloaded and saved position data from the HORIZONS web site for a whole year's worth of simulation, from 1 Jan 2012 to 1 Jan 2013. The data is saved in csv format in a separate file for each planet and is located in a subdirectory in the source code folder for this simulation. Note that the HORIZONS system is frequently updated as new measurement data is incorporated. The implication is that if you download data at a different time you may not obtain exactly the same figures to 16-digit accuracy. For most purposes, you wouldn't even notice the difference, though!

To compare our simulation with this data, we need to modify the code so that it can read in the data, process it, and then plot it together with the simulation data. With all these modifications, the code in **SolarSystem.as** is fairly lengthy. Also, much of the rest of the code is similar to that in

SolarSystemBasic.as. So we'll just show you the main structure with some of the added methods, letting you dig into the source file for details. Let's start with the init() method:

```
private function init():void{
      setupScaling();
      setupPlanetData();
      setInitialConditions();
      setupDataFile();
}
```

In addition to the previous method calls, init() now calls the setupDataFile() method, which in turn calls the loadFile() function that loads in a specified data file and triggers an event handler csvLoaded() when that is done.

```
private function setupDataFile():void{
      var file:String = 'planets_data/' + _planetNames[_ip-1] + '_XYZ.csv';
      loadFile(file);
}

private function loadFile(pFile:String):void{
      var dataLoader:URLLoader = new URLLoader();
      dataLoader.dataFormat = URLLoaderDataFormat.TEXT;
      dataLoader.addEventListener(Event.COMPLETE, csvLoaded);
      dataLoader.load(new URLRequest(pFile));
}
```

The csvLoaded() method sorts through the data and puts it into arrays for the position components:

```
private function csvLoaded(e:Event):void {
      _arrData = e.target.data.split(/\r/);
      for (var i:int=0; i<_arrData.length; i++) {
            _tArray[i] = i;
            var arr:Array = _arrData[i].split(",");
            _xArray[i] = arr[0]*1000/_scaleDist;
            _yArray[i] = arr[1]*1000/_scaleDist;
            _zArray[i] = arr[2]*1000/_scaleDist;
      }
      initSetup();
}
```

After all the data is sorted and put into the data arrays, csvLoaded() calls the initSetup() method, which looks like this:

```
private function initSetup():void{
      _sprite = new Sprite();
      addChild(_sprite);
      setupObjects();
      setupGraphs();
      plotData();
      simulate();
}
```

In addition to the previous setupObjects() and simulate() method calls, initSetup() calls the additional methods setupGraphs() and plotData(), which do exactly what their names suggest. We won't go into the details of the code in these methods, but do take a look at the source code file. There is also a line of code in the simulate() method that plots the corresponding simulated position (x, y, and z components relative to the Sun on three separate graphs). You can choose which planet's data you want to load and plot by setting the value of the **_ip** private variable at the beginning of the code.

Okay, after all that hard work it's now time to run the code and see the results. But first, put a comment before the line of code that calls the **simulate()** method in **initSetup()**. This will only plot NASA's data and won't run our simulation. If you run the code you'll see something like in Figure 16-11, in which we selected **_ip** = 4 to plot data for Mars.

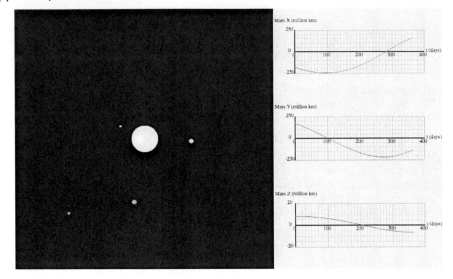

Figure 16-11. Initial planet positions and NASA's 1-year trajectory data for Mars

Now uncomment the line that calls **simulate()** and run the code once more. Again, bear in mind that you might need to wait for a few seconds before you see anything on the stage. You should now see something like in Figure 16-12.

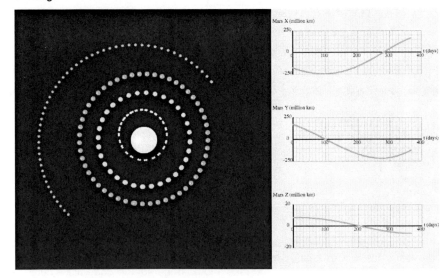

Figure 16-12. Planets' trajectories in a 1-year simulation with our code

The simulated trajectories now look more realistic with proper initial conditions. Note in particular the characteristic eccentricity of Mercury's orbit. On the right side you can now see plots of the position components from the simulation. But where are the plots of NASA's data gone? If you look carefully, you'll see that our simulated plots are sitting right on top of them! Note that we have modified the public `plot()` method of the **Graph** class to include line thickness and alpha parameters and have made the lines representing the simulated values transparent and thicker than the lines corresponding to the NASA data. Repeat the simulation plotting the positions of different planets and you'll see the same thing. You cannot distinguish between the two sets of plots at this resolution. Not bad, eh?

Although we have neglected a whole host of things such as the gas giants (especially Jupiter, the largest planet and the closest to the four terrestrial planets) asteroids, and relativistic effects, the results look pretty good. Of course, NASA's simulation has all these and a lot more, together with much more advanced numerical methods, which make it much more accurate. It would be interesting to run the simulation longer or reduce the timestep to see at what point it starts to show visible differences compared with the NASA data. There are, of course small differences, and bearing in mind that 1 px on the screen is a million km in reality, they may be significant in absolute terms. Nevertheless, while you may not necessarily be able to use this simulation to send your homemade space probe to Mars, you can most certainly use it to teach school kids or college students a thing or two about how the solar system works.

Other things to do

There are lots of ways in which you could develop or extend this simulation. The most obvious (and most straightforward) improvement would be to add in the four outer planets. You could also add in interactivity, dynamic scaling, animation, and so on. The file **SolarSystemAnimated.as** incorporates some basic animation into the last version of the simulation that you can no doubt develop further.

There is also a whole host of 3D features waiting to be exploited here. Our Sun and planets are just 2D **Ball** objects, so you can think of replacing them with 3D balls instead, perhaps with actual images of the planets wrapped on them. Then you could add functionality to rotate and scale the view. Perhaps you could even show the planets spinning when they are close up. We'll leave you to it.

Summary

With the completion of this book you now have a powerful set of tools at your disposal that will help you build more realistic and more engaging games and animations as well as some pretty powerful simulations. From the simple bouncing ball simulation of Chapter 1, you've come a long way, indeed!

Let's have a quick recap of all the ground covered in this book. In Part I, you went through a good deal of background material in ActionScript, math, and physics to establish the key concepts and techniques relating to physics-based motion and simulation.

Part II covered the basic laws of motion, and you encountered a wide variety of forces, building lots of examples that showed the interesting types of motion they produce.

In Part III, you simulated systems consisting of multiple particles or extended objects, including particle collisions, rigid bodies, and deformable bodies.

Finally, in Part IV you looked into how to create more complex simulations that require greater attention to numerical accuracy or that involve 3D or scale modeling. That's a lot of stuff.

This final chapter provided just a tiny glimpse of the possibilities that lie ahead for bringing all that physics together and putting it to use. We hope you will continue to have some serious fun with these projects as well as many others that you'll build from scratch. Just don't forget to share!

Index

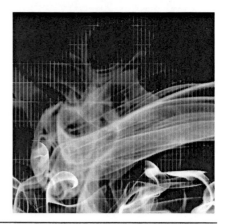

CPSIA information can be obtained at www.ICGtesting.com
Printed in the USA
LVOW050942231011

251664LV00004B/2/P